THE ESSENTIAL HISTORY OF
LEEDS UNITED

ANDREW MOURANT

FOREWORD BY PETER LORIMER

Acknowledgements

In ten years of writing about Leeds United, many ex players, managers and other key figures have been good enough to answer my questions. For their contributions to this book, I should like to thank Len Browning, David Cochrane, Bobby Forrest, Aubrey Powell and Harold Williams for illuminating the 1940s and 1950s. Valuable insights into modern times and running the club have come from Peter Ridsdale, Paul Hart and Eddie Gray. Ron Deaton has been an invaluable contact and Mark Evans worked far beyond the call of duty with his statistical contributions. Thanks also to Adrian Besley and Kathie Wilson at designsection and Peter 'Stix' Lockwood at Leeds United.

Copyright © 2000, 2002 Headline Book Publishing

The right of Andrew Mourant to be identified as the Author of the Work has been asserted by him in accordance with the Copyright, Designs and Patents Act 1988.

First published in 2000
by HEADLINE BOOK PUBLISHING
for WHSmith, Greenbridge Road, Swindon SN3 3LD

First published in paperback in 2002

10 9 8 7 6 5 4 3 2 1

ISBN 0 7553 1170 1
Design by designsection, Frome, Somerset
All photographs supplied by Colorsport
except pages 6tl, 68, 79, 96, 131, 181, 183, 187, 188, 196, 199, 202, 207, 209, 211, 212, 213, 215, 218, 219, 221 & 224

Printed and bound in Great Britain by Clays Ltd, St Ives PLC, Bungay, Suffolk

HEADLINE BOOK PUBLISHING
A division of Hodder Headline
338 Euston Road
London NW1 3BH

www.headline.co.uk
www.hodderheadline.com

Contents

Foreword
By Peter Lorimer

Leeds United have always been special to me. My association with the club goes back to the early 1960s – I was just 15 when I made my first-team debut.

I was lucky to be at the club during the greatest years in its history. It was a joy to be part of Don Revie's magnificent side and there was a great family spirit at Elland Road.

Having also experienced some of the not so good times, I have been thrilled to watch the resurgence of Leeds United, first under Howard Wilkinson then David O'Leary and now Terry Venables. These are exciting times to be a Leeds fan: a great crop of young players is growing up together, just like we did in the Revie era. Living and working close to Elland Road, as I do, I've enjoyed sharing in the supporters' enthusiasm.

I feel confident that this is a trophy-winning side in the making and am sure that for Leeds United even better times lie ahead.

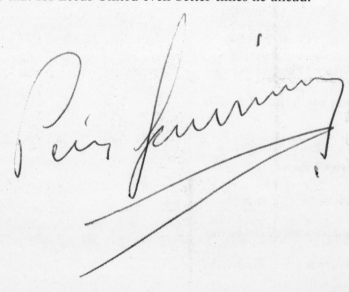

Leeds in celebration: (clockwise from top left) Peter Lorimer and Allan Clarke; Jack Charlton, Ray Hankin, Eric Cantona, Billy Bremner.

Chapter One: 1904-1919
The Leeds City Story

Were it not for financial skulduggery and scandal, Leeds United would probably not exist. Any team representing Yorkshire's capital would almost certainly have continued to bear the name of its original professional club, Leeds City. But no-one can legislate for an outfit that seals its own fate by underhand dealing and defying the game's governing body. That was to be Leeds City's lot. Fourteen years after joining the Second Division, the club was wiped out.

It had been a long haul to get football going in Leeds. The West Riding of Yorkshire was rugby territory with many teams attached to local churches. By 1877, when early efforts were first made to establish a soccer team in Hunslet, the game was thriving elsewhere across the country. Yet in Leeds, teams withered soon after they flowered: the Football League was formed in 1888 but it took a further six years for sufficient teams to emerge in the West Riding to create a local league.

Football had staggered on intermittently at Hunslet but the club had no ground of its own. Having disbanded in 1902 to concentrate on fund-raising, its future, and that of association football in Leeds, turned on the demise two years later of Holbeck Rugby Club, which played at Elland Road. The men behind Hunslet, quick to seize an opportunity, became the catalyst of a meeting held at the Griffin Hotel calling on interested parties to establish an association club in the city – an idea dependent on renting Holbeck's ground with the option to buy.

Here was the cohesiveness, the ambition and intent, that had been lacking in previous attempts to foster football in Leeds. The plight of Holbeck rugby was soccer's good fortune. There was now a firm footing and a view of the future with which to attract players. The new club, as if in keeping with the high aspirations, was to be known as Leeds City.

The club's first directors, men such as the clothier Norris Hepworth and iron founder Joseph Henry, convinced the Football League that

Leeds City would be a worthy addition. The team had played its first season in the West Yorkshire League; its first match at Elland Road on 15 October 1904, a 2-0 defeat by Hull City, was watched by around 3,000 fans. And while the club struggled, finishing 11th, the future was the thing. Election to the Football League on 29 May 1905 would enable the squad to be transformed and heralded a new professionalism.

The team embarked on its first season in the Second Division having appointed Gilbert Gillies, formerly with Chesterfield, as secretary-manager in March 1905. The opening game of the 1905-6 campaign, a 1-0 defeat against Bradford City at Valley Parade, drew 15,000 spectators. The Leeds line-up, wearing blue and gold, had been assembled from far and wide: Burton United; Blackburn Rovers; Woolwich Arsenal; yet had the coherence to compete at a higher level.

After defeats in their two first matches, City lost only one of the following nine. A first victory came in their fourth outing, on 16 September at Leicester Fosse, secured by the game's only goal from left winger Harry Singleton.

It seemed to act as a tonic: a week later, Leeds recorded their first win at Elland Road, a 3-1 over Hull, watched by a crowd of 13,654. They finished sixth and had much to build on. That they lost their way in 1906-7 was due in part to a tragedy on the field: the death of centre forward David Wilson during the home match against Burnley on 27 October.

A former soldier who had fought in the Boer War, Wilson, bought from Hull City, made a striking impact initially but then lost form and complained about a shortage of breath in the weeks before his death. He had been a heavy smoker and during the Burnley match left the pitch soon after half-time, feeling ill. But he forced himself to return because Leeds were 1-0 down and struggling.

Wilson lasted scarcely two more minutes. He took himself off once more and died in the dressing room shortly afterwards. Amid the shock and distress of a team-mate's death, City's fortunes temporarily slumped. They lost the next five games and slumped to tenth by the end of the season.

Stumbling inconsistency coloured the fortunes of Leeds City for the next five years, and crowds fluctuated wildly: a home game against Bradford City on 1 February 1908 attracted 35,000; the next fixture at Elland Road against Derby two weeks later, 8,000. There was, however, one demoralizing constant: an acute lack of money.

Financial Crisis

The Leeds board had terminated Gillies' contract in March 1908, appointing as successor Frank Scott-Walford, manager of Brighton and Hove Albion and an engineer by training. But Scott-Walford fared no better. Leeds slid down the Second Division table, finishing 12th in 1908 and 1909; then 17th in 1910. By the end of 1911-12, as

Great Matches

FOOTBALL LEAGUE DIVISION TWO	Leicester, 16 September 1905
Leicester Fosse 0 Leeds City 1	Estimated Attendance 5,000

Singleton

It was a landmark – a win for City at last. 'They have progressed by stages and fully justified their right to be in the second division' said the *Yorkshire Post*. 'In a fine and open game, Leeds showed perhaps greater skill than they have in previous matches. Morris, Hargraves and Watson were a dashing triplet inside. In general smartness, they showed themselves to be the home team's superiors.'

A fluky goal on 35 minutes decided the outcome. As City put pressure on the Fosse goal, the ball fell to outside left Harry Singleton. His softish shot deceived the advancing Leicester goalkeeper and the ball rolled into the net. 'The ball either had a lot of twist on it or the ground was uneven,' reported the *Leeds Mercury*.

City, under pressure for much of the second half, owed much to goalkeeper Harry Bromage who 'kept out several hot drives'. The Mercury caught the celebratory mood. 'By an exceedingly fine display all round, the spell of ill-luck and disappointment has been broken.'

Leicester Fosse: Smith, Ashby, Oakes, Morgan, Bannister, Pollock, Durrant, Moody, Cox, Gould, Hodgkinson.

Leeds City: Bromage, McDonald, Ray, Morgan, Stringfellow, Henderson, Parnell, Watson, Hargraves, Morris, Singleton.

City ended up 19th and were forced to seek re-election, the club's financial crisis reached a head. With debts exceeding £13,000, and an appeal for fresh capital at the start of the season falling largely on deaf ears, a receiver was called in.

Scott-Walford, who always bought players as cheaply as he could, resigned. The club was in dire straits but re-election offered the chance of fresh start. Much would rest on the new manager; and City found exactly the right man: Herbert Chapman, blessed with a sure touch, self-confidence, new ideas, and firm grasp of what was needed.

Chapman was never a great player: a workaday forward who had roamed among several clubs; but had achieved early managerial success, taking Northampton to the Southern League title in 1909. He made an immediate impact at Elland Road by signing established professionals rather than the cut-price possibles hired by his predecessor.

And while early results during 1912-13 were inconsistent, there was a new vigour about Leeds City. They finished sixth, the best position since their first season; the average crowd rose from less than 8,000 to 13,000. The club recorded a profit of £383, the first since its inaugural season in the League when it ended up £122 in the black.

Herbert Chapman's glory days – at Huddersfield, then at Arsenal – were to come. Leeds City were early beneficiaries of his enlightened approach: he consulted players when plotting tactics; he instituted team talks; and introduced golf, for relaxation, into the training routine. He rejuvenated players he had inherited, such as centre forward Billy McLeod, who plundered 54 League goals in two seasons, and signed accomplished defenders such as full back Fred Blackman from Huddersfield Town. In 1913-14, the last full season before the Great War, Chapman's team finished fourth and just two points behind promoted Bradford Park Avenue.

The Demise of Leeds City

In August 1914, a syndicate of businessmen headed by Joseph Connor, president of the West Riding FA, bought Leeds City from the receiver. This looked like the basis for financial stability yet after a strong showing in 1913-14, City faltered, finishing 15th in the last season of Football League matches before competition was suspended because of the war. No-one, however, could have dreamed that Leeds would be robbed of its football team not by the decimation of young men on the battlefield but through administrative malpractice, managerial incompetence and malice.

It took a man with a grudge to precipitate Leeds City's demise; though trouble had been brewing long before summer 1919 when full back Charlie Copeland contacted the FA to tell what he knew of

Great Matches

FOOTBALL LEAGUE DIVISION TWO   **Elland Road, 29 November 1913**
                                      Estimated Attendance 14,000

Leeds City 8   Nottingham Forest 0

McLeod 4
Price 2
Hampson
Speirs

It looked like a rout and it was: confidence surged through Leeds City as Herbert Chapman's reconstruction took effect. 'Let it be said they deserved every one of the goals – they worked hard and their forwards were great opportunists,' reported the *Leeds Mercury*. 'They could have won by ten had not Foley missed a penalty and McLeod not touched the ball with his hand when he had only Hanna to beat.'

Even against a stiff wind, Leeds went 3-0 up within half an hour. This was the day that almost everything went right: at times, Chapman's team looked like supermen. 'The City forwards, especially McLeod and Price, were a brilliant lot who displayed fire and resolution in their attacks,' said the Mercury.

It was a record score for Leeds City. 'Hopes of supporters will naturally dwell all the more lovingly on promotion prospects,' said the *Yorkshire Post*. As for Forest, they deserved credit for perseverance but lacked the firepower ever to trouble the City defence in which Copeland and Affleck had been 'a puissant pair of backs' .

Leeds City: Hogg, Copeland, Affleck, Law, Hampson, Foley, Bainbridge, Speirs, McLeod, Price, Sharpe.

Nottingham Forest: Hanna, Dudley, Gibson, Armstrong, Mercer, Meedham, Firth, Bell, Jones, Derrick, Banks.

Referee: J. Butterfield (London).

The 1914-15 Leeds City team. City finished 15th in the last pre-war season.
A Leeds City side would never again compete in a full league season.

alleged illegal payments to players during wartime. Herbert Chapman's departure to the Barnbow munitions factory meant that his assistant, George Cripps, took control and picked the team. But Cripps had the confidence of neither the players, who at one time threatened to go on strike, nor of the chairman, Joseph Connor. Yet for all that he was held in low esteem, when Chapman came back in 1918 to reclaim the top job, Cripps, rather than retreat gracefully, chose to sue for wrongful dismissal.

Copeland meanwhile had a grievance about money. He wanted £6 a week but had only been offered an increase with strings: extra cash depended on him gaining a regular first team place. Otherwise, he had to settle for a basic £3.10 shillings a week. Copeland claimed that such a deal would have left him poorer than when he joined Leeds City in 1912. His method of revenge, tipping off the FA with whispers about illicit payments, set in motion a chain of calamitous events.

Much mystery still surrounds what happened. What, exactly, did Copeland know? How significant was it that Copeland's solicitor, James

Bromley, a former Leeds director, also represented George Cripps? And what ultimately became of a bundle of documents that Cripps, as part of his settlement, was requested to hand over to club directors in the offices of Leeds City's solicitor, Alderman William Clarke?

Cripps had told James Bromley about the illegal payments; but it was when Copeland spilled the beans that the crisis began, and a joint inquiry, conducted by the Football Association and the Football League was held in September 1919.

The documents were crucial; the inquisitors' determination to get them matched only by the club's refusal to yield them. Yet there was a feeling that the storm could be ridden out. On the day that Leeds City was due to learn its fate, the *Yorkshire Post* anticipated 'a satisfactory arrangement being made for the continuance of the club'.

Leaving in Style

Despite the impending catastrophe, City had made a sound start in the first postwar Division Two campaign. They were to depart the League in style, beating Wolves 4-2 at Molineux on 4 October 1919. 'The smashing defeat of Wolverhampton Wanderers on their own ground was... a veritable eye-opener to those at the match,' reported the *Leeds Mercury*.

It was a grand swansong for centre forward Billy McLeod who, having served City so well for 13 years, signed off with a hat-trick. The *Yorkshire Post* recorded the 'direct drives of the master shooter' and that 'real genius allowed him to score' when in a hopeless position, as the Mercury relished McLeod's equalizer – 'one of his special twisters' – while celebrating 'unquestionably a brilliant victory'.

But three days later, on 7 October 1919, the *Yorkshire Post* was struggling to digest the shock of Leeds City's suspension for a repeated failure to disclose the relevant papers. Joseph Henry, the Lord Mayor, had intervened to try to save the club by offering the directors' resignations. But the inquiry team was unmoved and ordered Leeds City's expulsion from the Football League unless all the documentary evidence was produced.

As this never saw the light, the conclusion that Leeds City had things to hide was inescapable. More ignominy followed with an order that four directors, along with Chapman and Cripps, should be suspended indefinitely from involvement in the professional game. The League president, John McKenna, did not mince words. 'We will have no nonsense... Leeds were defiant and could only be defiant through one cause, fear of the papers giving away certain secrets.'

Those secrets remain. Meanwhile the players no longer had a club. The League's hard line led to an outcome as pathetic as it was bizarre: a ceremonial auctioning of footballing flesh at the Metropole Hotel on 17 October; City men bid for and knocked down as if they were cattle: Billy McLeod, veteran of almost 300 appearances and scorer of 170 goals, realized £1,000 when sold to Notts County; Tommy Lamph went to Manchester City for £800; while lesser lights such as William Short, an inside forward who played only five games, slipped away to Hartlepools United for a mere £200. Going, going, gone: it seemed an apposite metaphor for the plight of Leeds City.

Chapter Two: 1920-39
Out of the Ashes – United

Football in Leeds was not to be killed off by the machinations of the city's only professional club. As the human assets were being dispersed across the country, committed fans and businessmen began working towards a revival. A meeting at the Salem Hall, instigated by Leeds solicitor and former City vice-chairman Alf Masser, voted to enrol members of a supporters' club. The mood had been indignant. 'After the courageous intervention of the Lord Mayor, the punishment meted out to the City was rather like hanging a lad for stealing his first apple,' Masser declared.

Advertisements were to be placed in the press to try to recruit a team. Former City full back Dick Ray, a member of the seven man committee, was elected secretary-manager. There was abundant goodwill towards this enterprise, which had the blessing of the FA; but anger among football fans in Leeds at the eagerness of Port Vale to profit from City's sins by lobbying intensely – before City's fate was confirmed – to take their place in the League.

Things moved rapidly: within a fortnight of the auction at the Metropole, a new club, Leeds United, had been constituted and confirmed as members of the Midland League. Within just seven months, on 31 May 1920, Leeds United was elected to the Second Division.

That things happened so quickly was due, in part, to the unexpected stimulus of J. Hilton Crowther, chairman of neighbouring Huddersfield Town. Crowther had lots of money, big ambition and saw greater potential for success in Leeds than at Huddersfield. His first plan, for amalgamation, had caused a furore in Huddersfield and much legal wrangling before Crowther was bought out.

When finally he moved to Elland Road, Crowther brought with him Arthur Fairclough, his ally and secretary-manager, a football man with an excellent pedigree – he had taken Barnsley to two FA Cup finals.

Arthur Fairclough became Leeds United's secretary-manager in 1920.

There were solid foundations for the optimism: an appeal for share capital had raised £10,000; and there was an option to buy Elland Road for £5,500 and extend its capacity to 60,000.

On the eve of Leeds United's re-entry to League football, the Yorkshire Post speculated that within three years the club might make the First Division. As for Alf Masser, his dream was 'to find the name of Leeds inscribed indelibly on the rolls of the Football Association as the city which passed through fire, was cleansed, and given a fair and sporting chance to rehabilitate itself'.

Building United from Scratch

A new club; a new team; and new colours: the City blue and gold were jettisoned in favour of blue and white stripes. Fairclough's recruits were a mix of players from local junior clubs and solid professionals. His was, essentially, a team built from the back: the most significant signing Jim Baker, a centre half bought from Huddersfield and a defensive linchpin in United's first two seasons.

A team of mixed abilities took to the field on 28 August 1920 as Leeds United played their first game in the Second Division against – of all teams – Port Vale. The eleven were: Billy Down (from Ashington), Bert Duffield (Castleford Town), Arthur Tillotson (Castleford Town), Robert Musgrove (Durham City), Jim Baker (Huddersfield), Jimmy Walton (West Stanley), George Mason (Frickley Colliery), Ernie Goldthorpe (Bradford City), Robert Thompson (Durham City), John Lyon (Hull City) and Jerry Best (Newcastle United). There was a sharp imbalance of experience; and before long, many comings and going: more than 30 players were used in cup and league during United's first season.

Nothing would have been sweeter than victory at Port Vale. It was not to be: Leeds lost 2-0. But after a 2-1 home defeat against South

Shields watched by 16,958, Fairclough's men had a second chance to get at Port Vale. A week after defeat in The Potteries, Leeds exacted revenge, winning 3-1 at Elland Road with goals from Matt Ellson and Jerry Best. 'Their success greatly pleased the 15,000 spectators and atoned for the defeat sustained at Hanley,' reported the *Leeds Mercury*. The best of United had been seen after the interval; 'forwards ably supported by half backs; the shooting forceful and usually accurate'.

Early games suggested that United were at least good enough to survive. Defensively they were adequate: up front, short of a cutting edge. But 14th place with 38 points from 42 games was a fair achievement; defence the rock on which Fairclough built as, the following season, he lifted Leeds to eighth and then seventh in 1922-23. Jim Baker had been joined at the back by Ernie Hart, a burly young defender signed from Doncaster during the early trawl for players.

A new era dawns: The Leeds United squad of 1920-21.

Hart became one of the pre-war greats at Elland Road; he played more than 440 League games and was capped eight times for England.

Leeds United's talismans were stout defenders: right back Bert Duffield became another ever-present and created an excellent understanding with Jimmy Frew, his left-sided counterpart. While there were no scoring wizards, there was, by 1923-24, enough potency from inside forwards Percy Whipp, signed from Sunderland the previous season, Jack Swan and centre forward Joe Richmond to push Leeds up among the promotion contenders. Seven straight wins saw them top by November; another six match-winning burst from January to March kept up the momentum.

Yet for all that Leeds United were on the threshold of great things, the public appeared unmoved. Only in the climactic weeks did gates creep over 20,000; and only when promotion was there to be won, at home against Stockport on 21 April, did the crowd become, in the words of the *Yorkshire Post*, 'more demonstrative than perhaps any that has been assembled in this ground since the war'. There was good cause for their belated display of fervour, for out of the ashes of Leeds City, United, a team without flamboyant stars, tradition or big money, had made it to the First Division.

No set of players had worked harder; and a 1-0 home win over Nelson five days later gave Fairclough's men the silverware they deserved. The Second Division Championship was a precious achievement; for another 40 years were to elapse before any more trophies were held aloft at Elland Road.

'Lend us a Fiver'

The First Division was a land of richer teams and wilier players. Survival would entail Leeds drawing on all reserves of team spirit. But as they fought out an honourable 1-1 draw against Sunderland in the opening game of 1924-25, drawing to Elland Road a record League crowd of 33,722, an old distracting problem, lack of finance, had resurfaced. J. Hilton Crowther, whom Leeds United owed £54,000, wanted £35,000 of it back. That Saturday evening supporters were

Great Matches

FOOTBALL LEAGUE DIVISION TWO **Elland Road, 21 April 1924**

Leeds United 4 **Stockport County 0** **Estimated Attendance 21,622**

Swan 2

Richmond

Harris

Leeds' 4-0 demolition of Stockport, achieved through 'the extraordinary tenacity of the home players and their effective tackling', took them to new heights. But this promotion victory was much more of a tussle than the score suggests – a gruelling game in which the Stockport front line looked constantly threatening.

Even though Leeds went a goal up in 10 minutes when Jack Swan headed in a centre from Joe Harris and two up shortly after half-time with Swan's second from an opening fashioned by centre forward Joe Richmond, Fairclough's team had to hang on grimly.

The third, and best goal, finally allowed Leeds to breathe more easily in the last quarter of an hour: right winger Walter Coates' trickery took him past the Stockport defence and his pass to the unmarked Richmond was gleefully converted. When, two minutes from time, outside right Joe Harris rushed forward to head home a neat centre from Percy Whipp, the celebrations began in earnest.

It says much for Stockport's spirit that the *Leeds Mercury*'s report was preoccupied as much with the Leeds defenders as the forwards. 'Down kept goal magnificently; Baker was on the top of his form and he and Hart broke up many promising movements by the Stockport front line.'

Leeds United: Down, Duffield, Menzies, Baker, Hart, Smith, Coates, Whipp, Richmond, Swan, Harris.

Stockport County: Hardy, Richardson, Reid, Meads, Cockburn, Wilson, Critchley, Swan, Simms, White, Edgley.

called to a meeting and implored to join the 'Lend us a Fiver' fund-raising campaign.

Team improvements would depend on Fairclough's shrewd use of limited resources. It was to be a rocky season after mid-November when, following a five-match unbeaten run and lying comfortably in mid-table, United's form fluctuated crazily. Three new recruits in March, Willis Edwards, Tom Jennings and Russell Wainscoat, were for the future rather than short-term reinforcements. Determinedly, Leeds clung on in the First Division, finishing 18th, but survival had been a close run thing.

Their position at the end of 1925-26, 19th, suggested another backs to the wall campaign. Yet they gained two points more – 36 instead of 34 – and would have finished higher but for a dismal run in April. Moreover, there was comfort to be drawn from the performances of the bedded-in trio of Jennings, Wainscoat and Edwards.

Jennings, a strong predatory centre forward had, like many of his kind, benefited from an amendment to the rules that meant a player could not be offside if two (rather than three) opponents were closer to their own goal-line when the ball was last played. An instinctive scorer, Jennings, who had joined Leeds United from Raith Rovers, gave a cutting edge the team had lacked.

In his first full season at Elland Road, he was the only ever-present and scored 27 goals, easily surpassing previous records. His flow was interrupted only when bouts of illness forced him out of the side. Jennings became Leeds United's top pre-war marksman with 112 goals in 167 matches before moving to Chester in 1931.

Jennings' regular partner at inside left, Russell Wainscoat, had been signed from Middlesbrough for £2,000. Despite injuries he was a consistent, lively forward, his qualities recognized by the award of an England cap against Scotland in 1929. He served Leeds well, scoring 87 goals in 215 appearances, before he too left in 1931, joining Hull City.

As for Edwards, a wing half and former miner signed from Chesterfield, he was a player who combined impeccable talent with gentle manners. In Willis Edwards' game, timing and technique were everything: the ability to out-pass and outwit, his weapons. England selectors soon got the message: a year after his debut for Leeds, Edwards was called up by his country against Wales for the first of his 16 caps.

There was now top class talent to bolster the endeavour that had sustained Leeds. Bobby Turnbull, signed in the 1925 close season, provided another attacking option on the right wing, blessed with the precious ability to run at defenders. Yet still the team functioned in fits and starts. More ability, more strength in depth was needed.

The redoubtable Jim Baker left during 1925-26, and Jennings made hay in the following campaign, scoring ten goals in three games as Leeds beat Arsenal (4-1), Liverpool (4-2), and Blackburn (4-1) during an early season purple patch. However, the defence appeared less than the sum of its parts. Jennings had broken records with three successive hat-tricks but goals poured in at the other end, despite the best efforts of keeper Jim Potts.

As if believing that attack was the best method of defence, Fairclough broke the club transfer record by paying Hearts £5,600 for Scotland international inside forward John White. The stakes, First Division survival, could not have been higher, but while White would, in time, give good service, his arrival was not enough to stave

50 Greatest Players

WILLIS EDWARDS Right half

Joined Leeds: March 1925   **From:** Chesterfield

Debut: v Newcastle United, 21 March 1925

Appearances: 444   **Goals:** 6

Left Leeds: 1939 (retired)

Honours won with Leeds: 16 England caps

Willis Edwards' supreme ball control marked him out as one of the finest wing halves in his generation. Few, if any, were his equal when it came to simultaneously trapping and passing.

'That straight through ball or diagonal pass of his asks to be carried on', wrote Leeds Mercury journalist Herbert Campbell, savouring Edwards' masterful return from injury in a 1-1 draw against Aston Villa in 1931. 'I do not know many players who can meet a ball from any position and hold it like Edwards does.'

His control could switch the focus of play instantly. The constant probing ball pushed through sweetly to front-runners was a trademark. He could be firm, and tackle hard when needed, but Edwards is best remembered for his instinctive creativity. He later became assistant trainer, then manager in 1947, before returning to his former role following a difficult season after relegation. He died in 1988 aged 85.

Record signing John White joined in February 1927 and went on to score 36 goals in his three seasons with Leeds.

off relegation. After three roller-coaster seasons, Leeds United had to start all over again.

They were to do so without Arthur Fairclough, who resigned along with assistant Bill Norman. Fairclough felt he had exhausted all the possibilities at Elland Road. Yet there was continuity in 1927-28: Dick Ray, secretary-manager from the inception of Leeds United, returned to take over, determined to keep the club's star players. 'The enforced return... to the Second Division has awakened a new spirit... there is a feeling that United's setback is only temporary,' declared the *Yorkshire Post*.

A Victorious Salvo

An emphatic 5-1 win at South Shields on opening day augured well. But it took more than three months for the men Ray had fought so hard to keep to click into consistent winning ways. United's 5-0 win at home to Chelsea on 10 December heralded a dazzling burst of seven straight wins, the last a 4-1 home victory over Southampton and auspicious also for marking the opening of the new Lowfields Road stand.

Leeds scored 24 and conceded only four in this victorious salvo. Jennings was running amok, aided and abetted by Wainscoat, White, Turnbull and new signing Charlie Keetley, a centre forward plucked from local football in Derbyshire. One of five footballing brothers, Keetley, a natural finisher, made a scoring debut in Leeds' 3-0 home victory against South Shields on New Year's Eve. It was an excellent omen: in 160 League appearances for Leeds, Keetley scored 108 goals and came close to international honours.

50 Greatest Players

TOM JENNINGS Centre forward

Joined Leeds: March 1925   **From:** Raith Rovers

Debut: v Sheffield Utd, 14 March 1925

Appearances: 174   **Goals:** 117

Left Leeds: June 1931   **For:** Chester

Honours won with Leeds: None

Tom Jennings was signed to galvanize Leeds' attack as the team struggled to maintain First Division status. He did that and more, becoming the club's most prolific pre-war marksman.

A sturdy determined striker, who was hard to knock off the ball, Jennings benefited from the change in the offside law in 1925. His 35 goals in 41 league matches during 1926-27 included hat-tricks in three consecutive games. Jennings maintained a prodigious strike rate throughout his time at the club and if blood poisoning and other illnesses hadn't interrupted his run of games his tally of goals would have been even more impressive.

Successive defeats by Bristol City and Hull brought Leeds to earth but immediately they eased back into a winning rhythm and a 12-match unbeaten sequence. The last of these, a 3-2 win at Chelsea before a crowd of more than 47,000, was enough to guarantee promotion at the first time of asking. Despite being denied the Championship by Manchester City, 1-0 victors at Elland Road four days later, there was still enormous pride at Leeds' achievement, and its manner.

In winning at Chelsea, the *Yorkshire Post* noted 'exchanges that were extraordinarily fast and keen and reached a high standard of cleverness'. Leeds had scored 98 goals, and if the goals deficit – 49 – seemed high, a handful of off-days, such as the end of season 5-1 defeat at Stoke when promotion had been won, were mainly to blame.

The 1928-29 season was a new landmark: the first that Leeds United competed with the elite and held their own. The impetus of recent success appeared to spill over: the first four matches unbeaten; just two defeats in the opening 12 games; Wainscoat and Keetley firing in the goals. Such was Willis Edwards' quality, he had been made

England captain, and joined in the England team by Ernie Hart and Russell Wainscoat. For the rest of 1928-29, they were horribly inconsistent, living off the fat of their early purple patch. Five defeats in the last six games plunged them into 13th place; a torrid fortnight in February saw them lose 8-2 at Newcastle then 5-0 at Burnley. Injuries and temporary loss of form could explain some of the calamities, but Dick Ray was left with much to ponder.

Ray refrained from wholesale changes though added to the squad. Among the newcomers was left back Jack Milburn, one of a famous footballing dynasty from Ashington, Northumberland, whose brother George had already appeared at right back for Leeds; and whose other younger brother Jim would also become a mainstay at Elland Road. Between them, the three Milburns, full backs all, would make 750 appearances for Leeds over 24 years. Jim departed to Bradford in 1952, but the following year his nephew Jack Charlton made his debut, sustaining the family connection at Leeds for a further two decades.

From making his debut in the 2-1 home victory over Everton on 16 September 1929, Jack Milburn became an almost immovable fixture

for the next ten years. There was much more assurance about Leeds United in 1929-30: the defence, though still sometimes aberrant, more secure; the attack more productive.

As Leeds surged up the table in early November after an eight-match unbeaten run that included seven victories, they looked to have arrived as First Division heavyweights. Jennings, although in and out of the team, maintained his strike rate; Wainscoat was at his peak and Keetley's return towards the end of the season after illness brought a heady rush of ten goals in eight games.

Dick Ray took Leeds straight back to Division One in 1927-28.

The old inconsistency put paid to any fancies Leeds might have of becoming Champions. But by finishing fifth, there was a sense of a platform in place from which a title challenge might be launched. Instead, in 1930-31, all the old frailties returned which, along with disruptive injuries, meant the team fought a losing battle against relegation.

The spectre of debt was looming once more: the club owed around £30,000 and was paying crippling rates of interest. When John White was sold back to Hearts for £2,500, there was no money for reinforcing the team. An injury to George Reed, who, during three seasons at left half, had been a solid component of the team, meant Ray gambling on a young newcomer, Wilf Copping. Little in Copping's early displays suggested he was a Titan in the making. In 1930-31, the illustrious half back line of Willis Edwards, Ernie Hart and Wilf Copping came together for the first time, yet looked a far from awesome combination.

Falling Attendances

These were depressed and depressing times at Elland Road: home gates slumped from a high of more than 30,000 for the derby with Huddersfield on 27 September 1930 to 5,572 for the home match with Leicester on 18 February 1931. With crowds frequently below 10,000, an unforeseeable change of form, fortune and Dick Ray's ingenuity would be needed to rescue things.

But Leeds United's habit of bouncing back didn't desert them. The core of the team remained, albeit that Tom Jennings had departed for Chester. Left winger Tom Cochrane, who had first played in 1928-29, had sometimes been brilliant, at others anonymous; but in the Second Division found his best form. Likewise Billy Furness, playing alongside Cochrane at inside left and signed from non-league football in 1929. Jimmy Potts continued seeing off pretenders to his goalkeeping spot: Jack Milburn, Copping, Hart and Edwards; Wainscoat and Keetley: all had stayed put. After a wobbly start to 1931-32, United found their Second Division legs and soared up the table with nine successive League victories from 26 September to 21 November. Even if their form was never quite as convincing thereafter, this rush of points propelled the team towards promotion.

Leeds finished second. Crowds were still low, rarely exceeding 15,000; but a return to the First Division meant fans could dream that all things were possible. Dick Ray still had a genius for unearthing diamonds in non-league football. Arthur Hydes, recruited from the Barnsley area in 1931, made few appearances in Leeds' promotion season yet took to the First Division as if born to it. The defence, meanwhile, was becoming a fearsome unit.

Support in 1932-33 remained bewilderingly fickle. Yet over Christmas, more than 112,000 poured through the turnstiles to watch Leeds United's two clashes with Herbert Chapman's Arsenal. The second of these was at Elland Road, interest whipped up not only by a prospect of seeing the Champions elect but by Leeds' superb 2-1 victory at Highbury on Boxing Day.

For Leeds' previous home game against Bolton on Christmas Eve, the crowd was 15,634; for the Arsenal, the spectators numbered 56,976. Trains, taxis and trams were packed; dozens watched precariously from the roof of a local pub. The match was goalless; but no anti-climax: Leeds pressed hard while their robust defence had few problems in snuffing out the Gunners' attack.

The unyielding style of the Leeds defence tended to linger in an opponent's memory. Fifty years after the event, Joe Mercer recalled his debut for Everton at Leeds on 18 April 1933. 'I played against Potts, Milburn, Willis Edwards, Hart and Copping, and they kicked the stocking tops off everybody.'

They resumed in much the same way in 1933-34 though injury meant Willis Edwards was frequently absent. Arthur Hydes was as sharp as previously; though when he was injured, Ray was forced to use Irish winger Harry Duggan as an auxiliary centre forward. Another season of trademark inconsistency was most notable for a record home League victory, 8-0 against Leicester

Russell Wainscoat won his single England cap against Scotland in 1929.

City, just eight days after the team had crashed 5-1 at Tottenham.

The team finished ninth with 42 points. But when Copping, whose thunderous displays had made him a folk hero, left for Arsenal in the close season and brought Leeds a much-needed £6,000, there was no obvious replacement. Copping had been a tenacious warrior, a one-off, whose departure was one of many headaches faced by Dick Ray in 1934-35.

His injury-hit squad toiled and stuttered, scrambling enough points near the end to finish 18th and cling on in the top flight. But there had been some defensive horrors: a record 8-1 defeat by Stoke City; a 7-1 hammering at Chelsea; a 6-3 beating at West Bromwich. Besides Wilf Copping, another stalwart had left:

Wilf Copping was sorely missed after his departure to Arsenal in 1934.

goalkeeper Jimmy Potts, for years a reassuring figure, had joined Port Vale after more than 260 appearances in league and cup.

Ray had been an excellent servant. But, as Arthur Fairclough found, the club's finances restricted room for manoeuvre in the transfer market. Both worked minor miracles procuring and developing unsung talent but by the end of 1934-35, Ray felt he had little more to offer and moved to Bradford City.

His successor, Billy Hampson, had a long playing career with Newcastle and managed Carlisle United before coming to Elland Road. Hampson imported new blood such as former England goalkeeper Albert McInroy from Sunderland and George Brown, a centre forward

Great Matches

FOOTBALL LEAGUE DIVISION ONE Highbury, 26 December 1932
Attendance 55,876

Arsenal 1   **Leeds United 2**
Hulme   Keetley 2

While a match for any First Division side, few gave Leeds much chance at Highbury. But Arsenal, six points clear at the top, were jolted by a thrilling performance from Dick Ray's men who took the game to the home side.

The Gunners had an early warning of what might be to come when outside right Johnny Mahon found space and centred only for Charlie Keetley to squander an excellent chance. Leeds began applying intense pressure and in a seven-minute spell forced five corners; yet with the game goalless at half-time, had nothing to show for their efforts.

That all changed four minutes after the interval with what the *Leeds Mercury* described as 'a perfect picture goal'. Outside left Tom Cochrane centred from by the goal-line for Keetley to score after a neat exchange of passes with Mahon.

Leeds faced a test of character and endurance when Jack Milburn's unlucky deflection of a shot from Hulme gave Arsenal the equalizer. But Dick Ray's men continue to press: Mahon hit a post before picking up a loose ball bobbling near the Arsenal goal and then hooking it across for Keetley to score.

This was a magnificent result: Leeds played well to a man and of the much-fêted Arsenal attack, only Bastin had caused problems.

Arsenal: Moss, Mayle, Hapgood, Hill, Roberts, John, Hulme, Jack, Lambert, James, Bastin.

Leeds United: Potts, Milburn G, Milburn J, Stacey, Hart, Copping, Mahon, Hydes, Keetley, Furness, Cochrane.

from Burnley. He also began making best use of the young talent he had inherited, notably right back Bert Sproston, who was rejected as a teenager by Huddersfield Town and discovered by Dick Ray playing non-league football in Cheshire for Sandbach Ramblers. Under Hampson, Sproston swiftly became a first-team regular and a stylish defender, winning the first of 11 caps for England against Wales in Cardiff in October 1937.

50 Greatest Players

WILF COPPING Left half

Joined Leeds: March 1929   **From:** Middlecliffe Rovers

Debut: v Portsmouth, 30 August 1930

Appearances: 183   **Goals:** 4

Left Leeds: 1934   **For:** Arsenal

Re-joined Leeds: March 1939   **Left Leeds:** 1942 (retired)

Honours won with Leeds: 7 England caps

In any hall of fame of hard men, Copping belongs at the top table. A strong cleft chin, often left unshaven before a big match, and stony unblinking eyes were indications that he should not be trifled with.

His exhortation was 'Get stuck in'; and if ever there was a man for practising what he preached, it was Wilf Copping. When he broke his nose in one game, he shooed away the trainer, set the nose himself and carried on playing, holding a sponge to stem the bleeding. Friends and foe referred to him ironically as 'Smiler'.

It was in the 1932-33 campaign that Copping made his name. At the end of the season he won his first cap for England, against Italy in Rome. Eighteen months later, in November 1934, as the same two countries clashed in what became known as the notorious 'Battle of Highbury', Copping was in his element, treating Italians to the delights of his two-footed tackle and buffeting shoulder-charge. He had, by then, decamped to the all-conquering Arsenal, though returned to Elland Road in 1939 with legendary status assured.

Copping retired in 1942 and after the war became a trainer at Southend, Bristol City and Coventry. He died in 1980.

It said much for Hampson's first transitional season that Leeds recovered a mid-table position, finishing 11th. 1935-36 marked the end of another era, Ernie Hart's 14-year domination of the centre half spot. Defensive nightmares followed Hart's departure to Mansfield as Hampson's injury-ravaged squad dug in for a battle against relegation. Leeds finished 19th in 1936-37 with the worst away record in their history, 19 defeats, a solitary win and a draw.

During the absences of Arthur Hydes, the team had struggled for goals. In the dour battle for survival, the form of inside left Eric Stephenson, another Dick Ray protégé who seized his chance when in

Great Managers –1927-35

DICK RAY

Dick Ray had been a full back in the Leeds City team in their first season in the Football League in 1905. In the newly formed Leeds United he was originally made secretary-manager although moved aside to assist Arthur Fairclough until 1923 when he left to manage Doncaster Rovers.

Ray returned at the beginning of the 1927-28 season to take over the newly-relegated team from Fairclough. He managed to take them back to the top flight and to fifth place in 1930. Finding themselves back in Division Two in 1931, once again he took Leeds back to the First and again threatened the established clubs notably with a victory over Herbert Chapman's Arsenal at Highbury.

Ray proved that even with limited finance, Leeds could compete with the best in the land. He built a strong team with meagre resources through a keen eye for a bargain, signing Arthur Hydes and Wilf Copping from non-league football, and fostering the talents of players like Willis Edwards, Jennings and Wainscoat. Ray resigned in 1935.

the first team, provided hope for the future. Like Sproston, Stephenson made rapid progress and in 1938 followed the Leeds right back into the England team. War brought an abrupt and savage end to what might have been a great career: Stephenson was killed in action in Burma in 1944.

Hampson had mixed fortunes with his signings but owed much to South African born Gordon Hodgson, aged 34 when he joined Leeds from Aston Villa for £1,500 in March 1937. In the short term, Hodgson's goals and vitality helped ensure survival; and in 1937-38, in a more settled team, he led the front line superbly scoring 25 goals in 36 League matches. Such was his form, confidence and fitness that Hampson felt able to offload the injury-hit Arthur Hydes to Newport.

Hodgson was regarded with affection by former team-mates. Welsh inside forward Aubrey Powell, who made his debut as an 18-year-old against Middlesbrough on Christmas Day 1936, recalls the South African's protective instincts. 'He was very good in the air, very strong and looked after you on the field. At corner kicks, he'd say "I'll go in there – you stay out on the edge of the area". He'd always help you out.'

There was little, however, Hodgson could have done to prevent Powell's career almost coming to a premature end after the young Welshman was felled by a violent tackle at Preston that left him with a compound fracture of the leg. The injury put one of Leeds' most promising players out of the game for over a year. Doctors had feared Powell might never play again.

The tale of a season in which Leeds finished ninth again revolved around inconsistency. The mirage of a First Division Championship had appeared at Christmas when Leeds lay second, only to melt away with a barren

50 Greatest Players

ERNIE HART Centre half

Joined Leeds: 1920   **From:** Woodlands Wesleyans

Debut: v Stockport County, 19 February 1921

Appearances: 472   **Goals:** 15

Left Leeds: August 1936   **For:** Mansfield

Honours won with Leeds: Division 2 Championship 1924;

8 England caps

Ernie Hart was the focal point of Leeds United's defence for almost 15 years. He read the game superbly, developed a fine understanding with fellow half backs Willis Edwards and Wilf Copping, and was a much better ball player than the average centre half.

Given the chance, he loved to delegate defensive responsibilities and join the attack. In Leeds' 2-0 home victory over Chelsea at Elland Road in November 1932, the *Mercury* remarked on Hart's masterly attacking game. 'His baffling footwork and accurate passing, and above all his generalship... was the dominating force in the whole game. Where is there a better centre half?'

In Leeds' 1-0 home win against Everton the following season, Hart was lauded for 'standing out alone from other centre halves, sharing in attacks on all parts of the front but showing reserves of power enabling him to get across the field and stop danger'.

Some contemporaries felt Hart deserved more than the eight caps he won for England – the first came against Wales in 1921; but his cause may not have been helped by a month-long ban in 1933 after he was sent off for swearing at the referee during a West Riding Cup final against Huddersfield. Hart eventually left for Mansfield in 1936 but re-established his connection with Leeds by working as a scout. He died in 1954 aged 52.

run in February and March. The team's capacity for boomeranging in and out of form had been characteristic throughout the 1930s.

Yet by the eve of war, Leeds United could be satisfied with the playing achievements of almost 20 years. They had been well-managed by men able to make much out of little. From unknown players, plying their trade in minor leagues, some fine international footballers had been created. Yet if few clubs had a paying public so fickle, the fans were entitled to question Leeds United's ambition: shortly after the club made a profit of almost £4,000 in 1937-38, it disposed of Bert Sproston, unable to resist the £9,500 dangled by Tottenham Hotspur. A financial crisis, immediate or pending, always cast its shadow.

50 Greatest Players

BERT SPROSTON Full back

Joined Leeds: May 1933   **From:** Sandbach

Debut: v Chelsea, 23 December 1933

Appearances: 140   **Goals:** 1

Left Leeds: June 1938   **For:** Tottenham

Honours won with Leeds: 8 England caps

Bert Sproston rose rapidly from non-league right back to England international. While Leeds United had some fierce players in the ranks – like George and Jack Milburn, and Wilf Copping – Sproston was a stylish defender blessed with great pace.

Team-mates have vivid memories of his speed. 'He was very quick on the turn, at running back and recovering to catch the winger – he always amazed me,' Aubrey Powell recalls. 'There was nothing hard about him – he was a good footballer.'

Sproston had joined Leeds as an 18-year-old. After three eye-catching seasons, he made his England debut against Wales, and was in the team notoriously ordered by the FA to perform a Nazi salute before kicking-off the international in Germany in 1938.

Lack of money – forever Leeds' problem – forced the sale of Sproston to Spurs for a near record £9,500 in June 1938. Within six months he moved to Manchester City; and later worked at Bolton, as trainer and scout.

Chapter Three: 1939-61
The Major and the Gentle Giant

How might Leeds United have fared but for the Second World War? Would a continuous flow of new talent have replaced marketable assets such as Bert Sproston? The side had plenty of spine: Wilf Copping was back, 30, when war was declared; unyielding, fit and possibly good for five more years; while Tom Holley, a commanding centre half who joined Leeds from Sunderland in 1936, was 26, young enough to resume playing in peacetime. Wing halves Jimmy Makinson, 26, and Bobby Browne, 27, had a lot left in them, though never the natural gifts of Edwards and Copping.

But Eric Stephenson, whose star rose so quickly, was widely admired and the sort of player that Leeds might have cashed in; as was Aubrey Powell, 21, at the outbreak of war; and outside right David Cochrane, who made his debut aged 17 against Derby County in March 1938 after signing from Portadown for £2,000. Rich clubs would have hungered for Cochrane's pace and skill: he and Powell had an excellent understanding on the right flank.

The 1939-40 League season ran for a week before war was declared and the programme suspended. Leeds started poorly: three 1-0 defeats left them propping up the division. In the last of these, at home to Sheffield United, right back Jim Milburn made his debut, only for his League career to go on hold for six years.

With contracts suspended and players liable for conscription, there began various regional competitions and knock-out tournaments. Elland Road had the air of a barracks after being requisitioned by the War Office for administrative purposes. The Regional League north-east division, in which Leeds found themselves playing, was disrupted for two months from early January to March by one of the coldest winters of the century. By 1940-41, as the so-called phoney war ended and military conflict intensified, United's ranks were swollen by a bewildering number of guest players: 37 wore the colours that season; more than 50 during 1941-42; over 70 in 1942-43. At times, the football, logistics and organization bordered on the farcical.

Leeds players called up to serve their country included the ill-fated Eric Stephenson, Wilf Copping, Bobby Browne, Tom Holley, Jim Milburn and Aubrey Powell. When the war ended, United's ranks still contained Powell, Cochrane, Milburn and Holley. But after enormous social upheaval, damage to grounds and with players still in uniform, a full League programme did not resume until 1946-47, though the FA Cup, with all ties two-legged, was reinstated. In 1945-46, Leeds played as one of 22 clubs in the Football League northern section. The team, still reliant on guest players, finished bottom after a series of defensive nightmares: an 8-2 defeat at Preston; 9-4 at Bradford. These were a bad omen.

Dismal League Resumption

Record crowds, long starved of public entertainment, flocked to see Hampson's team in meaningful action. They were sorely disappointed. Having crash-landed in the northern section competition, results grew ever worse in 1946-47. An abysmal collapse in the New Year brought only one victory. Leeds were manifestly the worst team in the division: their points total, 18, a record low; their away form, one draw and 20 defeats, the worst in history.

Every football club had endured six years of disruption – why had Leeds come off worst? For David Cochrane, the answer was simple. 'We didn't have enough good players.' But Aubrey Powell felt the statistics painted an unduly lurid picture. 'You couldn't put your finger on what was different,' he said. 'In some games we were very unlucky; we'd hit the post one minute then the other team would break away and score. After we'd played Wolves at Elland Road and lost 1-0, Billy Wright said "I can't understand what you're doing down there at the bottom".'

Wolves had finished third, a point behind Champions Liverpool; and in a third of matches, Leeds had lost only by the odd goal. The habit of defeat, however, seemed impossible to shrug off. Historically Leeds were always buoyant after relegation. But in 1947-48, still in a nose-dive, they finished 18th in Division Two, their lowest since entering the League.

Billy Hampson had quit after Leeds tumbled out of the First Division, serving briefly as chief scout. Willis Edwards, assistant trainer at the time, took over. Edwards was a benevolent figure but lacked the leadership qualities needed to effect a revival. He could be credited with giving centre forward Albert Wakefield a chance, which Wakefield repaid with 21 League goals in 37 games. But there was little else for the crowds, still consistently above 20,000, to cling to. After a year in charge, Edwards resigned, resuming as assistant trainer and staying at Elland Road for another 10 years.

While the club stumbled between financial crises, Sam Bolton, a wealthy

Elland Road hero Willis Edwards returned after the War as assistant trainer and spent a year as manager.

haulier and lifelong fan, was elected chairman in 1949. Among Bolton's first, most urgent jobs, was to find a manager who might stop the rot. The board's appointment of a controversial maverick, 64-year-old Major Frank Buckley, could be construed as desperation, inspiration, or a mixture of both.

For all that he was an egocentric self-publicist, Buckley was a consummate football man. A much-travelled centre half who had won a cap for England against Northern Ireland in 1914, he reached the rank of Major during the First World War. His principal managerial achievements had been at Wolves in the 1930s, whom he had transformed from Division Two strugglers into one of the country's strongest sides, League runners-up in 1938 and 39, when they were also FA Cup finalists.

At Wolves, Buckley had earned a reputation for being money-conscious and hatching profitable transfer deals. Leeds United's parlous financial state was one of his main concerns when Sam Bolton persuaded him to move from Notts County to Elland Road.

The Major's methods and peremptory military manners came as a shock to some. Aubrey Powell, who had heard alarming stories on the football grapevine about his abrasive style, was soon at odds. 'Billy Hampson and Willis Edwards were gentlemen, but Buckley had me in his office and said "I will make you loyal to this club". I told him that I always had been loyal,' Powell recalls. After this tart exchange and questioning of his commitment, Powell transferred to Everton for £10,000 in June 1948.

Yet if confrontation came naturally to the Major, often it worked in Leeds United's best interests. He looked to recruit players he knew, and to young talent. His immediate priorities were cutting costs and ensuring Leeds did not slide out of the Second Division.

New regulars for 1948-49 included a Scottish right back, Jimmy Dunn, wing half Tommy Burden, whom Buckley had known as a teenager at Wolves and was signed from Chester on Willis Edwards' recommendation, and a young centre forward, Len Browning.

Results in his first season were mediocre – Leeds finished 15th – but Buckley arrested the downward spiral. Burden was a shrewd, stabilizing influence, Dunn a solid right back; and Browning proved his worth with 13 goals in 24 League matches. As Buckley's hunt for youthful talent continued, Jack Pickard, United's scout in South Wales, invited a strapping teenager called John Charles, on Swansea Town's ground staff but untried in the first team, for a trial at Elland Road. Swansea's loss was Leeds United's monumental gain: Pickard had unearthed the greatest talent the Yorkshire club had ever known.

The postwar soccer boom showed no sign of abating. In 1949-50, Leeds United, tighter at the back though often lacking incisiveness up front, were pulling in 40,000 or more. The defensive unit of Dunn, Jim Milburn, right half Jim McCabe – signed from Middlesbrough in March 1948 – Charles and Burden had a solidity that had not been

Len Browning's strength and eye for goal earned him 44 goals in three seasons at Leeds, but Major Buckley surprisingly off-loaded him to Sheffield United in 1951.

seen for a long time. Six straight wins from late December to mid-February fostered dreams of promotion; and an FA Cup run worthy of the name kept the excitement bubbling.

For almost 30 years, Leeds' Cup form had been wretched and Wembley a distant utopia where it seemed they would never tread. More than 50,000 flocked to Elland Road for the fourth round against First Division Bolton Wanderers; a 1-1 draw played on a treacherously icy pitch. The heroics were reserved for the replay at Burnden Park where, on a quagmire and showing enormous resilience, Leeds overcame supposedly superior and often aggressive opponents 3-2 after extra-time.

Cup fever, a new phenomenon, saw 53,099 descend on Elland Road for the fifth round against Cardiff City, a less attritional contest which Leeds won 3-1 and was their passport for a quarter-final tie with

Arsenal at Highbury. They succumbed to a solitary goal from Reg Lewis but achieved a moral victory, digging in magnificently and harrying the Gunners until the last. 'We should never have lost,' says Len Browning. 'We could have gone on to win the Cup.'

The form of wingers David Cochrane and Harold Williams had much to do with rekindling Leeds as an attacking force. 'Cochrane was brilliant – he could dribble and was superb at crossing the ball,' says Browning. Williams joined Leeds having been their principal tormentor when Newport County won at Elland Road in the FA Cup third round a season earlier. Although his career was blighted by injuries, he gave Leeds excellent service until 1957, playing almost 230 games.

A late season dip in form wiped out prospects of returning to the First Division but, with Leeds finishing fifth, it was clear that Buckley was turning things around. The cup win at Bolton suggested that his fitness and training routines, some seemingly outlandish, were having an effect. He exhorted players to become two-footed, and had painful methods of ensuring that they learned to strike a ball properly. 'One exercise involved balancing a ball on bricks which were placed either side of it,' Len Browning recalls. 'You had to run up in gym shoes and then kick it. I missed – and I was off for a week.'

Buckley, then in his late 60s yet still vain about his own fitness, took a dim view of anyone who missed training, whatever the excuse. Bobby Forrest, an inside forward signed from Retford in December 1952, had found himself fog-bound one winter's day, unable to get a bus for his rail link from Doncaster to Leeds. 'Next day when I went in, he gave us a right roasting,' Forrest recalls. 'Then he said "D'you think you're fit?" He made a mark high on the wall and put his foot right up to it. He asked if I could reach it with my foot – and I couldn't.'

Sometimes the Major held dancing sessions on the pitch to improve co-ordination – 'a bloody comedy act' in the eyes of Harold Williams. Buckley became celebrated for trying to persuade players to take extract of monkey gland, the properties of which were said to enhance mental and physical powers. For the likes of Tommy Burden and Harold Williams, this was one eccentricity too many. Wartime service in the navy had made Williams heartily sick of injections – 'I didn't require needles up my backside to play football,' he says.

Major Buckley seemed almost the caricature of an army officer, rapping out orders as if on the parade ground, striding about Elland Road in brogues and Oxford bags, his small Welsh terrier, Bryn, beside him. While Leeds' best results drew extravagant praise from the

---

50 Greatest Players

DAVID COCHRANE Right winger

Joined Leeds: January 1937   **From:** Portadown

Debut: v Derby County, 26 March 1938

Appearances: 185   **Goals:** 32

Left Leeds: 1950 (retired)

Honours won with Leeds: 12 Northern Ireland caps

War interrupted a potent double act at Leeds: the almost telepathic understanding between right winger David Cochrane and inside forward Aubrey Powell.

Cochrane was an outside right of great natural talent, picked for Northern Ireland when only 18. 'He was very good on the ball and would always taken on full backs,' Powell recalls. 'He was very hard for defenders to read because he'd go close to them before switching direction – cutting inside as I went outside.'

Many of Cochrane's finest years were lost to war though during the hostilities he had games with several Irish clubs. He returned to Elland Road in peacetime, staying with Leeds until he retired from football – always exciting to watch even when playing in a struggling side.

---

manager, he was scathing when they fell below standard. One hapless reserve whose control the Major had found wanting was made to run about with a ball tied to his boot.

But for all his whims, Frank Buckley had been the man for a crisis. In 1950-51, Leeds again finished fifth, a season perhaps most significant for Buckley discovering that in John Charles, he had not only a brilliant centre half but potentially a devastating centre forward. Yet, as Charles recalls, he might never had been tried up front but for an injury crisis. 'The Major told me that he didn't have anyone else to put in. It was Easter Saturday and we got beaten 4-1 at

Manchester City. I hardly got a kick. But he said I'd have to play there again so he put me in against Hull City on Easter Monday. We won 3-0 and I scored twice. Next day, the Major said: "Well done, lad, you'll stay at centre forward".'

During 1951-52, Charles was absent from Elland Road for almost half the season doing National Service. The team finished sixth, yet

Great Matches

FA CUP FOURTH ROUND REPLAY   **Burnden Park, 1 February 1950**
Attendance 29,440

Bolton Wanderers 2   **Leeds United 3***

McShane   Dudley 2

Lofthouse   Browning

* after extra time

If any match demonstrated the progress Leeds had made under Buckley, this was it. Leeds had, at times, struggled to contain their First Division opponents during the 1-1 draw at Elland Road. The replay at Bolton, on a vile pitch covered in icy pools, was an unappetizing prospect.

For Leeds, this victory was all the more joyous because it looked, having lost a two-goal lead, as if the game would slip away. Leeds went 1-0 up after two minutes when Dudley finished a good passing move involving Burden and Williams. Crisp finishing by Dudley gave Leeds a two-goal lead on 48 minutes but by the 70th, Bolton had stormed back to wipe out the deficit.

Leeds held out for the rest of the 90 minutes and then rallied in extra-time. The decisive goal came when Dudley snapped up Browning's headed deflection from a Charles free kick. And what they had, they managed to hold.

Buckley was unstinting in his praise. 'I've seen some wonderful displays of cup football on bad pitches, but United's was the best ever. Their spirit was wonderful. The way they fought back from losing a 2-0 lead amazed even me.' The *Yorkshire Post*'s Richard Ulyatt was also impressed. 'United's defence was quicker to the man on the ball. John Charles played as if on a dry lawn, Milburn was the best full back and Burden the best wing half,' he wrote.

Bolton Wanderers: Hanson, Roberts, R. Banks, Barrass, Gillies, Howe, McShane, Moir, Lofthouse, Bradley, Langton.

Leeds United: Searson, Dunn, Milburn, McCabe, Charles, Burden, Cochrane, Iggleden, Browning, Dudley, Williams.

Referee: E. Plinston (Warrington).

there was the sense of a plateau having been reached. 'We were good but we needed one or two more players, particularly play-maker inside forwards,' says Len Browning. By mid-season, he had become another on Buckley's roll call of profitable deals, transferred to Sheffield United for £12,000 after being replaced, to his own puzzlement and that of some fans, by Frank Fidler, signed from Wrexham in 1950. Fidler's lifetime at centre forward lasted only until Charles returned to the fold.

It was widely believed that Buckley was getting a cut from his various deals. 'He told me that Sheffield United were keen,' says Browning. 'He also told me there was few pounds in it for me if I went, which was all very illegal. But I had no argument; I was out of the team and Sheffield United were a good side.'

John Charles playing 'as if on a dry lawn' in the FA Cup replay against Bolton.

Buckley's gift for selling at top price and finding good bargains remained constant. In 1949 he had signed wing half Eric Kerfoot for £3,000 from Stalybridge Celtic who became one of the most consistent players of the 1950s. A year earlier he had discovered Grenville Hair, a 17-year-old left back, playing local league football in Burton on Trent. In 1951-52, Hair had become a mainstay replacing Jim Milburn, long a pillar of Leeds' defence and one whose rasping tackles were not to be taken lightly. Most of Leeds' problems lay in attack where the only reliable finisher was Ray Iggleden, scorer of 19 goals in 41 League matches. No-one else managed double figures.

The incisive wing play of David Cochrane and Harold Williams had brought some of Leeds' most exhilarating moments under Buckley. But Cochrane, who lost many good years to the war, had retired early in 1950-51, and injuries beset Williams: a broken leg, sustained in November 1952 during the 2-2 draw at Everton, kept him out for the rest of the season. The 1952-53 campaign became one of turning points: John Charles' monumental presence at centre forward brought 26 goals in 42 League matches yet Leeds drifted down the table to tenth place. They were never promotion material and had just one away victory, at Plymouth Argyle, mid-season.

As the season ended, Major Buckley had reached 70. There few signs of any sharpness deserting him but he felt, as had his predecessors Arthur Fairclough and Dick Ray, that he had done as much at Leeds United as the meagre budget would allow. He was a mercurial innovator, something of a martinet, financially ingenious and often unpredictable. Football had never seen anything like him.

His successor, Raich Carter, was one of the finest inside forwards of the 1930s and 40s, blessed with a mastery of the ball and first capped for England in 1934 while playing for Sunderland. Carter made the last of 13 appearances in 1947 after moving to Derby, with whom he won the FA Cup in 1946. He had managed Hull City before being enticed to Elland Road. He had in common with Frank Buckley, as his new charges soon found out, an absolute confidence in his own ability.

Carter had inherited a sound, unfancy crop of players and, in John Charles, a genius that big clubs were clamouring to sign. Charles, in 1953-54, plundered 42 goals in 39 games.

From 1950-58 the reliable Eric Kerfoot missed only a handful of first-team games.

In all, the team scored 99 times; but without Charles at centre half conceded 81. Leeds needed two of him. Despite all previous scoring records having been smashed, they finished tenth, as in 1952-53.

Leeds United's shaky start to 1954-55 emphasized Carter's dilemma over John Charles; and matters came to a head following a shambolic 5-3 defeat at Bury. It was a match of recrimination and ramifications that led to the re-deployment of Charles at centre half and the departure of Tommy Burden.

Burden, a popular captain and able wing half, knew his own mind and had a strong sense of injustice. While used to Major Buckley, he had little time for Raich Carter. Burden's career at Elland Road – where he had commuted from his home in Somerset – ended after a shouting match that resulted from Leeds' erratic afternoon at Gigg Lane. 'Carter wouldn't let you argue,' says Burden. 'We'd conceded a

---

50 Greatest Players

ERIC KERFOOT Wing half

Joined Leeds: December 1949 **From:** Stalybridge Celtic

Debut: v Queens Park Rangers, 17 December 1949

Appearances: 349   **Goals:** 10

Left Leeds: July 1959   **For:** Chesterfield

Honours won with Leeds: None

Kerfoot, another bargain discovered by Major Frank Buckley, was a latecomer to league football – 25 when he arrived at Elland Road; 26 before he became a first-team regular. But the wait did him no harm at all: he became one of Leeds United's most solid, consistent wing halves.

In the mid-1950s, he was an ever-present for three consecutive seasons: good on the ball with an awareness and enthusiasm for the game that marked him out as a future captain. His distribution was excellent and, although slightly built, he was a driving force at the heart of the team. A quick cigarette before the game, nipped out and put into a matchbox, never seemed to damage Kerfoot's fitness.

Kerfoot prospered under Major Buckley and Raich Carter but had no time for the methods of Bill Lambton, and, towards the end of his career at Leeds, was at the centre of a players' rebellion before leaving for Chesterfield in 1959.

goal from a free kick at Bury and he was blaming the goalkeeper Jack Scott. I thought "This isn't fair," so I said "You're the one who's bloody well to blame". We fell out.'

The problem of where best to play Charles became overshadowed by efforts to keep him. He wanted to test himself in the First Division and put in a written transfer request. Arsenal and Cardiff immediately declared an interest, but the board resisted using Charles as a cash crop.

Charles accepted the rejection of his request with equanimity, resumed business at centre half and, after losing five of their first six matches, Leeds began storming up the table. While there was no substitute for Charles up front, Carter used to good effect other forwards he had inherited: Bobby Forest; George Meek, a diminutive Scottish winger who had arrived a few months earlier from Hamilton; Albert Nightingale, a tigerish player well able to take care of himself and sort out opponents; and a signing of his own, 32-year-old Harold Brook, who cost just £600 from Sheffield United.

Great Managers –1948-53

MAJOR FRANK BUCKLEY

Major Frank Buckley is one of football's legendary names. In the 1930s he transformed Wolves from Second Division mediocrity to championship runners-up. A brilliant assessor of potentially great young players, he excelled in the transfer market. Buckley also had a great tactical knowledge and an intuitive feel for the game.

After spells at Notts County and Hull, Major Buckley arrived at Leeds in 1948. Through a clearout of players, raising admission prices at Elland Road, and astute transfer dealing – Burden, Hair, Kerfoot were among his recruits – Buckley was to steady the club's fragile finances. But his real legacy to the club was discovering and nurturing the great John Charles.

An idiosyncratic character who would often turn up to training with his little Welsh terrier, Buckley enriched the club without bringing success on the park. After leaving Elland Road, the Major managed Walsall until retiring in June 1955.

Leeds finished 1954-55 with a rare surge that took them to fourth. But this upturn did not transfer seamlessly into the new campaign: while often good to watch, and winning more than they lost in the first two months, Carter's team was still undermined by defensive frailties. Nor were the goals flowing as he would have liked.

It was time for another gamble. Charles was thrown forward once again and Jack Charlton, a 20-year-old centre half who had played just two games in the previous three seasons, pitched in at number five. A long time would elapse before Charlton became a linchpin of a watertight defence but Charles immediately began devouring the opposition. Harold Williams, who had made a fine recovery from his broken leg, was stricken by injury once more, a damaged

Raich Carter and his team celebrate a 4-1 victory at Hull and the end of a nine-year exile from the First Division.

cruciate ligament, allowing Jack Overfield, a swift capable left winger capable of taking on defenders in twos and threes, into the side. Meek, on the right flank, lacked Overfield's trickery and Williams' craft, especially in crossing, but compensated with unstinting effort and boundless energy. Carter had also promoted to the first team wing half Archie Gibson, signed from Scotland in 1951. Gibson was a tireless competitor with a good touch who combined many of the qualities of Burden and Kerfoot.

With 1955-56 past the three-quarters stage, few would have backed Leeds to go up. A run of mid-season inconsistency seemed destined to keep them in the Second Division until a crushing 6-1 victory over

Fulham on 2 April sparked another late charge. On the back of six straight wins, Leeds finally regained First Division status, the crucial turning point a 2-1 defeat of promotion rivals Bristol Rovers at Elland Road, watched by almost 50,000 and where Leeds came from behind to win with goals from Charles and Overfield. A 4-1 win at Hull City in the last match of the season, witnessed by hordes of euphoric camp followers, was enough to clinch promotion.

John Charles had finally got to play at the top level. But with generosity of spirit, he insisted it had been a team effort. 'The four people in the middle, the wing halves and inside forwards did all the work; they were the bees,' he said. 'We gelled; there was a good team spirit. Nobody was any better than anyone else.'

This patently was not so. But others agree about the team spirit. 'It was one big laugh in the dressing room and John Charles was one of the lads,' says Bobby Forrest. These were, with a maximum wage still in force, unworldly, communal times: a Friday night out for Bobby Forrest was going to the cinema with Jimmy Dunn and sharing a packet of wine gums. On Sunday mornings, players left their team houses on the Heaths estate near Elland Road to have a hot bath at the ground; and then perhaps to play snooker.

Raich Carter kept faith with his united band as Leeds took on the First Division. Their 5-1 home win over Everton on opening day, while a great boost to morale, came at a price: Albert Nightingale, one of the industrious forwards lauded by Charles, took a blow on the knee that ended his League career after playing more than 130 games. Described by team-mates as a 'hard bugger', a 'character' and a 'crowd pleaser', he had enormous stamina, an eye for goal, and was renowned for looking after himself. Bobby Forrest, less ebullient, though able to pass a sweet ball, took his place for much of the season.

The team, despite its proneness to off-days, had soared towards the top of the table by late September, with Charles averaging a goal a game. Bobby Forrest, for one, found the higher level to his liking. 'In the Second Division you had to really battle but in the First you had more time to play,' he said.

But any delight the club directors may have felt at Leeds' form was soon tempered by a devastating fire that consumed the West Stand on the night of 18 September 1956. Kit, club records, office accommodation: all went up in smoke. For ensuing home games, players had to change at the sports ground of Petty's, a local printing firm, be bussed to the ground then pick their way through the wreckage of twisted metal to the pitch.

Great Matches

FOOTBALL LEAGUE DIVISION TWO **Boothferry Park, 28 April 1956**
Attendance 31,123

Hull City 1   **Leeds United 4**
Martin   Charles 2
         Brook 2

Raich Carter's players had lived on their nerves for a week. If it meant deliverance from the Second Division after nine years, any win would do; but, as time went on, Leeds summoned the emphatic style that had characterized their splendid run-in. Hull, however, who had spent the season battling to avoid relegation, never made it easy; and at times were the better side.

Once again, John Charles made the difference: his brilliant individual goal on five minutes, a run and shot from near the halfway line, gave Leeds a priceless early advantage. It didn't last long: when Hull equalized eight minutes later with a goal from Tommy Martin, Leeds were suddenly in a battle. Hull were not going to leave the Second Division quietly.

On the hour came the turning point: George Meek was felled in the penalty area and Charles thumped home the spot-kick. Having finally got a grip, Leeds cut loose: twice Charles prompted Meek to sweep down the wing, and from the diminutive winger's excellent work, Harold Brook was on hand to score the third and fourth in the 78th and 80th minutes.

Raich Carter was upbeat about the prospects. Apart from the mighty Charles, there was real cohesion in the side. 'I have a team which is young and at least seven or eight players will improve,' he said.

Hull City: Fisher, Harrison, Jensen, Davidson, Berry, Bulless, Stephens, Martin, Bradbury, Clarke, Fraser.
Leeds United: Wood, Dunn, Hair, Ripley, Charlton, Kerfoot, Meek, Charles, Brook, Williams, Overfield.
Referee: T. Wood (Bury).

The stand had been drastically under-insured. The damage was estimated at £100,000 and the fact that they were around £60,000 short came to dictate the next chapter of the club's history. Yet in the short term, Leeds continued to meet the First Division on equal terms: their vibrant form dipped after New Year but they finished eighth with 44 points, in a comfort zone from which they could expect to prosper.

Goalkeeper Roy Wood was virtually an ever-present in the mid-50s Leeds' line-up.

Inevitably the season seemed all about John Charles who had scored 38 goals in 40 matches. But Charles was finally to be on his way. A new West Stand had been priced at £130,000 and while Leeds had fended off all previous bids for their star, the Italian club Juventus had offered £65,000. The fire forced the directors' hands. Yet, although swayed by the prospect of receiving match bonuses up to £500 (almost a player's annual wage in England), Charles would have been content to stay. 'Leeds was my team – I loved the place,' he said.

Juventus wanted Charles as a centre forward but some team-mates felt he was better at centre half where he was indomitable in the air and he distributed the ball with such assurance. 'He had no weaknesses. He had two great feet. He did all the simple things, and he did them well,' says Harold Williams. 'In my view, there has never been any player as good.' Charles' record in Italy, three championships, a cup winner's medal and being voted Footballer of the Year, is strong supporting evidence.

John Charles took with him volumes of goodwill and a new scoring record: 157 in 327 matches. The 1957-58 season was to be a stern test of the journeymen colleagues of whom he spoke so warmly. There was an enormous hole to be filled but Raich Carter had only half the

Whether at centre half or centre forward,
John Charles' presence transformed the side.

money from the Charles deal for a replacement.

He gambled £12,000 on centre forward Hughie Baird, a prolific scorer with Airdrie who had played for Scotland the previous year. His tally of 20 goals in 39 League games was respectable enough but no-one else managed double figures. Bobby Forrest, the next highest scorer with seven, was no marksman. 'Goals weren't my strength at all,' he says. 'I took a bit of stick from the crowd and the game's all about confidence. I had some good games but I had some stinkers as well.'

While the doughty old rearguard was still doing its stuff, Charles was, as Carter had realized, irreplaceable. Statistics told the story: 73 goals conceded, exactly as in 1956-57 but only 51 scored compared with 72.

It seemed rough justice to blame Carter for Leeds' slide to 17th but the directors decided not to renew his contract. This was the first of several false moves that would plunge the club into crisis. Appointing coach Bill Lambton as Carter's successor, but at first only on a temporary basis, smacked of indecision. Lambton was, in time, confirmed in the job, yet within months had resigned, claiming he had been undermined by criticisms of his methods.

Lambton was the first postwar Leeds manager not to have achieved either playing or managerial success at the top level. He was a fitness fanatic and pre-war had been a goalkeeper on Nottingham Forest's books. Not everyone was convinced he knew much about football.

He was, in Jimmy Dunn's eyes, 'a bloody comedian who had no experience'; yet Bobby Forrest was grateful to Lambton for making him fitter. 'His philosophy was that you "trained hard and played light" – so we trained in track suits with thick trainers and a couple of pullovers,' Forrest says. 'But one silly thing he did was having us play five-a-sides in spiked shoes so we'd play the ball first time – we were all trying not to go too near anyone.'

Perhaps a macho sense of insecurity had led Lambton one day in training to take off his boots and tell players they didn't need them when crossing a ball. Whatever, the players' reaction was scornful. 'Eventually we had a meeting about him,' says Jimmy Dunn. 'It was a rebellion. It boiled down to the fact that he couldn't manage the club.'

New Faces

As discontent rumbled, Grenville Hair and Jack Overfield slapped in transfer requests. Lambton meanwhile, in search of his own men, imported inside forward Don Revie from Sunderland and, following Baird's departure to Aberdeen after little more than a season, Alan Shackleton, a centre forward from Burnley. Few could grumble about Shackleton's return of 16 goals in 28 League games. But the defence, populated by ageing rebels such as Dunn and Kerfoot, was growing creaky. New faces were appearing: Jimmy Ashall at right back, who had largely been confined to reserve football since signing as a teenager in 1955 and Wilbur Cush, a utility player bought from Glenavon for £7,000 in December 1957.

Revie's arrival had a more profound significance than anyone could have imagined. Short term, it hastened the departure of Bobby Forrest. 'Don took my place and I never got back in the team,' he says. 'I'd never wanted to go anywhere else but Bill Lambton called me into the office one day and said "I've got Notts County wanting to talk to you". Don had come in November 1958 and I joined County in March 1959.'

Revie, a player of greater pedigree though past his best, put in some stylish performances and was made team captain. But the team was labouring in the lower reaches and as disquiet with Lambton reached a crescendo, the manager resigned in March. After he had gone, citing 'interference from directors in my training methods', Leeds won three and drew one of their final four matches, a vital run of form that ensured 15th place and ultimate survival.

The struggle Leeds had in finding a new manager to replace Lambton typified the malaise that had enveloped Elland Road. Arthur Turner, manager of Headington United, was approached but preferred prospects in the Southern League. A trawl through the lower divisions eventually netted Jack Taylor, a full back in Frank Buckley's illustrious Wolves team of the 1930s, and then manager, without notable success, for almost a decade at Queen's Park Rangers.

Since the sacking of Raich Carter, there appeared to be an absence of any strategic planning – the club had muddled along. But at least it had hung on in the First Division. The new season, though, saw Leeds without two great stalwarts, Jimmy Dunn, veteran of 422 League matches, and Eric Kerfoot, who played 336.

As ever, Jack Taylor had a pittance with which to rebuild and his plans were undermined by a crop of injuries: Revie, Overfield, Hair, Cush and Meek were just some of the casualties during 1959-60. When Alan Shackleton, Taylor's main target man, left for Everton with the season two games old, Taylor's first priority was to find another centre forward. He quickly signed John McCole, a prolific scorer with Bradford City, and an instinctive finisher who maintained his good strike rate at Elland Road.

Without money to throw around, Leeds had, under Lambton, begun developing the talents of local teenagers. They also signed a Scotland schoolboy winger, Tommy Henderson, who had arrived in 1959, left because he was homesick, but returned in 1962. For Leeds, the most significant thing about Henderson was his friendship with another Scots hopeful, Billy Bremner. Bremner, who came from Stirling, had barely heard of Leeds United before Henderson's involvement with the Yorkshire club, and was expecting to join Celtic. Instead, he was plucked from under Celtic's nose by Leeds

50 Greatest Players

JOHN CHARLES Centre half/centre forward

Joined Leeds: 1948   **From:** Swansea Town

Debut: v Blackburn Rovers, 23 April 1949

Appearances: 327   **Goals:** 157

Left Leeds: May 1957   **For:** Juventus

Rejoined Leeds: August 1962

Left Leeds: October 1962   **For:** Roma

Honours won with Leeds: 24 Wales caps

When Major Buckley gave 17-year-old Swansea misfit John Charles a League debut at centre half in April 1949, few would have envisaged he had unearthed one of the world's best ever footballers.

Charles was a manager's dream: a colossus with a delicate touch: an infinite capacity for soaking up pressure; an exemplary team-mate. Whether played at centre half or centre forward he was peerless.

When Leeds were promoted to the First Division in 1956, Charles scored 29 times. Heading, shooting, tackling, positional awareness: he had it all. However the fire in 1956 that destroyed the West Stand forced his transfer to Juventus for a record £65,000. He won three Italian championship medals, was voted Italy's footballer of the year and starred in Wales' 1958 World Cup adventure before Revie brought him back to Leeds in August 1962 for £53,000.

But after five golden years in Italy, Charles, at 30, had little appetite for the grind of Second Division football or Les Cocker's arduous training methods. In 11 games he scored just three times before returning to Italy, signing for Roma for around £65,000 – business done quickly enough to prevent his legendary status being tarnished.

director Harry Reynolds who descended on the family home and exhorted him to come to Elland Road.

Don Revie, the wise old head, and Billy Bremner, the 17-year-old raw talent, first played together on 23 January 1960 in Leeds 3-1 victory at Stamford Bridge. Revie had taken Bremner under his wing, leading him on a pre-match walk to calm his nerves. Jack Taylor's team had been perennial strugglers but victory at Chelsea, the third in an unbeaten run of four matches, heralded the end of Leeds United's best winning sequence.

More young lads were being licked into shape by coach Syd Owen and trainer Les Cocker, whom Taylor had recruited from Luton Town. In among his dozens of charges were a handful of players who would become household names; but only after Leeds United had passed through one of their greatest crises. They were to emerge after Leeds had been relegated. The 1959-60 season held little cheer save for the precocious form of Bremner, McCole's goals and some sharp wing play by 20-year-old Chris Crowe, a former England youth international who had joined Leeds in 1954. But before the end, Crowe had jumped ship and signed for Blackburn Rovers for £25,000.

With relegation came the inevitable shake-out. It marked the end for Jack Overfield, sold to Sunderland, George Meek, despatched to Leicester and Wilbur Cush who returned to Portadown. New recruits included Eric Smith, a hard-tackling wing half from Celtic, and, in place of Overfield, ex-Sunderland man Colin Grainger. Meek's place at outside right was taken by Gerry Francis, a South African and among the first black players in Britain.

When relegated, Leeds had finished 21st with 34 points, They were never as adrift as in 1947 but the sense of hopelessness was no less marked. As Leeds made a fumbling start in Division Two, crowds plunged below 10,000. Injuries continued to plague the side: by the end of the season, 27 players had been tried. There was also a corrosive apathy at Elland Road. 'The players were undisciplined. That wasn't their fault – Taylor had let things go,' said Eric Smith.

Revie was among those infected by the widespread loss of form and confidence. He asked to be relieved of the team captaincy, which passed to left half Freddie Goodwin. But Revie's commitment remained and his intelligent

Plucked from under Celtic's nose, 17-year-old Billy Bremner made his debut in 1960.

views on the game had come to the attention of Harry Reynolds, a lifelong fan who had made his fortune through steel and was as shrewd as any man on the board.

By March 1961, Leeds were nearer the Third Division than the First. Four straight defeats were the final straw: Taylor was called before the board and told by Reynolds that he and the club should part company. He resigned on 13 March. With United all at sea and escape from a second successive relegation by no means assured, the need for a dynamic successor had never been more urgent.

Chapter Four: 1961-64
The Revie Revolution

Don Revie, at 33, also had a sense of his time being up at Elland Road, and was keen to try running a club himself. As Jack Taylor was being shown the door, Revie was applying for the vacant manager's job at Bournemouth. Harry Reynolds began writing a reference then paused. Why off-load one of Leeds United's most valuable assets? Reynolds never completed the letter. He got the board to offer Revie the Leeds job instead.

While Reynolds knew what he was doing, the public remained unconvinced. Many fans had wanted a bigger name. Instead of a charismatic leader, they had got a thinker. A foreword in the programme for Revie's first home match in charge, against Sheffield United on 25 March, gave a glimpse of the future. It spoke of Revie having 'many carefully formulated theories on how to get the best out of a team, and how to groom young players for the future'.

The new Leeds manager had always been a canny judge of whom he should listen to: planning and preparation had been drummed into him from his time with Middlesbrough Swifts and manager Bill Sanderson's Sunday tactics talks. Days after getting the Leeds job, Revie visited Old Trafford to seek practical advice from Matt Busby who told him to establish consistent coaching methods from the first team to the juniors.

Revie wanted to make a symbolic statement that would mark a break from the past and emphasize the club's ambition. So he changed the first-team strip from blue and gold to the plain all white of Real Madrid, Europe's greatest club side. But there were few similarities with Real Madrid on the pitch. Of nine remaining games in 1960-61, Revie's only victory was a 7-0 thrashing of doomed Lincoln City. The final home fixture, against Scunthorpe, drew fewer than 7,000. Leeds finished 14th, and there was no sign that things were going to be any better than under Jack Taylor. A monumental reconstruction job was needed.

Harry Reynolds – the Common Touch

Football club chairmen are rarely heroes. But the renaissance of Leeds United would never have happened without Harry Reynolds, a steel magnate brought up near Elland Road, who in his retirement lavished time and money on the club he had supported as a boy.

Reynolds, himself once a talented young footballer who had represented Leeds schoolboys, joined the board in 1955. He was a self-made man without formal education and began working life as a railway cleaner and fireman. When eventually he went into business, he built up a prosperous engineering and steel stockholding company from which he withdrew in 1959. He had seen what could be built up from almost nothing and dreamed of building Leeds into a great club.

Reynolds never forsook his common touch. He had a humane style, the principles of which he instilled in Don Revie. Everyone connected with Elland Road, from players' wives to cleaners, was made to feel important. Reynolds had also been quick to realize the demoralizing effect of penny-pinching. Once he took the chair, Leeds started to travel first class.

He was as persuasive as Revie in recruiting young players. Through a mixture of hard work, determination and charm they outmanoeuvred many a big club by luring some of the best talent to Elland Road. The success of their double-act was in convincing parents that their sons would be properly looked after.

Harry Reynolds succeeded Sam Bolton as chairman in December 1961 though for some time had been the board's most dynamic force. He put up around £50,000 – and other directors around £10,000 each – for Revie to strengthen the team. Sometimes on match days Reynolds could be found patrolling the turnstile queues and selling raffle tickets. He had even been known to step in among rowdy supporters on a train and restore order.

Arthritis eventually forced Reynolds to relinquish the job into which he had poured so much energy. By then he had realized his dream of making Leeds United a major force, and before his death in 1974, saw the team lift two League Championships, the FA Cup,

50 Greatest Players

DON REVIE Inside forward

Joined Leeds: November 1958   **From:** Sunderland

Debut: v Newcastle United, 29 November 1958

Appearances: 80   **Goals:** 12

Left Leeds: 1961 (became manager, left Leeds in 1974 to manage England)

Honours won with Leeds (as player): None

Middlesbrough-born Revie joined Leicester in 1944 where he developed as an inside forward before moving to Hull City five years later. Failing to impress manager Raich Carter, he moved to Manchester City in 1951 for £25,000 where 'the Revie Plan' inspired by the Hungarian international side utilized his positional awareness, passing ability and stamina as a deep-lying centre forward. Footballer of the year in 1955, Revie won six England caps and an FA Cup winner's medal before joining Sunderland in 1956. There his style and character soon put him out of favour with manager Allan Brown and in 1958, he signed for Leeds for £12,000. Still one of the most creative and skilful forwards around, he bolstered a struggling team and acted as a mentor to the younger players. He was a thoughtful, influential player but his destiny was to become a brilliant manager, drawing on all his talents and hard-learned lessons.

League Cup and the Fairs Cup. Without his money and paternalistic dedication, none of it would have been possible.

A Faltering Start

The team of 1961-62 began to bear Revie's stamp. But results suffered as the playing pattern was continually disrupted. The surprise return of John McCole to Bradford City in October robbed the team of its only recognized goalscorer. As an emergency, Jack Charlton was thrown up front mid-season; but he was no John Charles. Nor was inside forward Noel Peyton, in and out of the side since 1958, the sharp finisher they so badly needed. Injuries and loss of form forced Revie continually to tinker with the line-up; even to play himself.

The most consistent forward was Billy Bremner, playing either on the right wing or at inside right, and being carefully nurtured. Another

50 Greatest Players

BOBBY COLLINS Inside forward/midfielder

Joined Leeds: March 1962   **From:** Everton

Debut: v Swansea Town, 10 March 1962

Appearances: 167   **Goals:** 25

Left Leeds: February 1967   **Joined:** Bury

Honours won with Leeds: Division 2 Championship 1964; Footballer of the Year 1965; 3 Scotland caps

Collins' discontent with criticism from Everton manager Harry Catterick was Leeds' good fortune. Revie, desperate for an authoritative presence in his struggling side, was happy to pay the £25,000 that Collins cost Everton when signing from Celtic in 1958-59. The 5 foot 4 inch (1.60 m) formidable, sometimes frightening opponent, tackled like a demon, yet was a great player orchestrating the game and always liable to strike a defence-splitting long ball.

   With the grim struggle for Second Division survival won, Collins led Leeds on to the offensive and within three seasons marched them to the top of the First, an FA Cup final and into Europe. His renaissance became complete when recalled for Scotland in 1965. He was 35 when he broke a leg playing against Torino, yet recovered to make seven first-team appearances before being granted a free transfer to Bury.

source of hope was Albert Johanneson, the second, and more talented, of two black South African wingers signed by Leeds. Johanneson had much to learn about football and life in England, but his blistering pace and wonderful control would have graced any stage.

   The defence, with men such as Grenville Hair, Freddie Goodwin, Eric Smith and left back/wing half Willie Bell, signed from Queen's Park, was sturdy enough. But without authority and creative talent, the team was sinking fast. Revie was forced to buy in a hurry, though was sticking to his guns about youth. 'No player can possibly acquire the loyalty that all clubs need to the same degree as those that start with the club,' he said.

   Some signings seemed hard to fathom. Disquiet about the quality of cover in goal led Revie, on the recommendation of Stanley Matthews, to Tommy Younger, an overweight keeper aged 31 playing in Canada, formerly with Liverpool and Stoke, and a Scottish international. Younger arrived with a reputation for having a suspect temperament and fitness, though swore to do his best. Younger's word was his bond: he lost weight, wrested the goalkeeping slot from Alan Humphries and turned in some fine displays.

Revie tried to plug the gap left by McCole with Billy McAdams from Bolton, a former team-mate from Manchester City days, and a proven regular scorer. It wasn't the answer. With the season closing in and relegation to the Third Division looming,

Goalkeeper Tommy Younger's reputation as a slacker proved ill-founded.

Revie threw the dice again, signing centre forward Ian Lawson from Burnley for £20,000. But what he most needed was a commanding presence to inspire, bring order and pull threads together.

Revie's saviour, all 5 feet 4 (1.60 m) of him, was waiting over the Pennines at Everton: another Scotsman thought to be over the hill, yet consumed by the urge to prove everyone wrong. Bobby Collins, like the cavalry in some old Western, arrived at Elland Road just in time to lift the siege.

On the Brink of Division Three

If ever Collins had wanted a challenge, hauling Leeds United out of the relegation mire was it. He made an immediate impact scoring in Leeds' 2-0 home win over Swansea on 10 March 1962, the first victory for almost two months. But seven days later, Leeds, in the throes of a goalkeeping crisis, lost 4-1 at Southampton. With Tommy Younger ill and Alan Humphries unfit, Revie summoned 16-year-old Gary Sprake, one of his youthful protégés, brought to Elland Road by Jack Pickard, the scout who unearthed John Charles. It was an

50 Greatest Players

GRENVILLE HAIR Full back

Joined Leeds: November 1948 **From:** Newhall United

Debut: v Leicester City, 31 March 1951

Appearances: 474 **Goals:** 2

Left Leeds: May 1964 **For:** Wellington Town

Honours won with Leeds: None

Major Frank Buckley's unerring eye for young talent rarely failed him. Hair, whom Buckley spotted as a teenager playing local football in Burton on Trent, became one of the club's great mainstays through the 1950s and early 60s.

Hair was a full back of the old school who knew his trade and stuck to it. While he could pass, his role was to shut out the opposition. He was good in the air, and quick to anticipate danger. And, according to colleagues, could be a touch ruthless when needed.

He saw good and bad times during almost 16 years at Elland Road. Contemporaries held Hair in high esteem and some think had he been with a more fashionable club, he might been picked for England. He died an untimely death in March 1968 when, aged only 36 and managing Bradford City, he had a heart attack after supervising training.

unnerving debut for Sprake, flown down in haste on a chartered plane, but the defensive shambles could not be blamed on him alone. And then suddenly, amid the desperation, the defence began to tighten up. Collins had stiffened midfield and left back Cliff Mason, a last-minute signing from Sheffield United for £10,000, had an immediate impact. A less robust tackler than Grenville Hair, Mason had a good football brain and could anticipate probable sources of danger. Leeds were becoming meaner and smarter; and in the nick of time, for the relegation dogfight was intensifying.

A chronic inability to score still threatened their survival despite eight unbeaten matches after the Southampton debacle. But six of these were draws, and when Leeds headed off to St James' Park, for the final match against Newcastle, the stakes were enormous: if they lost, and Bristol Rovers won at Luton, Elland Road would be hosting Third Division football for the first time ever. In the event, Leeds won

Great Matches

FOOTBALL LEAGUE DIVISION TWO **St James' Park, 28 April 1962**
Attendance 21,708

Newcastle United 0 **Leeds United 3**
Johanneson
McAdams
Keith (o.g.)

With a swirling wind, on a bumpy pitch and the home team strangely absent-minded and error-prone, Leeds made their final push for survival. Yet ultimately, they survived, in the view of *Yorkshire Post* journalist Eric Stanger, with almost ridiculous ease. Newcastle had been inept hosts.

Still, the job had to be done. The astonishing thing was that with the stakes so high, Leeds played as if they didn't have a care in the world, even though it took 37 minutes to score as Johanneson's shot from McAdams' pass went in off the bar.

On 65 minutes Leeds scored a second from the same combination, McAdams heading home from Johanneson's lofted centre. A spectacular own-goal from Bobby Keith ten minutes later sealed things and ensured Leeds' survival.

Collins again was outstanding, driving his men forward, as was Willie Bell, playing as an auxiliary inside left; and Albert Johanneson had one of his finest games. But the key to survival was the vastly improved defence; Mason had been worth his weight in gold, and Charlton had rediscovered his best form.

It was a victory which, as Revie and Reynolds embraced in ecstatic relief, would alter the course of football history; though greeted satirically by a cartoon in the *Yorkshire Evening Post*. 'Aren't we lucky,' said one flat-capped fan to another. 'Now we can look forward to another exciting season of second-class soccer.' Little did cynics know what the future held.

Newcastle United: Hollins, Keith, Clish, Wright, Thompson, Turner, Day, Kerray, Thomas, Allchurch, Fell.

Leeds United: Younger, Hair, Mason, Goodwin, Charlton, Smith, Bremner, Collins, McAdams, Hawksby, Johanneson.

Referee: J. Fellows (Chorley).

with ease. A 3-0 scoreline included goals from Johanneson, McAdams and an own goal by Newcastle's Bobby Keith.

1962-63 was the season of the big freeze, the grand return of John Charles and the revival: above all, and in unspectacular fashion, the forging of English football's most durable backbone.

Bringing back Charles, now 31, from Juventus was an extravagant flourish that made headline news but little impact long-term. The great Welshman, signed for £53,000, twice the cost of any previous Leeds player, seemed lethargic and distracted. With the season less than three months old, he was sold back to Italy – and at a profit, for Roma were willing to pay £65,000.

Charles admits he was not the player of old. 'I had a bit of personal trouble at the time and it worried me,' he said. Nor did returning to Italy work out – 'I took a chance but I didn't really like it – I didn't care for Rome.'

Youthful Reserves

Amid the Charles episode, Leeds were faltering. Collective weaknesses shown in an early 2-1 home defeat against Bury drove Revie to make fundamental changes and draw on his youthful reserves. For the next game at Swansea on 8 September 1962, Gary Sprake, his confidence knocked after the trauma at Southampton, was recalled. Revie also gambled on a promising young centre forward, Rod Johnson. At right back and left half respectively, two more rookies were thrown in: Paul Reaney and Norman Hunter.

Sprake, Reaney, Charlton, Hunter; and, at inside right, Bremner: together for the first time and destined, collectively, to make around

3,500 appearances for Leeds United. Fourteen years later, Reaney, Bremner and Hunter were still turning out, in the evening of their Titanic careers. For Johnson, it was a different story. He scored on his debut – Leeds won 2-0 – but was injured and never held down a regular first-team place.

Norman Hunter was 18 and Paul Reaney 17: Revie had never intended bedding them

Jack Charlton, once a member of the awkward squad, matured into one of England's finest centre halves.

50 Greatest Players

ALBERT JOHANNESON Left winger

Joined Leeds: April 1961   **From:** South Africa

Debut: v Swansea Town, 8 April 1961

Appearances: 202   **Goals:** 67

Left Leeds: July 1970   **For:** York City

Honours won with Leeds: Division 2 Championship 1964

Johanneson had miraculous tricks in his boots and a devastating turn of speed. With more self-belief, he might have been one of the great left-sided flank players. He arrived in 1961 from South Africa with the club at a low ebb. There had been few black players in English football, and at times he suffered racial abuse from opposing players and fans.

Johanneson made an immediate impact on his debut, despatching a sweet centre for Jack Charlton to head home. He was a wizard in the driven Leeds team that won the Second Division Championship in 1963-64 and scored a masterpiece on Easter Monday 1964 against Newcastle United, controlling a long through pass and side-stepping three players before slipping the ball past the goalkeeper.

His career at Leeds was cut short first by injury, then by the emergence of Eddie Gray; and in 1970, he left for York City. If the rest of Johanneson's story is of a sad decline and fall into lonely alcoholism, he had earned his place in history as one of the rare footballers who offered something different. Johanneson died in September 1995.

into the side so soon, yet once in, they were never out. Meanwhile the failure of the John Charles experiment thrust an unexpected weight on Jim Storrie, a £15,000 signing from Airdrie. At under 5 feet 9 (1.64 m), Storrie was small for a centre forward; but he was a fearless, hustling committed team player and often hard to contain. His tally of 25 League goals in 1962-63 was the best since John Charles' in 1956.

As the season unfolded, the team began to look more settled. But Revie still went out on a limb with his young lads: at Southampton, on 29 September 1962, Peter Lorimer, at 15 years 289 days, became the youngest player ever to pull on a Leeds jersey. Lorimer had been run to ground by Revie and Reynolds at his family home in Dundee, woken in the middle of the night with alluring promises and a contract for signing. His feats in junior football had fuelled a gold rush of managers: Lorimer had scored 176 goals for his school.

Jimmy Greenhoff, another prodigy, was just 16 when he played at right half for the last two games of the season. By then, and after football had been frozen out for more than two months by one of the worst winters on record, Leeds had ploughed through a hectic schedule in style. A last-minute loss of form in May – three successive defeats – cost them the chance of promotion. It might have come too soon: the team had a strong spine but was still raw and rough at the edges.

More wise heads were needed. In the close season, Revie made another inspired purchase, paying FA Cup winners Manchester United £35,000 for outside right Johnny Giles. For all the success at Old Trafford, Giles felt under-valued and his antennae, even without Revie's hard sell, told him that things were stirring over in Leeds. His arrival solved another problem: Bremner had long clamoured for a more central role, and when, switched to number four, could unleash his talent in midfield.

Another piece of the jigsaw.
Snapping up Johnny Giles was
a Revie masterstroke.

Revie's class of 1963-64 had a ferocious will to win: with Collins and Bremner stoking the fires, it could hardly have been otherwise. The crowds – 30,000 or more – were flocking back. Sometimes the football wasn't pretty. Jim Storrie was the chief casualty of a bruising Christmas encounter at Sunderland and played just two more games all season; Freddie Goodwin's career ended when he broke a leg after colliding with John Charles in a third round FA Cup tie at Cardiff; and Jack Charlton missed a third of the campaign after injury in the home match with Charlton in November.

Great Matches

FOOTBALL LEAGUE DIVISION TWO

The Vetch Field, 11 April 1964
Attendance 14,321

Swansea Town 0   **Leeds United 3**
Peacock 2
Giles

It looked all over well before half-time: two goals from Alan Peacock and one from Johnny Giles meant Leeds were going up. The prospect of Swansea, battling against relegation, scoring three, or more, against the meanest defence in the division was unthinkable.

This was among the finest of Leeds United's 12 away wins during the 1963-64 season. Sharp finishing by Peacock and Giles, gave Leeds the cushion they needed. In the second half, Leeds retreated, with Collins and Terry Cooper, making his debut on the left wing, playing deeper as Swansea pressed feverishly, forcing Sprake into several fine saves.

Euphoria swept the Leeds camp at full-time. It signalled a remarkable transformation in fortunes; also a fine debut by Cooper who showed great spirit and composure.

The champagne, however, had not been put on ice: Revie was not a man to tempt fate. So he and his players still had work to do after full-time, scouring the pubs of Swansea in search of bubbly to sustain them on the train ride home.

Swansea Town: Dwyer, R. Evans, Hughes, Johnson, Purcell, Williams, Jones, Draper, Thomas, McLaughlin, B. Evans.

Leeds United: Sprake, Reaney, Bell, Bremner, Charlton, Hunter, Giles, Weston, Peacock, Collins, Cooper.

Referee: N. Matthews (Bicester).

By Christmas, Revie's men were top, locked in a promotion battle with Sunderland and Preston. But in the New Year, Leeds began sagging for the want of a cutting edge up front, where Ian Lawson and Don Weston, signed in December 1962 from Rotherham, were doing the donkey work. While Weston was quick and Lawson an industrious target man, the goals were drying up. In his anxiety for more clout, Revie lavished £55,000, a record for Leeds, on Middlesbrough's Alan Peacock.

Peacock's aerial threat and ability to link up with play were priceless. His career was blighted by injury, but when fit Peacock, an

England international, was a formidable centre forward. He was the right man at the right time: by early March, his powerful presence was helping Leeds shrug off their stuttering form. Revie's men had won six and drawn one of the previous seven matches before the bandwagon descended on Swansea on 11 April. Victory at the Vetch Field would mean promotion.

The Championship duly followed. And when Leeds clinched the title with a 2-0 victory at Charlton, they had broken many a record: most points in a season (63), most away victories (12) and fewest defeats (three). The revolution was underway: Revie's Leeds were ready for anything and anybody.

18-year-old Gary Sprake's 17 clean sheets in 1963-64 were instrumental in Leeds' record-breaking season.

Chapter Five: 1964-70
Bruises and Brilliance

'We were young, we were cocky and we weren't the most attractive to watch.' Such was Billy Bremner's honest view of the team – during their promotion season, he and his colleagues received more cautions than any other. But Revie was determined there should be no let-up: the Leeds manager's talk in 1964-65 was of winning the league.

Nothing was left to chance. Syd Owen had begun the ritual of studying opponents in minute detail and drawing up detailed dossiers on every player. Revie came to regard these almost as religious tracts; his players less so. They relied more on a one for all and all for one mentality, repaying hostilities with interest and breathing down the neck of the referee; but on skill also.

Straight wins over Aston Villa, Champions Liverpool, and Wolves made Leeds the unexpected early front runners, and seemed to justify Revie's decision to stick with the promotion squad. Their form then became erratic through September but by early October, a 3-2 win at Stoke, marked by Jimmy Greenhoff's first league goal, set Leeds off on a prodigious run that would propel them to the threshold of the League Championship and FA Cup double.

As ever, there was turbulence along the way. In October 1964, Revie, although only halfway through a three-year contract, almost defected to richer pastures at Everton. Following a demonstration by fans and an intervention by Harry Reynolds, recovering in hospital after a car crash, the Leeds United board gave Revie the rise he was angling for. After this messy business was settled the team began its run of storming form.

While an injury to Peacock meant that Leeds lacked their best target man for most of the season, Storrie, Johanneson, Collins and Giles provided ample goals. Controversy, meanwhile, was never far away. The First Division saw few games more rancorous than the battle at Goodison Park on 7 November 1964, which left almost everyone with wounds to lick and in which Everton's Sandy Brown was sent off in the first five minutes for a foul on Giles.

The score – 1-0 to Leeds – following a first-half header from Willie Bell was almost incidental. With fearsome tackles flying in and cushions being hurled from the stands on to the pitch, referee Roger Stokes took the teams off in the 35th minute to calm everyone down and restore order.

But if redneck tactics became habitual for Don Revie's men, so did winning – even in the FA Cup where their form had been so wretched over the years. With victories over Southport, Everton, Shrewsbury Town and Crystal Palace, Leeds reached the semi-final for the first time, drawing Manchester United, their rivals for the League title.

Victory at Old Trafford

Matt Busby could have been forgiven for thinking that he had spilled too many secrets in his tutorial with the apprentice Leeds manager four years earlier. Revie had repaid him by winning 1-0 at Old Trafford on 5 December, and then, after two heavyweight contests, putting Manchester United out of the FA Cup.

These matches showed Leeds in all their colours. The first, at Hillsborough, had been one of many dour, spoiling goalless draws associated with Revie's men, played on a gluepot of a pitch and shot through with fouls and niggles. The replay, at the City Ground, Nottingham, was a thriller, wherein Leeds survived a long onslaught, gradually wrested the initiative and won at the death with a flashing header from Billy Bremner. Leeds had shown nerve, character, strength and technique: all their best qualities.

By 1965 Jack Charlton had already seen ten seasons in the first team and was the senior player in the side.

But Manchester United had the last laugh. In a summit meeting at Elland Road on 17 April, a match watched by more than 52,000 and on which the destiny of the League title was to rest, Revie's men seemed gripped with apprehension. It was a taut, cagey encounter, but in losing to a daisycutter of a shot from John Connelly, Leeds took a knockout blow. While statistics suggest the title race was close to the end, with Manchester United winning only on goal average, that defeat, followed two days later by a 3-0 beating at Sheffield Wednesday, killed off hopes of the double.

Revie's tense demeanour and brooding superstitious nature sometimes infected his players. Physically and mentally, some were in poor shape for the FA Cup final against Liverpool. Although Leeds had achieved so much so quickly, the team and its fans were unused to moving in high places. As the team coach drove along Wembley way Jack Charlton noted that Leeds supporters seemed almost invisible; the precincts of Wembley dominated by Liverpool's red. He was filled with a sense of foreboding.

A 2-1 defeat after extra time epitomized the so-near-yet-so-far nature of Leeds United's finest season. Bobby Collins' selection as Footballer of the Year was a testimony to everyone's achievement. For the next decade, the team would contest one or more of the domestic and European trophies: the strongest, sternest and eventually the most fluent side in the land, yet often undone by outrageous ill-fortune, or aberrations at crucial times.

In 1965-66, the First Division knew what to expect. With one new key signing, winger Mike O'Grady bought from Huddersfield for £30,000, Revie's team plunged into a new Championship race. This was, until Christmas, a serious contest with old

Willie Bell and Gary Sprake defy the Liverpool attack in December 1965.

Great Matches

FA CUP FINAL

Wembley, 1 May 1965
Attendance 100,000

Liverpool 2   Leeds United 1*
Hunt   Bremner
St John
*after extra time

This was an enormous milestone for Leeds United but a crushing disappointment: the second game in a fortnight that had seemed too big to handle. Liverpool left back Gerry Byrne played with a broken collar bone while for Leeds, Jim Storrie was nowhere near fully fit. The day was overcast and the surface greasy: Albert Johanneson might have thrived on it yet seemed more inhibited than anyone.

The likes of Hunter, Charlton and Sprake emerged with most credit, for while Liverpool dominated the first 90 minutes, Leeds hung on and shut them out. But in the third minute of extra-time, what had long seemed inevitable happened as Byrne's cross found Roger Hunt unmarked who headed in from close range.

Leeds looked sunk, yet seven minutes later they fashioned their one golden moment: a crossfield ball from Hunter was headed by Charlton into the path of Bremner who, with a panache that Leeds had so badly lacked, thumped a first-time shot past Lawrence.

But Liverpool scented more blood and Leeds were again undone by the combination of cross and header: Ian St John scoring from Ian Callaghan's centre. Only nine minutes of extra time remained and as Wembley resounded to Liverpudlian anthems, the stuffing had been knocked out of Bobby Collins and co. For Jack Charlton, it had been 'a performance so out of keeping with our ability that it hurt'.

Liverpool: Lawrence, Lawler, Byrne, Strong, Yeats, Stevenson, Callaghan, Hunt, St John, Smith, Thompson.

Leeds United: Sprake, Reaney, Bell, Bremner, Charlton, Hunter, Giles, Storrie, Peacock, Collins, Johanneson.

Referee: W. Clements (West Bromwich).

adversaries Liverpool. Then Shankly's men won at Elland Road on 28 December, nullifying Leeds' 1-0 victory at Anfield the previous day. From that point, realistic expectations of winning the League began melting away.

In the Inter-Cities Fairs Cup, where cultures and temperaments collided, Leeds became sucked into their usual quota of storms and

'Don't let the occasion become bigger than you,' warned Revie before leading his team out in the 1965 FA Cup final. His young side, however, seemed overawed.

heroics. In the second leg of their opening tie, against Torino, came a defining moment of their season: a shattering tackle on Bobby Collins by defender Poletti that left the Leeds skipper with a broken leg.

Collins had been the heart and soul of Leeds United for three and a half years as cunning prompter and pugnacious competitor. With a need to re-shape forced upon him, Revie moved Johnny Giles to inside left and drafted in Peter Lorimer at number eight. With the likes of Hunter and Bremner, Leeds did not want for motivators. Battling for most of the second half with ten men, they had held out for a 0-0 draw, with Gary Sprake a superb last line of defence, as he would be in future European sieges.

February saw Leeds in the third round and drawn against the Spanish team Valencia. As the first leg at Elland Road boiled over into violence, the referee took off both sides to cool down: an experience that seemed to follow Revie's Leeds around. Charlton, made captain in Collins' absence, was fouled once too often, threw a punch at left back Bidagany and the pair were sent off. Later, the Spaniards' inside forward Sanchez-Lage was dismissed for kicking Jim Storrie.

A 1-1 home draw did not inspire confidence that Leeds would survive the return leg. But they were becoming masters of shutting out the opposition in hostile territory. When Charlton and company concentrated on disciplined defence and ignored provocation, their growing maturity was plain to see. They stole the match, and the tie, with a goal from Mike O'Grady

On New Year's Day 1966 17-year-old Eddie Gray, another fresh face from the production line of youthful talent, made a scoring debut in Leeds' 3-0 home win over Sheffield Wednesday. Gray was, of all the Revie protégés, the most sought after, having dazzled hordes of scouts with his wing play when playing for Scotland schoolboys.

Although tried in several forward positions early in his career, Gray would eventually settle at number 11, a slot with which Revie was continuing to experiment. Terry Cooper, who had played only a handful of games since joining Leeds in 1961, was one option but despite good control seemed too easily subdued by full backs. His unconventional and unfulfilled footballing talent was seemingly difficult to accommodate; and he might have been sold but for the ploy of converting him into a full back in place of Willie Bell, who in September 1967 transferred to Leicester. From that point onwards, Terry Cooper experienced a meteoric rise in fortune.

Another young face emerged from the junior ranks: Paul Madeley, a tall, lean, phlegmatic footballer who appeared willing and able to play almost anywhere. First Division defences meanwhile were making painful acquaintance with Peter Lorimer, who had arrived in the team to stay: his 13 goals invaluable as Alan Peacock sustained an injury in the 2-0 defeat at Sunderland in January that ruled him out for the rest of the season.

In fact there was little football left for Peacock at Elland Road. He went through agonies to recover his fitness from a series of cartilage injuries but the knee persisted in giving out. He was to play a smattering of games in 1966-67; then only three more after

50 Greatest Players

ALAN PEACOCK Centre forward

Joined Leeds: February 1964 **From:** Middlesbrough

Debut: v Norwich City, 9 February 1964

Appearances: 65   **Goals:** 31

Left Leeds: October 1967   **For:** Plymouth Argyle

Honours won with Leeds: Division 2 Championship 1964;
2 England caps

Peacock played relatively few games for Leeds but his
influence was enormous. During 1963-64, his goals, eight in
14 matches, and his presence as probably the best header of
ball in the country, revitalized a stuttering attack and Leeds'
faltering challenge for the Second Division title.

Peacock was playing well enough to add two more England caps to the four he won
at Middlesbrough when his career was undone by a knee injury. A player of Peacock's
bravery, who, although not especially mobile, was gifted at converting half-chances,
proved extremely hard to replace. He and Jim Storrie formed a good partnership: many
of Storrie's goals came from Peacock's aerial knock-downs at the far post.

An unassuming player, Peacock had a long and painful struggle to regain fitness but it
was not to be and he took part in just three more league matches after moving to
Plymouth in 1967.

transferring to Plymouth Argyle at the end of the season: a sad end
for one of most fearless attackers of his generation.

Liverpool had left the rest of the First Division trailing by the end
of February, and after fourth round defeat in the FA Cup at Chelsea,
Leeds' priority became Europe adventures. Having collected the
scalps of Torino, S.C. Leipzig, Valencia and Ujpest Dozsa, Leeds were
in the semi-finals, facing Spanish opposition again in Real Zaragoza.

Zaragoza were a wicked combination of thuggery and brilliance.
In Spain, Giles had risen to the bait, sent off for retaliation near the
end after being clattered throughout. Yet Leeds had escaped with a
1-0 deficit, the only goal a penalty; and their reward for wiping that
out with a 2-1 win at Elland Road was home advantage for the play-off.
But, with Revie's men seemingly caught cold, Zaragoza got down to

some football, scything through the Leeds defence three times in 13 minutes. There was no way back: Jack Charlton's second-half goal was too little too late.

The final game of 1965-66, a 1-1 draw at Old Trafford, featured a lively return by Bobby Collins, a rare headed goal by Paul Reaney and secured Leeds second place, though with 55 points, six fewer than in the previous season. Although it had been a time of consolidation, there was a sense that Leeds United would not budge easily from the top end of the First Division – or so it seemed.

Yet in the first four months of 1966-67, the men capable of such defensive heroics had sunk to mid-table, and, within a fortnight in November, been thrashed 7-0 by West Ham in the League Cup and

---

50 Greatest Players

WILLIE BELL Full back

Joined Leeds: July 1960   **From:** Queen's Park

Debut: v Leyton Orient, 7 September 1960

Appearances: 260   **Goals:** 18

Left Leeds: September 1967   **For:** Leicester

Honours won with Leeds: Division 2 Championship 1964;

2 Scotland caps

When Willie Bell arrived at Elland Road, he was a pedestrian midfielder and Leeds were a struggling side. By the time he left, Bell had been converted to left back, capped for Scotland and was a member of a Don Revie team on its way to greatness.

Solid industrious players like Bell were the backbone of the Leeds revival. While less composed than Grenville Hair, whom he replaced, Bell was as tenacious as they come; the man for the moment.

As a fierce tackler, Bell was in good company with the likes of Reaney, Collins, Bremner and Hunter. He was notably brave in the air, and deployed as the spare man at the back to attack the ball at corners and free kicks. What he lacked in pace and natural ability, Bell more than made up for with energy and a willingness to improve his game. After leaving when supplanted by Terry Cooper, Bell's varied career included managing Birmingham City and coaching in America.

5-0 at Liverpool in the League. These were the worst results since the beginning of the Revie era. The Leeds manager was not amused.

Injuries didn't help. Mike O'Grady missed two thirds of the season; Charlton and Giles were in and out; and only five players managed more than 30 league games, compared with nine the previous season.

But by the beginning of December, Leeds had re-established a winning habit; and if not with quite the conviction of potential League Champions, enough to keep their season alive with vigorous campaigns in both FA Cup and Fairs Cup.

The FA Cup had an enormous allure for Leeds supporters. By round five, Leeds had chalked up confident victories against Crystal Palace and West Bromwich and drawn old enemies Sunderland. After a 1-1 draw played at Roker Park in front of more than 55,000, Leeds officials had no time to make the replay all ticket. The result: 57,892 poured into Elland Road, the biggest gate in the club's history.

In places, the ground was dangerously full: 18 were injured when a crush barrier collapsed on the Lowfields Road terrace. The match, resumed after a 15 minute delay, was another 1-1 stalemate; and the second replay, at Hull, a spiteful encounter in which, amid the skirmishes, Sunderland's George Herd and George Mulhall were sent off. A Giles penalty three minutes from time, and inevitably the focus of bitter controversy, saw Leeds win 2-1.

The Goal that Never Was

Leeds' 1-0 quarter-final victory over Manchester City at Elland Road was a peaceable oasis between the rancour of that fifth round and a traumatic semi-final against Chelsea at Villa Park. That game would have two pivotal moments: the brilliance of Chelsea's goal, a flying header from Tony Hateley after a mesmerizing dribble down the left by Charlie Cooke; and the notorious goal that never was: a rasping shot thumped by Peter Lorimer into the Chelsea net with only two minutes remaining.

Revie would often despair of match officials whose decisions contrived to undermine his team's hard work. Giles, by no means in haste, had rolled a short kick for Lorimer to unleash goalwards while referee Ken

Burns continued to usher back Chelsea's defensive wall. But as Burns was unready for the kick, he disallowed the goal.

And so another big game involving Leeds was played out to the sounds of fury and indignant post mortems. It was, perhaps, no wonder that an 'us against the rest of the world' mentality had grown up that forged in them a determination never to go down without a fight.

A season older and wiser, they set about the Fairs Cup once more and reached the final. Lessons learned in a previous feud with Valencia were put to best use as, in the third round and with a patched-up side, Leeds once more disposed of the Spaniards, 3-1 on aggregate. Revie rated the disciplined 2-0 victory in Spain as his side's best in Europe.

It had been tighter against Bologna in round four – 1-1 on aggregate over two legs and the outcome resolved on a toss of coin; but easier in the semi-final when a hat-trick before half-time from reserve centre-forward Rod Belfitt spurred Leeds on to a 4-2 home leg victory over Kilmarnock. When they drew the second leg in Scotland 0-0, it was 24 May, the last act of a sprawling season in which Leeds had finished fourth with 55 points.

The Fairs Cup final would be one of the first milestones of 1967-68; and all too soon for Revie's team which, without close season reinforcements and unsettled by injury, made a faltering start with one point from the first three matches.

If ever a contest underlined Leeds' paucity of attacking options, the final against Dinamo Zagreb was it. They were undone during a rocky period mid-way through the away leg, conceding two goals without reply. At Elland Road, Paul Reaney operated as an emergency right winger; Leeds huffed and puffed, but when attacking relied far too much on aimless high balls. It was 0-0 on the night; a 2-0 defeat on aggregate. They scarcely landed a punch.

Revie had stubbornly refused to buy just to appeal to the public. But in late September, and with his attacking options grinding to a halt, he signed Mick Jones from Sheffield United for £100,000. Having also installed Terry Cooper at left back, suddenly the team had a new vitality. Jones made his debut at home in the 3-2 home win over

Leicester City and to extraordinary effect: a *Daily Telegraph* reporter marvelled as Leeds 'attacked with such careless abandon that their usually resolute defence quivered.'

It was Chelsea's misfortune to be next up at Elland Road just as Leeds had started to get their eye in, using the part-timers of Spora Luxembourg for target practice in a 9-0 Fairs Cup win. Chelsea, in disarray and without a manager after the departure of Tommy Docherty, were subjected to one of the most devastating offensives from any Leeds team in history. Whipped on by Bremner, about to start a four weeks suspension, they came at Chelsea from all angles: 3-0 up after 14 minutes; by full-time, 7-0 winners, and, including Chelsea's hapless Hinton, seven different scorers.

Jones, although mixing up the attack nicely, had not been scoring much himself. But when he played, Leeds got their best results; and when he was out injured for six weeks in November and December, their form wobbled. His return just before Christmas coincided with a scintillating run in the league, six straight wins including back-to-back 5-0 victories over Fulham and Southampton.

Billy Bremner puts the finishing touch to the 7-0 rout of Chelsea at Elland Road.

The team found itself battling on four fronts: League, FA Cup, League Cup and Fairs Cup; and from mid-December, Leeds went almost four months unbeaten. Almost 52,000 poured into Elland Road for the summit meeting with Manchester City on 23 March, which Leeds won 2-0 with goals from Charlton and Giles, fuelling dreams that they might take the Championship.

But after a 3-2 defeat at relegation-threatened Stoke one month later, Leeds began coming off the rails. Within four days, they had lost a second successive FA Cup semi-final, to Everton at Old Trafford. Progress in the cup had been achieved in typical combative fashion: home victories over Nottingham Forest, Bristol City – in which Gary Sprake was sent off – and Sheffield United, were all from the school of hard knocks.

The semi-final was in similar bruising vein, but Leeds, their minds and bodies growing weary after a gruelling season, were undone by a

50 Greatest Players

MICK JONES Centre forward

Joined Leeds: September 1967   **From:** Sheffield United

Debut: v Leicester City, 23 September 1967

Appearances: 313   **Goals:** 111

Left Leeds: 1975 (retired through injury)

Honours won with Leeds: Division 1 Championship 1969, 1974; Fairs Cup winner 1968, 1971; FA Cup winner 1972; 1 England cap

Jones was never the most sophisticated centre forward. But he made Herculean efforts to improve his game and when his raw edges had been rounded, was wonderfully effective.

While Jones had made a fair impact at Bramall Lane, scoring more than 60 goals in five seasons and winning two England caps, Revie began by arranging special training sessions for him. He had soon added the knack of shielding the ball under pressure to his strength, endless stamina and courage that bordered on recklessness. By the time Allan Clarke arrived in 1969, Jones was a wonderful foil.

Few defenders mastered Jones in an aerial battle. The bravery with which he hurled himself into the fray made him difficult to subdue; but also put him at risk of injury. The sight of him struggling up to the royal box for his Cup winners medal in 1972, arm strapped, epitomized a selfless career that was ended three years later by a knee injury.

Great Matches

LEAGUE CUP FINAL

Wembley, 2 March 1968
Attendance 97,887

Arsenal 0   Leeds United 1
Cooper

Victory was everything: Leeds United's outlook had become shaped by too many high-profile failures for any Corinthian spirit to prevail. Their form in the League Cup's seven-year history had been poor; their passage to the 1968 final, unspectacular. But having got to Wembley, their goal was to expunge the memory of defeat, not to win friends.

It was a chilly overcast day. Arsenal, Leeds' opponents, lagged behind in football evolution terms, but could make a fight of almost anything. And it didn't take much to reduce Leeds to a kicking match, which is what much of the match became. Potential match-winners were thin on the ground: Jones cup-tied, Giles below par recovering from flu and Greenhoff carrying a knee injury. It left Paul Madeley to lead the attack at number nine.

The goal, on 17 minutes, was of rare beauty yet, inevitably, surrounded in controversy. As Eddie Gray's corner swung in from the left, Arsenal goalkeeper Jim Furnell claimed he had been impeded by Jack Charlton and Paul Madeley. Meanwhile, Peter Simpson weakly headed clear only for Terry Cooper's left foot volley to scorch into the net.

Most of the rest of action was bruising acrimony. But Leeds had won – and nor had it felt like an away game: the fans were much more vociferous than against Liverpool in 1965. It was, above all, the first major trophy in the club's 48-year history. With that psychological hurdle overcome, many more should follow. That was the optimists' theory – but with Revie's Leeds, things were never so simple.

Arsenal: Furnell, Storey, McNab, McLintock, Simpson, Ure, Radford, Jenkins (Neill), Graham, Sammels, Armstrong.

Leeds United: Sprake, Reaney, Cooper, Bremner, Charlton, Hunter, Greenhoff, Lorimer, Madeley, Giles, Gray (Belfitt).

Referee: L. J. Hamer (Norwich).

mad moment three minutes from half-time: Sprake, harassed by centre forward Joe Royle, despatched a feeble clearance to Jimmy Husband whose goal-bound shot was handled on the line by Charlton. Johnny Morrissey's penalty decided the outcome.

A week later, Leeds played their brightest football for some time against Liverpool at Elland Road but with a defensive brittleness that allowed Bill Shankly's team to come from 1-0 down to win 2-1 and kill any lingering Championship hopes. Leeds were, once again, to finish fourth, behind Manchester United, Manchester City and Liverpool in what had been a riveting four-horse Championship battle.

But no other team had had anything like Leeds' workload – 64 games in all competitions. After Spora Luxembourg, whom Leeds had used for target practice and beaten 16-0 on aggregate, the Fairs Cup threw up sterner challenges from Partizan Belgrade, Hibernian, Glasgow Rangers and Dundee en route to a final, which, like the previous one, was to be played early the following season.

The schedule had told Revie much about the levels of punishment his regular players could take; and what the reserves were capable of. Midfielder Mick Bates, a stand-in for Giles, was stylish and capable; perhaps only a lack of devil stood between him and a more illustrious career. Terry Hibbitt, whose misfortune was to be eclipsed by Eddie Gray, was a sparky left winger who thrived when transferred to Newcastle United.

Yet the well of talent was not inexhaustible, and there was dismay when early in 1968-69 Revie sold Jimmy Greenhoff to Birmingham City. Greenhoff, a beautifully mobile and intelligent forward with a powerful shot, had, like Terry Cooper, been hard to accommodate regularly in the first team. Even so, it seemed profligate to let go such a fine young player. And like Hibbitt, Greenhoff flourished elsewhere, notably at Stoke City and Manchester United.

A substitute in the first match of Leeds' two-legged Inter-Cities Fairs Cup final against Ferencvaros, Jimmy Greenhoff had left when the denouement was played out in Hungary five weeks later. Elland Road was half empty on 7 August, when much of Leeds was on holiday and many others chose to watch television. But a solitary goal bundled in from close range by Mick Jones shortly before half-time left the game finely balanced, and gave both teams hope. It made for a memorable night in Hungary.

Despite impressing for Leeds, Jimmy Greenhoff's career would flourish at Stoke City.

Great Matches

INTER-CITIES FAIRS CUP FINAL	Nep Stadium, Budapest, 11 September 1968 Attendance 76,000

Ferencvaros 0   Leeds United 0*
*Leeds won 1-0 on aggregate

This was one of the legendary rearguard actions. The Nep stadium was filled to bursting with 76,000 fans but only 50 or so had travelled from Leeds. Revie's team had not only to play 11 men but also a wildly partisan home crowd.

They drew on all their hard-learned lessons. 'It was an occasion that required an amount of equipoise and calm of mind, Leeds had it and Ferencvaros, with all the attack and the wind at their backs, lacked it,' said Geoffrey Green of *The Times*.

Leeds were pinned back not only in their own half but in their own penalty area. Yet they never lost concentration, and two forays up front almost brought a goal: Lorimer's deflected shot was beaten away and Jones headed O'Grady's free kick against the bar.

Sprake, as a last line of defence, was magnificent. Of all the saves he made, perhaps most miraculous was a dive to keep out Novak's free-kick when the view in front of him was blotted out by a ten-man defensive barrier. But every Leeds man, all of whom ran their hearts out, played heroically. For all the undignified brawls preceding it, Leeds' first European trophy had been won with courage and honour.

Ferencvaros: Geczi, Pancsis, Havasi, Juhasz, Sxucs, Szoke (Kraba), Varga, Albert, Rakori, Katona, Novak.

Leeds United: Sprake, Reaney, Cooper, Bremner, Charlton, Hunter, O'Grady, Lorimer, Jones, Madeley, Hibbitt (Bates).

Referee: G. Schulenberg (West Germany).

When Leeds flew home in triumph they were top of the League. They won seven of their first eight League matches though often less commandingly than results implied, and sorely missed the injured Johnny Giles. They lost for the first time at the end of September, comprehensively beaten 3-1 away at Manchester City; and three weeks later were ripped apart by Burnley at Turf Moor who won 5-1 on a day when every trick seemed to work for them.

Yet from that mid-October day, and looking frighteningly vulnerable, Leeds rallied and remained unbeaten for the rest of the League season. The Championship had become a consuming priority for them and few tears were shed over early exits from the League and FA Cups at the hands of Crystal Palace and Sheffield Wednesday respectively. But winning in the Inter-Cities Fairs Cup seemed a harder habit to shake off: Leeds had trooped back and forth to Liege, Napoli and Hanover before losing their fourth round tie in March 3-0 on aggregate to Ujpest Dozsa.

Eleven days earlier, Leeds had, in a tigerish 5-1 demolition of Stoke City at the Victoria Ground, showed what they could do when they cut loose. Mike O'Grady's performances on the right wing had earned him an England recall; while Eddie Gray produced similar flair on the left. Reaney, Hunter and Charlton were rock solid; and Bremner, skippering midfield with demonic energy, was almost impossible to outrun or outwit.

Yet several performances on the run-in were governed by a desperate fear of blowing up. Leeds had became masters of time-wasting when on top, playing keep-ball among themselves or hogging the ball down near the corner flag. Such were the features of a tense ill-tempered encounter with Arsenal at Highbury on 12 April, where Gary Sprake, having punched Gunners' centre forward Bobby Gould, was miraculously lucky not to be sent off; and where good fortune continued to hold as Leeds fed off centre half Ian Ure's defensive howlers for both goals to earn themselves a 2-1 victory.

With three games to go, only Liverpool and, less realistically, Everton could deny Revie's men – and Leeds faced away games with both. Another mighty defensive display at Goodison, watched by 59,000, shut out Harry Catterick's pretenders, the 0-0 draw effectively ending their interest in the title.

Leeds' Championship challenge had been plotted in meticulous detail; watertight defence the key. Although Leeds were much criticized, Liverpool, their principal rivals, scored fewer and conceded fewer: both sides were arch exponents of method football, where individual flair was subordinated for the greater good.

Leeds won the League with a record number points, 67. Revie's methods had paid in every sense: the miserable days of debt were gone; and the ground, with the roofing and improvement of the Kop, was at last catching up with the team's success.

Great Matches

FOOTBALL LEAGUE DIVISION ONE   **Anfield, 30 April 1969**
                                                Attendance 53,750

Liverpool 0   Leeds United 0

A point needed: a draw would do – circumstances under which Don Revie's team had come to excel. But the opponents were Liverpool, equally tough, durable and experienced in big games. And victory would keep the home team's championship hopes alive.

The sight and sound of the Kop in full cry had unnerved many a lesser team but Leeds, having held the fort in Budapest, could survive anywhere. If Liverpool had a weakness, it was, like Leeds, their lack of a striker with a rapier thrust. Whipped on by the gale of sound, they charged furiously but two golden chances, both falling to young Alun Evans, were spurned.

Bremner and co. steadied themselves, broke out and lifted the siege with raids into enemy territory. As a contest in hard running and organization, it was without equal. But Liverpool could not find a spark of genius with which to breach the Leeds defence.

At last the title had come to Elland Road. Leeds had, without question, deserved it; and after watching the trophy lifted from under their noses the Kop was memorably generous in acclaiming the achievement.

Liverpool: Lawrence, Lawler, Strong, Smith, Yeats, Hughes, Callaghan, Graham, Evans, St John, Thompson.

Leeds United: Sprake, Reaney, Cooper, Bremner, Charlton, Hunter, O'Grady, Madeley, Jones, Giles, Gray.

Referee: A Dimond (Harlow).

There was money to spend on the best players. And with Leeds competing in the European Cup, the squad needed strengthening, above all in attack, where still too little was being created through the lack of a partner for Mick Jones. Enter Allan Clarke from Leicester, at £165,000, Britain's most expensive footballer.

Clarke had put himself in the shop window in the 1969 FA Cup final against Manchester City, where, in an attacking midfield role, he was the best player on show despite being on the losing side. At Fulham and Walsall, he had an excellent strike rate averaging more than a goal every two games. Just 23 when he signed for Leeds, Revie had bought a composed and complete finisher.

50 Greatest Players

JACK CHARLTON Centre half

Joined Leeds: 1950

Debut: v Doncaster Rovers, 25 April 1953

Appearances: 773   **Goals:** 96

Left Leeds: Summer 1973   **For:** Middlesbrough (as manager)

Honours won with Leeds: Division 1 Championship 1969; Division 2 Championship 1964; Fairs Cup winner 1968, 1971; FA Cup winner 1972; League Cup winner 1968; Footballer of the Year 1967; 35 England caps

When Jack Charlton came to Leeds and played a trial game in a blizzard, the die was cast: he was to remain at the club for more than 20 years.

Early on, he had to live in the shadow of John Charles. Yet after Leeds won promotion to the First Division in 1956, Charlton started to attract attention as a swift, strong-running defender and a crisp tackler. However, in a struggling side he was noted for his in-built bad habits and reluctance to take advice. Only when taken firmly in hand by Don Revie did he become a linchpin of the meanest defence in the country. He gained his first England cap in March 1965, two months before his 30th birthday; and 15 months later was in the team that won the World Cup final. He had become a star turn, voted Footballer of the Year in 1967 – a giant at the back and a talismanic auxiliary attacker, causing turmoil in opposing defences either when standing on the goal-line at corners or surging from deep as defenders parted in confusion before him.

After leaving in 1973, he became a celebrated manager of Middlesbrough, Sheffield Wednesday and Newcastle; then the Republic of Ireland whom he took to the quarter-finals of the World Cup in 1990 and the last 16 in 1994.

There was, however, one seemingly inexplicable departure from Elland Road: Mike O'Grady was sold to Wolves for £80,000. Memories were still fresh of O'Grady's vibrant displays and the player was bemused by Revie's apparent eagerness to get rid of him. It was an unhappy move for O'Grady, whose career, dogged by injury, never recovered.

With an opening day 3-1 win over Spurs at White Hart Lane on 9 August, in which Clarke scored, Leeds exuded confidence and class. But their form over the next month stuttered, and Everton quickly emerged as serious rivals for the title. Leeds' unbeaten League run, which had stretched back to the Burnley debacle in

50 Greatest Players

JOHNNY GILES Midfielder

Joined Leeds: August 1963   **From:** Manchester United

Debut: v Bury, 31 August 1963

Appearances: 527   **Goals:** 115

Left Leeds: Summer 1975   **For:** West Bromwich Albion

Honours won with Leeds: Division 1 Championship 1969, 1974; Division 2 Championship 1964; Fairs Cup winner 1968, 1971; FA Cup winner 1972; League Cup winner 1968; 32 Republic of Ireland caps

In 1963, Johnny Giles had won the FA Cup with Manchester United, yet felt unappreciated, his prospects limited and uneasy among ill-assorted personalities. Leeds offered a fresh start and the hum of optimism; and Giles could provide a sometimes naïve team with the guile it needed.

After two seasons he switched from the right wing to inside left after Bobby Collins broke his leg. Part of the most feared midfield in the land, he displayed a peerless ingenuity at creating time and space before delivering long balls of shattering accuracy.

Giles could dispense physical aggression with the best; yet had a cool head that made him a master tactician and ideal penalty-taker. When teams were on their knees, Giles often supervised their extermination: his insolent flicked back-heel when Leeds were 7-0 up against Southampton in 1972 is an indelible image of Revie's team at its cruel best.

The directors ignored Revie's advice to appoint Giles as his successor in 1974 and eventually, Giles became manager at West Bromwich and of the Republic of Ireland.

October 1968, finally ended at Goodison Park on 30 August 1969 when Everton won 3-2, torturing Leeds with brilliant wing play and finishing.

But toward the end of October, Leeds got cracking. In consecutive home victories against Nottingham Forest (6-1) and Ipswich (4-0), Leeds showed a collective flair and lust for attack that had been lacking the previous season. They broke all previous scoring records, putting ten past Lyn Oslo in the home leg of their first round European Cup ties, winning 16-0 on aggregate. By the end of November, they had brushed Ferencvaros aside in round two with awesome style and power in what the Russian referee described as 'the best exhibition of football I have ever seen in Europe'.

Yet there was a sense in Leeds – partly justified, part paranoia – that still they weren't taken seriously by some of the metropolitan media.

Fresh from exacting revenge by beating Everton 2-1 at Elland Road on 27 December, Leeds travelled to Chelsea, who were also having a fine season. Leading 2-1 at half-time, and looking comfortable, Dave Sexton's men were subjected to a 45-minute master class in the extermination of upstarts. With brilliant link-up play and smashing passes from all angles, Leeds scored five. It was a watershed: smart Londoners could no longer deny the collective brilliance of this team.

But, long before the days of big squads, the same warriors were doing battle week in week out. And the games were getting bigger, compressed into a

Johnny Giles became an ever-growing influence as the 60s progressed.

season truncated by the demands of the 1970 World Cup. The stakes got higher: in March, after its winter break, the European Cup resumed. By the end of the month, the dream of a magnificent treble, League, FA Cup and European Cup, was starting to look distinctly possible.

Leeds had reached the semi-final of the European Cup by ousting Standard Liege 1-0 on aggregate in two stirring trials of strength and skill. They were jostling Everton at the top of the League. They reached the FA Cup semi-final knocking out Swansea Town, Sutton United, Mansfield Town and Swindon Town. Manchester United were their first first heavyweight opponents.

Nine games were crammed into March. If Leeds could have avoided two cup semi-final replays, they might have drawn breath, recovered from knocks and been spared the exhaustion through which the season was to founder. But, the semi-final became an epic in three acts: the first, a 0-0 draw at Hillsborough where, despite a late onslaught, Leeds failed to crack the United defence. The replay, at Villa Park on a night of torrential rain, remained stubbornly goalless after extra-time and intense Manchester pressure.

Three days later, the two sides were once more locked in combat at Burnden Park, Bolton. If any man could make the crucial difference, it was Billy Bremner, the Footballer of the Year. One chance, the ball falling to him off Mick Jones' leg in the ninth minute, a swing of the left leg and Bremner flashed home the only goal of a tie that lasted an epic 300 minutes.

Some commentators began to fear for them. Geoffrey Green of *The Times* reflected: 'They say Leeds relish hard work; that the expense of energy seems an eternal delight. But surely there must be a limit.'

There was, and it had been reached. In the next home match with Southampton, Leeds lost 3-1, squandering an early lead through a grotesque sequence of errors and misfortunes; and any realistic chance of catching Everton. To conserve what strength his players had left, Revie sent out a team of reserves for the next match at Derby, scheduled just two days before a European Cup semi-final with Celtic. Leeds lost 4-1 and were later fined £5,000 by the League for fielding a weakened team.

Peter Lorimer was one of Revie's reliables throughout the glory years.

But there was an air of fallibility even about the A-team, especially with the enforced absence through injury of Hunter. At Elland Road, Celtic, showing the vibrancy that had deserted Revie's team, caught out Leeds with the only goal after two minutes, leaving another mountain to climb at Hampden Park. And they would now be without Paul Reaney, who broke his leg in a meaningless League match at West Ham just 24 hours afterwards. In the words of a correspondent from *The Times*: 'The gods who watch over the brave were asleep last night, and while they nodded Leeds United suffered one more sickening blow.'

They had, at least, the luxury of a week's respite between a 2-1 home victory over Burnley and the FA Cup final against Chelsea. And while events were to prove that Leeds' powers of recuperation were enormous, durable opponents had a way of finding their Achilles heel.

Down in Hampden's bowl, with Celtic roared on by 136,000 fans, the biggest crowd in European Cup history, Leeds were entitled to think the world was against them. When Bremner struck from

50 Greatest Players

MIKE O'GRADY Winger

Joined Leeds: October 1965   **From:** Huddersfield

Debut: v Northampton Town, 16 October 1965

Appearances: 121   **Goals:** 16

Left Leeds: September 1969   **For:** Wolves

Honours won with Leeds: Division 1 Championship 1969;
1 England cap

O'Grady made a striking impact in Leeds schoolboy soccer yet
was allowed to slip away to local rivals Huddersfield before
Don Revie signed him for £30,000 in 1965.

At Leeds Road, O'Grady made such rapid progress that he
was awarded an England cap against France shortly after he had turned 20. Though
thwarted by injury to start with at Elland Road, in the championship season of 1968-
69 he flourished, often the
most potent attacker in the Leeds team and ever eager to take on defenders.

In this confident vein of form, O'Grady earned an England recall; yet the following
season, having shone so brightly in a title-winning side, found himself injured, out of
favour and was transferred to Wolves.

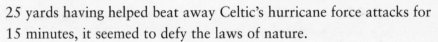

25 yards having helped beat away Celtic's hurricane force attacks for
15 minutes, it seemed to defy the laws of nature.

It was too good to last. Mick Jones gashed a leg and had to be taken
off. Two minutes after half-time, John Hughes headed the equalizer.
Leeds' misfortunes were compounded as, a few minutes later, Sprake
was injured in a collision with the marauding Hughes, and had to be
carried off. The first act of substitute keeper David Harvey following
another Celtic attack was to pick Bobby Murdoch's shot out of the net.

The European adventure was over: Leeds had lost 3-1 on aggregate.
Minds and bodies now had to be coaxed into readiness for the
FA Cup final replay. Two remaining League matches against Manchester
City and Ipswich were lost and forgotten about. Leeds had eight free
days before their date with Chelsea at Old Trafford in the first
FA Cup final replay for 58 years.

Great Matches

FA CUP FINAL   **Wembley, 11 April 1970**
                                                    Attendance 100,000

Chelsea 2   Leeds United 2*

Houseman   Charlton

Hutchinson   Jones

* after extra time

At last Leeds were to flaunt their talents at Wembley. That the best team didn't, in the end, win, was symptomatic of a tragic season. Leeds dug into all their reserves of strength and creativity yet could not subdue Chelsea's indomitable spirit.

The heavily-sanded pitch played a bit part in this marvellous contest. Leeds' first goal, a close-range header from Jack Charlton, never bounced as the Chelsea defence might have expected. The surface did not lend itself to good football, yet Eddie Gray's sorcery on the left wing and torture of right back David Webb has become one of the legendary Wembley performances.

With Bremner and Giles fizzing in midfield, most of the fine football came from Leeds. But so did crucial mistakes: Sprake let squirt under his body a long-range shot from Peter Houseman, giving Chelsea an unexpected equalizer before half-time. For all Leeds' command, this aberration emphasized their fallibility.

In the second half, Chelsea once more gave most of the ground. Just seven minutes remained when Mick Jones struck a goal with his left foot after Clarke's header rebounded from the bar. Game over, it seemed.

But not so. Chelsea kept harrying and Leeds, too intent on disputing a free kick conceded by Charlton on 86 minutes, allowed themselves to be undone once more. As the ball sailed over from the left, Ian Hutchinson sprang unmarked into the air and headed past Sprake.

The pitch caught up with everyone in extra-time and the final minutes of a riveting final, with the balance of power swinging to and fro, were played out in slow motion by exhausted men.

Chelsea: Bonetti, Webb, McCreadie, Hollins, Dempsey, Harris (Hinton), Baldwin, Houseman, Osgood, Hutchinson, Cooke.

Leeds United: Sprake, Madeley, Cooper, Bremner, Charlton, Hunter, Lorimer, Clarke, Jones, Giles, Gray.

Referee: E. Jennings (Stourbridge).

Twenty minutes into the game and Jack Charlton's headed goal ignites one of the most memorable FA Cup finals ever seen at Wembley.

This was a match of X-certificate tackles and spasmodic brilliance: more of a legend even than the magnificent encounter at Wembley. As theatre, it was, for Leeds fans, a tragedy full of dark moments where early optimism generated by Mick Jones' superb first-half goal ebbed and gave way to despair; where fatal flaws were exposed; and where David Webb, Eddie Gray's stooge at Wembley, struck the killer blow as Chelsea inexorably wrested the initiative.

Webb's coup de grace in extra-time had seemed inevitable after Osgood's brilliant headed equalizer 12 minutes from time. By then, Leeds were being overrun in midfield. In the light of earlier ferocious exchanges, it was a miracle that both teams finished with 11 men; yet if any team had been softened up, it was Leeds. Their last-minute efforts to retrieve the match, and the season, were frenzied but blunt-edged. This was the most shattering defeat of all. Leeds had, in the words of one commentator, 'like Sisyphus, pushed three boulders almost to the top of three mountains only to see them back in the valley'.

Don Revie with the Manager of the Year trophy which he won in 1969 and 1970.

Chapter Six: 1970-74
One Game Too Many?

There was widespread sympathy for Leeds but the self-pity was soon over and done with. Revie told the players to go away on holiday and start all over again. And that's what they did; and for every other season during his reign. The players, although reaching their peak, continued to be put through the hoops. 'Over the years, a good 70 per cent of the lads played in games where they shouldn't have done,' said Billy Bremner. 'I remember being put in for a cup game against Sunderland when I had done my knee ligaments the previous Saturday. A week for knee ligaments is impossible.'

Peter Lorimer has similar memories. 'When you're fresh you can carry an injury; when you're tired, you can't,' he said. 'I saw the boss tell the doctor a player would be alright when I'm sure the doctor didn't think he was fit.'

The punishing 1969-70 season left Paul Madeley too drained to join the England World Cup squad in place of Paul Reaney. When the new domestic campaign began, injured absentees such as Giles and Gray reduced attacking options. But there was good news when Reaney, one of the great quiet hard men, returned on 12 October for the game at West Bromwich looking as fresh as if he'd never been away.

Despite the absences of Giles and Gray, normal service was resumed. Leeds, mixing moods of brilliance and aggression, won their first five matches and settled into a metronome-like pattern of victories. By New Year, they had lost only once, 3-0 at Stoke in September, when collectively off-colour. More often they showed a superiority that marked them out from all other teams. Of their 1-0 victory over Manchester City at Elland Road on 28 November the *Sunday Times* wrote: 'Leeds normally field seven or eight brilliant players and their whole squad does not include a weak performer. Quality and ability are at the root of their consistency.'

If there was a weakness, it was Gary Sprake's occasional lapses of concentration. Three weeks earlier at Crystal Palace, Sprake had let sail through his arms a long-range drifting shot from John Sewell, giving Palace the most unlikely equalizer, and with only five minutes left. It looked at the time merely like a point dropped; in the end it would proved crucial.

The Biggest Cup Shock Ever

Leeds, as ever, had much else to see to: the Fairs Cup, where they were making steady progress, and the FA Cup, which had slipped so agonizingly from their grasp. Having laboured to beat Rotherham in round three then won easily at Swindon in round four, a fifth round tie at Colchester was surely an open door to the quarter-final.

But Revie seemed unduly nervous. In veteran striker Ray Crawford, Colchester had a man given to causing turmoil in the Leeds defence. And Leeds habitually made heavy weather of games against lesser sides – it took a replay to dispatch Rotherham. Had confidence been knocked the previous week when old adversaries Liverpool inflicted on Revie's men their first home League defeat of the season? Whatever, Leeds were stunningly out of sorts at Layer Road.

Perhaps one key was the absence of Bremner, plagued by injury during the latter part of the season. But with Leeds 3-0 down after 54 minutes, the greatest FA Cup shock of modern times was unfolding. A late rally with goals from Giles and Hunter was not enough. Crawford, with two goals, had once more been Leeds' nemesis.

Yet their League form, despite the occasional hiccup, was still that of potential Champions. But with Arsenal equally consistent, defeats for Revie's men, although few, suddenly came to matter. Nerves began jangling when they went down 3-1 at Stamford Bridge on 27 March. When Leeds faced West Bromwich Albion at Elland Road on 17 April, Arsenal, four points behind but with three games in hand, were much too close for comfort.

There was an edginess about Leeds long before referee Ray Tinkler's notorious intervention, or lack of it, sealed their downfall. A horribly misdirected pass by Jack Charlton had allowed Albion to score a breakaway goal on 19 minutes and stoked up anxiety. With neither Gray nor Bremner fully fit, the team was a shadow of its usual self.

Then, with 20 minutes left, Tinkler overruled a linesman who had flagged Colin Suggett offside as Albion made an ambush. The attack continued in surreal fashion before Tony Brown squared to Jeff Astle who scored. As the 36,000 inside Elland Road howled their anger, Tinkler was accosted by a handful of enraged fans who had invaded the pitch. His decision had cost Leeds the match and possibly the title.

Leeds players and fans are enraged as referee Ray Tinkler confirms the West Bromwich Albion goal. 'It cost us nine months hard work,' Revie said afterwards.

But while Arsenal had the initiative, winning two games in hand and going top on goal average, Leeds did not collapse. A week later, at The Dell, they gave Southampton short shrift and won 3-0 – an ideal tonic for Arsenal's visit to Leeds two days later.

This was as intense a cut and thrust summit meeting as Elland Road had known. As the second half ticked away, Bremner and co. began turning the screw. As Leeds worked up to a frenzied finale, Clarke stabbed a shot goalwards and Charlton bundled the ball against the post for it to rebound off a defender into the net. In the 89th minute, amid pandemonium, Arsenal's inexorable victory charge had been halted.

Leeds could only give it their best shot and hope. Their final victory, a 2-0 home win over Nottingham Forest, was a valedictory show of energy and invention by a team back to its best. But Arsenal had been winning too long for defeat at Elland Road to knock them off their stride. In another electrified battle, at White Hart Lane with bitter rivals Tottenham, they got the victory they needed to secure the Championship.

Meanwhile, in Europe, Leeds had disposed of Sarpsborg, Dynamo Dresden, Sparta Prague and Vitoria Setubal in low-key games but a semi-final against Liverpool rekindled old passions. A headed goal from Billy Bremner in the Anfield leg was enough to take Leeds through to the final against Juventus, 1-0 on aggregate.

The trophy was hard-won, though the football much more creative than in Leeds' previous finals. The leg in Italy became a two-act drama; a deluge of rain had caused abandonment of the first after 50 minutes. Forty-eight hours later, the teams contested a classic match, with Leeds twice retrieving a deficit to draw 2-2. The second equalizer, smashed home by Mick Bates just after coming on as substitute, was the finest moment in his career.

With away goals now counting double in the event of level scores, Leeds had a whip hand for the return at Elland Road on 2 June; their

Allan Clarke scores to give Leeds a 1-0 lead in the early minutes of the Fairs Cup final second leg against Juventus at Elland Road.

grip tightened when, after 11 minutes, Clarke scored with a superb snapshot on the turn. Anastasi, then the world's costliest footballer, equalized six minutes later; and the game swung end to end, yet with Leeds usually in control. It was, after recent uproar, shocks and disappointments, a richly satisfying way to end the season.

Injuries and loss of form to key players saw Leeds make a rocky start to 1971-72. As punishment for pitch invasion amid the West Bromwich fiasco, they had to play their first four 'home' matches at Huddersfield, Hull and Hillsborough. During a spluttering early run, Leeds contrived to get knocked out of the UEFA (formerly the Fairs) Cup in the first round, squandering a 2-0 lead from the away leg with SK Lierse by losing 4-0 at Elland Road. They had held the trophy barely three months.

A preoccupation for Revie was strengthening the squad. He had a fondness for dynamic midfielders; five seasons earlier he had tried – and failed – to woo Alan Ball from Blackpool. His latest target, West Bromwich Albion's Asa Hartford, was in the Bremner/Ball mould, and set to sign when a medical examination revealed evidence of a heart condition. Revie wasn't prepared to run the risk: Manchester City were, and Hartford flourished at Maine Road.

Without new faces, seemingly unsure of where they were going, Leeds were barely above mid-table by early October and much the poorer without the injured Mick Jones. Then, after a dismal 3-1 defeat at Coventry on 9 October, Revie's men started remembering their lines. After home victories over Manchester City and Everton, they travelled to Manchester United, the First Division leaders. Lorimer's booming 30-yard shot in the fourth minute decided the match and became a turning point in the season; the two teams on escalators going in opposite directions.

Back to their Best

Less than four months later, the gulf in class between them was brutally exposed. Early in 1972, Leeds were hitting new heights. Jones was back – how badly he'd been missed – and Gray. Peter Lorimer

50 Greatest Players

GARY SPRAKE Goalkeeper

Joined Leeds: 1962   **From:** Juniors

Debut: v Southampton, 17 March 1962

Appearances: 507

Left Leeds: October 1973   **For:** Birmingham City

Honours won with Leeds: Division 1 Championship 1969; Fairs Cup 1968, 1971; League Cup 1968; Division 2 Championship 1964; 32 Wales caps

Gary Sprake's career was tempestuous from the day he was airlifted to Southampton as a 16-year-old to make his debut as an emergency reserve. Leeds lost 4-1 and relegation threatened. Convinced by Revie to stick it out, he found himself in the team within six months – where he stayed for the next ten years.

Sprake was a magnificent athletic keeper, a natural and spectacular shot-stopper, but he suffered from flashes of temper, a tendency to lose concentration and to blunder on the big occasion. Better to remember him for his heroics in the 1968-69 season when he often stood between Leeds and defeat, against Ferencvaros in the second leg of the Fairs Cup final and his vital saves in the championship decider at Anfield. Eventually ousted by his understudy David Harvey he joined Birmingham in October 1973, retiring with a back injury two years later.

was playing the best football of his career. Suddenly, the team had supreme balance; all its parts in perfect working order.

Results in the FA Cup were ample evidence. Leeds had brushed off Bristol Rovers 4-1 in round three then in round four shut out Liverpool in a 0-0 draw at Anfield, enabling Allan Clarke to prise open Shankly's men with two goals in the replay. In round five, Leeds' 2-0 victory at Cardiff was, in the words of one reporter, 'as smooth as cream'.

This was to herald a magnificent month. On 19 February, a fortnight after Leeds' elegant disposal of Cardiff, Manchester United, a shadow of the poised team that once led the division, were devoured at Elland Road by a Leeds team playing as if driven by a lust for frail flesh. But a 5-1 victory, for all its gorgeous satisfaction, had not sated appetites. A fortnight later, Southampton became sacrificial lambs and ritually humiliated as Leeds, seven goals up, played a mocking game of keep-ball.

50 Greatest Players

TERRY COOPER Left winger/left back

Joined Leeds: May 1961   **From:** Juniors

Debut: v Swansea Town, 11 April 1964

Appearances: 350   **Goals:** 11

Left Leeds: March 1975   **For:** Middlesbrough

Honours won with Leeds: Division 1 Championship 1969; Fairs Cup winner 1968, 1971; League Cup 1968; 15 England caps

Terry Cooper joined Leeds in 1961, having been with Wolves as a junior, yet took six years to claim a regular first-team place. Then, at the start of 1967-68, Don Revie converted him from left winger to left back. The conversion was an instant success: as a winger, he lacked the sharpness to shrug off the close attentions of defenders. At full back his superb passes and overlapping wing play helped illuminate the 1967-68 season. His sweetly volleyed goal brought Leeds their first major trophy, the League Cup, and by 1970, Cooper was playing in the World Cup finals in Mexico.

But a broken left shin sustained at Stoke in April 1972 cast gloom over the remainder of his Leeds career. After a painful recovery, he played only a handful more games for Leeds before transferring to Middlesbrough in 1975. He went on to play more than 250 games for Boro, Bristol City, Bristol Rovers and Doncaster Rovers.

Yet Leeds were never more eloquent than in the FA Cup sixth round tie against Tottenham at Elland Road. As an exhibition of controlled aggression, flair and team-work, few watching had seen anything like it. Yet it was a real contest: Spurs were more potent than previous visitors, and at the end Leeds, for all their majesty, were hanging on for their 2-1 win.

But what a show they gave. For Robert Oxby of the *Daily Telegraph*, Leeds produced 'an awe-inspiring and quicksilver grace that had a majesty and scope unequalled in Britain since real Madrid beat Eintracht in 1960'. The critics, to Revie's delight, had been seduced.

While tilting at Wembley, Leeds were, inevitably, enmeshed in the race for the Championship. But away from Elland Road, lapses and

Great Matches

THE CENTENARY FA CUP FINAL

Wembley, 6 May 1972
Attendance 100,000

Arsenal 0   Leeds United 1
Clarke

Some finals, like wines from awkward vintages, deserve reappraisal. For a long time, this one was harsh and unwelcoming: McNab and George for Arsenal, Hunter and Bremner for Leeds were all booked in the first half-hour. With Arsenal intent on the role of destroyers, Leeds' first job was to assert themselves and, being a team for all seasons, they were able to win a kicking match as well as a football contest.

But when Allan Clarke struck after 53 minutes, a closed-up game suddenly blossomed. It was as if the splendour of his goal, a flying header connecting with Mick Jones' centre from near the right-hand corner flag, served to remind everyone that this was meant to be a great occasion.

The football began to flow. Charlie George smote the Leeds bar, his chance created through a series of deft Arsenal passes. But Leeds, their tensions evaporated, started playing with majesty: Lorimer crashed a shot against the base of a post; Clarke had earlier headed against the bar. Yet Arsenal, though outclassed, were only ever a goal away from parity; and it took Paul Reaney on the goal-line to preserve Leeds' slender lead by blocking a volley from Alan Ball.

Rather than kill the game with defensive possession, as of old, Leeds never stopped pressing for a second goal. But as Mick Jones led another assault near the end, he collided with Arsenal goalkeeper Geoff Barnett and dislocated his elbow. It was a punishing price to pay for a great victory.

Arsenal: Barnett, Rice, McNab, Storey, McLintock, Simpson, Armstrong, Ball, George, Radford (Kennedy), Graham.

Leeds United: Harvey, Reaney, Madeley, Bremner, Charlton, Hunter, Lorimer, Clarke, Jones, Giles, Gray.

Referee: D. Smith (Gloucester).

dropped points were causing tension. Perhaps weary from their exertions in retrieving a two-goal deficit to draw 2-2 at West Ham on Good Friday, Leeds were out of sorts at Derby the following day. They lost 2-0, a defeat that would cost them dear. Beautiful though Leeds were to watch, their iron grip was not quite what it once was.

And now for the double? Bremner and the team celebrate winning the FA Cup against Arsenal.

And the fates were always on hand to mug them: the pleasure of a 3-0 victory over Stoke City on 8 April marred by Terry Cooper breaking a leg – an injury that effectively ended his career at Elland Road. Leeds could ill afford the loss of his talents. Madeley's ability to slot in anywhere – during 1971-2 he filled five positions and played in every League and Cup match – had never been so important.

When Leeds played Birmingham City in the FA Cup semi-final at Hillsborough, they were back in the old swinging rhythm. Birmingham, Second Division big shots on the verge of promotion, were blown away in the first half-hour by goals from Jones and Lorimer. Thereafter, Leeds swaggered around as they pleased, sealing the game with a third from Mick Jones on 65 minutes. Their reward: a final against Arsenal. Neutrals feared a war of attrition.

Just two days after the final, Leeds were scheduled to play at Wolves, needing just a draw to take the title. The Football League refused any re-scheduling, saying it would interfere with preparations for England's European Nations Cup and Wolves' UEFA Cup final. There was no mercy from the fixture list.

No one expected a subtle FA Cup final. It did, however, contain more golden moments than some dared hope for.

Celebrations were much more muted among the players than the throngs of Leeds fans, who had turned this into one of the most raucous finals ever. For pursuit of the double was only half-done and there were walking wounded. Jones, who, his arm heavily strapped, had struggled valiantly up to the royal box for his winner's medal, was a non-starter for Molineux; Gray and Clarke were doubtful but played anyway. Without them, the attack would have been threadbare.

More than 53,000, half of them Leeds camp followers, descended on Wolverhampton that hectic Monday night. But it was another game too far – just – for Revie's men. The atmosphere galvanised Wolves players who were much fresher and played for pride with a vengeance. Leeds, needing only a draw to take the League title and become possibly the finest double winners of all time, went two down with just over 20 minutes left to goals from Francis Munro and Derek Dougan.

But Bremner, for one, was not done. Straight after Dougan's strike, from a brilliant passing move involving Madeley and Giles, he fired

home from close range. The game became a siege, a saga of penalty claims turned down, desperate defence from Wolves and brilliant saves by Phil Parkes. It was a defeat that meant Derby County were Champions; and that once more, the greatest prize had been snatched from Revie's ill-starred troopers.

Reshaping the Team

It was time now for Revie to think seriously about reshaping his team. Mick Jones, like Eddie Gray, was injury-prone; and Jack Charlton, at 37, on borrowed time. Reinforcements finally began to appear: left back Trevor Cherry and centre half Roy Ellam were signed from Huddersfield;

'I don't think he had a single weakness.' Coach Syd Owen on Paul Madeley.

and Joe Jordan, a raw young centre forward, signed from Morton on the recommendation of Bobby Collins.

It was time, at last, to make David Harvey first-choice goalkeeper. Gary Sprake, who had enormous natural talent and produced many match-saving heroic performances, had also made too many mistakes for comfort while Harvey, emerging from Sprake's shadow towards the end of 1971-72, had hardly put a foot wrong.

In 1972-73 Leeds remained the same old Leeds, competing for everything. But there was a stronger smell of fallibility about them than normal. Revie never resolved who should play at centre half: Roy Ellam, who was not really up to the Leeds standard, was one of four players tried at number five.

Bremner began the season carrying an injury. Some journalists suggested that he was over the hill but most changed their tune in the autumn as Leeds clicked into a regular winning rhythm. This began in began in fine style when, after successive defeats by Newcastle and Liverpool, Leeds thrashed Derby, the Champions, 5-0. 'Bremner is far from an extinct volcano – the eruptions of energy less spectacular but the subtlety even clearer to see,' reported the *Observer*.

Three weeks later Revie's men exacted a degree of revenge for events in May: Leeds' 2-0 win over Wolves at Molineux was cool, collected and bordering on the arrogant. By New Year, the Championship became a three-horse race involving Leeds, Liverpool and Arsenal, but as Liverpool constantly nudged in front, Leeds became distracted by other matters: defence of the FA Cup, and a first challenge for the European Cup-Winners' Cup was serious business.

They insisted on making things difficult for themselves. Fierce encounters brought a flurry of bookings and mid-season suspensions for Bremner and Hunter. League form began to suffer as tensions, rarely far from the surface, brought about ill-tempered matches. At Derby on 3 March, a spectacle of 50 fouls, endless feuds and arguments ended in Leeds' favour, a 3-2 victory with two penalties and a predator's goal from Allan Clarke. It had been a wild introduction to the First Division for Gordon McQueen, making his debut.

On 17 March, Leeds returned to the Baseball Ground for a sixth round FA Cup tie. This was a better-behaved game, the result

50 Greatest Players

EDDIE GRAY Left winger

Joined Leeds: January 1963   **From:** School

Debut: v Sheffield Wednesday, 1 January 1966

Appearances: 579   **Goals:** 69

Left Leeds: October 1985   **For:** Whitby Town

Re-joined Leeds: 1995 (as coach)

Honours won with Leeds: Division 1 championship 1969; Fairs Cup winner 1968; FA Cup winner 1972; League Cup winner 1968; 12 Scotland caps

Three days before his 18th birthday, former Scotland schoolboy international Eddie Gray made a stylish scoring debut and helped invigorate his team in the latter half of 1966-67. Despite an injury-dogged career, Gray's wing play made Leeds sparkle. His performance against Wembley against Chelsea in 1970 was the stuff of schoolboy fantasy and his meandering runs and goals will live long in the memory.

A key figure in the 1968-69 championship side, Gray was robbed of a second Championship medal after receiving the worst attentions of Manchester United defenders in 1973. For the next few years his appearances were sporadic, before Allan Clarke converted him into a full back – a position Gray found 'ridiculously easy'.

He was appointed player-manager following Leeds' traumatic relegation in 1982 but was sacked – many felt unjustly – in 1985. He returned to Elland Road in 1995 as a youth team coach and is now assistant manager.

snatched by a goal from Peter Lorimer on the half-hour, from which point Leeds rediscovered their old knack of closing down and shutting out the opposition to ensure a victory.

They made stealthy progress in the European Cup-Winners' Cup, knocking out Ankaragucu and Carl Zeiss Jena before a quarter-final in March against Rapid Bucharest. The home leg, won 5-0, showed Leeds capable of blitzing serious opposition while exercising self-restraint when assailed by the Romanians' reckless tackling. After an 8-1 aggregate win, two mean semi-final matches against Hajduk Split made for a grim anti-climax. The crucial action centred on Allan Clarke, whose run and decisive first-half goal transcended the spoiler of a first leg at Elland Road before he got sent off for retaliation.

Billy Bremner and Johnny Giles: two of the greatest footballers of their generation.

By then, 25 April 1973, Liverpool were uncatchable at the top of the division but Leeds had reached Wembley for their second successive FA Cup final. The semi against Wolves at Maine Road was a match of thrills and frenzied pressure from both sides. Amid Leeds' second-half bombardment of the Wolves' defence, Bremner, once again, stole the match, barging home a ball hooked into the goal mouth by Peter Lorimer.

Leeds' opponents at Wembley were Second Division Sunderland, improbable semi-final conquerors of Arsenal. Revie's men were the hottest favourites in living memory despite suffering three successive League defeats on the run-in. Yet while on Wearside there was a sense of fiesta, FA Cup final day found Revie in irritable, superstitious mood, 'more uptight than I'd ever seen him', according to Eddie Gray. The manager's mood became infectious.

Eleven days after the debacle at Wembley, Leeds seemed gripped by apprehension when arriving in Salonika for the European Cup-Winners' Cup final against AC Milan. Injuries and suspension deprived them of

Bremner, Clarke, Giles and Eddie Gray, their cutting edge and creative force. Revie's patched-up team included Terry Yorath, Gray's younger brother Frank, and Mick Bates. Moreover there were rumours it might not be Revie's team much longer, for he had travelled to Greece while mulling over another offer to manage Everton.

As events unfolded, it looked as if Leeds were playing not against 11 men but 12, such was the partiality of Greek referee Christos

Great Matches

FA CUP FINAL   **Wembley, 5 May 1973**
                                                    Attendance 100,000

Sunderland 1   Leeds United 0
Porterfield

The pre-match psychological battle had been won by Sunderland, with Bob Stokoe, their track-suited manager full of wisecracks and jibes at the expense of his old enemy Don Revie. But if Revie's team, contrastingly stiff and in suits, had the air of men who knew that few neutrals wanted them to win, almost everyone thought they would. Leeds were used to the rest of the world being against them. And the early exchanges suggested that being the people's favourites would not be enough for Sunderland.

But when they finally broke out and Harvey tipped an innocuous shot from Vic Halom over the bar, the match took a dramatic turn. From the corner Halom flicked on, and with the Leeds defence on its heels, Ian Porterfield smashed the ball home.

Leeds, 1-0 down against the run of play, continued to play the better football. But the hallmark of this final was a superhuman save on 65 minutes that denied Leeds their equalizer as they attacked with hurricane force. Reaney's inviting centre, headed goalwards by Trevor Cherry and beaten away by goalkeeper Jim Montgomery, fell to Lorimer. But, as the man with the fiercest shot in the land let fly, Montgomery launched himself off the ground and nudged the ball on to the underside of the bar.

This was a match that defied all understanding; a day when men with enormous heart, buoyed by overwhelming support, conquered superior skill.

Leeds United: Harvey, Reaney, Cherry, Bremner, Madeley, Hunter, Lorimer, Clarke, Jones, Giles, Gray (Yorath).

Sunderland: Montgomery, Malone, Guthrie, Horswill, Watson, Pitt, Kerr, Hughes, Halom, Porterfield, Tueart.

Referee: K. Burns.

Michas towards the Italians. The tone was set from the fourth minute when Madeley was penalized for what many thought a fair tackle. The resulting indirect free kick from Chiarugi was deflected and squirted into the Leeds net off the foot of the post.

This, the scruffiest of goals, settled the shabbiest of matches. For most of the rest of it, Leeds laid siege to the Milan goal, three times denied what looked like clear penalties, while Italian defenders, seemingly with diplomatic immunity, scythed down Revie's men. Two minutes from the end, Hunter could take no more, sent off as he lashed out after being hacked down by Rivera. The match, and Leeds' sorry season, had disintegrated.

Now a chorus of voices was suggesting that a great team was in irreversible decline. The time was up for Jack Charlton, who, when in his late 20s, looked unlikely to win anything – let alone a World Cup winner's medal. As he departed to manage Middlesbrough, critics wondered how long Bremner, Giles and Hunter could carry on. 'This may be the breaker's yard for Leeds United's most successful combination,' wrote Eric Todd of *The Guardian*. Gary Sprake, supplanted by David Harvey, had also left, transferred to Birmingham City for £100,000.

For reasons described as 'personal', Revie eschewed Everton's offer, driven perhaps to have one more go at proving the critics wrong. There was promising new blood: Joe Jordan was a skilful, potent, aggressive centre forward; and Gordon McQueen, 21 and bought for £30,000 from St Mirren in September 1972, looked as if he might measure up at centre half. Eddie Gray's younger brother Frank, who came to Leeds in 1970 when 17, was a richly talented passer of the ball. Terry Yorath, who had served most of his six years at Elland Road in the reserves, was industrious, hard-tackling and versatile.

Norman Hunter drives forward in the 1973 FA Cup final defeat by Sunderland.

One thing was clear: Leeds needed to get a grip on their discipline. Hunter and Cherry were each booked eight times during 1972-73 and there had been a fistful of cautions for others. As the FA imposed a £3,000 fine, to be suspended only if the team improved its behaviour, Leeds tried to clean up their image, appointing their first full-time public relations officer.

But the summer break had a miraculously recuperative effect. The football Leeds produced in the early autumn once more had onlookers groping for superlatives. After a seventh straight win at Southampton, John Arlott, reporting for the *Guardian*, saw Revie's men. 'Wearing the white strip of a blameless life – it was all so controlled – so free from the aura of violence they used to generate.'

And so it seemed a curious perversion of the past that, in the next game, a declining Manchester United team brought violence to Elland

---

50 Greatest Players

ALLAN CLARKE Inside forward

Joined Leeds: June 1969   **From:** Leicester City

Debut: v Manchester City (Charity Shield) 2 August 1969

Appearances: 366   **Goals:** 151

Left Leeds: June 1978   **For:** Barnsley

Honours won with Leeds: Division 1 Championship 1974; Fairs Cup winner 1971; FA Cup winner 1972; 19 England caps

When Don Revie broke the British transfer record by paying Leicester £165,000 for Clarke, few questioned that he had bought the best. One of five Staffordshire-born footballing brothers, he learned his passing craft as a midfielder at Fulham with Haynes and Cohen and honed his goalscoring skills at Leicester.

His composure was absolute. He had great acceleration, was a fine header of the ball and became a chilling executioner anywhere near goal. He also learned to become a complete team player and admits that without Mick Jones much of what he achieved would have been impossible. After Clarke left Elland Road in 1978, he began a promising stint in management, winning promotion with Barnsley before taking charge at Leeds in 1980. Sadly, a traumatic second season ended in relegation and his managerial career never recovered.

50 Greatest Players

NORMAN HUNTER Left half

Joined Leeds: October 1960   **From:** Juniors

Debut: v Swansea Town, 5 September 1962

Appearances: 726   **Goals:** 21

Left Leeds: October 1976   **For:** Bristol City

Honours won with Leeds: Division 1 Championship 1969, 1974; Division 2 Championship 1964; Fairs Cup winner 1968, 1971; FA Cup winner 1972; League Cup winner 1968; 28 England caps

Once Norman Hunter bit your legs, the memory stayed with you. He was an indefatigable hard man who hardly ever had a bad game. His speed and anticipation were often a last line of defence when others had been dragged out of position. In 1974 he was voted PFA Player of the Year. Hunter was a gifted footballer, awesome when spraying long balls around the field and with excellent close control. He also had a lethal left-foot shot.

At 33, he left Leeds United for Bristol City where, despite having done everything in the game, he saw the move as a fresh challenge. There he made 100 league appearances and came to be as revered at Ashton Gate as he had been at Elland Road.

Road. In a roughhouse of a 0-0 draw, they were the first team to prise a point out of Leeds during the season. Amid brutal exchanges, Eddie Gray sustained an injury at the hands of the United defence and would play only one more match in the rest of the season.

This hard-fought draw marked the end of Leeds' early season cakewalk. The next run of games was more closely contested, but Leeds held on unbeaten, deriving great satisfaction from a 1-0 home win over Champions Liverpool, their goal the fruit of a brilliant passing move finished off by a header from Mick Jones. They seemed buoyed up again: victories at Elland Road over West Ham (4-1) and Coventry (3-0) moved Alan Dunn of the *Guardian* to declare that 'Leeds players were finding levels of understanding that were other-worldly'.

Revie was starting to dream once more. 'The romantic in me hopes we might go the whole season without losing a single match,' he said;

Norman Hunter and referee Clive Thomas were familiar with each other's reputations.

though Ipswich had knocked them out of the League Cup, and by December, they had been relieved from further bother in the UEFA Cup after losing 3-2 on aggregate to Vitoria Setubal. By then, with a 3-0 demolition of Ipswich, Leeds had equalled Liverpool's modern-day record of 19 League matches unbeaten from the start of the season.

Everyone craved to knock them off their perch. There were 22 matches down, 20 to go, when Leeds arrived at Birmingham City on 29 December. More than 50,000 saw the Blues come within three minutes of lowering Leeds' colours. Both sides were under excruciating pressure as Madeley played a long ball to Lorimer down the right. As Lorimer crossed, Jordan closed in for the kill, driving the ball firmly past his old team-mate Gary Sprake.

On pitches less accommodating than in the early autumn, some results had to be ground out. By February, Giles had been absent four months, injured, and Leeds once more left most of football dumbfounded when beaten 1-0 by Bristol City at Elland Road in an FA Cup fifth round replay. Never was the Irishman's skill and cunning more badly needed as the run-in beckoned and Liverpool began chipping away what had once looked an impregnable lead.

Revie gambled on Giles for the 30th League match of the season, at Stoke. There was no Jones, McQueen, Reaney or Gray; Cooper's fitness was still in doubt though he was pressed into service as Giles' groin injury flared up once more. Stoke, 2-0 down after 19 minutes to goals from Bremner and Clarke, scented a way back. By half-time they had equalized; and on 67 minutes became the first team to put three goals past Leeds in a League match when Denis Smith crashed home a header from a corner.

50 Greatest Players

BILLY BREMNER Forward/right half

Joined Leeds: December 1959   **From:** Juniors

Debut: v Chelsea, 23 January 1960

Appearances: 773   **Goals:** 115

Left Leeds (as player): September 1976   **For:** Hull City

Honours won with Leeds: Division 1 Championship 1969, 1974; Division 2 Championship 1964; Fairs Cup winner 1968, 1971; FA Cup winner 1972; League Cup winner 1968; Footballer of the Year 1970; 54 Scotland caps

Bremner was the complete footballer, the ultimate captain who never let up. He was a source of exquisite passes and flashing goal-bound volleys. But, Leeds could have lost him: Revie had to persuade the homesick Stirling-born Bremner to stay and threatened to resign when the Leeds directors contemplated selling him.

After making an impressive debut when aged 17 and notwithstanding suspensions and injuries, Bremner was a fixture in the side for nearly 17 years. He was made captain in 1968 and was elected Footballer of the Year in 1970.

Bremner's belligerent combativeness sometimes worked against him. He was easily provoked and struggled to subdue his wilder instincts. Technically, though, he was without a weakness. His nerve invariably held for the big occasions – the indefatigable Bremner could be relied upon for decisive strikes such as in the FA Cup semi-finals of 1970 and 73.

In 1965 Bremner won the first of 54 caps for Scotland but his international career ended abruptly following a brawl outside a Copenhagen nightclub in 1975. In September 1976, he was sold to Hull City for £35,000 and returned to manage Leeds from 1985 to 1988. Although he was eventually sacked, his love for Leeds United was undimmed. The statue erected outside Elland Road following his untimely death from a heart attack in 1997 is a permanent reminder of Bremner's brilliance and fighting spirit.

A volatile match grew ever wilder; the tackles furious; the Leeds dissent more strident. Gone, in defeat, were the mild manners and control of the early season. Fluency and confidence gave way to desperation. Revie's men scratched four points out of the next six after 1-1 draws with Leicester and Newcastle and a scuffling 1-0 win at Manchester City but on 16 March lost 1-0 at Liverpool, beaten by Steve Heighway's goal seven minutes from the end of a long rearguard action.

If the Stoke defeat was a blow, this was unnerving: Liverpool, now six points behind, had two games in hand. Next up at Elland Road

50 Greatest Players

PAUL MADELEY Utility player

Joined Leeds: May 1962   **From:** Amateur football

Debut: v Manchester City, 11 January 1964

Appearances: 725   **Goals:** 34

Left Leeds: November 1980 (retired)

Honours won with Leeds: Division 1 Championship 1969, 1974; Fairs Cup winner 1968, 1971; FA Cup winner 1972; League Cup winner 1968; 24 England caps

There has rarely been a more versatile footballer than Paul Madeley. Born in Leeds, he made his debut aged 19 at centre half and in the subsequent 18 years at Elland Road, he was deployed in every position except goalkeeper.

A man of athleticism, precise passes, admirable balance and anticipation – he was a master at winning back possession. There were few more enthralling sights than a 'turbo-charged' Madeley turning defence into attack. He also had great self-control: in a team of volatile temperaments, the phlegmatic Madeley was cautioned only twice.

It took a brave man to decline a place in the Mexico 1970 World Cup squad but the exhausted Madeley did so, believing he would only be a makeweight. Ramsey respected his decision, awarding him his first cap the following year. Madeley gave Leeds many more years of excellent service before retiring in 1980.

were Burnley; but with confidence, composure and discipline shot to pieces, Leeds crashed 4-1. Another week; another calamity for Leeds, beaten 3-1 at West Ham after being a goal up. The unthinkable was happening: they could be overhauled by Liverpool. They were no longer in control of their destiny.

But while they weren't to know it, the worst was over. As onlookers sensed a disastrous meltdown, Leeds began recovering their grip by beating Derby 2-0 at Elland Road on 6 April. Two days later, after six straight wins, Liverpool lost 1-0 at Sheffield United. Both teams were now wobbling; each drew their next two matches.

Leeds' date with Sheffield United at Bramall Lane forced Revie's men to draw on all their strength and character. With the game goalless at half-time, news filtered through that Liverpool were 4-0 up against Manchester City. In the second half, Leeds went for broke, using the half-fit Mick Jones as a battering ram as they pummelled the Sheffield defence. Their 2-0 victory, with goals from Peter Lorimer, one a penalty, owed as much to brute force as to skill. It meant that the outcome of the Championship was now back in

---

Great Matches

FOOTBALL LEAGUE DIVISION ONE   **Elland Road, 20 April 1974**
Attendance 44,015

Leeds United 3   **Ipswich Town 2**

Lorimer   Talbot

Bremner   Hamilton

Clarke

Leeds finally staggered over the finishing line to claim the title. But against Ipswich, as for much of the last three months, they subjected their fans to emotional torture. And as at Stoke, they contrived to squander a two-goal lead.

Leeds' first goal was a fine one: McQueen's excellent pass to Lorimer who rifled home the chance. And when Lorimer's low free kick deflected upwards for Bremner to head a smart second goal, Leeds had carte blanche to take control. But Ipswich rallied: by half-time, 2-0 was 2-1; and then 2-2 as Bryan Hamilton equalized on 55 minutes.

Elland Road, scenting another debacle, grew fretful. Then, as Don Revie roared for more urgency, rumours swept the terraces that Liverpool were losing to Everton. Twenty minutes remained as Reaney made a foray down the right and crossed. Lorimer's header wrong-footed the Ipswich defence and Clarke pushed the ball home. 'Handball' cried Ipswich manager Bobby Robson. 'Goal' said the referee. Things could never be straightforward.

The noise thundered; everything seemed to vibrate. But Liverpool were not losing; they had drawn 0-0. Yet all the delirium at Elland Road suggested the title was won. As indeed it had been, though no-one at the time could have known it.

Leeds United: Harvey, Reaney, Cherry, Bremner, McQueen, Hunter, Lorimer, Clarke, Jones, Madeley, Gray.

Ipswich Town: Cooper, Burley, Mills, Morris, Hunter, Beattie, Hamilton, Talbot, Johnson, Osborne, Woods.

Referee: K. Baker (Rugby).

Leeds' hands as Ipswich visited for the last, melodramatic home match of the season.

Their victory over the East Anglians proved too much for Liverpool. Even if Leeds were to lose their last match at Queens Park Rangers, Shankly's men would be forced to win their three remaining games. Four days later, Arsenal visited Anfield, were subjected to the usual ferocious pressure, yet stole the match with a goal from Ray Kennedy. Leeds had been delivered the Championship on a plate

What a difference a week made. Like men reprieved, Leeds went out to celebrate before 35,353, the biggest crowd ever to pack Loftus Road; and with all the poise and calm assurance of old, clinching the match with a clinical individual goal from Allan Clarke. It was the good times revisited. But within weeks, these were to come to an abrupt and unexpected end.

League Champions 1973-74: Back row (left to right): Madeley, E. Gray, Letheran, Reaney, Harvey, Cherry, Hunter, McQueen, Jones, Jordan, Clarke, Ellam.
Front row: Bates, F. Gray, Lorimer, Bremner, Cooper, Yorath.

Chapter Seven: 1974-82
From European Cup to Division Two

The Championship had been won; the critics confounded; but sooner rather than later, Revie would have to face the trauma of rebuilding, dispensing with legends such as Bremner and Hunter. And while a chance to win the European Cup was tantalizing, more so was the prospect of managing England.

With Joe Mercer's caretaker spell as England manager coming to its end, Don Revie went after the job and got it. He cleared his desk at Elland Road at once, and without sentimentality, recommending that Johnny Giles replace him. But the Leeds board, armed with compensation from the FA, had other ideas.

New manager Brian Clough leads out his Leeds team in the 1974 Charity Shield.

Maurice Lindley, Revie's assistant, took charge until, to the astonishment of all, the directors hired Brian Clough, a trenchant critic of the Leeds' bad habits, foul play and gamesmanship. Clough was still banging the same drum in the club programme before the first home match of 1974-75 against Queens Park Rangers. 'The club has to be sold to the public because what they achieved on the field was not enough to win over the public's hearts. People have begrudged them their success,' he wrote.

His 44-day tenure of the post, which began in July 1974, became the stuff of soap opera. When Clough arrived from Brighton, he informed the players that all their hard-won medals had been won by cheating. He left, possibly chastened, but undoubtedly richer.

Clough brought with him his former trainer Jimmy Gordon – Les Cocker had followed Revie to the England set-up – and two trusted Derby players, midfielder John McGovern and centre forward John O'Hare. He also paid Nottingham Forest £250,000 for their quixotic inside forward Duncan McKenzie.

Suddenly there was an unhappy cocktail of personalities at Elland Road. Most of the players had only ever known Revie and his methods. Some of Clough's views came as an insult. 'The atmosphere was terrible,' Eddie Gray recalls. 'I honestly think if things had continued, the club would gave struggled to survive that year.'

Clough, who had long criticized Leeds' behavioural standards, took a dim view of Bremner's sending off at Wembley following a fracas with Kevin Keegan in the 1974 Charity Shield match with Liverpool.

Great Managers –1961-74

DON REVIE

Not only Leeds' but one of English football's greatest ever managers. Many who saw Leeds' rise from Division Two no-hopers to become one of Europe's elite would put Revie in that category. Through his playing days at Leicester, Hull, Manchester City, Sunderland and of course, Leeds, Revie had developed a deep understanding of the game, a fascination with tactics and a indefatigable desire to win.

Loyal to his players, unafraid to adopt new ideas, cynical where necessary, Revie was the master. He displayed genius in the transfer market as the signings of Bobby Collins and Johnny Giles prove; his introduction of young players – Reaney, Bremner, Lorimer and others – was timed to perfection; and he had an ability to get the best out of less naturally talented players such as Charlton and Cherry. Some might criticize his sides' cautious or aggressive approach or failure to win where it mattered, but no-one can deny his achievements. For nearly a decade Leeds dominated English football and walked tall in Europe. Revie left Leeds to become England manager in 1974, but fell into disgrace three years later, walking out to manage the United Arab Emirates. He died in 1989 after suffering for three years with motor neurone disease.

If early results had been good, things might have been different. John McGovern, standing in for Bremner, whose Wembley tantrums had earned an 11-match suspension, soon had the Leeds fans on his back. Some saw him as a usurper of the number four shirt. By early September, Leeds were languishing in 19th place, with one win from first six matches. Only a late goal from Peter Lorimer staved off League Cup defeat by Third Division Huddersfield. Hunter and Clarke, as well as Bremner, were suspended; Gray and Jones were long-term injuries.

Clough was in dire need of moral support. But Peter Taylor, his old assistant at Derby and Brighton, chose to stay at the Goldstone Ground. Syd Owen, the Leeds coach, had little time for his new manager and conscientiously avoided him. Clough himself was frequently absent. As mutiny stirred, two anti-Clough members of the board, Sam Bolton and Percy Woodward, called a players' meeting to clear the air. The players said their piece, some more forcefully than others; although few now care to dwell on their contributions.

On 12 September 1974, an emergency board meeting was held after which Clough was sacked, handsomely compensated, and left declaring that it was 'a sad day for Leeds United'. His managerial talent was indisputable but his cocky, iconoclastic style jarred with

Billy Bremner follows Kevin Keegan off the field after their dismissal in the 1974 Charity Shield. Bremner was given a £500 fine and an 11-match suspension.

veteran internationals who had seen and won almost everything. 'The Leeds United club and the happiness of Leeds United players must come first,' said chairman Manny Cussins.

For the Leeds board, it had been a costly and humiliating episode. Even a match programme admitted that it had shown up the club 'in a bad and reactionary light', though denied that 'player power' had done for Clough. Once more, Maurice Lindley was called upon to hold the fort. Cussins favoured appointing Johnny Giles as Clough's successor; but without the unanimous backing of the board, Giles suspected the job might be a poisoned chalice and did not pursue the position.

Armfield Recruited

Besides a good manager, Leeds United needed a healer. Three weeks later, the directors recruited Jimmy Armfield, who had won the Third Division Championship with Bolton and been one of England's most distinguished full backs, capped 43 times. Armfield had a calm, affable temperament and unlike Clough was the last person to cause gratuitous offence.

And by the time he arrived, there were signs that Leeds were out of the sick bay. Immediately after Clough had left, they lost again, 2-1, at Burnley, but the following week thrashed Sheffield United 5-1 at Elland Road. They also dealt summarily with FC Zurich in the European Cup first round, winning the home leg 4-1. In the prevailing climate all Clough's new hands, O'Hare, McGovern and McKenzie, had been dropped: McGovern, indeed, had played for the last time the previous week in the 1-1 draw with Luton.

Armfield was to rebuild thoughtfully and without rancour. He bought no new players in 1974-75 and had to contend with the loss through injury of Mick Jones, all season, and Norman Hunter throughout the winter. He quickly made use of McKenzie's deft talents while releasing O'Hare and McGovern to join Clough at his new club, Nottingham Forest.

Slowly Leeds hauled themselves off the floor but only to a mid-table comfort zone. For the first time in ten years, they failed to contest the

50 Greatest Players

PETER LORIMER Winger/midfielder

Joined Leeds: May 1962   **From:** Juniors

Debut: v Southampton, 29 September 1962

Appearances: 685   **Goals:** 238

Left Leeds: March 1979   **For:** Toronto Blizzards

Rejoined Leeds: December 1983   **From:** Vancouver Whitecaps

Left Leeds: December 1985   **For:** Whitby Town

Honours won with Leeds: Division 1 Championship 1969, 1974; FA Cup 1972; Fairs Cup 1968, League Cup 1968, 1971; 21 Scotland caps

Although the youngest ever Leeds debutant at 15 years 289 days, Lorimer had to wait another three years for a chance to establish a regular first-team place. Soon he became a sensation.

Not just the hardest shot in the land, Lorimer had great stamina, sublime passing ability and could cross superbly from the right. He was an outstanding figure as Leeds scaled new heights in 1971-2 and during Scotland's 1974 World Cup campaign. But many will remember him for his disallowed goals, thunderbolts against Chelsea in the 1967 FA Cup semi-final and Bayern Munich in the 1975 European Cup final.

At 32, Lorimer supplanted Charles as Leeds' record scorer, before leaving for Toronto Blizzards. In 1983, he returned as a midfielder, helping tend Eddie Gray's young prospects. He is now a media pundit and runs the Commercial Hotel, a pub near Elland Road.

Championship, finishing ninth. But much else was happening: Europe and the FA Cup thrust Leeds centre-stage.

A fourth round draw with Southern League Wimbledon whetted the appetites of those looking for the mighty to fall. Once more, Leeds, already removed from the League Cup after a 3-0 defeat by Fourth Division Chester, flirted with humiliation. Wimbledon held the Champions to a 0-0 draw at Elland Road, and lost the replay only through a Dave Bassett own goal. For Leeds, dismayed onlookers as Dickie Guy saved Peter Lorimer's penalty in the first game, it was a reminder of their fallibility.

Cup fever was building up. More than 46,000 watched Wimbledon at Elland Road; and 45,000 the replay at Selhurst Park. In round five

Leeds were, again, conquerors of Derby County, 1-0 winners at the Baseball Ground, then in the quarter-final paired with League front-runners Ipswich Town. This marathon tie, in four instalments, drew a record 38,010 to Portman Road, while the replay attracted the first 50,000 crowd in four years to Elland Road. Only after two more replays, at Leicester, did Ipswich squeeze through, 3-2 victors.

They were rising stars who had dragged some of the old resilient best out of Leeds. In the European Cup there was a memory bank of lessons on which to draw. They beat FC Zurich 5-3 on aggregate in round one; Ujpest Dosza 5-1 in round two against whom, during a spiteful first leg in Budapest, Duncan McKenzie marked his European debut by being sent off; and in round three, Anderlecht 4-0, where a 3-0 win in the first, fog-bound leg at Elland Road proved decisive.

The semi-final against Barcelona attracted the third 50,000 plus crowd to Leeds in less than a month. While Elland Road, by Barcelona's Nou Camp standards, was no football cathedral, profits from the Revie era helped replace the primitive Scratching Shed with the imposing 7,700 capacity South Stand.

Peter Lorimer built a reputation for packing the hardest shot in the land.

Injuries had forced key adjustments on Armfield. Reserve goalkeeper David Stewart, drafted in after David Harvey injured his foot in a car crash, had been gratifyingly reliable cover while Frank Gray showed versatility by dropping in at left back. Terry Cooper had struggled in vain to reclaim his place and was transferred to Middlesbrough in March 1975 for £50,000.

Monumental Encounters

Stewart and Gray came of age during the monumental encounters with Barcelona. In the first, a taut thriller at Elland Road, Leeds attacked fervently and played most of the football, subduing, for the most part, Johan Cruyff, reputedly Europe's greatest player. But between fine goals from Bremner and Clarke, Leeds conceded an equalizer midway through the second half. Two-one was a fragile lead to take to Barcelona.

Fragile, but enough. A goal on seven minutes from Lorimer, thumped home with incomparable force, was the perfect start, dampening the spirits of the 110,000 home crowd. Leeds took the heat out of the game until the 70th minute but then Barcelona fashioned an equalizer

through Clares. When, shortly after, McQueen was sent off for throwing a punch at the same player, Leeds were in momentary disarray. While the last 20 minutes were a time for cool heads, Leeds owed their passage to the final, above all, to inspired goalkeeping from David Stewart in the midst of an unrelenting Barcelona offensive.

Whole-hearted but often maligned, Terry Yorath was to inherit Giles' number ten shirt.

Great Matches

EUROPEAN CUP FINAL   **Parc des Princes, Paris, 28 May 1975**
                                Attendance 48,374

Bayern Munich 2   Leeds United 0
Roth
Müller

This, the biggest match in Leeds United's history, contained all the tragedy, ugliness and misfortune that had stalked the Revie era. Veterans such as Reaney, Bremner, Hunter and Giles had hoped to claim Europe's top prize before fading away.

Bayern had great men: defender Franz Beckenbauer and Gerd Müller, one of Europe's most potent strikers. But for much of the match the Germans seemed content to sit back as Leeds came forward at full throttle, taking advantage of disruption caused to Bayern through first-half injuries to Andersson and Hoeness.

Jordan and Clarke marauded, causing continual problems, and Bayern lived closed to the edge. A handball and a foul by Beckenbauer on Clarke seemed to merit penalties. On the balance of play, Leeds should have led at half-time. Then, on 67 minutes came a dreadful turning point. Leeds, it seemed, had finally got their just reward as a thunderous volley from Lorimer scorched past Sepp Maier into the net. But it was, to general mystification, disallowed because other team-mates were adjudged offside although they were clearly not interfering with play.

The vagaries of officialdom once more knocked the stuffing out of Leeds. Bayern seized on their distracted state and struck with classic counter-attacking goals from Roth and Müller. The match, and with it Revie's dream of emulating Real Madrid, was over. The last desperate minutes were played out to a background of drunken Leeds fans rioting in the stands, the harbinger of a grim new era.

Bayern Munich: Maier, Durnberger, Andersson (Weiss), Schwarzenbeck, Beckenbauer, Roth, Tortensson, Zobel, Müller, Hoeness (Wunder), Kapellman.

Leeds United: Stewart, Reaney, F. Gray, Bremner, Madeley, Hunter, Lorimer, Clarke, Jordan, Giles, Yorath (E. Gray).

Referee: M. Kitabdjian (France).

Revie had watched defeat in the final as a TV pundit, as distraught as if Leeds had still been his team. In a way, it still was, carrying the baggage of the past; though now the time had come for his old-stagers to move on.

Johnny Giles was first to go, departing for West Bromwich to become player-manager. The number ten shirt, worn with such distinction by Giles and Bobby Collins before him, went to Terry Yorath. He was a willing industrious player, more skilful than the boorish elements in the Leeds crowd gave him credit for. In the end, these helped drive Yorath away but he made a sound contribution in 1975-76, where, mid-season, Leeds played scintillating football and shot towards the top of the League.

Some of their best moments came from Duncan McKenzie, a box of tricks capable of most things except consistency. But a dip in form from late January expunged any hopes of a serious title challenge while early exits from the League and FA Cups made for a tame end to the season.

50 Greatest Players

TONY CURRIE Midfielder

Joined Leeds: August 1976   **From:** Sheffield United

Debut: v West Bromwich Albion, 21 August 1976

Appearances: 124   **Goals:** 16

Left Leeds: May 1979   **For:** Queens Park Rangers

Honours won with Leeds: 10 England caps

Tony Currie was an artist rather than enforcer: a dazzling individualist, cantering around midfield, spraying delectable passes and unleashing fearsome banana shots. Unlike Revie's men he perhaps lacked the stomach for drudgery, but he was no soft touch. He had strength and determination to win the ball and then throw defences into turmoil with muscular goalward runs or through inch-perfect passes.

Signed from Sheffield United for £240,000, Currie gave Leeds hope, especially for much of the 1978-79 season in which the team finished fifth. Despite his talents, inconsistency, evident in some of Leeds' more mundane matches, is blamed for his paltry number of England caps. When for family reasons he agreed a move to Queens Park Rangers at the end of 1978-79, Leeds cast around in vain for a creative force to replace him.

Masterful in the air, Gordon McQueen was a mainstay of the Leeds defence for five years.

Leeds had finished fifth – in normal circumstances good enough to secure a UEFA Cup place. But the savage finale of the European Cup final had put the club in the dock, facing a four-year ban from any European contest. And while Armfield's reasoned intervention helped reduce this to two years, horizons at Elland Road were narrowed during that time.

In 1976-77, Armfield's stealthy rebuilding continued. By early autumn, the two great icons and the pillars on which glory years had been built, Hunter and Bremner, had departed for Bristol City and Hull. Trevor Cherry, sturdy and increasingly authoritative, took over the number four shirt and the captaincy, and Paul Madeley slotted in at number six. One joy was the return to fitness and form of Eddie Gray, who had an almost uninterrupted run at number 11; and another, the arrival of playmaker Tony Currie. Terry Yorath, unappreciated by many and disillusioned, was sold to Coventry for £125,000.

The team was to struggle desperately for goals. McKenzie, after two impish seasons, departed for Anderlecht, while Allan Clarke was lost to the Leeds team for half the campaign through injury. Jordan had a heavy, sometimes frustrating burden to shoulder up front.

League performances were fitful: Leeds kept their powder dry for the FA Cup. They were at their exhilarating best in flattening

Great Matches

FA CUP FIFTH ROUND Elland Road, 26 February 1977

Attendance 47,731

Leeds United 1   Manchester City 0
Cherry

The pitch was like a pudding; the match had been in danger of being called off. Sometimes the action was tentative; at others more like unarmed combat. This, though it had some exquisite moments, was miles from a football classic. What distinguished it was the volcanic atmosphere; the potential for explosion; the eruptive climax.

City spent much of the first half defending in depth. Currie floated while Jordan clattered about the pitch in street fighter mode. Brian Kidd for City and Eddie Gray for Leeds each hit the bar while Dennis Tueart failed to capitalize on a collision between David Harvey and Gordon McQueen.

At half-time it had been an absorbing encounter though crying out to be seized by the throat. In the second half, Leeds began pounding towards Joe Corrigan's goal in front of the Kop. When on 55 minutes Joe Jordan crossed from the right and Clarke's header scorched towards the net, waves of supporters began tumbling down the terraces to acclaim the lead. Then Corrigan materialized out of the blue and with a giant hand flipped the ball away.

It was 0-0 with four minutes left; but still a sense that something could happen. As Eddie Gray launched the ball diagonally upfield, Jordan's downward header was met by Trevor Cherry. His first effort was blocked by a City defender; the second, though hit far from cleanly, despatched into the net. Never would such numbers congregate again at Elland Road for so raucous a victory celebration.

Leeds United: Harvey, Reaney, Hampton, Cherry, McQueen, Madeley, F. Gray, Clarke, Jordan, Currie, E. Gray.

Manchester City: Corrigan, Clements, Donachie, Doyle, Watson, Power, Conway, Kidd, Royle, Hartford, Tueart.

Referee: W.T. Gow (Swansea).

Norwich with a five goal first-half blitz in round three; had a storming 2-1 win at Birmingham City in round four where Frank Gray roamed midfield to wonderful effect; then overturned Manchester City at Elland Road in round five, a match of uncontainable excitement.

For the quarter-final at Wolverhampton, Division Two leaders, there was a change of mood and a match neatly controlled, the result secured by Eddie Gray's first-half goal. History suggested that Leeds might vanquish Manchester United in the semi-final at Hillsborough, but the Reds were playing vibrant football and caught Leeds on the chin twice in ten minutes with goals from Jimmy Greenhoff and Steve Coppell – blows that Leeds, despite restoring order and scoring a second-half penalty, never shrugged off.

Support ebbed away, with crowds for the final few home matches barely struggling over 20,000 as Leeds sank to tenth. In 1977-78 there was more of the same: inconsistency in the League with interest sustained by a run to the League Cup semi-final. But there, defeat by Brian Clough's Nottingham Forest was all the more miserable for emphasizing the chasm in class between victors and vanquished.

A run of six wins out of eight before Christmas had given hopes of better things. Armfield had pepped up the attack, still depleted by the absence through injury of Clarke, by recruiting striker Ray Hankin from Burnley for £170,000 and Scottish international outside left Arthur Graham from Aberdeen for £125,000. Hankin, a battering ram of a player, scored 20 goals in 33 League outings, and Graham's buoyant displays on the left flank soon made him a favourite. In November 1977, he bought midfielder Brian Flynn, also from Burnley, for £175,000. Flynn was energetic and combative, able to strike good long passes: in the Bremner mould though lacking that player's genius.

But there were ominous signs of discontent among the likes of Joe Jordan and Gordon McQueen. 'After the European Cup final and that team breaking up, I wanted to try and win things and I didn't think we were going to do that,' said Jordan. By January 1978, he was sold to Manchester United for £350,000, soon followed by McQueen who netted £495,000, a record transfer deal between two English clubs.

These were becoming unhappy times. Hooliganism, the bane of many a club, was infecting Leeds with a particular virulence. The third round FA Cup tie with Manchester City contained wretched

50 Greatest Players

GORDON McQUEEN Defender

Joined Leeds: September 1972 **From:** St Mirren

Debut: v Derby County, 3 March 1973

Appearances: 172   **Goals:** 19

Left Leeds: February 1978   **For:** Manchester United

Honours won with Leeds: Division 1 Championship 1974; 17 Scotland caps

Having failed to make the grade with Liverpool or Glasgow Rangers, McQueen found himself in modest surroundings at St Mirren before Don Revie bought him in 1972 for £30,000. Despite being six feet three and a half, he was comfortable on the ball – and emerged as a fine successor to Jack Charlton. With his arrival as a regular in 1973-74, Leeds began their 29-match unbeaten run, some brilliant football and a League Championship.

McQueen was dominant in the air, energetic when covering and with surging runs turned defence into attack. He matured with astonishing speed, winning his first Scottish cap just 15 months after his debut. An achilles injury restricted appearances in 1975-6, and in 1978, McQueen's ambitious nature took him to Manchester United where five years later he won an FA Cup winner's medal.

scenes: first an unseemly spat between McQueen and Harvey; then City goalkeeper Joe Corrigan being attacked by a member of the crowd as his team went 2-0 up. With such supporters, Leeds hardly needed enemies. Punishment beckoned: the FA ordered all cup-ties to be played away for three years; though subsequently the ban was imposed only through 1978-79.

McQueen's departure left a large hole in defence. In March, Armfield signed Paul Hart, a craggy young defender from Blackpool who also had been pursued by Everton. After a torrid first few games, characterized by own goals and blunders, Hart soon got the measure of the First Division.

Leeds finished ninth, respectable enough, but in summer 1978, Armfield was sacked by a board impatient for success. His football expertise was unquestionable; he made some good buys; but he was probably too mild-mannered to restore the club's fortunes. 'I always

50 Greatest Players

JOE JORDAN Centre forward

Joined Leeds: October 1970 **From:** Morton

Debut: v Arsenal, 11 September 1971

Appearances: 215 **Goals:** 48

Left Leeds: January 1978 **For:** Manchester United

Honours won with Leeds: Division 1 Championship 1974;
27 Scotland caps

With a recommendation from Morton manager and
Leeds old boy, Bobby Collins, Revie had no hesitation
in speculating on Morton's raw and uncut 18-year-old
Joe Jordan. As cover for injury-prone Jones, Jordan quickly
made the grade. He used his height and strength in the air to master more experienced
opponents, though his ferocity on the pitch together with his toothless snarl was belied
by his soft-spoken manner off it. Like Jones, he was full of direct running, though more
antagonistic; and always eager for possession, well able to hold the ball under pressure.

Within two years, Jordan had won his first Scottish cap and in 1974 went to the
World Cup Finals. He left Leeds in 1978 in search of greater things, finding success
first at Manchester United and then AC Milan before going on to become manager at
Hearts and Bristol City.

got the impression he never enjoyed the job,' said Eddie Gray.
'I don't think he liked laying down the law but the hassle is part and
parcel of everything.'

Armfield's was not the only departure. Two others from the great
past, Allan Clarke and Paul Reaney, also moved on: Reaney, a stalwart
for almost 16 years now approaching 34, to Bradford City on a free
transfer and Clarke, nearing 32, to Barnsley as player-manager.

As Armfield's successor, Leeds appointed someone who did have a
record of being ruthless when needed, the former Celtic boss Jock
Stein. Stein, a giant among managers and sore at having been kicked
upstairs in favour of Billy McNeil, arrived to a hero's welcome. But
within 44 days he had gone, lured away when offered the job of
Scotland team manager. Stein's rapid exit left everyone at Leeds

Duncan McKenzie, a box of tricks capable of most things except consistency.

deflated. 'I always got the feeling that coming here was just a stop-gap and that he was waiting for the phone call from Scotland,' said Gray. 'We never really got to know him.' Supporters who took Stein's first column in the club programme at face value were entitled to feel short-changed. 'My aim is to build up to the success level that Leeds United are associated with, and if I did not think that possible, then I would not have taken the job,' he wrote. 'I also want to establish a close contact with you, the supporters of Leeds United.'

Once more, Maurice Lindley became caretaker until, in October, directors recruited Sunderland manager Jimmy Adamson, who previously had an excellent track record of finding and developing players when in charge at Burnley. Leeds had made a patchy start but, with stability, results started flowing their way.

Striker John Hawley, an £80,000 close season buy from Hull City, astonished many with his unflashy composure and the ease with which he adapted. Suddenly, with goals flying in from the likes of Hawley, Hankin and Graham, with Currie and Flynn an effective double-act in midfield, and with Hart, Madeley, Cherry and Frank Gray coherent at the back, Leeds looked a well-oiled machine and were playing football as good as anyone's.

Mid-season, they embarked on an unbeaten run of 16 League matches. Their 3-3 draw with West Bromwich Albion, the other form team, in round four of the FA Cup, was a fiesta of vibrant attacking play, one of the most exhilarating matches of 1978-79. By late January, expectations simmered as Leeds again reached the semi-final of the League Cup. Southampton, less formidable opponents than Nottingham Forest the previous year, looked there for the taking; but Leeds contrived to squander a two-goal lead at Elland Road drawing 2-2, and then, for all their frenetic pressure, lose 1-0 at The Dell.

Defeat at West Bromwich in the FA Cup fourth round replay a month later stopped the season in its tracks. While Leeds finished fifth, other defeats by Manchester United, 4-1 at Old Trafford, and 3-0 at home by Champions Liverpool in the last match of 1978-79, were uncomfortable reminders of how easily they could be brushed aside by old rivals. Liverpool's stroll to victory gave them 68 points, eclipsing Leeds' record points total of 67. A piece of proud history from the Revie era had been surrendered with precious little fight.

With 20 goals in 33 matches Ray Hankin proved a good short-term purchase.

Great Managers –1974-78

JIMMY ARMFIELD

A former full back with Blackpool and England, Armfield had proved his managerial credentials by winning the Third Division championship with Bolton. However after the Clough fiasco, Armfield's equable temperament was another big factor in his favour.

Armfield's task was a difficult one: dismantling the ageing Revie side and still maintaining a Championship challenge. Nevertheless he enjoyed some success; in taking the club to the European Cup final for the first time (Armfield, below left, and the Leeds bench watch the match against Bayern Munich); finding room for crowd-pleasers like McKenzie and Currie and bringing a stability that subsequent events proved did not come naturally to the club. Despite finishing in the top ten of the First Division every season, the Leeds directors were used to greater things and Jimmy Armfield was sacked.

The close season departure of Tony Currie was widely lamented. Midfield creators of his calibre were rare; without him, Elland Road became a grimmer place. Frank Gray, who had no great desire to leave, was also sold, joining Nottingham Forest for £500,000. Hawley, after one splendid season, soon followed, taken to Sunderland in a player exchange deal with Wayne Entwistle. Of the newcomers, most was expected of Alan Curtis, signed from Swansea for £400,000 and regarded as the best striker outside the First Division.

Luck did not go with Curtis. Two goals on his debut at Bristol City promised much but he was injured mid-season having managed only

Tony Currie paraded a rare combination of strength, balance and exquisite skill.

four League goals in 22 outings. Indeed, injuries played havoc with whatever strategy Adamson had. By mid-November, with results worsening by the week, and crowds falling below 20,000, there was a sense of disillusionment unseen at Leeds since the pre-Revie era. The shock of a 7-0 thrashing by Arsenal in the first round of the League Cup had been hard to shrug off; while a 4-0 aggregate defeat at the hands of the Romanian student team Universitatae Craiova in round two of the UEFA Cup heaped on further humiliation.

It took a 17-year-old debutant striker who cost the club nothing to inject life into the season. Terry Connor, thrown on as Leeds were toiling at home to West Bromwich on 17 November, scored a fine match-winning individual goal and played with a verve and confidence that could galvanize less spirited players around him. But he could not, alone, dictate the destiny of a disjointed team where confidence was palpably fragile.

Signings such as full back Kevin Hird, bought by Adamson from Blackburn for £350,000 the previous season, were industrious and

50 Greatest Players

PAUL REANEY Right back

Joined Leeds: October 1961   **From:** Juniors

Debut: v Swansea Town, 8 September 1962

Appearances: 748   **Goals:** 9

Left Leeds: June 1978   **Joined:** Bradford City

Honours won with Leeds: Division 1 Championship 1969, 1974;
Division 2 Championship 1964; Fairs Cup winner 1968, 1971; FA Cup winner 1972;
League Cup winner 1968; 3 England caps

Paul Reaney's famous last-ditch clearances of goal-bound shots made him a folk hero
at Elland Road. He was the complete stopper, tackling with gusto and adept also at
overlapping down the right and knocking over teasing centres. Reaney had such speed
and stamina he could quickly resume defensive duties. His one defect was, perhaps,
that he was not the strongest kicker of a ball.

He arrived at Leeds in 1961 aged 17, made the first team the next year and stayed
there for almost 17 years. There was no better man-marker: 'As usual, Best found
himself playing rabbit to Reaney's stoat,' said the *Yorkshire Post* in 1968 as Leeds
secured a 0-0 draw at Old Trafford en route to the championship.

A broken leg sustained at West Ham in April 1970 cost him a place in the
1970 England World Cup squad; but he was, typically, back in less than six months.
He transferred to Bradford City in 1978, later playing in Australia, and, after returning
to England, worked as a coach.

committed but lacked the calibre of their illustrious predecessors.
It didn't take much for the crowd to get on Hird's back though his
nerve was strong enough to accept the role of penalty-taker. Brian
Greenhoff arrived from Manchester United in August 1979 less than
fully fit and prone to further injury. There were high hopes of Gary
Hamson, a vigorous hard-running midfielder signed from Sheffield
United for £140,000, but he lacked Currie's inspirational spark.
Derek Parlane, signed towards the season's end from Glasgow Rangers
for £200,000, managed just three goals in 11 games.

The form of Connor and young goalkeeper John Lukic, who had
supplanted David Harvey, were two reasons to cheer in an otherwise

Allan Clarke returned to Elland Road as manager, but always faced an uphill struggle.

dreary season. A third was Leeds' unexpected display of passion and style on the final day when they outran and outplayed Championship pretenders Manchester United during a 2-0 win at Elland Road; a victory that allowed fans to dream of a revival.

Adamson Quits

But after four defeats in the first five games of 1980-81, Adamson's head was on the block. As supporters turned their venom upon him, the Leeds manager cut his losses and quit in September 1980. There had been protests the previous season: police had to break up a demonstration after a dismal 0-0 draw with Coventry in March. Like Armfield, Adamson knew his football; but he too had lacked self-assertiveness. Players were fond of him rather than fearfully respectful and had found his lack of daily involvement disconcerting. 'When Jimmy was talking to us on Saturday, I got the impression he never really knew what had been going on in the week,' said Eddie Gray. Paul Hart agrees. 'He didn't work with us enough. I liked it when he did – he brought the best out of me. He gave me confidence and calmed me down.'

There followed the ritual of Maurice Lindley acting as caretaker before Allan Clarke returned to Elland Road from Barnsley. Unlike Adamson and Armfield, Clarke, a hero of the Revie era, had behind him an enormous fund of goodwill, and, with promises to deliver a trophy within three years, made noises the fans liked to hear.

He brought with him his Barnsley backroom staff of Martin Wilkinson, assistant manager, and Barry Murphy, coach. With Leeds showing all-round weakness, Clarke made the defence his priority. Somehow he had also to engender some spirit: few displays were ever more supine than the 5-0 home defeat by Arsenal on 8 November 1980, a dismal finale to Paul Madeley's great career at Elland Road.

This was the nadir: slowly thereafter, Clarke's team began grinding out results as a solid defence shaped up. Brian Greenhoff recovered from injury and Eddie Gray was successfully converted to left back. Cherry and Hart looked sound and Lukic was emerging as the best young goalkeeper in the country. But recovery was often painful to watch. Early exits from both League and FA Cups robbed the season of any

spice and crowds frequently dipped below 20,000.

The statistics, 39 goals scored all season, reflected the unappetizing football. Winger Carl Harris, for years a fringe player after his scoring debut against Ipswich in 1975, was top marksman with ten League goals. No-one else managed more than five. But Clarke's priority had been to perform a rescue, and having hauled Leeds up into ninth place, he had done so.

Frank Gray, in his first spell at Leeds, pays close attention to Tottenham's Ian Moores.

Remoulding the Team

He then began remoulding the team. Alan Curtis had already been sold back to Swansea for £165,000. During 1981-82, Clarke also off-loaded Argentinian midfielder Alex Sabella, bought from Sheffield United for a £400,000 fee by Jimmy Adamson just before he resigned, but never a favourite of the new Leeds manager. Wide midfielder Jeff Chandler was another Adamson new recruit, bought from Blackpool for £100,000 in 1979, who struggled in difficult times. He was sold to Bolton.

Frank Gray, now a regular for Scotland and winner of a European Cup medal during his two-year sojourn at Forest, was brought back to Elland Road and deployed in midfield. Clarke's most spectacular purchase was the England and West Brom winger Peter Barnes, for a club record £930,000. It was a costly mistake for club and player; and hard to fathom Clarke's strategy, for midfield and central attack had needed strengthening the most.

There were signs of trouble from day one of 1981-82. Leeds were blown apart by newly-promoted Swansea City, 5-1 victors after a second-half rout which, with the score 1-1 at half-time, few foresaw. A one-off, some thought; but within the month Clarke's team had crashed 4-0 at Coventry and Manchester City. By October, they were in the relegation zone. Clarke, desperate for a seasoned campaigner, signed Kenny Burns from Nottingham Forest to steady things at the back. Burns, a striker converted to defence and voted Footballer of the Year in 1978, had been a formidable operator, and a winner at Forest. Clarke hoped for more of the same at Leeds.

For a while, results stabilized. From mid-October, Leeds won five and drew two of the next nine League matches, a run that ended with a modicum of revenge when beating Swansea 2-0 at Elland Road on 16 January. But, following a 1-0 fourth round FA Cup defeat at Spurs, things went horribly wrong: six games without a goal, and five defeats. By mid-March, Leeds were in the quicksand. Clarke's latest foray into the transfer market smacked more of the gambler than the strategist, the exchange of utility player Byron Stevenson for Birmingham striker Frank Worthington.

50 Greatest Players

FRANK GRAY Midfielder/full back

Joined Leeds: Summer 1970   **From:** Juniors

Debut: v Leicester City, 10 February 1973

Appearances: 404   **Goals:** 35

Left Leeds: July 1979   **For:** Nottingham Forest

Re-joined Leeds: May 1981   **Left:** July 1985 **For:** Sunderland

Honours won with Leeds: 25 Scotland caps

He was eight years younger, but, like Eddie, Frank Gray was a natural: quick, a superb passer, an excellent reader of the game who did simple things well. Equally comfortable at full back or in midfield where he could be wonderfully creative, Frank had an unflappable temperament which made him the ideal penalty-taker. He won a European Cup medal with Nottingham Forest, while of the 32 caps he won for Scotland, half were awarded after he returned to a struggling Leeds side destined for the Second Division.

Frank Gray was quite the opposite of a malcontent, seemingly content to drop anchor at left back in a side going nowhere. 'He should have pushed himself... been harder on himself,' says brother Eddie. Nevertheless, in Leeds' darkest hours, it was some small comfort still to have such an able and elegant player in the ranks.

Stevenson, a contemporary of Harris – both were from South Wales and had signed for Leeds in 1973 – served a long apprenticeship on the periphery of the first team in defence and midfield but never looked convincing at the top level. Worthington, by contrast, was an old master, with sublime control and awareness. But he was 33, and his appetite for a desperate scrap questionable.

Despite their parlous position, several players seemed blasé. 'Some would say "we're too good to go down",' Eddie Gray recalls. 'I would say "You're not too good – it happened to Man United." They didn't care enough about getting beaten.' Terry Connor, whose glorious early blaze had been snuffed out by injuries and loss of form, became dispirited by monotonous training routines and Allan Clarke's lack of experienced back-up. 'Possibly too many senior players had too much of a say – you got the feeling they weren't pulling in his direction,' he said.

Most of the players of whom Paul Hart had once been in awe had gone. 'With respect to everyone who came in, no one had star quality,' he said. 'Perhaps we were trying to do things on the cheap. The mixture wasn't quite right. Allan did well for us at the start – we were in the bottom four when he came and he pulled us up by the boot straps. The bottom line is that it comes down to the players. I think we've got to take a lot of the blame.'

Peter Barnes, who hadn't come cheap, too often languished on the left wing with an air of being disengaged. A tantalizing glimpse of what might have been came near the season's end as Leeds, perilously close to relegation, astounded everyone by winning 4-1 at Aston Villa. Barnes, on the night, displayed the wizardry that had caused so much excitement when he had burst on to the scene with Manchester City and England.

But it was only Leeds' second League victory in 16 outings. There would be just one more, a frenetic 2-1 home win scrambled against Brighton: goals from Hamson and Hird, after Leeds had gone 1-0 down, triggered uproarious celebrations and offered a whiff of hope for the last match three days later at the Hawthorns where West Bromwich were also facing relegation.

On a wild night, where 6,000 Leeds fans penned in the Smethwick End filled the air with menace, second-half goals from Cyrille Regis and Steve Mackenzie effectively consigned Leeds to the Second Division. With the game up and Clarke's team running on empty the hooligans took charge; and as attempts at a pitch invasion were repelled by police officers wielding batons, they turned their destructive lust on the stadium, the cars and the streets outside.

When Stoke City beat West Bromwich 3-0 at the Victoria Ground two nights later, the survival of both Midlands clubs was ensured and, after 17 years in the top flight, Leeds fell through the trapdoor into Division Two. Few exits ever had a more shameful accompaniment.

Chapter Eight: 1982-90
An Eight-year Exile

Deep in the red and with supporters leaving in droves, the outlook for Leeds United was bleak. Allan Clarke paid the penalty for relegation and was dismissed. Without money to attract a big name, the board improvised, appointing, to the surprise of many, Eddie Gray as player-manager – 'a cheap but hopeful option' according to a former chief executive Peter Nash. Gray had the players' respect and knew the game at the highest level. Back in 1974, when on the sidelines injured, Don Revie had him coaching young players. With no money to buy their way out of the Second Division, Leeds United's need to groom youthful talent was paramount.

But old hands with lucrative contracts were in no hurry to leave, as Jimmy Lumsden, a reserve forward from the Revie era whom Gray knew from schooldays and brought in as assistant manager, recalls. 'The first thing the chairman asked us is who we would get rid of because the wages were high and the club was in horrendous debt.'

Lumsden soon realized that some senior pros did not have their heart in it. Gray began trying young hopefuls such as Aidan Butterworth, a quick, hustling young striker in the Terry Connor mould, and who became Connor's partner for some of the season. While Butterworth finished top scorer with 11, this proved a lightweight combination. Before the season's end, Connor left, exchanged for Brighton's Andy Ritchie.

Connor was Leeds to the core: playing for his home town club all he ever wanted. 'It hurt an awful lot,' he said. For all that there is little sentiment in football, Jimmy Lumsden was sensitive to Connor's distress. 'Getting rid of him was one of the saddest things we ever did,' he said. 'But without any money, we had to try to wheel and deal. He didn't have the best touch but made up for that with effort and commitment.'

These were essential qualities for a side serious about fighting its way out of the Second Division. But another battler, midfielder Gary Hamson, had been badly injured during the debacle at West Bromwich, and made only one appearance all season. Hamson proved hard to replace: Leeds' poverty was exposed when they recruited Neil McNab, another forceful midfielder, from Brighton on loan but could afford neither the £65,000 fee nor his wages.

Yet, to the end of October, Leeds had looked promotion possibles, though victory margins were rarely emphatic. 'We should have murdered that league and gone straight back up – we had enough about us,' said Paul Hart. Enough, perhaps, except for a killer instinct and appetite for the struggle: half Leeds' 42 League games in 1982-83 were drawn, and they finished eighth.

While much of what happened on the field was forgettable, violent events off it made lurid headlines. The hooligans who sacked West Bromwich on that overcast night in May 1982 reappeared on a hot August Saturday afternoon in Cleethorpes for Leeds' first Division Two fixture at Grimsby. Trouble followed the club home and away; and when Kevin Keegan was struck by a ball-bearing thrown during Leeds' 3-1 home win over Newcastle, the FA ordered closure of the Kop for two matches.

A Leeds man at heart, Terry Connor was exchanged for Brighton's Andy Ritchie in 1983 after relegation.

It was the last thing Leeds needed: the second of these, a home match with Shrewsbury on 18 December, attracted just 8,741, the lowest League crowd at Elland Road for almost 20 years. Six weeks earlier a doom-laden front cover programme editorial warned: 'The mindless actions of a

50 Greatest Players

ARTHUR GRAHAM Left winger

Joined Leeds: July 1977   **From:** Aberdeen

Debut: v Newcastle United, 20 August 1977

Appearances: 260   **Goals:** 47

Left Leeds: August 1983   **Joined:** Manchester United

Honours won with Leeds: 10 Scotland caps

Leeds were past their best when Graham joined in summer 1977 and he was often at the heart of their best moments in this difficult period. Aged only 24, he had won an FA Cup medal with Aberdeen when just 17 and had already made 240 appearances for the Dons.

Favouring the left flank, Graham was a quick, stocky player, with a low centre of gravity. He could as easily move inside and unleash a shot as deliver a teasing cross from the by-line. He had a sharp eye for goal and scored hat-tricks against Valetta in the UEFA Cup and Birmingham and Wolves in the league.

Graham stayed one season after relegation before moving to Manchester United for £50,000. He gave a number of stirring performances at Old Trafford before moving to Bradford City where he later became coach and assistant manager.

minority of the club's so-called supporters have placed an enormous degree of uncertainty over this great club.'

By the end of 1982-83, Gray's reconstruction was underway. The Ritchie/Connor trade-off was not the only surprise: John Lukic, after 146 consecutive appearances, was dropped when he asked for a transfer and sold to Arsenal for £125,000 during the close season. He was replaced by the familiar, comforting figure of David Harvey, now 34, who had spent more than three years in Canada with Vancouver Whi tecaps. Brian Flynn moved on, loaned to his old club Burnley, whom he later re-joined permanently for a fee of £60,000; as did Paul Hart who went to Nottingham Forest for £40,000. Just before 1983-84 got underway, Arthur Graham departed, sold to Manchester United for £50,000. There was also a change in the boardroom: Leslie Silver took over as chairman from Manny Cussins who continued to serve as vice-chairman.

50 Greatest Players

BRIAN FLYNN Midfielder

Joined Leeds: November 1977 **From:** Burnley

Debut: v Norwich City, 5 November 1977

Appearances: 177   **Goals:** 11

Left Leeds: March 1982   **To:** Burnley

Honours won with Leeds: 31 Wales caps

Flynn, another in the tradition of diminutive Leeds midfielders, was a good foil for the stylish, occasionally languid Tony Currie. He buzzed, hustled, harried, could strike a long ball and hit a wicked shot though never had quite the guile and craft of his legendary predecessors, Collins, Giles and Bremner.

These were hard acts to follow; though Flynn had good times in his spell at Leeds. There were occasions, particularly during 1978-79, when he and Leeds looked to be going places, but a side that had promised much suffered grievously when Currie, its creative genius, departed. Flynn, for all his fizzing industry, found it hard to strike sparks off more mundane colleagues; and sometimes the ferocity of his tackling caused stormy scenes.

When Leeds were relegated in 1982 Flynn rejoined his old club, Burnley. He has, since 1989, been manager of Wrexham where, during his long tenure, Flynn has enjoyed great success in the FA Cup including victory over Arsenal.

What next? wondered many Leeds fans. Peter Barnes was back after a 12-month loan spell with Spanish club Real Betis; but the line-up for 1983-84 was populated by unfamiliar names and faces, among them midfielders Andy Watson from Aberdeen, John Donnelly from Dumbarton and striker George McCluskey from Celtic. They too were cheap but hopeful options.

Gray made use of his home-grown players: Gwyn Thomas, a hustling midfielder; Martin Dickinson, a quick central defender; and an outstanding young prospect in midfielder John Sheridan, who made his debut as an 18-year-old in November 1982, and whose great gifts, passing and reading the game, had unaccountably been discarded by Manchester City.

As 1983-84 progressed, others of high calibre joined him: full backs Neil Aspin and Denis Irwin, Scott Sellars, another slight young midfielder with delicate skills; and Tommy Wright, a sharp nib of a striker who beat a quick confident path to goal. But in the early months, Leeds United looked as ill-assorted a crew as ever wore a white shirt, devoid of heart and leadership. There were unimaginable humiliations including a 5-1 beating at Shrewsbury in October. In the FA Cup third round, after three attempts at conquering Scunthorpe United, Leeds ended up losing 4-2.

But as the year turned, League results perked up, an improvement that coincided with the return to his old stamping ground of Peter Lorimer. The swift winger of old was patrolling midfield, passing on his know-how to Sellars and Sheridan, protégés little more than half his age. Save for a 5-0 defeat at Champions-elect Chelsea near the season's end, the defence had been much tighter. Tenth place and 60 points was a far better outcome than had looked likely mid-autumn.

Four straight wins at the start of 1984-85, the fruit of deft, incisive football, set fans dreaming of the First Division. But defeats in the following three woke up everyone to Leeds' frailty. 'We were asking two teenagers to run the show in the middle of the park,' said Jimmy Lumsden. 'They were brave, they accepted the ball in any situation and were as comfortable on it as any young lads could be. Eddie had faith in them. A lot of people, myself included, might have waited.'

More old hands had moved on: Kenny Burns, the previous season; then Kevin Hird and Peter Barnes. But with money still tight, Gray's only close season deal was to spend £20,000 on Andy Linighan, a six feet four central defender from Hartlepool. Watson, Donnelly and McCluskey had not adapted, and all left, but Linighan was one bargain who did fit in.

After two mid-term changes, signing goalkeeper Mervyn Day for £30,000 from Aston Villa to replace David Harvey, and striker Ian Baird for £75,000 from Southampton, Leeds found form that took them to the threshold of promotion. Baird's aggression and ability to rough up defences gave the attack an abrasive edge it had lacked.

50 Greatest Players

DAVID HARVEY Goalkeeper

Joined Leeds: Summer 1963   **From:** Juniors

Debut: v West Bromwich Albion, 13 October 1965

Appearances: 447

Left Leeds: January 1980   **For:** Partick Thistle

Re-joined Leeds: March 1983   **From:** Vancouver Whitecaps

Left Again: February 1985 (retired)

Honours won with Leeds: Division 1 Championship 1974; FA Cup 1972;

16 Scotland caps

Born in Leeds, David Harvey made his debut for the club aged 17, but spent most of the next seven seasons as Gary Sprake's understudy. Though a transfer request was rejected, it was not until the end of 1971-72 that Harvey finally got his chance. He kept soundly in the FA Cup final victory over Arsenal and belatedly laid claim to the number one shirt.

Harvey may have lacked Sprake's instinctive flair, but he had courage, excellent concentration and sharp reflexes. He could be indecisive on crosses but his general reliability inspired confidence in defenders. A Scottish father entitled him to international consideration and he won acclaim for his displays in the 1974 World Cup. In 1979 he left for Vancouver Whitecaps; yet returned in 1983 as captain of Eddie Gray's young team, staying for two years.

His match-winning goals meant that on the last day of the 1984-85 season, a win at Birmingham City might have taken Leeds back to Division One.

Birmingham were already promoted. But what, for them, was meant to be a farewell celebration descended into an orgy of hooliganism. Martin Kuhl's goal, the only one of the game, triggered violent scenes among Leeds fans who already had been sacking the Tilton Road end. The match was suspended for more than half an hour; and what resumed was an inhibited, unreal contest. Worse was to come: as the Leeds mob pushed and shoved its way out of the exits, a supporting wall collapsed and a teenage boy was killed. This, on the day of the fire at Bradford City which killed 56, was among football's grimmest hours.

Leeds finished seventh, four points short of promotion. Arguably, this was a team unready for the First Division and it was hard to imagine where the money would come for reinforcements. Straitened finances had forced the club to sell Elland Road to the city council for £2.5 million, and remain there on a 125-year lease. Yet many young players had proved themselves, and Gray felt able to sell on his brother Frank to Sunderland for £100,000. In his quest for a dynamic midfield presence, he spent £200,000 on Ian Snodin, an England under-21 defender playing under Billy Bremner at Doncaster Rovers.

Snodin and Bremner were to be reunited more quickly than anyone might have imagined. After early inconsistency – though save for a 6-2 drubbing at Stoke results had not been disastrous – Gray was, to widespread astonishment and dismay, sacked in October 1985. The directors were suddenly impatient for success; though one, Brian Woodward, resigned over Gray's dismissal. There was unrest among the players too; the board's strategy seemed hard to follow. In a statement to fans, Leslie Silver spoke of 'the deep debt of gratitude owed to Gray... but that it was mutually agreed to be in the best interests of Eddie and the club that his role as team manager should be ended'. Supporters found these platitudes hard to swallow.

But appointing Bremner in Gray's place mollified many. His style would be to pack the side with moderately-priced experienced professionals. The old guard, Lorimer and Harvey, were soon on their way; but much of Gray's young talent also went, and cheaply: Scott Sellars sold to Blackburn for £20,000; Denis Irwin given a free transfer to Oldham; Terry Phelan destined for a fine career with Manchester City went free to Swansea. Andy Linighan (£55,000) and Tommy Wright (£80,000) also headed to Oldham.

New recruits included Brendan Ormsby, signed for £65,000 from Aston Villa, and David Rennie, £50,000 from Leicester. But Leeds fans were to endure a season worse than any they had known under Gray. Crowds at Elland Road struggled to reach 10,000 as the team

Mervyn Day enjoyed an Indian summer in his career after he joined Leeds from Aston Villa in 1984-85.

toiled in the lower reaches, and it took three straight wins in April to vanquish fears of relegation. Away matches, following the Birmingham riot, had been made all ticket, with games at Carlisle and Wimbledon watched by meagre crowds of around 3,500.

The case for Bremner looked scarcely more convincing during the first half of 1986-87 when, by mid-season, Leeds lay just above mid-table and went into Christmas off the back of a 7-2 drubbing at Stoke. Close season reinforcements had included centre half Jack Ashurst, signed from Carlisle for £35,000; full backs Bobby McDonald from Oxford for £25,000 and Peter Haddock from Newcastle for £45,000; and striker Keith Edwards, a prolific scorer with Sheffield United, for £125,000. Others arrived later: midfielder Mark Aizlewood (£200,000) and John Pearson (£72,000) from Charlton, and left back Micky Adams from Coventry for £110,000.

Bremner financed this hectic trading by accepting an irresistible offer for Ian Snodin whom he sold to Everton for £840,000. What sort of broth all the new ingredients might make was anyone's guess. Yet from the New Year Leeds ran into their most consistent form under Bremner's management, buoyed by an FA Cup run that began in unpromising circumstances with a bumpy 2-1 win over non-league Telford United in round three.

The pitch had been semi-frozen; the critical difference Ian Baird's control and finishing. But thereafter Leeds grew in confidence in disposing of Swindon, QPR and Wigan Athletic while marching towards a semi-final encounter with Coventry City at Hillsborough.

Crowds were returning, often around 20,000 as the team's fortunes improved. The defensive unit of Aspin, Ashurst, Ormsby and McDonald looked solid: Bremner had acquired eager, honest, competent players; and John Sheridan, Leeds' creative spark, was free of injury and in grand form. Baird remained the cutting edge up front; though late season, and in crucial matches, began getting support from Edwards.

Play-off Drama

The season 1986-87 saw play-offs introduced to determine final promotion and relegation places. It gave Leeds, and others, much more to play for. Good home form propelled Bremner's men into fourth place and the play-off melting pot where, in the semi-finals, theatrical late strikes by Keith Edwards in each leg did for Oldham.

The final, against First Division Charlton, became a battle of wills and nerve. In the three games it took to decide matters, Leeds were Charlton's equal in every department except durability. Each side had won 1-0 on home territory, matches that were cagey rather than explosively exciting. A third encounter, at St Andrew's, Birmingham, produced good football amid the tension, yet reached extra-time goalless before Sheridan broke the deadlock with a searing free kick. Enough to finish off most sides; but Charlton were survivors and snatched back the game at the death with goals from Peter Shirtliff.

For Bremner, this stunning outcome recalled many a near miss in the Revie era. Yet the season appeared to mark a decisive turning point, creating the belief that before long, Leeds would resume business in Division One. But, as with Eddie Gray's last season, the team was unable to sustain the momentum: Leeds scored only seven in their first 13 matches and by mid-October were in the lower reaches, mulling over the indignity of a 6-3 defeat at Plymouth. Andy Ritchie had been sold to Oldham for £50,000; Ian Baird was injured and Keith Edwards out of form.

Others on the sick list included Aizlewood, Pearson and Ormsby, whose career never recovered from an injury he sustained in the play-off

Great Matches

FA CUP SEMI-FINAL

Hillsborough, 12 April 1987
Attendance 51,372

Coventry City 3   Leeds United 2*

Gynn	Rennie
Houchen	Edwards
Bennett	

* after extra time

The stakes were higher than just a place at Wembley. Leeds United, public enemy number one in the eyes of many, were taking part in their biggest set-piece match for 10 years. It asked several questions: was the so-called sleeping giant stirring? And would the hordes of travelling Leeds fans be controllable?

The score tells of a match lost but rarely can the vanquished have exacted as much consolation from defeat. This was a magnificent semi-final; Bremner's men were primed to a level of performance that almost transcended their abilities, storming Coventry's defences from the kick-off. Rennie's crashing headed goal from Micky Adams' corner on 14 minutes was an electrifying climax to sustained pressure.

Leeds held that lead almost for an hour, contesting every ball; pouring forward when the chance arose. That they lost the initiative was due to an unfortunate error when Ormsby, as brave and committed as anyone, conceded possession near the by-line allowing winger Dave Bennett to cross and Micky Gynn to equalize.

The signs then were that Leeds had shot their bolt. Coventry, appearing to have the legs of them, pressed; and a goal from Keith Houchen looked enough to take them to Wembley. But with Coventry still pressing, there were gaps at the back and with little more than five minutes left, Andy Ritchie got away, found substitute Keith Edwards alone up front; and Edwards' header looped past Ogrizovic into the net.

It was an exhilarating moment. But in the end, Coventry were the more measured, and Dave Bennett's goal in the first half of extra-time was decisive – just. Leeds staved off exhaustion and fought to the last; Edwards, still fresh, forcing a superb save from Ogrizovic that denied Leeds a replay. The fans, mercifully, had chosen to mark a great occasion by behaving themselves.

Coventry City: Ogrizovic, Burrows, Downs, McGrath, Kilcline, Peake, Bennett, Phillips, Regis, Houchen, Pickering (Gynn).

Leeds United: Day, Aspin, Adams, Stiles, (Haddock), Ashurst, Ormsby, Ritchie, Sheridan, Pearson (Edwards) Baird, Rennie.

Referee: R.G. Milford (Bristol).

Manager Billy Bremner celebrates, but in a frustrating echo of the Revie era his teams failed at the last hurdle.

denouement at Birmingham. As the season unfolded, Bremner pitched in a couple of his younger charges: Bob Taylor, a 19-year-old striker signed from Hordern Colliery Welfare, and a snappy midfielder whose juvenile appearance belied an appetite for combat in midfield. David Batty, a player after Bremner's heart, and carefully nurtured by the Leeds boss, had arrived to stay.

Bremner, unlike Gray, survived a poor early autumn and in November results picked up, a six-match winning sequence through December to New Year putting Leeds in the promotion frame. Games with old rivals brought crowds flocking back: 34,000 watched the 2-0 home win over Middlesbrough at Elland Road on 28 December; 36,000 the derby with Bradford City four days later.

Bremner's Reign Ends

But they could not keep the consistency going. Hopes of promotion were effectively snuffed out after a home defeat by Champions-elect Millwall on 6 April 1988. Leeds finished seventh, eight points away from a promotion place. Another shaky start would bring Bremner's three-year reign to an end and cause Leeds United's directors to contemplate the future as they have never done before. Fans blamed the board rather than a popular manager for creating the latest state of flux. After his sacking on 13 October 1988, Bremner found himself shaking hands with devotees who flocked to Elland Road to wish him well, whereas days earlier, after a 1-0 defeat at Elland Road by Watford, a hostile crowd had massed outside, demanding the head of Leslie Silver.

Bremner had scented malaise at Elland Road three years earlier. He found the club in a mess and that attempting to manage was 'like trying to sweep up dead leaves in a gale'. His successor, Sheffield Wednesday boss Howard Wilkinson, Leeds' eighth manager in 14 years, was no more impressed. He deplored the dilapidated training ground next to Elland Road; the run-down changing rooms; the stadium 'with an aura of an old museum where... aspirations for the future appeared to grow dim'.

Yet Sheffield Wednesday, with its tight wage structure and reluctance to spent big money in the transfer market, was, in Wilkinson's eyes, critically short of ambition. That was what led him to abandon a middling First Division club for the rudderless Second Division ship at Leeds. He called upon the directors to gamble; announcing that with unstinting financial backing for the top wages and the best players, he would aim to take Leeds up within two years.

Silver and colleagues bit the bullet and hired Wilkinson on the basis of his costly action plan. Almost as soon as he was installed, Wilkinson banished all memorabilia of the Revie era, which he regarded as an invitation to look dotingly on the past

Andy Ritchie, scorer of 44 goals in his four seasons at Elland Road.

rather than inspiration. Norman Hunter, whom Bremner had recruited as a coach, was also shown the door. Wilkinson brought his own staff from Hillsborough, including, as assistant, Mick Hennigan.

Wilkinson's preoccupations were many: results, of course, but also improving the club's image and poor disciplinary record. Soon he was blending Bremner's imports: centre half Noel Blake and winger Vince Hilaire who came from Portsmouth along with Ian Baird, who had been sold and then re-signed; and full back Gary Williams. Mid-season, Wilkinson made low-key signings of his own: midfielder Andy Williams from Rotherham and full back Mike Whitlow from non-league Witton Albion. Results got better and striker Bobby Davison, whom Bremner signed from Derby for £350,000 in 1987-88, formed a lively partnership with Baird. Early in April, Leeds scented the promotion play-offs until successive defeats by Crystal Palace and Plymouth brought them to earth.

But their stumbling run-in had been partially eclipsed by Wilkinson's most spectacular signing to date, Gordon Strachan, suddenly surplus to requirements at Old Trafford.

It was the first test for Leeds United's blank cheque policy; and Strachan was, according to Wilkinson, stunned by the extravagant terms on offer. A rival bid from Sheffield Wednesday manager Ron Atkinson forced up the price from £200,000 to £300,000 but Leeds were prepared to pay whatever. Strachan became a leader in the Bobby Collins mould; central to the new Leeds. Meanwhile poignant memories of the old Leeds resurfaced with the death in May 1989 of Don Revie. Revie had been struck down by motor neurone disease, his muscles wasting away over three years. It was a distressing end to a tempestuous career in which, for all his mercenary wanderings, Leeds stayed closest to his heart. Revie had, during Eddie Gray's reign, acted as a consultant at Elland Road. 'He would offer advice but not as if he were telling you how to do your job,' said Jimmy Lumsden. 'We held him in high respect.'

Money, as with Revie, also talked loud to Strachan. But it was not, he claims, the only factor. 'It was the first time for a long while that

I felt someone really believed in me as a player. I got a great buzz from that,' he said. Wilkinson's confidence was not misplaced: Strachan was a catalytic, inspirational signing.

With less fanfare striker Carl Shutt, another Sheffield Wednesday old boy, had arrived from Bristol City in exchange for Bob Taylor, yet marked his debut with a hat-trick against Bournemouth. Shutt was, however, destined to be a squad player, often a willing substitute when fresh legs were needed. It was in the close season, after Leeds finished tenth, that Wilkinson made more waves, selling John Sheridan for £650,000 to Nottingham Forest and buying Vinnie Jones from Wimbledon for the same money. Leeds fans who believed in the beauty of football were bemused: Sheridan, despite a fiery temper, had barely put a foot wrong in six years while Jones, the shaven-haired former hod carrier, was a hooligans' icon.

Wilkinson, however, detected that beneath the surface of the 'media monster' was a footballer striving to get out. He wanted Jones' uncompromising gee-up presence as back-up for Strachan; and spent a further £600,000 invigorating the squad by signing right back Mel Sterland from Glasgow Rangers, a robust defender with exuberant attacking instincts and a rasping shot.

He had signed Chris Fairclough from Tottenham before the 1989 deadline, and he forged a good understanding in central defence with Peter Haddock. Haddock was a player's player, composed under pressure and an excellent reader of the game, his career cut short by injury just as he seemed to be approaching his peak. Other in-comers were winger John Hendrie who cost £500,000 from Newcastle and veteran centre half John McClelland signed from Watford for £150,000. The disfavoured Aizlewood meanwhile was sold to Bradford City for £200,000.

The hype around Leeds had become enormous but the first match of 1989-90, a 5-2 defeat at Newcastle, suggested parts of the machine were not properly joined up. Jones had, that day, been a voluble spectator on the bench but was picked for the next match and for every other in the campaign. Four days later, Leeds shrugged off their

Former Sheffield Wednesday and Rangers full back Mel Sterland was quick to shine in Howard Wilkinson's new look team.

thumping at Newcastle with a 2-1 home win over Middlesbrough, and began a 16-match unbeaten run that was halted by a 4-3 defeat at Leicester City on 11 November. Leeds' recent tradition of prospering in December continued but in the New Year, results became too patchy for comfort. Promotion was a jostling three-horse race involving Newcastle and Sheffield Wednesday; and Howard Wilkinson detected that his players had become more intent on avoiding defeat than winning.

Extra ingredients were needed. Mid-season, he sold Ian Baird to Middlesbrough for £500,000 and imported trusted former servant Lee Chapman from Nottingham Forest for £400,000. More bite was added to midfield with the arrival of Chris Kamara from Stoke for £150,000. Some fans looked askance at Wilkinson's switch of Chapman for Baird but Wilkinson stood by his man; 'single-minded; astute; fairly thick-skinned; all the attributes of a great goalscorer'.

As ever, there were injury problems: the left back spot appeared jinxed, while Hendrie's season was blighted by a violent tackle inflicted

50 Greatest Players

GORDON STRACHAN Midfielder

Joined Leeds: March 1989   **From:** Manchester United

Debut: v Portsmouth, 25 March 1989

Appearances: 245   **Goals:** 45

Left Leeds: March 1995   **For:** Coventry City

Honours won with Leeds: Division 1 Championship 1992; Division 2 Championship 1990; Footballer of the Year 1991; 8 Scotland caps

As Revie had brought the disenchanted Bobby Collins from Everton 26 years earlier, so Wilkinson lured Strachan from Manchester United. The effect was to be similar.

Strachan had languished on the right wing at Old Trafford where his relationship with Alex Ferguson had grown uneasy. He was 32, but fitter and faster than men ten years his junior. In 1989-90, he played in every league game and went on to make 104 successive appearances. When Howard Wilkinson made him captain, Strachan became the creative focal point, evoking memories of Billy Bremner. Though his tackling was less rasping, he was Bremner's equal in passing and shooting, and in his ability to read the game and switch directions of play. He also shared Bremner's gift of finding some way through when a game seemed lost. Although often playing in pain from sciatica, Strachan's performances earned him a recall to the Scotland team and saw him voted Footballer of the Year in 1991.

On leaving Leeds in 1995 he became assistant manager at Coventry City, but his playing days were still not over. As his 40th year loomed, the ageing maestro still had the legs to turn out in emergencies. Strachan became manager at Coventry and then at Southampton.

by Swindon's Jon Gittens. But after New Year came a growing sense that Leeds would gain promotion; that at last they could clamber out of Division Two. A 4-2 victory over Oxford on 10 March, achieved after Wilkinson's men had been 2-0 down, showed their capacity for bouncing back. The rousing 4-0 win over Sheffield United on 16 April, Easter Monday, put promotion and the Second Division title in sight.

But nothing was ever won easily at Leeds. Nine days later, a 2-1 home defeat by Barnsley began spreading apprehension. Nerves were stretched almost to breaking point in the game with Leicester at Elland Road on 28 April when, after Mel Sterland put Leeds in front, Gary McAllister's ferocious equalizer threatened to bring everyone's

Gordon Strachan, the catalyst of the championship-winning Leeds team.

hopes crashing down. It was a night for digging in; for a crowd at fever pitch to roar the team home; and for Strachan to trump McAllister's effort with a blistering late winner. 'That day there was an atmosphere that I don't think I'll ever feel again – a oneness with the team and supporters,' Strachan said.

Yet results elsewhere meant that Leeds, to be sure of any reward, had to win their last game, at Bournemouth. Police had long feared that this fixture, scheduled for a May bank holiday, was a time bomb. The sun beat down; the hordes descended; and the stakes were enormous: Leeds' promotion; Bournemouth's survival in Division Two. For the Dorset constabulary, it was the worst scenario possible.

The chief constable's fears were justified: a weekend of mayhem ensued. While thousands without tickets swarmed around Dean Court, the 10,000 inside witnessed a tentative encounter on a hard dry pitch. Bournemouth were short on fight and craft but the match needed to be won. Leeds dominated but lacked a cutting edge. Then early in the second half, Kamara broke down the right and picked out the unmarked Chapman with his centre, and Chapman's header zipped emphatically into the net. One strike was decisive. Leeds United were Champions. Deliverance, after eight years, was theirs at last.

50 Greatest Players

MEL STERLAND Full back

Joined Leeds: July 1989   **From:** Glasgow Rangers

Debut: v Newcastle United, August 19 1989

Appearances: 146   **Goals:** 20

Left Leeds: February 1994 (retired through injury)

Honours won with Leeds: Division 1 Championship 1992

Howard Wilkinson could have fielded almost a complete team recruited from his Sheffield Wednesday old boys. They varied in ability but Sterland was one of the best. He arrived at Elland Road after just four months with Scottish champions Rangers and became the finest right back to play for Leeds since Paul Reaney. Fans appreciated his vigour and commitment; his genial temperament; his capacity to excite. Sterland had a fearsome shot that brought valuable goals, notably from free kicks; and his long throw-ins caused many a defensive tremor in the opposition penalty area.

Sometimes Sterland's attacking instincts left him out of position, leaving him vulnerable to quick wingers. But his overall contribution to the Leeds renaissance was immense, and he would doubtless have given more had injury not forced him out of the game.

Promotion at last! Mel Sterland (left), Vinnie Jones (centre) and Chris Fairclough (right) lead the dressing room celebrations.

Chapter Nine: 1990-96
Champions and Contenders

Wilkinson turned out to be the most systematic manager seen at Leeds since Don Revie. He had a background not only in football – as a winger with Sheffield Wednesday and Brighton – but in education. A PE graduate of Sheffield University, Wilkinson had taught; qualified as an FA coach; managed the England Under 21s; and declined an offer by Bobby Robson to be England number two.

He believed in planning; tactics; leaving nothing to chance. His thoroughness impressed Gary McAllister, signed in the close season for £1 million from Leicester City. Nothing, McAllister found, escaped his new boss: Wilkinson had dossiers, Revie-style, on the opposition whose tactics would be copied by Leeds reserves in pre-match training routines so the first team would know exactly what to expect.

Wilkinson's rigorous fitness programme came as a shock to McAllister's system, as it did also to centre half Chris Whyte, signed from West Bromwich for £450,000. The other big transfer had been re-signing goalkeeper John Lukic for £1 million from Arsenal. Mervyn Day had kept splendidly during the promotion season but age was against him serving Leeds long-term.

The craft and guile that McAllister brought to Leeds epitomized Wilkinson's ambitions for the club.

The biggest shock, at least to the fans, was Wilkinson's decision to sell Vinnie Jones who had done everything expected of him and behaved better than many had feared. But buying McAllister was an indicator of higher aspirations; and Wilkinson feared Jones could become an unsettling presence if not guaranteed a first-team place. Many eyes were caught by the midfield quartet assembled by Wilkinson: the perpetual motion of Strachan; the tigerish David Batty; the craft of McAllister, who just weeks earlier had threatened to be Leeds' nemesis; and Gary Speed, a lithe, athletic young Welshman, excellent in the air and adept at losing markers who, like Batty, emerged through the junior ranks.

Batty versus Gascoigne. By 1990 the young Leeds midfielder was proving a handful for even the most gifted of opponents.

Opening Day Victory

After their opening salvo in the First Division, Leeds could have been forgiven for wondering what the fuss was about: 3-0 up at Everton and strolling. Everton pulled two back but victory on the opening day was an enormous boost to morale. The first game at Elland Road was against Manchester United; and they ran the old enemy close in a 0-0 draw. It was quickly apparent that Leeds would do far more than merely survive: a run of eight wins and two draws in November and December put them in sight of the Championship. McAllister, after early teething troubles, found his shooting range and men on his wavelength: Strachan was irrepressible; and the central defensive duo of Whyte and Fairclough – Leeds' player of the year during the promotion season – was working well. Chapman had become a better goalscorer and braver target man than anyone apart from Wilkinson might have imagined.

It took a 3-0 defeat by Liverpool at Anfield on New Year's Day to remind Leeds that they were still pretenders. Indifferent League form in early 1991 coincided with slogging heavyweight encounters in both the Rumbelows and the FA Cup: Leeds succumbed in the former to Manchester United in the semi-final; and in the latter, after a four-match marathon fourth round, to Arsenal, Champions in the making. While on their jaded off-days, they were fallible against lesser opposition, Leeds had proved they could tussle with the best and provide great entertainment.

Wilkinson had described the Leeds United of the 1980s as England's most hated team, a slur for which hooligan followers were largely responsible. But many of these had melted away; and the football had blossomed: Gordon Strachan had been voted Footballer of the Year. For once, the club was at ease with itself and the world.

Amid the delight though, there were some losers. An injury incurred during the League Cup semi-final had ended the career of Peter Haddock, the quiet central defender whom Wilkinson rated his pick of the Leeds team during 1989-90. 'I can't think of anyone who asked so little and has given so much,' Howard Wilkinson said of him later. An ankle injury sustained at Coventry in November 1990 also put a stop to Chris Kamara's feisty Indian summer.

Wilkinson was to finally sort out the left back slot by paying Chelsea £1.3 million for the stylish Tony Dorigo; then stiffened midfield with the £900,000 purchase of Steve Hodge from Nottingham Forest. He also brought from Southampton the Wallace twins, striker Rod and defender Ray, in a £1.7 million package. Rod Wallace, mobile, elastic, with fearsome pace and control, was to oust Carl Shutt as 1991-92 progressed. It became Hodge's fate largely to

50 Greatest Players

JOHN LUKIC Goalkeeper

Joined Leeds: December 1978 **From:** Juniors

Debut: v Valetta, 3 October 1979

Appearances: 399

Left Leeds: August 1983   **For:** Arsenal

Rejoined Leeds: August 1990   **Left Leeds:** Summer 1996 **For:** Arsenal

Honours won with Leeds: Division 1 Championship 1992; Charity Shield 1992

Lukic had two spells at Leeds: one as the precocious young talent who, at 18, eclipsed David Seaman and ousted David Harvey. He went on to play 146 consecutive games. The other was as the finished article, when he returned from Highbury in 1990 and became one of the few players to win championship medals with two consecutive clubs.

At 6 feet 4 in (1.92 m), Lukic, born of Yugoslavian parentage, was a towering figure who quickly learned to command the penalty area. He was brave, agile, athletic and unflappable. Lukic first made an impact in a declining Leeds side. He was, though, prone to the occasional unforced error, and the Leeds defence became a less certain place after changes to the back-pass law. Lukic returned to Arsenal in 1996 and was replaced by Nigel Martyn.

kick his heels on the bench, his effectiveness reduced by a nagging calf injury; yet his first full match, on 21 September 1991, against Liverpool at Elland Road, saw him score the only goal of a game that took Leeds' unbeaten start to nine matches. No less important, it reinforced a belief that they could conquer the best.

After that, Leeds never dropped out of the top two. A last-gasp goal scored by Crystal Palace at Selhurst Park ten days later ended the unbeaten run yet failed to break up confidence or rhythm. A win at Oldham on 26 October put Leeds on top of the League for the first time in 17 years. They were not to lose another League match for four months. The 4-1 win at Aston Villa on 24 November was an almost flawless exhibition of passing and finishing, and a tribute to high levels of fitness; the 6-1 victory at Hillsborough over flu-stricken Sheffield Wednesday on 12 January 1992 a merciless assault on sickly prey. But there was no escaping the old bête noire, Manchester

United, who, with games in hand, had a marked advantage at the top by the New Year. Within a week, Leeds found themselves playing Alex Ferguson's team in both League and FA Cup. Two big matches: two home defeats for Wilkinson's men, and possibly a decisive statement about which was the better of the two Uniteds. Loss of pride wasn't the only problem: Chapman had fractured a wrist during the FA Cup game and was to miss the next four matches. He and Wallace had become a potent partnership up front. Chapman's absence, as scorer and target man, underlined Wilkinson's paucity of options.

He needed something different to shake into the cocktail. Thirty-five miles down the road at Hillsborough, Eric Cantona, a talented

50 Greatest Players

DAVID BATTY Midfielder

Joined Leeds: July 1985   **From:** Juniors

Debut: v Swindon Town, 21 November 1987

Appearances: 359   **Goals:** 4

Left Leeds: November 1993 **For:** Blackburn Rovers.

Rejoined: December 1998   **From:** Newcastle United

Honours won with Leeds: Division 1 Championship 1992; 19 England caps

Born and reared in the city, David Batty watched from the terraces at Elland Road before signing on as trainee. He had been a small boy during the glory days; and still looked that way – though was 18 – when Billy Bremner gave him his first-team debut.

Batty appealed to Bremner. He was belligerent, committed and snapped into tackles with enough bite to knock the stuffing out of bigger and older men. As he harassed and buzzed and made forward runs, Batty was a key component of the Championship team, and at 21 he became an England international.

Frustrated by the defensive role he was expected to play, Batty was sold to Blackburn for £2.7 million, becoming a focal point of Rovers' drive towards the Championship. He then followed Dalglish to Newcastle coming near to Championship glory for a third time. But as Leeds revived and Newcastle disintegrated, Batty was lured back to Leeds by David O'Leary. While his old role as enforcer to be seriously disrupted by injuries, he defied almost everyone's expectations by regaining his place in 2001.

displaced Frenchman with a flawed temperament, had spent a week having trials with Sheffield Wednesday. Cantona's reputation for wizardry was matched by a predilection for tantrums and walking away from clubs that incurred his displeasure. Hard winter weather had restricted training and Wednesday manager Trevor Francis wanted a second week to inspect Cantona before gambling £1.1 million of his club's money. The French striker was not amused. On 31 January 1992 he was about to depart in a huff from his hotel when Howard Wilkinson, who had seen Cantona only on video, caught up with events. One long telephone call later, a deal was struck: Wilkinson persuaded Cantona to sign on loan until the end of the season, and Leeds would pay his club Nimes £100,000 with a view to making the transfer permanent.

Carl Shutt scored five goals in the last six league games of 1990-91.

It was an extraordinary coup. Of Cantona's first training session, Wilkinson wrote: 'Eric lifted the proceedings to a higher level with a series of devastating flicks and passes.' But the early evidence suggested that Cantona, for all his eagerness to impress, was not match fit. He made his debut as a substitute against Oldham at Boundary Park on 8 February 1992. Leeds lost 2-0; only their second League defeat of the season. In the next game at Everton, a 1-1 draw, Cantona started but had an undistinguished game. Leeds were sailing into a rocky patch: looming were ignominious defeats – 4-1 at Queen's Park Rangers and 4-0 at Manchester City.

Wilkinson was bemused by the speed at which Cantona established his phenomenal rapport with the Leeds fans. The Frenchman's first goal, in the 2-0 home win over Luton on 29 February, triggered rapturous celebrations. An ankle injury to Sterland, incurred during

Leeds' 3-1 win at Tottenham the following week, forced Wilkinson to reshape the team and he gave Cantona four consecutive starts. The Frenchman's performances were uneven: he was the most impressive Leeds player in the 0-0 draw against West Ham at Elland Road on 28 March, hard working, covering the pitch, giving the best passes; but at Maine Road on 4 April, hopelessly anonymous.

Manchester City's four goals looked to have sunk any lingering Championship hopes. But City were the last team to do their Manchester neighbours any favours. Four days later they went to Old Trafford, trailed 1-0 at half-time, had Neil Pointon sent off, yet contrived an equalizer that robbed United of two points. Alex Ferguson's men were starting to suffer from altitude sickness.

Cantona Unleashed

The next Saturday, Cantona, unleashed from the bench during Leeds' home game against Chelsea, scored a magician's goal during the 3-0 victory. But Wilkinson had decided that the team could not revolve around him: his role was to be that of exotic supersub. The Leeds manager had other things to think about, among them the hole at right back, which he filled with Jon Newsome, bought from Sheffield Wednesday along with David Wetherall for £250,000.

At Anfield on Easter Saturday, Leeds went into a defensive shell and chiselled out a 0-0 draw. 'A point won,' declared Wilkinson, mindful of recent horrors elsewhere. Both Uniteds were at home on Monday and looked likely victors: Manchester against Nottingham Forest and Leeds against Coventry. But in matches choreographed by the demands of television, Manchester United went first, laboured, and lost 2-1; while Leeds, buoyed by the unexpected turn of events, toiled but won 2-0. The second goal, a harshly-awarded penalty for handball, also saw Coventry defender Lloyd McGrath sent off. The win hauled Wilkinson's men back to the top and its nature suggested the luck was flowing their way.

The extent to which Manchester United's nerves were frayed became manifest when, two days later, they lost 1-0 at West Ham, for whom relegation beckoned. Suddenly, the destiny of the Championship rested in Leeds' hands: a point ahead of Manchester United; each with two games to play; a scenario that was unimaginable three weeks earlier.

On Sunday 28 April, with both in action, it fell to Leeds to go first. At noon, amid a feverish atmosphere, they joined battle with Sheffield United at Bramall Lane. The sun glared and in a swirling wind the ball bobbled about the pitch. A madhouse game unfolded, strewn with errors and own goals, throbbing with melodrama. A goal from Alan Cork on 28 minutes was cancelled out by Strachan's quick-thinking on half-time, his free kick bobbling off Rod Wallace into the net. As Leeds gathered composure in the second half, Newsome's stooping header, a wonderful connection to McAllister's free kick,

50 Greatest Players

LEE CHAPMAN Centre forward

Joined Leeds: January 1990   **From:** Nottingham Forest

Debut: v Blackburn Rovers, 13 January 1990

Appearances: 177   **Goals:** 81

Left Leeds: August 1993   **For:** Portsmouth

Rejoined Leeds: January 1996 **From:** Ipswich (loan)

Left: February 1996   **For:** Ipswich

Honours won with Leeds: Division 1 Championship 1992

Leeds' challenge for the Second Division title was starting to flag when Howard Wilkinson brought Lee Chapman to Elland Road. Chapman, at 30, having wandered around several clubs, was not universally welcomed by the fans. But he proved an inspired purchase and a great bargain.

He got a goal on his debut, a 2-1 win at Blackburn, and scored regularly thereafter. Other strikers have been blessed with greater natural ability but Chapman's positional sense, intelligence, bravery and ability to hold the ball up made him an ideal target man.

Chapman finished Leeds' first season back in Division One as the League's top scorer in all competitions, a fitting reward for his willingness to chase any cause and get in where it hurt. His understanding of Wilkinson's expectations and willingness to work hard brought prizes that have eluded more stylish but less committed strikers.

gave them the lead, a glimpse of the League title, and the game the flash of grandeur it had lacked.

Twenty-five minutes remained but within two, the tone had been lowered. A Sheffield corner swung in from the left; the defence failed to clear and Lee Chapman, willing but ill-fated, turned John Pemberton's shot over his own goal-line. What might happen next was anyone's guess; and with 13 minutes remaining, the Mad Hatter moment arrived. Sheffield United defender David Barnes lofted a high ball toward his own goal; Cantona and Wallace chased it but were beaten by Brian Gayle who looped a header over his own keeper and into the net. This low farce meant Leeds, although they didn't yet know it, were Champions.

Manchester United had to face Liverpool three hours later. They travelled to Anfield like men condemned, crestfallen after events at Sheffield. Liverpool, their bitter rivals, became executioners, shooting them down with goals from Ian Rush and Mark Walters. Anfield rejoiced. Meanwhile, the speed at which Wilkinson had won English football's great domestic prize had astounded everyone.

Indeed it had come, as later he was to reflect, perhaps too quickly. Leeds savoured their title moment with a leisurely 1-0 victory over

The Leeds squad celebrate after bringing home the championship for the first time in 18 years.

Norwich at Elland Road and a victory parade through the city. They were popular Champions though Wilkinson became irritated by comparisons made between his team and that of Don Revie. Soon he was plotting the new season. Expectations were for a vigorous defence of the title and a good run in the European Cup.

Wilkinson had strengthened the squad by signing David Rocastle from Arsenal for £2 million. Rocastle, strong in the tackle, with a good touch and a powerful shot looked, on his day, the complete midfielder, a robust figure and possible long-term replacement for Gordon Strachan. Scott Sellars, the subtle left-sided midfielder groomed by Eddie Gray, was also re-signed, Wilkinson paying Blackburn Rovers £900,000.

In the FA Charity Shield, Liverpool and Leeds atoned for their disgrace at Wembley 18 years earlier with a display of lusty attacking football that was, in the main, good-natured. Leeds won 4-3, and Cantona scored a hat-trick. It helped convince Wilkinson that, with some modifications, he might accommodate Chapman and Cantona up front. As the season proper kicked off, Cantona was back in the starting line-up, though his preference was playing between the midfield and front men, a style that Leeds did not use.

Alarm bells soon began to sound; early results were inconsistent. A 4-1 defeat at Middlesbrough in the third match of the season was as bad as any performance under Wilkinson; yet the 5-0 demolition of Tottenham at Elland Road three days later showed Leeds, and hat-trick man Eric Cantona, apparently back to their best.

Matters were not helped by a flare-up of Strachan's sciatica: for the first seven League matches, he sat on the bench. As the chivvying captain who pulled together all the threads, he was badly missed. But by mid-September, and the start of Leeds' European Cup adventure against Stuttgart, he was back, if not completely fit.

The two games against Stuttgart, however, were, once more, much ado about Cantona. With Leeds 1-0 down in Germany and trying to restore order within the ranks, who but Cantona, pulling up with a hamstring problem, would play a reckless crossfield ball instead of clearing to safety? Wilkinson watched aghast as the Germans, gifted possession, broke away and scored a second. A few minutes later Stuttgart were 3-0 up and, for Leeds, the position looked hopeless. But a benign twist of fate determined otherwise, the unexpected outcome of a stunning performance in the home leg at Leeds.

Yet bureaucracy, rather than heroic sweat, was to save Leeds' day. Stuttgart had broken UEFA rules by fielding four instead of the maximum three foreigners permitted. The battle was on for Leeds' reinstatement. UEFA would do no better than grant them a third match, on neutral territory in Barcelona, but this secured Leeds' passage to the second round, and a tie with Glasgow Rangers. The row seemed to take the wind out Stuttgart. Barely more than 7,000 rattled around the 120,000 capacity Nou Camp but with Leeds fans having the vocal edge, the players poured forward as if at Elland Road. They won 2-1, a victory delivered by Carl Shutt who broke away and scored the decisive goal just after replacing Cantona.

In the League, Leeds continued to splutter. Defensive vulnerability could not just be explained by the replacement of Sterland with Newsome. The inconsistency of Cantona and his uneasy partnership with Chapman was causing tension. Rocastle, meanwhile, grew dismayed at being kept out by Strachan.

Leeds fans had been excluded from the European Cup game at Ibrox, as would be the Scots from Elland Road. But the hostile cacophony that greeted Wilkinson's team was silenced within the first minute by a fabulous goal from Gary McAllister. A Leeds corner; a weak headed clearance; and McAllister's volley screamed into the net. With away goals counting double if the scores were level, this one looked worth its weight in gold.

Yet there was no escaping the aberrations to which Leeds had become prone. Rangers still seemed half stunned and had barely threatened when they won a corner. As it sailed over, Lukic, dazzled by the floodlights, punched the ball into his own net. The crowd rediscovered its voice, Rangers their swagger and emerged victorious from an impassioned second half, given a 2-1 lead by Ally McCoist. Rangers had the slenderest of leads but a psychological advantage.

Great Matches

EUROPEAN CUP	**Elland Road, September 30 1992**
FIRST ROUND SECOND LEG	**Attendance 20,457**
Leeds United 4 **Vfb Stuttgart 1**	
Speed	Buck
McAllister (pen)	
Cantona	
Strachan	

If all was lost after the encounter in Germany, no-one had confided in Strachan and co. In need of luck as well as inspiration, Leeds resurrected their championship form and set about the German champions with gusto.

The crowd caught the mood as Wilkinson's men attacked on all fronts. The first goal on 17 minutes typified their wit and style: Strachan's chip; Cantona's knockdown and a sweet volley from Speed. But when Buck shot through a crowded area on 33 minutes to equalize, it seemed inevitable that the earlier good work would count for nothing.

Leeds did not appear to recognize when they were beaten. Shortly before half-time, McAllister scored from a penalty and on the hour, Cantona stoked up the fires by latching onto a rebounding ball and lobbing deftly into the net.

Elland Road was a cauldron of noise and expectation. When Chapman headed home Strachan's corner on 79 minutes, Stuttgart were in turmoil. In the 11 manic minutes both teams were to go close. One more goal would have given Leeds a place in European Cup history. It never came, but UEFA had another twist in store...

Leeds United: Lukic, Sellars, Dorigo, Batty, Fairclough, Whyte, Strachan, Cantona, Chapman, Wallace, Speed.

Vfb Stuttgart: Immel, Schafer, Frontzeck, Dubajic, Struntz, Buchwald, Buck, Sverrisson, Walter (Knup), Gaudino (Simakic), Kogl.

Referee: K. Nielsen (Denmark).

Back in Yorkshire, Howard Wilkinson's relations with Cantona grew increasingly fraught. After the game in Glasgow, to which the Frenchman contributed little, Wilkinson dropped him for the League match at Queens Park Rangers. When Cantona turned up for a team talk wearing, instead of the sober pre-match attire of collar and tie, the most garish clothing he could muster, it was one act of disrespect too many. Wilkinson exploded and sent the Frenchman home.

This was the beginning of the end: six weeks later, Cantona, to the consternation of Leeds fans, would be wearing Manchester United

Gary Speed challenges Ally McCoist in the European Cup tie against Rangers.

Eric Cantona: mercurial presence or talented misfit? Wilkinson answered the dilemma by selling the Frenchman to Manchester United.

colours. He played, and scored, in the return against Rangers but Leeds by then were 2-0 down and on their way out. Depressed and deflated, Leeds trooped off to Maine Road three days later, on 7 November, and suffered their second four-goal hammering by City in seven months. This was Cantona's last appearance in a white shirt.

No one, least of all Wilkinson, seemed able to explain Leeds' swings of form and mood. Two weeks after their humiliation at Maine Road, they produced their best League display of 1992-93 beating Arsenal 3-0 at Elland Road. There was a run-out for David Rocastle who, with the rest of the team, showed something like his true form. It might have been a platform for relaunching the season. But the next fortnight brought defeats at Chelsea and Nottingham Forest; and by the first week in December, it became obvious Leeds had lost their grip on the Championship. A month later things were no better; and nor was Wilkinson's diagnosis very clear. In programme notes he drew an analogy between Leeds' inexplicable misfortunes and the illness ME. 'Nobody is totally sure what the disease is and it is particularly difficult to diagnose. But the symptoms are painfully apparent and provoke a lack of energy and drive.'

Aftershocks from Cantona's transfer were still being felt. 'The Euro defeat left us as flat as a pancake,' wrote Gary McAllister in his football biography *Captain's Log*. 'We were in trouble and we needed players to kick, bite and scratch to help us through a difficult season. Everyone knows that's not Eric's game.' Strachan, too, had sympathy with Wilkinson's decision. 'He couldn't relate to Lee Chapman and Chappy found it hard to understand him,' he said. 'There were lots of places where Cantona just didn't produce.'

New Back-Pass Law

It was Strachan's belief also that a change in the back-pass law, preventing goalkeepers from handling the ball, created more difficulties for defenders such as Chris Whyte and Chris Fairclough than for others more skilled at retaining possession. When Howard Wilkinson wrote *Managing to Succeed* in 1992, the new rule had yet to be tested in the League. But it had been in the 1991 European Youth Championships and Wilkinson disliked what he saw. 'Instead of improving the game and forcing defenders to turn with the ball, FIFA have inadvertently encouraged more long-ball football,' he said. Strachan felt that the back-pass change 'killed the side'. Certainly the defence was jittery and alarmingly prone to conceding late goals.

Wilkinson continued tinkering with the side but his gift of buying appropriate players seemed temporarily to have deserted him. Frank Strandli, a young Norwegian striker, was signed for £250,000 in January from IK Staart, but never made the grade and departed the following season. After early exits from both cups and unable to win away all season, Leeds, from early February, were on the fringes of a relegation battle. And yet there were occasional reminders of what they had been: a bravura 5-2 victory over high-flying Blackburn on 10 April did much to stave off fears of the drop.

Youth Cup Winners

Any cause for optimism lay at the grass roots. Leeds won the FA Youth Cup, beating Manchester United over two legs in matches that drew more than 60,000 fans. The more talented Manchester youngsters had been hustled out of things by Leeds who played their hearts out. 'We won it tactically,' says Paul Hart, who had returned to Elland Road as director of the youth academy. Long term, the Manchester crop, including Gary and Phil Neville, David Beckham, Paul Scholes and Keith Gillespie, bloomed, while of the physically stronger Leeds team, only striker Noel Whelan became an established Premiership player.

As Wilkinson rebuilt in 1993-94, a fresh face did emerge from the youth ranks. Gary Kelly, who did not play in the Youth Cup final, had already had a taste of first-team football. Kelly had started life as a centre forward, his talent and willingness plain to see. But he had become unsettled and homesick. 'Gary was on the verge of saying he'd had enough when, pre-season, Howard said "I'm going to try him at full back",' recalls Hart. 'I was surprised it worked out so well.'

Kelly became an admirable replacement for Mel Sterland, whose career had been ended by injury. Lee Chapman, who had laboured up front with little reward or support in 1992-93, moved to Portsmouth; and Chris Whyte, who after two excellent seasons had such a torrid time in defence, went to Birmingham. Wilkinson's big money signing was Brian Deane, a Leeds-born striker from Sheffield United for £2.7 million; as defensive cover, he acquired David O'Leary who had spent 20 years in Arsenal colours. O'Leary's pedigree was unquestionable but, at 35, he did not look the most ambitious signing. An achilles tendon injury restricted him to 10 League appearances.

There were other new faces: goalkeeper Mark Beeney signed from Brighton for £350,000 as cover for Lukic; and then later, David White from Manchester City, swopped for David Rocastle; and utility player John Pemberton from Sheffield United.

Signs of Recovery

One win in the first five League matches of 1993-94 seemed to herald another season of suffering. But after a 4-0 home defeat by Norwich, came signs of a recovery. The misery of more than a season without an away win ended on 11 September at Southampton as Leeds cantered towards an assured 2-0 victory. It began a 13-match unbeaten run in the League. Rod Wallace, fit and back in form, was working well alongside Deane; and Leeds looked more secure than at any time since 1991-92.

David Wetherall, chemistry finals behind him, had been pitched into central defence following injury to O'Leary and looked comfortable. McAllister, an ever-present, was near his creative best. Wilkinson, under some financial pressure, decided to sell Batty to Blackburn Rovers for £2.7 million. But, with a dip in form in January and early February, came the season's embarrassment, FA Cup defeat at Elland Road by Oxford United in a fourth round replay. Yet Leeds emerged from this bad patch, finished fifth and made hay with a 5-0 win at relegated Swindon on the final day.

Few forwards were braver than Lee Chapman in the early 90s.

It had been a substantial improvement. With the 17,000 capacity East Stand fully open, crowds of 40,000 watched the games against Newcastle, Liverpool and Manchester United. But home defeat by the latter, closing in on a second successive Championship, emphasized the gulf between Wilkinson's men and the old enemy. And for Wilkinson, the burdensome legacy of 1991-92 was that the demand for more silverware remained high.

Strachan had already seen off one pretender, David Rocastle, for the number four shirt. He had kept playing longer than he wanted, yet even when ageing and not fully fit, Strachan's presence and example, like that of Bremner before him, had counted for so much. But Wilkinson needed a new authority figure; and with this in mind signed Carlton Palmer from Sheffield Wenesday for £2.6 million. Strachan would depart mid-season. Batty would come to be missed.

Palmer was to buttress central defence though he had made his name as a ball-winning midfielder. Wilkinson hired yet another old Wednesdayite, Nigel Worthington, as further defensive cover. He also made two intriguing signings from South Africa, each costing £250,000: striker Phil Masinga from Mamelodi Sundowns and central defender Lucas Radebe from Kaizer Chiefs. Mid-season saw another African import, Tony Yeboah from Eintracht Frankfurt for £3.4 million. Wilkinson had long been tracking the Ghanaian striker who had scored 68 times in 123 games in the Bundesliga.

Gary Speed in action against Sheffield United's John Pemberton in September 1993. Leeds would sign the Blades' defender two months later.

The flourish with which Leeds finished 1994-95 propelled them once more to fifth place and into the UEFA Cup. There were some familiar tales: cup embarrassment against Third Division Mansfield Town who drummed Wilkinson's men out of the Coca-Cola competition in the second round. Only a late equaliser from David Wetherall spared Leeds similar humiliation in the FA Cup at Walsall. It needed extra-time, and a rapid hat-trick from Phil Masinga, to dispose of the Saddlers in the replay.

To every fan's frustration, Leeds once more capitulated to Manchester United in the FA Cup, beaten 3-1 in round five at Old Trafford. But the match had a milestone: Tony Yeboah's first goal, an almost diffident effort that crept in. However untidy it was, Yeboah had found his range. Before long he was scoring from all angles.

There was a sense that Leeds' season might peter out tamely until a stylish 3-0 win at Chelsea triggered a storming run-in wherein the team lost only once in the final 13 matches. Brian Deane, not everyone's idea of a top-drawer striker, had given good service when free of injury, particularly when playing out wide. The habit of scoring, rather than conceding goals, at the death was now with Leeds, as they secured crucial points in home games against Champions-elect Blackburn Rovers, Aston Villa and Norwich. Deane's equalizer against Tottenham in the last match of 1994-95, when he dashed from his own half past a clutch of defenders to drive the ball home, gave Leeds the point needed to ensure UEFA Cup qualification and satisfaction all round.

In the glow of late summer, Leeds' new season held much promise. By the end, fans were baffled and disillusioned. The early performances of 1995-96 had been a feast; those at the end, hard tack. No one, least of all Howard Wilkinson, seemed able to finger what had gone awry.

Yeboah began scoring explosively, his extravagant volleys against Liverpool and Wimbledon the signature of a man in peak form. The winner against Liverpool on 21 August, voted *Match of the Day*'s goal of the season, became the brightest memory of 1995-96. Others were soon to fade: his stylish hat-trick in Monaco, as Leeds embarked on their UEFA Cup campaign, put into perspective as, in round two, a crushing 8-3 aggregate defeat by PSV Eindhoven exposed the tactical naivety that had come with too little European football.

Too often, Gary McAllister toiled alone as midfield creator. The newer defenders looked like journeymen: Paul Beesley, signed close season for £250,000 from Sheffield United, and in October, Richard Jobson for £1 million from Oldham Athletic both struggled to settle in. As injuries compelled Wilkinson to mix and match at the back, defensive horrors unknown since his arrival at Elland Road occurred: the 6-2 defeat at Sheffield Wednesday on 16 December and a 5-0 thrashing at Anfield a month later.

With Yeboah's goals and supply drying up, Wilkinson, the Leeds board breathing down his neck, cast around for new blood. In November, he made his big splash, paying Parma £4.5 million for Tomas Brolin. A record fee for Leeds but it was, for player and manager, an ill-fated deal. Brolin, who showed stirring form for

Victory over Manchester United in the FA Youth Cup in 1992-3 was an indication that Howard Wilkinson's youth policy was bearing fruit and a catalyst for attracting some of the best young players anywhere.

Sweden in the 1994 World Cup, was palpably unfit. Then, in what looked a desperate hunt for another quick fix, Wilkinson re-engaged Lee Chapman. There was a sense of the absurd when, in his first appearance against West Ham on 13 January, Chapman, now 36, lasted just 22 minutes before being sent off for leading with the elbow.

Supporters wondered why, with Masinga and Yeboah absent on African Nations Cup duty, Wilkinson had sold Noel Whelan to Coventry for £2 million. Whelan, strong, mobile and confident and Leeds to the core, had never clamoured to leave. 'We were relying an awful lot on the chairman's money,' says Paul Hart. 'There were economic reasons for selling Whelan. It was a good price.'

Progress in the Coca-Cola Cup helped keep fans interested. Only in beating Champions Blackburn en route to the semi-final had Wilkinson's men looked convincing: their earlier passage had been marked by scrambling performances against Notts County and Reading. But the 5-1 aggregate win over Birmingham City had been emphatic. Supporters found it hard to believe the club was Wembley bound for the first time in 23 years. Success though had its price: Dorigo's hamstring injury forced him out for the rest of the season.

Leeds had also made grinding progress in the FA Cup; and, as March arrived, it was conceivable they might become Wembley finalists twice

Beaten all ends up. Villa's Dwight Yorke takes command against Leeds in the 1996 Coca-Cola Cup final.

over. By the end of the month, reality caught up with everyone. In the televized FA Cup quarter-final against Liverpool, Wilkinson's men, mindful of January's 5-0 hammering at Anfield, were pitifully timid. The 0-0 draw was among the most sterile ever between these old rivals; and in the replay at Anfield, Leeds scarcely offered an attack worthy of the name. They were overrun in the second half and beaten 3-0.

50 Greatest Players

GARY SPEED Midfielder

Joined Leeds: June 1988   **From:** Juniors

Debut: v Oldham Athletic, 6 May 1989

Appearances: 312   **Goals:** 57

Left Leeds: June 1996   **For:** Everton

Honours won with Leeds: Division 2 Championship 1990;
Division 1 Championship 1992; 35 Wales caps

Gary Speed is a professional's player whose finest years at
Leeds were his early ones after Howard Wilkinson had made him
a regular during the Second Division Championship season of 1989-90. Speed, who
joined Leeds from school, quickly made an impact as an attacking left-sided midfielder
with pace, a willingness to receive the ball in tight situations and an eye for goal.

Although not the tallest player – 5 feet 9 in – Speed has remarkable ability in the
air, timing jumps perfectly to win most duels. Managers have appreciated Speed's
willingness to play anywhere and honest endeavour; though some feel Wilkinson
persisted with him too long after he lost form and confidence. Speed left Elland Road
in 1996, and continued giving good service at Everton and Newcastle.

This was poor form to take to the Coca-Cola Cup final against
Aston Villa. Less than two months earlier, Leeds had lost 3-0 at Villa
Park when Wilkinson, desperate to shake the team out of its lethargy,
pitched in youngsters: Alan Maybury, Rob Bowman and Andy Couzens,
the latter two graduates of the FA Youth Cup winning team.

No one imagined that a Wembley appearance would not rouse the
senior pros into giving their all. But their display was shockingly
supine. Save for young Andy Gray on the left wing, Leeds were
ponderous, inhibited and sluggish while Villa, 3-0 victors, were lively,
outgoing and sharp. It was a non-contest; and Leeds' lack of fight
caused supporters to turn on Wilkinson at full-time. 'That game and
the aftermath were the low points of my career,' he reflected
afterwards. Old warriors like Peter Lorimer were stunned by the tame
surrender. 'The team didn't really seem to care and accepted defeat,'
he said. 'There was no real battler. That's what hurt the fans'.

The Brolin experiment had failed. At the end of 1995-96 he departed on loan to FC Zurich; and thence to his old club, Parma. After the Coca-Cola Cup final, Yeboah was injured, out for the rest of the season. More youngsters appeared fitfully: Mark Ford, a combative midfielder; Ian Harte, a young Irish defender, the nephew of Gary Kelly. But whatever combination Wilkinson tried, things failed to improve. In April came five successive defeats: relegation form mitigated only by nobly stubborn resistance against Manchester United at Old Trafford, where Leeds lost 1-0 and Lucas Radebe played in goal after Mark Beeney was sent off. Alex Ferguson mischievously suggested that Wilkinson had been sold short in other games. As for the early optimism, nine points from the first three matches turned out to be the deposit that saved Leeds from relegation rather than points in the bank for a Championship challenge.

After a wretched season came a chaotic summer. The resignation in April 1996 of 71-year-old chairman Leslie Silver on health grounds triggered a bitter boardroom battle and the evolution of the club into a plc. Wilkinson could only look on helplessly as his planned close season shopping spree stalled.

Silver, who had made his fortune in paint manufacturing, had joined the board in 1981 and became chairman in 1984. However, he knew that the business complexities of modern football meant the part-time non-executive figurehead had grown obsolete. 'With the development of the Premier League, the job is substantially more demanding. We are now moving to a £20 million turnover,' he said.

Following such a dismal campaign, the name of George Graham had been linked with Elland Road. Bill Fotherby, the acting chairman, was quick to scotch such nonsense. 'There is no question of George Graham coming to Leeds, and I want to make that very clear,' he told the *Yorkshire Evening Post* on 11 April. 'Howard Wilkinson is our manager and one of the most able men there is.'

But the fortunes of the team, and the sales of McAllister to Coventry for £3.5 million and Gary Speed to Everton, became almost a sideshow as a battle for control of the club took centre stage. There were two parties: the London-based media group Caspian and Conrad, a sports

50 Greatest Players

GARY McALLISTER Midfielder

Joined Leeds: Summer 1990   **From:** Leicester City

Debut: v Everton, 25 August 1990

Appearances: 294   **Goals:** 45

Left Leeds: July 1996   **For:** Coventry City

Honours won with Leeds: Division 1 Championship 1992; 41 Scotland caps

In April 1990, on a night of excruciating tension at Elland Road, a fiendish strike by Leicester midfielder McAllister nearly put paid to Leeds' promotion hopes. Howard Wilkinson took note and swiftly recruited him for Leeds' campaign in the top flight.

Although initially lacking in confidence the 26-year-old soon became a central figure as Wilkinson put a greater emphasis on skill. He was a supreme passer and had the trademark of the best midfielders: the ability and willingness to receive the ball in tight situations; to create time; to assume responsibility. In 1990 he was called up for Scotland, eventually becoming captain. As Leeds fell from grace, McAllister still shone, but his self-confidence was vulnerable. Hostility from the Hampden Park crowd resulted in his premature international retirement.

For someone who was so admired, McAllister's departure to Coventry in 1996 was distressingly acrimonious: he left days after publicly promising to remain at Leeds. But his career flourished at Highfield Road and he enjoyed an Indian Summer at Liverpool before retiring as a player in 2002.

and leisure group. Fotherby and Silver backed the Caspian bid but Peter Gilman, the third major shareholder, was vehemently opposed. 'It stinks for the fans and under-values the club,' he declared.

On 3 July, the club announced that Caspian had bought Leeds United for £35 million. They had promised Wilkinson funds 'beyond people's wildest imaginings.' Wilkinson, with £12 million to spend on players, belatedly went shopping, paying Charlton Athletic £2.6 million for 19-year-old Lee Bowyer, making him Britain's most expensive teenager. But Gilman then began high court proceedings, claiming that the projected deal breached an agreement made by the three major shareholders that any sale must be approved unanimously. Caspian did not take final control until the end of July. For Wilkinson, rebuilding became 'like trying to pick my crop two months after everyone picks theirs'.

Bowyer, though, proved a brilliant signing, as did goalkeeper Nigel Martyn, bought from Crystal Palace for £2.25 million as replacement for John Lukic, who returned to Arsenal. But there were mixed feelings about lavishing £4.5 million to bring Lee Sharpe from Manchester United; and a sense that Wilkinson's fondness for ageing workhorses had again got the better of him when Ian Rush arrived on a free transfer from Liverpool; and then Mark Hateley from Rangers.

Spirit was willing but defensive flesh weak in the first game of 1996-97, a 3-3 draw at Derby where horrible mistakes meant that Leeds twice threw away a winning advantage. Two dismal home performances at Elland Road, defeat by Sheffield Wednesday and a scruffy 1-0 victory over Wimbledon, resurrected growls of discontent. These subsided after Ian Harte's headed goal brought a 1-0 victory at Blackburn where Leeds had played some of the neat passing football to which Wilkinson claimed he had been converted.

But three days after that balmy night in Blackburn, Wilkinson, Leeds' longest-serving manager since Revie, was out of a job. The word humiliation hardly did justice to the 4-0 home defeat inflicted by Manchester United on 7 September. Caspian, the new owners, had no loyalty to Wilkinson. They could look to 1995-96 in making the case that the Leeds manager had lost his way and his ability to motivate his players.

For Wilkinson, until then never sacked, dismissal was a terrible shock. He blamed fans for turning on his players; though he departed 'without bitterness'. Then, presciently, he added: 'Possibly the most galling part... is that I won't have the chance to see the kids come through the youth ranks. Five or six are class acts, believe me.'

Bill Fotherby described the decision to sack Wilkinson as 'the hardest of his life – like tearing a piece of my body away'. But Fotherby also confessed to having lost confidence in the Leeds manager and a feeling that Wilkinson had stayed 'a little too long'. As for a successor, it was time for George Graham, in whom five months earlier Fotherby denied having any interest, to step forward from where he had been lurking with intent.

Chapter Ten: 1996-2000
The Arsenal Connection

George Graham had been out of football for 18 months, sacked from Arsenal in February 1995 after receiving money from an agent, the so-called 'bungs', for transfer deals that brought John Jensen and Pal Lydersen to Highbury.

Following his appointment on 10 September 1996, Graham appointed David O'Leary as his assistant. He also made comforting noises about hard work, total commitment and re-building from the back. Whatever misgivings there were, Graham's record of achievement at Arsenal was formidable: two League Championships; the FA Cup; the League Cup and the European Cup-Winners' Cup. Graham too had misgivings – principally about his inheritance from Howard Wilkinson. 'I've been very surprised by the lack of numbers and experience in the first-team squad – for a club of our size, it's simply not good enough,' he said.

A patched-up, injury-hit side took the field at Coventry for Graham's first game in charge, a 2-1 defeat where old boys Whelan and McAllister caught the eye as creators and executioners while for Leeds, only Martyn excelled as a last line of defence.

Another grim campaign beckoned: concentration on defence and a goals famine. But there were solid figures around whom Graham could build: Gary Kelly, a model of consistency and fitness at right back; also Lucas Radebe, injured and then overlooked by Wilkinson.

With the celebrated midfield of Strachan, Batty, McAllister and Speed all departed, Bowyer, at 19, had the

George Graham (left) replaced Howard Wilkinson as manager in September 1996.

Great Managers – 1988-96

HOWARD WILKINSON

Like his more illustrious predecessor Don Revie, Howard Wilkinson took over a Leeds side struggling at the foot of the Second Division and moulded a team of Championship winners. The former Sheffield Wednesday and Brighton winger, teacher and England under-21 coach, had already won promotion with Notts County and Sheffield Wednesday when he dropped a division to take over at Leeds.

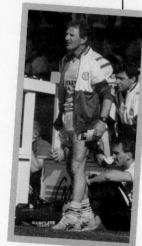

Thorough and often able to raise players' performances, Wilkinson maintained strong discipline and his teams were supremely well-organized. In addition he showed an ability to make key signings – Strachan, Cantona, McAllister – at the right times and backed them up with the canny imports of Vinnie Jones, Chris Whyte, Lee Chapman, Tony Dorigo and others. Wilkinson also made significant changes at the club, installing a new youth system and training facilities. Having taken Leeds to a League Championship, into Europe and to the Coca Cola Cup final in his six years at the club, he was sacked early in the 1996-7 season. He is now the FA's technical director.

mantle of creator thrust upon him. But Graham felt several of the young players brought on by Wilkinson were not up to scratch – 'Good but nowhere near good enough for the Premiership'. In time, Andy Gray, Mark Ford, Andy Couzens, Mark Tinkler and others were released.

Up front, Rush toiled honestly but often had to forage for the ball himself. Hateley made little impact and left mid-season. More perplexing was Tony Yeboah's fall from grace. The knee injury; a struggle for fitness; lost confidence and a sense that Graham did not fancy him: all made Yeboah a shadow of what he had been a year earlier. Yeboah's departure became inevitable when, substituted during the 1-0 defeat at Tottenham on 15 March 1997, he showed his disgust by ripping off his shirt and hurling it towards the Leeds dugout.

Yeboah's disillusionment was complete as Leeds' once adoring fans turned on him. But his frustrations had long been simmering.

'Despite the fact that I had recovered from injury, Mr Graham refused to give me a decent run in the team. We did talk over the situation but that didn't provoke any change,' Yeboah told one journalist. Of Howard Wilkinson's three African recruits, only Lucas Radebe was to build a career at Elland Road. Phil Masinga had played too few games to get his work permit renewed and left for the Swiss club FC Gallen.

The hunt for new defenders continued. Liverpool's John Scales flirted with Leeds but went to Tottenham, for £4 million. Graham instead buttressed his back line from the bargain basement, paying Oldham £400,000 for Gunnar Halle, and the Dutch team FC Volendam £1.1 million for Robert Molenaar. They had different styles – the burly Molenaar something of a Desperate Dan figure while Halle was tidy and unobtrusive, with good awareness and positional sense. Both, in their different ways, did a fine job: Graham's failure to woo Scales was money well saved.

50 Greatest Players

TONY DORIGO Left back

Joined Leeds: July 1991   **From:** Chelsea
Debut: v Nottingham Forest, 20 August 1991
Appearances: 209   **Goals:** 6
Left Leeds: August 1997   **For:** Torino
Honours won with Leeds: Division 1 Championship 1992;
Charity Shield 1992; 9 England caps

Tony Dorigo was a footballing defender. Speed and an ability to time tackles were his greatest assets – many forwards given a few yards start found it not enough to shrug off Dorigo. But his game also had intelligence: he was excellent at anticipating danger, intercepting, and turning defence into attack with balls short or long.

Dorigo had an outstanding first season – Leeds won the Championship and he was voted supporters' player of the year. He was exciting to watch, whether overlapping on the flank, from where he could knock in teasing crosses, or striking the ball with venom from 25 yards. Dorigo proved an excellent servant for Leeds and was, in a world of histrionics and violent behaviour, the model of decorum.

That his team survived in the Premiership was due to its knack of beating other strugglers. The highlights, amid a series of painful performances, were isolated: a sterling 2-0 victory over Chelsea on 1 December, in which Rush scored his first goal in Leeds colours; a smash and grab FA Cup fourth round win at Arsenal; and uncharacteristically sparkling football in a 2-2 draw at Sheffield Wednesday towards the end of the season.

Dour and Functional?

'So much money; so little talent' mourned the *Yorkshire Evening Post* after the drab goalless game against Blackburn on 7 April. Graham had caused some amusement when claiming 'It's not my style to be dour and functional' – his side scored only 28 league goals, and whenever they went a goal down never retrieved the match. The £2.25 million spent on Nigel Martyn looked a priceless investment – in Bill Fotherby's eyes, Martyn was the difference between survival and relegation. Attacking reinforcements were hopefuls rather than proven achievers: Derek Lilley from Morton for £700,000 and winger Pierre Laurent from Bastia for £250,000. Neither made an impact.

Among the ill-fated of 1996-97 was Leeds United's chief executive Robin Launders, a victim of dissatisfaction with the club's commercial operation. But while much of the football had been torture to watch, average crowds at Elland Road had grown to around 35,000. Through all the battles of attrition, the team had finished 11th. Meanwhile the next generation of young players had won the FA Youth Cup; and those in the know had an inkling that Harry Kewell, Stephen McPhail, Jonathan Woodgate and Matthew Jones might go further than the school of 1993.

In the close season, Graham began shopping seriously. David Hopkin, a combative goal-scoring midfielder, arrived from Crystal Palace for £3.25 million, a hero following his last-gasp winner in the London club's play-off final against Sheffield United. With Brian Deane sold to back to Sheffield United for £1.5 million after scoring just five times in 1996-97, Graham's priority was to find a potent, affordable striker: almost a contradiction in terms. Potential bargains, Graham hoped, lay within the less fashionable clubs of Europe. The Dutchman Jimmy Floyd Hasselbaink had scored 27 goals in 1996-97 for the Portuguese side Boavista; 20 the previous season for relegated Campomairorense. At £2 million, he looked a good bet for Leeds.

When watching Hasselbaink, Graham's eye had also been caught by Bruno Ribeiro, a combative left-sided midfielder with Vitoria Setubal. Graham spent £500,000 on Ribeiro and a similar amount early in the close season for Glasgow Rangers' full back David Robertson. He further stiffened midfield with Alf-Inge Haaland, recruited from Nottingham Forest for £1.6 million. Carlton Palmer, increasingly a target for boorish elements of the Leeds crowd, had been sold to Southampton for £1 million.

While in 1996-97 fans grew resigned to performances of numbing tedium, in 1997-98 Leeds became a team of many moods. Graham's carefully-laid defensive plans often went astray, but the team became infinitely more watchable. Hopkin, in the early stages, did much to pep them up and Hasselbaink, despite his glowering persona and predilection for moaning at team-mates, proved a magnificent acquisition, striking sparks off Rod Wallace. The team had, by Christmas, exceeded its tally of Premiership goals for 1996-97.

David Hopkin with John Salako. Hopkin's arrival in the summer of 1997 immediately added fire to the Leeds midfield. He transferred to Bradford City in Summer 2000.

Where the previous season there had been over-caution, now there was madness. The match at Blackburn on 14 September which Leeds won 4-3, yielded seven goals before half-time. Such were its thrills and spills that Graham, perhaps with a tinge of self-mockery declared: 'It sent shivers down my spine.' Yet six days later, a 1-0 home defeat inflicted by Leicester had about it the air of hangover. Critics accused Leeds of a lack of intelligence, except, that was, for young Harry Kewell, who, on as substitute, produced the most perceptive passes of the match.

Kewell was the first graduate of the 1997 FA Youth Cup winning side to claim a regular first-team place. Following the 1-0 win at Tottenham on 1 November, a match in which Leeds had been utterly dominant, Graham hinted that others might follow. 'A lot more real quality kids are a year or so from playing in the first team,' he said. It was prediction more resoundingly accurate than Graham could ever have realized; but possibly because their breakthrough was not at his instigation.

Another week; another game of wild excitement and atrocious defending: Leeds, 3-0 down at home to Derby after 33 minutes thundered back to win 4-3. Now in the top four, they were to stay in the upper reaches. And there were times when Graham could be proud of his team's defences. At Stamford Bridge on 13 December 1997, in a wild match that began decorously with a minute's silence

for the death of Billy Bremner, Leeds were reduced to nine men before half-time by the sendings-off of Haaland and Kelly. But although besieged by Chelsea's cosmopolitan wizards, the nine held out for a 0-0 draw. Bremner would have been proud of them.

Mark Ford in FA Youth Cup action against Manchester United's Robbie Savage. Ford would be one of the first of Wilkinson's youngsters to make the first team, but fell short of Graham's expectations.

While Graham persisted in talking down the team's achievements, Leeds were showing form that might get them into Europe; and having the luck of the draw in the FA Cup. After modest opponents in shape of Oxford United, Grimsby Town and Birmingham City, next up at Elland Road were Wolves. An open invitation to reach the semi-finals was, in Leeds' tradition of inglorious cup defeats, spurned. A shapeless match burst into life only in the last eight minutes, turning on a fine goal for the First Division visitors from Leeds-born Don Goodman, and a penalty miss, two minutes from time, by Jimmy Floyd Hasselbaink.

Two seasons earlier, exit in the sixth round precipitated a shocking nosedive. This time Leeds bounced back in style, crushing Blackburn Rovers 4-0 at Elland Road; and then, a few days later, Derby 5-0 at the Baseball Ground.

50 Greatest Players

ROD WALLACE Forward

Joined Leeds: May 1991   **From:** Southampton

Debut: v Nottingham Forest, August 20 1991

Appearances: 245   **Goals** 67

Left Leeds: July 1998   **For:** Glasgow Rangers

Honours won with Leeds: Division 1 Championship 1992

On his day, with the right people playing around him, few strikers looked more potent than Rod Wallace. He formed an excellent understanding with Lee Chapman after arriving at Elland Road with twin brother Ray in a £1.7 million deal and, in a memorable first season, showed electric pace, mobility and an elasticity that allowed him to control almost any ball.

With greater consistency – like most strikers, he suffered injuries or loss of form – Wallace would surely have achieved full international recognition: speed and the technique that enables him to skip away from defenders at will are the gold standard. Virtuoso goals in the Championship celebration win over Norwich in May 1992 and his goal of the season at Tottenham in 1995 were out of the top drawer. After transferring to Rangers, he found the Scottish Premier League a happy hunting ground before returning to the English scene.

Near Disaster

Yet Leeds were unaccountably feeble in their next outing at West Ham losing 3-0 on 31 March. The result, however, was overshadowed by a near disaster on the team's flight home from Stansted airport where the pilot was forced to abort take-off, the plane overshot the runway and the front undercarriage collapsed. It said much for the skill and courage of the pilot that of 40 passengers and four crew, only two were slightly injured.

George Graham had not been on board, opting to stay overnight in London. Among the abiding media images was the paternal calm shown by David O'Leary. Soon it became clear that, for personal and professional motives, Graham had his eyes on a return to the capital. The sight of O'Leary, shepherding and protecting Leeds players in troubled times, would, in time, become familiar.

Leeds had finished fifth and qualified again for the UEFA Cup. While sometimes dour and scratchy, at other times their exuberance confounded critics; and perhaps even Graham himself. Hasselbaink had been a steal at £2 million: hungry for possession; holding up the ball; taking up good positions; dangerous not only as a sharpshooter but when spinning off defenders, sprinting down the flanks and crossing for others to inflict damage. Kewell's vision, touch, skill and stamina were becoming increasingly prominent. Wallace had combined well; but Leeds were destined to lose him: out of contract and unwilling to re-sign, he left for Glasgow Rangers. It once more raised questions about the Leeds strike-force during 1998-99.

Jimmy Floyd Hasselbaink; top-scorer in both his seasons at Elland Road.

Graham, having hit the jackpot with Hasselbaink, engaged another powerful black Dutch front runner, Clyde Wijnhard, from Willem II, for the new campaign. Martin Hiden, an elegant, capable right-sided Austrian defender signed the previous February from Rapid Vienna, had slotted in neatly; and, with injury to David Robertson, Ian Harte seized his chance at left back. Harte, like his uncle Gary Kelly, came from tenacious Irish stock. Once drafted in, he soon eclipsed Danny Granville, signed for £1.6 million from Chelsea. Kelly's legendary durability had, for once, been undermined by injury; and he was to miss the whole season.

The season began with Leeds struggling to find a rhythm and Graham dampening expectations. 'I don't think we are as good as the big boys yet,' he opined after a nondescript 1-1 home draw with Aston Villa on 19 September. But by then, his thoughts were straying to the managerial vacancy at White Hart Lane, where, by a piquant coincidence, Leeds were due to play their next match. Sitting alongside chairman Peter Ridsdale, George Graham cut an impassive figure. Ridsdale exuberantly celebrated each of Leeds goals; but Graham's allegiances, as he watched Spurs retrieve a 3-1 deficit to equalize in injury time, were harder to fathom.

It was, indeed, Graham's last match as Leeds United's manager; a curious occasion where supporters from both teams directed abuse at him, those of Spurs reviling him for a long association with Arsenal. While not a man to inspire gratitude, Graham had, in two seasons, stopped the rot at Leeds and effected a revival. What dismayed supporters were his morale-sapping expressions of doubt and apparent lack of will to drive Leeds further forward.

When Graham jumped ship, Leeds set out to woo Martin O'Neill from Leicester City. But the Leicester board would not entertain an approach. O'Leary, in temporary charge, at first denied any

Brian Deane scored 38 goals in 168 appearances for Leeds between August 1993 and September 1997.

desire for the job. But events – the intractability of Leicester directors and the burgeoning goodwill towards him – changed matters. It became clear on the night of 29 September as Leeds despatched Maritimo from the UEFA Cup 4-1 on penalties in the Madeiran evening sunshine, that a bond between players and caretaker manager was forming.

O'Leary had an abundance of talent with which to work, not least the young players that Graham, despite singing their praises, seemed reluctant to blood. McPhail was recalled to the frame, and Jonathan Woodgate, a young central defender full of confidence and composure, called up. Within nine months, Woodgate, who made a faultless debut in the 1-1 draw at Nottingham Forest on 17 October, vaulted from reserve football to the full England team. Injuries dictated that McPhail's appearances, characterized by ingenious, precise passing, were fitful; but his time was not far away.

Any lingering doubts O'Leary had about taking charge were probably banished in Italy where Leeds, squaring up to the sophisticates of Roma, were cast as vanquished heroes in their 1-0 UEFA Cup defeat. It was a proving ground for the imperturbable McPhail, from whose telling balls Ribeiro and Halle hit the post; and told O'Leary much about the defence's stomach for coping with a bombardment after Ribeiro was sent off with half an hour left on the clock.

As McPhail and Woodgate bedded in, striker Alan Smith entered the arena on 14 November 1998 with Leeds a goal down at Anfield and 15 minutes left. Smith's first act in Premiership football, within seconds of coming on as substitute, was to race forward and score. Two late goals from Hasselbaink gave Leeds the points and buoyed them up for when Charlton, struggling and brittle, came to Leeds the following week. Kewell ran riot; Smith re-enacted his party piece of coming off the bench to score and Bowyer, who two months earlier had been disparaged by one reporter as a harrying spoiler, was fêted for being 'foot-perfect in midfield... an England candidate' in Leeds' 4-1 win.

Another week, another youngster: goalkeeper Paul Robinson, a debutant the previous month in a game against Chelsea at Elland Road, had made his mark at Manchester United when substituting for Nigel Martyn. Robinson, like everyone else, seemed unawed by Old Trafford: Leeds lost 3-2 a match that could have gone either way. The real cost was not only Martyn's injury but long-term damage inflicted on Hiden's knee ligaments after his studs got caught in the turf.

Seven of the team that ran West Ham ragged six days later were 21 or under. While Leeds' 4-0 victory was joyous stuff, reinforcements were needed for sterner challenges and a long season. Leeds prepared to celebrate the £4.4 million homecoming of David Batty, whose sale, Peter Ridsdale admitted, had been forced by the bank and who, in O'Leary's mind, 'should never have been allowed to leave.' David Batty's hunger to play for Leeds left few in doubt that it was the ideal move.

He returned in typical style in the 2-0 home win against Coventry on 14 December, booked after five minutes for a fiendish tackle on George Boateng; and forced to leave the field 20 minutes from time clutching his ribs. Injury-free for so much of his early career, Batty, whose presence Leeds craved when the going got tough, was destined to become a frequent long-term casualty.

Pre-Christmas, Leeds were a little short of living with the best. As the year turned, hiccups of inconsistency reminded romantics that O'Leary's juvenile cavaliers were unready to make some fantastic assault on the Championship. It was as king-makers that their role lay.

Leeds finished fourth and had everything to look forward to. Neutrals were beguiled by their youthful talent and the demonstrations of team spirit. The close season priority for O'Leary and Ridsdale was to get the cream of the talent under long-term contract. All went well until it came to dealing with Jimmy Floyd Hasselbaink.

After four prolific seasons in Portugal and England, Hasselbaink, and his agent, knew his worth. But Ridsdale was not prepared to shatter the wages structure by entertaining the £40,000 a week being demanded. It all struck a sour note with the Leeds fans, who, after singing eulogies to the Dutch striker at Coventry in the last game of

Great Matches

FA PREMIER LEAGUE   Elland Road, 11 May 1999

Leeds United 1   Arsenal 0   Attendance 40,124

Hasselbaink

Victory for the Gunners would give them a hand on the Championship; for Leeds, pride in beating the team widely regarded as superior to Manchester United. It would be a litmus test of progress under O'Leary. Yet if Leeds won, by their hand the title might be delivered to Old Trafford. An unpalatable thought; much for the home fans to mull over.

Arsenal arrived as fêted guests. The early minutes were tepid, enlivened principally by a long-distance lob from Batty that almost fooled Seaman; there was little to suggest that the match would ignite into a rip-roaring, gladiatorial contest. But tackles suddenly grew sterner; politeness wore thin; and conflicts began. Battles started breaking out: Batty and Bowyer versus Vieira and Petit; Alan Smith going for Tony Adams' jugular.

There were hair-raising escapes: Overmars' cross-shot just beating the far post; Martyn clearing from Adams off the line. Then when Keown brought down Smith, Harte smacked a penalty against the bar. Names began entering the referee's notebook thick and fast.

Art and conflict rolled on unabated into the second half, the tempo, the passion, the fusillade of near misses unstinting. The tricky Kanu came on, but whenever the first line of the Leeds defence was breached, the last held firm. Radebe was a colossus.

Only four minutes remained when Kewell, a scourge of Arsenal throughout, found unaccustomed room on the left, and leaving Dixon in his wake, looped over a teasing cross for Hasselbaink who had got in front of Vivas. His diving header crashed into the net and Arsenal were undone, defeated in the league for the first time since December. A present for Manchester United; but Leeds had repelled the hungriest and the best when the stakes were high. And that was what mattered most.

Leeds United: Martyn, Haaland, Woodgate, Radebe, Harte, Batty, Hopkin, Bowyer, Kewell, Smith, Hasselbaink.

Arsenal: Seaman, Dixon, Winterburn (Vivas), Vieira, Keown, Adams, Parlour (Diawara), Anelka, Petit, Bergkamp, Overmars (Kanu).

Referee: G. Willard (Worthing).

1998-99, turned on him vehemently in a pre-season friendly at Birmingham. This turned out to be Hasselbaink's last game. Rather than have him stew discontentedly in the reserves, Leeds sold him to Atletico Madrid for £12 million.

His departure had been half expected. Leeds had already outlaid £5 million on Michael Bridges, a stylish young striker unable to claim a regular first-team place at Sunderland. Darren Huckerby, a box of tricks from Coventry, was also signed for £5 million to bolster the front line. Danny Mills arrived from Charlton Athletic for £4 million as cover at right back; Michael Duberry for £5 million from Chelsea in central defence. Eirik Bakke, a rangy Norwegian midfielder, was signed from Sogndal, and proved a snip at £1 million. Meanwhile David Wetherall, ousted by the emergence of Jon Woodgate, was sold to Bradford City along with Gunnar Halle. Bruno Ribeiro left for Sheffield United; Danny Granville for Manchester City.

The first month of 1999-2000 saw some uneven performances: a dreary 0-0 draw at home to Derby on opening day; and two weeks later, a 2-1 home defeat by Liverpool wherein Leeds looked bereft of ideas and vulnerable especially to the power and pace of Titi Camara.

---

50 Greatest Players

HARRY KEWELL Forward

Joined Leeds: July 1995   **From:** New South Wales Academy, Australia

Debut: v Middlesbrough, 30 March 1996

Appearances: 201   **Goals:** 47

Honours won with Leeds: FA Youth Cup 1997; 20 Australia caps

When Harry Kewell arrived in England as a 16-year-old from the New South Wales academy for an informal trial at Elland Road, he played at full back. Kewell had written to other clubs but only Leeds took him up. They were counting their blessings.

Kewell could, it seemed, play anywhere and do anything. He inflicts much of his damage from the left side of midfield, his weaving runs scintillating examples of the flank player's art: the balance perfect; the surefootedness absolute although not extravagant.

Against Aston Villa in January 2000 he typically combined his technical gifts with cheek and surprise. Within 10 seconds of the second half kicking off, Kewell had the ball in Villa's net: from chest to knee; a darting run and a vicious 30-yard strike. It was a party piece that few would have dared and fewer could have brought off.

In 1999-2000, Kewell's talents achieved widespread acclaim and he was voted Young Player of the Year. With application – and luck – Kewell could become a great player. He missed much of 2001-02 with an Achilles injury and rarely looked at his fittest after returning. Leeds were usually the poorer without his cutting edge.

But between times, there had been a 3-0 win at Southampton, graced by a stylish hat-trick from Michael Bridges. Bridges, plunged into regular action sooner than O'Leary had intended, was a revelation, showing splendid poise, control and a finishing ability that Sunderland never fully exploited.

By the end of August, Leeds snapped into a regular winning habit, providing thrills and making waves. Once more, they were at the heart of colourful and rumbustious games, coming back from 2-1 down to win 4-3 at Coventry on 11 September; spilling a lead in the last minute to draw 4-4 at Everton on 24 October. Gary Kelly had recovered from his lost season, back in typically swift-running, unobtrusive style: good news for everyone except his replacement Danny Mills.

The UEFA Cup campaign became peppered with political rows, matches of high drama and tension; and then, in its final throes, marred irredeemably by tragedy. It landed Leeds in strange places under curious circumstances: an away leg with Partizan Belgrade played in Holland; and, when the biting winter stopped play in Moscow, a Russian 'home' leg in Bulgaria, accompanied by much sniping from the Spartak camp.

Against the likes of Spartak Moscow, who landed in the UEFA Cup after being jettisoned from the European Champions League, Leeds could be judged as a team of international stature. Their contest was unnervingly tight, yet a satisfying examination of Leeds' credentials. In Sofia, O'Leary's team had surrendered the advantage given by Kewell's opening goal, scored from a preposterously acute angle, and returned to Elland Road 2-1 down. Thus they remained until the 84th minute of the home leg when McPhail whipped in a corner that was met by Radebe's crashing header. One strike and Spartak were out.

But by then, some onlookers had misgivings about Leeds' lack of cover in key positions. While man for man their first team was the equal of any, Leeds were to rue the loss of David Batty with a calf injury; his appearance against Bradford City on 20 November was his last of the campaign. Eirik Bakke, rather than Hopkin, emerged to fill the breach: another young man destined for a swifter football education than had originally been planned. The role of enforcer could not be learned overnight but Bakke gave it his best shot. He was also a sweet passer, had an eye for goal and was effective in the air. A mid-term investment of £3.75 million in Jason Wilcox from Blackburn Rovers came not a moment too soon, giving Leeds another forceful presence down the left and Kewell the option to roam.

Young, naïve and stretched the talent may have been but O'Leary's men were fit, fast and adept at snatching priceless points with late goals. On successive Sundays, they plundered last-gasp 1-0 victories over Southampton and Derby. They went into Christmas looking the only plausible challengers to Manchester United, only to emerge hungover by defeats at Arsenal (2-0), whose midfield dynamos Vieira and Petit were returning to fitness, then at home to Aston Villa on 3 January (2-1).

First Division opposition in the FA Cup provided a welcome break. On 9 January Leeds travelled to Manchester City, twice went a goal down, then grabbed the game by the collar and won 5-2, polishing off

50 Greatest Players

LUCAS RADEBE Central defender

Joined Leeds: August 1994   **From:** Kaizer Chiefs

Debut: v Mansfield Town, September 1994 (Coca Cola Cup)

Appearances: 219   **Goals:** 3

Honours won with Leeds: 39 South Africa caps

Lucas Radebe was a gangling centre half when signed from South Africa along with striker Phil Masinga in August 1994. Howard Wilkinson had paid Kaizer Chiefs £250,000 for Radebe which, in view of his evolution into a world class defender, must rank alongside the purchase of Gordon Strachan as Wilkinson's greatest transfer coup.

Radebe's home debut could hardly have been less auspicious – as substitute in one Leeds United's most embarrassing displays of the 90s, a home Coca-Cola Cup defeat by Mansfield Town in September 1994. A cruciate knee ligament injury arrested his progress but in time Radebe got to grips with the English game. He developed good positional sense and strength in the air. He has an excellent temperament, times tackles beautifully and his distribution is sound. When the occasion demands, he is a tenacious man-marker. His career, as captain of Leeds and South Africa, blossomed under David O'Leary only to be thwarted for another two seasons by injury.

City in swashbuckling style. This, was, however, to be the last carefree moment of Leeds United's season.

Within days, news broke that Jonathan Woodgate and Lee Bowyer, pivotal players in excellent form, had been arrested and questioned by police in connection with an alleged assault on an Asian student outside a Leeds nightclub. Following extensive enquiries into the attack, both were charged – as also were Michael Duberry, reserve striker Tony Hackworth and two of Woodgate's friends. As legal proceedings dragged on for almost two years, a pall of notoriety and uncertainty once more hung over a club that had striven to improve its public image.

In February the pressures intensified. Preoccupied by Europe and the Premiership, a fourth round FA Cup defeat at Aston Villa had mattered little. More alarming was that beneath Leeds, Chelsea, Liverpool and Arsenal were starting to stir. At Anfield on 5 February, Leeds were outgunned and outrun by a Liverpool team in imperious form. Nerves were frayed and self-control in short supply during the home match with Spurs a week later. Lee Bowyer's wild challenge on Stephen Clemence precipitated a mass brawl that led to both clubs being fined £150,000 by the FA.

Leeds were unusually subdued when Manchester United arrived for a Sunday lunchtime showdown on 20 February; and, without Radebe and Batty, lacking authoritative old hands. Matthew Jones, another

The trial of Jonathan Woodgate and Lee Bowyer was front-page news for the best part of two years.

bright face of the future, was drafted in for only his second start of the season though he had played impressively against the Champions at Elland Road the previous season. It was, for the most part, a cagey game. But Andy Cole made and then took his opportunity brilliantly whereas the width of the crossbar had kept out Bakke's header. Then, in the 82nd minute, Bowyer, with the goal at his mercy after Smith's shot rebounded off a post, blazed over the bar from five yards out.

The Reds' procession to another Premiership title was not yet cut and dried. Leeds, in the top two since September, were to battle on for another month while still campaigning in Europe. But the fourth round

Great Matches

UEFA CUP FOURTH ROUND   **Elland Road, 9 March 2000**
Leeds United 1   AS Roma 0   **Attendance 39,149**
Kewell

There could have been no greater contrast to Leeds' gung-ho display of folly against PSV Eindhoven four seasons earlier than this model performance of discipline and control. After a 0-0 draw in Rome, the tie was precariously balanced: the desire of each to win tempered by fear of making a crucial mistake.

Kewell, identified by the Italians as Leeds' principal threat, was singled out for special treatment. It took time for him to recover from having his leg raked by Aldair; but he did and proved uncontainable, creating space, making unnerving runs and probing passes.

Leeds built patiently. On the hour, Kewell stroked the ball into Bowyer's path but he pulled a decent chance wide. Six minutes later, Bowyer found Kewell to devastating effect: an adroit sidestep and a searing shot from 25 yards by the young prodigy produced a magisterial goal fit to settle a heavyweight contest.

Roma retaliated feverishly but without drawing blood, thwarted by defending that was, by turns, brave and methodical. In injury time, Vincent Candela, epitomizing Roma's deep frustration, was sent off for butting Huckerby. Leeds had been the supreme copyists; the style of their victory classically Italian.

Leeds United: Martyn, Kelly, Harte, Haaland, Radebe, Bakke (Jones), Bowyer, McPhail, (Huckerby), Wilcox, Bridges (Smith), Kewell.

AS Roma: Antonioli, Zago, Aldair, Mangone, Rinaldi, Nakata, Di Francesco, Tomasi, Candela, Totti, Delvecchio.

Referee: J.M Garcia-Aranda (Spain).

UEFA Cup battle with AS Roma, conquerors of O'Leary's team the previous season, was a vivid illustration of how much they had grown up.

In the quarter-final, the tie with Slavia Prague was effectively settled by Leeds' 3-0 win at Elland Road. More draining was the ritual of returning from foreign parts in the small hours of Friday morning to try to catch up Manchester United on Sunday afternoon. Until mid-March,

Leeds stuck at the task well. But there was a palpable weariness about them after trooping back from Prague, 2-1 losers in the second leg. With little let-up in Manchester United's winning streak, a Sunday trip to Leicester City, hustlers and spoilers extraordinary, was the last thing O'Leary's young team wanted.

They toiled, lost 2-1 and in defeat were forced to concede the Championship. Six days later, on April Fools day, leg-weary, low on morale and short of ideas, Leeds were a feeble echo of their vibrant selves in losing 1-0 at home to Chelsea. Fans were forced to confront the previously unimaginable: that, after having given so much, Leeds might run out of steam and fail to qualify for the Champions League.

It bode ill for the UEFA Cup semi-final against Galatasaray. But even had they been in the best form, it is hard to imagine how the team might have recovered its equilibrium and set about its task after Leeds fans Kevin Speight and Chris Loftus were stabbed to death in downtown Istanbul the day before the match. Amid the sulphurous atmosphere of the Ali Sami Yen stadium, where official expressions of condolence were perfunctory and the locals ritualistically hostile, Leeds looked vulnerable and distracted. Poor marking allowed Sukur to score in 12 minutes; and in keeping with Leeds' ill-fortune, Galatasaray's second goal, bundled over the line by de Olivera, arrived just on half-time.

Yet Leeds did do more than go through the motions. In the second half they made, and spurned, several chances. But above all, everyone connected with Leeds simply wanted to escape. Peter Ridsdale had witnessed the trauma at close quarters, rushing to hospital to support injured survivors of the brawl, among them Chris Loftus' brother. It was clear to Ridsdale that if Turkish fans came to Elland Road for the replay, the outcome for public order in Leeds could be catastrophic. Leeds lobbied UEFA successfully for a ban, despite Turkish demands that the second leg be held at a neutral venue.

Around Elland Road the dead were mourned with flowers, scarves and cards. A sense of bereavement enveloped Leeds United for the next two weeks. The players, emotionally, were still off balance; and while they made a fight of the Sunday game with Aston Villa, a week later, Leeds were thrashed 4-0 by Arsenal at Elland Road. 'Meltdown' screamed the tabloids. As the return clash with Galatasaray loomed, the world's media gathered alongside the curious, the vengeful and legions of true fans still struggling to reconcile their emotions.

Inside Elland Road the atmosphere was ugly and fractured. Galatasaray players, bearing their own floral tributes and donning black armbands, seemed able to shrug off the hostility. Hagi's sixth-minute penalty killed the contest. The match was a 2-2 draw; the Leeds goals were from Bakke; and Kewell and Emre were sent off, each the victim of pitiful refereeing. But for Leeds, the overriding priority was simply to get matters over and done with.

Although still stalked by frailties, Leeds rediscovered better form in their next League match, at Newcastle. They let slip a 2-0 lead, drawing 2-2; but a sense that the worst was over was confirmed a

50 Greatest Players

NIGEL MARTYN Goalkeeper

Joined Leeds: July 1996   **From:** Crystal Palace

Debut: v Derby County, 17 August 1996

Appearances: 273

Honours won with Leeds: 19 England caps

Rarely was £2.25 million better spent. Although plying his trade in the First Division, everyone in the game knew how good a goalkeeper Nigel Martyn was. And while, during eight years at Leeds, Howard Wilkinson's transfer dealings veered from the brilliant to the bizarre, buying Martyn belongs emphatically in the former category.

From the outset he proved a commanding presence, imposing authority on a defence badly in need of bolstering. Martyn was pivotal to George Graham's 'build from the back' philosophy. He had an outstanding first season and was, some believe, all that stood between Leeds and relegation from the Premiership in 1996-97.

As a shot stopper he usually excels; his anticipation is spot on and he rarely flaps at crosses. But it has been his misfortune to wobble at the highest level, and while in the late 1990s Martyn looked to be England's number one, the odd aberration weighed against him in the battle with David Seaman for pole position during the 2002 World Cup.

week later in the 3-0 win at ailing Sheffield Wednesday, where David Hopkin scored in the first minute. Four days later, a 3-1 home victory over relegation victims Watford confirmed that the trauma was over; the patient convalescing nicely. Resignation gave way to renewed hope. Third place, and Champions League qualification beckoned once more, as Liverpool, who had thrashed Leeds with such aplomb two months earlier, were having their own end-of-season crisis.

With draws against Everton and West Ham, Leeds staggered, rather than marched, into third place. There had been a meltdown but at Anfield, not Elland Road. In a fateful, tumultuous campaign, the club, chairman, manager, players and fans had come together in adversity. While 1999-2000 brought Leeds much of what had been hoped for – the prospect of dining at Europe's top table; full houses at Elland Road; the continued flowering of fine young players – rarely had a season given so many shocks to the system.

50 Greatest Players

LEE BOWYER Midfielder

Joined Leeds: July 1996   **From:** Charlton Athletic
Debut: v Derby County, 17 August 1996
Appearances: 244   **Goals:** 52
Honours won with Leeds: None

Lee Bowyer is in the tradition of great Leeds midfielders: combative, compact and with a wide range of skills.

At £2.6 million, Bowyer became Britain's most expensive teenager when, aged 19, he signed for Leeds from Charlton. He was bought by Howard Wilkinson but had hardly got into his stride before Wilkinson was sacked. Wilkinson's successor George Graham seemed to have an ambivalent attitude towards the young star. But he blossomed under David O'Leary; and his ability to sustain form during his trial in January 2001, facing serious charges relating to the assault of a student, was miraculous.

Bowyer can hustle, tackle, link play, pass, and score. He has phenomenal stamina, giving the impression he could motor forever up and down the field. There have been many calls for him to receive a full England cap; though some feel he must rein in his aggression before being granted the honours his talents merit.

Chapter Eleven: 2000-02
Trials and Tribulations

If ever a team needed recuperation, it was that of David O'Leary. Yet unwelcome baggage from the previous campaign would burden Leeds into the new season and beyond. Emotions were pulled in all directions: 2000-01 was, even by Leeds United standards, a year of extremes.

The immediate goal, qualifying for the group stages of the European Champions League, had to be realized amid an injury list that cast its shadow for months. Batty was plagued by Achilles tendon trouble and there were doubts he would ever play again. There would be no sign of Kewell, another Achilles tendon victim, until early December; Steven McPhail, the third Achilles victim, would make just a handful of appearances; Michael Bridges would be fated to miss almost two seasons through an ankle injury; an Achilles injury snuffed out Michael Duberry's season.

New blood, powerful pivotal figures, were needed: and O'Leary's principal summer signings, centre forward Mark Viduka, signed for £6 million from Celtic, and ball-winning midfielder Olivier Dacourt for £7.2 million from Lens, looked robust, convincing additions to the squad. Mercifully, they were not to join the ranks of the long-term wounded. The other key close season recruit, Dominic Matteo, also arrived complete with injury, but once he made his debut, became a vital component of a sorely tried defence. O'Leary also augmented the coaching staff, recruiting Brian Kidd, former manager of Blackburn Rovers and assistant at Manchester United, as director of youth development.

The Return of Alan Smith

The season began early, and tempestuously. TSV 1860 Munich stood between Leeds and the pot of gold that was the Champions League. Leeds won the first leg 2-1 but at the cost of seeing Dacourt and Bakke

50 Greatest Players

MARK VIDUKA Centre forward

Joined Leeds: Summer 2000   **From:** Celtic

Debut: v TSV 1860 München, 9 August 2000

Appearances: 95   **Goals:** 38

Honours won with Leeds: 2 Australia caps

On his day, Mark Viduka ranks among the best centre forwards Leeds United have ever had. Powerfully built, with immense body strength, he is a great focal point, invaluable at holding up the ball and bringing others into play. Yet his touch is surprisingly delicate; his close control often – though not invariably – excellent.

After a slow start disrupted by the demands of playing for Australia in the Olympics, Viduka got his eye in to spectacular effect. His solo four-goal mission against Liverpool in November 2000 was a fine display of the striker's art; but he thrived also on the big European stage. He has combined particularly well with Alan Smith.

Sometimes, perhaps when not fully fit, Viduka looks sluggish and heavy legged: infuriatingly so to the fans who know only too well his true capabilities. But when in form and in the mood, few are more difficult customers for Premiership defenders than Mark Viduka.

sent off. The bright spot was Alan Smith's return to ebullient form after a protracted ankle injury; the blot, a goal conceded in injury time that changed Leeds' position from comfort to one of insecurity.

Smith, for much of 1999-2000 a forgotten man, soon reminded the world of his abundant qualities, good and bad. He helped send Everton packing from Elland Road in the first Premiership game of the season with two smart headed goals; and shone four days later in the away leg of the qualifier against 1860 Munich, showing composure and strength to score the only goal of the match, one destined to shape the rest of Leeds United's season.

Elation at reaching the group stages of the Champions League was tempered by the enormity of the task that lay ahead, as seeding plunged Leeds into a group with Barcelona, the Turkish club Besiktas, and AC Milan. Leeds' visit to Barcelona, the biggest beast in the jungle, came in mid-September with the team's pool of fit players threadbare: no Bakke; no Woodgate; and Viduka, the spearhead of their attack, was playing for Australia in the Olympics. O'Leary's frail and incomplete side was slaughtered at the Nou Camp by the likes of Rivaldo, Patrick Kluivert and Marc Overmars; a 4-0 defeat and injury to Lucas Radebe souvenirs of a torrid evening.

Then, a season that had started to disintegrate prematurely following Leeds 2-1 home defeat by Ipswich four days later, took its first unexpected twist. Their spirits somehow revived, Leeds snapped into life against AC Milan the following week. They chivvied and pressed, keeping the ball much better; the crowd content to settle for an honourable point when Lee Bowyer pushed forward with two minutes remaining, shot from distance, and the Brazilian goalkeeper Dida dropped the shot and saw it dribble into the goal. It was a victory sent from heaven.

Besiktas caused further upheaval in the group by beating Barcelona; but when they came to Elland Road, proved accommodating visitors. Leeds tore into them from the start; ran out 6-0 winners; and suddenly the group was turned on its head.

O'Leary's side wobbled through autumn, never so bereft of first choice talent as for the game against Manchester United at Old Trafford in October, where absentees included Martyn, Mills, Radebe, Harte, Bakke, Dacourt, Batty, Kewell and Bridges. Defeat – 3-0 – had seemed inevitable; as did further humiliation at the hands of Liverpool at Elland Road two weeks later when Leeds found themselves 2-0 down in rapid time. But Viduka suddenly found form and fitness following his return from the Olympics in Australia, and astounded all with his wizardry: a delicate chip; a powerful header; a mazy run and drive; a clever lob bringing four goals, one more than the eleven from Anfield could muster.

It was an intoxicating result to take to Milan, where just a point was needed to make the second phase of the Champions League, and with it £10 million of assured income. A near-post header by Matteo from a Lee Bowyer corner on half time, Matteo's first, and probably his most priceless goal for his new club, gave Leeds a breathing space.

Milan equalised but everyone was happy: Barcelona, two months earlier the torturers of O'Leary's patched up team, had fallen spectacularly and were out of the competition.

One Strip, Two Teams

Even allowing for the ravages of injuries, two teams appeared to be inhabiting the Leeds strip: European conquerors and domestic fumblers; a team that could beat AC Milan but not Bradford City or West Ham; nor Tranmere Rovers, who in October, had knocked Leeds out of the Worthington Cup 3-2. O'Leary grew sick of being confronted by the paradox. 'It became tiresome to be asked every week whether we could transfer our European form into the Premiership... I couldn't freshen the team up – I had no options,' he said.

Amid the dismay when, on 18 November, Leeds lost at home to West Ham for the first time in more than 20 years, the excellence of Rio Ferdinand, whom Leeds had long courted, was appreciated more than usual. A week later, Leeds broke all transfer records and paid the Hammers £18 million for the elegant young central defender.

But if there were no doubting the statement of intent, performances on the pitch continued to baffle. Leeds' reward for surviving their first, punishing, Champions League group, was to be thrust into another lion's den alongside Real Madrid, Lazio and Anderlecht. It seemed like a conspiracy. Real Madrid, playing Leeds at their injury-hit weakest, were too strong at Elland Road, winning 2-0, but among the stand-ins goalkeeper Paul Robinson was growing in stature, his quality epitomized by a brilliant fingertip save from Raul.

Once more elimination beckoned; once more Leeds rallied. The team that ventured to play Lazio in Rome on 5 December was in far better shape: the muscularity of Dacourt and Bakke restored to midfield; Woodgate fitter; poise and confidence restored throughout. Ten minutes from time, Viduka and Smith combined exquisitely to steal the game: the Australian's clever backheel driven unerringly low by his young partner into the Lazio net. It was a choice moment; one that sustained optimism through the winter.

Finally the sick bay began to empty. For the home match with Sunderland on 16 December, the season half over, O'Leary had more or less his top team: Kewell made his first start; and at 2-0 up, the game won, David Batty, whose Achilles problem had proved excruciatingly complicated, returned to a hero's welcome. The squad had been further strengthened by the arrival of Irish striker Robbie Keane, a misfit under the new regime at Inter Milan, for a down payment of £1 million and a further £11 million to follow at the season's end. The spending spree was driven by optimism, funded on future expectations of Leeds' continued participation in the Champions League.

But results refused to flow Leeds' way. Successive defeats by Aston Villa and Newcastle around Christmas, and a 1-1 draw with Middlesbrough on New Year's Day, much more obdurate opponents under Terry Venables, dragged Leeds down to thirteenth place. Their match at Manchester City on 13 January was spoken of as a relegation battle. But City were in far worse disarray, and Leeds won a largely wretched game 4-0 – the margin flattered – aided by two late goals from Keane.

But the 3-1 home defeat by Newcastle that followed suggested Leeds' had yet to solve their chronic inability to exploit territorial superiority. O'Leary plunged into a depression; yet from this nadir, Leeds' miserably inconsistent form was to improve dramatically, the sense of disillusionment banished once everyone got over Liverpool's 2-0 FA Cup fourth round victory at Elland Road on 27 January.

More Champions League football rekindled appetites. The management of Anderlecht, Leeds' next opponents, sharpened the edge of O'Leary's men by dismissing them as 'little more than a pub team'. The first 45 minutes at Elland Road was forgettable but the second epitomised Leeds' indestructible character. Having fallen a goal behind, they equalized though a ballistic free kick from Ian Harte; and snatched the game at the death, Bowyer latching on to a pass from Smith and smashing an angled drive past goalkeeper Milojevic.

Great European Run

Bowyer's propensity for concocting late drama was becoming legendary; the world marvelling at his fitness and mental strength. He had rushed 50 miles from Hull Crown Court, where he was standing trial on charges of affray and grievous bodily harm relating to the assault of the Asian student Sarfraz Najeib, seemingly immune from the weight of the proceedings that were having so traumatic effect on his co-defendant Woodgate. Defeat, meanwhile, failed to puncture the

Great Matches

CHAMPIONS LEAGUE QUARTER-FINAL	Elland Road, 4 April 2001
Leeds United 3 Deportivo La Coruña 0	Attendance 35,508

Harte
Smith
Ferdinand

'Three-nil to the weakest team.' With uncontainable glee, the chorus of Leeds' fans threw back the jibe in the face of the Deportivo management: for the masters were not, as had been feared, the sophisticated technicians from Spain but the advanced apprentices from Yorkshire.

It was a brilliant, unrelenting show by O'Leary's men, redolent of their triumph against Anderlecht. From the earliest minutes – Smith's clever angled pass almost putting in Bowyer; Kewell's shimmering run and flashing shot across goal, Leeds thrust in from all sides. In the 27th minute came their first reward: a free kick on the lip of 'D' curled high into the net with masterful precision by Harte.

Leeds kept coming. They deserved more than 1-0 at half time; and Deportivo had overturned many a deficit. But not this time. Another fluid move; Dacourt to Harte down the left, who overlapped and sent over a perfect cross for Alan Smith to score with a downward header. And still they did not let-up. Harte's corner from the left in the 66th minute was flapped at by Deportivo goalkeeper Molina and found the head of Ferdinand.

Deportivo woke up, but too late. As they grasped the initiative near the end, Martyn was forced to make fine saves to protect Leeds' monumental advantage and keep the 'weakest team' flying high.

Leeds United: Martyn, Mills, Ferdinand, Matteo, Harte, Bowyer, Batty, Dacourt, Kewell (Wilcox 84), Viduka, Smith.

Deportivo la Coruña: Molina, Manuel Pablo, Cesar Sampaio, Naybet, Romero, Scaloni (Tristan, 72), Emerson, Duscher (Valeron 54), Fran (Pandiani 72), Djalminha, Makaay.

Referee: G Veissiere (France).

hubris of Anderlecht coach Aime Anthuenis, who predicted a walkover for his team in the home match. So foolish a remark helped catalyse one of Leeds' finest hours in Europe: they ripped the Belgian side apart, 3-0 up at half time; 4-1 winners at the final whistle.

In this grand manner, Leeds qualified for the quarter-finals; their final group matches against Real Madrid in Spain (lost 3-2) and at home to Lazio (drawn 3-3) were merely exercises in maintaining pride and providing entertainment. On

Anderlecht coach Aime Anthuenis whose comments spurred United to a 4-1 win.

the home front, the game of catch-up became paramount, at least until Leeds' clash with Deportivo La Coruña on 4 April. After victory over Anderlecht, Leeds embarked on their best run of form through late February and March: confident 2-1 winners at Tottenham; robbed only by a linesman's flag of a win over Manchester United at Elland Road; vigorous away victories at Charlton (2-1), and Sunderland (2-0).

From the fringes of a relegation battle, Leeds had shot up to third place. It was just the form to take into their Champions League quarter-final with Deportivo, unfashionable, yet one of the most formidable teams in Europe. Deportivo had though, like Anderlecht, grossly underestimated the men from Elland Road.

The momentum carried on with a home victory over Southampton three days later. But as the Leeds team went about its work that Saturday afternoon, it knew nothing of the bombshell being concocted by the Sunday Mirror: that, with the jury out considering verdicts on the players allegedly involved in the assault on Sarfraz Najeib, the paper would run an interview with a family member alleging the attack had a racial element. This damning allegation, directly at odds with the trial judge's summing up to jurors, brought proceedings to a screeching halt. It resulted in a contempt charge against the Mirror, and the need for a retrial. So irresponsible a piece of journalism was the last thing Leeds had needed. The case against Hackworth had been dropped through lack of evidence; and Duberry and Woodgate had been cleared by the jury of conspiracy to pervert the course of justice. But other serious charges would hang over Bowyer and Woodgate until the year's end.

Yet Good Friday, with the media and legal storm barely subsided, brought a 2-1 victory for Leeds over Liverpool at Anfield, the least Leeds deserved for their dominance. Once more, a dogfight beckoned with Houllier's team for third place and Champions League qualification. Leeds though had unfinished business in Spain with Deportivo, whose glimpse of form in the final minutes at Elland Road was a foretaste of what awaited them. On home territory, urged on by Djalminha's 9th minute penalty following a foul by Kewell, Deportivo besieged the Leeds goal, yet were thwarted by Martyn, desperate defending and good luck, drawing blood again only in the 73rd minute when Diego Tristan fired home a low shot from a quickly-taken free kick. 'This was the first time I sensed apprehension among my players,' said O'Leary afterwards. 'They seemed to be handicapped by the awareness they were so near the semi-finals.'

But the mauling in La Coruña did not herald an incipient collapse. Atonement for the first wayward half of the season continued with victories at West Ham – Rio Ferdinand appearing embarrassed at scoring against his old club – and at home to Chelsea, snatched late by goals from Keane and Viduka. In the Champions League, Valencia remained the last obstacle between Leeds, the final, and a triumph that, after defeat by Barcelona almost nine months earlier, looked unimaginable.

Valencia came to Elland Road well organized and in no mood to collapse. The match was a taut, tactical affair, never loosened by a goal though Mendieta, Valencia's brilliant midfielder, hit the bar in the first half, as did Bowyer in the second. Ferdinand rescued Leeds at the death, heading out from under the bar, allowing Leeds to travel to Spain intact. Between times, though, was the unwelcome prospect of a game with Arsenal. Batty was suspended; and some players were unusually tentative. Leeds' 2-1 defeat was their first in the Premiership since losing to Newcastle in January.

Then, out of the blue, Leeds were mugged by UEFA's snap decision to suspend Bowyer for the Champions League semi-final second leg – punishment for violent conduct after he appeared to have stamped on Valencia's Sanchez. Bowyer, whose marauding box-to-box play was so vital to the team, was a grave loss. The haunting figure of Sanchez struck all too early in Spain, deflecting Valencia's first goal with his arm in the 16th minute. One-nil down at half time, the game could be salvaged; but Leeds, perhaps finally overwhelmed by their combined misfortunes and having too few fresh legs, crumbled afterwards, first

backing off Sanchez, allowing him to fire a low shot past Martyn; and then succumbing to a powerful left-foot drive from Mendieta. Near the end, Alan Smith vented his frustration with a two-footed challenge on Vincente, and got himself sent off. So petulant a finale ill-fitted Leeds' magnificent European campaign.

In the end, poor Premiership form before January cost them dear. Liverpool won the scrap for third place, despite Leeds' gluttonous 6-1 victory at Valley Parade over doomed neighbours Bradford City, and a 3-1 home win over Leicester on the last day

Gaizka Mendieta spurred Valencia on to victory over Leeds in the Champions League semi-final.

of the season. The club had gone for broke; but the team pulled up just too short. If the sums of money swirling around belonged to 21st-century football showbiz, emotionally there were echoes of the Revie era.

Great Expectations

Still expectations were high for 2001-2002. The football world saw a squad of fine young players, bonded through competing against the best. In theory, the likes of Kewell, Smith, and Ferdinand could only improve. Some felt the absence of a second successive Champions League campaign might free Leeds up to win the Premiership. Several commentators saw them as favourites.

For the first half of the season no one team seemed capable of grabbing the title race by the collar. A 2-0 win for Leeds at Charlton on 16 September put them top; and even if there were a sense of O'Leary's team misfiring intermittently, they went unbeaten in the Premiership until 18 November when they lost 2-0 at Sunderland. But Leeds were not to lose again before their madly profligate 4-3 home defeat by Newcastle United on 22 December in which they squandered a 3-1 lead. Yet after New Year's Day, they sat atop the Premiership once more, the 3-0 defeat of West Ham at Elland Road their silkiest home performance of the season.

There lay no hint, in victory over West Ham, of the turbulence that had preceded it; nor of that to come. The wilder young men of Leeds had got stuck in as quickly as the second match back in August, Mills and Bowyer sent off against Arsenal at Highbury. But although it was a fractious night, Leeds produced their bravest display of the campaign, clinging on to win 2-1. Yet such concentration was palpably absent in early stages of the UEFA Cup: a deplorable 1-0 defeat in Madeira by Maritimo in the first round first leg; the scramble to survive having once led 4-1 at Elland Road against Troyes in the second leg but conceding a late goal against ten men, and then losing 3-2 in France. A 4-3 aggregate victory over Grasshoppers of Zurich also lacked the conviction of Leeds' European Champions

League campaign: it was as if, even subconsciously, playing in Europe's second string competition had induced a sense of anti-climax.

Meanwhile the club continued to astonish with its enormous – reckless, some felt – expenditure on new players, one that anticipated nothing less than re-entry to the Champions League. Further aggression was recruited to midfield in October with the purchase for £7 million of 22-year-old Seth Johnson from Derby, an investment for the future rather than immediate use. He was followed in November by Liverpool striker Robbie Fowler, priced at £11 million, a Scouser at heart but at 26, with England ambitions still intense, no longer content to languish on the bench. He came with the right words to hand: 'Leeds are as good as anyone in Europe right now... it's a change I need.'

The purchases of Seth Johnson (top) and Robbie Fowler in 2001 continued Leeds' huge investment in new players.

Leeds United on Trial

The two transfers brought Leeds' spending to £96 million since O'Leary's arrival, whereas outgoing players, Jimmy Floyd Hasselbaink (to Chelsea), David Wetherall and David Hopkin (Bradford City), Danny Granville, Alfe-Inge Haaland and Darren Huckerby (all to Manchester City), and Matthew Jones (to Leicester) had netted around £29 million. Under a 25-year bond scheme, or 'securitization', launched in September 2001, Leeds had borrowed

£60 million from institutional investors secured through future receipts and repayable over 25 years. To the sceptics and the nervous, Ridsdale replied: 'This is a plc committing on behalf of our shareholders to invest in quality people... it makes sense to fund their purchase.' Leeds' operating profit of £10.1 million for 2001 – turnover up 65 per cent to £86.3 million – had become a £12.7 million loss thanks to the pursuit of costly players.

In December, legal proceedings against Lee Bowyer and Jonathan Woodgate following the assault on Sarfraz Najeib, which had sprawled across three seasons, reached their conclusion: Bowyer acquitted of affray and causing grievous bodily harm; Woodgate guilty only of affray and ordered to perform 100 hours community

service. But acrimony rumbled on: O'Leary himself creating aftershocks with the tactless publication of his book *Leeds United on Trial*; Bowyer in dispute and placed on the transfer list by refusing to accept a fine of four weeks wages or perform extra community duty as punishment for being drunk in Leeds city centre when Sarfraz Najeib was assaulted.

And then, on 6 January 2002, came another explosive day; though its incendiary nature was not of Leeds' making. The inflammable atmosphere surrounding their third round FA Cup draw with Cardiff City had been fuelled by the Welsh club's chairman Sam Hammam, who brought to the pitch his talents as cheerleader of the good, the bad and the ugly. That Leeds crashed to defeat, 2-1, after Viduka put them ahead in 12 minutes, was eclipsed by a post-match pitch invasion and inquests into the conduct of Hammam, his stewards and moronic elements of the Cardiff crowd. On a bad Sunday outing for the potential Champions, Alan Smith had, yet again, been sent off. Old demons had been stirred up: indiscipline and an incorrigible weakness against lesser opposition in Cup competitions.

A Turn for the Worse

Defeat at Cardiff proved fatally difficult to shrug off. Rot set in: Leeds did not win another football match for two months; the nature of their UEFA Cup defeat by PSV Eindhoven on 21 February, falling to a last-minute goal in the home leg at Elland Road, symbolic of having tumbled the wrong side of fortune. As they sunk to sixth place, rivals Arsenal, Liverpool, Manchester United and Newcastle burst clear at the top. Qualification for the Champions League looked a forlorn hope; and nor could a return to the UEFA Cup be taken for granted. Sights were lowered; gratitude for small mercies a commodity more commonly seen.

What seemed most telling was the emphatic margin by which Leeds were beaten by old foes; few defeats more wounding than the 4-0 trouncing by Liverpool at Elland Road on 3 February. At the end of this sterile run, a goalless draw with Everton, Leeds fans sought a scapegoat and picked on Brian Kidd, promoted senior coach almost a year earlier, whose principal crime, in the eyes of chauvinists, was to come from Manchester.

But then the fixture list relented, and served Leeds a succession of strugglers. A 2-0 victory against Ipswich halted the slide; the first of five wins in

Harry Kewell failed to produce his best form during 2001-02; Leeds fans hope that this will change in 2002-03.

seven matches, the last of which, against Aston Villa, and set against other results, assured Leeds of a place in the 2002-03 UEFA Cup. It remained arithmetically possible to grasp a qualifying place in the Champions League, but the pallid, sterile nature of Leeds' penultimate home match, a 1-0 defeat by Fulham, suggested some players felt their season's work was done.

There was the small satisfaction, following victories at Derby and at home to Middlesbrough, of beating Chelsea to fifth place. Although the club had, at times, shown signs of tearing itself apart, Ferdinand, as player and captain, had been more or less impeccable; and while Smith got enmeshed in too many brawls, he had also exhibited technical excellence, a willingness to toil anywhere and the continued ability to score crucial goals. The solidity of Matteo and Batty was reassuring; the fitful form of Kewell and Keane less so.

Financial Reality

But there was also the abrupt awakening to financial reality. Failure to reach the Champions League, and the implications for Leeds United's acutely sensitive financial position, meant that the big buyers suddenly needed to sell. Bowyer, so often a tower of strength during his trial – though less potent after his acquittal – had a wage demand of almost £40,000 a week rejected, and grew restless. He seemed, to the dismay of many fans, a prime candidate to be cashed in.

A crisis of confidence within the club's support was the last thing needed. The Leeds board said that 'crown jewels' – the likes of Ferdinand, Viduka and Kewell – would not be for sale. But unforeseeable events, forever waiting to derail Leeds United's plans, intervened once more. Ferdinand, arguably England's finest player in the 2002 World Cup, had developed a taste for the world stage and become a magnet for some of Europe's most acquisitive big clubs. Suddenly the genial young central defender from Peckham seemed bigger than Leeds United. Mixed messages emanated from Elland Road about whether he would stay or go.

If Ferdinand's departure to Manchester United was felt inevitable, David O'Leary, summarily sacked by his chairman, became the most unexpected casualty of the tremors that shook Elland Road daily. O'Leary had, in four years, taken Leeds to 4th, 3rd, 4th and 5th place and plotted their enthralling assault on the Champions League. But in a plc driven by the need to churn profits, not keeping them there consistently, rather than the failure to win domestic trophies, did for him.

Leeds tried once more to lure their old favourite, Martin O'Neill. But O'Neill was not to be prised away from Celtic. As the press peddled various alternatives, Peter Ridsdale took a jet to Spain to persuade Terry Venables that his real mission in life was to effect a revival at Elland Road rather than that of television pundit.

The announcement that Terry Venables was to take over at Elland Road came as a surprise to many – but his experience may turn out to be just what is needed.

There had been very little money – smart or otherwise – put on Venables. In his favour, he had charisma, talent; the experience gained from coaching, among others, England, Barcelona and Spurs. Gary Lineker, who played under him at Barcelona, reckoned him the best boss he had had: perpetually inventive, able to extract the best from players. Any unease related to Venables' copious baggage: too many fingers in a surfeit of pies; a tendency not to stay anywhere too long. The hope of Leeds fans was that, at 59, Venables might decide the time had come to drop anchor, at least for as long as his gifts as coach and motivator might endure.

Chapter Twelve: In the 21st Century
Behind the Scenes at Leeds United

Elland Road in the mid 1950s: a bleak ground of few comforts; the barrel-roofed west stand; the primitive scratching shed; swathes of terracing open to wind and rain. Players living in modest club houses on the Heaths Estate opposite, over the shop. A good night out a trip to the cinema and a packet of wine gums. John Charles, one of the great players in the world, paid, like his colleagues, a few pounds a week, his earning power throttled by the egalitarian maximum wage. A club run on a shoestring, a financial crisis always round the corner. 'Lend us a fiver.' A history of getting out the begging bowl.

By the 1980s, the club had boomed and bust. While in the black during the Revie era, relegation to the Second Division in 1982 was a financial catastrophe. The maximum wage had been swept away in 1961 and players were free to negotiate their own pay. Most were comfortably off; some wealthy. Poor crowds; yet an obligation to pay high salaries: it couldn't add up. In 1985, the club was forced to sell Elland Road to the city council for £2.5 million.

Football was, by then, much more commercially aware, club shops were stacked with replica kit and memorabilia, and the club earning some revenue from terrestrial television. But most clubs were run in time-honoured fashion, their fate in the hands of a godfather chairman or a few plutocratic directors. Up until 1996, Leeds United had just three major shareholders. But for Leeds, and every big club, Sky television money effected a revolution. In 1992, the top clubs ring-fenced themselves into the FA Premier League to secure the lion's share. Staying in the elite, though, was expensive; the economies of scale immense.

Leeds United's takeover in 1996 by Caspian, the media group, and its evolution into a plc and Leeds Sporting, brought modern business practices to Elland Road. Leslie Silver, the last of the self-made

Elland Road may see the last of Leeds United in 2004 if the team relocates to Skelton.

millionaire chairmen, realized when he resigned in 1997 that football had become too big a business to be run in the old-fashioned way. He joined the board in 1981 when the club was broke. 'In those days, you were talking of £200,000 making a big difference. Now you are talking of millions not making a difference,' he said in a valedictory interview. 'The chairmanship needs professionalism and high quality management.'

Ten-Year Plan

Yet Leeds began facing up to the future when Howard Wilkinson arrived in 1988. He was as much of a strategist as Revie with a broader range of management skills. One plank of Revie thinking he revived – which in the past had been turned to in adversity rather than built into the structure of the club – was the need to find and develop young players. Then, the Sky-manipulated Premiership and mass influx of foreigners dining at the trough was almost four years away.

The resultant youth policy at Leeds has, apart from the Championship win of 1992, became Wilkinson's most celebrated legacy.

Wilkinson saw it as a ten-year plan. When Paul Hart was recruited as director of the Leeds youth academy in early 1993, much still needed to be done. 'Howard said at the time that we were about 37th in the league in terms of youth development,' said Hart. 'He wanted to get to the top three. Maybe we hadn't been as competitive as we could be but we'd just won the League and felt confident, so we threw everything behind it.

'The real catalyst was winning the FA Youth Cup. People sat up and took notice. That victory allowed me to get into people's houses – we had the FA Youth Cup win on our cv. We invited parents in or went to see them and persuaded them we could develop their sons. Out of that Cup success came our latest bunch; the Kewells and the McPhails. We shopped a lot in Ireland and we had a contact in Sydney, Australia, who brought us Harry Kewell through a scholarship.'

Even in the early 1990s, the facilities were limited. 'I was screaming for more pitches and Howard wanted better,' said Hart. Moves began to create a purpose-built training ground and hostel at Thorp Arch, near Wetherby, which cost £3 million. It opened in summer 1996, and is where all Leeds United teams are coached and trained.

Finding Tomorrow's Stars

In establishing the youth set-up, Wilkinson decreed that the academy director should be responsible not to the first-team manager but to the chairman. 'That was common sense: it meant that if Howard went, it couldn't be interfered with,' said Hart. It did, however, create tension between Hart, who left Leeds in 1997, and Wilkinson's successor, George Graham.

Alan Smith is the pride of Leeds' youth academy.

50 Greatest Players

ALAN SMITH Striker

Joined Leeds: Summer 1998   **From:** Juniors

Debut: v Liverpool, 14 November 1998

Appearances: 140   **Goals:** 36

Honours won with Leeds: 3 England caps

In a hostile world, where all fine strikers need an edge, Alan Smith has an abundance, possibly an excess. He is revered for his talents and a commitment to his home city team that seems to transcend an ambition for riches and trophies. Smith wants to win but, like his fellow citizen David Batty, above all for Leeds.

Smith has all the raw material: tremendous body strength; a deft touch and fine control; and is never overawed: witness his first goal, poked home within seconds of making his debut at Liverpool. He can throw top-class defenders by the speed of his turn; and keeps a cool head when advancing on goal. Few players run harder for the general cause.

But the excess of edge; his ability to create or become sucked into conflagrations, can spoil things. Smith is needed to make waves on the pitch, rather than to kick his heels in the stands, suspended and in disgrace.

Wilkinson's plan has produced the likes of Ian Harte, Harry Kewell, Stephen McPhail, Paul Robinson, Jonathan Woodgate, Alan Smith and Matthew Jones. 'I'm not surprised by how they've developed,' says Paul Hart. 'We worked hard with them... at mental strength, standards, expectations, dealing with situations; not allowing standards to fall.' Eddie Gray, who fostered much young talent when managing Leeds in the 1980s, returned to Elland Road in 1995 to help out. 'If you're good enough, you're old enough,' Gray says. 'I took Woodgate to a tournament in Dallas when he was only 15, just coming on to the staff. He came up against a group of Brazilians that had played for the under-21 side and acquitted himself very well.'

Howard Wilkinson was voted manager of the year after 1991-92 Championship season.

Trawling for the likes of Woodgate is as sophisticated a process as it is unrelenting. Contacts; scouts; knocking on the door; that much would have been recognizable to Revie and it still happens. But new rules restrict the recruitment of boys who live more than 90 minutes drive from the club, depending on their age. Unable to bring over boys from Ireland, whence came Harte, Kelly and McPhail, until they reach 15, Leeds established formal links with Home Farm, a renowned source of young talent, and developed joint initiatives intended to benefit both clubs. A similar link was created with the Lanzie centre of excellence in Glasgow; and a partnership developed with Oldham Athletic.

The Supporter-Chairman

The success of the class of 1997 did much to rehabilitate Leeds United's image. There were compelling business and social reasons for Leeds to cast off the image of bête noire. Peter Ridsdale, Leeds-born and a lifelong fan, joined the board in the 1980s when the club was public enemy number one. 'You get emotionally attached; you pretend the negative sides don't exist,' he says, 'But it was very difficult at times because of the hooliganism and the racial element.' Ridsdale had, unlike previous self-made chairman, forged a career in large public

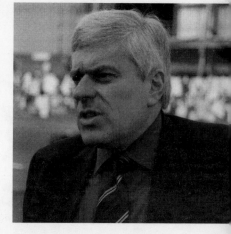

companies, and held senior positions within the Burton Group when, after a chance meeting with directors, he was invited to join the board after agreeing that Burton would sponsor the team. 'We thought as sponsors, we might be able to do the sort of things we expected the club to do within the community.'

When Caspian took over in 1996, many felt a metropolitan media company could not be trusted to put football interests first; that these could not be reconciled with the requirement to satisfy shareholders. Making Ridsdale chairman

Peter Ridsdale joined the Leeds board in the 1980s, and became chairman in 1996-97.

– an unpaid one at first – was an adroit move. 'They were keen to have someone with a Leeds background and a real feel for the club,' he said. Even when living in Surrey, he trekked north for every home match, introducing his son to Leeds as a four-week-old babe in arms.

In June 1999, Ridsdale became more hands-on, appointed chairman of Leeds Sporting plc, now Leeds United plc. Already the club had been working alongside the city council towards greater community involvement, establishing links with inner city schools; offering evening facilities for schoolchildren or mature adults learning computer or literacy skills.

Loyalty breeds Loyalty

Ridsdale believes that a profitable, well-run club best serves the interests of the city and supporters. 'If you're driving every element of the business hard to generate income for the club, the manager has transfer funds to spend on the right players and you get the right facilities,' he says. Yet he feels too few clubs have cared about the fans. 'The effect a successful football club has on people's lives is enormous. But spectators aren't a single mass; they are 40,000 individuals; each has to be treated as an individual.'

Leeds United fans can be proud of the club and look forward to an exciting future.

With Ridsdale's guidance, the club has shown a deft touch in its mix of public relations, and business acumen, by cutting the cost of tickets for early rounds of the UEFA Cup. This resulted in full houses for games that historically drew sparse crowds. Season ticket prices were frozen, and when new sponsors for 2000-01 were found, this was announced before Christmas so that fans buying replica kit and other memorabilia as presents realized their wares had a limited shelf life. Ridsdale's view is that if you treat people as if you care, you get the loyalty back.

Loyalty to Leeds United has been exploited in various enterprises unrelated to football. A travel company, based opposite the ground, contributed £7 million in its first year, 1999-2000. A financial services arm sells motor insurance, mortgages and credit cards. A large hospitality suite caters for conferences and banquets. A publishing arm has been created.

In 1999, to the alarm of fans that distrust the long-term stratagems of Rupert Murdoch, BSkyB bought a 10 per cent stake in Leeds United. But Ridsdale saw it as merely as another source of growing the club's profit from new joint media ventures of which Leeds United would receive 70 per cent. Interim results for Leeds Sporting plc for the six months ending 31 December 1999 saw the operating profit leap 89 per cent to £6.4 million. Average crowds for the same period rose from 33,174 to 39,044. Season ticket sales were up 30 per cent; TV and broadcasting fees up from £4.7 million to £7 million.

Yet the potential price of failure, bringing with it the spectre of decimated revenues, is horrifying. And failure for Leeds, whose top players gobble up more than £30,000 a week in wages, constituted the inability to qualify for the Champions League in successive seasons and cash in on TV revenues. With a deficit of almost £67 million on transfer dealings from the O'Leary era, suddenly Leeds' stars, notably Rio Ferdinand, became, whatever their contractual terms, vulnerable to predators.

At the end of 1999-2000, Ridsdale described elaborate plans to redevelop Elland Road, adding 5,000 seats to the West Stand and creating a complex by the ground with an exhibition arena, a theatre and hotels. But this regenerative plan has now been superseded. In September 2001 fans were consulted about abandoning the club's roots and moving across the city to a new 50,000 capacity stadium at Skelton, near the M1. While unsavoury extremists reacted by sending Ridsdale hate mail, 87 per cent of season ticket holders – a majority at which the Leeds chairman professed astonishment – voted in favour.

50 Greatest Players

RIO FERDINAND Central defender

Joined Leeds: November 2000 **From:** West Ham United

Debut: v Leicester City, 2 December 2000

Appearances: 73   **Goals:** 3

Left Leeds: July 2002   **For:** Manchester United

Honours won with Leeds: 20 England caps

Rio Ferdinand arrived as a prodigy and left Elland Road, in some minds, as the best central defender in the world. His masterful performances for England in the World Cup 2002 would have surprised no one who watched him regularly during his last, unfulfilled season at Leeds.

What singled him out was the hunger always to learn. In that respect, his former manager David O'Leary, one of the finest defenders of his generation, was the ideal mentor. Ferdinand's occasional errors became fewer; while his innate positional sense and the perfect timing of tackles, became standard.

He was given his head to develop that precious skill, moving the ball neatly out of defence; becoming a springboard for attack, much in the mould of his predecessor at West Ham, Bobby Moore; finding the time to look up and swiftly assess the best options. It was a combination of assets that made him, much to the chagrin of Leeds' fans everywhere, available to the highest bidder.

Ridsdale justified the logic of the move in the unsentimental language of big business. 'A new stadium is easier to deliver because you can get a sponsorship deal on it; you can sell the existing ground; and there would be no disruption to income when building it,' he said. 'With the existing stadium you would have to do it piecemeal; it would take twice as long; and you wouldn't get the same level of sponsorship.'

The plan is for Skelton to be ready for 2004-05. Almost a century of memories are destined to be left behind. But so turbulent has been Leeds United's recent history, anything is possible. It remains to be seen what comes to fruition and what may unravel.

THE ESSENTIAL HISTORY OF LEEDS UNITED

CLUB STATISTICS

The Leeds United Directory

- Formed in 1919 as Leeds United after disbandment (by FA order) of Leeds City (formed 1905).
- Joined Midland League in October 1919.
- Turned professional in 1920.
- Elected to Football League Division 2 on 31 May 1920.
- Became Public Limited Company in 1996.
- Ground: Elland Road.

Honours

League Division 1 champions: 1968-69, 1973-74, 1991-92. Runners-up: 1964-65, 1965-66, 1969-70, 1970-71, 1971-2.
Division 2 champions: 1923-24, 1963-64, 1989-90. Runners-up: 1927-28, 1931-32, 1955-56.
FA Cup winners: 1972. Runners-up: 1965, 1970, 1973.
League Cup winners: 1968. Runners-up: 1996.
European Cup runners-up:1974-75.
European Cup-Winners' Cup runners-up: 1972-73.
European Fairs Cup winners: 1967-68, 1970-71.

European Competitions

European Cup: 1969-70 (semi-final), 1974-75 (runners-up), 1992-93 (round 2).
Champions League: 2000-2001 (semi-final)
European Cup-Winners' Cup: 1972-73 (runners-up).
UEFA Cup: 1971-72 (round 1), 1973-74 (round 3), 1979-80 (round 2), 1995-96 (round 2), 1998-99 (round 2), 1999-2000 (semi-final), 2001-2002 (round 4).
Inter-Cities Fairs Cup: 1965-66 (semi-final), 1966-67 (runners-up), 1967-68 (winners), 1968-69 (quarter-final), 1970-71 (winners).

Records

- Record victory: 10-0 v Lyn (Oslo), (h) European Cup 1st Round 1st Leg, 17 September 1969.
- Record League win: 8-0 v Leicester City (h) Division 1, 7 April 1934.
- Record FA Cup win: 8-1 v Crystal Palace (h) Round 3, 11 January 1930.
- Record defeat: 1-8 v Stoke City, Division 1, 27 August 1934.
- Points gained in season (2pts): 67, Division 1, 1968-69; (3pts): 85 Division 2, 1989-90.
- Most League goals in season: 98, Division 2, 1927-28.
- Highest League scorer in season: John Charles, 42, Division 2, 1953-54.
- Most senior appearances: Jack Charlton, 773 (1952-73).
- Most League goals: Peter Lorimer 168 (1965-79 and 1983-86).
- Most League goals in a game: 5, Gordon Hodgson v Leicester City, Division 1, 1 October 1938.
- Most capped player (with club): Billy Bremner, 54 for Scotland.
- Youngest League player: Peter Lorimer, aged 15 years 289 days v Southampton, (h) Division 2, 29 September 1962.

Jack Charlton holds the record for most senior Leeds appearances.

- Oldest League player: Eddie Burbanks, aged 41 years, 23 days v Hull City, (a) Division 2, 24 April, 1954.
- Record signing: £18 million for Rio Ferdinand from West Ham United, November 2000.
- Record sale: £30 million for Rio Ferdinand to Manchester United, July 2002.
- Record attendance: 57,892 v Sunderland, FA Cup 5th Round replay, 15 March 1967.
- Record attendance (all-seater stadium): 40,287 v Newcastle United, 22 December, 2001.
- Record receipts: Everton v Tottenham Hotspur, FA Cup semi-final, 9 April 1995.
- Most first-class matches played in one season: 64 (42 League, 5 FA Cup, 7 League Cup, 12 Inter-Cities Fairs Cup) in 1967-68.

Sequences

Longest League runs
- Undefeated League matches: 34 (1968-69).
- Undefeated start to season: 29 (1973-74).
- Undefeated home League matches: 39 (1968-70).
- Undefeated away League matches: 17 (1968-69).
- Successive League wins: 9 (1931-32).
- Successive League defeats: 6 (1995-96).
- Successive home League wins: 12 (1968-69).
- Without a League win: 17 (1946-47).
- Without a home win: 10 (1982).
- Without an away win: 26 (1939-47).

50 Greatest Players

The merits of players from different eras, playing in teams with varying degrees of success, are difficult to judge. We all place different values on loyalty, consistency, entertainment value and determination. My selection unscientifically takes all of these into account, combining those I have enjoyed watching and those who emerge as key figures in the club's history. I'm sure no two Leeds supporters would come up with an identical all-time top 50 players, but I hope my choice will inspire reminiscences and debate. (Please note that the appearance totals below and in the Great Player boxes include appearances as substitute.)

No. 1 John Charles (Centre half/centre forward) – 327 appearances, 157 goals. A legend in England, Wales and Italy, 'the Gentle Giant' was Leeds' best ever striker and defender (see page 52).

No. 2 Billy Bremner (Inside forward/right half) – 773 appearances, 115 goals. Skilful and ferocious, Bremner was the ultimate captain, driving Leeds through the glory years (see page 111).

No. 3 Norman Hunter (Left half) – 726 appearances, 21 goals. A fearsome reputation for tackling eclipsed his considerable footballing skills (see page 109).

No. 4 Gordon Strachan (Midfielder) – 245 appearances, 45 goals. The creative focal point of the 1991-92 championship season, Strachan proved that talent needn't fade with age (see page 154).

No. 5 Johnny Giles (Midfielder) – 527 appearances, 115 goals. His midfield partnership with Bremner was one of the greatest of all time. Giles combined brains, brawn and ball control to orchestrate Leeds' greatest displays (see page 85).

No. 6 Harry Kewell (Forward) – 201 appearances, 47 goals. Voted the Young Player of the Year in 2000 after setting the league ablaze with audacious goals and breathtaking skills (see page 193).

No. 7 Eddie Gray (Left winger) – 579 appearances, 69 goals. Fast, stylish and inventive, Gray was the quintessential winger, but his career was unfortunately dogged by injury (see page 104).

No. 8 Paul Madeley (Utility player) – 725 appearances, 34 goals. A unique player whose complete skills endorsed his versatility as he served Leeds in every outfield position (see page 112).

No. 9 Willis Edwards (Right Half) – 444 appearances, 6 goals. A loyal servant of the club whose supreme control and passing abilities ensured Edwards' place in England's half back line (see page 21).

No. 10 Nigel Martyn (Goalkeeper) – 272 appearances. Dominant in his area and an excellent shot-stopper, Martyn has been consistently dependable and is arguably the best in the land (see page 199).

No. 11 Allan Clarke (Inside forward) – 366 appearances, 151 goals. The cool executioner's acceleration, control and poise made him the spearhead of Revie's team (see page 108).

No. 12 Lucas Radebe (Central defender) – 188 appearances, 3 goals. Resolute at the back and an excellent man-marker South Africa's captain soon made a name for himself at Leeds (see page 195).

No. 13 Mick Jones (Centre forward) – 313 appearances, 111 goals. The perfect attacking foil for Allan Clarke whose strike rate proves he was a great goalscorer in his own right (see page 78).

No. 14 Bobby Collins (Inside forward/midfielder) – 167 appearances, 25 goals. The 'Little General' was a master tackler and passer who resurrected his own career and Leeds' fortunes in the early Revie years (see page 58).

No. 15 Jack Charlton (Centre half) – 773 appearances, 96 goals. A giant in defence and more than a nuisance when sent up front, Jack was Leeds' and England's hero (see page 84).

No. 16 Terry Cooper (Left winger/left back) – 350 appearances, 11 goals. Converted from winger to become a potent attacking full back and part of England's great 1970 team (see page 99).

No. 17 Ernie Hart (Centre half) – 472 appearances, 15 goals. The ball-playing defender was one of the formidable 30s half back line and a focal point of Leeds' defence for nearly 15 years (see page 31).

No. 18 Tony Currie (Midfielder) – 124 appearances, 16 goals. Strong and skilful, Currie's style was characterized by an ambling grace (see page 123).

No. 19 Wilf Copping (Left half) – 183 appearances, 4 goals. One of the hardest tacklers of his day, Copping was an Elland Road hero in two spells at the club (see page 29).

No. 20 Gary McAllister (Midfielder) – 294 appearances, 45 goals. With supreme control and incisive passing, he was the linchpin of Leeds' 1991-92 title-winning side (see page 179).

No. 21 Peter Lorimer (Winger/midfielder) – 685 appearances, 238 goals. Leeds' youngest ever debutant and record goalscorer left memories galore in nearly 20 seasons at Elland Road (see page 119).

No. 22 David Batty (Midfielder) – 357 appearances, 4 goals. The Leeds-born fighter was of the old school. Though tough and committed, he never lacked creative skill (see page 161).

No. 23 Tom Jennings (Centre forward) – 174 appearances, 117 goals. A determined, direct striker with a prodigious strike rate (see page 23).

No. 24 David Harvey (Goalkeeper) – 447 appearances. Waited seven seasons to display his courage, concentration and sharp reflexes in Leeds' 70s triumphs (see page 144).

No. 25 Paul Reaney (Right back) – 748 appearances, 9 goals. Superb tackler and man-marker Reaney was a rock in Revie's defence (see page 133).

No. 26 Joe Jordan (Centre forward) – 215 appearances, 48 goals. The Scottish international used his height and strength to maximum effect in the late Revie era (see page 128).

No. 27 Lee Bowyer (Midfielder) – 244 appearances, 52 goals. All-round midfielder with a great engine and aggression to spare (see page 200).

No. 28 Alan Smith (Striker) – 147 appearances, 38 goals. Prolific striker whose loyalty and commitment to the Leeds cause are both his strength and his weakness (see page 220).

No. 29 Rio Ferdinand (Central defender) – 73 appearances, 3 goals. Regarded by many as the best central defender in the world (see page 224).

No. 30 Tony Dorigo (Full back) – 209 appearances, 6 goals. An exciting, overlapping left back with pace and fine tackling ability (see page 183).

No. 31 Frank Gray (Midfielder/full back) – 404 appearances, 35 goals. A great reader of the game at the back and a wonderfully creative midfielder who served Leeds and Scotland well (see page 137).

No. 32 Bert Sproston (Full back) – 140 appearances, 1 goal. Leeds enjoyed the blossoming talents of this stylish international defender (see page 32).

No. 33 Mark Viduka (Centre forward) – 95 appearances, 38 goals. Powerful Australian striker with surprisingly delicate touch (see page 76).

No. 34 Gordon McQueen (Defender) – 172 appearances, 19 goals. Dominant in the air and comfortable on the ball, an essential member of the 1973-74 Championship-winning side (see page 127).

No. 35 Mel Sterland (Full back) – 146 appearances, 20 goals. Vigour, commitment and a fearsome shot made him a favourite in his injury-curtailed career (see page 156).

No. 36 John Lukic (Goalkeeper) – 399 appearances. In two spells, his command of the area inspired his defences with confidence (see page 160).

No. 37 Gary Sprake (Goalkeeper) – 507 appearances. The athletic and often heroic shot-stopper's reputation was tarnished by high-profile mistakes (see page 98).

No. 38 Albert Johanneson (Left wing) – 202 appearances, 67 goals. The South African's wing play was a highlight of the mid-60s side (see page 63).

No. 39 Lee Chapman (Centre forward) 177 appearances, 81 goals. An ideal target man whose goals helped win both First and Second Division championships (see page 164).

No. 40 Alan Peacock (Centre forward) – 65 appearances, 31 goals. His goals and aerial ability won him England caps and Elland Road acclaim (see page 73).

No. 41 Rod Wallace (Forward) – 245 appearances, 67 goals. Possessed a fantastic ability to skip past defenders and score virtuoso goals (see page 187).

No. 42 Mike O'Grady (Winger) – 121 appearances, 16 goals. Became the scourge of defenders in Leeds' 1969 championship campaign (see page 89).

No. 43 Arthur Graham (Left winger) – 260 appearances, 47 goals. With accurate crosses and powerful shots, Graham made a strong impact in his time at Elland Road (see page 141).

No. 44 David Cochrane (Right winger)– 185 appearances, 32 goals. Great natural talent set the Northern Irishman apart from most wingers of his day (see page 39).

No. 45 Willie Bell (Full back) – 260 appearances, 18 goals. Tenacious, brave and dedicated to Leeds' cause, Bell was a vital element in Revie's early years (see page 74).

No. 46 Gary Speed (Midfielder) – 312 appearances, 57 goals. Welsh international and accomplished left-sided player who was always a threat in the air (see page 177).

No. 47 Eric Kerfoot (Wing half) – 349 appearances, 10 goals. A driving force who was an ever-present for three consecutive seasons (see page 43).

No. 48 Brian Flynn (Midfielder) – 177 appearances, 11 goals. A fine midfield dynamo with a wicked shot, Flynn was a great foil to Tony Currie (see page 142).

No. 49 Grenville Hair (Full back) – 474 appearances, 2 goals. A great servant of the club, he was a defensive mainstay through the 50s and 60s (see page 60).

No. 50 Don Revie (Inside forward) – 80 appearances, 12 goals. In the twilight of his career he retained the positional awareness, passing ability and stamina that had won him honours (see page 57).

Results and Tables 1905-2002

Norman Hunter and Gordon McQueen: often inpenetrable in the centre of Leeds' defence.

The following pages include details of every official match played by Leeds United Football Club since their participation in Football League Division Two in 1920-21 as well as those of their fore-runners Leeds City Football Club (who joined the Football League in 1905 and were expelled in October 1919).

Each season has its own page and is dated at the top. League matches appear first, followed by individual cup competitions. The opponents played at home are written in capital letters, and appear in upper and lower case for away games. The date of the match, the score, the Leeds United (or City) goalscorers and the match attendance are also included. Full league and cup and European competition appearances and the goalscorers are featured separately. The final league table is included at the bottom of each page as well as a Fact File which notes particularly interesting facts and figures for the season as well as any notable transfers etc.

During the World Wars the official Football League programme was suspended. The results of matches played during the years 1915-18 and 1939-45 are not included. There was a huge amount of football played during the wartime years but teams were greatly disrupted with many players called up to fight and others guesting for various different teams all over the country. For these reasons, wartime football statistics, though interesting, are not regarded as 'official'. In both the League & Cup Appearances and Goalscorers tables the category 'other' includes matches in the FA Charity Shield, the Full Members Cup and the Zenith Data Systems Cup.

Leeds City Season 1905-06

Football League Division 2

DATE	OPPONENTS	SCORE	GOALSCORERS	ATTENDANCE
Sep 2	Bradford City	L 0-1		15,000
Sep 9	WEST BROMWICH ALBION	L 0-2		6,802
Sep 11	LINCOLN CITY	D 2-2	Drain 2	3,000
Sep 16	Leicester Fosse	W 1-0	Singleton	5,000
Sep 23	HULL CITY	W 3-1	R Morris 2, Hargraves	13,654
Sep 30	Lincoln City	W 2-1	Parnell (pen), Hargraves	3,000
Oct 14	Port Vale	L 0-2		1,500
Oct 21	BARNSLEY	W 3-2	R Morris, Hargraves, Stacey o.g.	12,000
Nov 11	GRIMSBY TOWN	W 3-0	Hargraves 2, Stringfellow	7,000
Nov 13	Burton United	D 1-1	Parnell	1,500
Nov 25	CHELSEA	D 0-0		20,000
Dec 2	Gainsborough Town	L 1-4	Watson	2,000
Dec 9	BRISTOL CITY	D 1-1	Morgan	15,000
Dec 23	GLOSSOP NORTH END	W 1-0	Hargraves	9,000
Dec 26	Stockport County	L 1-2	Singleton	5,000
Dec 30	BRADFORD CITY	L 0-2		22,000
Jan 1	Blackpool	W 3-0	R Morris, Wilson, Singleton	3,000
Jan 6	West Bromwich Albion	L 1-2	Wilson	2,553
Jan 15	Manchester United	W 3-0	Watson, Wilson, Singleton	6,000
Jan 20	LEICESTER FOSSE	W 4-1	Murray, Drain, Watson, Hargraves	8,000
Jan 27	Hull City	D 0-0		10,000
Feb 3	BURNLEY	D 1-1	Watson	7,129
Feb 10	Chesterfield	W 2-0	R Morris, Singleton	4,000
Feb 17	PORT VALE	W 3-1	Wilson, Hargraves, Parnell	9,000
Feb 24	Barnsley	L 0-3		5,000
Feb 27	CHESTERFIELD	W 3-0	Wilson 2, Murray (pen)	2,000
Mar 3	CLAPTON ORIENT	W 6-1	Wilson 4, Hargraves, Parnell	8,000
Mar 10	Burnley	L 3-4	Wilson 2, Singleton	5,000
Mar 17	Grimsby Town	D 1-1	Murray	3,000
Mar 24	BURTON UNITED	W 2-1	Watson, Singleton	5,000
Mar 29	Clapton Orient	D 0-0		1,000
Mar 31	Chelsea	L 0-4		15,000
Apr 7	GAINSBOROUGH TOWN	W 1-0	Hargraves	12,000
Apr 13	STOCKPORT COUNTY	D 1-1	Lavery	10,000
Apr 14	Bristol City	L 0-2		12,000
Apr 16	BLACKPOOL	W 3-0	Hargraves 2, Watson	10,000
Apr 21	MANCHESTER UNITED	L 1-3	Lavery	10,000
Apr 28	Glossop North End	W 2-1	Parnell, Wilson	1,500

FA Cup

Oct 7	MORLEY	(Rd 1) W 11-0	Hargraves 4, Watson 2, R Morris 4, Parnell	3,000
Oct 28	MEXBOROUGH	(Rd 2) D 1-1	Hargraves	4,000
Nov 2	Mexborough	(R) D 1-1	Parnell	3,000
Nov 6	MEXBOROUGH	(2R) W 3-1	Watson, R Morris, Hargraves	5,000
Nov 22	Hull City	(Rd 3) D 1-1	Hargraves	3,000
Nov 29	HULL CITY	(R) L 1-2	Parnell	7,000

League & Cup Appearances

PLAYER	LEAGUE	CUP COMPETITION FA CUP	TOTAL
Bromage	35	6	41
Clay		1	1
Drain	9	1	10
Freeborough	2		2
George	5		5
Hargraves	28	6	34
Henderson	35	5	40
Howard	1		1
Lavery	8		8
McDonald	25	6	31
Ray	27	5	32
Morgan	35	6	41
Morris J	9		9
Morris R	25	6	31
Murray	23		23
Parnell	37	6	43
Singleton	37	6	33
Stringfellow	13	3	16
Swift	1		1
Walker	15	3	18
Watson	30	6	36
Whitley	3		3
Wilson D	15		15

Goalscorers

PLAYER	LEAGUE	CUP COMPETITION FA CUP	TOTAL
Hargraves	12	7	19
Wilson D	13		13
Morris R	5	5	10
Parnell	5	3	8
Watson	5	3	8
Singleton	7		7
Drain	3		3
Murray	3		3
Lavery	2		2
Morgan	1		1
Stringfellow	1		1
Opps' o.gs.	1		1

Fact File

Leeds City took the field in their opening Football League game in blue and gold shirts with white shorts.

MANAGER: Gilbert Gillies
CAPTAIN: Dick Ray
TOP SCORER: Fred Hargraves
BIGGEST WIN: 11-0 v Morley, 7 October 1905, FA Cup Round 1
HIGHEST ATTENDANCE: 22,000 v Bradford City, 30 December 1905, lost 0-2, League

Final Division 2 Table

		P	W	D	L	F	A	Pts
1	BRISTOL C	38	30	6	2	83	28	66
2	MANCHESTER U	38	28	6	4	90	28	62
3	CHELSEA	38	22	9	7	90	37	53
4	WBA	38	22	8	8	79	36	52
5	HULL C	38	19	6	13	67	54	44
6	LEEDS CITY	38	17	9	12	59	47	43
7	LEICESTER FOSSE	38	15	12	11	53	48	42
8	GRIMSBY T	38	15	10	13	46	46	40
9	BURNLEY	38	15	8	15	42	53	38
10	STOCKPORT CO	38	13	9	16	44	56	35
11	BRADFORD C	38	13	8	17	46	60	34
12	BARNSLEY	38	12	9	17	60	62	33
13	LINCOLN C	38	12	6	20	69	72	30
14	BLACKPOOL	38	10	9	19	37	62	29
15	GAINSBOROUGH T	38	12	4	22	44	57	28
16	GLOSSOP	38	10	8	20	49	71	28
17	BURSLEM PORT VALE	38	12	4	22	49	82	28
18	CHESTERFIELD T	38	10	8	20	40	72	28
19	BURTON U	38	10	6	22	34	67	26
20	CLAPTON ORIENT	38	7	7	24	35	78	21

Season 1906-07

Football League Division 2

DATE	OPPONENTS	SCORE	GOALSCORERS	ATTENDANCE
Sep 1	BRADFORD CITY	D 1-1	Lavery	20,000
Sep 8	West Bromwich Albion	L 0-5		15,504
Sep 10	LINCOLN CITY	D 1-1	Cubberley	5,000
Sep 15	LEICESTER FOSSE	D 1-1	Jefferson	11,000
Sep 22	Nottingham Forest	L 0-3		5,000
Sep 29	Lincoln City	D 1-1	Jefferson	4,000
Oct 6	Burton United	W 2-0	Lavery, Watson	3,000
Oct 13	GRIMSBY TOWN	W 4-3	Watson 2, D Murray (pen), Lavery	10,000
Oct 20	Port Vale	W 2-1	Lavery, Parnell	4,000
Oct 27	BURNLEY	L 0-1		14,000
Nov 3	Chesterfield	L 0-1		3,000
Nov 10	Barnsley	L 0-3		4,000
Nov 17	CHELSEA	L 0-1		8,000
Nov 24	Wolverhampton W	L 2-3	Lavery, D Murrray (pen)	4,500
Dec 1	CLAPTON ORIENT	W 3-2	Watson, Parnell, McLeod	10,000
Dec 5	Blackpool	L 0-1		2,000
Dec 8	Gainsborough Town	L 0-1		3,000
Dec 15	STOCKPORT COUNTY	W 6-1	McLeod, Lavery 3, Watson 2	8,000
Dec 22	Hull City	L 1-2	Lavery	10,000
Dec 29	Bradford City	D 2-2	McLeod, T Wilson	17,000
Jan 1	Glossop North End	L 0-2		1,000
Jan 5	WEST BROMWICH ALBION	W 3-2	McLeod 2, Jefferson	14,000
Jan 19	Leicester Fosse	D 2-2	McLeod, Kirk	8,000
Jan 26	NOTTINGHAM FOREST	L 1-4	McLeod	14,000
Feb 2	BLACKPOOL	D 1-1	Jefferson	7,000
Feb 9	BURTON UNITED	W 3-1	McLeod 2, Parnell	7,000
Feb 16	Grimsby Town	L 0-4		4,000
Feb 23	PORT VALE	W 2-0	Parnell, Watson	7,000
Mar 2	Burnley	W 2-1	Harwood, T Wilson	5,000
Mar 9	CHESTERFIELD	W 1-0	McLeod	10,500
Mar 16	BARNSLEY	W 2-1	McLeod, Watson	14,000
Mar 23	Chelsea	L 0-2		25,000
Mar 30	WOLVERHAMPTON W	W 2-0	Watson, Cubberley	15,000
Apr 1	GLOSSOP NORTH END	L 1-4	McEwan o.g.	8,000
Apr 6	Clapton Orient	D 1-1	Lavery	6,000
Apr 13	GAINSBOROUGH TOWN	W 4-0	Cubberley, Lavery 2, McLeod	3,000
Apr 20	Stockport County	D 2-2	Kennedy, McLeod	3,000
Apr 27	HULL CITY	D 2-2	McLeod 2	7,000

FA Cup

Jan 12	Bristol City	(Rd 1) L 1-4	McLeod	14,000

League & Cup Appearances

PLAYER	LEAGUE	CUP COMPETITION FA CUP	TOTAL
Clark	24		24
Cubberley	20		20
Freeborough	20		20
George	3		3
Hargraves	33	1	34
Harwood	1		1
Henderson	15		15
Jefferson	9	1	10
Kennedy	35	1	36
Kirk	8	1	9
Lavery	27	1	28
Morgan	6		6
Morris J	1		1
Murray D	23	1	24
Murray W	8		8
Parnell	33		33
Pickard	2		2
Ray	11	1	12
Singleton	8		8
Walker	11		11
Watson	28	1	29
Whitley	4		4
Wilson D	6		6
Wilson T	20	1	21

Goalscorers

PLAYER	LEAGUE	CUP COMPETITION FA CUP	TOTAL
McLeod	15	1	16
Lavery	12		12
Watson	9		9
Jefferson	4		4
Parnell	4		4
Cubberley	3		3
Murray D	2		2
Wilson T	2		2
Harwood	1		1
Kennedy	1		1
Kirk	1		1
Opps' o.gs.	1		1

Fact File

David Wilson died in the Elland Road dressing room after leaving the pitch during the second half of the Burnley match in October.

MANAGER: Gilbert Gillies

CAPTAIN: Dick Ray

TOP SCORER: Billy McLeod

BIGGEST WIN: 6-1 v Stockport County, 15 December 15 1906, League

HIGHEST ATTENDANCE: 25,000 v Chelsea, 23 March 1907, lost 0-2, League

MAJOR TRANSFERS IN: Billy McLeod from Lincoln City

Final Division 2 Table

		P	W	D	L	F	A	Pts
1	NOTTINGHAM F	38	28	4	6	74	36	60
2	CHELSEA	38	26	5	7	80	34	57
3	LEICESTER FOSSE	38	20	8	10	62	39	48
4	WBA	38	21	5	12	83	45	47
5	BRADFORD C	38	21	5	12	70	53	47
6	WOLVERHAMPTON W	38	17	7	14	66	53	41
7	BURNLEY	38	17	6	15	62	47	40
8	BARNSLEY	38	15	8	15	73	55	38
9	HULL	38	15	7	16	65	57	37
10	LEEDS CITY	38	13	10	15	55	63	36
11	GRIMSBY T	38	16	3	19	57	62	35
12	STOCKPORT CO	38	12	11	15	42	52	35
13	BLACKPOOL	38	11	11	16	33	51	33
14	GAINSBOROUGH T	38	14	5	19	45	72	33
15	GLOSSOP	38	13	6	19	53	79	32
16	BURSLEM PORT VALE	38	12	7	19	60	83	31
17	CLAPTON ORIENT	38	11	8	19	45	67	30
18	CHESTERFIELD T	38	11	7	20	50	66	29
19	LINCOLN C	38	12	4	22	46	73	28
20	BURTON U	38	8	7	23	34	68	23

Season 1907-08

Football League Division 2

DATE	OPPONENTS	SCORE	GOALSCORERS	ATTENDANCE
Sep 2	GLOSSOP NORTH END	W 2-1	Lavery, Tustin o.g.	4,000
Sep 7	Leicester Fosse	D 2-2	Watson, McLeod	10,000
Sep 9	CLAPTON ORIENT	W 5-2	Watson 2, Croot, Lavery 2	6,000
Sep 14	Blackpool	W 3-2	Watson, Lavery, Parnell	6,000
Sep 21	Stoke	L 1-2	Parnell	10,000
Sep 28	WEST BROMWICH ALBION	W 1-0	McLeod	24,000
Oct 5	Bradford City	L 0-5		27,000
Oct 12	HULL CITY	W 3-2	McLeod 2, Watson	15,000
Oct 19	Derby County	L 1-6	Atkin o.g.	10,000
Oct 26	LINCOLN CITY	W 2-1	Parnell, McLeod	10,000
Nov 2	Fulham	L 0-2		20,000
Nov 9	BARNSLEY	D 1-1	McLeod	11,000
Nov 16	Chesterfield	L 3-4	Thomas 2, Parnell	4,000
Nov 23	BURNLEY	D 2-2	Croot, McLeod	7,000
Nov 30	Oldham Athletic	L 2-4	McLeod, Gemmell	8,000
Dec 14	GRIMSBY TOWN	W 4-1	McLeod, Croot 2, Murray	5,000
Dec 21	Wolverhampton W	L 0-2		5,000
Dec 25	Stockport County	L 1-2	McLeod	8,000
Dec 28	GAINSBOROUGH TOWN	D 0-0		8,000
Jan 1	Glossop North End	W 2-0	Croot, McLeod	2,000
Jan 4	LEICESTER FOSSE	D 0-0		10,000
Jan 18	STOKE	L 0-1		10,000
Jan 25	West Bromwich Albion	L 0-1		8,000
Feb 1	BRADFORD CITY	L 0-1		35,000
Feb 8	Hull City	L 1-4	McLeod	9,000
Feb 15	DERBY COUNTY	W 5-1	Murray, Croot, Lavery, McLeod 2	8,000
Feb 22	Lincoln City	L 0-5		1,000
Feb 29	FULHAM	L 0-1		10,000
Mar 7	Barnsley	W 3-1	Jefferson, McLeod, Croot	5,000
Mar 14	CHESTERFIELD	D 0-0		6,000
Mar 21	Burnley	L 0-1		7,000
Mar 28	OLDHAM ATHLETIC	L 1-2	Parnell	15,000
Apr 4	Clapton Orient	D 0-0		8,000
Apr 11	Grimsby Town	L 0-2		6,000
Apr 17	STOCKPORT COUNTY	W 3-0	Gemmell, McLeod (pen), Croot	12,000
Apr 18	WOLVERHAMPTON W	W 3-1	Parnell, Gemmell, Watson	10,000
Apr 20	BLACKPOOL	D 1-1	Lavery	7,000
Apr 22	Gainsborough Town	L 1-2	McLeod	3,500

FA Cup

Jan 11	Oldham Athletic	(Rd 1) L 1-2	Parnell	14,000

League & Cup Appearances

PLAYER	LEAGUE	CUP COMPETITION FA CUP	TOTAL
Bates	3		3
Bromage	10		10
Croot	38	1	39
Cubberley	29	1	30
Freeborough	2		2
Gemmell	16	1	17
Hargraves	2		2
Henderson	25		25
Hynds	37	1	38
Jefferson	8		8
Kay	31	1	32
Kennedy	8	1	9
Lavery	21		21
McLeod	36	1	37
Murray D	34	1	35
Parnell	34	1	35
Pickard	2		2
Naisby	28	1	29
Thomas	9	1	10
Thorpe	9		9
Tompkins	11		11
Watson	25		25

Goalscorers

PLAYER	LEAGUE	CUP COMPETITION FA CUP	TOTAL
McLeod	16		16
Parnell	6	1	7
Croot	6		6
Lavery	6		6
Watson	6		6
Gemmell	3		3
Murray D	2		2
Thomas	2		2
Jefferson	1		1
Opps' o.gs.	2		2

Fact File

At the end of March the Leeds board declined to extend manager Gilbert Gillies contract and Frank Scott-Walford took over.

MANAGER: Gilbert Gillies

CAPTAIN: Bob Watson

TOP SCORER: Billy McLeod

BIGGEST WIN: 5-1 v Derby County, 15 Febraury 1908, League

HIGHEST ATTENDANCE: 35,000 v Bradford City, 1 February 1908, lost 0-1, League

MAJOR TRANSFERS IN: Fred Croot from Glossop

Final Division 2 Table

		P	W	D	L	F	A	Pts
1	BRADFORD C	38	24	6	8	90	42	54
2	LEICESTER FOSSE	38	21	10	7	72	47	52
3	OLDHAM ATH	38	22	6	10	76	42	50
4	FULHAM	38	22	5	11	82	49	49
5	WBA	38	19	9	10	61	39	47
6	DERBY CO	38	21	4	13	77	45	46
7	BURNLEY	38	20	6	12	67	50	46
8	HULL C	38	21	4	13	73	62	46
9	WOLVERHAMPTON W	38	15	7	16	50	45	37
10	STOKE	38	16	5	17	57	52	37
11	GAINSBOROUGH T	38	14	7	17	47	71	35
12	LEEDS CITY	38	12	8	18	53	65	32
13	STOCKPORT CO	38	12	8	18	48	67	32
14	CLAPTON ORIENT	38	11	10	17	40	65	32
15	BLACKPOOL	38	11	9	18	51	58	31
16	BARNSLEY	38	12	6	20	54	68	30
17	GLOSSOP	38	11	8	19	54	74	30
18	GRIMSBY T	38	11	8	19	43	71	30
19	CHESTERFIELD T	38	6	11	21	46	92	23
20	LINCOLN C	38	9	3	26	46	83	21

Season 1908-09

Football League Division 2

DATE	OPPONENTS		SCORE	GOALSCORERS	ATTENDANCE
Sep 5	TOTTENHAM HOTSPUR	W	1-0	Rodger	20,000
Sep 7	CLAPTON ORIENT	D	0-0		8,000
Sep 12	HULL CITY	W	2-0	Rodger, Bowman	12,000
Sep 14	BARNSLEY	W	2-0	McLeod 2	8,000
Sep 19	DERBY COUNTY	L	2-5	McLeod 2 (1 pen)	20,000
Sep 26	Blackpool	L	0-1		5,000
Oct 3	Chesterfield	L	0-2		7,000
Oct 10	Glossop North End	D	0-0		4,000
Oct 17	STOCKPORT COUNTY	W	2-1	McLeod, Molyneux o.g.	8,500
Oct 24	West Bromwich Albion	L	1-2	McLeod	13,554
Oct 31	BIRMINGHAM	W	2-0	McLeod, Rodger	15,000
Nov 7	Gainsborough Town	D	1-1	McLeod	4,000
Nov 14	GRIMSBY TOWN	W	4-1	Gemmell 2, McLeod 2	8,000
Nov 21	Fulham	W	1-0	McLeod	18,000
Nov 28	BURNLEY	D	1-1	Bowman	14,000
Dec 12	WOLVERHAMPTON W	W	5-2	McLeod, Gemmell 3, Guy	14,000
Dec 19	Oldham Athletic	L	0-6		8,000
Dec 25	Bolton Wanderers	L	0-2		19,400
Dec 26	BOLTON WANDERERS	L	1-2	Joynes	15,000
Jan 1	Barnsley	L	1-2	Guy	6,500
Jan 2	Tottenham Hotspur	L	0-3		16,000
Jan 9	Hull City	L	1-4	McLeod	7,000
Jan 23	Derby County	L	1-5	Bowman	7,000
Jan 30	BLACKPOOL	W	1-0	Bowman	8,000
Feb 13	GLOSSOP NORTH END	W	3-1	Croot, Burnett, Gemmell	10,000
Feb 20	Stockport County	L	0-1		6,000
Feb 27	WEST BROMWICH ALBION	D	1-1	McLeod	12,000
Mar 13	GAINSBOROUGH TOWN	L	0-2		7,000
Mar 20	Grimsby Town	W	1-0	Gemmell	5,500
Mar 27	FULHAM	W	2-0	Bowman, Guy	10,000
Apr 3	Burnley	D	0-0		5,000
Apr 9	CHESTERFIELD	W	3-0	Rodger, Gemmell, Bowman	10,000
Apr 10	BRADFORD PARK AVENUE	L	0-3		11,000
Apr 12	Birmingham	L	0-1		3,000
Apr 13	Clapton Orient	D	0-0		3,000
Apr 17	Wolverhampton W	L	1-2	McLeod	7,000
Apr 24	OLDHAM ATHLETIC	W	3-0	Burnett, Croot, Dougal	4,500
Apr 27	Bradford Park Avenue	L	0-2		6,000

FA Cup

Jan 16	Oldham Athletic	(Rd 1) D	1-1	McLeod	7,000
Jan 20	OLDHAM ATHLETIC	(R) W	2-0	McLeod (pen), Guy	19,047
Feb 6	WEST HAM UNITED	(Rd 2) D	1-1	Burnett	31,471
Feb 11	West Ham United*	(R) L	1-2	Bowman	13,000
Jan 10	Liverpool	L	0-3		39,000

*After extra time.

League & Cup Appearances

PLAYER	LEAGUE	CUP COMPETITION FA CUP	TOTAL
Bates	12		12
Bowman	15	1	16
Bromage	4		4
Burnett	18	4	22
Croot	37	4	41
Cubberley	27	4	31
Cunningham	1		1
Dougal	10		10
Gemmell	28	4	32
Guy	18	4	22
Hamilton	21	4	25
Joynes	15	1	16
Kennedy	15		15
McAllister	32	4	36
McDonald	14		14
McLeod	22	2	24
Morris	9		9
Murray D	3		3
Naisby	33	4	37
Rodger	25		25
Watson	28	4	32
White	31	4	35

Goalscorers

PLAYER	LEAGUE	CUP COMPETITION FA CUP	TOTAL
McLeod	15	2	17
Gemmell	8		8
Bowman	6	1	7
Guy	3	1	4
Rodger	4		4
Burnett	2	1	3
Croot	1		1
Dougal	1		1
Joynes	1		1
Opps' o.gs.	1		1

Fact File

The seven consecutive defeats in December and January was the worst run in Leeds City's short history.

MANAGER: Frank Scott-Walford
CAPTAIN: Bob Watson
TOP SCORER: Billy McLeod
BIGGEST WIN: 5-2 v Wolves, 12 December 1908, League
HIGHEST ATTENDANCE: 20,000 v Tottenham Hotspur, 5 September 1908, won 1-0, League; 20,000 v Derby County, 19 September 1908, lost 2-5, League

Final Division 2 Table

		P	W	D	L	F	A	Pts
1	BOLTON W	38	24	4	10	59	28	52
2	TOTTENHAM H	38	20	11	7	67	32	51
3	WBA	38	19	13	6	56	27	51
4	HULL C	38	19	6	13	63	39	44
5	DERBY CO	38	16	11	11	55	41	43
6	OLDHAM ATH	38	17	6	15	55	43	40
7	WOLVERHAMPTON W	38	14	11	13	56	48	39
8	GLOSSOP	38	15	8	15	57	53	38
9	GAINSBOROUGH T	38	15	8	15	49	70	38
10	FULHAM	38	13	11	14	58	48	37
11	BIRMINGHAM	38	14	9	15	58	61	37
12	LEEDS CITY	38	14	7	17	43	53	35
13	GRIMSBY T	38	14	7	17	41	54	35
14	BURNLEY	38	13	7	18	51	58	33
15	CLAPTON ORIENT	38	12	9	17	37	49	33
16	BRADFORD PA	38	13	6	19	51	59	32
17	BARNSLEY	38	11	10	17	48	57	32
18	STOCKPORT CO	38	14	3	21	39	71	31
19	CHESTERFIELD T	38	11	8	19	37	67	30
20	BLACKPOOL	38	9	11	18	46	68	29

Season 1909-10

Football League Division 2

DATE	OPPONENTS	SCORE	GOALSCORERS	ATTENDANCE
Sep 1	LINCOLN CITY	W 5-0	Gemmell 2, Halligan 2, Morris	6,000
Sep 4	Hull City	L 1-3	Halligan	10,000
Sep 11	DERBY COUNTY	W 2-1	Croot, Halligan	12,000
Sep 18	Stockport County	D 0-0		7,000
Sep 25	GLOSSOP NORTH END	L 1-2	McLeod	12,000
Oct 2	Birmingham	W 2-1	Halligan 2	14,000
Oct 9	WEST BROMWICH ALBION	L 0-1		7,500
Oct 16	Oldham Athletic	L 1-2	Halligan	10,000
Oct 23	BARNSLEY	L 0-7		8,000
Oct 30	Fulham	L 1-5	Halligan	14,000
Nov 6	BURNLEY	W 1-0	Halligan	7,000
Nov 13	BRADFORD PARK AVENUE	L 2-3	McLeod 2	10,000
Nov 20	Wolverhampton W	L 0-5		5,500
Nov 27	GAINSBOROUGH TOWN	D 0-0		3,000
Dec 4	Grimsby Town	L 1-3	Halligan	3,000
Dec 11	MANCHESTER CITY	L 1-3	McLeod	5,000
Dec 18	Leicester Fosse	L 2-6	McLeod, Halligan	12,000
Dec 25	CLAPTON ORIENT	W 2-1	Roberts, McLeod	6,000
Dec 27	BLACKPOOL	W 3-2	McLeod, Roberts 2	10,000
Dec 28	Lincoln City	D 0-0		8,000
Jan 1	Blackpool	L 1-3	Halligan	4,000
Jan 8	HULL CITY	D 1-1	Gemmell	10,000
Jan 22	Derby County	L 0-1		7,000
Feb 5	Glossop North End	L 1-2	Roberts	1,000
Feb 12	BIRMINGHAM	W 2-1	Roberts, Croot	10,000
Feb 26	OLDHAM ATHLETIC	L 3-5	McLeod, Mulholland, Croot (pen)	6,000
Mar 5	STOCKPORT COUNTY	L 0-2		5,000
Mar 7	West Bromwich Albion	L 1-3	McLeod	6,800
Mar 12	FULHAM	D 2-2	Croot 2 (1 pen)	4,000
Mar 17	Barnsley	D 1-1	McLeod	2,000
Mar 19	Burnley	L 0-3		4,000
Mar 26	Bradford Park Avenue	L 2-4	Croot (pen), McLeod	12,000
Mar 28	Clapton Orient	W 2-0	McLeod 2	7,000
Apr 2	WOLVERHAMPTON W	W 1-0	McLeod	5,000
Apr 9	Gainsborough Town	L 0-2		3,000
Apr 16	Grimsby Town	W 3-1	Croot 2 (1 pen), McLeod	5,000
Apr 23	Manchester City	L 0-3		15,000
Apr 30	LEICESTER FOSSE	D 1-1	McLeod	2,000

FA Cup

Jan 15	Sunderland	(Rd 1) L 0-1		18,000

League & Cup Appearances

PLAYER	LEAGUE	CUP COMPETITION FA CUP	TOTAL
Ackerley	2		2
Affleck	25	1	26
Astill	1		1
Beren	3		3
Bridgett	1		1
Bromage	35	1	36
Burnett	2		2
Croot	34	1	35
Cubberley	35	1	36
Dougal	15		15
Gemmell	23	1	24
Halligan	24	1	26
Hamilton	3		3
Hogg	1		1
Horsley	20	1	21
Joynes	7		7
McAllister	21	1	22
McLeod	28	1	29
Morris	24		24
Mulholland	22		22
Naisby	2		2
Pickard	4		4
Price	8		8
Roberts	24	1	25
Stockton	3		3
Tydlesley	6	1	7
Watson	17		17
White	28		28

Goalscorers

PLAYER	LEAGUE	CUP COMPETITION FA CUP	TOTAL
McLeod	14		14
Halligan	12		12
Croot	8		8
Roberts	5		5
Gemmell	3		3
Morris	1		1
Mulholland	1		1

Fact File

Elland Road staged this year's FA Cup semi-final between Barnsley and Everton.

MANAGER: Frank Scott-Walford

CAPTAIN: Bob Watson

TOP SCORER: Billy McLeod

BIGGEST WIN: 5-0 v Lincoln City, 1 September 1909, League

HIGHEST ATTENDANCE: 15,000 v Manchester City, 23 April 1910, lost 0-3, League

Final Division 2 Table

		P	W	D	L	F	A	Pts
1	MANCHESTER C	38	23	8	7	81	40	54
2	OLDHAM ATH	38	23	7	8	79	39	53
3	HULL C	38	23	7	8	80	46	53
4	DERBY CO	38	22	9	7	72	47	53
5	LEICESTER FOSSE	38	20	4	14	79	58	44
6	GLOSSOP	38	18	7	13	64	57	43
7	FULHAM	38	14	13	11	51	43	41
8	WOLVERHAMPTON W	38	17	6	15	64	63	40
9	BARNSLEY	38	16	7	15	62	59	39
10	BRADFORD PA	38	17	4	17	64	59	38
11	WBA	38	16	5	17	58	56	37
12	BLACKPOOL	38	14	8	16	50	52	36
13	STOCKPORT CO	38	13	8	17	50	47	34
14	BURNLEY	38	14	6	18	62	61	34
15	LINCOLN C	38	10	11	17	42	69	31
16	CLAPTON ORIENT	38	12	6	20	37	60	30
17	LEEDS CITY	38	10	7	21	46	80	27
18	GAINSBOROUGH T	38	10	6	22	33	75	26
19	GRIMSBY T	38	9	6	23	50	77	24
20	BIRMINGHAM	38	8	7	23	42	78	23

Season 1910-11

Football League Division 2

DATE	OPPONENTS	SCORE	GOALSCORERS	ATTENDANCE
Sep 3	BLACKPOOL	L 1-2	Enright	12,000
Sep 10	Glossop North End	L 1-2	Enright	8,000
Sep 17	LINCOLN CITY	L 0-1		8,000
Sep 24	Huddersfield Town	L 2-3	Croot (pen), McLeod	7,500
Oct 1	BIRMINGHAM	D 1-1	Gillespie	8,000
Oct 8	West Bromwich Albion	L 0-2		10,000
Oct 15	HULL CITY	W 1-0	Gillespie	8,000
Oct 22	Fulham	L 1-2	Gillespie	11,000
Oct 29	BRADFORD PARK AVENUE	W 2-0	McLeod, Gillespie	13,000
Nov 5	Burnley	L 1-4	McLeod	8,000
Nov 12	GAINSBOROUGH TOWN	W 4-0	Enright, Gillespie 2, McLeod	5,000
Nov 19	Bolton Wanderers	L 0-3		10,000
Nov 26	Stockport County	W 4-0	Gillespie 2, McLeod, Bridgett	4,000
Dec 3	DERBY COUNTY	W 3-2	Morris, Roberts 2	10,000
Dec 10	Barnsley	L 0-4		4,000
Dec 17	LEICESTER FOSSE	L 2-3	Enright, Morris	5,000
Dec 24	Wolverhampton W	L 1-3	Gillespie	6,000
Dec 26	CHELSEA	D 3-3	Roberts, Croot, McLeod	18,000
Dec 27	CLAPTON ORIENT	W 1-0	Mulholland	10,000
Dec 31	Blackpool	W 2-1	McLeod, Bridgett	1,000
Jan 7	GLOSSOP NORTH END	L 0-2		10,000
Jan 21	Lincoln City	D 1-1	Enright	5,000
Jan 28	HUDDERSFIELD TOWN	W 5-2	Croot 2(1 Pen), McLeod 2, Mulholland	10,000
Feb 4	Birmingham	L 1-2	McLeod	15,000
Feb 11	West Bromwich Albion	W 3-1	McLeod, Mulholland, Enright	10,700
Feb 18	Hull City	D 1-1	Enright	6,000
Feb 25	FULHAM	W 3-1	Croot (pen), Enright, Mulholland	6,000
Mar 4	Bradford Park Avenue	W 2-0	Croot (pen), Mulholland	12,000
Mar 18	Gainsborough Town	W 2-1	Enright, Roberts	4,000
Mar 25	BOLTON WANDERERS	W 1-0	Mulholland	15,000
Mar 27	BURNLEY	D 0-0		5,500
Apr 1	STOCKPORT COUNTY	W 4-0	McLeod 2, Mulholland 2	9,000
Apr 8	Derby County	D 2-2	Croot (pen), Mulholland	5,000
Apr 14	Chelsea	L 1-4	McLeod	5,000
Apr 15	BARNSLEY	D 0-0		10,000
Apr 17	Clapton Orient	L 0-1		6,000
Apr 22	Leicester Fosse	L 1-2	Croot	5,000
Apr 29	WOLVERHAMPTON W	W 1-0	Enright	6,000

FA Cup

Jan 14	BRIGHTON	(Rd 1) L 1-3	Roberts	17,000

League & Cup Appearances

PLAYER	LEAGUE	CUP COMPETITION FA CUP	TOTAL
Affleck	37	1	38
Bridgett	8	1	9
Bromage	25	1	26
Creighton	38	1	39
Croot	30		30
Cubberley	34	1	35
Cunningham	3		3
Enright	37	1	38
Foley	4		4
Gillespie	18		28
Harkins	31	1	32
Hogg	13		13
Horsley	9		9
Kelly	3		3
McLeod	35	1	36
Morris	36	1	37
Mulholland	21	1	22
Roberts	35	1	36
White	1		1

Goalscorers

PLAYER	LEAGUE	CUP COMPETITION FA CUP	TOTAL
McLeod	13		13
Enright	9		9
Gillespie	9		9
Mulholland	9		9
Croot	8		8
Roberts	5	1	6
Bridgett	2		2
Morris	2		2

Fact File

Leeds lost all of their first four matches this season.

MANAGER: Frank Scott-Walford
CAPTAIN: George Affleck
TOP SCORER: Billy McLeod
BIGGEST WIN: 5-2 v Huddersfield Town, 28 January 1911, League
HIGHEST ATTENDANCE: 50,000 v Chelsea, 14 April 1911, lost 1-4, League

Final Division 2 Table

		P	W	D	L	F	A	Pts
1	WBA	38	22	9	7	67	41	53
2	Bolton W	38	21	9	8	69	40	51
3	Chelsea	38	20	9	9	71	35	49
4	Clapton Orient	38	19	7	12	44	35	45
5	Hull C	38	14	16	8	55	39	44
6	Derby Co	38	17	8	13	73	52	42
7	Blackpool	38	16	10	12	49	38	42
8	Burnley	38	13	15	10	45	45	41
9	Wolverhampton W	38	15	8	15	51	52	38
10	Fulham	38	15	7	16	52	48	37
11	Leeds City	38	15	7	16	58	56	37
12	Bradford PA	38	14	9	15	53	55	37
13	Huddersfield T	38	13	8	17	57	58	34
14	Glossop	38	13	8	17	48	62	34
15	Leicester Fosse	38	14	5	19	52	62	33
16	Birmingham	38	12	8	18	42	64	32
17	Stockport Co	38	11	8	19	47	79	30
18	Gainsborough T	38	9	11	18	37	55	29
19	Barnsley	38	7	14	17	52	62	28
20	Lincoln C	38	7	10	21	28	72	24

Season 1911-12

Football League Division 2

DATE	OPPONENTS	SCORE	GOALSCORERS	ATTENDANCE
Sep 2	Nottingham Forest	L 1-2	McLeod	10,000
Sep 4	Burnley	L 2-4	McLeod, Enright	15,000
Sep 9	CHELSEA	D 0-0		15,000
Sep 16	Clapton Orient	L 1-2	McLeod	13,000
Sep 23	BRISTOL CITY	W 3-1	Croot, Enright, McLeod	10,000
Sep 30	Birmingham	L 3-4	Enright, Roberts, Croot	10,000
Oct 7	HUDDERSFIELD TOWN	W 2-0	McLeod, Enright	12,000
Oct 14	Blackpool	L 0-3		4,000
Oct 21	GLOSSOP NORTH END	W 2-1	Mulholland, Croot	6,000
Oct 28	Hull City	L 0-1		10,000
Nov 4	BARNSLEY	W 3-2	McLeod, Mulholland 2	12,000
Nov 11	Bradford Park Avenue	D 1-1	Croot (pen)	13,000
Nov 18	FULHAM	L 0-2		8,000
Nov 25	Derby County	L 2-5	McLeod, Roberts	12,000
Dec 4	GRIMSBY TOWN	L 1-2	McLeod	3,000
Dec 9	BURNLEY	L 1-5	Gillespie (pen)	10,000
Dec 16	Wolverhampton W	L 0-5		8,000
Dec 23	LEICESTER FOSSE	W 2-1	Enright 2	6,000
Dec 25	GAINSBOROUGH TOWN	D 0-0		9,000
Dec 26	Gainsborough Town	L 1-2	Mulholland	6,000
Dec 30	NOTTINGHAM FOREST	W 3-1	Mulholland 2, Enright	8,000
Jan 6	Chelsea	L 2-4	McLeod, Foley	10,000
Jan 20	CLAPTON ORIENT	L 0-2		5,000
Jan 23	Grimsby Town	W 2-1	Johnson, Enright	3,000
Jan 27	Bristol City	L 1-4	Croot (pen)	7,000
Feb 10	Huddersfield Town	W 2-1	Mulholland 2	8,000
Feb 17	BLACKPOOL	W 1-0	Enright	6,000
Feb 24	Glossop North End	L 1-2	Mulholland	3,000
Mar 2	HULL CITY	D 0-0		8,000
Mar 16	BRADFORD PARK AVENUE	L 1-2	Foley	10,000
Mar 23	Fulham	L 2-7	Enright, Mulholland	3,000
Mar 30	DERBY COUNTY	L 0-1		4,500
Apr 5	BIRMINGHAM	D 0-0		5,000
Apr 6	STOCKPORT COUNTY	D 1-1	Enright	4,000
Apr 11	Barnsley	W 4-3	McLeod 2, Croot (2 pen)	3,000
Apr 15	Stockport County	D 3-3	McLeod 2, Mulholland	3,000
Apr 20	WOLVERHAMPTON W	D 1-1	McLeod	5,000
Apr 27	Leicester Fosse	L 1-2	Enright	10,000

FA Cup

Jan 13	Glossop North End	(Rd 1) W 1-0	Roberts	21,000
Feb 3	WEST BROMWICH ALBION	(Rd 2) L 0-1		21,320

League & Cup Appearances

PLAYER	LEAGUE	CUP COMPETITION FA CUP	TOTAL
Affleck	37	2	39
Bridgett	3		3
Campbell	1		1
Clarkin	1		1
Croot	32	2	34
Creighton	28	2	30
Cubberley	20		20
Enright	34	2	36
Foley	9	1	10
Fortune	1		1
Gillespie	6		6
Harkins	32	2	34
Heaney	2		2
Hogg	8		8
Johnson	7		7
Kelly	1		1
McDaniel	1		1
McLeod	31	1	32
Moran	24	2	26
Morris	37	2	39
Mulholland	35	2	37
Murphy	18	1	19
Reinhardt	12	1	13
Roberts	38	2	40

Goalscorers

PLAYER	LEAGUE	CUP COMPETITION FA CUP	TOTAL
McLeod	14		14
Enright	12		12
Mulholland	11		11
Croot	7		7
Roberts	2	1	3
Foley	2		2
Gillespie	1		1
Johnson	1		1

Fact File

Finishing 19th, Leeds City were forced to seek re-election to the Football League.

MANAGER: Frank Scott-Walford

CAPTAIN: George Affleck

TOP SCORER: Billy McLeod

BIGGEST WIN: 4-3 v Barnsley, 11 April 1912, League

HIGHEST ATTENDANCE: 15,000 v Burnley, 4 September 1911, lost 2-4, League; 15,000 v Chelsea, 9 September 1911, drew 0-0, League

Final Division 2 Table

		P	W	D	L	F	A	Pts
1	DERBY CO	38	23	8	7	74	28	54
2	CHELSEA	38	24	6	8	64	34	54
3	BURNLEY	38	22	8	8	77	41	52
4	CLAPTON ORIENT	38	21	3	14	61	44	45
5	WOLVERHAMPTON W	38	16	10	12	57	33	42
6	BARNSLEY	38	15	12	11	45	42	42
7	HULL C	38	17	8	13	54	51	42
8	FULHAM	38	16	7	15	66	58	39
9	GRIMSBY T	38	15	9	14	48	55	39
10	LEICESTER FOSSE	38	15	7	16	49	66	37
11	BRADFORD PA	38	13	9	16	44	45	35
12	BIRMINGHAM	38	14	6	18	55	59	34
13	BRISTOL C	38	14	6	18	41	60	34
14	BLACKPOOL	38	13	8	17	32	52	34
15	NOTTINGHAM F	38	13	7	18	46	48	33
16	STOCKPORT CO	38	11	11	16	47	54	33
17	HUDDERSFIELD T	38	13	6	19	50	64	32
18	GLOSSOP	38	8	12	18	42	56	28
19	LEEDS CITY	38	10	8	20	50	78	28
20	GAINSBOROUGH T	38	5	13	20	30	64	23

Season 1912-13

Football League Division 2

DATE	OPPONENTS	SCORE	GOALSCORERS	ATTENDANCE
Sep 7	Fulham	L 0-4		20,000
Sep 14	BARNSLEY	W 2-0	Robertson, Croot (pen)	15,000
Sep 21	Bradford Park Avenue	W 1-0	Cubberley	18,000
Sep 28	WOLVERHAMPTON W	D 2-2	McLeod, Croot (pen)	20,000
Oct 5	Leicester Fosse	D 1-1	Robertson	10,000
Oct 12	STOCKPORT COUNTY	W 2-1	McLeod 2	15,000
Oct 19	Preston North End	L 2-3	McLeod, Enright	9,000
Oct 26	BURNLEY	W 4-1	Robertson 2, McLeod, Cubberley	10,000
Nov 2	Hull City	L 2-6	McLeod, Croot (pen)	12,000
Nov 9	GLOSSOP NORTH END	W 4-0	McLeod 3, Foley	12,000
Nov 16	Clapton Orient	L 0-2		10,000
Nov 23	LINCOLN CITY	D 2-2	Robertson, Lintott	15,000
Nov 30	Nottingham Forest	W 2-1	Robertson, Roberts	8,000
Dec 7	BRISTOL CITY	D 1-1	Robertson	10,000
Dec 14	Birmingham	D 2-2	McLeod 2	21,000
Dec 21	HUDDERSFIELD TOWN	L 0-3		15,000
Dec 25	GRIMSBY TOWN	L 1-2	Cubberley	15,000
Dec 26	BLACKPOOL	L 0-2		8,000
Dec 28	FULHAM	L 2-3	Bainbridge, Price	10,000
Jan 1	Blackpool	W 3-0	Croot, Bainbridge, McLeod	5,000
Jan 4	Barnsley	L 0-2		5,000
Jan 18	BRADFORD PARK AVENUE	W 2-0	Foley, Spiers	10,000
Jan 25	Wolverhampton W	D 2-2	Bainbridge, McLeod	8,000
Feb 8	LEICESTER FOSSE	W 5-1	Price 2, Spiers, Fenwick, McLeod	10,000
Feb 15	Stockport County	L 0-6		7,000
Feb 22	PRESTON NORTH END	W 5-1	Affleck (pen), Fenwick 2, Bainbridge, Foley	18,000
Mar 1	Burnley	D 2-2	McLeod, Spiers	12,000
Mar 8	HULL CITY	W 1-0	McLeod	20,000
Mar 15	Glossop North End	L 1-2	McLeod	2,000
Mar 21	Grimsby Town	L 2-3	McLeod 2	8,000
Mar 22	CLAPTON ORIENT	W 3-1	Spiers 2, McLeod	6,000
Mar 24	Bury	D 1-1	McLeod	10,000
Mar 25	BURY	W 4-2	McLeod 3, Spiers	17,000
Mar 29	Lincoln City	D 3-3	Spiers, McLeod, Croot	9,000
Apr 5	NOTTINGHAM FOREST	W 1-0	McLeod	20,000
Apr 12	Bristol City	D 1-1	Spiers	15,000
Apr 19	BIRMINGHAM	W 4-0	Spiers 2, McLeod, Foley	8,000
Apr 26	Huddersfield Town	L 0-1		8,000

FA Cup

Jan 15	Burnley	(Rd 1) L 2-3	McLeod, Foley	13,109

League & Cup Appearances

PLAYER	LEAGUE	CUP COMPETITION FA CUP	TOTAL
Affleck	19	1	20
Allan	14	1	15
Bainbridge	24	1	25
Bridgett	1		1
Broughton	4		4
Copeland	20		20
Croot	32	1	33
Cubberley	16		16
Enright	6		6
Fenwick	5		5
Ferguson	17		17
Foley	36	1	37
Gibson	5		5
Hogg	14	1	15
Law	35	1	36
Lintott	38	1	39
McLeod	38	1	39
Moran	1		1
Price	12		12
Roberts	11		11
Robertson	27	1	28
Scott	24		24
Speirs	19	1	20

Goalscorers

PLAYER	LEAGUE	CUP COMPETITION FA CUP	TOTAL
McLeod	26	1	27
Speirs	10		10
Robertson	7		7
Croot	5		5
Foley	4	1	5
Bainbridge	4		4
Cubberley	3		3
Fenwick	3		3
Price	3		3
Affleck	1		1
Enright	1		1
Lintott	1		1
Roberts	1		1

Fact File

An FA Cup replay at Elland Road between Bradford City and Barnsley saw chaos descend with the Leeds stadium ill-equipped to deal with the 45,000 spectators who turned up to watch the game.

MANAGER: Herbert Chapman

CAPTAIN: George Affleck

TOP SCORER: Billy McLeod

BIGGEST WIN: 5-1 v Leicester Fosse, 8 February 1913, League

HIGHEST ATTENDANCE: 21,000 v Birmingham, 14 December 1912, drew 2-2, League

MAJOR TRANSFERS IN: Billy Scott from Everton, Evelyn Lintott and Jimmy Speirs from Bradford City, Jimmy Robertson from Barrow

Final Division 2 Table

		P	W	D	L	F	A	Pts
1	PRESTON NE	38	19	15	4	56	33	53
2	BURNLEY	38	21	8	9	88	53	50
3	BIRMINGHAM	38	18	10	10	59	44	46
4	BARNSLEY	38	19	7	12	57	47	45
5	HUDDERSFIELD T	38	17	9	12	66	40	43
6	LEEDS CITY	38	15	10	13	70	64	40
7	GRIMSBY T	38	15	10	13	51	50	40
8	LINCOLN C	38	15	10	13	50	52	40
9	FULHAM	38	17	5	16	65	55	39
10	WOLVERHAMPTON W	38	14	10	14	56	54	38
11	BURY	38	15	8	15	53	57	38
12	HULL C	38	15	6	17	60	55	36
13	BRADFORD PA	38	14	8	16	60	60	36
14	CLAPTON ORIENT	38	10	14	14	34	47	34
15	LEICESTER FOSSE	38	13	7	18	49	65	33
16	BRISTOL C	38	9	15	14	46	72	33
17	NOTTINGHAM F	38	12	8	18	58	59	32
18	GLOSSOP	38	12	8	18	49	68	32
19	STOCKPORT CO	38	8	10	20	56	78	26
20	BLACKPOOL	38	9	8	21	39	69	26

Season 1913-14

Football League Division 2

DATE	OPPONENTS	SCORE	GOALSCORERS	ATTENDANCE
Sep 6	GLOSSOP NORTH END	W 3-0	Speirs, McLeod 2	8,000
Sep 13	Stockport County	L 1-2	McLeod	10,000
Sep 20	BRADFORD PARK AVENUE	W 5-1	Speirs, Price, Bainbridge 2, McLeod	23,000
Sep 27	Notts County	L 0-4		12,000
Oct 4	LEICESTER FOSSE	W 2-1	Bainbridge, Price	18,000
Oct 11	Wolverhampton W	W 3-1	Speirs 2, Sharpe (pen)	10,000
Oct 18	HULL CITY	L 1-2	Speirs	20,000
Oct 25	Barnsley	W 4-1	Speirs 2, Price, McLeod	12,000
Nov 1	BURY	W 2-1	Price, Speirs	20,000
Nov 8	Huddersfield Town	D 1-1	Turner	9,000
Nov 15	LINCOLN CITY	W 1-0	McLeod	12,000
Nov 22	Blackpool	D 2-2	Hampson, Croot	5,000
Nov 29	NOTTINGHAM FOREST	W 8-0	McLeod 4, Price 2, Hampson, Speirs	14,000
Dec 6	The Arsenal	L 0-1		18,000
Dec 13	GRIMSBY TOWN	W 4-1	McLeod 2, Hampson, Price	10,000
Dec 20	Birmingham	W 2-0	McLeod, Sharpe	15,000
Dec 25	FULHAM	W 2-1	McLeod, Hampson	30,000
Dec 26	Fulham	W 1-0	McLeod	25,000
Dec 27	Glossop North End	D 1-1	Bainbridge	2,000
Jan 3	STOCKPORT COUNTY	W 5-1	Speirs, Jackson 2, McLeod, Sharpe	10,000
Jan 17	Bradford Park Avenue	L 1-3	McLeod	32,184
Jan 24	NOTTS COUNTY	L 2-4	Sharpe, Hampson	25,000
Feb 7	Leicester Fosse	L 1-5	Speirs	4,000
Feb 14	WOLVERHAMPTON W	W 5-0	McLeod 3, Speirs, Sharpe	10,000
Feb 21	Hull City	L 0-1		18,000
Feb 28	BARNSLEY	W 3-0	McLeod, Sharpe 2 (1 pen)	20,000
Mar 2	Clapton Orient	L 1-3	Hampson	7,000
Mar 7	Bury	D 1-1	Jackson	12,000
Mar 14	HUDDERSFIELD TOWN	W 5-1	Hampson, McLeod 3, Speirs	14,000
Mar 21	Lincoln City	L 0-1		8,000
Mar 28	BLACKPOOL	W 2-1	McLeod, Hampson	12,000
Apr 4	Nottingham Forest	L 1-2	Law	6,000
Apr 10	Bristol City	D 1-1	McLeod	20,000
Apr 11	THE ARSENAL	D 0-0		25,000
Apr 13	BRISTOL CITY	W 1-0	Turner	12,000
Apr 14	CLAPTON ORIENT	D 0-0		12,000
Apr 18	Grimsby Town	W 1-0	Price	9,000
Apr 25	BIRMINGHAM	W 3-2	Price, Stuart o.g., McLeod	10,000

FA Cup

Jan 10	Gainsborough Town	(Rd 1) W 4-2	Jackson 2, Law, McLeod	14,000
Jan 31	West Bromwich Albion	(Rd 2) L 0-2		29,733

League & Cup Appearances

PLAYER	LEAGUE	CUP COMPETITION FA CUP	TOTAL
Affleck	38	2	40
Bainbridge	15	2	17
Blackman	14		14
Copeland	23	1	24
Croot	10		10
Dougherty	1		1
Foley	38	2	40
Hampson	36	2	38
Hogg	36	2	38
Jackson	22	2	24
Johnson	1		1
Lamph	1		1
Law	35	2	37
Lintott	5	1	6
McLeod	37	2	39
Peart	1		1
Price	35		35
Scott	2		2
Sharpe	35	2	37
Speirs	29	2	31
Turner	4		4

Goalscorers

PLAYER	LEAGUE	CUP COMPETITION FA CUP	TOTAL
McLeod	27	1	28
Speirs	12		12
Price	9		9
Hampson	8		8
Sharpe	7		7
Jackson	3	2	5
Bainbridge	4		4
Law	1	1	2
Turner	2		2
Croot	1		1
Stuart	1		1
Opps' o.gs.	1		1

Fact File

Leeds City appealed unsuccessfully against the result of the match at Clapton Orient, goalkeeper Billy Scott claiming it was too dark to see the last two goals he conceded.

MANAGER: Herbert Chapman

CAPTAIN: John Hampson

TOP SCORER: Billy McLeod

BIGGEST WIN: 8-0 v Nottingham Forest, 29 November 1913, League

HIGHEST ATTENDANCE: 32,184 v Bradford, 17 January 1914, lost 1-3, League

MAJOR TRANSFERS IN: Ivan Sharpe from Derby County, John Hampson from Northampton, Fred Blackman from Huddersfield Town

Final Division 2 Table

		P	W	D	L	F	A	Pts
1	Notts Co	38	23	7	8	77	36	53
2	Bradford PA	38	23	3	12	71	47	49
3	The Arsenal	38	20	9	9	54	38	49
4	Leeds City	38	20	7	11	76	46	47
5	Barnsley	38	19	7	12	51	45	45
6	Clapton Orient	38	16	11	11	47	35	43
7	Hull C	38	16	9	13	53	37	41
8	Bristol C	38	16	9	13	52	50	41
9	Wolverhampton W	38	18	5	15	51	52	41
10	Bury	38	15	10	13	39	40	40
11	Fulham	38	16	6	16	46	43	38
12	Stockport Co	38	13	10	15	55	57	36
13	Huddersfield T	38	13	8	17	47	53	34
14	Birmingham	38	12	10	16	48	60	34
15	Grimsby T	38	13	8	17	42	58	34
16	Blackpool	38	9	14	15	33	44	32
17	Glossop	38	11	6	21	51	67	28
18	Leicester Fosse	38	11	4	23	45	61	26
19	Lincoln C	38	10	6	22	36	66	26
20	Nottingham F	38	7	9	22	37	76	23

Season 1914-15

Football League Division 2

DATE	OPPONENTS	SCORE	GOALSCORERS	ATTENDANCE
Sep 2	Fulham	L 0-1		8,000
Sep 5	Stockport County	L 1-3	Sharpe	5,000
Sep 9	Fulham	L 0-1		5,000
Sep 12	HULL CITY	L 2-3	Speirs, Jackson	8,000
Sep 19	BLACKPOOL	W 2-0	McLeod, Goodwin (pen)	8,000
Sep 26	Clapton Orient	L 0-2		9,000
Oct 3	THE ARSENAL	D 2-2	Goodwin (pen), Speirs	10,000
Oct 10	Derby County	W 2-1	Speirs, McLeod	5,000
Oct 17	LINCOLN CITY	W 3-1	McLeod, Speirs 2	10,000
Oct 24	Birmingham	L 3-6	Sharpe 2, Speirs	8,000
Oct 31	GRIMSBY TOWN	W 5-0	McLeod 2, Speirs, Bainbridge, Jackson	5,000
Nov 7	Huddersfield Town	L 0-1		14,000
Nov 14	BRISTOL CITY	D 1-1	McLeod	8,000
Nov 21	Bury	D 0-0		6,000
Nov 28	PRESTON NORTH END	D 0-0		7,000
Dec 5	Nottingham Forest	L 1-3	Speirs	3,000
Dec 12	LEICESTER FOSSE	W 7-2	Bainbridge 2, McLeod 2, Price 3	5,000
Dec 19	Barnsley	L 1-2	Sharpe	3,000
Dec 25	Glossop North End	W 3-0	Jackson 2, McLeod	1,000
Dec 26	GLOSSOP NORTH END	W 3-0	Bainbridge, Price, McLeod	6,000
Jan 2	STOCKPORT COUNTY	L 1-3	Speirs	7,000
Jan 16	Hull City	W 6-2	McLeod 5, Sharpe	5,000
Jan 23	Blackpool	L 0-1		6,000
Feb 3	CLAPTON ORIENT	L 0-1		4,000
Feb 6	The Arsenal	L 0-2		10,000
Feb 13	DERBY COUNTY	L 3-5	Edmondson, Speirs, Sharpe	5,000
Feb 20	Lincoln City	W 1-0	Edmondson	4,000
Feb 27	BIRMINGHAM	W 2-0	Jackson, Price	7,000
Mar 6	Grimsby Town	W 5-2	Edmondson, Jackson, Sharpe, Goodwin, Price	4,000
Mar 13	HUDDERSFIELD TOWN	W 1-0	Sharpe	12,000
Mar 20	Bristol City	L 0-1		5,000
Mar 27	BURY	W 2-1	McLeod, Price	6,000
Apr 3	Preston North End	L 0-2		5,000
Apr 5	Wolverhampton W	L 1-5	McLeod	15,000
Apr 6	WOLVERHAMPTON W	L 2-3	McLeod, Price	5,000
Apr 10	NOTTINGHAM FOREST	W 4-0	Price 3, Sharpe	4,000
Apr 17	Leicester Fosse	L 1-5	Jackson	3,000
Apr 24	BARNSLEY	L 0-2		5,000

FA Cup

Jan 9	Derby County	(Rd 1) W 2-1	McLeod, Sharpe	9,417
Jan 30	Queens Park Rangers	(Rd 2) L 0-1		10,000

League & Cup Appearances

PLAYER	LEAGUE	CUP COMPETITION FA CUP	TOTAL
Affleck	24	2	26
Bainbridge	18	2	20
Blackman	30	2	32
Copeland	1		1
Cowen	2		2
Cowen	2		2
Croot	5		5
Edmondson	5		5
Foley	35	2	37
Green	1		1
Goodwin	19		19
Hampson	28	1	29
Hogg	24	2	26
Jackson	32	2	34
Lamph	2		2
Law	35	2	37
Lawrence	6		6
McLeod	31	2	33
McQuillan	20		20
Peart	6	1	7
Price	24		24
Richardson	2		2
Rothwell	1		1
Sharpe	26	2	28
Speirs	25	2	27
Wainwright	2		2
Walker	14		14

Goalscorers

PLAYER	LEAGUE	CUP COMPETITION FA CUP	TOTAL
McLeod	18	1	19
Price	11		11
Sharpe	9	1	10
Speirs	10		10
Jackson	7		7
Bainbridge	4		4
Edmondson	3		3
Goodwin	3		3

Fact File

In August 1914 a syndicate of businessmen bought the club back from the Official Receiver.

MANAGER: Herbert Chapman

CAPTAIN: John Hampson

TOP SCORER: Billy McLeod

BIGGEST WIN: 7-2 v Leicester Fosse, 12 December 1914, League

HIGHEST ATTENDANCE: 15,000 v Wolverhampton Wanderers, 5 April 1915, lost 1-5, League

Final Division 2 Table

		P	W	D	L	F	A	PTS
1	DERBY CO	38	23	7	8	71	33	53
2	PRESTON NE	38	20	10	8	61	42	50
3	BARNSLEY	38	22	3	13	51	51	47
4	WOLVERHAMPTON W	38	19	7	12	77	52	45
5	THE ARSENAL	38	19	5	14	69	41	43
6	BIRMINGHAM	38	17	9	12	62	39	43
7	HULL C	38	19	5	14	65	54	43
8	HUDDERSFIELD T	38	17	8	13	61	42	42
9	CLAPTON ORIENT	38	16	9	13	50	48	41
10	BLACKPOOL	38	17	5	16	58	57	39
11	BURY	38	15	8	15	61	56	38
12	FULHAM	38	15	7	16	53	47	37
13	BRISTOL C	38	15	7	16	62	56	37
14	STOCKPORT CO	38	15	7	16	54	60	37
15	LEEDS CITY	38	14	4	20	65	64	32
16	LINCOLN C	38	11	9	18	46	65	31
17	GRIMSBY T	38	11	9	18	48	76	31
18	NOTTINGHAM F	38	10	9	19	43	77	29
19	LEICESTER FOSSE	38	10	4	24	47	88	24
20	GLOSSOP	38	6	6	26	31	87	18

Season 1919-20

Football League Division 2

DATE	OPPONENTS	SCORE	GOALSCORERS	ATTENDANCE
Aug 30	Blackpool	L 2-4	McLeod 2	10,000
Sep 3	COVENTRY CITY	W 3-0	McLeod 2, Bainbridge	8,000
Sep 6	BLACKPOOL	W 1-0	Edmondson	10,000
Sep 11	Coventry City	W 4-0	McLeod 2, Edmondson, Bainbridge	12,000
Sep 13	HULL CITY	L 1-2	Bainbridge	10,000
Sep 20	Hull City	D 1-1	Edmondson	8,000
Sep 27	WOLVERHAMPTON W	D 1-1	Price (pen)	12,000
Oct 4	Wolverhampton W	W 4-2	Lamph, McLeod 3	15,000

Remaining fixtures undertaken by Port Vale after Leeds City were expelled from the Football League.

League & Cup Appearances

PLAYER	LEAGUE	TOTAL
Affleck	2	2
Bainbridge	7	7
Edmondson	6	6
Foley	5	5
Goodwin	1	1
Hampson	7	7
Hopkins	7	7
Kirton	1	1
Lamph	8	8
Lounds	8	8
Millership	8	8
McLeod	8	8
Short	5	5
Price	7	7
Walker	8	8

Goalscorers

PLAYER	LEAGUE	TOTAL
McLeod	9	9
Bainbridge	3	3
Edmondson	3	3
Lamph	1	1
Price	1	1

Fact File

Billy McLeod, the brightest star of Leeds City's short history, bade farewell to their League status with a hat-trick against Wolves. He was sold to Notts County as Leeds City were auctioned off.

MANAGER: Herbert Chapman
CAPTAIN: John Hampson
TOP SCORER: Billy McLeod
BIGGEST WIN: 4-0 v Coventry City, September 11 1919, League
HIGHEST ATTENDANCE: 15,000 v Wolverhampton Wanderers, 4 October 1919, won 4-2, League

Final Division 2 Table*

		P	W	D	L	F	A	PTS
1	TOTTENHAM H	42	32	6	4	102	32	70
2	HUDDERSFIELD T	42	28	8	6	97	38	64
3	BIRMINGHAM	42	24	8	10	85	34	56
4	BLACKPOOL	42	21	10	11	65	47	52
5	BURY	42	20	8	14	60	44	48
6	FULHAM	42	19	9	14	61	50	47
7	WEST HAM U	42	19	9	14	47	40	47
8	BRISTOL C	42	13	17	12	46	43	43
9	SOUTH SHIELDS	42	15	12	15	58	48	42
10	STOKE	42	18	6	18	60	54	42
11	HULL C	42	18	6	18	78	72	42
12	BARNSLEY	42	15	10	17	61	55	40
13	PORT VALE	42	16	8	18	59	62	40
14	LEICESTER C	42	15	10	17	41	61	40
15	CLAPTON ORIENT	42	16	6	20	51	59	38
16	STOCKPORT CO	42	14	9	19	52	61	37
17	ROTHERHAM CO	42	13	8	21	51	83	34
18	NOTTINGHAM F	42	11	9	22	43	73	31
19	WOLVERHAMPTON W	42	10	10	22	55	80	30
20	COVENTRY C	42	9	11	22	35	73	29
21	LINCOLN C	42	9	9	24	44	101	27
22	GRIMSBY T	42	10	5	27	34	75	25

*LEEDS CITY WERE NOT INCLUDED IN THE FINAL TABLE AS THEY DID NOT FULFIL ALL THEIR FIXTURES.

Leeds United Season 1920-21

Football League Division 2

DATE	OPPONENTS	SCORE	GOALSCORERS	ATTENDANCE
Aug 28	Port Vale	L 0-2		19,000
Sep 1	SOUTH SHIELDS	L 1-2	Armitage	16,958
Sep 4	PORT VALE	W 3-1	Best, Ellson 2	15,000
Sep 8	South Shields	L 0-3		15,000
Sep 11	Leicester City	D 1-1	Ellson	16,000
Sep 18	LEICESTER CITY	W 3-1	Ellson, Goldthorpe 2 (1 pen)	11,000
Sep 25	Blackpool	L 0-1		8,000
Oct 2	BLACKPOOL	W 2-0	Walton, Mason	10,000
Oct 9	Sheffield Wednesday	L 0-2		20,000
Oct 16	SHEFFIELD WEDNESDAY	W 2-0	Thompson, Ellson	15,000
Oct 23	Hull City	W 1-0	Thompson	10,000
Oct 30	HULL CITY	D 1-1	Ellson	20,000
Nov 6	Stoke	L 0-4		10,000
Nov 13	STOKE	D 0-0		15,000
Nov 27	Coventry City	D 1-1	Lyon	18,000
Dec 1	COVENTRY CITY	W 4-0	Thompson 2, Ellson, Mason	10,000
Dec 4	Notts County	W 2-1	Lyon 2	14,000
Dec 11	NOTTS COUNTY	W 3-0	Thompson 3	12,000
Dec 18	Birmingham	L 0-1		20,000
Dec 25	FULHAM	D 0-0		25,000
Dec 27	Fulham	L 0-1		30,000
Jan 1	BIRMINGHAM	W 1-0	Baker (pen)	24,000
Jan 8	ROTHERHAM	W 1-0	Ellson	18,000
Jan 15	Wolverhampton W	L 0-3		20,000
Jan 22	WOLVERHAMPTON W	W 3-0	Thompson 2, Lyon	14,000
Jan 29	WEST HAM UNITED	L 1-2	Thompson	15,000
Feb 5	West Ham United	L 0-3		23,000
Feb 12	Stockport County	L 1-3	Thompson	9,000
Feb 19	STOCKPORT COUNTY	L 0-2		20,000
Feb 26	Clapton Orient	L 0-1		17,000
Mar 5	CLAPTON ORIENT	W 2-1	Musgrove, Baker (pen)	18,000
Mar 12	Bury	D 1-1	Howarth	10,000
Mar 19	BURY	W 1-0	Musgrove	16,000
Mar 26	BRISTOL CITY	L 0-1		20,000
Mar 28	Cardiff City	L 0-1		30,000
Mar 29	CARDIFF CITY	L 1-2	Howarth	20,000
Apr 2	Bristol City	D 0-0		24,000
Apr 9	BARNSLEY	D 0-0		13,000
Apr 16	Barnsley	D 1-1	Howarth	12,000
Apr 23	NOTTINGHAM FOREST	D 1-1	Howarth	12,000
Apr 30	Nottingham Forest	L 0-1		8,000
May 7	Rotherham	W 2-0	Howarth 2 (1 pen)	10,000

FA Cup

Sep 11	BOOTHTOWN	(1QR) W 5-2	Armitage 2, O'Doherty 3	1,500
Sep 25	Leeds Steelworks	(2QR) W 7-0	Butler 3, Thompson, Hart, O'Doherty, Waterhouse	3,000

Leeds withdrew from the competition after the second Qualifying Round.

League & Cup Appearances

PLAYER	LEAGUE	CUP COMPETITION FA CUP	TOTAL
Armitage	6	1	7
Baker	42		42
Best	11		11
Boardman	4		4
Brock	6		6
Butler	1	2	3
Coope		2	2
Cooper		2	2
Down	42		42
Duffield	42		42
Ellson	36		36
Frew	36		36
Goldthorpe	6		6
Hart	5	2	7
Hill	7	1	8
Howarth	11		11
Jacklin		2	2
Lamph	6		6
Lyon	33		33
Mason	35		35
McGee		1	1
Musgrove	36		36
O'Doherty		2	2
Powell	3		3
Rodgerson	3		3
Sharpe	1		1
Smelt	1	1	2
Stuart	1	2	3
Thompson	23	2	25
Tillotson	2		2
Walton	41		41
Waterhouse		2	2
Wood	22		22

Goalscorers

PLAYER	LEAGUE	CUP COMPETITION FA CUP	TOTAL
Thompson	11	1	12
Ellson	8		8
Howarth	6		6
O'Doherty		4	4
Armitage	1	2	3
Butler		3	3
Lyon	3		3
Musgrove	3		3
Baker	2		2
Goldthorp	2		2
Mason	2		2
Best	1		1
Hart		1	1
Walton	1		1
Waterhouse		1	1

Fact File

Leeds United's colours for their first League season were blue and white striped shirts and white shorts.

MANAGER: Arthur Fairclough

CAPTAIN: Jim Baker

TOP SCORER: Robert Thompson

BIGGEST WIN: 7-0 v Leeds Steelworks, 25 September 1920, FA Cup, 2nd Qualifying Round

HIGHEST ATTENDANCE: 30,000 v Fulham, 27 December 1920, lost 0-1, League; 30,000 v Cardiff City, 28 March 1921, lost 0-1, League

MAJOR TRANSFERS IN: Tommy Howarth from Bristol City, Jack Swan from Huddersfield

Final Division 2 Table

		P	W	D	L	F	A	Pts
1	BIRMINGHAM	42	24	10	8	79	38	58
2	CARDIFF C	42	24	10	8	59	32	58
3	BRISTOL C	42	19	13	10	49	29	51
4	BLACKPOOL	42	20	10	12	54	42	50
5	WEST HAM U	42	19	10	13	51	30	48
6	NOTTS CO	42	18	11	13	55	40	47
7	CLAPTON ORIENT	42	16	13	13	43	42	45
8	SOUTH SHIELDS	42	17	10	15	61	46	44
9	FULHAM	42	16	10	16	43	47	42
10	SHEFFIELD W	42	15	11	16	48	48	41
11	BURY	42	15	10	17	45	49	40
12	LEICESTER C	42	12	16	14	39	46	40
13	HULL C	42	10	20	12	43	53	40
14	LEEDS UNITED	42	14	10	18	40	45	38
15	WOLVERHAMPTON W	42	16	6	20	49	66	38
16	BARNSLEY	42	10	16	16	48	50	36
17	PORT VALE	42	11	14	17	43	49	36
18	NOTTINGHAM F	42	12	12	18	48	55	36
19	ROTHERHAM CO	42	12	12	18	37	53	36
20	STOKE	42	12	11	19	46	56	35
21	COVENTRY C	42	12	11	19	39	70	35
22	STOCKPORT CO	42	9	12	21	42	75	30

Season 1921-22

Football League Division 2

DATE	OPPONENTS	SCORE	GOALSCORERS	ATTENDANCE
Aug 27	PORT VALE	W 2-1	Howarth, Walton	18,000
Aug 29	Bristol City	D 0-0		16,000
Sep 3	Port Vale	W 1-0	Howarth	18,000
Sep 5	BRISTOL CITY	W 3-0	Howarth 2, Moore	18,000
Sep 10	BLACKPOOL	D 0-0		18,000
Sep 17	Blackpool	W 3-1	Howarth, Wood, Mason	15,000
Sep 24	CLAPTON ORIENT	W 2-0	Wood, Howarth	20,000
Oct 1	Clapton Orient	L 2-4	Howarth (pen), Moore	20,000
Oct 8	SOUTH SHIELDS	D 0-0		20,000
Oct 15	South Shields	W 1-0	Howarth	15,000
Oct 22	STOKE	W 1-2	Howarth	10,000
Oct 29	Stoke	L 0-3		15,000
Nov 5	BRADFORD PARK AVENUE	D 3-0	Howarth (pen), Armitage, Mason	18,000
Nov 12	Bradford Park Avenue	W 1-0	Howarth	20,000
Nov 19	Hull City	L 0-1		12,800
Nov 26	HULL CITY	L 0-2		20,000
Dec 3	Notts County	W 1-4	Howarth	12,000
Dec 10	NOTTS COUNTY	W 1-1	Moore	16,000
Dec 17	CRYSTAL PALACE	L 0-0		10,000
Dec 24	Crystal Palace	L 2-1	Swan, Moore	10,000
Dec 26	SHEFFIELD WEDNESDAY	L 1-1	Swan	20,540
Dec 27	Sheffield Wednesday	D 1-2	Howarth	25,000
Dec 31	ROTHERHAM COUNTY	D 0-2		12,000
Jan 14	Rotherham County	W 0-1		6,000
Jan 21	WEST HAM UNITED	D 0-0		7,000
Jan 28	West Ham United	D 1-1	Armitage	20,000
Feb 4	BURY	W 2-0	Armitage, Poyntz	5,000
Feb 11	Bury	L 1-2	Armitage	10,000
Feb 20	LEICESTER CITY	W 3-0	Poyntz 3	5,000
Feb 25	Leicester City	D 0-0		14,000
Mar 4	DERBY COUNTY	W 2-1	Swan 2	12,000
Mar 11	Derby County	L 0-2		9,000
Mar 18	Coventry City	L 0-1		15,000
Mar 25	COVENTRY CITY	W 5-2	Armitage 2, Swan 3	10,000
Apr 1	Barnsley	D 2-2	Swan, Armitage	12,660
Apr 8	BARNSLEY	W 4-0	Swan 2, Gittins o.g., Poyntz	10,000
Apr 14	FULHAM	W 2-0	Poyntz, Coates	20,000
Apr 15	Wolverhampton W	D 0-0		10,000
Apr 17	Fulham	W 1-0	Armitage	20,000
Apr 22	WOLVERHAMPTON W	D 0-0		7,000
Apr 29	Nottingham Forest	L 0-1		16,000
May 6	NOTTINGHAM FOREST	D 0-0		10,000

FA Cup

Jan 7	Swindon Town	(Rd 1) L 1-2	Swan	16,000

League & Cup Appearances

PLAYER	LEAGUE	CUP COMPETITION FA CUP	TOTAL
Armitage	31	1	32
Baker	42	1	43
Clark	10		10
Coates	20		20
Down	1		1
Duffield	37	1	38
Ellson	1		1
Frew	23		23
Gascoigne	6		6
Hart	32		32
Howarth	28	1	29
Jacklin	3		3
Mason	17	1	18
Moore	27	1	28
Potts	1		1
Powell	2		2
Poyntz	15		15
Robson	3		3
Rodgerson	24	1	25
Sherwin	28	1	29
Swan	22	1	23
Walton	17	1	18
Whalley	38	1	39
Wood	34		34

Goalscorers

PLAYER	LEAGUE	CUP COMPETITION FA CUP	TOTAL
Howarth	13		13
Swan	10	1	11
Armitage	8		8
Poyntz	6		6
Moore	3		3
Mason	2		2
Wood	1		1
Walton	1		1
Opps' o.g.	1		1

Final Division 2 Table

		P	W	D	L	F	A	Pts
1	NOTTINGHAM F	42	22	12	8	51	30	56
2	STOKE	42	18	6	8	60	44	52
3	BARNSLEY	42	22	8	12	67	52	52
4	WEST HAM U	42	20	8	14	52	39	48
5	HULL C	42	19	10	13	51	41	48
6	SOUTH SHIELDS	42	17	12	13	43	38	46
7	FULHAM	42	18	9	15	57	38	45
8	LEEDS UNITED	42	16	13	13	48	38	45
9	LEICESTER C	42	14	17	11	39	34	45
10	SHEFFIELD W	42	15	14	13	47	50	44
11	BURY	42	15	10	17	54	55	40
12	DERBY CO	42	15	9	18	60	64	39
13	NOTTS CO	42	12	15	15	47	51	39
14	CRYSTAL PALACE	42	13	13	16	45	51	39
15	CLAPTON ORIENT	42	15	9	18	43	50	39
16	ROTHERHAM CO	42	14	11	17	32	43	39
17	WOLVERHAMPTON W	42	13	11	18	44	49	37
18	PORT VALE	42	14	8	20	43	57	36
19	BLACKPOOL	42	15	5	22	44	57	35
20	COVENTRY C	42	12	10	20	51	60	34
21	BRADFORD PA	42	12	9	21	46	62	33
22	BRISTOL C	42	12	9	21	37	58	33

Fact File

For the second successive season, Jim Baker was an ever-present in the Leeds team.

MANAGER: Arthur Fairclough
CAPTAIN: Jim Baker
TOP SCORER: Tommy Howarth
BIGGEST WIN: 4-0 v Barnsley, 8 April 1922, League
HIGHEST ATTENDANCE: 25,000 v Sheffield Wednesday, 27 December 1921, lost 1-2, League

Season 1922-23

Football League Division 2

DATE	OPPONENTS	SCORE	GOALSCORERS	ATTENDANCE
Aug 26	BLACKPOOL	D 1-1	Swan	18,000
Aug 28	Southampton	W 1-0	Swan	16,000
Sep 2	Blackpool	L 0-1		15,000
Sep 4	SOUTHAMPTON	W 1-0	Harris	6,000
Sep 9	STOCKPORT COUNTY	W 2-0	Walton, Armitage	12,000
Sep 16	Stockport County	L 1-2	Armitage	14,000
Sep 23	BRADFORD CITY	W 1-0	Harris	20,000
Sep 30	Bradford City	W 2-0	Swan, Harris	22,000
Oct 7	Clapton Orient	L 0-3		14,000
Oct 14	CLAPTON ORIENT	D 0-0		15,000
Oct 21	LEICESTER CITY	D 0-0		12,000
Oct 28	Leicester City	L 1-2	Harris	20,000
Nov 4	WEST HAM UNITED	W 3-1	Whipp 3 (1 pen)	12,000
Nov 11	West Ham United	D 0-0		14,000
Nov 18	SOUTH SHIELDS	L 0-1		12,000
Nov 25	South Shields	W 2-0	Whipp, Poyntz	18,000
Dec 2	WOLVERHAMPTON W	W 1-0	Walton	14,000
Dec 9	Wolverhampton W	W 1-0	Hart	16,000
Dec 16	Coventry City	W 2-1	Richmond 2	12,000
Dec 23	COVENTRY CITY	W 1-0	Whipp	10,000
Dec 25	Bury	D 1-1	Whipp	20,000
Dec 26	BURY	D 0-0		27,000
Dec 30	Port Vale	W 2-1	Whipp 2	8,000
Jan 6	PORT VALE	W 2-1	Whipp 2	15,000
Jan 20	Manchester United	D 0-0		25,000
Jan 27	MANCHESTER UNITED	L 0-1		25,000
Feb 10	Barnsley	L 0-1		11,000
Feb 17	SHEFFIELD WEDNESDAY	D 0-0		14,000
Feb 24	Barnsley	D 1-1	Swan	8,000
Mar 3	HULL CITY	D 2-2	Swan 2	12,000
Mar 10	Hull City	L 1-3	Swan	14,000
Mar 17	Crystal Palace	L 0-1		15,000
Mar 19	Sheffield Wednesday	L 1-3	Powell	11,000
Mar 24	CRYSTAL PALACE	W 4-1	Whipp, Swan, Powell, Sherwin	8,000
Mar 30	ROTHERHAM COUNTY	W 2-0	Powell, Whipp	12,000
Mar 31	Fulham	L 0-3		16,000
Apr 2	Rotherham County	L 1-3	Harris (pen)	10,000
Apr 7	FULHAM	D 1-1	Whipp	10,000
Apr 14	Notts County	L 0-1		10,000
Apr 21	NOTTS COUNTY	W 3-0	Whipp 2, Powell	8,000
Apr 28	Derby County	W 1-0	Noble	5,000
May 5	DERBY COUNTY	W 1-0	Powell (pen)	4,000

FA Cup

Jan 13	Portsmouth	(Rd 1) D 0-0		26,046
Jan 17	PORTSMOUTH	(R) W 3-1	Whipp, Armitage, Swan	21,240
Feb 3	Bolton Wanderers	(Rd 2) L 1-3	Swan	43,389

League & Cup Appearances

PLAYER	LEAGUE	CUP COMPETITION FA CUP	TOTAL
Armand	7		7
Armitage	11	3	14
Baker	42	3	45
Bell T	1		1
Clark	3		3
Coates	1		1
Dark	3		3
Duffield	41	3	44
Frew	33	3	36
Gascoigne	11		11
Harris	39	3	42
Hart	41	3	44
Howarth	6		6
Mason	13		13
Noble	28	3	31
Potts	9		9
Powell	12		12
Poyntz	14		14
Richmond	5		5
Robson	7		7
Sherwin	28	3	31
Smith	2		2
Swan	23	2	25
Walton	11	1	12
Whalley	42	3	45
Whipp	29	3	32

Goalscorers

PLAYER	LEAGUE	CUP COMPETITION FA CUP	TOTAL
Whipp	15	1	16
Swan	8	2	10
Harris	5		5
Powell	5		5
Walton	2		2
Armitage	2	1	3
Richmond	2		2
Hart	1		1
Noble	1		1
Poyntz	1		1
Sherwin	1		1

Fact File

Percy Whipp scored a hat-trick on his debut against West Ham.

MANAGER: Arthur Fairclough

CAPTAIN: Jim Baker

TOP SCORER: Percy Whipp

BIGGEST WIN: 4-1 v Crystal Palace, 24 March 1923, League

HIGHEST ATTENDANCE: 47,000 v Bolton Wanderers, 3 February 1923, lost 1-3, FA Cup, Round 2

MAJOR TRANSFERS IN: Percy Whipp from Sunderland, Joe Richmond from Durham

Final Division 2 Table

		P	W	D	L	F	A	Pts
1	Notts Co	42	23	7	12	46	34	53
2	West Ham U	42	20	11	11	63	38	51
3	Leicester C	42	21	9	12	65	44	51
4	Manchester U	42	17	14	11	51	36	48
5	Blackpool	42	18	11	13	60	43	47
6	Bury	42	18	11	13	55	46	47
7	Leeds United	42	18	11	13	43	36	47
8	Sheffield W	42	17	12	13	54	47	46
9	Barnsley	42	17	11	14	62	51	45
10	Fulham	42	16	12	14	43	32	44
11	Southampton	42	14	14	14	40	40	42
12	Hull C	42	14	14	14	43	45	42
13	South Shields	42	15	10	17	35	44	40
14	Derby Co	42	14	11	17	46	50	39
15	Bradford C	42	12	13	17	41	45	37
16	Crystal Palace	42	13	11	18	54	62	37
17	Port Vale	42	14	9	19	39	51	37
18	Coventry C	42	15	7	20	46	63	37
19	Clapton Orient	42	12	12	18	40	50	36
20	Stockport Co	42	14	8	20	43	58	36
21	Rotherham Co	42	13	9	20	44	63	35
22	Wolverhampton W	42	9	9	24	42	77	27

Season 1923-24

Football League Division 2

DATE	OPPONENTS	SCORE	GOALSCORERS	ATTENDANCE
Aug 25	Stoke	D 1-1	Noble	12,000
Aug 27	CRYSTAL PALACE	W 3-0	Fullam, Noble, Whipp	10,000
Sep 1	STOKE	D 0-0		12,900
Sep 5	Crystal Palace	D 1-1	Whipp	8,000
Sep 8	Leicester City	L 0-2		18,000
Sep 15	LEICESTER CITY	L 1-2	Swan	15,000
Sep 22	Hull City	W 2-1	Swan 2,	11,500
Sep 29	HULL CITY	W 5-2	Richmond 3, Swan, Harris	12,000
Oct 6	Clapton Orient	W 1-0	Richmond	25,000
Oct 13	CLAPTON ORIENT	W 1-0	Harris	15,000
Oct 20	Port Vale	W 1-0	Richmond	10,000
Oct 27	PORT VALE	W 3-0	Swan 2, Richmond	12,000
Nov 3	BRADFORD CITY	W 1-0	Whipp	17,000
Nov 10	Bradford City	D 0-0		25,000
Nov 17	BARNSLEY	W 3-1	Swan 2, Whipp	12,000
Nov 24	Barnsley	W 3-1	Harris, Richmond 2	12,000
Dec 1	MANCHESTER UNITED	D 0-0		20,000
Dec 8	Manchester United	L 1-3	Whipp	30,000
Dec 15	BURY	L 1-2	Whipp (pen)	17,000
Dec 22	Bury	L 0-3		10,000
Dec 25	Oldham Athletic	D 2-2	Richmond 2	17,000
Dec 26	OLDHAM ATHLETIC	W 5-0	Swan 2, Richmond, Whipp 2	12,000
Jan 5	South Shields	L 0-2		10,000
Jan 19	Sheffield Wednesday	D 0-0		18,000
Jan 26	SHEFFIELD WEDNESDAY	W 1-0	Swan	15,000
Feb 9	COVENTRY CITY	W 3-1	Armand, Richmond, Harris	11,239
Feb 16	Bristol City	W 1-0	Swan	14,000
Feb 27	SOUTH SHIELDS	W 2-1	Whipp, Armand	8,000
Mar 1	Southampton	W 1-0	Hart	8,000
Mar 8	SOUTHAMPTON	W 3-0	Shelley o.g., Swan, Harris	15,000
Mar 10	Coventry City	L 1-2	Sherwin	6,000
Mar 15	FULHAM	W 3-0	Swan 2, Coates	18,000
Mar 19	BRISTOL CITY	D 0-0		8,000
Mar 22	Fulham	W 2-0	Fullam, Whipp	17,000
Mar 29	BLACKPOOL	D 0-0		25,000
Apr 5	Blackpool	D 1-1	Richmond	14,000
Apr 12	DERBY COUNTY	D 1-1	Whipp	20,000
Apr 18	Stockport County	D 1-1	Richmond	15,000
Apr 19	Derby County	L 0-2		21,622
Apr 21	STOCKPORT COUNTY	W 4-0	Swan 2, Richmond, Harris	22,500
Apr 26	NELSON	W 1-0	Coates	20,000
May 3	Nelson	L 1-3	Swan	10,000

FA Cup

Jan 12	STOKE	(Rd 1)	W 1-0	Whipp	26,500
Feb 2	West Ham United	(Rd 2)	D 1-1	Coates	30,123
Feb 6	WEST HAM UNITED	(R)	W 1-0	Whipp	31,071
Feb 23	Aston Villa	(Rd 3)	L 0-3		51,600

League & Cup Appearances

PLAYER	LEAGUE	CUP COMPETITION FA CUP	TOTAL
Allen	2		2
Armand	7	1	8
Baker J W	36	4	40
Baker L H	10		10
Bell A	1		1
Coates	18	3	21
Down	32	4	36
Duffield	38	4	42
Frew	4		4
Fullam	7		7
Gascoigne	3		3
Harris	41	4	45
Hart	29	4	33
Johnson	3		3
Lambert	1		1
Mason	10		10
Menzies	17	1	18
Noble	21		21
Powell	4		4
Richmond	34	4	38
Sherwin	30	4	34
Smith	9		9
Speak	23	3	26
Swan	36	4	40
Whalley	7		7
Whipp	39	4	43

Goalscorers

PLAYER	LEAGUE	CUP COMPETITION FA CUP	TOTAL
Swan	18		18
Richmond	15		15
Whipp	10	2	12
Harris	6		6
Coates	2	1	3
Armand	2		2
Fullam	2		2
Noble	2		2
Hart	1		1
Sherwin	1		1

Final Division 2 Table

		P	W	D	L	F	A	Pts
1	LEEDS UNITED	42	21	12	9	61	35	64
2	BURY	42	21	9	12	63	35	51
3	DERBY CO	42	21	9	12	75	42	51
4	BLACKPOOL	42	18	13	11	72	47	49
5	SOUTHAMPTON	42	17	14	11	52	31	48
6	STOKE	42	14	18	10	44	42	46
7	OLDHAM ATH	42	14	17	11	45	52	45
8	SHEFFIELD W	42	16	12	14	54	51	44
9	SOUTH SHIELDS	42	17	10	15	49	50	44
10	CLAPTON ORIENT	42	14	15	13	40	36	43
11	BARNSLEY	42	16	11	15	57	61	43
12	LEICESTER C	42	17	8	17	64	54	42
13	STOCKPORT CO	42	13	16	13	44	52	42
14	MANCHESTER U	42	13	14	15	52	44	40
15	CRYSTAL PALACE	42	13	13	16	53	65	39
16	PORT VALE	42	13	12	17	50	66	38
17	HULL C	42	10	17	15	46	51	37
18	BRADFORD C	42	11	15	16	35	48	37
19	COVENTRY C	42	11	13	18	52	68	35
20	FULHAM	42	10	14	18	45	56	34
21	NELSON	42	10	13	19	40	74	33
22	BRISTOL C	42	7	15	20	32	65	29

Fact File

Seven straight wins in the autumn sent Leeds to the top of the table.

MANAGER: Arthur Fairclough

CAPTAIN: Jim Baker

TOP SCORER: Jack Swan

BIGGEST WIN: 5-0 v Oldham Athletic, 26 December 1923, League

HIGHEST ATTENDANCE: 51,600 v Aston Villa, 23 February 1924, lost 0-3, FA Cup, Round 3

Season 1924-25

Football League Division 1

DATE	OPPONENTS	SCORE	GOALSCORERS	ATTENDANCE
Aug 30	SUNDERLAND	D 1-1	Swan	33,722
Sep 1	Notts County	L 0-1		16,000
Sep 6	Cardiff City	L 0-3		30,000
Sep 10	NOTTS COUNTY	D 1-1	Swan	18,000
Sep 13	PRESTON NORTH END	W 4-0	Swan 2, Thom, Harris	20,000
Sep 17	EVERTON	W 1-0	Thom	22,000
Sep 20	Burnley	D 1-1	Thom	23,000
Sep 27	HUDDERSFIELD TOWN	D 1-1	Swan	41,800
Oct 4	BIRMINGHAM	L 0-1		24,000
Oct 11	West Bromwich Albion	L 1-3	Robson	21,332
Oct 18	TOTTENHAM HOTSPUR	W 1-0	Whipp	23,000
Oct 25	Blackburn Rovers	W 3-2	Robson 2, Swan	20,000
Nov 1	WEST HAM UNITED	W 2-1	Richmond (pen), Swan	17,000
Nov 8	Sheffield United	D 1-1	Swan	30,000
Nov 15	NEWCASTLE UNITED	D 1-1	Whipp	30,000
Nov 22	Liverpool	L 0-1		20,000
Nov 29	NOTTINGHAM FOREST	D 1-1	Robson	20,000
Dec 6	Bury	L 0-1		15,000
Dec 13	MANCHESTER CITY	L 0-3		15,000
Dec 20	The Arsenal	L 1-6	Whipp	30,000
Dec 25	ASTON VILLA	W 6-0	Whipp 3, Swan 2, Hart	24,000
Dec 26	Aston Villa	L 1-2	Swan	50,000
Dec 27	Sunderland	L 1-2	Richmond	18,000
Jan 3	CARDIFF CITY	D 0-0		19,000
Jan 17	Preston North End	W 4-1	Whipp 2, Powell 2	15,000
Jan 24	BURNLEY	L 0-2		15,000
Jan 31	Huddersfield Town	L 0-2		12,000
Feb 7	Birmingham	D 0-0		20,000
Feb 14	WEST BROMWICH ALBION	L 0-1		18,500
Feb 28	BLACKBURN ROVERS	D 1-1	Noble	17,000
Mar 7	West Ham United	D 0-0		15,000
Mar 9	Tottenham Hotspur	L 1-2	Armand	12,000
Mar 14	SHEFFIELD UNITED	D 1-1	Harris	25,000
Mar 21	Newcastle United	L 1-4	Wainscoat	15,000
Mar 28	LIVERPOOL	W 4-1	Wainscoat, Armand, Harris, Jennings	25,000
Apr 4	Nottingham Forest	L 0-4		5,000
Apr 10	Bolton Wanderers	L 0-1		25,000
Apr 11	BURY	W 1-0	Jennings	25,000
Apr 14	BOLTON WANDERERS	W 2-1	Wainscoat, Jennings	30,000
Apr 18	Manchester City	L 2-4	Wainscoat, Whipp	14,000
Apr 25	THE ARSENAL	W 1-0	Whipp	20,000
May 2	Everton	L 0-1		10,000

FA Cup

Jan 10	Liverpool	(Rd 1) L 0-3		39,000

League & Cup Appearances

PLAYER	LEAGUE	CUP COMPETITION FA CUP	TOTAL
Armand	14	1	15
Atkinson	13		13
Baker J W	29		29
Baker L H	1		1
Clark	3		3
Coates	8		8
Down	21	1	22
Duffield	39		39
Duxbury	3		3
Edwards	9		9
Graver	3		3
Harris	42	1	43
Hart	37	1	38
Jennings	10		10
Johnson	6		6
Martin	2		2
Mason	5		5
Menzies	40	1	41
Moore	6		6
Noble	11		11
Powell	7		7
Richmond	17		17
Robson	17	1	18
Russell	9		9
Sherwin	12	1	13
Smith	15	1	16
Speak	5	1	6
Swan	27	1	28
Thom	7		7
Wainscoate	9		9
Whipp	35	1	36

Goalscorers

PLAYER	LEAGUE	CUP COMPETITION FA CUP	TOTAL
Swan	11		11
Whipp	10		10
Robson	4		4
Wainscoat	4		4
Harris	3		3
Jennings	3		3
Thom	3		3
Armand	2		2
Powell	2		2
Richmond	2		2
Hart	1		1
Noble	1		1

Fact File

Edwards, Jennings and Wainscoat all made their debuts against Newcastle in March. All would be regulars for the next five seasons.

MANAGER: Arthur Fairclough

CAPTAIN: Jim Baker

TOP SCORER: Jack Swan

BIGGEST WIN: 6-0 v Aston Villa, 25 December 1924, League

HIGHEST ATTENDANCE: 50,000 v Aston Villa, 25 December 1924, lost 1-2, Division 1

MAJOR TRANSFERS IN: Russell Wainscoat from Middlesbrough, Willis Edwards from Chesterfield, Tom Jennings from Raith Rovers

Final Division 1 Table

		P	W	D	L	F	A	Pts
1	Huddersfield T	42	21	16	5	69	28	58
2	WBA	42	23	10	9	58	34	56
3	Bolton W	42	22	11	9	76	34	55
4	Liverpool	42	20	10	12	63	55	50
5	Bury	42	17	15	10	54	51	49
6	Newcastle U	42	16	16	10	61	42	48
7	Sunderland	42	19	10	13	64	51	48
8	Birmingham	42	17	12	13	49	53	46
9	Notts Co	42	16	13	13	42	31	45
10	Manchester C	42	17	9	16	76	68	43
11	Cardiff C	42	16	11	15	56	51	43
12	Tottenham H	42	15	12	15	52	43	42
13	West Ham U	42	15	12	15	62	60	42
14	Sheffield U	42	13	13	16	55	63	39
15	Aston Villa	42	13	13	16	58	71	39
16	Blackburn R	42	11	13	18	53	66	35
17	Everton	42	12	11	19	40	60	35
18	Leeds United	42	11	12	19	46	59	34
19	Burnley	42	11	12	19	46	75	34
20	The Arsenal	42	14	5	23	46	58	33
21	Preston NE	42	10	6	26	37	74	26
22	Nottingham F	42	6	12	24	29	65	24

Season 1925-26

Football League Division 1

DATE	OPPONENTS	SCORE	GOALSCORERS	ATTENDANCE
Aug 29	Notts County	L 0-1		18,155
Aug 31	BOLTON WANDERERS	W 2-1	Jennings, Harris	24,188
Sep 5	ASTON VILLA	D 2-2	Jennings 2	29,501
Sep 7	Bolton Wanderers	L 0-1		23,343
Sep 12	Leicester City	W 3-1	Jennings, Turnbull 2	23,592
Sep 16	NEWCASTLE UNITED	W 2-0	Jennings, Jackson	21,291
Sep 19	WEST HAM UNITED	W 5-2	Whipp, Jennings, Wainscoat 2	16,433
Sep 26	The Arsenal	L 1-4	Wainscoat	32,531
Oct 3	MANCHESTER UNITED	W 2-0	Jennings, Wainscoat	26,265
Oct 10	Liverpool	D 1-1	Wainscoat	30,088
Oct 17	HUDDERSFIELD TOWN	L 0-4		33,008
Oct 24	Everton	L 2-4	Jennings, Wainscoat	28,660
Oct 31	BURY	L 2-3	Hart, Jackson	15,008
Nov 7	Blackburn Rovers	D 2-2	Hart, Jennings	9,190
Nov 14	CARDIFF CITY	W 1-0	Turnbull	19,360
Nov 21	Sheffield United	L 0-1		22,327
Nov 28	WEST BROMWICH ALBION	L 0-1		14,774
Dec 5	Birmingham	L 1-2	Jennings	13,435
Dec 12	MANCHESTER CITY	L 3-4	Armand 2 (1pen), Chadwick	18,762
Dec 19	Tottenham Hotspur	L 2-3	Armand 2 (1pen)	19,200
Dec 25	BURNLEY	D 2-2	Turnbull, Whipp	23,325
Dec 26	Burnley	L 3-6	Whipp, Armand, Jennings	22,207
Jan 1	Sunderland	W 3-1	Armand (pen), Townsley, Jennings	29,527
Jan 2	NOTTS COUNTY	W 2-1	Armand (pen), Whipp	14,615
Jan 23	LEICESTER CITY	W 1-0	Chadwick	19,569
Jan 30	West Ham United	L 2-4	Jennings 2	17,246
Feb 3	Aston Villa	L 1-3	Jennings	11,573
Feb 6	THE ARSENAL	W 4-2	Jennings 3, Chadwick	26,239
Feb 13	Manchester United	L 1-2	Jennings	29,584
Feb 20	LIVERPOOL	D 1-1	Jennings	24,158
Feb 27	Huddersfield Town	L 1-3	Wainscoat	26,248
Mar 6	EVERTON	D 1-1	Wainscoat	18,163
Mar 13	Bury	W 2-1	Armand, Jennings	15,226
Mar 20	BLACKBURN ROVERS	W 2-1	Fell, Armand	22,419
Mar 27	Cardiff City	D 0-0		18,300
Apr 3	SHEFFIELD UNITED	W 2-0	Jennings, Turnbull	26,262
Apr 5	Newcastle United	L 0-3		16,666
Apr 6	SUNDERLAND	L 0-2		27,345
Apr 10	West Bromwich Albion	L 0-3		11,358
Apr 17	BIRMINGHAM	D 0-0		12,186
Apr 27	Manchester City	L 1-2	Jennings	42,475
May 1	TOTTENHAM HOTSPUR	W 4-1	Turnbull, Jennings 2, Whipp	16,158

FA Cup

Jan 9	Middlesbrough	(Rd 1) L 1-5	Armand (pen)	29,000

League & Cup Appearances

PLAYER	LEAGUE	CUP COMPETITION FA CUP	TOTAL
Allen	35	1	36
Armand	17	1	18
Atkinson	23	1	24
Baker	9		9
Chadwick	14		14
Duffield	6		6
Edwards	40	1	41
Fell	7		7
Harris	4		4
Hart	26		26
Jackson	30	1	31
Jennings	42	1	43
Johnson	29	1	30
Kirkpatrick	7		7
Mears	1		1
Menzies	35	1	36
Potts	12		12
Reed	1		1
Roberts	1		1
Sissons	6		6
Smith	6		6
Thornton	1		1
Townsley	21	1	22
Turnbull	37	1	38
Wainscoat	25		25
Whipp	27	1	28

Goalscorers

PLAYER	LEAGUE	CUP COMPETITION FA CUP	TOTAL
Jennings	25		25
Armand	9	1	10
Wainscoat	8		8
Turnbull	5		5
Whipp	5		5
Chadwick	3		3
Hart	2		2
Jackson	2		2
Harris	1		1
Fell	1		1
Townsley	1		1

Final Division 1 Table

		P	W	D	L	F	A	Pts
1	HUDDERSFIELD T	42	23	11	8	92	60	57
2	THE ARSENAL	42	22	8	12	87	63	52
3	SUNDERLAND	42	21	6	15	96	80	48
4	BURY	42	20	7	15	85	77	47
5	SHEFFIELD U	42	19	8	15	102	82	46
6	ASTON VILLA	42	16	12	14	86	76	44
7	LIVERPOOL	42	14	16	12	70	63	44
8	BOLTON W	42	17	10	15	75	76	44
9	MANCHESTER U	42	19	6	17	66	73	44
10	NEWCASTLE U	42	16	10	16	84	75	42
11	EVERTON	42	12	18	12	72	70	42
12	BLACKBURN R	42	15	11	16	91	80	41
13	WBA	42	16	8	18	79	78	40
14	BIRMINGHAM	42	16	8	18	66	81	40
15	TOTTENHAM H	42	15	9	18	66	79	39
16	CARDIFF C	42	16	7	19	61	76	39
17	LEICESTER C	42	14	10	18	70	80	38
18	WEST HAM U	42	15	7	20	63	76	37
19	LEEDS UNITED	42	14	8	20	64	76	36
20	BURNLEY	42	13	10	19	85	108	36
21	MANCHESTER C	42	12	11	19	89	100	35
22	NOTTS CO	42	13	7	22	54	74	33

Fact File

Leeds needed to beat Tottenham on the last game of the season to retain their First Division status.

MANAGER: Arthur Fairclough

CAPTAIN: Jim Baker

TOP SCORER: Tom Jennings

BIGGEST WIN: 5-2 v West Ham United, 19 September 1925, League

HIGHEST ATTENDANCE: 42,000 v Manchester City, 27 April 1926, lost 2-1, League

Season 1926-27

Football League Division 1

DATE	OPPONENTS	SCORE	GOALSCORERS	ATTENDANCE
Aug 28	BOLTON WANDERERS	L 2-5	Wainscoat, Turnbull	23,699
Aug 30	CARDIFF CITY	D 0-0		14,242
Sep 4	Manchester United	D 2-2	Jennings, Wainscoat (pen)	26,338
Sep 6	Cardiff City	L 1-3	Whipp	13,653
Sep 11	DERBY COUNTY	W 1-0	Jennings	17,411
Sep 15	ASTON VILLA	W 3-1	Armand, Jennings, Sissons	13,792
Sep 18	Sheffield United	L 0-1		19,940
Sep 25	THE ARSENAL	W 4-1	Jennings 3, Wainscoat	20,544
Oct 2	Liverpool	W 4-2	Jennings 4	30,942
Oct 9	BLACKBURN ROVERS	W 4-1	Jennings 4	16,304
Oct 16	Leicester City	L 2-3	Jennings 2 (1 pen)	27,753
Oct 23	EVERTON	L 1-3	Jennings	24,867
Oct 30	Huddersfield Town	L 1-4	Jennings	29,679
Nov 6	SUNDERLAND	D 2-2	Jennings, Duggan	15,667
Nov 13	West Bromwich Albion	W 4-2	Mitchelll 2, Whipp, Armand	10,269
Nov 20	BURY	W 4-1	Jennings 3, Mitchell	18,332
Nov 27	Birmingham	L 0-2		19,707
Dec 4	TOTTENHAM HOTSPUR	D 1-1	Armand	24,470
Dec 11	West Ham United	L 2-3	Armand, Menzies	20,924
Dec 18	SHEFFIELD WEDNESDAY	W 4-1	Edwards, Jennings, Mitchell, Whipp	20,722
Dec 27	NEWCASTLE UNITED	L 1-2	Jennings	48,590
Dec 28	Aston Villa	L 1-5	Armand	43,963
Jan 1	Newcastle United	L 0-1		51,343
Jan 15	Bolton Wanderers	L 0-3		19,149
Jan 22	MANCHESTER UNITED	L 2-3	Jennings 2 (1 pen)	16,816
Feb 5	SHEFFIELD UNITED	D 1-1	Jennings	18,348
Feb 12	The Arsenal	L 0-1		25,961
Feb 19	Derby County	L 0-1		14,597
Feb 23	LIVERPOOL	D 0-0		13,776
Feb 26	Blackburn Rovers	L 1-4	White	16,149
Mar 5	LEICESTER CITY	D 1-1	Jennings	21,420
Mar 12	Everton	L 1-2	Jennings	57,440
Mar 19	HUDDERSFIELD TOWN	D 1-1	Turnbull	36,364
Mar 26	Sunderland	L 2-6	Wainscoat 2	12,288
Apr 2	WEST BROMWICH ALBION	W 3-1	Jennings 2, Wainscoat	20,176
Apr 9	Bury	L 2-4	Wainscoat, Jennings	12,489
Apr 15	Burnley	L 2-3	Turnbull, Jennings	21,099
Apr 16	BIRMINGHAM	W 2-1	Turnbull, Jennings	18,703
Apr 19	BURNLEY	L 0-2		18,740
Apr 23	Tottenham Hotspur	L 1-4	Jennings	17,745
Apr 30	WEST HAM UNITED	W 6-3	Turnbull, White, Wainscoat 4	10,997
May 7	Sheffield Wednesday	L 0-1		12,027

FA Cup

DATE	OPPONENTS		SCORE	GOALSCORERS	ATTENDANCE
Jan 8	SUNDERLAND	(Rd 3)	W 3-2	Jennings 2 (1 pen), Duggan	31,000
Jan 29	BOLTON WANDERERS	(Rd 4)	D 0-0		42,694
Feb 2	Bolton Wanderers	(R)	L 0-3		46,686

League & Cup Appearances

PLAYER	LEAGUE	CUP COMPETITION FA CUP	TOTAL
Allen	22	1	23
Armand	18	2	20
Atkinson	11		11
Chadwick	2		2
Duggan	8	1	9
Edwards	37	3	40
Fell	6		6
Hart	5		5
Jackson	8		8
Jennings	41	3	44
Kirkpatrick	3		3
Mears	1	1	2
Menzies	30	2	32
Mitchell	23	3	26
Potts	42	3	45
Reed	22	3	25
Roberts	34	3	37
Robinson	4		4
Sissons	16	1	17
Townsley	42	3	45
Turnbull	31	1	32
Wainscoat	25	2	27
Whipp	15		15
White	16	1	17

Goalscorers

PLAYER	LEAGUE	CUP COMPETITION FA CUP	TOTAL
Jennings	35	2	37
Wainscoat	8		8
Armand	5		5
Turnbull	5		5
Mitchell	4		4
Whipp	3		3
Duggan	1	1	2
White	2		2
Edwards	1		1
Menzies	1		1
Sisson	1		1

Fact File

In the autumn, Tom Jennings scored three successive hat-tricks, but Leeds were relegated after the defeat at Tottenham in April.

MANAGER: Arthur Fairclough

CAPTAIN: Jimmy Potts

TOP SCORER: Tom Jennings

BIGGEST WIN: 6-3 v West Ham United, 30 April 1927, League

HIGHEST ATTENDANCE: 57,440 v Everton, 12 March 1927, lost 2-1, League

MAJOR TRANSFERS IN: John White from Hearts, Bobby Turnbull from Bradford Park Avenue

Final Division 1 Table

		P	W	D	L	F	A	Pts
1	NEWCASTLE U	42	25	6	11	96	58	56
2	HUDDERSFIELD T	42	17	17	8	76	60	51
3	SUNDERLAND	42	21	7	14	98	70	49
4	BOLTON W	42	19	10	13	84	62	48
5	BURNLEY	42	19	9	14	91	80	47
6	WEST HAM U	42	19	8	15	86	70	46
7	LEICESTER C	42	17	12	13	85	70	46
8	SHEFFIELD U	42	17	10	15	74	86	44
9	LIVERPOOL	42	18	7	17	69	61	43
10	ASTON VILLA	42	18	7	17	81	83	43
11	THE ARSENAL	42	17	9	16	77	86	43
12	DERBY CO	42	17	7	18	86	73	41
13	TOTTENHAM H	42	16	9	17	76	78	41
14	CARDIFF C	42	16	9	17	55	65	41
15	MANCHESTER U	42	13	14	15	52	64	40
16	SHEFFIELD W	42	15	9	18	75	92	39
17	BIRMINGHAM	42	17	4	21	64	73	38
18	BLACKBURN R	42	15	8	19	77	96	38
19	BURY	42	12	12	18	68	77	36
20	EVERTON	42	12	10	20	64	90	34
21	LEEDS UNITED	42	11	8	23	69	88	30
22	WBA	42	11	8	23	65	86	30

Season 1927-28

Football League Division 2

DATE	OPPONENTS	SCORE	GOALSCORERS	ATTENDANCE
Aug 27	South Shields	W 5-1	Wainscoat, Mitchell, White 2, Jennings	9,826
Aug 29	BARNSLEY	D 2-2	White, Jennings	21,219
Sep 3	SOUTHAMPTON	W 2-0	Wainscoat 2	19,479
Sep 10	NOTTINGHAM FOREST	W 4-0	Turnbull, Jennings, Wainscoat, Mitchell	19,748
Sep 17	Manchester City	L 1-2	Jennings	40,931
Sep 24	HULL CITY	W 2-0	Jennings, Wainscoat	21,943
Sep 26	Barnsley	L 1-2	Mitchell	13,038
Oct 1	Preston North End	L 1-5	White	16,966
Oct 8	SWANSEA TOWN	W 5-0	Jennings 2 (1 pen), Turnbull, White 2	18,697
Oct 15	Fulham	D 1-1	White	16,704
Oct 22	Grimsby Town	L 2-3	Jennings, Wainscoat	11,909
Oct 29	OLDHAM ATHLETIC	W 1-0	Mitchell	17,615
Nov 5	Notts County	D 2-2	Jennings 2	9,866
Nov 12	Reading	W 6-2	Wainscoat, Turnbull 2, White 2, Jennings	17,257
Nov 19	Blackpool	W 2-0	Mitchell 2	9,008
Nov 26	WEST BROMWICH ALBION	L 1-2	Townsley	23,690
Dec 3	Clapton Orient	L 1-2	Mitchell	12,838
Dec 10	CHELSEA	W 5-0	Jennings 4, White	22,059
Dec 17	Bristol City	W 2-1	Wainscoat, White	18,326
Dec 24	STOKE CITY	W 5-1	Jennings 2, White, Turnbull, Hart	12,889
Dec 26	PORT VALE	W 2-1	Wainscoat, White	18,869
Dec 27	Port Vale	W 3-0	Wainscoat, Jennings 2	32,275
Dec 31	SOUTH SHIELDS	W 3-0	Turnbull, Wainscoat, Keetley	12,752
Jan 7	Southampton	W 4-1	White 2, Wainscoat, Keetley	13,966
Jan 21	Nottingham Forest	D 2-2	White, Keetley	13,133
Jan 28	BRISTOL CITY	W 3-2	Keetley 3	15,534
Feb 4	Hull City	L 1-3	Jennings	12,502
Feb 11	PRESTON NORTH END	L 2-4	Wainscoat 2	24,276
Feb 18	Swansea Town	D 1-1	Jennings	13,444
Feb 25	FULHAM	W 2-1	White, Wainscoat	17,358
Mar 3	GRIMSBY TOWN	D 0-0		23,567
Mar 10	Oldham Athletic	W 1-0	Keetley	22,029
Mar 17	NOTTS COUNTY	W 6-0	Keetley 3, Turnbull, Armand, White	17,643
Mar 24	Reading	W 1-0	Keetley	13,098
Mar 31	BLACKPOOL	W 4-0	Wainscoat 2, Mitchell, Armand	19,630
Apr 7	West Bromwich Albion	W 1-0	Turnbull	23,644
Apr 9	Wolverhampton W	D 0-0		25,251
Apr 10	WOLVERHAMPTON W	W 3-0	Keetley 2, White	29,821
Apr 14	CLAPTON ORIENT	W 4-0	Keetley 3, White	22,884
Apr 21	Chelsea	W 3-2	Keetley 2, White	47,562
Apr 25	MANCHESTER CITY	L 0-1		48,470
May 5	Stoke City	L 1-5	Wainscoat	12,401

FA Cup

Jan 14	Manchester City	(Rd 3) L 0-1		50,473

League & Cup Appearances

PLAYER	LEAGUE	CUP COMPETITION FA CUP	TOTAL
Allen	13		13
Armand	2		2
Atkinson	5		5
Baker	2		2
Coutts	1		1
Edwards	32	1	33
Hart	30	1	31
Jennings	26	1	27
Johnson	4		4
Keetley	16		16
Menzies	33	1	34
Mitchell	42	1	43
Potts	38	1	39
Reed	42	1	43
Roberts	7		7
Robinson	1		1
Sissons	8		8
Stacey	2		2
Townsley	42	1	43
Turnbull	34	1	35
Wainscoat	41	1	42
White	41	1	42

Goalscorers

PLAYER	LEAGUE	CUP COMPETITION FA CUP	TOTAL
Jennings	21		21
White	21		21
Keetley	18		18
Wainscoat	18		18
Turnbull	9		9
Mitchell	8		8
Armand	2		2
Hart	1		1
Townsley	1		1

Final Division 2 Table

		P	W	D	L	F	A	Pts
1	MANCHESTER C	42	25	9	8	100	59	59
2	LEEDS UNITED	42	25	7	10	98	49	57
3	CHELSEA	42	23	8	11	75	45	54
4	PRESTON NE	42	22	9	11	100	66	53
5	STOKE C	42	22	8	12	78	59	52
6	SWANSEA T	42	18	12	12	75	63	48
7	OLDHAM ATH	42	19	8	15	75	51	46
8	WBA	42	17	12	13	90	70	46
9	PORT VALE	42	18	8	16	68	57	44
10	NOTTINGHAM F	42	15	10	17	83	84	40
11	GRIMSBY T	42	14	12	16	69	83	40
12	BRISTOL C	42	15	9	18	76	79	39
13	BARNSLEY	42	14	11	17	65	85	39
14	HULL C	42	12	15	15	41	54	39
15	NOTTS CO	42	13	12	17	68	74	38
16	WOLVERHAMPTON W	42	13	10	19	63	91	36
17	SOUTHAMPTON	42	14	7	21	68	77	35
18	READING	42	11	13	18	53	75	35
19	BLACKPOOL	42	13	8	21	83	101	34
20	CLAPTON ORIENT	42	11	12	19	55	85	34
21	FULHAM	42	13	7	22	68	89	33
22	SOUTH SHIELDS	42	7	9	26	56	111	23

Fact File

A win at Chelsea ensured Leeds' promotion but defeat at home against Manchester City effectively cost them the Championship.

MANAGER: Dick Ray
CAPTAIN: Jimmy Potts
TOP SCORER: Tom Jennings
BIGGEST WIN: 6-0 v Notts County, 17 March 1928, League
HIGHEST ATTENDANCE: 50,473 v Manchester City, 4 April 1928, lost 1-0, FA Cup, Round 3

Season 1928-29

Football League Division 1

DATE	OPPONENTS	SCORE	GOALSCORERS	ATTENDANCE
Aug 25	ASTON VILLA	W 4-1	Keetley 3, Wainscoat	26,588
Aug 27	BURY	W 3-1	Armand, Wainscoat 2	18,354
Sep 1	Leicester City	D 4-4	Keetley 2, Turnbull, Armand	27,507
Sep 8	MANCHESTER UNITED	W 3-2	Wainscoat, Keetley, Armand	28,723
Sep 15	Huddersfield Town	L 1-6	Wainscoat (pen)	39,869
Sep 22	Liverpool	D 1-1	Wainscoat	37,417
Sep 29	WEST HAM UNITED	W 4-1	Jennings 2, Wainscoat, White	29,423
Oct 6	Newcastle United	L 2-3	Wainscoat, Jennings	39,166
Oct 13	BURNLEY	W 2-1	White, Jennings	29,565
Oct 20	MANCHESTER CITY	W 4-1	White 3, Wainscoat	32,866
Oct 27	Everton	W 1-0	Wainscoat	41,504
Nov 3	PORTSMOUTH	W 3-2	Wainscoat, Jennings, White	29,022
Nov 10	Bolton Wanderers	L 1-4	Turnbull	16,308
Nov 17	SHEFFIELD WEDNESDAY	L 0-2		25,519
Nov 24	Derby County	W 4-3	White, Keetley, Mitchell, Wainscoat	16,601
Dec 1	SUNDERLAND	L 0-3		30,082
Dec 8	Blackburn Rovers	W 1-0	Keetley	17,333
Dec 15	ARSENAL	D 1-1	Keetley	20,293
Dec 22	Birmingham	L 1-5	Turnbull	16,057
Dec 25	CARDIFF CITY	W 3-0	Keetley, White, Hart	28,188
Dec 26	Cardiff City	L 1-2	Turnbull	20,409
Dec 29	Aston Villa	L 0-1		31,565
Jan 1	Bury	D 2-2	Turnbull, Wainscoat	21,696
Jan 5	LEICESTER CITY	W 4-3	Keetley 3, Turnbull	18,870
Jan 19	Manchester United	W 2-1	Keetley, Hart	21,995
Feb 2	LIVERPOOL	D 2-2	Done o.g., Jennings	18,780
Feb 9	West Ham United	L 2-8	Wainscoat, Jennings	18,055
Feb 16	NEWCASTLE UNITED	D 0-0		16,036
Feb 23	Burnley	L 0-5		13,506
Mar 2	Manchester City	L 0-3		33,921
Mar 9	EVERTON	W 3-1	Keetley 3	22,459
Mar 16	Portsmouth	W 2-0	Mitchell, Wainscoat	17,700
Mar 30	Sheffield Wednesday	L 2-4	Wainscoat, Keetley	30,655
Apr 1	Sheffield United	D 1-1	Keetley	20,400
Apr 2	SHEFFIELD UNITED	W 2-0	Jennings, White	20,119
Apr 6	DERBY COUNTY	D 1-1	Mitchell	19,985
Apr 13	Sunderland	L 1-2	Keetley	12,208
Apr 20	BLACKBURN ROVERS	L 0-1		17,201
Apr 27	Arsenal	L 0-1		21,465
Apr 29	BOLTON WANDERERS	D 2-2	Wainscoat 2	12,877
May 1	HUDDERSFIELD TOWN	L 1-2	Jennings	17,291
May 4	BIRMINGHAM	L 0-1		8,151

FA Cup

Jan 12	Exeter City	(Rd 3) D 2-2	Keetley, Menzies	13,500
Jan 16	EXETER CITY	(R) W 5-1	Wainscoat, Reed, Cochrane, Keetley, Lowton o.g.	23,000
Jan 26	Huddersfield Town	(Rd 4) L 0-3		53,700

League & Cup Appearances

PLAYER	LEAGUE	CUP COMPETITION FA CUP	TOTAL
Armand	9		9
Buck	8		8
Cochrane	11	2	13
Edwards	29	3	32
Firth	1		1
Gribben	3		3
Hart	35	3	38
Jennings	17		17
Keetley	29	3	32
Longden	3		3
McNestry	3		3
Menzies	38	3	41
Milburn G W	5		5
Mitchell	30	1	31
Potts	39	2	41
Reed	39	3	42
Roberts	6		6
Stacey	6		6
Townsley	38	3	41
Turnbull	39	3	42
Underwood	1		1
Wainscoat	39	3	42
White	28	3	31
Wilson G M	3		3
Wilson J	3	1	4

Goalscorers

PLAYER	LEAGUE	CUP COMPETITION FA CUP	TOTAL
Keetley	20	2	22
Wainscoat	18	1	19
Jennings	9		9
White	9		9
Turnbull	6		6
Armand	3		3
Mitchell	3		3
Hart	2		2
Cochrane		1	1
Menzies		1	1
Reed		1	1
Opps' o.gs.	1	1	2

Fact File

With 18 points from 24 by the end of October, Leeds appeared to be Championship contenders, but their form was to drop off.

MANAGER: Dick Ray

CAPTAIN: Jimmy Potts

TOP SCORER: Charlie Keetley

BIGGEST WIN: 5-1 v Exeter City, 16 January 1929, FA Cup, Round 3 replay

HIGHEST ATTENDANCE: 53,700 v Huddersfield Town, 4 April 1929, lost 0-3, FA Cup, Round 4

MAJOR TRANSFERS IN: Wilf Copping from Middlecliffe Rovers

Final Division 1 Table

		P	W	D	L	F	A	Pts
1	SHEFFIELD W	42	21	10	11	86	62	52
2	LEICESTER C	42	21	9	12	96	67	51
3	ASTON VILLA	42	23	4	15	98	81	50
4	SUNDERLAND	42	20	7	15	93	75	47
5	LIVERPOOL	42	17	12	13	90	64	46
6	DERBY CO	42	18	10	14	86	71	46
7	BLACKBURN R	42	17	11	14	72	63	45
8	MANCHESTER C	42	18	9	15	95	86	45
9	ARSENAL	42	16	13	13	77	72	45
10	NEWCASTLE U	42	19	6	17	70	72	44
11	SHEFFIELD U	42	15	11	16	86	85	41
12	MANCHESTER U	42	14	13	15	66	76	41
13	LEEDS UNITED	42	16	9	17	71	84	41
14	BOLTON W	42	14	12	16	73	80	40
15	BIRMINGHAM	42	15	10	17	68	77	40
16	HUDDERSFIELD T	42	14	11	17	70	61	39
17	WEST HAM U	42	15	9	18	86	96	39
18	EVERTON	42	17	4	21	63	75	38
19	BURNLEY	42	15	8	19	81	103	38
20	PORTSMOUTH	42	15	6	21	56	80	36
21	BURY	42	12	7	23	62	99	31
22	CARDIFF C	42	8	13	21	43	59	29

Season 1929-30

Football League Division 1

DATE	OPPONENTS	SCORE	GOALSCORERS	ATTENDANCE
Aug 31	Arsenal	L 0-4		41,855
Sep 7	ASTON VILLA	W 4-1	Roberts 2, (2 pen), Longden, Jennings	23,649
Sep 11	Everton	D 1-1	Turnbull	24,098
Sep 14	Huddersfield Town	L 0-1		28,287
Sep 16	EVERTON	W 2-1	Wainscoat, Jennings	16,667
Sep 21	Sheffield Wednesday	W 2-1	Turnbull, Wainscoat	21,353
Sep 23	PORTSMOUTH	W 1-0	White	14,027
Sep 28	BURNLEY	W 3-0	Wainscoat, Hart, White	26,676
Oct 5	Sunderland	W 4-1	Mangnall 2, Wainscoat, Turnbull	23,503
Oct 12	BOLTON WANDERERS	W 2-1	Turnbull, Mangnall	29,749
Oct 19	BIRMINGHAM	W 1-0	Turnbull	20,067
Oct 26	Leicester City	D 2-2	Mitchell, Mangnall	27,242
Nov 2	GRIMSBY TOWN	W 6-0	White, Wainscoat 2, Turnbull, Mangnall, Reed	24,013
Nov 9	Sheffield United	L 2-3	Turnbull, Mangnall	25,359
Nov 16	WEST HAM UNITED	L 1-3	Wainscoat	18,582
Nov 23	Liverpool	L 0-1		30,643
Nov 30	MIDDLESBROUGH	L 1-2	Reed	19,508
Dec 7	Blackburn Rovers	L 1-2	Mitchell	13,504
Dec 14	NEWCASTLE UNITED	W 5-2	Wainscoat, Longden 2, Jennings 2	21,097
Dec 21	Manchester United	L 1-3	Longden	15,054
Dec 25	DERBY COUNTY	W 2-1	Longden, Wainscoat	25,360
Dec 26	Derby County	L 0-3		30,307
Dec 28	ARSENAL	W 2-0	Jennings 2	29,167
Jan 4	Aston Villa	W 4-3	Jennings 2, White, Wainscoat	32,476
Jan 18	HUDDERSFIELD TOWN	L 0-1		40,789
Feb 1	Burnley	W 3-0	Duggan, Jennings 2	12,505
Feb 8	SUNDERLAND	W 5-0	Cochrane, Wainscoat 2, Jennings, Longden	22,377
Feb 15	Bolton Wanderers	L 2-4	Jennings, Duggan	18,104
Feb 22	Birmingham	L 0-1		17,703
Mar 1	LEICESTER CITY	L 1-2	Jennings	18,486
Mar 8	Grimsby Town	W 2-1	Firth, Jennings	16,591
Mar 15	SHEFFIELD UNITED	D 2-2	Turnbull, Wainscoat	7,569
Mar 22	West Ham United	L 0-3		18,351
Mar 29	LIVERPOOL	D 1-1	Wainscoat	14,178
Apr 5	Middlesbrough	D 1-1	Keetley	14,136
Apr 9	SHEFFIELD WEDNESDAY	W 3-0	Keetley	3,950
Apr 12	BLACKBURN ROVERS	W 4-2	Longden, Keetley, Hart, Mitchell	15,451
Apr 19	Newcastle United	L 1-2	Keetley	23,066
Apr 21	Manchester City	L 1-4	Keetley	23,578
Apr 22	MANCHESTER CITY	W 3-2	Turnbull, Keetley, Wainscoat	16,636
Apr 26	MANCHESTER UNITED	W 3-1	Keetley 2, Firth	10,596
May 3	Portsmouth	D 0-0		13,925

FA Cup

DATE	OPPONENTS		SCORE	GOALSCORERS	ATTENDANCE
Jan 11	CRYSTAL PALACE	(Rd 3)	W 8-1	Turnbull, White 2, Jennings 2, Wainscoat 3	31,418
Jan 25	West Ham United	(Rd 4)	L 1-4	Jennings	34,000

Fact File

Leeds achieved their highest League placing so far and did the 'double' over champions Sheffield Wednesday.

MANAGER: Dick Ray

CAPTAIN: Jimmy Potts

TOP SCORER: Russell Wainscoat

BIGGEST WIN: 8-1 v Crystal Palace, 11 January 1930, FA Cup, Round 3

HIGHEST ATTENDANCE: 41,855 v Arsenal, 31 August 1929, lost 0-4, League

MAJOR TRANSFERS OUT: David Mangnall to Huddersfield

League & Cup Appearances

PLAYER	LEAGUE	CUP COMPETITION FA CUP	TOTAL
Cochrane	6		6
Duggan	9		9
Edwards	39	2	41
Firth	10		10
Hart	30	2	32
Jennings	23	2	25
Johnson	26		26
Keetley	3		3
Longden	23		23
Mangnall	9		9
Menzies	14		14
Millburn G W	6		6
Millburn J	38	2	40
Mitchell	33	2	35
Potts	16	2	18
Reed	37	2	39
Roberts	31	2	33
Stacey	3		3
Townsley	9		9
Turnbull	35	2	37
Underwood	4		4
Wainscoat	40	2	42
White	17	2	19

Goalscorers

PLAYER	LEAGUE	CUP COMPETITION FA CUP	TOTAL
Wainscoat	15	3	18
Jennings	14	3	17
Turnbull	9	1	10
Keetley	8		8
Longden	7		7
Mangnall	6		6
White	4	2	6
Mitchell	3		3
Duggan	2		2
Firth	2		2
Hart	2		2
Reed	2		2
Roberts	2		2
Cochrane	1		1

Final Division 1 Table

		P	W	D	L	F	A	Pts
1	SHEFFIELD W	42	26	8	8	105	57	60
2	DERBY CO	42	21	8	13	90	82	50
3	MANCHESTER C	42	19	9	14	91	81	47
4	ASTON VILLA	42	21	5	16	92	83	47
5	LEEDS UNITED	42	20	6	16	79	63	46
6	BLACKBURN R	42	19	7	16	99	93	45
7	WEST HAM U	42	19	5	18	86	79	43
8	LEICESTER C	42	17	9	16	86	90	43
9	SUNDERLAND	42	18	7	17	76	80	43
10	HUDDERSFIELD T	42	17	9	16	63	69	43
11	BIRMINGHAM	42	16	9	17	67	62	41
12	LIVERPOOL	42	16	9	17	63	79	41
13	PORTSMOUTH	42	15	10	17	66	62	40
14	ARSENAL	42	14	11	17	78	66	39
15	BOLTON W	42	15	9	18	74	74	39
16	MIDDLESBROUGH	42	16	6	20	82	84	38
17	MANCHESTER U	42	15	8	19	67	88	38
18	GRIMSBY T	42	15	7	20	73	89	37
19	NEWCASTLE U	42	15	7	20	71	92	37
20	SHEFFIELD U	42	15	6	21	91	96	36
21	BURNLEY	42	14	8	20	79	97	36
22	EVERTON	42	12	11	19	80	92	35

Season 1930-31

Football League Division 1

DATE	OPPONENTS	SCORE	GOALSCORERS	ATTENDANCE
Aug 30	PORTSMOUTH	D 2-2	Turnbull, Keetley	15,900
Sep 3	Derby County	L 1-4	Wainscoat	13,924
Sep 6	Arsenal	L 1-3	Furness	40,828
Sep 8	MANCHESTER CITY	W 4-2	Cochrane, Keetley 3 (1 pen)	12,295
Sep 13	BLACKBURN ROVERS	W 4-2	Keetley, Duggan, Furness, Wainscoat	11,837
Sep 17	Manchester City	L 0-1		17,051
Sep 20	Blackpool	W 7-3	Furness 2, Cochrane 2, Keetley 2 (1 pen), Turnbull	25,473
Sep 27	HUDDERSFIELD TOWN	L 1-2	Wainscoat	30,625
Oct 4	SUNDERLAND	L 0-3		16,378
Oct 11	Leicester City	L 0-4		19,405
Oct 18	Liverpool	L 0-2		25,637
Oct 25	MIDDLESBROUGH	W 7-0	Mitchell, Duggan 2, Wainscoat 2, Jennings 2	18,116
Nov 1	Newcastle United	L 1-4	Jennings	13,534
Nov 8	SHEFFIELD WEDNESDAY	L 2-3	Jennings, Hart	22,040
Nov 15	West Ham United	D 1-1	Wainscoat	16,612
Nov 22	CHELSEA	L 2-3	Wainscoat, Duggan	13,602
Nov 29	Grimsby Town	L 0-2		6,783
Dec 6	BOLTON WANDERERS	W 3-1	Turnbull, Wainscoat, Keetley	7,595
Dec 13	Aston Villa	L 3-4	Turnbull, Keetley 2	26,272
Dec 20	MANCHESTER UNITED	W 5-0	Wainscoat, Turnbull 3, Furness	11,282
Dec 25	Birmingham	W 1-0	Furness	24,991
Dec 26	BIRMINGHAM	W 3-1	Keetley, Furness 2	12,381
Dec 27	Portsmouth	D 1-1	Keetley	18,530
Jan 1	Manchester United	D 0-0		9,875
Jan 17	Blackburn Rovers	L 1-3	Hydes	11,975
Jan 28	BLACKPOOL	D 2-2	Hart, Turnbull	7,750
Jan 31	Huddersfield Town	L 0-3		13,044
Feb 7	Sunderland	L 0-4		25,765
Feb 18	LEICESTER CITY	L 1-3	Duggan	5,572
Feb 21	LIVERPOOL	L 1-2	Wainscoat	15,570
Feb 28	Middlesbrough	L 0-5		15,707
Mar 7	NEWCASTLE UNITED	W 1-0	Turnbull (pen)	6,845
Mar 11	ARSENAL	L 1-2	Turnbull (pen)	12,212
Mar 14	Sheffield Wednesday	L 1-2	Wainscoat	14,562
Mar 21	WEST HAM UNITED	W 3-0	Turnbull (pen), Alderson 2	11,611
Mar 28	Chelsea	L 0-1		25,446
Apr 4	GRIMSBY TOWN	D 0-0		14,951
Apr 6	Sheffield United	D 1-1	Copping	12,948
Apr 7	SHEFFIELD UNITED	W 4-0	Keetley 2, Thorpe o.g., Wainscoat	13,315
Apr 11	Bolton Wanderers	L 0-2		15,438
Apr 18	ASTON VILLA	L 0-2		10,388
May 2	DERBY COUNTY	W 3-1	Keetley 2, Green	11,190

FA Cup

Jan 10	HUDDERSFIELD TOWN	(Rd 3) W 2-0	Hydes, Furness	41,103
Jan 24	NEWCASTLE UNITED	(Rd 4) W 4-1	Furness, Wainscoat 2, Mitchell	40,261
Feb 14	Exeter City	(Rd 5) L 1-3	Mitchell	19,130

League & Cup Appearances

PLAYER	LEAGUE	CUP COMPETITION FA CUP	TOTAL
Alderson	4		4
Brown	1		1
Cochrane T	28	3	31
Copping	42	3	45
Danskin	1		1
Duggan	12		12
Edwards	40	3	43
Firth	2		2
Furness	37	3	40
Green	3		3
Hart	36	3	39
Hornby	10		10
Hydes	2	2	4
Jennings	8		8
Johnson	4		4
Keetley	29	1	30
Longden	2		2
Menzies	13		13
Milburn GW	22	3	25
Milburn J	41	3	44
Mitchell	14		14
Potts	38	3	41
Roberts	5		5
Townsley	7		7
Turnbull	27	3	30
Underwood	1		1
Wainscoat	33	3	36

Goalscorers

PLAYER	LEAGUE	CUP COMPETITION FA CUP	TOTAL
Keetley	16		16
Wainscoat	12	2	14
Turnbull	11		11
Furness	8	2	10
Duggan	5		5
Jennings	4		4
Cochrane T	3		3
Mitchell	1	2	3
Alderson	2		2
Hart	2		2
Hydes	1	1	2
Copping	1		1
Green	1		1
Opps' o.gs.	1		1

Final Division 1 Table

		P	W	D	L	F	A	Pts
1	ARSENAL	42	28	10	4	127	59	66
2	ASTON VILLA	42	25	9	8	128	78	59
3	SHEFFIELD W	42	22	8	12	102	75	52
4	PORTSMOUTH	42	18	13	11	84	67	49
5	HUDDERSFIELD T	42	18	12	12	81	65	48
6	DERBY CO	42	18	10	14	94	79	46
7	MIDDLESBROUGH	42	19	8	15	98	90	46
8	MANCHESTER C	42	18	10	14	75	70	46
9	LIVERPOOL	42	15	12	15	86	85	42
10	BLACKBURN R	42	17	8	17	83	84	42
11	SUNDERLAND	42	16	9	17	89	85	41
12	CHELSEA	42	15	10	17	64	67	40
13	GRIMSBY T	42	17	5	20	82	87	39
14	BOLTON W	42	15	9	18	68	81	39
15	SHEFFIELD U	42	14	10	18	78	84	38
16	LEICESTER C	42	16	6	20	80	95	38
17	NEWCASTLE U	42	15	6	21	78	87	36
18	WEST HAM U	42	14	8	20	79	94	36
19	BIRMINGHAM	42	13	10	19	55	70	36
20	BLACKPOOL	42	11	10	21	71	125	32
21	LEEDS UNITED	42	12	7	23	68	81	31
22	MANCHESTER U	42	7	8	27	53	115	22

Fact File

Blackpool managed a draw in their final match of the season – one point was enough to send Leeds down to Division 2.

MANAGER: Dick Ray

CAPTAIN: Jimmy Potts

TOP SCORER: Charlie Keetley

BIGGEST WIN: 7-0 v Middlesbrough, 25 October 1930, League

HIGHEST ATTENDANCE: 41,103 v Huddersfield Town, 10 January 1931, drew 1-1, League

Season 1931-32

Football League Division 2

DATE	OPPONENTS	SCORE	GOALSCORERS	ATTENDANCE
Aug 29	Swansea Town	W 2-0	Firth, Green	16,175
Aug 31	Port Vale	W 2-1	Wainscoat, Green	16,874
Sep 5	BARNSLEY	L 0-1		13,078
Sep 7	MILLWALL	L 0-1		8,388
Sep 12	Notts County	D 1-1	Cochrane	12,630
Sep 14	Millwall	W 3-2	Keetley, Furness, Cochrane	11,844
Sep 19	PLYMOUTH ARGYLE	D 0-0		10,782
Sep 26	Bristol City	W 2-0	Furness, Keetley	9,157
Oct 3	OLDHAM ATHLETIC	W 5-0	Keetley 3, Cochrane 2	12,336
Oct 10	Bury	W 4-1	Firth, Duggan, Hart, Keetley	16,353
Oct 17	WOLVERHAMPTON W	W 2-1	Furness, Keetley	13,825
Oct 24	Charlton Athletic	W 1-0	Furness	11,303
Oct 31	STOKE CITY	W 2-0	Cochrane, Furness	15,524
Nov 7	Manchester United	W 5-2	Duggan, Firth 2, Keetley, Furness	9,512
Nov 14	PRESTON NORTH END	W 4-1	Firth 2, Furness, Keetley	15,439
Nov 21	Burnley	W 5-0	Cochrane 2, Furness, Firth 2	12,767
Nov 28	CHESTERFIELD	D 3-3	Keetley 2, Furness	13,483
Dec 5	Nottingham Forest	D 3-3	Keetley 2, Furness	12,214
Dec 12	Tottenham Hotspur	W 1-0	Green	15,689
Dec 19	Southampton	L 1-2	Duggan	11,736
Dec 25	Bradford Park Avenue	L 0-3		32,421
Dec 26	BRADFORD PARK AVENUE	W 3-2	Duggan, Keetley 2	34,005
Jan 2	SWANSEA TOWN	W 3-2	Keetley, Firth, Danskin	12,885
Jan 16	Barnsley	W 2-0	Keetley, Firth	9,136
Jan 23	NOTTS COUNTY	D 2-2	Keetley 2	14,562
Jan 30	Plymouth Argyle	L 2-3	Firth, Hydes	28,426
Feb 6	BRISTOL CITY	W 1-0	Firth	10,677
Feb 13	Oldham Athletic	L 1-2	Keetley	6,496
Feb 20	BURY	W 1-0	Firth	13,748
Feb 27	Wolverhampton W	D 1-1	Cochrane	34,520
Mar 5	CHARLTON ATHLETIC	W 2-0	Firth, Keetley	11,092
Mar 12	Stoke City	W 4-3	Bennett 2, Keetley, Hornby	17,981
Mar 19	MANCHESTER UNITED	L 1-4	Bennett	13,644
Mar 26	Preston North End	D 0-0		12,151
Mar 28	Bradford City	L 1-4	Bennett	22,354
Mar 29	BRADFORD CITY	D 1-1	Hydes	18,277
Apr 2	Burnley	W 3-1	Cochrane, Furness, Hydes	13,037
Apr 9	Chesterfield	D 1-1	Duggan	11,992
Apr 16	NOTTINGHAM FOREST	D 1-1	J Milburn (pen)	12,195
Apr 23	Tottenham Hotspur	L 1-3	Furness	17,285
Apr 30	SOUTHAMPTON	W 1-0	Keetley	13,401
May 7	PORT VALE	L 0-2		9,588

FA Cup

Jan 9	Queens Park Rangers	(Rd 3) L 1-3	J Milburn (pen)	41,097

League & Cup Appearances

PLAYER	LEAGUE	CUP COMPETITION FA CUP	TOTAL
Bennett	10	1	11
Cochrane T	41	1	42
Copping	40	1	41
Danskin	4	1	5
Duggan	35	1	36
Edwards	28	1	29
Firth	33	1	34
Furness	25		25
Green	9		9
Hart	38		38
Hornby	11		11
Hydes	8		8
Keetley	37	1	38
Menzies	28	1	29
Milburn G W	12		12
Milburn J	42	1	43
Moore	10	1	11
Neal	2		2
Potts	32		32
Stacey	9		9
Turbull	1		1
Wainscoat	3		3
Wilkinson	2		2

Goalscorers

PLAYER	LEAGUE	CUP COMPETITION FA CUP	TOTAL
Keetley	23		23
Firth	14		14
Furness	12		12
Cochrane T	9		9
Duggan	5		5
Bennett	4		4
Green	3		3
Hydes	3		3
Milburn J	1	1	2
Danskin	1		1
Hart	1		1
Hornby	1		1
Wainscoat	1		1

Fact File

Nine straight victories in the autumn saw Leeds topping the table.

MANAGER: Arthur Fairclough

CAPTAIN: Jimmy Potts

TOP SCORER: Charlie Keetley

BIGGEST WIN: 5-0 v Oldham Athletic, 3 October 1931, League

HIGHEST ATTENDANCE: 41,109 v Queens Park Rangers, 9 January 1932, lost 1-3, FA Cup, Round 3

MAJOR TRANSFERS IN: Billy Furness from Unsworth Colliery

MAJOR TRANSFERS OUT: Russell Wainscoat to Hull City

Final Division 2 Table

		P	W	D	L	F	A	Pts
1	WOLVERHAMPTON W	42	24	8	10	115	49	56
2	LEEDS UNITED	42	22	10	10	78	54	54
3	STOKE C	42	19	14	9	69	48	52
4	PLYMOUTH ARG	42	20	9	13	100	66	49
5	BURY	42	21	7	14	70	58	49
6	BRADFORD PA	42	21	7	14	72	63	49
7	BRADFORD C	42	16	13	13	80	61	45
8	TOTTENHAM H	42	16	11	15	87	78	43
9	MILLWALL	42	17	9	16	61	61	43
10	CHARLTON ATH	42	17	9	16	61	66	43
11	NOTTINGHAM F	42	16	10	16	77	72	42
12	MANCHESTER U	42	17	8	17	71	72	42
13	PRESTON NE	42	16	10	16	75	77	42
14	SOUTHAMPTON	42	17	7	18	66	77	41
15	SWANSEA T	42	16	7	19	73	75	39
16	NOTTS CO	42	13	12	17	75	75	38
17	CHESTERFIELD	42	13	11	18	64	86	37
18	OLDHAM ATH	42	13	10	19	62	84	36
19	BURNLEY	42	13	9	20	59	87	35
20	PORT VALE	42	13	7	22	58	89	33
21	BARNSLEY	42	12	9	21	55	91	33
22	BRISTOL C	42	6	11	25	39	78	23

Season 1932-33

Football League Division 1

DATE	OPPONENTS	SCORE	GOALSCORERS	ATTENDANCE
Aug 27	DERBY COUNTY	L 0-2		16,344
Aug 29	Blackpool	L 1-2	Roper	20,313
Sep 3	Blackburn Rovers	D 1-1	Cochrane	13,010
Sep 5	BLACKPOOL	W 3-1	Keetley, Copping, Furness	9,171
Sep 10	HUDDERSFIELD TOWN	D 1-1	Keetley	23,882
Sep 17	SHEFFIELD WEDNESDAY	W 3-2	Keetley 2, Duggan	17,977
Sep 24	West Bromwich Albion	W 1-0	Keetley	26,497
Oct 1	BIRMINGHAM	D 1-1	Duggan	14,193
Oct 8	Sunderland	D 0-0		9,651
Oct 15	MANCHESTER CITY	W 2-1	Hydes, J Milburn (pen)	16,898
Oct 22	Sheffield United	D 0-0		13,842
Oct 29	WOLVERHAMPTON W	W 2-0	O'Grady, Hydes	11,486
Nov 5	Liverpool	W 1-0	Duggan	25,464
Nov 12	LEICESTER CITY	D 1-1	Hydes	12,426
Nov 19	Portsmouth	D 3-3	J Milburn (pen), Furness, Cochrane	17,579
Nov 26	CHELSEA	W 2-0	Hydes 2	19,709
Dec 3	Newcastle United	L 1-3	Hydes	20,965
Dec 10	ASTON VILLA	D 1-1	Hydes	23,794
Dec 17	Middlesbrough	W 1-0	Keetley	9,341
Dec 24	BOLTON WANDERERS	W 4-3	Hydes 2, Keetley, Furness	15,804
Dec 26	Arsenal	W 2-1	Keetley 2	55,876
Dec 27	ARSENAL	D 0-0		56,796
Dec 31	Derby County	L 1-5	Keetley	13,375
Jan 7	BLACKBURN ROVERS	W 3-1	Furness, Keetley, Mahon	14,043
Jan 21	Huddersfield Town	D 2-2	O'Grady, Furness	18,619
Feb 4	WEST BROMWICH ALBION	D 1-1	Hydes	19,696
Feb 8	Sheffield Wednesday	L 0-2		9,585
Feb 11	Birmingham	L 1-2	Hydes	22,157
Feb 22	SUNDERLAND	L 2-3	Hydes, Duggan	7,971
Mar 4	SHEFFIELD UNITED	L 1-3	Hydes	13,448
Mar 11	Wolverhampton W	D 3-3	Keetley 3	24,901
Mar 18	LIVERPOOL	W 5-0	Bradshaw o.g., Mahon 2, Hydes, Duggan	12,268
Mar 25	Leicester City	L 1-3	Furness	13,669
Apr 1	PORTSMOUTH	L 0-1		9,839
Apr 5	Manchester City	D 0-0		16,789
Apr 8	Chelsea	L 0-6		31,095
Apr 15	NEWCASTLE UNITED	W 6-1	Fowler 2, Mahon 2, Copping, Hydes	14,967
Apr 17	Everton	W 1-0	Hydes	21,265
Apr 18	EVERTON	W 1-0	Duggan	19,663
Apr 22	Aston Villa	D 0-0		21,238
Apr 29	MIDDLESBROUGH	L 0-1		9,006
May 6	Bolton Wanderers	L 0-5		10,048

FA Cup

Jan 14	Newcastle United	(Rd 3) W 3-0	Hydes 3		47,554
Jan 28	Tranmere Rovers	(Rd 4) D 0-0			20,000
Feb 1	TRANMERE ROVERS	(R) W 4-0	J Milburn (pen), Mahon, Cochrane, Hydes		25,000
Feb 18	Everton	(Rd 5) L 0-2			58,073

League & Cup Appearances

PLAYER	LEAGUE	CUP COMPETITION FA CUP	TOTAL
Cochrane T	30	4	34
Copping	39	4	43
Duggan	28	1	29
Edwards	23	4	27
Firth	5		5
Fowler	6		6
Furness	42	4	46
Green	5		5
Hart	39	4	43
Hornby	3		3
Hydes	39	4	43
Keetley	24	3	27
Mahon	22	3	25
Milburn G W	42	4	46
Milburn J	42	4	46
Moore	12		12
Neal	3		3
O'Grady	8	1	9
Potts	30	4	34
Roper	1		1
Stacey	19		19

Goalscorers

PLAYER	LEAGUE	CUP COMPETITION FA CUP	TOTAL
Hydes	16	4	20
Keetley	14		14
Duggan	6		6
Furness	6		6
Mahon	5	1	6
Cochrane T	2	1	3
Milburn J	2	1	3
Copping	2		2
Fowler	2		2
O'Grady	2		2
Roper	1		1
Opps' o.gs.	1		1

Fact File

Leeds beat Champions Arsenal at Highbury on Boxing Day and then drew with Herbert Chapman's side the following day in front of Elland Road's then biggest ever crowd.

MANAGER: Dick Ray
CAPTAIN: Jimmy Potts
TOP SCORER: Arthur Hydes
BIGGEST WIN: 6-1 v Newcastle United, 15 April 1932, League
HIGHEST ATTENDANCE: 58,073 v Everton, 18 February 1932, lost 0-2, FA Cup, Round 5

Final Division 1 Table

		P	W	D	L	F	A	PTS
1	ARSENAL	42	25	8	9	118	61	58
2	ASTON VILLA	42	23	8	11	92	67	54
3	SHEFFIELD W	42	21	9	12	80	68	51
4	WBA	42	20	9	13	83	70	49
5	NEWCASTLE U	42	22	5	15	71	63	49
6	HUDDERSFIELD T	42	18	11	13	66	53	47
7	DERBY CO	42	15	14	13	76	69	44
8	LEEDS UNITED	42	15	14	13	59	62	44
9	PORTSMOUTH	42	18	7	17	74	76	43
10	SHEFFIELD U	42	17	9	16	74	80	43
11	EVERTON	42	16	9	17	81	74	41
12	SUNDERLAND	42	15	10	17	63	80	40
13	BIRMINGHAM	42	14	11	17	57	57	39
14	LIVERPOOL	42	14	11	17	79	84	39
15	BLACKBURN R	42	14	10	18	76	102	38
16	MANCHESTER C	42	16	5	21	68	71	37
17	MIDDLESBROUGH	42	14	9	19	63	73	37
18	CHELSEA	42	14	7	21	63	73	35
19	LEICESTER C	42	11	13	18	75	89	35
20	WOLVERHAMPTON W	42	13	9	20	80	96	35
21	BOLTON W	42	12	9	21	78	92	33
22	BLACKPOOL	42	14	5	23	69	85	33

Season 1933-34

Football League Division 1

DATE	OPPONENTS	SCORE	GOALSCORERS	ATTENDANCE
Aug 26	Blackburn Rovers	L 2-4	Hydes, Cochrane	10,130
Aug 28	MIDDLESBROUGH	W 5-2	Hydes 4, Roper	10,896
Sep 2	NEWCASTLE UNITED	W 3-0	J Milburn (pen), Cochrane, Hydes	17,721
Sep 9	Huddersfield Town	D 0-0		18,976
Sep 16	Derby County	L 1-3	Hydes	16,584
Sep 23	WEST BROMWICH ALBION	W 3-0	Hydes 2, G Shaw o.g.	17,364
Sep 30	Birmingham	L 0-4		21,566
Oct 7	SHEFFIELD WEDNESDAY	W 2-1	Fowler 2	16,165
Oct 14	Manchester City	W 1-0	Fowler	22,413
Oct 21	PORTSMOUTH	W 1-0	Fowler	18,255
Oct 28	Sunderland	L 2-4	Fowler, Keetley	14,578
Nov 4	ASTON VILLA	L 2-4	Hornby, Furness (pen)	20,148
Nov 11	Liverpool	L 3-4	Hydes, Fowler, Duggan	26,181
Nov 18	TOTTENHAM HOTSPUR	D 0-0		19,681
Nov 25	Leicester City	D 2-2	Duggan, Hydes	14,022
Dec 2	STOKE CITY	W 2-0	Keetley, Hydes	12,601
Dec 9	Sheffield United	L 1-2	Furness	11,113
Dec 16	WOLVERHAMPTON W	D 3-3	Keetley 2, Duggan	11,013
Dec 23	Chelsea	D 1-1	Keetley	18,157
Dec 25	ARSENAL	L 0-1		33,192
Dec 26	Arsenal	L 0-2		22,817
Dec 30	BLACKBURN ROVERS	W 4-0	Hydes 3, Furness	10,722
Jan 1	Middlesbrough	L 1-2	Hydes	16,071
Jan 6	Newcastle United	L 0-2		21,587
Jan 20	HUDDERSFIELD TOWN	D 1-1	J Milburn (pen)	24,957
Jan 31	DERBY COUNTY	L 0-2		11,790
Feb 3	West Bromwich Albion	W 3-0	Roper, Mahon 2	13,343
Feb 10	BIRMINGHAM	W 1-0	Furness	14,753
Feb 24	MANCHESTER CITY	W 3-1	Firth, Mahon, Furness	15,761
Feb 26	Sheffield Wednesday	W 2-0	Firth, Keetley	6,546
Mar 7	Portsmouth	L 1-2	Copping	10,568
Mar 10	SUNDERLAND	W 3-1	Cochrane, Duggan, Furness	7,333
Mar 24	LIVERPOOL	W 5-1	Mahon, Firth 2, Duggan 2	12,907
Mar 30	EVERTON	D 2-2	Duggan 2	19,951
Mar 31	Tottenham Hotspur	L 1-5	Keetley	29,574
Apr 2	Everton	L 0-2		25,624
Apr 7	LEICESTER CITY	W 8-0	Duggan 2, Mahon 2, Furness 2, Firth 2	11,871
Apr 14	Stoke City	W 2-1	Duggan, Firth	16,262
Apr 21	SHEFFIELD UNITED	D 1-1	Holmes o.g.	10,815
Apr 28	Wolverhampton W	L 0-2		5,571
Apr 30	Aston Villa	L 0-3		9,849
May 5	CHELSEA	W 3-1	Mahon, Firth, Cochrane	6,092

FA Cup

Jan 13	PRESTON NORTH END	(Rd 3)	L	0-1	29,158

League & Cup Appearances

PLAYER	LEAGUE	CUP COMPETITION FA CUP	TOTAL
Cochrane	41	1	42
Copping	38	1	39
Duggan	33	1	34
Edwards	15		15
Firth	18	1	19
Fowler	9		9
Furness	41	1	42
Green	2		2
Hart	33	1	34
Hornby	19	1	20
Hydes	19		19
Keetley	15	1	16
Mahon	18		18
Milburn G W	37	1	38
Milburn J	41	1	42
Moore	42	1	43
Neal	1		1
Roper	14		14
Sproston	5		5
Stacey	12		12
Turner	8		8
Wilkinson	1		1

Goalscorers

PLAYER	LEAGUE	CUP COMPETITION FA CUP	TOTAL
Hydes	16		16
Duggan	11		11
Firth	8		8
Furness	8		8
Keetley	7		7
Mahon	7		7
Fowler	6		6
Cochrane	4		4
Milburn J	2		2
Roper	2		2
Copping	1		1
Hornby	1		1
Opps' o.gs.	2		2

Fact File

Leeds' record home win, 8-0 over Leicester City, was achieved without regular strikers Keetley and Hydes.

MANAGER: Dick Ray
CAPTAIN: Wilf Copping
TOP SCORER: Arthur Hydes
BIGGEST WIN: 8-0 v Leicester City, 7 April 1934, League
HIGHEST ATTENDANCE: 33,192 v Arsenal, 25 December 1933, lost 0-1, League

Final Division 1 Table

		P	W	D	L	F	A	Pts
1	ARSENAL	42	25	9	8	75	47	59
2	HUDDERSFIELD T	42	23	10	9	90	61	56
3	TOTTENHAM H	42	21	7	14	79	56	49
4	DERBY CO	42	17	11	14	68	54	45
5	MANCHESTER C	42	17	11	14	65	72	45
6	SUNDERLAND	42	16	12	14	81	56	44
7	WBA	42	17	10	15	78	70	44
8	BLACKBURN R	42	18	7	17	74	81	43
9	LEEDS UNITED	42	17	8	17	75	66	42
10	PORTSMOUTH	42	15	12	15	52	55	42
11	SHEFFIELD W	42	16	9	17	62	67	41
12	STOKE C	42	15	11	16	58	71	41
13	ASTON VILLA	42	14	12	16	78	75	40
14	EVERTON	42	12	16	14	62	63	40
15	WOLVERHAMPTON W	42	14	12	16	74	86	40
16	MIDDLESBROUGH	42	16	7	19	68	80	39
17	LEICESTER C	42	14	11	17	59	74	39
18	LIVERPOOL	42	14	10	18	79	87	38
19	CHELSEA	42	14	8	20	67	69	36
20	BIRMINGHAM	42	12	12	18	54	56	36
21	NEWCASTLE U	42	10	14	18	68	77	34
22	SHEFFIELD U	42	12	7	23	58	101	31

Season 1934-35

Football League Division 1

DATE	OPPONENTS	SCORE	GOALSCORERS	ATTENDANCE
Aug 25	MIDDLESBROUGH	L 2-4	Mills 2	15,949
Aug 27	Stoke City	L 1-8	Hornby	24,568
Sep 1	Blackburn Rovers	D 1-1	J Milburn (pen)	12,316
Sep 3	STOKE CITY	W 4-2	Cochrane, Mahon, Furness, Duggan	8,932
Sep 8	ARSENAL	D 1-1	Furness	29,447
Sep 15	Portsmouth	D 0-0		17,470
Sep 22	LIVERPOOL	L 0-3		10,877
Sep 29	HUDDERSFIELD TOWN	W 2-0	Duggan 2	12,298
Oct 6	West Bromwich Albion	L 3-6	J Milburn (pen), Duggan, Mahon	15,843
Oct 13	SHEFFIELD WEDNESDAY	D 0-0		16,860
Oct 20	EVERTON	W 2-0	Hydes, Furness	16,731
Oct 27	Grimsby Town	L 2-3	Hydes 2	10,940
Nov 3	CHELSEA	W 5-2	McAulay o.g., Furness, Hydes, Mahon	13,295
Nov 10	Wolverhampton W	W 2-1	J Milburn (pen), Mahon	13,602
Nov 17	SUNDERLAND	L 2-4	Duggan, Furness	24,141
Nov 24	Leicester City	L 0-1		12,785
Dec 1	DERBY COUNTY	W 4-2	Furness 2, Hydes 2	16,565
Dec 8	Aston Villa	D 1-1	Hydes	31,682
Dec 15	PRESTON NORTH END	D 3-3	Hornby, Duggan 2	13,342
Dec 22	Tottenham Hotspur	D 1-1	Furness	23,662
Dec 25	MANCHESTER CITY	L 1-2	J Milburn (pen)	24,810
Dec 26	Manchester City	L 0-3		51,387
Dec 29	Middlesbrough	D 3-3	Hydes 2, Mahon	15,615
Jan 5	BLACKBURN ROVERS	W 5-1	Hydes 3, Firth, Furness	13,832
Jan 19	Arsenal	L 0-3		37,026
Feb 2	Liverpool	L 2-4	Hydes 2	21,201
Feb 9	Huddersfield Town	L 1-3	Mahon	18,413
Feb 20	WEST BROMWICH ALBION	W 4-1	J Milburn (pen), Mahon 2, Duggan	7,408
Feb 23	Sheffield Wednesday	L 0-1		19,591
Mar 2	PORTSMOUTH	W 3-1	Hydes 2, G.W Milburn	13,450
Mar 6	Everton	D 4-4	Hydes 2, Stephenson 2	10,441
Mar 9	GRIMSBY TOWN	W 3-1	Hodgson o.g., Hydes, J Milburn (pen)	15,458
Mar 16	Chelsea	L 1-7	J Kelly	35,698
Mar 23	WOLVERHAMPTON W	D 1-1	Hornby	9,001
Mar 30	Sunderland	L 0-3		19,118
Apr 6	LEICESTER CITY	L 0-2		12,086
Apr 13	Derby County	W 2-1	Furness 2	11,041
Apr 19	BIRMINGHAM	D 1-1	Furness	14,786
Apr 20	ASTON VILLA	D 1-1	Furness	16,234
Apr 22	Birmingham	L 1-3	Furness	18,008
Apr 27	Preston North End	W 2-0	Duggan, Hydes	11,758
May 4	TOTTENHAM HOTSPUR	W 4-3	Furness 2, Hydes, Hart	7,668

FA Cup

Jan 12	BRADFORD PARK AVENUE (Rd 3)	W 4-1	Hydes 2, Furness, Mahon	35,444
Jan 26	Norwich City	(Rd 4) D 3-3	Mahon, Duggan, Cochrane	13,710
Jan 30	NORWICH CITY	(R) L 1-2	Hydes	27,269

League & Cup Appearances

PLAYER	LEAGUE	CUP COMPETITION FA CUP	TOTAL
Abel	1		1
Cochrane T	41	3	44
Daniels	1		1
Duggan	35	2	37
Edwards	28	2	30
Firth	7	1	8
Furness	34	2	36
Hart	27	1	28
Hornby	34		34
Hydes	30	3	33
Keetley	1		1
Kelly J	10	1	11
Kelly J M	2		2
Mahon	32	3	35
McDougall	11	3	14
Milburn G W	17		17
Milburn J	41	3	44
Mills	16		16
Moore	14	3	17
Neal	9	3	12
Roper	3		3
Savage	27		27
Sproston	25	3	28
Stephenson	4		4
Turner	5		5
Wilcockson	4		4
Worsley	3		3

Goalscorers

PLAYER	LEAGUE	CUP COMPETITION FA CUP	TOTAL
Hydes	22	3	25
Furness	16	1	17
Duggan	9	1	10
Mahon	8	2	10
Milburn J	6		6
Hornby	3		3
Mills	2		2
Stephenson	2		2
Cochrane T	1	1	2
Firth	1		1
Hart	1		1
Kelly J	1		1
Milburn GW	1		1
Opps' o.gs.	2		2

Fact File

Leeds took the lead in the tenth minute of the match at Chelsea on 16 March only to let in seven.

MANAGER: Dick Ray/Billy Hampson

CAPTAIN: Jock McDougall

TOP SCORER: Arthur Hydes

BIGGEST WIN: 5-1 v Blackburn Rovers, 5 January 1934, League

HIGHEST ATTENDANCE: 37,026 v Arsenal, 19 January 1935, lost 0-3, League

MAJOR TRANSFERS OUT: Wilf Copping to Arsenal, Jimmy Potts to Port Vale

Final Division 1 Table

		P	W	D	L	F	A	Pts
1	ARSENAL	42	23	12	7	115	46	58
2	SUNDERLAND	42	19	16	7	90	51	54
3	SHEFFIELD W	42	18	13	11	70	64	49
4	MANCHESTER C	42	20	8	14	82	67	48
5	GRIMSBY T	42	17	11	14	78	60	45
6	DERBY CO	42	18	9	15	81	66	45
7	LIVERPOOL	42	19	7	16	85	88	45
8	EVERTON	42	16	12	14	89	88	44
9	WBA	42	17	10	15	83	83	44
10	STOKE C	42	18	6	18	71	70	42
11	PRESTON NE	42	15	12	15	62	67	42
12	CHELSEA	42	16	9	17	73	82	41
13	ASTON VILLA	42	14	13	15	74	88	41
14	PORTSMOUTH	42	15	10	17	71	72	40
15	BLACKBURN R	42	14	11	17	66	78	39
16	HUDDERSFIELD T	42	14	10	18	76	71	38
17	WOLVERHAMPTON W	42	15	8	19	88	94	38
18	LEEDS UNITED	42	13	12	17	75	92	38
19	BIRMINGHAM	42	13	10	19	63	81	36
20	MIDDLESBROUGH	42	10	14	18	70	90	34
21	LEICESTER C	42	12	9	21	61	86	33
22	TOTTENHAM H	42	10	10	22	54	93	30

Season 1935-36

Football League Division 1

DATE	OPPONENTS	SCORE	GOALSCORERS	ATTENDANCE
Aug 31	Stoke City	L 1-3	J Milburn (pen)	22,552
Sep 4	BIRMINGHAM	D 0-0		13,271
Sep 7	BLACKBURN ROVERS	L 1-4	Hydes	14,514
Sep 11	Birmingham	L 0-2		14,298
Sep 14	Chelsea	L 0-1		35,270
Sep 18	ARSENAL	D 1-1	J Kelly	24,283
Sep 21	LIVERPOOL	W 1-0	J Milburn (pen)	17,931
Sep 28	Grimsby Town	W 1-0	J Kelly	11,236
Oct 5	HUDDERSFIELD TOWN	D 2-2	J Milburn (pen), Brown	33,224
Oct 12	WEST BROMWICH ALBION	D 1-1	J Milburn (pen)	21,657
Oct 19	Middlesbrough	D 1-1	J Milburn (pen)	12,256
Oct 26	ASTON VILLA	W 4-2	Brown 2, J Kelly 2	19,358
Nov 2	Wolverhampton W	L 0-3		22,243
Nov 9	SHEFFIELD WEDNESDAY	W 7-2	J Kelly, Cochrane, Duggan 3, Edwards, J Milburn (pen)	19,897
Nov 16	Portsmouth	D 2-2	Duggan, Furness	15,120
Nov 23	BOLTON WANDERERS	W 5-2	Duggan, Brown 2, J Kelly, Furness	22,973
Nov 30	Brentford	D 2-2	Cochrane, Brown	23,914
Dec 7	DERBY COUNTY	W 1-0	Brown	21,331
Dec 14	Everton	D 0-0		28,901
Dec 21	PRESTON NORTH END	L 0-1		17,749
Dec 26	Sunderland	L 1-2	J Milburn (pen)	25,296
Dec 28	STOKE CITY	W 4-1	Brown 2, J Kelly, J Milburn (pen)	18,621
Jan 4	Blackburn Rovers	W 3-0	Duggan, Brown, J Kelly	13,110
Jan 18	CHELSEA	W 2-0	Brown, Furness	18,999
Feb 1	GRIMSBY TOWN	L 1-2	Hodgeson o.g.	24,212
Feb 8	Huddersfield Town	W 2-1	J Kelly, Brown	20,862
Feb 19	West Bromwich Albion	L 2-3	Furness, Stephenson	7,939
Feb 22	MIDDLESBROUGH	L 0-1		21,055
Feb 29	Sheffield Wednesday	L 0-3		6,316
Mar 7	BRENTFORD	L 1-2	Brown	10,509
Mar 14	Aston Villa	D 3-3	Furness, Brown, J Kelly	37,382
Mar 18	Liverpool	L 1-2	Brown	16,210
Mar 21	PORTSMOUTH	W 1-0	J Milburn (pen)	13,031
Mar 28	Bolton Wanderers	L 0-3		21,289
Apr 4	WOLVERHAMPTON W	W 2-0	Hydes, J Kelly	10,754
Apr 10	Manchester City	W 3-1	Hydes 2, J Kelly	17,175
Apr 11	Derby County	L 1-2	J Kelly	15,585
Apr 13	MANCHESTER CITY	D 1-1	Furness	38,773
Apr 18	EVERTON	W 3-1	J Kelly, Brown 2	13,738
Apr 22	SUNDERLAND	W 3-0	Brown (pen), J Kelly, Cochrane	16,682
Apr 25	Preston North End	L 0-5		10,927
May 2	Arsenal	D 2-2	Furness (pen), Hydes	25,920

FA Cup

DATE	OPPONENTS	SCORE	GOALSCORERS	ATTENDANCE
Jan 11	Wolverhampton W	D 1-1	McDougall	39,176
Jan 15	WOLVERHAMPTON W	W 3-1	J Kelly, Cochrane, Duggan	35,637
Jan 28	BURY	W 3-2	Brown 2, Duggan	19,633
Feb 15	Sheffield United	L 1-3	Furness	68,287

League & Cup Appearances

PLAYER	LEAGUE	CUP COMPETITION FA CUP	TOTAL
Armes	7	1	8
Brown	33	4	37
Browne	25	4	29
Cane	10		10
Carr	2		2
Cochrane	40	4	44
Duggan	29	3	32
Edwards	39	4	43
Furness	34	4	38
Hargreaves	2		2
Hart	4		4
Hornby	11		11
Hydes	10		10
Kelly J	34	4	38
Kelly JM	2		2
Mahon	4		4
Makinson	3		3
McDougall	29	4	33
McInroy	41	4	45
Milburn GW	5		5
Milburn J	39	4	43
Neal	5		5
Savage	1		1
Sproston	40	4	44
Stephenson	10		10
Turner	3		3

Goalscorers

PLAYER	LEAGUE	CUP COMPETITION FA CUP	TOTAL
Brown	18	2	20
Kelly J	15	1	16
Milburn J	10		10
Furness	7	1	8
Duggan	6	2	8
Hydes	5		5
Cochrane	3	1	4
Stephenson	1		1
Edwards	1		1
McDougall		1	1
Opps' o.gs.	1		1

Fact File

Leading goalscorer, George 'Mickey' Brown, had just one full season at Elland Road. He joined from Aston Villa having been Huddersfield's star striker in their 1920s heyday.

MANAGER: Billy Hampson

CAPTAIN: Jock McDougall

TOP SCORER: George 'Mickey' Brown

BIGGEST WIN: 7-2 v Sheffield Wednesday, 9 November 1935, League

HIGHEST ATTENDANCE: 68,287 v Sheffield United, 15 February 1936, lost 1-3, FA Cup Round 5

MAJOR TRANSFERS IN: Albert McInroy from Sunderland, George Brown from Burnley

MAJOR TRANSFERS OUT: Ernie Hart to Mansfield

Final Division 1 Table

		P	W	D	L	F	A	Pts
1	SUNDERLAND	42	25	6	11	109	74	56
2	DERBY CO	42	18	12	12	61	52	48
3	HUDDERSFIELD T	42	18	12	12	59	56	48
4	STOKE C	42	20	7	15	57	57	47
5	BRENTFORD	42	17	12	13	81	60	46
6	ARSENAL	42	15	15	12	78	48	45
7	PRESTON NE	42	18	8	16	67	64	44
8	CHELSEA	42	15	13	14	65	72	43
9	MANCHESTER C	42	17	8	17	68	60	42
10	PORTSMOUTH	42	17	8	17	54	67	42
11	LEEDS UNITED	42	15	11	16	66	64	41
12	BIRMINGHAM	42	15	11	16	61	63	41
13	BOLTON W	42	14	13	15	67	76	41
14	MIDDLESBROUGH	42	15	10	17	84	70	40
15	WOLVERHAMPTON W	42	15	10	17	77	76	40
16	EVERTON	42	13	13	16	89	89	39
17	GRIMSBY T	42	17	5	20	65	73	39
18	WBA	42	16	6	20	89	88	38
19	LIVERPOOL	42	13	12	17	60	64	38
20	SHEFFIELD W	42	13	12	17	63	77	38
21	ASTON VILLA	42	13	9	20	81	110	35
22	BLACKBURN R	42	12	9	21	55	96	33

Season 1936-37

Football League Division 1

DATE	OPPONENTS	SCORE	GOALSCORERS	ATTENDANCE
Aug 29	CHELSEA	L 2-3	J Milburn 2 (1 pen)	19,379
Sep 2	Manchester City	L 0-4		24,726
Sep 5	Stoke City	L 1-2	Stephenson	19,193
Sep 9	MANCHESTER CITY	D 1-1	Hargreaves	13,933
Sep 12	CHARLTON ATHLETIC	W 2-0	Edwards, Brown	13,789
Sep 16	Portsmouth	L 0-3		12,222
Sep 19	Grimsby Town	L 1-4	Betmead o.g.	11,217
Sep 26	LIVERPOOL	W 2-0	Furness, Hargreaves	16,861
Oct 3	Huddersfield Town	L 0-3		18,654
Oct 10	Birmingham	L 1-2	Hydes	23,833
Oct 17	EVERTON	W 3-0	Thomson, Stephenson, Hydes	16,861
Oct 24	Bolton Wanderers	L 1-2	Thomson	20,411
Oct 31	BRENTFORD	D 3-1	Armes, Stephenson, Hydes	21,498
Nov 7	Arsenal	L 1-4	Thomson	32,535
Nov 14	PRESTON NORTH END	W 1-0	Hydes	15,651
Nov 21	Sheffield Wednesday	W 2-1	Hydes 2	18,411
Nov 28	MANCHESTER UNITED	W 2-1	Stephenson, Thomson	17,610
Dec 5	Derby County	L 3-5	Buckley 2, Hydes	15,557
Dec 19	Sunderland	L 1-2	Ainsley	23,633
Dec 25	MIDDLESBROUGH	W 5-0	Hydes, Ross o.g., Ainsley 2, Buckley	30,647
Dec 26	Chelsea	L 1-2	Hydes	27,761
Dec 28	Middlesbrough	L 2-4	Hydes, Powell	14,191
Jan 2	STOKE CITY	W 2-1	Buckley, Ainsley	13,506
Jan 9	Charlton Athletic	L 0-1		26,760
Jan 23	GRIMSBY TOWN	W 2-0	Hydes, Furness	11,752
Jan 30	Liverpool	L 0-3		11,252
Feb 6	HUDDERSFIELD TOWN	W 2-1	Edwards, Mountford o.g.	28,930
Feb 13	BIRMINGHAM	L 0-2		13,674
Feb 27	BOLTON WANDERERS	D 2-2	Edwards, Furness	15,090
Mar 3	Everton	L 1-7	Hodgson	17,064
Mar 6	Brentford	L 1-4	Powell	16,588
Mar 13	ARSENAL	L 3-4	Thomson, Hodgson, Buckley	25,148
Mar 20	Preston North End	L 0-1		18,050
Mar 27	SHEFFIELD WEDNESDAY	D 1-1	Ainsley	20,776
Mar 29	West Bromwich Albion	L 0-3		31,247
Mar 30	WEST BROMWICH ALBION	W 3-1	Hodgson 2, Stephenson	16,016
Apr 3	Manchester United	D 0-0		34,429
Apr 10	DERBY COUNTY	W 2-0	Stephenson, Hodgson	20,228
Apr 17	Wolverhampton W	L 0-3		13,688
Apr 21	WOLVERHAMPTON W	L 0-1		14,220
Apr 24	SUNDERLAND	W 3-0	Furness, Hodgson, J Milburn (pen)	22,234
May 1	PORTSMOUTH	W 3-1	Furness, Kelly, J Milburn (pen)	15,034

FA Cup

Jan 16	Chelsea	(Rd 3) L 0-4		34,589

League & Cup Appearances

PLAYER	LEAGUE	CUP COMPETITION FA CUP	TOTAL
Ainsley	13	1	14
Armes	20		20
Brown	4		4
Browne	16		16
Buckley	30	1	31
Cane	27	1	28
Cochrane T	2		2
Duggan	1		1
Edwards	35	1	36
Furness	27		27
Gadsby	1		1
Hargreaves	10		10
Hodgson	13		13
Holley	7		7
Hydes	19	1	20
Kelly J	10		10
Makinson	5		5
McDougall	12		12
McInroy	26		26
Milburn G W	16	1	17
Milburn J	38		38
Mills	31	1	32
Powell	11	1	12
Savage	16	1	17
Sproston	23	1	24
Stephenson	22		22
Tomson	16		16
Trainor	2	1	3
Turner	9		9

Goalscorers

PLAYER	LEAGUE	CUP COMPETITION FA CUP	TOTAL
Hydes	11		11
Hodgson	6		6
Stephenson	6		6
Ainsley	5		5
Buckley	5		5
Furness	5		5
Milburn J	4		4
Edwards	3		3
Hargreaves	2		2
Powell	2		2
Armes	1		1
Brown	1		1
Kelly J	1		1
Opps' o.gs.	3		3

Fact File

At the age of 34, Gordon Hodgson scored on his debut in the defeat at Everton on 3 March.

MANAGER: Billy Hampson

CAPTAIN: Jock McDougall

TOP SCORER: Arthur Hydes

BIGGEST WIN: 5-0 v Middlesbrough, 25 December 1936, League

HIGHEST ATTENDANCE: 34,589 v Chelsea, 16 January 1937, lost 0-4, FA Cup Round 3

MAJOR TRANSFERS IN: Gordon Hodgson from Aston Villa

MAJOR TRANSFERS OUT: Bert Sproston to Tottenham Hotspur

Final Division 1 Table

		P	W	D	L	F	A	Pts
1	MANCHESTER C	42	22	13	7	107	61	57
2	CHARLTON ATH	42	21	12	9	58	49	54
3	ARSENAL	42	18	16	8	80	49	52
4	DERBY CO	42	21	7	14	96	90	49
5	WOLVERHAMPTON W	42	21	5	16	84	67	47
6	BRENTFORD	42	18	10	14	82	78	46
7	MIDDLESBROUGH	42	19	8	15	74	71	46
8	SUNDERLAND	42	19	6	17	89	87	44
9	PORTSMOUTH	42	17	10	15	62	66	44
10	STOKE C	42	15	12	15	72	57	42
11	BIRMINGHAM	42	13	15	14	64	60	41
12	GRIMSBY T	42	17	7	18	86	81	41
13	CHELSEA	42	14	13	15	52	55	41
14	PRESTON NE	42	14	13	15	56	67	41
15	HUDDERSFIELD T	42	12	15	15	62	64	39
16	WBA	42	16	6	20	77	98	38
17	EVERTON	42	14	9	19	81	78	37
18	LIVERPOOL	42	12	11	19	62	84	35
19	LEEDS UNITED	42	15	4	23	60	80	34
20	BOLTON W	42	10	14	18	43	66	34
21	MANCHESTER U	42	10	12	20	55	78	32
22	SHEFFIELD W	42	9	12	21	53	69	30

Season 1937-38

Football League Division 1

DATE	OPPONENTS	SCORE		GOALSCORERS	ATTENDANCE
Aug 28	Charlton Athletic	D	1-1	Hodgson	30,979
Sep 1	CHELSEA	W	2-0	Armes, Barber o.g.	18,858
Sep 4	PRESTON NORTH END	D	0-0		22,513
Sep 8	Chelsea	L	1-4	Hodgson	17,300
Sep 11	Grimsby Town	D	1-1	Hodgson	9,328
Sep 15	PORTSMOUTH	W	3-1	Hodgson 2, Ainsley	12,579
Sep 18	HUDDERSFIELD TOWN	W	2-1	Milburn (pen), Armes	33,200
Sep 25	LIVERPOOL	W	2-0	Armes, Ainsley	21,477
Oct 2	West Bromwich Albion	L	1-2	Milburn (pen)	25,609
Oct 9	BIRMINGHAM	W	1-0	Ainsley	20,698
Oct 16	Everton	D	1-1	Armes	26,035
Oct 23	WOLVERHAMPTON W	L	1-2	Buckley	13,304
Oct 30	Leicester City	W	4-2	Hodgson 2, Milburn (pen), Buckley	18,833
Nov 6	BLACKPOOL	D	1-1	Buckley	18,438
Nov 13	Derby County	D	2-2	Thomson, Hodgson	15,966
Nov 20	BOLTON WANDERERS	D	1-1	Hodgson	23,687
Nov 27	Arsenal	L	1-4	Stephenson	34,350
Dec 4	SUNDERLAND	W	4-3	Stephenson 3, Hodgson	15,349
Dec 11	Brentford	D	1-1	Hodgson	18,184
Dec 18	MANCHESTER CITY	W	2-1	Stephenson, Buckley	22,144
Dec 25	MIDDLESBROUGH	W	5-3	Hodgson 2, Buckley, Stephenson, Thomson	37,020
Dec 27	Middlesbrough	L	0-2		34,640
Jan 1	CHARLTON ATHLETIC	D	2-2	Stephenson, Buckley	26,433
Jan 15	Preston North End	L	1-3	Thomson	14,032
Jan 26	GRIMSBY TOWN	D	1-1	Buckley	10,512
Jan 29	Huddersfield Town	W	3-0	Armes, Buckley, Thomson	16,677
Feb 5	Liverpool	D	1-1	Hodgson	34,468
Feb 12	WEST BROMWICH ALBION	W	1-0	Hodgson	21,819
Feb 19	Birmingham	L	2-3	Hodgson, Thomson	20,403
Feb 26	EVERTON	D	4-4	Hodgson 4	23,497
Mar 5	Wolverhampton W	D	1-1	Sproston	38,849
Mar 12	LEICESTER CITY	L	0-2		19,839
Mar 19	Blackpool	L	2-5	Ainsley, Hodgson	18,029
Mar 26	DERBY COUNTY	L	0-2		19,911
Apr 2	Bolton Wanderers	D	0-0		18,492
Apr 9	ARSENAL	L	0-1		29,365
Apr 16	Sunderland	D	0-0		21,450
Apr 18	Stoke City	W	1-0	Mould o.g.	25,114
Apr 19	STOKE CITY	W	2-1	Ainsley, Stephenson	17,896
Apr 23	BRENTFORD	W	4-0	Hodgson 3, Ainsley	17,840
Apr 30	Manchester City	L	2-6	Hodgson, Buckley	26,732
May 7	Portsmouth	L	0-4		29,571

FA Cup

Jan 8	CHESTER	(Rd 3) W	3-1	Armes, Buckley 2	37,155
Jan 22	Charlton Athletic	(Rd 4) L	1-2	Hodgson	50,516

League & Cup Appearances

PLAYER	LEAGUE	CUP COMPETITION FA CUP	TOTAL
Ainsley	26	2	28
Armes	39	2	41
Browne	31		31
Buckley	35	2	37
Cochrane T	1		1
Edwards	3		3
Francis	1		1
Goldberg	3		3
Hargreaves	7		7
Hodgson	36	2	38
Holley	24		24
Kane	14	2	16
Kelly D	4		4
Kelly J	5		5
Makinson	40	2	42
Milburn J	42	2	44
Mills	12	2	14
Savage	32	2	34
Sproston	37	2	39
Stephenson	38	2	40
Thomson	19		19
Trainor	1		1
Turner	2		2
Twomey	10		10

Goalscorers

PLAYER	LEAGUE	CUP COMPETITION FA CUP	TOTAL
Hodgson	25	1	26
Buckley	9	2	11
Stephenson	8		8
Ainsley	6		6
Armes	5	1	6
Thomson	5		5
Milburn Jack	3		3
Opps' o.gs.	2		2

Fact File

Eric Stephenson made his England debut against Scotland in April. His death during the Second World War would rob Leeds of one of its most promising young players.

MANAGER: Billy Hampson
CAPTAIN: Tom Holley
TOP SCORER: Gordon Hodgson
BIGGEST WIN: 4-0 v Brentford, 23 April 1938, League
HIGHEST ATTENDANCE: 50,516 v Charlton Athletic, 22 January 1938, lost 1-2, FA Cup, Round 4

Final Division 1 Table

		P	W	D	L	F	A	Pts
1	ARSENAL	42	21	10	11	77	44	52
2	WOLVERHAMPTON W	42	20	11	11	72	49	51
3	PRESTON NE	42	16	17	9	64	44	49
4	CHARLTON ATH	42	16	14	12	65	51	46
5	MIDDLESBROUGH	42	19	8	15	72	65	46
6	BRENTFORD	42	18	9	15	69	59	45
7	BOLTON W	42	15	15	12	64	60	45
8	SUNDERLAND	42	14	16	12	55	57	44
9	LEEDS UNITED	42	14	15	13	64	69	43
10	CHELSEA	42	14	13	15	65	65	41
11	LIVERPOOL	42	15	11	16	65	71	41
12	BLACKPOOL	42	16	8	18	61	66	40
13	DERBY CO	42	15	10	17	66	87	40
14	EVERTON	42	16	7	19	79	75	39
15	HUDDERSFIELD T	42	17	5	20	55	68	39
16	LEICESTER C	42	14	11	17	54	75	39
17	STOKE C	42	13	12	17	58	59	38
18	BIRMINGHAM	42	10	18	14	58	62	38
19	PORTSMOUTH	42	13	12	17	62	68	38
20	GRIMSBY T	42	13	12	17	51	68	38
21	MANCHESTER C	42	14	8	20	80	77	36
22	WBA	42	14	8	20	74	91	36

The Essential History of Leeds United

Football League Division 1

DATE	OPPONENTS	SCORE	GOALSCORERS	ATTENDANCE
Aug 27	PRESTON NORTH END	W 2-1	Hodgson, Buckley	19,255
Aug 31	BIRMINGHAM	W 2-0	Ainsley, Buckley	13,578
Sep 3	Charlton Athletic	L 0-2		30,383
Sep 5	Stoke City	D 1-1	Hodgson	16,052
Sep 10	BOLTON WANDERERS	L 1-2	Hodgson	20,381
Sep 17	Huddersfield Town	W 1-0	Hodgson	19,793
Sep 24	Liverpool	L 0-3		32,197
Oct 1	LEICESTER CITY	W 8-2	Hodgson 5, Cochrane, Milburn (pen), Hargreaves	15,001
Oct 8	Middlesbrough	W 2-1	Armes, Hodgson	23,009
Oct 15	WOLVERHAMPTON W	W 1-0	Thomson	25,860
Oct 22	Everton	L 0-4		30,747
Oct 29	PORTSMOUTH	D 2-2	Ainsley, Rowe o.g.	18,055
Nov 5	Arsenal	W 3-2	Stephenson 2, Buckley	39,092
Nov 12	BRENTFORD	W 3-2	Hodgson 2, Buckley	22,555
Nov 19	Blackpool	W 2-1	Hodgson, Hargreaves	16,612
Nov 26	DERBY COUNTY	L 1-4	Buckley	34,158
Dec 3	Grimsby Town	L 2-3	Armes, Powell	11,202
Dec 10	SUNDERLAND	D 3-3	Ainsley, Hargreaves, Powell	20,853
Dec 17	Aston Villa	L 1-2	Hargreaves	28,990
Dec 24	Preston North End	L 0-2		18,424
Dec 26	CHELSEA	D 1-1	Edwards	27,586
Dec 27	Chelsea	D 2-2	Hodgson, Stephenson	32,692
Dec 31	CHARLTON ATHLETIC	W 2-1	Hodgson, Cochrane	18,774
Jan 14	Bolton Wanderers	D 2-2	Hodgson, Goslin o.g.	14,893
Jan 28	LIVERPOOL	D 1-1	Hodgson	13,679
Feb 4	Leicester City	L 0-2		12,618
Feb 11	MIDDLESBROUGH	L 0-1		18,273
Feb 18	Wolverhampton W	L 1-4	Sutherland	31,977
Feb 25	EVERTON	L 1-2	Ainsley	21,728
Mar 8	Portsmouth	L 0-2		14,469
Mar 11	ARSENAL	W 4-2	Stephenson (pen), Powell, Hodgson, Hargreaves	22,160
Mar 18	Brentford	W 1-0	Hargreaves	21,480
Mar 25	BLACKPOOL	W 1-0	Cochrane	21,818
Apr 1	Derby County	L 0-1		11,278
Apr 7	Manchester United	D 0-0		35,564
Apr 8	GRIMSBY TOWN	L 0-1		19,700
Apr 10	MANCHESTER UNITED	W 3-1	Ainsley, Hodgson, Buckley	13,771
Apr 15	Sunderland	L 1-2	Ainsley	10,913
Apr 19	HUDDERSFIELD TOWN	W 2-1	Hodgson, Powell	12,006
Apr 22	ASTON VILLA	W 2-0	Hargreaves 2	14,241
Apr 29	Birmingham	L 0-4		12,522
May 6	STOKE CITY	D 0-0		12,048

FA Cup

Jan 17	BOURNEMOUTH	(Rd 3) W 3-1	Stephenson, Hargreaves, Cochrane	10,114
Jan 21	HUDDERSFIELD TOWN	(Rd 4) L 2-4	Hodgson, Cochrane	43,702

League & Cup Appearances

PLAYER	LEAGUE	CUP COMPETITION FA CUP	TOTAL
Ainsley	20		20
Armes	13		13
Browne	16		16
Buckley	16		16
Cochrane D	27	2	29
Copping	12		12
Dunderdale	3		3
Edwards	20	2	22
Gadsby	37	2	39
Goldberg	16		16
Hampson	2		2
Hargreaves	26	2	28
Henry	2		2
Hodgson	32	2	34
Holley	37	2	39
Kane	5		5
Makinson	20		20
Milburn J	22	2	24
Mills	8		8
Parry	6	2	8
Powell	28	2	30
Savage	3	2	5
Scaife	9		9
Stephenson	34	2	36
Sutherland	3		3
Thomson	6		6
Twomey	39		39

Goalscorers

PLAYER	LEAGUE	CUP COMPETITION FA CUP	TOTAL
Hodgson	20	1	21
Hargreaves	8	1	9
Ainsley	6		6
Buckley	6		6
Stephenson	4	1	5
Cochrane D	3	2	5
Powell	4		4
Armes	2		2
Edwards	1		1
Milburn J	1		1
Sutherland	1		1
Thomson	1		1
Opps' o.gs.	2		2

Fact File

For the second time in six seasons Leeds ran in eight goals against Leicester City.

MANAGER: Billy Hampson

CAPTAIN: Tom Holley

TOP SCORER: Arthur Hydes

BIGGEST WIN: 8-2 v Leicester City, 1 October 1938, League

HIGHEST ATTENDANCE: 43,702 v Huddersfield Town, 21 January 1939, lost 2-4, FA Cup Round 4

MAJOR TRANSFERS IN: Wilf Copping from Arsenal, David Cochrane from Portadown

MAJOR TRANSFERS OUT: George Brown to Darlington

Final Division 1 Table

		P	W	D	L	F	A	Pts
1	EVERTON	42	27	5	10	88	52	59
2	WOLVERHAMPTON W	42	22	11	9	88	39	55
3	CHARLTON ATH	42	22	6	14	75	59	50
4	MIDDLESBROUGH	42	20	9	13	93	74	49
5	ARSENAL	42	19	9	14	55	41	47
6	DERBY CO	42	19	8	15	66	55	46
7	STOKE C	42	17	12	13	71	68	46
8	BOLTON W	42	15	15	12	67	58	45
9	PRESTON NE	42	16	12	14	63	59	44
10	GRIMSBY T	42	16	11	15	61	69	43
11	LIVERPOOL	42	14	14	14	62	63	42
12	ASTON VILLA	42	15	11	16	71	60	41
13	LEEDS UNITED	42	16	9	17	59	67	41
14	MANCHESTER U	42	11	16	15	57	65	38
15	BLACKPOOL	42	12	14	16	56	68	38
16	SUNDERLAND	42	13	12	17	54	67	38
17	PORTSMOUTH	42	12	13	17	47	70	37
18	BRENTFORD	42	14	8	20	53	74	36
19	HUDDERSFIELD T	42	12	11	19	58	64	35
20	CHELSEA	42	12	9	21	64	80	33
21	BIRMINGHAM	42	12	8	22	62	84	32
22	LEICESTER C	42	9	11	22	48	82	29

Season 1945-46

Football League (North)

DATE	OPPONENTS	SCORE	GOALSCORERS	ATTENDANCE
Aug 25	Chesterfield	L 1-3	Hindle	7,229
Sep 1	CHESTERFIELD	L 1-3	Short	7,339
Sep 8	BARNSLEY	L 1-2	Powell	8,561
Sep 13	Stoke City	L 1-2	Hindle	6,882
Sep 15	Barnsley	L 2-3	Henry, Hindle	10,055
Sep 22	Everton	W 2-0	Grainger, Henry	19,711
Sep 29	EVERTON	L 2-3	Short, Hindle	13,541
Oct 6	BOLTON WANDERERS	W 2-1	Grainger, Hindle	11,836
Oct 13	Bolton Wanderers	L 0-6		17,770
Oct 20	PRESTON NORTH END	W 2-1	Dutchman, Henry	11,782
Oct 27	Preston North End	L 2-8	Chew, Henry	12,344
Nov 3	BURNLEY	L 1-2	Ainsley	11,387
Nov 10	Burnley	W 3-2	Ainsley, Henry, Short	6,925
Nov 17	MANCHESTER UNITED	D 3-3	Ainsley, Short, Henry	12,013
Nov 24	Manchester United	L 1-6	Whalley o.g.	21,312
Dec 1	SUNDERLAND	W 4-2	Ainsley, Grainger, Stelling o.g., Dutchman	9,509
Dec 8	Sunderland	L 1-5	Grainger	10,106
Dec 15	SHEFFIELD UNITED	L 2-4	J W Stevens, Henry	10,401
Dec 22	Sheffield United	L 2-6	Ainsley, Grainger	14,926
Dec 25	MIDDLESBROUGH	W 1-0	Grainger	12,217
Dec 26	Middlesbrough	L 1-4	Ainsley	23,019
Dec 29	STOKE CITY	D 0-0		22,219
Jan 12	BLACKPOOL	L 1-2	Ainsley	14,372
Jan 19	Blackpool	L 2-4	Ainsley 2	8,734
Jan 26	Grimsby Town	L 2-3	Ainsley, Henry	10,105
Feb 2	LIVERPOOL	W 3-0	Henry 2 (1 pen), Ainsley	11,881
Feb 9	BURY	D 3-3	Hindle 2, Ainsley (pen)	13,474
Feb 16	Bury	L 1-3	Grainger	8,623
Feb 23	Blackburn Rovers	D 0-0		6,048
Mar 2	BLACKBURN ROVERS	L 1-4	Ainsley (pen)	10,752
Mar 9	Grimsby Town	D 2-2	Henry, Heaton	8,000
Mar 16	Bradford Park Avenue	L 4-9	Ainsley 2, McGraw, Grainger	11,302
Mar 23	Manchester City	L 1-5	Heaton	20,000
Mar 30	MANCHESTER CITY	L 1-3	Price	10,000
Apr 6	NEWCASTLE UNITED	L 0-3		14,000
Apr 10	Liverpool	D 1-1	Grainger	10,620
Apr 13	Newcastle United	D 1-1	Ainsley	25,000
Apr 20	HUDDERSFIELD TOWN	W 3-2	Briggs o.g., Powell, Heaton	15,000
Apr 22	SHEFFIELD WEDNESDAY	L 0-1		14,000
Apr 23	Sheffield Wednesday	L 0-2		14,000
Apr 27	Huddersfield Town	L 2-3	Ainsley 2	4,622
May 1	BRADFORD PARK AVENUE	W 3-2	Hindle, Ainsley 2	10,000

FA Cup

Jan 5	MIDDLESBROUGH	(Rd 3) D 4-4	Henry, Ainsley, Hardwick o.g., Short	18,000
Jan 9	Middlesbrough	(R) L 2-7	Grainger, Ainsley	23,878

League & Cup Appearances

PLAYER	LEAGUE	CUP COMPETITION FA CUP	TOTAL
Ainsley	28	2	30
Alberry	1		1
Barton	4		4
Batey	8		8
Blair	1		1
Browne	4		4
Buckley	1		1
Burbanks	2		2
Butterworth	18	2	20
Chew	6		6
Coyne	24	2	26
Crookes	1		1
Duffy	15		15
Dutchman	3		3
Duthoit	17	2	19
Fearnley	4		4
Gadsby	6	2	8
Glackin	1		1
Goldberg	7		7
Grainger	35	2	37
Heaton	19		19
Henry	30	2	32
Hindle	33	2	35
Hodgson	36	2	38
Holley	28	1	29
Hudson	7		7
Iceton	2		2
Jones E	1		1
Jones S	11		11
Knight	6		6
Laidman	3		3
McGraw	5		5
Milburn Jack	3		3
Milburn Jim	10		10
Moule	3		3
Oliver	1		1
Parker	2		2
Powell	12		12
Price	21	1	22
Short	11	2	13
Smith	11		11
Stevens A	1		1
Stevens JW	11		11

Goalscorers

PLAYER	LEAGUE	CUP COMPETITION FA CUP	TOTAL
Ainsley	20	2	22
Henry	11	1	12
Grainger	9	1	10
Hindle	8		8
Short	4	1	5
Heaton	3		3
Dutchman	2		2
Powell	2		2
Chew	1		1
Price	1		1
Stevens JW	1		1
Alberry	1		0
Opps' o.gs.	3	1	4

Fact File

In the last of the wartime regional leagues, Leeds finished bottom, using over 40 players as they returned from military service. This did not affect their League Division 1 position when matches resumed in 1946-47.

MANAGER: Billy Hampson
CAPTAIN: Tom Holley
TOP SCORER: George Ainsley
BIGGEST WIN: 3-0 v Liverpool, 2 February 1946, Football League (North)
HIGHEST ATTENDANCE: 25,000 v Newcastle United, 13 April 1946, drew 1-1, Football League (North)

Final Football League (North) Table

		P	W	D	L	F	A	Pts
1	SHEFFIELD U	42	27	6	9	112	62	60
2	EVERTON	42	23	9	10	88	54	55
3	BOLTON W	42	20	11	11	67	45	51
4	MANCHESTER U	42	19	11	12	98	62	49
5	SHEFFIELD W	42	20	8	14	67	60	48
6	NEWCASTLE U	42	21	5	16	106	70	47
7	CHESTERFIELD	42	17	12	13	68	49	46
8	BARNSLEY	42	17	11	14	76	68	45
9	BLACKPOOL	42	18	9	15	94	92	45
10	MANCHESTER C	42	20	4	18	78	75	44
11	LIVERPOOL	42	17	9	16	80	70	43
12	MIDDLESBROUGH	42	17	9	16	75	87	43
13	STOKE C	42	18	6	18	88	79	42
14	BRADFORD PA	42	17	6	19	71	84	40
15	HUDDERSFIELD T	41	17	4	21	90	89	38
16	BURNLEY	42	13	10	19	63	84	36
17	GRIMSBY T	42	13	9	20	61	89	35
18	SUNDERLAND	42	15	5	22	55	83	35
19	PRESTON NE	42	14	6	22	70	77	34
20	BURY	42	12	10	20	60	85	34
21	BLACKBURN R	42	11	7	24	60	111	29
22	LEEDS UNITED	42	9	7	26	66	118	25

Season 1946-47

Football League Division 1

DATE	OPPONENTS	SCORE	GOALSCORERS	ATTENDANCE
Aug 31	Preston North End	L 2-3	Grainger 2	25,311
Sep 4	CHARLTON ATHLETIC	L 0-2		22,857
Sep 7	SHEFFIELD UNITED	D 2-2	Powell, Henry	28,543
Sep 14	Chelsea	L 0-3		57,184
Sep 16	Stoke City	L 2-5	Ainsley 2	21,141
Sep 21	BOLTON WANDERERS	W 4-0	Cochrane, Ainsley, Short 2	25,739
Sep 25	Charlton Athletic	L 0-5		16,488
Sep 28	Liverpool	L 0-2		51,042
Oct 5	HUDDERSFIELD TOWN	W 5-0	Ainsley 3, Powell, Short	30,622
Oct 12	GRIMSBY TOWN	W 1-0	Powell	28,877
Oct 19	Wolverhampton W	L 0-1		40,113
Oct 26	BLACKBURN ROVERS	L 0-1		28,683
Nov 2	Portsmouth	L 1-4	Ainsley	25,984
Nov 9	EVERTON	W 2-1	Powell, Short	22,992
Nov 16	Arsenal	L 2-4	Ainsley 2	36,377
Nov 23	BLACKPOOL	W 4-2	Powell 2, Ainsley, Grainger	25,829
Nov 30	Brentford	D 1-1	Cochrane	20,352
Dec 7	SUNDERLAND	D 1-1	Cochrane	25,784
Dec 14	Aston Villa	L 1-2	Powell	29,410
Dec 21	DERBY COUNTY	L 1-2	Henry (pen)	21,320
Dec 25	MIDDLESBROUGH	D 3-3	Milburn, Short, Cochrane	28,742
Dec 26	Middlesbrough	L 0-3		45,336
Dec 28	PRESTON NORTH END	L 0-3		33,433
Jan 4	Sheffield United	L 2-6	Cochrane, Ainsley	31,947
Jan 18	CHELSEA	W 2-1	Henry (pen), Cochrane	37,884
Feb 1	LIVERPOOL	L 1-2	Grainger	25,430
Feb 3	Bolton Wanderers	L 0-2		6,278
Feb 22	WOLVERHAMPTON W	L 0-1		30,313
Mar 1	Blackburn Rovers	L 0-1		28,371
Mar 22	ARSENAL	D 1-1	Grainger	32,190
Mar 29	Blackpool	L 0-3		14,501
Apr 5	BRENTFORD	L 1-2	Henry (pen)	23,962
Apr 7	Manchester United	L 1-3	Cochrane	41,912
Apr 8	MANCHESTER UNITED	L 0-2		15,528
Apr 12	Sunderland	L 0-1		30,429
Apr 19	ASTON VILLA	D 1-1	Clarke	22,291
Apr 26	Derby County	L 1-2	Powell	10,994
May 3	STOKE CITY	L 1-2	Short	21,714
May 10	Huddersfield Town	L 0-1		20,596
May 17	Grimsby Town	L 1-4	Short	10,795
May 24	PORTSMOUTH	L 0-1		14,097
May 26	Everton	L 1-4	Powell	21,001

FA Cup

Jan 11	West Bromwich Albion	(Rd 3) L 1-2	Ainsley	31,007

League & Cup Appearances

PLAYER	LEAGUE	CUP COMPETITION FA CUP	TOTAL
Ainsley	28	1	29
Bannister	23		23
Batey	8		8
Browne	19		19
Browning	1		1
Clarke	14		14
Cochrane	38	1	39
Fearnley	9		9
Gadsby	16	1	17
Goldberg	12		12
Grainger	32	1	33
Heaton	14		14
Henry	36	1	37
Hindle	11		11
Hodgkinson	1		1
Hodgson	19		19
Holley	39	1	40
Kane	1		1
Martin	8	1	9
Milburn Jim	36	1	37
Powell	34	1	35
Price	6		6
Short	32	1	33
Twomey	14	1	15
Willingham	11		11

Goalscorers

PLAYER	LEAGUE	CUP COMPETITION FA CUP	TOTAL
Ainsley	11	1	12
Powell	9		9
Cochrane	7		7
Short	7		7
Grainger	5		5
Henry	4		4
Clarke	1		1
Milburn Jim	1		1

Final Division 1 Table

		P	W	D	L	F	A	Pts
1	LIVERPOOL	42	25	7	10	84	52	57
2	MANCHESTER U	42	22	12	8	95	54	56
3	WOLVERHAMPTON W	42	25	6	11	98	56	56
4	STOKE C	42	24	7	11	90	53	55
5	BLACKPOOL	42	22	6	14	71	70	50
6	SHEFFIELD U	42	21	7	14	89	75	49
7	PRESTON NE	42	18	11	13	76	74	47
8	ASTON VILLA	42	18	9	15	67	53	45
9	SUNDERLAND	42	18	8	16	65	66	44
10	EVERTON	42	17	9	16	62	67	43
11	MIDDLESBROUGH	42	17	8	17	73	68	42
12	PORTSMOUTH	42	16	9	17	66	60	41
13	ARSENAL	42	16	9	17	72	70	41
14	DERBY CO	42	18	5	19	73	79	41
15	CHELSEA	42	16	7	19	69	84	39
16	GRIMSBY T	42	13	12	17	61	82	38
17	BLACKBURN R	42	14	8	20	45	53	36
18	BOLTON W	42	13	8	21	57	69	34
19	CHARLTON ATH	42	11	12	19	57	71	34
20	HUDDERSFIELD T	42	13	7	22	53	79	33
21	BRENTFORD	42	9	7	26	45	88	25
22	LEEDS UNITED	42	6	6	30	45	90	18

Fact File

Leeds recorded the lowest ever points total in Division 1.

MANAGER: Billy Hampson

CAPTAIN: Tom Holley

TOP SCORER: George Ainsley

BIGGEST WIN: 5-0 v Huddersfield Town, 5 October 1946, League

HIGHEST ATTENDANCE: 57,184 v Chelsea, 14 September 1946, lost 0-3, League

Season 1947-48

Football League Division 2

DATE	OPPONENTS	SCORE	GOALSCORERS	ATTENDANCE
Aug 23	LEICESTER CITY	W 3-1	Short, Ainsley 2	26,519
Aug 27	Barnsley	L 0-3		23,440
Aug 30	Southampton	W 2-1	Smith o.g., Wakefield	21,023
Sep 3	BARNSLEY	W 4-1	Wakefield 2, Short, Cochrane	36,501
Sep 6	Fulham	L 2-3	Short, Wakefield	26,247
Sep 10	PLYMOUTH ARGYLE	W 5-0	Short, Powell 3, Heaton (pen)	29,396
Sep 13	COVENTRY CITY	W 2-1	Powell 2	30,462
Sep 17	Plymouth Argyle	L 0-1		21,126
Sep 20	Newcastle United	L 2-4	Wakefield, Cochrane	57,275
Sep 27	BIRMINGHAM CITY	L 0-1		37,135
Oct 4	West Bromwich Albion	L 2-3	Heaton, Wakefield	30,479
Oct 11	DONCASTER ROVERS	D 0-0		34,775
Oct 18	Nottingham Forest	L 0-1		22,380
Oct 25	BRADFORD PARK AVENUE	W 2-0	Wakefield 2	31,532
Nov 1	Cardiff City	D 0-0		36,851
Nov 8	SHEFFIELD WEDNESDAY	D 2-2	Wakefield 2	32,547
Nov 15	Tottenham Hotspur	L 1-3	Cochrane (pen)	41,563
Nov 22	MILLWALL	W 2-1	Powell 2	24,160
Nov 29	Chesterfield	L 0-3		15,501
Dec 6	WEST HAM UNITED	W 2-1	Short, Martin	21,866
Dec 13	Bury	D 1-1	Wakefield	13,104
Dec 20	Leicester City	L 0-2		22,252
Dec 26	LUTON TOWN	L 0-2		28,597
Dec 27	Luton Town	L 1-6	Cochrane	16,964
Jan 3	SOUTHAMPTON	D 0-0		23,794
Jan 17	FULHAM	L 0-1		29,640
Jan 24	NEWCASTLE UNITED	W 3-1	Cochrane, Wakefield 2	30,367
Jan 31	Coventry City	W 2-1	Wakefield 2	22,269
Feb 14	Birmingham	L 1-5	Chisholm	39,955
Feb 21	WEST BROMWICH ALBION	W 3-1	Hindle, Pemberton o.g., Chisholm	22,333
Feb 28	Doncaster Rovers	L 0-3		26,569
Mar 6	NOTTINGHAM FOREST	D 2-2	Powell, Wakefield	27,018
Mar 13	Bradford Park Avenue	L 1-3	Powell	21,060
Mar 20	CARDIFF CITY	W 4-0	Chisholm 2, Powell, Short	34,276
Mar 26	Brentford	L 0-3		30,538
Mar 27	Sheffield Wednesday	L 1-3	Short	38,736
Mar 29	BRENTFORD	D 1-1	Bannister (pen)	26,775
Apr 3	TOTTENHAM HOTSPUR	L 1-3	Wakefield	24,891
Apr 10	Millwall	D 1-1	Chisholm	21,426
Apr 17	CHESTERFIELD	W 3-0	Hindle, Chisholm, Wakefield	28,794
Apr 24	West Ham United	L 1-2	Chisholm	13,594
May 1	BURY	W 5-1	Wakefield 3, Cochrane 2	17,573

FA Cup

Jan 10	Blackpool	(Rd 3)	L 0-4		28,500

League & Cup Appearances

PLAYER	LEAGUE	CUP COMPETITION FA CUP	TOTAL
Ainsley	2		2
Bannister	8		8
Bullions	24	1	25
Chisholm	17		17
Cochrane	38	1	39
Dunn	15		15
Fearnley	6		6
Gadsby	24	1	25
Grainger	5		5
Heaton	24		24
Henry	6		6
Hindle	21	1	22
Hodgkinson	1		1
Hodgson	1		1
Holley	23	1	24
Ingham	1		1
Kirby	8		8
Martin	35	1	36
McCabe	10		10
Milburn	34	1	35
Morton	1		1
Powell	39	1	40
Short	21		21
Twomey	35	1	36
Wakefield	37	1	38
Willingham	24	1	25
Windle	2		2

Goalscorers

PLAYER	LEAGUE	CUP COMPETITION FA CUP	TOTAL
Wakefield	21		21
Powell	10		10
Chisholm	7		7
Cochrane	7		7
Short	7		7
Ainsley	2		2
Heaton	2		2
Hindle	2		2
Bannister	1		1
Martin	1		1
Opps' o.gs.	2		2

Fact File

Albert Wakefield marked his debut with a goal against Southampton in August and ended the season as the club's top scorer.

MANAGER: Willis Edwards (to April)/Major Frank Buckley
CAPTAIN: Tom Holley
TOP SCORER: Albert Wakefield
BIGGEST WIN: 5-0 v Plymouth Argyle, 10 September 1947, League
HIGHEST ATTENDANCE: 57,275 v Newcastle United, 20 September 1947, lost 2-4, League

Final Division 2 Table

		P	W	D	L	F	A	PTS
1	BIRMINGHAM C	42	22	15	5	55	24	59
2	NEWCASTLE U	42	24	8	10	72	41	56
3	SOUTHAMPTON	42	21	10	11	71	53	52
4	SHEFFIELD W	42	20	11	11	66	53	51
5	CARDIFF C	42	18	11	13	61	58	47
6	WEST HAM U	42	16	14	12	55	53	46
7	WBA	42	18	9	15	63	58	45
8	TOTTENHAM H	42	15	14	13	56	43	44
9	LEICESTER C	42	16	11	15	60	57	43
10	COVENTRY C	42	14	13	15	59	52	41
11	FULHAM	42	15	10	17	47	46	40
12	BARNSLEY	42	15	10	17	62	64	40
13	LUTON T	42	14	12	16	56	59	40
14	BRADFORD PA	42	16	8	18	68	72	40
15	BRENTFORD	42	13	14	15	44	61	40
16	CHESTERFIELD	42	16	7	19	54	55	39
17	PLYMOUTH ARG	42	9	20	13	40	58	38
18	LEEDS UNITED	42	14	8	20	62	72	36
19	NOTTINGHAM F	42	12	11	19	54	60	35
20	BURY	42	9	16	17	58	68	34
21	DONCASTER R	42	9	11	22	40	66	29
22	MILLWALL	42	9	11	22	44	74	29

Season 1948-49

Football League Division 2

DATE	OPPONENTS	SCORE	GOALSCORERS	ATTENDANCE
Aug 21	Leicester City	L 2-6	Chisholm, Short	34,937
Aug 25	BRENTFORD	D 0-0		26,625
Aug 28	LUTON TOWN	W 2-0	Chisholm 2	25,463
Sep 1	Brentford	W 3-1	Milburn (pen), Short, Chisholm	19,212
Sep 4	COVENTRY CITY	W 4-1	Chisholm 2, Short 2	29,557
Sep 8	TOTTENHAM HOTSPUR	D 0-0		37,640
Sep 11	Sheffield Wednesday	L 1-3	Cochrane	31,735
Sep 13	Tottenham Hotspur	D 2-2	Milburn, Cochrane	33,793
Sep 18	LINCOLN CITY	W 3-1	Wakefield, Milburn (pen), Cochrane	33,963
Sep 25	Chesterfield	L 1-3	Wakefield	15,150
Oct 2	WEST BROMWICH ALBION	L 1-3	Marsh	33,706
Oct 9	Bradford Park Avenue	D 1-1	Chisholm	25,587
Oct 16	SOUTHAMPTON	D 1-1	Cochrane	34,959
Oct 23	Barnsley	D 1-1	Browning	26,010
Oct 30	GRIMSBY TOWN	W 6-3	Burden 2, Milburn (pen), Heaton, Chisholm, Browning	33,581
Nov 6	Nottingham Forest	D 0-0		24,237
Nov 13	FULHAM	D 1-1	Browning	26,240
Nov 20	Plymouth Argyle	L 1-2	Heaton	24,752
Dec 4	Cardiff City	L 1-2	Browning	31,973
Dec 11	QUEENS PARK RANGERS	L 1-2	Burden	26,420
Dec 18	LEICESTER CITY	W 3-1	Heaton 2, Chisholm	22,600
Dec 25	West Ham United	L 2-3	Holley, Browning	20,660
Dec 26	WEST HAM UNITED	L 1-3	Chisholm	32,577
Jan 1	Luton Town	D 0-0		15,310
Jan 15	Coventry City	L 1-4	Browning	23,670
Jan 22	SHEFFIELD WEDNESDAY	D 1-1	Cochrane	42,053
Jan 29	BLACKBURN ROVERS	W 1-0	McMorran	32,963
Feb 5	Lincoln City	D 0-0		18,060
Feb 12	BURY	L 0-1		27,063
Feb 19	CHESTERFIELD	W 1-0	Browning	29,362
Mar 5	BRADFORD PARK AVENUE	W 4-2	Browning 2, Iggleden, Cochrane	22,477
Mar 12	Southampton	L 1-2	Webber o.g.	25,736
Mar 19	BARNSLEY	W 4-1	Moss, McMorran, Browning 2	29,701
Mar 26	Grimsby Town	L 1-5	Browning	15,848
Apr 2	NOTTINGHAM FOREST	W 1-0	Iggleden	23,932
Apr 6	West Bromwich Albion	L 0-1		28,662
Apr 9	Fulham	L 0-1		23,961
Apr 16	PLYMOUTH ARGYLE	W 1-0	Browning	24,326
Apr 18	Bury	L 1-3	McMorran	15,305
Apr 23	Blackburn Rovers	D 0-0		18,873
Apr 30	CARDIFF CITY	D 0-0		19,945
May 7	Queens Park Rangers	L 0-2		16,730

FA Cup

Jan 8	NEWPORT COUNTY	(Rd 3) L 1-3	Browning	31,500

League & Cup Appearances

PLAYER	LEAGUE	CUP COMPETITION FA CUP	TOTAL
Bannister	5		5
Browning	24	1	25
Bullions	10	1	11
Burden	35	1	36
Charles	3		3
Chisholm	23		23
Cochrane	37	1	38
Depear	4	1	5
Dunn	37	1	38
Edwards	2		2
Fearnsley	13	1	14
Heaton	21	1	22
Hindle	11		11
Holley	32		32
Iggleden	16		16
Ingham	1		1
Lomas	1		1
Marsh	4	1	5
Martin	4		4
McAdam	20		20
McCabe	37	1	38
McMorran	12		12
Milburn	42	1	43
Moss	8		8
Rudd	12		12
Searson	18		18
Short	7		7
Twomey	10		10
Wakefield	12		12
Williams J	1		1

Goalscorers

PLAYER	LEAGUE	CUP COMPETITION FA CUP	TOTAL
Browning	13	1	14
Chisholm	10		10
Cochrane	6		6
Heaton	4		4
Milburn	4		4
Short	4		4
Burden	3		3
McMorran	3		3
Iggleden	2		2
Wakefield	2		2
Holley	1		1
Marsh	1		1
Moss	1		1
Opps' o.gs.	1		1

Fact File

The great John Charles made his Leeds debut on 23 April 1949 away at Blackburn Rovers.

MANAGER: Major Frank Buckley

CAPTAIN: Tom Holley

TOP SCORER: Len Browning

BIGGEST WIN: 6-3 v Grimsby Town, 30 October 1948, League

HIGHEST ATTENDANCE: 42,053 v Sheffield Wednesday, 22 January 1948, drew 1-1, League

MAJOR TRANSFERS IN: Harold Williams from Newport County, Tommy Burden from Chester

Final Division 2 Table

		P	W	D	L	F	A	Pts
1	FULHAM	42	24	9	9	77	37	57
2	WBA	42	24	8	10	69	39	56
3	SOUTHAMPTON	42	23	9	10	69	36	55
4	CARDIFF C	42	19	13	10	62	47	51
5	TOTTENHAM H	42	17	16	9	72	44	50
6	CHESTERFIELD	42	15	17	10	51	45	47
7	WEST HAM U	42	18	10	14	56	58	46
8	SHEFFIELD W	42	15	13	14	63	56	43
9	BARNSLEY	42	14	12	16	62	61	40
10	LUTON T	42	14	12	16	55	57	40
11	GRIMSBY T	42	15	10	17	72	76	40
12	BURY	42	17	6	19	67	76	40
13	QPR	42	14	11	17	44	62	39
14	BLACKBURN R	42	15	8	19	53	63	38
15	LEEDS UNITED	42	12	13	17	55	63	37
16	COVENTRY C	42	15	7	20	55	64	37
17	BRADFORD PA	42	13	11	18	65	78	37
18	BRENTFORD	42	11	14	17	42	53	36
19	LEICESTER C	42	10	16	16	62	79	36
20	PLYMOUTH ARG	42	12	12	18	49	64	36
21	NOTTINGHAM F	42	14	7	21	50	54	35
22	LINCOLN C	42	8	12	22	53	91	28

Season 1949-50

Football League Division 2

DATE	OPPONENTS	SCORE		GOALSCORERS	ATTENDANCE
Aug 20	QUEENS PARK RANGERS	D	1-1	Milburn (pen)	31,589
Aug 22	West Ham United	L	1-3	Rudd	24,728
Aug 27	Preston North End	D	1-1	Burden	31,378
Aug 31	WEST HAM UNITED	D	2-2	Cochrane, Dudley	29,732
Sep 3	SWANSEA TOWN	L	1-2	Dudley	29,767
Sep 5	Sheffield United	W	1-0	Browning	22,126
Sep 10	Tottenham Hotspur	L	0-2		48,274
Sep 14	SHEFFIELD UNITED	L	0-1		23,199
Sep 17	Southampton	L	1-2	P Harrison	23,214
Sep 24	COVENTRY CITY	D	3-3	McMorran, Dudley, Cochrane	22,590
Oct 1	Luton Town	L	0-1		15,291
Oct 8	CARDIFF CITY	W	2-0	Dudley, Browning	25,523
Oct 15	Blackburn Rovers	W	1-0	Dudley	22,038
Oct 22	BRENTFORD	W	1-0	Dudley	27,342
Oct 29	Hull City	L	0-1		47,638
Nov 5	SHEFFIELD WEDNESDAY	D	1-1	Williams	33,733
Nov 12	Plymouth Argyle	W	2-1	Frost, Charles (pen)	21,923
Nov 19	CHESTERFIELD	D	0-0		24,409
Nov 26	Bradford Park Avenue	W	2-1	Dudley, Frost	18,401
Dec 3	LEICESTER CITY	D	1-1	P Harrison	26,768
Dec 10	Bury	L	0-2		13,381
Dec 17	Queens Park Rangers	D	1-1	Dudley	13,256
Dec 24	PRESTON NORTH END	W	3-1	Browning, Dudley, Quigley o.g.	41,303
Dec 26	Barnsley	D	1-1	Milburn	27,017
Dec 27	BARNSLEY	W	1-0	Williams	47,817
Dec 31	Swansea Town	W	2-1	Williams, Browning	23,192
Jan 14	TOTTENHAM HOTSPUR	W	3-0	Cochrane 2, Iggleden	50,476
Jan 21	SOUTHAMPTON	W	1-0	Williams	38,646
Feb 4	Coventry City	W	4-0	Williams 2, Iggleden, Browning	22,990
Feb 18	LUTON TOWN	W	2-1	Browning, Iggleden	37,263
Feb 25	Cardiff City	L	0-1		28,423
Mar 11	Brentford	D	0-0		22,231
Mar 18	HULL CITY	W	3-0	Williams, McMorran, Milburn (pen)	49,465
Mar 25	Sheffield Wednesday	L	2-5	Browning, Williams	50,485
Apr 1	BRADFORD PARK AVENUE	D	0-0		31,062
Apr 7	Grimsby Town	L	0-2		22,511
Apr 8	Leicester City	D	1-1	McMorran	33,881
Apr 10	GRIMSBY TOWN	W	1-0	Milburn (pen)	17,991
Apr 15	PLYMOUTH ARGYLE	D	1-1	Williams	24,132
Apr 22	Chesterfield	L	1-3	Dudley	11,346
Apr 26	BLACKBURN ROVERS	W	2-1	Dunn, Williams	12,538
Apr 29	BURY	W	4-1	Dudley 2, Moss, Cochrane	8,913

FA Cup

Jan 7	Carlisle United	(Rd 3) W	5-2	Browning, Dudley 2, Williams, Cochrane	22,832
Jan 28	BOLTON WANDERERS	(Rd 4) D	1-1	Williams	51,488
Feb 1	Bolton Wanderers	(R) W	3-2	Dudley 2, Browning	29,440
Feb 11	CARDIFF CITY	(Rd 5) W	3-1	Williams, Cochrane, Iggleden	53,099
Mar 4	Arsenal	(Rd 6) L	0-1		62,273

League & Cup Appearances

PLAYER	LEAGUE	CUP COMPETITION FA CUP	TOTAL
Bannister	8		8
Browning	29	5	34
Bullions	1		1
Burden	42	5	47
Casey	4		4
Charles	42	5	47
Cochrane	29	5	34
Dudley	38	5	43
Dunn	40	5	45
Frost	9		9
Harrison P	4		4
Harrison R	2		2
Hilton	1		1
Iggleden	16	3	19
Ingham	1		1
Kerfoot	9		9
McAdam	4		4
McCabe	27	5	32
McMorran	26	2	28
Milburn	36	5	41
Moss	8		8
Rudd	6		6
Searson	42	5	47
Taylor	3		3
Wilkins	3		3
Williams HT	32	5	37

Goalscorers

PLAYER	LEAGUE	CUP COMPETITION FA CUP	TOTAL
Dudley	12	4	16
Williams HT	10	3	13
Browning	7	2	9
Cochrane	5	2	7
Iggleden	3	1	4
Milburn	4		4
McMorran	3		3
Frost	2		2
Harrison P	2		2
Burden	1		1
Charles	1		1
Dunn	1		1
Moss	1		1
Rudd	1		1
Opps' o.gs.	1		1

Final Division 2 Table

		P	W	D	L	F	A	Pts
1	TOTTENHAM H	42	27	7	8	81	35	61
2	SHEFFIELD W	42	18	16	8	67	48	52
3	SHEFFIELD U	42	19	14	9	68	49	52
4	SOUTHAMPTON	42	19	14	9	64	48	52
5	LEEDS UNITED	42	17	13	12	54	45	47
6	PRESTON NE	42	18	9	15	60	49	45
7	HULL C	42	17	11	14	64	72	45
8	SWANSEA T	42	17	9	16	53	49	43
9	BRENTFORD	42	15	13	14	44	49	43
10	CARDIFF C	42	16	10	16	41	44	42
11	GRIMSBY T	42	16	8	18	74	73	40
12	COVENTRY C	42	13	13	16	55	55	39
13	BARNSLEY	42	13	13	16	64	67	39
14	CHESTERFIELD	42	15	9	18	43	47	39
15	LEICESTER C	42	12	15	15	55	65	39
16	BLACKBURN R	42	14	10	18	55	60	38
17	LUTON T	42	10	18	14	41	51	38
18	BURY	42	14	9	19	60	65	37
19	WEST HAM U	42	12	12	18	53	61	36
20	QPR	42	11	12	19	40	57	34
21	PLYMOUTH ARG	42	8	16	18	44	65	32
22	BRADFORD PA	42	10	11	21	51	77	31

Fact File

In their best ever FA Cup run, Leeds reached the quarter-finals before losing 1-0 to Arsenal at Highbury.

MANAGER: Major Frank Buckley

CAPTAIN: Tommy Burden

TOP SCORER: Frank Dudley

BIGGEST WIN: 4-0 v Coventry City, 4 February 1950, League

HIGHEST ATTENDANCE: 62,273 v Arsenal, 4 March 1950, lost 0-1, FA Cup, Round 6

MAJOR TRANSFERS IN: Eric Kerfoot from Stalybridge Celtic

Season 1950-51

Football League Division 2

DATE	OPPONENTS	SCORE	GOALSCORERS	ATTENDANCE
Aug 19	DONCASTER ROVERS	W 3-1	Dudley 2, Browning	40,208
Aug 21	Coventry City	L 0-1		30,213
Aug 26	Brentford	W 2-1	Williams, Burden	20,381
Aug 30	COVENTRY CITY	W 1-0	Browning	28,938
Sep 2	BLACKBURN ROVERS	L 0-1		32,799
Sep 7	Swansea Town	L 2-4	Dudley, Browning	19,501
Sep 9	Southampton	L 0-2		25,806
Sep 16	BARNSLEY	D 2-2	Browning, Williams	37,633
Sep 23	Sheffield United	D 2-2	Dudley, Hughes	28,872
Sep 30	LUTON TOWN	W 2-1	Dudley, Browning	21,209
Oct 7	BURY	D 1-1	Williams	28,859
Oct 14	Preston North End	L 0-2		35,578
Oct 21	CHESTERFIELD	W 2-0	Browning, Iggleden	23,032
Oct 28	Queens Park Rangers	L 0-3		15,935
Nov 4	MANCHESTER CITY	D 1-1	Dudley	30,764
Nov 11	Leicester City	W 5-1	Burden, Dudley 3, Williams	26,573
Nov 18	NOTTS COUNTY	L 0-1		29,728
Nov 25	Grimsby Town	D 2-2	Browning 2	15,561
Dec 2	BIRMINGHAM CITY	W 3-0	Milburn, Browning, Burden	23,355
Dec 9	Cardiff City	L 0-1		23,716
Dec 16	Doncaster Rovers	D 4-4	Harrison 2, Dudley, Browning	16,745
Dec 23	BRENTFORD	W 1-0	Dudley	19,839
Dec 25	West Ham United	L 1-3	Harrison	19,519
Dec 26	WEST HAM UNITED	W 2-0	Browning 2	33,162
Jan 13	SOUTHAMPTON	W 5-3	Williams, Browning 3, Burden	29,253
Jan 20	Barnsley	W 2-1	Milburn (pen), Glover o.g.	21,967
Feb 3	SHEFFIELD UNITED	W 1-0	Browning	28,438
Feb 10	Blackburn Rovers	L 1-2	Harrison	25,496
Feb 17	Luton Town	W 3-2	Iggleden, Stevenson, Browning	13,323
Feb 24	Bury	W 1-0	Stevenson	13,517
Mar 3	PRESTON NORTH END	L 0-3		42,114
Mar 10	Chesterfield	L 0-1		9,856
Mar 17	QUEENS PARK RANGERS	D 2-2	Milburn, Browning	18,094
Mar 23	Hull City	L 0-2		46,701
Mar 24	Manchester City	L 1-4	Harrison	35,149
Mar 26	HULL CITY	W 3-0	Charles 2, Stevenson	27,887
Mar 31	LEICESTER CITY	W 2-1	Burden 2	14,397
Apr 7	Notts County	D 0-0		23,466
Apr 14	GRIMSBY TOWN	W 1-0	Charles	15,524
Apr 21	Birmingham City	W 1-0	Stevenson	23,809
Apr 28	CARDIFF CITY	W 2-0	Iggleden, Hollyman o.g.	14,765
May 5	SWANSEA TOWN	W 2-0	Iggleden, Browning	11,213

FA Cup

Jan 6	MIDDLESBROUGH	(Rd 3) W 1-0	Browning	45,583
Jan 27	Manchester United	(Rd 4) L 0-4		55,434

League & Cup Appearances

PLAYER	LEAGUE	CUP COMPETITION FA CUP	TOTAL
Browning	34	2	36
Burden	39	2	41
Charles	34	2	36
Cochrane	2		2
Dudley	26	2	28
Dunn	40	2	42
Frost	1		1
Hair	2		2
Harrison	30	2	32
Hughes	11		11
Iggleden	23	1	24
Kerfoot	31		31
Kirk	9		9
McCabe	28	2	30
McNeish	1		1
Milburn	42	2	44
Miller	9	1	10
Moss	7		7
Scott	17		17
Searson	25	2	27
Stevenson	13		13
Vickers	2		2
Williams	36	2	38

Goalscorers

PLAYER	LEAGUE	CUP COMPETITION FA CUP	TOTAL
Browning	19	1	20
Dudley	11		11
Burden	6		6
Williams	5		5
Harrison	5		5
Iggleden	4		4
Stevenson	4		4
Milburn	3		3
Charles	3		3
Hughes	1		1
Opps' o.gs.	2		2

Fact File

John Charles was tried at centre forward in the home game against Manchester City in November.

MANAGER: Major Frank Buckley

CAPTAIN: Tommy Burden

TOP SCORER: Len Browning

BIGGEST WIN: 5-1 v Leicester City, 11 November 1950, League

HIGHEST ATTENDANCE: 55,434 v Manchester United, 27 January 1951, lost 0-4, FA Cup, Round 4

MAJOR TRANSFERS IN: Frank Fidler from Wrexham

Final Division 2 Table

		P	W	D	L	F	A	Pts
1	PRESTON NE	42	26	5	11	91	49	57
2	MANCHESTER C	42	19	14	9	89	61	52
3	CARDIFF C	42	17	16	9	53	45	50
4	BIRMINGHAM C	42	20	9	13	64	53	49
5	LEEDS UNITED	42	20	8	14	63	55	48
6	BLACKBURN R	42	19	8	15	65	66	46
7	COVENTRY C	42	19	7	16	75	59	45
8	SHEFFIELD U	42	16	12	14	72	62	44
9	BRENTFORD	42	18	8	16	75	74	44
10	HULL C	42	16	11	15	74	70	43
11	DONCASTER R	42	15	13	14	64	68	43
12	SOUTHAMPTON	42	15	13	14	66	73	43
13	WEST HAM U	42	16	10	16	68	69	42
14	LEICESTER C	42	15	11	16	68	58	41
15	BARNSLEY	42	15	10	17	74	68	40
16	QPR	42	15	10	17	71	82	40
17	NOTTS CO	42	13	13	16	61	60	39
18	SWANSEA T	42	16	4	22	54	77	36
19	LUTON T	42	9	14	19	57	70	32
20	BURY	42	12	8	22	60	86	32
21	CHESTERFIELD	42	9	12	21	44	69	30
22	GRIMSBY T	42	8	12	22	61	95	28

Season 1951-52

Football League Division 2

DATE	OPPONENTS	SCORE	GOALSCORERS	ATTENDANCE
Aug 18	BRENTFORD	D 1-1	Browning	20,268
Aug 22	Birmingham City	D 1-1	Stevenson	17,081
Aug 25	Doncaster Rovers	L 0-2		22,222
Aug 29	BIRMINGHAM CITY	D 1-1	Iggleden	15,098
Sep 1	EVERTON	L 1-2	Miller	16,873
Sep 8	Southampton	D 0-0		19,682
Sep 12	CARDIFF CITY	W 2-1	Hughes, Milburn	12,860
Sep 15	SHEFFIELD WEDNESDAY	W 3-2	Browning 2, Tyrer	20,016
Sep 22	West Ham United	L 0-2		19,464
Sep 29	Rotherham United	L 2-4	Iggleden 2	21,352
Oct 6	SHEFFIELD UNITED	W 3-1	Iggleden 2, Mills	26,915
Oct 13	Barnsley	L 1-3	Iggleden	15,565
Oct 20	HULL CITY	W 2-0	Iggleden, Harrison	24,656
Oct 27	Blackburn Rovers	W 3-2	Harrison, Fidler, Iggleden	20,631
Nov 3	QUEENS PARK RANGERS	W 3-0	Iggleden, Fidler, Williams	22,875
Nov 10	Notts County	W 2-1	Fidler, Kerfoot	25,307
Nov 17	LUTON TOWN	D 1-1	Iggleden	27,405
Nov 24	Bury	W 2-1	Fidler, Iggleden	11,836
Dec 1	SWANSEA TOWN	D 1-1	Mills	26,235
Dec 8	Coventry City	L 2-4	Williams, Kerfoot	14,621
Dec 15	Brentford	L 1-2	Mills	17,957
Dec 22	DONCASTER ROVERS	D 0-0		21,793
Dec 25	Leicester City	W 2-1	Iggleden, Mills	24,498
Dec 26	LEICESTER CITY	W 2-1	Fidler 2	29,422
Dec 29	Everton	L 0-2		37,616
Jan 5	SOUTHAMPTON	D 1-1	Fidler	25,319
Jan 19	Sheffield Wednesday	W 2-1	Iggleden 2	42,354
Jan 26	WEST HAM UNITED	W 3-1	Milburn, Kirk, Iggleden	32,297
Feb 9	ROTHERHAM UNITED	W 3-0	Stewart, Milburn, Iggleden	47,985
Feb 16	Sheffield United	L 0-3		36,265
Mar 1	BARNSLEY	W 1-0	Mills	32,221
Mar 8	Hull City	L 2-3	Stewart, Williams	28,767
Mar 15	BLACKBURN ROVERS	W 1-0	Iggleden	29,226
Mar 22	Queens Park Rangers	D 0-0		15,195
Mar 29	NOTTS COUNTY	W 1-0	Barritt	12,867
Apr 5	Luton Town	L 1-2	Iggleden	11,460
Apr 11	Nottingham Forest	D 1-1	Williams	28,808
Apr 12	BURY	W 2-1	Mills 2	23,004
Apr 14	NOTTINGHAM FOREST	D 0-0		26,511
Apr 19	Swansea Town	L 1-4	Williams	18,206
Apr 26	COVENTRY CITY	W 3-1	Dorman o.g., Kerfoot, Fidler	16,322
May 3	Cardiff City	L 1-3	Iggleden	45,925

FA Cup

Jan 12	Rochdale	(Rd 3)	W 2-0	Kirk 2	21,475
Feb 2	BRADFORD CITY	(Rd 4)	W 2-0	Milburn, Iggleden	50,645
Feb 23	CHELSEA	(Rd 5)	D 1-1	Milburn	52,328
Feb 27	Chelsea	(R)	D 1-1	Kirk	60,851
Mar 3	Chelsea*	(2nd R)	L 1-5	Mills	30,504

*Played at Villa Park, Birmingham.

League & Cup Appearances

PLAYER	LEAGUE	CUP COMPETITION FA CUP	TOTAL
Barritt	6		6
Browning	9		9
Burden	40	5	45
Charles	18	5	23
Dunn	36	5	41
Fidler	17	1	18
Finlay	1		1
Hair	27	5	32
Harrison	31		31
Hudson	4		4
Hughes	10	2	12
Iggleden	41	5	46
Kerfoot	34	5	39
Kirk	25	5	30
McCabe	14		14
Milburn	17	2	19
Miller	4		4
Mills	25	3	28
Mollatt	4		4
Ross	5		5
Scott	12		12
Searson	19	5	24
Stevenson	3		3
Stewart	7	2	9
Taylor	11		11
Tyrer	5		5
Williams	37	5	42

Goalscorers

PLAYER	LEAGUE	CUP COMPETITION FA CUP	TOTAL
Iggleden	19	1	20
Mills	7	1	8
Fidler	8		8
Williams	5		5
Milburn	2	2	4
Kirk	1	3	4
Browning	3		3
Kerfoot	3		3
Harrison	2		2
Stewart	2		2
Hughes	1		1
Stevenson	1		1
Miller	1		1
Tyrer	1		1
Barritt	1		1
Opps' o.gs.	1		1

Fact File

John Charles returned from National Service to take his place in the team against Southampton in January.

MANAGER: Major Frank Buckley

CAPTAIN: Tommy Burden

TOP SCORER: Ray Iggleden

BIGGEST WIN: 3-0 v Queens Park Rangers, 3 November 1951, League
3-0 v Rotherham United, 9 February 1952, League

HIGHEST ATTENDANCE: 60,851 v Chelsea, 27 February 1952, drew 1-1, FA Cup, Round 5

MAJOR TRANSFERS OUT: Len Browning to Sheffield United

Final Division 2 Table

		P	W	D	L	F	A	Pts
1	SHEFFIELD W	42	21	11	10	100	66	53
2	CARDIFF C	42	20	11	11	72	54	51
3	BIRMINGHAM C	42	21	9	12	67	56	51
4	NOTTINGHAM F	42	18	13	11	77	62	49
5	LEICESTER C	42	19	9	14	78	64	47
6	LEEDS UNITED	42	18	11	13	59	57	47
7	EVERTON	42	17	10	15	64	58	44
8	LUTON T	42	16	12	14	77	78	44
9	ROTHERHAM U	42	17	8	17	73	71	42
10	BRENTFORD	42	15	12	15	54	55	42
11	SHEFFIELD U	42	18	5	19	90	76	41
12	WEST HAM U	42	15	11	16	67	77	41
13	SOUTHAMPTON	42	15	11	16	61	73	41
14	BLACKBURN R	42	17	6	19	54	63	40
15	NOTTS CO	42	16	7	19	71	68	39
16	DONCASTER R	42	13	12	17	55	60	38
17	BURY	42	15	7	20	67	69	37
18	HULL C	42	13	11	18	60	70	37
19	SWANSEA T	42	12	12	18	72	76	36
20	BARNSLEY	42	11	14	17	59	72	36
21	COVENTRY C	42	14	6	22	59	82	34
22	QPR	42	11	12	19	52	81	34

Season 1952-53

Football League Division 2

DATE	OPPONENTS	SCORE	GOALSCORERS	ATTENDANCE
Aug 23	Huddersfield Town	L 0-1		35,230
Aug 28	Bury	D 2-2	Iggleden, Langley	12,274
Aug 30	PLYMOUTH ARGYLE	D 1-1	Rundle o.g.	25,067
Sep 3	BURY	W 2-0	Iggleden, Langley	14,623
Sep 6	Rotherham United	L 1-3	Iggleden	14,900
Sep 10	BIRMINGHAM CITY	L 0-1		14,133
Sep 13	FULHAM	W 2-0	Smith, Mills	18,371
Sep 17	Birmingham City	D 2-2	Hastie 2	18,371
Sep 20	West Ham United	D 2-2	Iggleden, Tyrer	22,437
Sep 24	SOUTHAMPTON	D 1-1	Iggleden	13,299
Sep 27	LEICESTER CITY	L 0-1		19,724
Oct 4	Notts County	L 2-3	Iggleden, Southwell o.g.	22,836
Oct 11	Sheffield United	L 1-2	Nightingale	33,683
Oct 18	BARNSLEY	W 4-1	Nightingale 2, Charles, Mills	22,155
Oct 25	Lincoln City	D 1-1	Charles	15,491
Nov 1	HULL CITY	W 3-1	Charles 3	25,538
Nov 8	Blackburn Rovers	D 1-1	Charles	22,510
Nov 22	Everton	D 2-2	Charles 2	28,664
Nov 29	BRENTFORD	W 3-2	Charles 3	16,077
Dec 6	Doncaster Rovers	D 0-0		15,744
Dec 13	SWANSEA TOWN	W 5-1	Charles 2 (1 pen), Nightingale, Iggleden 2	21,065
Dec 20	HUDDERSFIELD TOWN	W 2-1	Iggleden, Charles	34,365
Dec 26	Luton Town	L 0-2		19,480
Dec 27	LUTON TOWN	D 2-2	Charles, Langley	31,634
Jan 3	Plymouth Argyle	W 1-0	Iggleden	22,149
Jan 17	ROTHERHAM UNITED	W 4-0	Charles 3, Nightingale	24,048
Jan 24	Fulham	L 1-2	Tyrer	21,210
Feb 7	WEST HAM UNITED	W 3-2	Iggleden, Charles 2	17,680
Feb 14	Leicester City	D 3-3	Meek, Charles 2	21,754
Feb 21	NOTTS COUNTY	W 3-1	Burden, Iggleden, McCall	22,922
Feb 28	SHEFFIELD UNITED	L 0-3		39,858
Mar 7	Barnsley	D 2-2	Charles, McCall	11,536
Mar 14	LINCOLN CITY	W 2-1	Meek 2	18,293
Mar 21	Hull City	L 0-1		25,387
Mar 28	BLACKBURN ROVERS	L 0-3		10,644
Apr 4	Nottingham Forest	L 1-2	Nightingale	18,734
Apr 6	Southampton	D 2-2	Nightingale 2	17,704
Apr 11	EVERTON	W 2-0	Forrest, Meek	15,363
Apr 16	Swansea Town	L 2-3	Meek, Charles	21,262
Apr 18	Brentford	D 3-3	Charles 2, Forrest	12,783
Apr 22	NOTTINGHAM FOREST	W 2-1	Burden, Kerfoot	11,497
Apr 25	DONCASTER ROVERS	D 1-1	Kerfoot	12,715

FA Cup

Jan 10	Brentford	(Rd 3) L 1-2	Charles	22,650

League & Cup Appearances

PLAYER	LEAGUE	CUP COMPETITION FA CUP	TOTAL
Burden	42	1	43
Charles	40	1	41
Charlton	1		1
Dunn	42	1	43
Fidler	5		5
Forrest	6		6
Hair	40	1	41
Hastie	4		4
Iggleden	38	1	39
Kerfoot	39	1	40
Langley	9		9
Marsden	7		7
McCabe	22	1	23
McCall	16		16
Meek	28	1	29
Mills	9		9
Mollatt	3		3
Nightingale	26	1	27
Scott	42	1	43
Smith	2		2
Stewart	2		2
Tyrer	21	1	22
Williams	18		18

Goalscorers

PLAYER	LEAGUE	CUP COMPETITION FA CUP	TOTAL
Charles	26	1	27
Iggleden	12		12
Nightingale	8		8
Meek	5		5
Langley	3		3
Mills	2		2
Hastie	2		2
Tyrer	2		2
Burden	2		2
McCall	2		2
Forrest	2		2
Kerfoot	2		2
Smith	1		1
Opps' o.gs.	2		2

Fact File

In October 1952 John Charles once again answered the call to play in Leeds' forward line and scored 14 goals in 10 games.

MANAGER: Major Frank Buckley
CAPTAIN: Tommy Burden
TOP SCORER: John Charles
BIGGEST WIN: 5-1 v Swansea Town, 13 December 1952, League
HIGHEST ATTENDANCE: 39,858 v Sheffield United, 28 February 1953, lost 0-3, League

Final Division 2 Table

		P	W	D	L	F	A	Pts
1	SHEFFIELD U	42	25	10	7	97	55	60
2	HUDDERSFIELD T	42	24	10	8	84	33	58
3	LUTON T	42	22	8	12	84	49	52
4	PLYMOUTH ARG	42	20	9	13	65	60	49
5	LEICESTER C	42	18	12	12	89	74	48
6	BIRMINGHAM C	42	19	10	13	71	66	48
7	NOTTINGHAM F	42	18	8	16	77	67	44
8	FULHAM	42	17	10	15	81	71	44
9	BLACKBURN R	42	18	8	16	68	65	44
10	LEEDS UNITED	42	14	15	13	71	63	43
11	SWANSEA T	42	15	12	15	78	81	42
12	ROTHERHAM U	42	16	9	17	75	74	41
13	DONCASTER R	42	12	16	14	58	64	40
14	WEST HAM U	42	13	13	16	58	60	39
15	LINCOLN C	42	11	17	14	64	71	39
16	EVERTON	42	12	14	16	71	75	38
17	BRENTFORD	42	13	11	18	59	76	37
18	HULL C	42	14	8	20	57	69	36
19	NOTTS CO	42	14	8	20	60	88	36
20	BURY	42	13	9	20	53	81	35
21	SOUTHAMPTON	42	10	13	19	68	85	33
22	BARNSLEY	42	5	8	29	47	108	18

Season 1953-54

Football League Division 2

DATE	OPPONENTS	SCORE	GOALSCORERS	ATTENDANCE
Aug 19	NOTTS COUNTY	W 6-0	Charles 4, Williams, Nightingale	18,432
Aug 22	ROTHERHAM UNITED	W 4-2	Charles 3, Nightingale	24,309
Aug 27	Swansea Town	L 3-4	Charles, Nightingale, Burbanks	26,408
Aug 29	Leicester City	L 0-5		21,984
Sep 2	SWANSEA TOWN	W 3-2	Nightingale, Charles 2	20,949
Sep 5	STOKE CITY	D 1-1	Charles	27,571
Sep 7	Plymouth Argyle	D 1-1	Charles	20,356
Sep 12	Fulham	W 3-1	Charles 2, Williams	26,044
Sep 16	PLYMOUTH ARGYLE	D 1-1	Williams	20,621
Sep 19	WEST HAM UNITED	L 1-2	Charles	28,635
Sep 26	Lincoln City	L 0-2		17,979
Oct 3	Birmingham City	D 3-3	Charles, Iggleden, Kerfoot	26,434
Oct 10	BRISTOL ROVERS	D 3-3	Forrest 3	19,386
Oct 17	Brentford	L 1-2	Charles	18,329
Oct 24	DERBY COUNTY	W 3-1	Charles 2, Nightingale	26,430
Oct 31	Blackburn Rovers	D 2-2	Williams, Nightingale	25,272
Nov 7	DONCASTER ROVERS	W 3-1	Nightingale 3,	26,830
Nov 14	Bury	D 4-4	Charles 3, Nightingale	11,915
Nov 21	OLDHAM ATHLETIC	W 2-1	Forrest, Nightingale	26,747
Nov 28	Everton	L 1-2	Charles	55,970
Dec 5	HULL CITY	D 0-0		21,070
Dec 12	Notts County	L 0-2		17,552
Dec 19	Rotherham United	W 4-2	Charles 3 (1 pen), Iggleden	13,145
Dec 25	Nottingham Forest	L 2-5	Nightingale, Charles	19,725
Dec 26	NOTTINGHAM FOREST	L 0-2		22,135
Jan 2	LEICESTER CITY	W 7-1	Iggleden 3, Williams, Charles, Nightingale, Tyrer	21,532
Jan 16	Stoke City	L 0-4		26,794
Jan 23	FULHAM	L 1-2	Charles	20,170
Feb 6	West Ham United	L 2-5	Iggleden, McCall	15,585
Feb 13	LINCOLN CITY	W 5-2	Charles 3, Iggleden, Nightingale	15,325
Feb 20	BIRMINGHAM CITY	D 1-1	Burden	22,803
Feb 27	Bristol Rovers	D 1-1	Nightingale	26,846
Mar 6	BRENTFORD	W 4-0	Charles 2, Nightingale, Williams	16,501
Mar 13	Derby County	W 2-0	Forrest 2	12,773
Mar 20	BLACKBURN ROVERS	W 3-2	McCall, Nightingale, Charles (pen)	24,915
Mar 27	Oldham Athletic	L 2-4	Williams, Charles	18,067
Apr 3	EVERTON	W 3-1	Williams, Forrest, Kerfoot	22,581
Apr 10	Doncaster Rovers	D 0-0		12,472
Apr 16	Luton Town	D 1-1	Charles	16,129
Apr 17	BURY	L 3-4	Charles 2 (1 pen), Forrest	17,156
Apr 19	LUTON TOWN	W 2-1	Charles 2 (1 pen)	13,930
Apr 24	Hull City	D 1-1	Charles	18,619

FA Cup

Jan 9	Tottenham Hotspur	(Rd 3) D 3-3	Iggleden, Charles, Ramsey o.g.	41,465
Jan 13	TOTTENHAM HOTSPUR	(R) L 0-1		35,023

League & Cup Appearances

PLAYER	LEAGUE	CUP COMPETITION FA CUP	TOTAL
Burbanks	13		13
Burden	40	2	42
Charles	39	2	41
Davies	1		1
Dawson	1		1
Dunn	41	2	43
Flynn	1		1
Forrest	10		10
Hair	42	2	44
Iggleden	31	2	33
Kerfoot	42	2	44
Marsden	28	2	30
McCabe	14		14
McCall	18		18
Mollatt	5		5
Nightingale	39	2	41
Scott	26	2	28
Tyer	13	2	15
Webb	2		2
Wheatley	6		6
Williams	37	2	39
Willis	3		3
Wood	10		10

Goalscorers

PLAYER	LEAGUE	CUP COMPETITION FA CUP	TOTAL
Charles	42	1	43
Nightingale	17		17
Iggleden	7	1	8
Forrest	8		8
Williams	8		8
Kerfoot	2		2
McCall	2		2
Tyrer	1		1
Burden	1		1
Burbanks	1		1
Opps' o.gs.		1	1

Fact File

John Charles set the record for a Leeds goalscorer with 42 League goals in one season – a record that still stands today.

MANAGER: Raich Carter
CAPTAIN: Tommy Burden
TOP SCORER: John Charles
BIGGEST WIN: 7-1 v Leicester City, 2 January 1954, League
HIGHEST ATTENDANCE: 55,970 v Everton, 28 November 1953, lost 1-2, League

Final Division 2 Table

		P	W	D	L	F	A	Pts
1	LEICESTER C	42	23	10	9	97	60	56
2	EVERTON	42	20	16	6	92	58	56
3	BLACKBURN R	42	23	9	10	86	50	55
4	NOTTINGHAM F	42	20	12	10	86	59	52
5	ROTHERHAM U	42	21	7	14	80	67	49
6	LUTON T	42	18	12	12	64	59	48
7	BIRMINGHAM C	42	18	11	13	78	58	47
8	FULHAM	42	17	10	15	98	85	44
9	BRISTOL R	42	14	16	12	64	58	44
10	LEEDS UNITED	42	15	13	14	89	81	43
11	STOKE C	42	12	17	13	71	60	41
12	DONCASTER R	42	16	9	17	59	63	41
13	WEST HAM U	42	15	9	18	67	69	39
14	NOTTS CO	42	13	13	16	54	74	39
15	HULL C	42	16	6	20	64	66	38
16	LINCOLN C	42	14	9	19	65	83	37
17	BURY	42	11	14	17	54	72	36
18	DERBY CO	42	12	11	19	64	82	35
19	PLYMOUTH ARG	42	9	16	17	65	82	34
20	SWANSEA T	42	13	8	21	58	82	34
21	BRENTFORD	42	10	11	21	40	78	31
22	OLDHAM ATH	42	8	9	25	40	89	25

Season 1954-55

Football League Division 2

DATE	OPPONENTS	SCORE	GOALSCORERS	ATTENDANCE
Aug 21	Hull City	W 2-0	Brook, Charles	32,971
Aug 25	ROTHERHAM UNITED	L 2-4	Charles 2	25,021
Aug 28	LINCOLN CITY	L 2-3	Toner, Vicers	22,326
Aug 30	Rotherham United	L 0-3		17,799
Sep 4	Bury	L 3-5	McCall, Charles, May o.g.	15,357
Sep 8	STOKE CITY	L 0-1		20,295
Sep 11	SWANSEA TOWN	W 5-2	Nightingale 3, Kerfoot, Brook	20,040
Sep 13	Stoke City	W 1-0	Forrest	19,311
Sep 18	NOTTINGHAM FOREST	D 1-1	Forrest	22,402
Sep 25	Ipswich Town	W 2-1	Williams, Nightingale	16,716
Oct 2	BIRMINGHAM CITY	W 1-0	Forrest	21,200
Oct 9	Derby County	W 4-2	Brook 2, McCall 2	20,214
Oct 16	WEST HAM UNITED	W 2-1	Ripley, Forrest	21,074
Oct 23	Bristol Rovers	L 1-5	Brook	24,568
Oct 30	PLYMOUTH ARGYLE	W 3-2	Williams, Nightingale, McCall	20,613
Nov 6	Port Vale	W 1-0	Nightingale	16,062
Nov 13	DONCASTER ROVERS	W 1-0	Ripley	15,757
Nov 20	Notts County	W 2-1	Nightingale 2	14,519
Nov 27	LIVERPOOL	D 2-2	Forrest, Charles (pen)	22,263
Dec 4	Blackburn Rovers	W 2-1	Nightingale 2	26,187
Dec 11	FULHAM	D 1-1	Charles	30,714
Dec 18	HULL CITY	W 3-0	Brook, Nightingale, Forrest	23,991
Dec 25	MIDDLESBROUGH	D 1-1	Forrest	26,344
Dec 27	Middlesbrough	L 0-1		45,271
Jan 1	Lincoln City	L 0-2		12,231
Jan 15	BURY	W 1-0	Lydon	8,954
Jan 22	Swansea Town	L 0-2		19,637
Feb 5	Nottingham Forest	D 1-1	Charles	14,074
Feb 12	IPSWICH TOWN	W 4-1	Brook 2, Vicers 2	12,038
Feb 26	DERBY COUNTY	W 1-0	Charles (pen)	16,994
Mar 2	Birmingham City	L 0-2		10,774
Mar 5	West Ham United	L 1-2	Forrest	19,664
Mar 12	BRISTOL ROVERS	W 2-0	Brook, Forrest	16,922
Mar 19	Plymouth Argyle	L 1-3	Brook	19,968
Mar 26	PORT VALE	W 3-0	Henderson, Ripley, Charles (pen)	8,831
Apr 2	Doncaster Rovers	W 1-0	Brook	12,740
Apr 8	Luton Town	D 0-0		25,775
Apr 9	NOTTS COUNTY	W 2-0	Brook, Nightingale	24,564
Apr 11	LUTON TOWN	W 4-0	Brook, Charles 2 (2 pen), Henderson	29,583
Apr 23	Liverpool	D 2-2	Meek, Brook	34,950
Apr 23	BLACKBURN ROVERS	W 2-0	Brook 2	39,208
Apr 30	Fulham	W 3-1	Smith o.g., Henderson, Nightingale	21,400

FA Cup

Jan 8	TORQUAY UNITED	(Rd 3) D 2-2	Kerfoot, Charles	28,150
Jan 12	Torquay United	(R) L 0-4		12,000

League & Cup Appearances

PLAYER	LEAGUE	CUP COMPETITION FA CUP	TOTAL
Brook	37	2	39
Burden	5		5
Charles	40	2	42
Charlton	1		1
Dunn	42	2	44
Forrest	25		25
Gibson	12		12
Hair	42	2	44
Henderson	9		9
Iggleden	4		4
Kerfoot	39	2	41
Lydon	4		4
Marsden	7	2	9
McCall	28	2	30
Meek	10		10
Mollatt	5		5
Nightingale	38	2	40
Ripley	25	2	27
Scott	14		14
Toner	7		7
Vickers	7		7
Webb	1		1
Williams	32	2	34
Wood	28	2	30

Goalscorers

PLAYER	LEAGUE	CUP COMPETITION FA CUP	TOTAL
Brook	16		16
Nightingale	13		13
Charles	11	1	12
Forrest	9		9
McCall	4		4
Vickers	3		3
Ripley	3		3
Henderson	3		3
Kerfoot	1	1	2
Williams	2		2
Toner	1		1
Lydon	1		1
Opps' o.gs.	2		2

Fact File

Despite five defeats in their first six games Leeds fought back to mount a promotion challenge.

MANAGER: Raich Carter

CAPTAIN: Eric Kerfoot

TOP SCORER: Harold Brook

BIGGEST WIN: 5-2 v Swansea Town, 11 September 1954, League

HIGHEST ATTENDANCE: 45,271 v Middlesbrough, 27 December 1954, lost 0-1, League

MAJOR TRANSFERS IN: Harold Brook from Sheffield United

MAJOR TRANSFERS OUT: Tommy Burden to Bristol City

Final Division 2 Table

		P	W	D	L	F	A	Pts
1	BIRMINGHAM C	42	22	10	10	92	47	54
2	LUTON T	42	23	8	11	88	53	54
3	ROTHERHAM U	42	25	4	13	94	64	54
4	LEEDS UNITED	42	23	7	12	70	53	53
5	STOKE C	42	21	10	11	69	46	52
6	BLACKBURN R	42	22	6	14	114	79	50
7	NOTTS CO	42	21	6	15	74	71	48
8	WEST HAM U	42	18	10	14	74	70	46
9	BRISTOL R	42	19	7	16	75	70	45
10	SWANSEA T	42	17	9	16	86	83	43
11	LIVERPOOL	42	16	10	16	92	96	42
12	MIDDLESBROUGH	42	18	6	18	73	82	42
13	BURY	42	15	11	16	77	72	41
14	FULHAM	42	14	11	17	76	79	39
15	NOTTINGHAM F	42	16	7	19	58	62	39
16	LINCOLN C	42	13	10	19	68	79	36
17	PORT VALE	42	12	11	19	48	71	35
18	DONCASTER R	42	14	7	21	58	95	35
19	HULL C	42	12	10	20	44	69	34
20	PLYMOUTH ARG	42	12	7	23	57	82	31
21	IPSWICH T	42	11	6	25	57	92	28
22	DERBY CO	42	7	9	26	53	82	23

Season 1955-56

Football League Division 2

DATE	OPPONENTS	SCORE	GOALSCORERS	ATTENDANCE
Aug 20	Barnsley	L 1-2	Brook	19,341
Aug 22	BURY	W 1-0	Henderson	19,722
Aug 27	MIDDLESBROUGH	W 2-0	Nightingale, Brook	22,535
Aug 30	Bury	L 0-1		11,674
Sep 3	Bristol City	W 1-0	Forrest	31,060
Sep 5	HULL CITY	W 1-0	Ripley	17,524
Sep 10	WEST HAM UNITED	D 3-3	Ripley, Nightingale, Meek	21,855
Sep 17	Port Vale	L 0-2		21,348
Sep 24	ROTHERHAM UNITED	W 4-1	Nightingale, Ripley 3	23,763
Oct 1	Swansea Town	D 1-1	Brook	29,477
Oct 8	NOTTINGHAM FOREST	W 3-0	Ripley, Brook, Charles	21,272
Oct 15	Sheffield Wednesday	L 0-4		27,640
Oct 22	LINCOLN CITY	W 1-0	Overfield	17,378
Oct 29	Bristol Rovers	L 1-4	Brook	24,575
Nov 5	STOKE CITY	W 1-0	Charles	21,261
Nov 12	Plymouth Argyle	L 3-4	Robertson o.g., Williams, Charles	19,122
Nov 19	LIVERPOOL	W 4-2	Overfield, Charles 2, Brook	22,596
Nov 26	Leicester City	L 2-5	Charles 2 (2 pen)	30,196
Dec 3	DONCASTER ROVERS	W 3-0	Hutchinson, Charles, Overfield	21,769
Dec 10	Blackburn Rovers	W 3-2	Overfield, Charles 2 (1 pen)	18,898
Dec 17	BARNSLEY	W 3-1	Hutchinson 2, Williams	23,493
Dec 24	Middlesbrough	L 3-5	Hutchinson, Charles, Vicers	19,416
Dec 26	NOTTS COUNTY	W 1-0	Brook	24,869
Dec 27	Notts County	L 1-2	Charles	23,910
Dec 31	BRISTOL CITY	W 2-1	Hutchinson, Brook	31,751
Jan 14	West Ham United	D 1-1	Charles	20,000
Jan 21	PORT VALE	D 1-1	Brook	23,680
Feb 11	SWANSEA TOWN	D 2-2	Charles (pen), Nightingale	20,089
Feb 25	SHEFFIELD WEDNESDAY	W 2-1	Charles, Forrest	43,268
Feb 28	Liverpool	L 0-1		21,068
Mar 3	Lincoln City	D 1-1	Charles (pen)	13,713
Mar 10	BLACKBURN ROVERS	L 1-2	Charles	28,380
Mar 17	Stoke City	L 1-2	Brook	22,784
Mar 24	PLYMOUTH ARGYLE	W 4-2	Brook, Nightingale, Charles 2	12,348
Mar 30	Fulham	W 2-1	Brook, Charles	25,459
Mar 31	Nottingham Forest	L 0-2		19,448
Apr 2	FULHAM	W 6-1	Charles 3, Nightingale 2, Brook	20,115
Apr 7	LEICESTER CITY	W 4-0	Overfield, Brook, Charles 2 (1 pen)	26,408
Apr 14	Doncaster Rovers	W 2-1	Charles, Nightingale	18,404
Apr 21	BRISTOL ROVERS	W 2-1	Charles, Overfield	49,274
Apr 23	Rotherham United	W 2-0	Nightingale 2	20,013
Apr 28	HULL CITY	W 4-1	Charles 2 (1 pen), Brook 2	31,123

FA Cup

Jan 7	CARDIFF CITY	(Rd 3) L 1-2	Brook	40,000

League & Cup Appearances

PLAYER	LEAGUE	CUP COMPETITION FA CUP	TOTAL
Ashall	6		6
Brook	32	1	33
Charles	41	1	42
Charlton	34	1	35
Dunn	42	1	43
Forrest	12		12
Gibson	27	1	28
Hair	34	1	35
Henderson	6		6
Hutchinson	11		11
Kerfoot	42	1	43
Marsden	2		2
Meek	26		26
Nightingale	26		26
Overfield	30	1	31
Ripley	19		19
Vickers	11	1	12
Williams	19	1	20
Wood	42	1	43

Goalscorers

PLAYER	LEAGUE	CUP COMPETITION FA CUP	TOTAL
Charles	29		29
Brook	16	1	17
Nightingale	10		10
Ripley	6		6
Overfield	6		6
Hutchinson	5		5
Forrest	2		2
Williams	2		2
Vickers	1		1
Henderson	1		1
Meek	1		1
Opps' o.gs.	1		1

Fact File

Leeds needed to win their last game – away to Hull City – to clinch promotion. They did it in style, winning 4-1.

MANAGER: Raich Carter

CAPTAIN: John Charles

TOP SCORER: John Charles

BIGGEST WIN: 6-1 v Fulham, 2 April 1956, League

HIGHEST ATTENDANCE: 49,274 v Bristol Rovers, 21 April 1956, won 2-1, League

Final Division 2 Table

		P	W	D	L	F	A	Pts
1	SHEFFIELD W	42	21	13	8	101	62	55
2	LEEDS UNITED	42	23	6	13	80	60	52
3	LIVERPOOL	42	21	6	15	85	63	48
4	BLACKBURN R	42	21	6	15	84	65	48
5	LEICESTER C	42	21	6	15	94	78	48
6	BRISTOL R	42	21	6	15	84	70	48
7	NOTTINGHAM F	42	19	9	14	68	63	47
8	LINCOLN C	42	18	10	14	79	65	46
9	FULHAM	42	20	6	16	89	79	46
10	SWANSEA T	42	20	6	16	83	81	46
11	BRISTOL C	42	19	7	16	80	64	45
12	PORT VALE	42	16	13	13	60	58	45
13	STOKE C	42	20	4	18	71	62	44
14	MIDDLESBROUGH	42	16	8	18	76	78	40
15	BURY	42	16	8	18	86	90	40
16	WEST HAM U	42	14	11	17	74	69	39
17	DONCASTER R	42	12	11	19	69	96	35
18	BARNSLEY	42	11	12	19	47	84	34
19	ROTHERHAM U	42	12	9	21	56	75	33
20	NOTTS CO	42	11	9	22	55	82	31
21	PLYMOUTH ARG	42	10	8	24	54	87	28
22	HULL C	42	10	6	26	53	97	26

Season 1956-57

Football League Division 1

DATE	OPPONENTS	SCORE	GOALSCORERS	ATTENDANCE
Aug 18	EVERTON	W 5-1	Overfield, Charles, Brook 3	31,379
Aug 23	Charlton Athletic	W 2-1	Charles 2	23,299
Aug 25	Tottenham Hotspur	L 1-5	Ripley	51,212
Aug 29	CHARLTON ATHLETIC	W 4-0	Forrest 2, Charles, Brook	34,444
Sep 1	CHELSEA	D 0-0		38,679
Sep 5	Manchester City	L 0-1		34,185
Sep 8	BOLTON WANDERERS	W 3-2	Meek, Charles, Brook	40,010
Sep 12	MANCHESTER CITY	W 2-0	Charles, Brook	35,068
Sep 15	Wolverhampton W	W 2-1	Charles 2	40,824
Sep 22	ASTON VILLA	W 1-0	Charles	35,388
Sep 29	Luton Town	D 2-2	Charles 2	20,949
Oct 6	Cardiff City	L 1-4	Forrest	38,333
Oct 13	BIRMINGHAM CITY	D 1-1	Ripley	34,460
Oct 20	Burnley	D 0-0		26,440
Oct 27	PRESTON NORTH END	L 1-2	Wilson o.g.	36,571
Nov 3	Newcastle United	W 3-2	McKenna 2, Charles	49,034
Nov 10	SHEFFIELD WEDNESDAY	W 3-1	Charles 3	31,857
Nov 17	Manchester United	L 2-3	McKenna, Charles (pen)	52,401
Nov 24	ARSENAL	D 3-3	Charles 2, Forrest	39,113
Dec 1	West Bromwich Albion	D 0-0		29,000
Dec 8	PORTSMOUTH	W 4-1	Charles 2, Ripley 2	29,866
Dec 15	Everton	L 1-2	Ripley	33,765
Dec 25	Blackpool	D 1-1	Brook	20,517
Dec 26	BLACKPOOL	W 5-0	Brook 3, Charles 2	22,689
Dec 29	Chelsea	D 1-1	Armstrong o.g.	43,860
Jan 12	Bolton Wanderers	L 3-5	Charles 2, Meek	25,705
Jan 19	WOLVERHAMPTON W	D 0-0		32,910
Feb 2	Aston Villa	D 1-1	Forrest	39,432
Feb 9	LUTON TOWN	L 1-2	Charles	25,646
Feb 16	CARDIFF CITY	W 3-2	McKenna, Charles, Forrest	21,695
Feb 23	Preston North End	L 0-3		14,036
Mar 2	TOTTENHAM HOTSPUR	D 1-1	Charles	33,895
Mar 9	Portsmouth	W 5-2	Charles 2, Crowe 2, Meek	23,596
Mar 11	BURNLEY	D 1-1	Charles	31,956
Mar 16	NEWCASTLE UNITED	D 0-0		32,541
Mar 26	Sheffield Wednesday	W 3-2	Charles 3	33,205
Mar 30	MANCHESTER UNITED	L 1-2	Charles	47,216
Apr 6	Arsenal	L 0-1		40,388
Apr 13	WEST BROMWICH ALBION	D 0-0		20,905
Apr 19	Sunderland	L 0-2		56,551
Apr 20	Birmingham City	L 2-6	Charles 2	30,642
Apr 22	SUNDERLAND	W 3-1	Charles 2, Brook	29,328

FA Cup

Jan 5	CARDIFF CITY	(Rd 3)	L 1-2	Charles	34,237

League & Cup Appearances

PLAYER	LEAGUE	CUP COMPETITION FA CUP	TOTAL
Brook	24	1	25
Charles	40	1	41
Charlton	21	1	22
Crowe	13		13
Dunn	42	1	43
Forrest	27	1	28
Gibson	40	1	41
Hair	42	1	43
Kerfoot	42	1	43
Marsden	21		21
McKenna	6		6
Meek	40	1	41
Nightingale	1		1
O'Brien	8		8
Overfield	42	1	43
Ripley	11		11
Wood	42	1	43

Goalscorers

PLAYER	LEAGUE	CUP COMPETITION FA CUP	TOTAL
Charles	38	1	39
Brook	11		11
Forrest	6		6
Ripley	5		5
McKenna	4		4
Meek	3		3
Crowe	2		2
Overfield	1		1
Opps' o.gs.	2		2

Fact File

On 18 September, a fire swept through the West Stand. The financial consequences of the blaze forced the sale of John Charles to Juventus.

MANAGER: Raich Carter

CAPTAIN: John Charles

TOP SCORER: John Charles

BIGGEST WIN: 5-0 v Blackpool, 26 December 1956, League

HIGHEST ATTENDANCE: 56,551 v Sunderland, 19 April 1957, lost 0-2, League

MAJOR TRANSFERS IN: George O'Brien from Dunfermline

MAJOR TRANSFERS OUT: Albert Nightingale (retired)

Final Division 1 Table

		P	W	D	L	F	A	Pts
1	MANCHESTER U	42	28	8	6	103	54	64
2	TOTTENHAM H	42	22	12	8	104	56	56
3	PRESTON NE	42	23	10	9	84	56	56
4	BLACKPOOL	42	22	9	11	93	65	53
5	ARSENAL	42	21	8	13	85	69	50
6	WOLVERHAMPTON W	42	20	8	14	94	70	48
7	BURNLEY	42	18	10	14	56	50	46
8	LEEDS UNITED	42	15	14	13	72	63	44
9	BOLTON W	42	16	12	14	65	65	44
10	ASTON VILLA	42	14	15	13	65	55	43
11	WBA	42	14	14	14	59	61	42
12	BIRMINGHAM C	42	15	9	18	69	69	39
13	CHELSEA	42	13	13	16	73	73	39
14	SHEFFIELD W	42	16	6	20	82	88	38
15	EVERTON	42	14	10	18	61	79	38
16	LUTON T	42	14	9	19	58	76	37
17	NEWCASTLE U	42	14	8	20	67	87	36
18	MANCHESTER C	42	13	9	20	78	88	35
19	PORTSMOUTH	42	10	13	19	62	92	33
20	SUNDERLAND	42	12	8	22	67	88	32
21	CARDIFF C	42	10	9	23	53	88	29
22	CHARLTON ATH	42	9	4	29	62	120	22

Season 1957-58

Football League Division 1

DATE	OPPONENTS	SCORE	GOALSCORERS	ATTENDANCE
Aug 24	Blackpool	L 0-3		26,700
Aug 26	Aston Villa	L 0-2		25,693
Aug 31	LEICESTER CITY	W 2-1	Baird (pen), Overfield	26,660
Sep 4	ASTON VILLA	W 4-0	Baird 2, O'Brien, Brook	22,685
Sep 7	Manchester United	L 0-5		50,842
Sep 11	LUTON TOWN	L 0-2		21,972
Sep 14	NOTTINGHAM FOREST	L 1-2	Overfield	25,566
Sep 18	Luton Town	D 1-1	Overfield	16,887
Sep 21	BOLTON WANDERERS	W 2-1	Meek, Baird	18,379
Sep 25	SUNDERLAND	W 2-1	Baird, Gibson	17,600
Sep 28	Arsenal	L 1-2	Brook	39,538
Oct 5	WOLVERHAMPTON W	D 1-1	Baird	28,635
Oct 12	Portsmouth	W 2-1	Baird, Brook	23,534
Oct 19	WEST BROMWICH ALBION	D 1-1	Forrest	24,614
Oct 26	Tottenham Hotspur	L 0-2		33,860
Nov 2	PRESTON NORTH END	L 2-3	Baird 2 (2 pen)	23,832
Nov 9	Sheffield Wednesday	L 2-3	Ripley, Forrest	21,469
Nov 16	MANCHESTER CITY	L 2-4	Kerfoot, Baird	23,855
Nov 23	Burnley	L 1-3	Baird (pen)	24,144
Nov 30	BIRMINGHAM CITY	D 1-1	Cush	21,358
Dec 7	Chelsea	L 1-2	Baird	17,038
Dec 14	NEWCASTLE UNITED	W 3-0	Forrest, Crowe, Overfield	23,363
Dec 21	BLACKPOOL	W 2-1	Cush, Forrest	32,411
Dec 26	Sunderland	L 1-2	Crowe	34,875
Dec 28	Leicester City	L 0-3		31,747
Jan 11	MANCHESTER UNITED	D 1-1	Baird	39,401
Jan 18	Nottingham Forest	D 1-1	Baird	23,368
Feb 1	Bolton Wanderers	W 2-0	Forrest, Cush	18,558
Feb 19	Wolverhampton W	L 2-3	Paton, Forrest	35,527
Feb 22	PORTSMOUTH	W 2-0	Baird 2	26,713
Mar 8	TOTTENHAM HOTSPUR	L 1-2	Baird	23,429
Mar 12	West Bromwich Albion	L 0-1		16,412
Mar 15	Preston North End	L 0-3		21,353
Mar 19	ARSENAL	W 2-0	Meek, Paton	25,948
Mar 22	BURNLEY	W 1-0	Meek	24,994
Mar 29	Manchester City	L 0-1		21,962
Apr 4	Everton	W 1-0	Baird	32,679
Apr 5	SHEFFIELD WEDNESDAY	D 2-2	Meek, Baird	26,212
Apr 7	EVERTON	W 1-0	Forrest	25,188
Apr 12	Birmingham City	D 1-1	O'Brien	23,112
Apr 19	CHELSEA	D 0-0		20,515
Apr 26	Newcastle United	W 2-1	Baird, O'Brien	32,594

FA Cup

Jan 4	Cardiff City	(Rd 3) L 1-2	Forrest	30,374

League & Cup Appearances

PLAYER	LEAGUE	CUP COMPETITION FA CUP	TOTAL
Ashall	9		9
Baird	39		39
Brook	9		9
Charlton	40	1	41
Crowe	19	1	20
Cush	21	1	22
Dunn	35	1	36
Forrest	24	1	25
Francis	1		1
Gibson	25	1	26
Hair	34	1	35
Kerfoot	42	1	43
Marsden	4		4
Meek	40	1	41
Nimmo	1		1
O'Brien	19		19
Overfield	36	1	37
Paton	11		11
Ripley	12		12
Wood	41	1	42

Goalscorers

PLAYER	LEAGUE	CUP COMPETITION FA CUP	TOTAL
Baird	20		20
Forrest	7	1	8
Meek	4		4
Overfield	4		4
Brook	3		3
O'Brien	3		3
Cush	3		3
Crowe	2		2
Paton	2		2
Ripley	1		1
Gibson	1		1
Kerfoot	1		1
Opps' o.gs.	0		0

Fact File

South African Gerry Francis made his debut against Birmingham in November. He was one of the first black players to play in the Football League.

MANAGER: Raich Carter/Bill Lambton

CAPTAIN: Wilbur Cush

TOP SCORER: Hugh Baird

BIGGEST WIN: 4-0 v Aston Villa, 4 September 1957, League

HIGHEST ATTENDANCE: 50,842 v Manchester United, 7 September 1957, lost 0-5, League

MAJOR TRANSFERS IN: Hughie Baird from Airdrie, Wilbur Cush from Glenavon

MAJOR TRANSFERS OUT: John Charles to Juventus

Final Division 1 Table

		P	W	D	L	F	A	Pts
1	WOLVERHAMPTON W	42	28	8	6	103	47	64
2	PRESTON NE	42	26	7	9	100	51	59
3	TOTTENHAM H	42	21	9	12	93	77	51
4	WBA	42	18	14	10	92	70	50
5	MANCHESTER C	42	22	5	15	104	100	49
6	BURNLEY	42	21	5	16	80	74	47
7	BLACKPOOL	42	19	6	17	80	67	44
8	LUTON T	42	19	6	17	69	63	44
9	MANCHESTER U	42	16	11	15	85	75	43
10	NOTTINGHAM F	42	16	10	16	69	63	42
11	CHELSEA	42	15	12	15	83	79	42
12	ARSENAL	42	16	7	19	73	85	39
13	BIRMINGHAM C	42	14	11	17	76	89	39
14	ASTON VILLA	42	16	7	19	73	86	39
15	BOLTON W	42	14	10	18	65	87	38
16	EVERTON	42	13	11	18	65	75	37
17	LEEDS UNITED	42	14	9	19	51	63	37
18	LEICESTER C	42	14	5	23	91	112	33
19	NEWCASTLE U	42	12	8	22	73	81	32
20	PORTSMOUTH	42	12	8	22	73	88	32
21	SUNDERLAND	42	10	12	20	54	97	32
22	SHEFFIELD W	42	12	7	23	69	92	31

Season 1958-59

Football League Division 1

DATE	OPPONENTS	SCORE	GOALSCORERS	ATTENDANCE
Aug 23	Bolton Wanderers	L 0-4		25,922
Aug 26	LUTON TOWN	D 1-1	Crowe (pen)	25,498
Aug 30	BURNLEY	D 1-1	Forrest	22,739
Sep 3	Luton Town	D 1-1	Baird	13,497
Sep 6	Preston North End	W 2-1	Baird (pen), Overfield	22,765
Sep 10	BIRMINGHAM CITY	D 0-0		25,228
Sep 13	LEICESTER CITY	D 1-1	Meek	23,487
Sep 17	Birmingham City	L 1-4	Forrest	24,068
Sep 20	Everton	L 2-3	Cush, Crowe	31,105
Sep 27	ARSENAL	W 2-1	Crowe (pen), Overfield	33,961
Oct 4	Manchester City	L 1-2	Leivers o.g.	31,989
Oct 11	Portsmouth	L 0-2		22,570
Oct 18	ASTON VILLA	D 0-0		21,088
Oct 25	Tottenham Hotspur	W 3-2	Cush, O'Brien, Overfield	38,691
Nov 1	MANCHESTER UNITED	L 1-2	Shackleton	48,574
Nov 8	Chelsea	L 0-2		33,357
Nov 15	BLACKPOOL	D 1-1	Crowe	29,252
Nov 22	Blackburn Rovers	W 4-2	Shackleton 3, Humphries	28,727
Nov 29	NEWCASTLE UNITED	W 3-2	Overfield, Crown, Scott o.g.	23,732
Dec 6	West Ham United	W 3-2	Crowe (pen), Overfield, Bond o.g.	22,022
Dec 13	NOTTINGHAM FOREST	W 1-0	Crowe	26,341
Dec 20	BOLTON WANDERERS	L 3-4	Crowe (pen), Gibson, Shackleton	28,534
Dec 26	West Bromwich Albion	W 2-1	Humphries, Crowe (pen)	34,878
Dec 27	WEST BROMWICH ALBION	L 0-1		44,929
Jan 3	Burnley	L 1-3	Shackleton	26,013
Jan 17	PRESTON NORTH END	L 1-3	Revie	22,043
Jan 31	Leicester City	W 1-0	Shackleton	23,376
Feb 7	EVERTON	W 1-0	Shackleton	18,200
Feb 14	Wolverhampton W	L 2-6	Shackleton, Overfield	26,790
Feb 21	MANCHESTER CITY	L 0-4		18,515
Feb 24	Arsenal	L 0-1		30,034
Feb 28	PORTSMOUTH	D 1-1	Cush	14,900
Mar 7	Aston Villa	L 1-2	Overfield	27,631
Mar 14	TOTTENHAM HOTSPUR	W 3-1	Crowe, Shackleton, Overfield	17,010
Mar 21	Manchester United	L 0-4		45,473
Mar 28	CHELSEA	W 4-0	O'Brien 2, Shackleton, Crowe	16,676
Mar 31	WOLVERHAMPTON W	L 1-3	Crowe	35,819
Apr 4	Blackpool	L 0-3		14,089
Apr 11	BLACKBURN ROVERS	W 2-1	Shackleton, Charlton	15,232
Apr 18	Newcastle United	D 2-2	Revie, Paton	19,321
Apr 22	Nottingham Forest	W 3-0	Shackleton 3	18,650
Apr 25	WEST HAM UNITED	W 1-0	Shackleton	11,257

FA Cup

Jan 10	Luton Town	(Rd 3)	L 1-5	Shackleton	18,354

League & Cup Appearances

PLAYER	LEAGUE	CUP COMPETITION FA CUP	TOTAL
Ashall	32	1	33
Baird	6		6
Burgin	16		16
Charlton	39	1	40
Crowe	35	1	36
Cush	36	1	37
Dunn	10		10
Forrest	15		15
Gibson	31	1	32
Hair	37	1	38
Humphries	23	1	24
Kemp	1		1
Kerfoot	16		16
Kilford	1		1
Marsden	2		2
McConnell	6		6
Meek	18		18
Mitchell	4		4
O'Brien	17		17
Overfield	35	1	36
Peyton	8		8
Revie	20	1	21
Shackleton	28	1	29
Wood	26	1	27

Goalscorers

PLAYER	LEAGUE	CUP COMPETITION FA CUP	TOTAL
Shackleton	16	1	17
Crowe	11		11
Overfield	8		8
Cush	3		3
O'Brien	3		3
Forrest	2		2
Baird	2		2
Humphries	2		2
Revie	2		2
Meek	1		1
Crown	1		1
Gibson	1		1
Charlton	1		1
Peyton	1		1
Opps' o.gs.	3		3

Fact File

Three wins and a draw in four games at the end of the season saved Leeds from relegation.

MANAGER: Bill Lambton

CAPTAIN: Wilbur Cush

TOP SCORER: Alan Shackleton

BIGGEST WIN: 4-0 v Chelsea, 28 March 1959, League

HIGHEST ATTENDANCE: 48,574 v Manchester United, 1 November 1958, lost 1-2, League

MAJOR TRANSFERS IN: Don Revie from Sunderland, Alan Shackleton from Burnley

MAJOR TRANSFERS OUT: Bobby Forrest to Notts County, Hughie Baird to Aberdeen

Final Division 1 Table

		P	W	D	L	F	A	Pts
1	WOLVERHAMPTON W	42	28	5	9	110	49	61
2	MANCHESTER U	42	24	7	11	103	66	55
3	ARSENAL	42	21	8	13	88	68	50
4	BOLTON W	42	20	10	12	79	66	50
5	WBA	42	18	13	11	88	68	49
6	WEST HAM U	42	21	6	15	85	70	48
7	BURNLEY	42	19	10	13	81	70	48
8	BLACKPOOL	42	18	11	13	66	49	47
9	BIRMINGHAM C	42	20	6	16	84	68	46
10	BLACKBURN R	42	17	10	15	76	70	44
11	NEWCASTLE U	42	17	7	18	80	80	41
12	PRESTON NE	42	17	7	18	70	77	41
13	NOTTINGHAM F	42	17	6	19	71	74	40
14	CHELSEA	42	18	4	20	77	98	40
15	LEEDS UNITED	42	15	9	18	57	74	39
16	EVERTON	42	17	4	21	71	87	38
17	LUTON T	42	12	13	17	68	71	37
18	TOTTENHAM H	42	13	10	19	85	95	36
19	LEICESTER C	42	11	10	21	67	98	32
20	MANCHESTER C	42	11	9	22	64	95	31
21	ASTON VILLA	42	11	8	23	58	87	30
22	PORTSMOUTH	42	6	9	27	64	112	21

Season 1959-60

Football League Division 1

DATE	OPPONENTS	SCORE	GOALSCORERS	ATTENDANCE
Aug 22	BURNLEY	L 2-3	Charlton, Cush (pen)	20,233
Aug 26	Leicester City	L 2-3	Crowe, Cush	24,790
Aug 29	Luton Town	W 1-0	Revie	15,822
Sep 2	LEICESTER CITY	D 1-1	Crowe	18,384
Sep 5	West Ham United	W 2-1	Crowe 2 (1 pen)	27,777
Sep 9	Manchester United	L 0-6		48,619
Sep 12	CHELSEA	W 2-1	Crowe 2	17,011
Sep 16	MANCHESTER UNITED	D 2-2	Cush, Crowe	34,048
Sep 19	West Bromwich Albion	L 0-3		26,364
Sep 26	NEWCASTLE UNITED	L 2-3	McCole, Revie	28,306
Oct 3	Birmingham City	L 0-2		25,301
Oct 10	EVERTON	D 3-3	Crowe (pen), Francis, McCole	19,122
Oct 17	Blackpool	D 3-3	McCole 2, Francis	22,301
Oct 24	BLACKBURN ROVERS	L 0-1		17,159
Oct 31	Bolton Wanderers	D 1-1	McCole	20,183
Nov 7	ARSENAL	W 3-2	Paton 2, McCole	21,617
Nov 14	Wolverhampton W	L 2-4	Crowe, Paton	21,546
Nov 21	SHEFFIELD WEDNESDAY	L 1-3	McCole	21,260
Nov 28	Nottingham Forest	L 1-4	Revie	21,366
Dec 5	FULHAM	L 1-4	McCole	18,846
Dec 12	Manchester City	D 3-3	Revie, Crowe, Gibson	19,715
Dec 19	Burnley	W 1-0	Overfield	17,398
Dec 26	TOTTENHAM HOTSPUR	L 2-4	McCole 2	36,037
Dec 28	Tottenham Hotspur	W 4-1	McCole 2, Cameron, Meek	54,170
Jan 2	LUTON TOWN	D 1-1	McCole	19,921
Jan 16	WEST HAM UNITED	W 3-0	Crowe, McCole, Meek	15,284
Jan 23	Chelsea	W 3-1	McCole 2, Paton	18,963
Feb 6	WEST BROMWICH ALBION	L 1-4	McCole (pen)	23,729
Feb 13	Newcastle United	L 1-2	Revie	16,148
Feb 27	Fulham	L 0-5		23,355
Mar 5	BLACKPOOL	L 2-4	McCole, Meek	23,127
Mar 9	BIRMINGHAM CITY	D 3-3	Revie 2, Bremner	8,557
Mar 19	MANCHESTER CITY	W 4-3	McCole 2 (2 pens), Bremner, Paton	32,545
Mar 26	Arsenal	D 1-1	Gibson	19,597
Apr 2	WOLVERHAMPTON W	L 0-3		29,492
Apr 9	Sheffield Wednesday	L 0-1		27,073
Apr 16	BOLTON WANDERERS	W 1-0	Charlton	19,272
Apr 18	Preston North End	D 1-1	Gibson	15,879
Apr 19	PRESTON NORTH END	W 2-1	Charlton, Francis	23,764
Apr 23	Everton	L 0-1		37,885
Apr 27	Blackburn Rovers	L 2-3	Meek, McCole	19,295
Apr 30	NOTTINGHAM FOREST	W 1-0	McCole (pen)	11,699

FA Cup

Jan 9	Aston Villa	(Rd 3) L 1-2	McCole	43,421

League & Cup Appearances

PLAYER	LEAGUE	CUP COMPETITION FA CUP	TOTAL
Ashall	38	1	39
Bremner	11		11
Burgin	32		32
Caldwell	10		10
Cameron	21	1	22
Charlton	41	1	42
Crowe	28	1	29
Cush	30	1	31
Francis	12		12
Gibson	34	1	35
Goodwin	10		10
Hair	32	1	33
Humphreys	3		3
Humphries	2		2
Kilford	4		4
McCole	33	1	34
McConnell	8		8
Meek	33	1	34
Overfield	16		16
Paton	20	1	21
Revie	35		35
Shackleton	2		2
Wood	7	1	8

Goalscorers

PLAYER	LEAGUE	CUP COMPETITION FA CUP	TOTAL
McCole	22	1	23
Crowe	11		11
Revie	7		7
Paton	5		5
Meek	4		4
Cush	3		3
Gibson	3		3
Charlton	3		3
Francis	3		3
Bremner	2		2
Cameron	1		1
Overfield	1		1
Opps' o.gs.	0		0

Fact File

Billy Bremner made his debut for Leeds at Chelsea in January 1960.

MANAGER: Jack Taylor

CAPTAIN: Don Revie/Wilbur Cush

TOP SCORER: John McCole

BIGGEST WIN: 4-0 v Tottenham Hotspur, 28 December 1959, League

HIGHEST ATTENDANCE: 54,170 4-0 v Tottenham Hotspur, 28 December 1959, League

MAJOR TRANSFERS IN: John McCole from Bradford City, Freddie Goodwin from Manchester United

MAJOR TRANSFERS OUT: Chris Crowe to Blackburn Rovers, Alan Shackleton to Everton

Final Division 1 Table

		P	W	D	L	F	A	Pts
1	BURNLEY	42	24	7	11	85	61	55
2	WOLVERHAMPTON W	42	24	6	12	106	67	54
3	TOTTENHAM H	42	21	11	10	86	50	53
4	WBA	42	19	11	12	83	57	49
5	SHEFFIELD W	42	19	11	12	80	59	49
6	BOLTON W	42	20	8	14	59	51	48
7	MANCHESTER U	42	19	7	16	102	80	45
8	NEWCASTLE U	42	18	8	16	82	78	44
9	PRESTON NE	42	16	12	14	79	76	44
10	FULHAM	42	17	10	15	73	80	44
11	BLACKPOOL	42	15	10	17	59	71	40
12	LEICESTER C	42	13	13	16	66	75	39
13	ARSENAL	42	15	9	18	68	80	39
14	WEST HAM U	42	16	6	20	75	91	38
15	EVERTON	42	13	11	18	73	78	37
16	MANCHESTER C	42	17	3	22	78	84	37
17	BLACKBURN R	42	16	5	21	60	70	37
18	CHELSEA	42	14	9	19	76	91	37
19	BIRMINGHAM C	42	13	10	19	63	80	36
20	NOTTINGHAM F	42	13	9	20	50	74	35
21	LEEDS UNITED	42	12	10	20	65	92	34
22	LUTON T	42	9	12	21	50	73	30

Season 1960-61

Football League Division 2

DATE	OPPONENTS	SCORE	GOALSCORERS	ATTENDANCE
Aug 20	Liverpool	L 0-2		43,041
Aug 24	BRISTOL ROVERS	D 1-1	McCole	11,330
Aug 27	ROTHERHAM UNITED	W 2-0	Hawksby, McCole	16,480
Aug 29	Bristol Rovers	D 4-4	Hawksby, Grainger, Peyton, McCole	18,864
Sep 3	Southampton	W 4-2	Grainger, Cameron, Francis, McCole	21,862
Sep 7	LEYTON ORIENT	L 1-3	Cameron	17,363
Sep 10	HUDDERSFIELD TOWN	L 1-4	Cameron (pen)	22,146
Sep 14	Leyton Orient	W 1-0	Revie	8,505
Sep 17	MIDDLESBROUGH	D 4-4	Stonehouse o.g., Goodwin, Cameron, McCole	17,799
Sep 24	Brighton & Hove Albion	L 1-2	McCole	16,276
Oct 1	IPSWICH TOWN	L 2-5	McCole 2	13,502
Oct 8	Sunderland	W 3-2	Peyton, Francis, McCole	22,296
Oct 15	PLYMOUTH ARGYLE	W 2-1	Grainger, Francis	12,229
Oct 22	Norwich City	L 2-3	Bremner 2	18,970
Oct 29	CHARLTON ATHLETIC	W 1-0	Grainger	14,014
Nov 5	Sheffield United	L 2-3	Cameron (pen), Francis	17,565
Nov 12	STOKE CITY	L 0-1		13,486
Nov 19	Swansea Town	L 2-3	McCole, Cameron	11,140
Dec 3	Lincoln City	W 3-2	McCole, Bremner, Peyton	5,678
Dec 10	PORTSMOUTH	D 0-0		9,421
Dec 17	LIVERPOOL	D 2-2	Murray, Bremner	11,929
Dec 24	Derby County	W 3-2	McCole, Bremner 2	15,185
Dec 27	DERBY COUNTY	D 3-3	McCole, Murray, Charlton	18,517
Dec 31	Rotherham United	W 3-1	McCole, Lambert o.g., Waterhouse o.g.	12,557
Jan 14	SOUTHAMPTON	W 3-0	Cameron, Francis 2	14,039
Jan 21	Huddersfield Town	W 1-0	McCole	18,938
Feb 4	Middlesbrough	L 0-3		16,593
Feb 10	BRIGHTON & HOVE ALBION	W 3-2	McCole, Charlton, Goodwin	12,598
Feb 18	Ipswich Town	L 0-4		13,124
Feb 25	SUNDERLAND	L 2-4	Smith, Bremner	15,136
Mar 4	Plymouth Argyle	L 1-3	Grainger	14,878
Mar 8	LUTON TOWN	L 1-2	Cameron (pen)	9,995
Mar 11	NORWICH CITY	W 1-0	Smith	11,294
Mar 18	Portsmouth	L 1-3	Charlton	16,230
Mar 25	SHEFFIELD UNITED	L 1-2	Shaw o.g.	13,688
Apr 1	Luton Town	D 1-1	Bremner	11,137
Apr 3	Scunthorpe United	L 2-3	Charlton 2 (1 pen)	8,725
Apr 8	SWANSEA TOWN	D 2-2	Charlton 2	11,862
Apr 15	Stoke City	D 0-0		7,130
Apr 22	LINCOLN CITY	W 7-0	McCole 2, Bell, Peyton, McConnell, Bremner, Drysdale o.g.	8,432
Apr 25	SCUNTHORPE UNITED	D 2-2	McCole 2	6,975
Apr 29	Charlton Athletic	L 0-2		9,081

FA Cup

Jan 7	Sheffield Wednesday	(Rd 3) L 0-2		34,281

League Cup

Sep 28	BLACKPOOL	(Rd 2) D 0-0		13,064
Oct 5	Blackpool	(Rd 2) W 3-1	Revie, McCole, Grainger	9,614
Nov 23	Chesterfield	(Rd 3) W 4-0	McCole, Cameron, Bremner, Peyton	2,021
Dec 5	Southampton	(Rd 4) L 4-5	Peyton, McCole, Charlton, Cameron (pen)	13,448

MANAGER: Jack Taylor/Don Revie

CAPTAIN: Freddie Goodwin

TOP SCORER: John McCole

BIGGEST WIN: 7-0 v Lincoln City, 22 April 1961, League

HIGHEST ATTENDANCE: 43,041 v Liverpool, 20 August 1960, lost 0-2, League

MAJOR TRANSFERS IN: Eric Smith from Celtic, Colin Grainger from Sunderland, Derek Mayers from Preston North End, Willie Bell from Queen's Park

MAJOR TRANSFERS OUT: Jack Overfield to Sunderland, George Meek to Leicester City, Wilbur Cush to Portadown

League & Cup Appearances

PLAYER	LEAGUE	CUP COMPETITION		TOTAL
		FA CUP	LC	
Ashall	4			4
Bell	5			5
Bremner	31	1	2	34
Burgin	10		1	11
Caldwell	10		2	12
Cameron	30	1	4	35
Carling	4		1	5
Charlton	41	1	4	46
Fitzgerald	8			8
Francis	31	1	3	35
Goodwin	36	1	4	41
Grainger	33	1	3	37
Hair	39	1	4	44
Hawksby	7			7
Humphreys	28	1	2	31
Johanneson	5			5
Jones	20	1	2	23
Kilford	10			10
Martin		1		1
McCole	35	1	4	40
McConnell	11			11
McGugan	1			1
Murraye	7			7
Peyton	23		3	26
Revie	14		3	17
Smith	18	1		19
Wright	1		1	2

Goalscorers

PLAYER	LEAGUE	CUP COMPETITION		TOTAL
		FA CUP	LC	
McCole	20		3	23
Cameron	8		2	10
Bremner	9		1	9
Charton	7		1	8
Grainger	5		1	6
Peyton	4		2	6
Francis	6			6
Hawksby	2			2
Revie	1		1	2
Goodwin	2			2
Murray	2			2
Smith	2			2
Bell	1			1
McConnell	1			1
Opps' o.gs.	4			4

Fact File

The home game against Middlesbrough in September saw Leeds play in all white (with blue trimmings) for the first time.

Final Division 2 Table

		P	W	D	L	F	A	Pts
1	IPSWICH T	42	26	7	9	100	55	59
2	SHEFFIELD U	42	26	6	10	81	51	58
3	LIVERPOOL	42	21	10	11	87	58	52
4	NORWICH C	42	20	9	13	70	53	49
5	MIDDLESBROUGH	42	18	12	12	83	74	48
6	SUNDERLAND	42	17	13	12	75	60	47
7	SWANSEA T	42	18	11	13	77	73	47
8	SOUTHAMPTON	42	18	8	16	84	81	44
9	SCUNTHORPE U	42	14	15	13	69	64	43
10	CHARLTON ATH	42	16	11	15	97	91	43
11	PLYMOUTH ARG	42	17	8	17	81	82	42
12	DERBY CO	42	15	10	17	80	80	40
13	LUTON T	42	15	9	18	71	79	39
14	LEEDS UNITED	42	14	10	18	75	83	38
15	ROTHERHAM U	42	12	13	17	65	64	37
16	BRIGHTON & HA	42	14	9	19	61	75	37
17	BRISTOL R	42	15	7	20	73	92	37
18	STOKE C	42	12	12	18	51	59	36
19	LEYTON ORIENT	42	14	8	20	55	78	36
20	HUDDERSFIELD T	42	13	9	20	62	71	35
21	PORTSMOUTH	42	11	11	20	64	91	33
22	LINCOLN C	42	8	8	26	48	95	24

Season 1961-62

Football League Division 2

DATE	OPPONENTS	SCORE	GOALSCORERS	ATTENDANCE
Aug 19	CHARLTON ATHLETIC	W 1-0	Bremner	12,916
Aug 22	Brighton & Hove Albion	W 3-1	Peyton, Bremner, Mayers	22,744
Aug 26	Liverpool	L 0-5		42,450
Aug 30	BRIGHTON & HOVE ALBION	D 1-1	Bremner	12,642
Sep 2	ROTHERHAM UNITED	L 1-3	McCole	12,610
Sep 6	Norwich City	L 0-2		26,860
Sep 9	Sunderland	L 1-2	McCole	30,737
Sep 16	STOKE CITY	W 3-1	McCole, Bremner, Peyton	9,578
Sep 20	NORWICH CITY	L 0-1		10,948
Sep 23	Bristol Rovers	L 0-4		13,676
Sep 30	PRESTON NORTH END	L 1-2	Charlton	9,360
Oct 7	Plymouth Argyle	D 1-1	McConnnell	10,144
Oct 14	HUDDERSFIELD TOWN	W 1-0	Charlton	19,162
Oct 21	Swansea Town	L 1-2	McConnell	11,091
Oct 28	SOUTHAMPTON	D 1-1	McConnell	10,145
Nov 4	Luton Town	L 2-3	Revie, Bremner (pen)	10,341
Nov 11	LEYTON ORIENT	D 0-0		7,967
Nov 18	Middlesbrough	W 3-1	Mayers, Bremner, Charlton	10,758
Nov 25	WALSALL	W 4-1	Charlton 2, Bremner (pen), Peyton	10,999
Dec 2	Derby County	D 3-3	Peyton, Mayers, Bell	16,408
Dec 16	Charlton Athletic	L 1-3	Bremner (pen)	9,459
Dec 23	LIVERPOOL	W 1-0	Bremner	17,214
Dec 26	SCUNTHORPE UNITED	L 1-4	Charlton	19,481
Jan 12	Rotherham United	L 1-2	McAdams	6,207
Jan 20	SUNDERLAND	W 1-0	Smith	17,763
Jan 27	NEWCASTLE UNITED	L 0-1		17,120
Feb 3	Stoke City	L 1-2	Peyton	21,935
Feb 10	BRISTOL ROVERS	D 0-0		9,108
Feb 20	Scunthorpe United	L 1-2	Mayers (pen)	9,186
Feb 24	PLYMOUTH ARGYLE	L 2-3	Charlton, Mayers	8,554
Mar 3	Huddersfield Town	L 1-2	Charlton	16,799
Mar 10	SWANSEA TOWN	W 2-0	Collins, McAdams	17,314
Mar 17	Southampton	L 1-4	Lawson	11,924
Mar 24	LUTON TOWN	W 2-1	Bremner 2	13,078
Mar 31	Leyton Orient	D 0-0		13,290
Apr 7	MIDDLESBROUGH	W 2-0	Hair, Gates o.g	16,116
Apr 9	Preston North End	D 1-1	Cunningham o.g	10,492
Apr 14	Walsall	D 1-1	Johanneson	9,005
Apr 20	Bury	D 1-1	Charlton	11,313
Apr 21	DERBY COUNTY	D 0-0		11,922
Apr 24	BURY	D 0-0		21,482
Apr 28	Newcastle United	W 3-0	Johanneson, McAdams, Keith o.g.	21,708

FA Cup

Jan 6	DERBY COUNTY	(Rd 3)	D 2-2	Peyton, Charlton	27,089
Jan 10	Derby County	(R)	L 1-3	McAdams	28,168

League Cup

Sep 13	BRENTFORD	(Rd 1)	W 4-1	McCole 4	4,517
Oct 4	HUDDERSFIELD TOWN	(Rd 2)	W 3-2	Bremner (pen), Charlton, McConnell	10,023
Dec 12	Rotherham United	(Rd 4)	D 1-1	Charlton	10,899
Dec 15	ROTHERHAM UNITED	(R)	L 1-2	Johanneson (pen)	6,385

League & Cup Appearances

PLAYER	LEAGUE	CUP COMPETITION		TOTAL
		FA CUP	LC	
Addy			1	1
Bell	23	2	3	28
Bremner	39	2	4	45
Cameron	7			7
Carling	1			1
Casey	3		1	4
Charlton	34	2	3	39
Collins	11			11
Francis	4			4
Goodwin	41	2	4	47
Hair	38	2	3	43
Hawksby	25		4	29
Humphreys	9		1	10
Johanneson	13		1	14
Jones	5		1	6
Kilford	6		2	8
Lawson	11			11
Mason	11			11
Mayers	20	2	2	24
McAdams	11	2		13
McCole	10		1	11
McConnell	23	2	3	28
Peyton	37	2	4	43
Revie	7			7
Smith	41	2	3	46
Sprake	1			1
Younger	31	2	3	36

Goalscorers

PLAYER	LEAGUE	CUP COMPETITION		TOTAL
		FA CUP	LC	
Charlton	9	1	2	12
Bremner	11		1	12
McCole	3		4	7
Peyton	5	1		6
Mayers	5			5
McAdams	3	1		4
McConnell	3		1	4
Johanneson	2		1	3
Revie	1			1
Smith	1			1
Bell	1			1
Hair	1			1
Collins	1			1
Lawson	1			1
Opps' o.gs.	3			3

Fact File

Bobby Collins scored on his debut against Swansea in March, Leeds first win for 2 months. They needed a last match victory to avoid relegation.

MANAGER: Don Revie

CAPTAIN: Freddie Goodwin

TOP SCORER: Jack Charlton

BIGGEST WIN: September 13, 1961 4-1 v Brentford, League Cup Round 1; November 25, 1961 4-1 v Walsall, Division 2

HIGHEST ATTENDANCE: August 26, 1961 42,450 v Liverpool, lost 0-5, Division 2

MAJOR TRANSFERS IN: Bobby Collins from Everton, Tommy Younger from Stoke City, Billy McAdams from Bolton Wanderers, Cliff Mason from Sheffield United, Ian Lawson from Burnley

MAJOR TRANSFERS OUT: John McCole to Bradford City

Final Division 2 Table

		P	W	D	L	F	A	Pts
1	LIVERPOOL	42	27	8	7	99	43	62
2	LEYTON ORIENT	42	22	10	10	69	40	54
3	SUNDERLAND	42	22	9	11	85	50	53
4	SCUNTHORPE U	42	21	7	14	86	71	49
5	PLYMOUTH ARG	42	19	8	15	75	75	46
6	SOUTHAMPTON	42	18	9	15	77	62	45
7	HUDDERSFIELD T	42	16	12	14	67	59	44
8	STOKE C	42	17	8	17	55	57	42
9	ROTHERHAM U	42	16	9	17	70	76	41
10	PRESTON NE	42	15	10	17	55	57	40
11	NEWCASTLE U	42	15	9	18	64	58	39
12	MIDDLESBROUGH	42	16	7	19	76	72	39
13	LUTON T	42	17	5	20	69	71	39
14	WALSALL	42	14	11	17	70	75	39
15	CHARLTON ATH	42	15	9	18	69	75	39
16	DERBY CO	42	14	11	17	68	75	39
17	NORWICH C	42	14	11	17	61	70	39
18	BURY	42	17	5	20	52	76	39
19	LEEDS UNITED	42	12	12	18	50	61	36
20	SWANSEA T	42	12	12	18	61	83	36
21	BRISTOL R	42	13	7	22	53	81	33
22	BRIGHTON & HA	42	10	11	21	42	86	31

Season 1962-63

Football League Division 2

DATE	OPPONENTS	SCORE	GOALSCORERS	ATTENDANCE
Aug 18	Stoke City	W 1-0	Storrie	27,118
Aug 22	ROTHERHAM UNITED	L 3-4	Storrie, Charles, Johanneson	14,119
Aug 25	SUNDERLAND	W 1-0	Bremner	17,753
Aug 28	Rotherham United	L 1-2	Charles	19,508
Sep 1	Huddersfield Town	D 1-1	Charles	34,946
Sep 5	BURY	L 1-2	Bremner	28,313
Sep 8	Swansea Town	W 2-0	Johnson, Bremner	17,696
Sep 15	CHELSEA	W 2-0	Johanneson 2	27,520
Sep 18	Bury	L 1-3	Storrie	18,876
Sep 22	Luton Town	D 2-2	Storrie, Collins	8,958
Sep 29	SOUTHAMPTON	D 1-1	Storrie	25,408
Oct 6	MIDDLESBROUGH	L 2-3	Hunter, Bremner	28,222
Oct 13	Derby County	D 0-0		14,246
Oct 20	NEWCASTLE UNITED	W 1-0	Johanneson	23,386
Oct 27	Walsall	D 1-1	Johanneson	7,353
Nov 3	NORWICH CITY	W 3-0	Storrie, Bell, Johanneson	15,919
Nov 10	Grimsby Town	D 1-1	Storrie	9,183
Nov 17	PLYMOUTH ARGYLE	W 6-1	Johanneson, Storrie 3, Collins, Bremner	15,301
Nov 24	Preston North End	L 1-4	Bell	13,145
Dec 1	PORTSMOUTH	D 3-3	Storrie, Collins, Johanneson	15,519
Dec 8	Cardiff City	D 0-0		11,334
Dec 15	STOKE CITY	W 3-1	Weston 3	19,331
Dec 22	Sunderland	L 1-2	Bremner	40,252
Mar 2	DERBY COUNTY	W 3-1	Weston, Storrie, Charlton (pen)	22,912
Mar 9	Newcastle United	D 1-1	Storrie	29,570
Mar 13	WALSALL	W 3-0	Johanneson, Storrie 2	17,077
Mar 23	Norwich City	L 2-3	Collins, Johanneson	26,154
Mar 30	GRIMSBY TOWN	W 3-0	Bremner, Collins 2	13,938
Apr 3	SCUNTHORPE UNITED	W 1-0	Bremner	15,783
Apr 6	Plymouth Argyle	L 1-3	Storrie	8,992
Apr 13	PRESTON NORTH END	W 4-1	Bremner 2, Storrie, Collins	16,016
Apr 15	Charlton Athletic	W 2-1	Charlton, Hunter	13,538
Apr 16	CHARLTON ATHLETIC	W 4-1	Weston, Henderson, Johanneson, Storrie	24,646
Apr 20	Portsmouth	L 0-3		7,773
Apr 23	Scunthorpe United	W 2-0	Lawson 2	7,794
Apr 27	CARDIFF CITY	W 3-0	Storrie 3	19,752
Apr 30	Chelsea	D 2-2	Lawson 2	24,387
May 4	LUTON TOWN	W 3-0	Storrie 2, Weston	23,781
May 6	Middlesbrough	L 1-2	Johanneson	17,365
May 11	HUDDERSFIELD TOWN	L 0-1		28,501
May 15	Southampton	L 1-3	Weston	11,619
May 18	SWANSEA TOWN	W 5-0	Storrie 2, Lawson, Collins, Johanneson	11,314

FA Cup

Mar 6	STOKE CITY	(Rd 3) W 3-1	Charlton, Reaney, Hair	36,873
Mar 16	Middlesbrough	(Rd 4) W 2-0	Storrie, Johanneson	39,672
Mar 19	Nottingham Forest	(Rd 5) L 0-3		36,392

League Cup

Sep 26	CRYSTAL PALACE	(Rd 2) W 2-1	Charlton, Storrie	
Oct 17	Blackburn Rovers	(Rd 3) L 0-4		7,680

League & Cup Appearances

PLAYER	LEAGUE	CUP COMPETITION		TOTAL
		FA CUP	LC	
Addy	2		1	3
Bell	32	3	1	36
Bremner	24			24
Charles	11			11
Charlton	38	3	1	42
Collins	41	3		44
Goodwin	8			8
Greenhoff	2			2
Hair	26	3	1	30
Hallett			1	1
Hawksby	5		2	7
Henderson	20	3		23
Hunter	36	3	2	41
Johanneson	41	3		44
Johnson	4		2	6
Lawson	6		2	8
Lorimer	1			1
Mason	20		2	22
Peyton	6		2	8
Reaney	35	3	1	39
Smith	6			6
Sprake	33	3	2	38
Storrie	38	3	2	43
Weston	15	3		18
Williamson	3			3
Wright	3			3
Younger	6			6

Goalscorers

PLAYER	LEAGUE	CUP COMPETITION		TOTAL
		FA CUP	LC	
Storrie	25	1	1	27
Johanneson	13	1		14
Bremner	10			10
Collins	8			8
Lawson	5			5
Charlton	2	1	1	4
Charles	3			3
Bell	2			2
Hunter	2			2
Weston	2			2
Hair		1		1
Henderson	1			1
Johnson	1			1
Reaney		1		1

Fact File

Against Southampton in September, Sprake, Reaney, Hunter and Lorimer played together for the first time – all were under 20 years of age (on his debut Lorimer was 15).

MANAGER: Don Revie

CAPTAIN: Bobby Collins

TOP SCORER: Jim Storrie

BIGGEST WIN: 6-1 v Plymouth Argyle, 17 November 1962, League

HIGHEST ATTENDANCE: 40,252 v Sunderland, 22 December 1962, lost 1-2, League

MAJOR TRANSFERS IN: John Charles from Juventus, Jim Storrie from Airdrie, Don Weston from Rotherham United

MAJOR TRANSFERS OUT: John Charles to Roma

Final Division 2 Table

		P	W	D	L	F	A	Pts
1	Stoke C	42	20	13	9	73	50	53
2	Chelsea	42	24	4	14	81	42	52
3	Sunderland	42	20	12	10	84	55	52
4	Middlesbrough	42	20	9	13	86	85	49
5	Leeds United	42	19	10	13	79	53	48
6	Huddersfield T	42	17	14	11	63	50	48
7	Newcastle U	42	18	11	13	79	59	47
8	Bury	42	18	11	13	51	47	47
9	Scunthorpe U	42	16	12	14	57	59	44
10	Cardiff C	42	18	7	17	83	73	43
11	Southampton	42	17	8	17	72	67	42
12	Plymouth Arg	42	15	12	15	76	73	42
13	Norwich C	42	17	8	17	80	79	42
14	Rotherham U	42	17	6	19	67	74	40
15	Swansea T	42	15	9	18	51	72	39
16	Portsmouth	42	13	11	18	63	79	37
17	Preston NE	42	13	11	18	59	74	37
18	Derby Co	42	12	12	18	61	72	36
19	Grimsby T	42	11	13	18	55	66	35
20	Charlton Ath	42	13	5	24	62	94	31
21	Walsall	42	11	9	22	53	89	31
22	Luton T	42	11	7	24	61	84	29

Season 1963-64

Football League Division 2

DATE	OPPONENTS	SCORE		GOALSCORERS	ATTENDANCE
Aug 28	ROTHERHAM UNITED	W	1-0	Weston	22,517
Aug 31	BURY	W	3-0	Collins, Storrie, Johanneson	26,041
Sep 3	Rotherham United	D	2-2	Charlton, Johanneson	14,178
Sep 7	Manchester City	L	2-3	Lawson, Johanneson	29,186
Sep 11	PORTSMOUTH	W	3-1	Storrie, Weston, Bremner	24,926
Sep 14	SWINDON TOWN	D	0-0		33,301
Sep 18	Portsmouth	D	1-1	Henderson	12,569
Sep 21	Cardiff City	D	0-0		16,117
Sep 28	NORWICH CITY	W	4-2	Weston 2, Johanneson, Collins (pen)	22,804
Oct 1	Northampton Town	W	3-0	Lawson, Weston, Collins	15,079
Oct 5	Scunthorpe United	W	1-0	Lawson	10,793
Oct 9	MIDDLESBROUGH	W	2-0	Hunter, Collins	36,919
Oct 12	Huddersfield Town	W	2-0	Giles, Weston	31,220
Oct 19	DERBY COUNTY	D	2-2	Charlton, Weston	29,864
Oct 26	Southampton	W	4-1	Lawson 2, Giles, Johanneson	18,036
Nov 2	CHARLTON ATHLETIC	D	1-1	Charlton	32,344
Nov 9	Grimsby Town	W	2-0	Lawson, Weston	12,194
Nov 16	PRESTON NORTH END	D	1-1	Johanneson	33,841
Nov 23	Leyton Orient	W	2-0	Collins, Johanneson	12,072
Nov 30	SWANSEA TOWN	W	2-1	Johanneson, Bell	21,870
Dec 7	Plymouth Argyle	W	1-0	Johanneson	9,918
Dec 14	NORTHAMPTON TOWN	D	0-0		21,108
Dec 21	Bury	W	2-1	Weston, Lawson	7,453
Dec 26	SUNDERLAND	D	1-1	Lawson	41,167
Dec 28	Sunderland	L	0-2		55,046
Jan 11	MANCHESTER CITY	W	1-0	Weston	33,737
Jan 18	Swindon Town	D	2-2	Giles, Hunter	19,015
Feb 1	CARDIFF CITY	D	1-1	Johanneson	28,039
Feb 8	Norwich City	D	2-2	Weston, Peacock	20,843
Feb 15	SCUNTHORPE UNITED	W	1-0	Johanneson	28,868
Feb 22	HUDDERSFIELD TOWN	D	1-1	Storrie	36,439
Mar 3	Preston North End	L	0-2		35,612
Mar 7	SOUTHAMPTON	W	3-1	Lawson, Collins, Johanneson	24,077
Mar 14	Middlesbrough	W	3-1	Lawson, Peacock, Giles	15,986
Mar 21	GRIMSBY TOWN	W	3-1	Lawson, Bremner, Peacock	25,351
Mar 27	Newcastle United	W	1-0	Giles	55,038
Mar 28	Derby County	D	1-1	Peacock	16,757
Mar 30	NEWCASTLE UNITED	W	2-1	Weston, Johanneson	40,105
Apr 4	LEYTON ORIENT	W	2-1	Giles, Weston	30,920
Apr 11	Swansea Town	W	3-0	Peacock 2, Giles	14,321
Apr 18	PLYMOUTH ARGYLE	D	1-1	Bell	34,725
Apr 25	Charlton Athletic	W	2-0	Peacock 2	21,323

FA Cup

Jan 4	CARDIFF CITY	(Rd 3) W	1-0	Bremner	13,932
Jan 25	EVERTON	(Rd 4) D	1-1	Lawson	48,286
Jan 28	Everton	(R) L	0-2		66,167

League Cup

Sep 26	MANSFIELD TOWN	(Rd 2) W	5-1	Lawson 2, Bell, Johanneson 2	29,843
Oct 22	SWANSEA TOWN	(Rd 3) W	2-0	Lawson, Storrie	10,748
Nov 27	Manchester City	(Rd 4) L	1-3	Weston	18,201

League & Cup Appearances

PLAYER	LEAGUE	CUP COMPETITION		TOTAL
		FA CUP	LC	
Bell	35	3	3	41
Bremner	39	3	1	43
Charlton	25		2	27
Collins	41	2	1	44
Cooper	2			2
Giles	40	3	2	45
Goodwin	12	1	1	14
Greenhoff	2		1	3
Hair	8		2	10
Hawksby		1	1	2
Henderson	2	3	2	7
Hunter	42	3	2	47
Johanneson	37	2	2	41
Lawson	24	3	2	29
Lorimer			1	1
Madeley	4	2		6
Peacock	14			14
Reaney	41	3	2	46
Smith			1	1
Sprake	41	3	3	47
Storrie	15		2	17
Weston	35	1	2	38
Williamson	1			1
Wright	2			2

Goalscorers

PLAYER	LEAGUE	CUP COMPETITION		TOTAL
		FA CUP	LC	
Lawson	11	1	3	15
Johanneson	13		1	14
Weston	13		1	14
Peacock	8			8
Giles	7			6
Collins	6			6
Storrie	3		1	4
Bell	2		1	3
Bremner	2	1		3
Charlton	3			3
Hunter	2			2
Henderson	1			1

Fact File

Leeds shattered Second Division records with most points in a season, most away victories and fewest defeats.

MANAGER: Don Revie

CAPTAIN: Bobby Collins

TOP SCORERS: Ian Lawson

BIGGEST WIN: 5-1 v Mansfield Town, 26 September 1963, League Cup, Round 2

HIGHEST ATTENDANCE: 66,167 v Everton, 28 January 1964, lost 0-2, FA Cup, Round 4 Replay

MAJOR TRANSFERS IN: Johnny Giles from Manchester United, Alan Peacock from Middlesbrough

Final Division 2 Table

		P	W	D	L	F	A	PTS
1	LEEDS UNITED	42	24	15	3	71	34	63
2	SUNDERLAND	42	25	11	6	81	37	61
3	PRESTON NE	42	23	10	9	79	54	56
4	CHARLTON ATH	42	19	10	13	76	70	48
5	SOUTHAMPTON	42	19	9	14	100	73	47
6	MANCHESTER C	42	18	10	14	84	66	46
7	ROTHERHAM U	42	19	7	16	90	78	45
8	NEWCASTLE U	42	20	5	17	74	69	45
9	PORTSMOUTH	42	16	11	15	79	70	43
10	MIDDLESBROUGH	42	15	11	16	67	52	41
11	NORTHAMPTON T	42	16	9	17	58	60	41
12	HUDDERSFIELD T	42	15	10	17	57	64	40
13	DERBY CO	42	14	11	17	56	67	39
14	SWINDON T	42	14	10	18	57	69	38
15	CARDIFF C	42	14	10	18	56	81	38
16	LEYTON ORIENT	42	13	10	19	54	72	36
17	NORWICH C	42	11	13	18	64	80	35
18	BURY	42	13	9	20	57	73	35
19	SWANSEA T	42	12	9	21	63	74	33
20	PLYMOUTH ARG	42	8	16	18	45	67	32
21	GRIMSBY T	42	9	14	19	47	75	32
22	SCUNTHORPE U	42	10	10	22	52	82	30

Season 1964-65

Football League Division 1

DATE	OPPONENTS	SCORE	GOALSCORERS	ATTENDANCE
Aug 22	Aston Villa	W 2-1	Johanneson, Charlton	28,000
Aug 26	LIVERPOOL	W 4-2	Yeats o.g., Weston, Bremner, Giles	36,005
Aug 29	WOLVERHAMPTON W	W 3-2	Storrie 2, Charlton	34,538
Sep 2	Liverpool	L 1-2	Collins	52,548
Sep 5	Sunderland	D 3-3	Storrie, Bell, Johanneson	48,858
Sep 7	Blackpool	L 0-4		26,310
Sep 12	LEICESTER CITY	W 3-2	Bremner 2 (1 pen), Johanneson	32,300
Sep 16	BLACKPOOL	W 3-0	Collins 2, Hunter	35,973
Sep 19	Chelsea	L 0-2		38,006
Sep 26	NOTTINGHAM FOREST	L 1-2	Storrie	32,776
Sep 30	FULHAM	D 2-2	Storrie 2	31,260
Oct 10	Stoke City	W 3-2	Storrie 2, Greenhoff	27,561
Oct 17	TOTTENHAM HOTSPUR	W 3-1	Belfitt, Giles, Bell (pen)	41,464
Oct 24	Burnley	W 1-0	Bell	24,329
Oct 31	SHEFFIELD UNITED	W 4-1	Collins, Storrie, Johanneson, Belfitt	33,357
Nov 7	Everton	W 1-0	Bell	43,605
Nov 11	ARSENAL	W 3-1	Charlton, Belfitt, Storrie	38,620
Nov 14	BIRMINGHAM CITY	W 4-1	Storrie, Charlton, Collins, Giles (pen)	32,030
Nov 21	West Ham United	L 1-3	Belfitt	28,150
Nov 28	WEST BROMWICH ALBION	W 1-0	Johnson	29,553
Dec 5	Manchester United	W 1-0	Collins	53,374
Dec 12	ASTON VILLA	W 1-0	Johanneson	27,399
Dec 19	Wolverhampton W	W 1-0	Johnson	17,126
Dec 26	BLACKBURN ROVERS	D 1-1	Storrie	45,341
Dec 28	Blackburn Rovers	W 2-0	Storrie, Johanneson	24,511
Jan 2	SUNDERLAND	W 2-1	Charlton, Hunter	43,808
Jan 16	Leicester City	D 2-2	Charlton, Johnson	23,230
Jan 23	CHELSEA	D 2-2	Storrie, Giles	47,109
Feb 6	Nottingham Forest	D 0-0		36,596
Feb 13	Arsenal	W 2-1	Giles, Weston	32,132
Feb 27	Tottenham Hotspur	D 0-0		42,202
Mar 13	Fulham	D 2-2	Peacock, Collins	24,704
Mar 15	BURNLEY	W 5-1	Collins 2, Charlton 2, Johanneson	38,506
Mar 20	EVERTON	W 4-1	Johanneson 2, Bremner, Peacock	29,701
Apr 3	WEST HAM UNITED	W 2-1	Peacock, Bremner	41,918
Apr 5	STOKE CITY	W 3-1	Weston 2, Greenhoff	38,133
Apr 12	West Bromwich Albion	W 2-1	Peacock 2	20,007
Apr 17	MANCHESTER UNITED	L 0-1		52,368
Apr 19	Sheffield Wednesday	L 0-3		39,054
Apr 20	SHEFFIELD WEDNESDAY	W 2-0	Storrie, Giles (pen)	45,065
Apr 24	Sheffield United	W 3-0	Storrie, Bremner, Peacock	32,928
Apr 26	Birmingham City	D 3-3	Giles (pen), Reaney, Charlton	16,644

FA Cup

Jan 9	SOUTHPORT	(Rd 3)	W 3-0	Greenhoff, Johanneson, Johnson	31,297
Jan 30	EVERTON	(Rd 4)	D 1-1	Storrie	50,051
Feb 2	Everton	(R)	W 2-1	Charlton, Weston	65,940
Feb 20	SHREWSBURY TOWN	(Rd 5)	W 2-0	Giles, Johanneson	47,740
Mar 10	Crystal Palace	(Rd 6)	W 3-0	Peacock 2, Storrie	45,384
Mar 27	Manchester United*	(SF)	D 0-0		65,000
Mar 31	Manchester United†	(R)	W 1-0	Bremner	46,300
May 1	Liverpool#	(F)	L 1-2	Bremner	100,000

*Played at Hillsborough, Sheffield. †Played at City Ground, Nottingham.
#Played at Wembley, result aet.

League Cup

Sep 23	HUDDERSFIELD TOWN	(Rd 2)	W 3-2	Hunter, Storrie, Belfitt	9,837
Oct 14	ASTON VILLA	(Rd 3)	L 2-3	Johanneson, Collins	10,656

MANAGER: Don Revie

CAPTAIN: Bobby Collins

TOP SCORER: Jim Storrie

BIGGEST WIN: 5-1 v Burnley, 15 March 1965, League

HIGHEST ATTENDANCE: 100,000 v Liverpool, 1 May 1965, lost 1-2, FA Cup final

League & Cup Appearances

PLAYER	LEAGUE	CUP COMPETITION		TOTAL
		FA CUP	LC	
Belfitt	8		2	10
Bell	34	7	2	43
Bremner	40	8		48
Charlton	39	8	2	49
Collins	39	8	1	48
Cooper	16	1	1	18
Giles	39	7		46
Greenhoff	8	1	1	10
Henderson	2	1		3
Hunter	41	8	2	51
Johanneson	30	1	2	33
Johnson	8	1	1	10
Lawson	3			3
Lorimer	1			1
Madeley	6		1	7
Peacock	10	4		14
Reaney	41	8		49
Sprake	41	8		49
Storrie	37	8	1	46
Weston	15	3		18
Williamson	1	2		3
Wright		2		2

Goalscorers

PLAYER	LEAGUE	CUP COMPETITION		TOTAL
		FA CUP	LC	
Storrie	16	2	1	19
Johanneson	9	2	1	12
Charlton	9	1		10
Collins	9		1	10
Bremner	6	2		8
Giles	7	1		8
Peacock	6	2		8
Belfitt	4		1	5
Weston	4	1		5
Bell	4			4
Johnson	3	1		4
Greenhoff	2	1		3
Hunter	2		1	3
Reaney	1			1
Opps' o.gs.	1			1

Fact File

Victories against Manchester United (FA Cup) and West Bromwich Albion (League) gave Leeds hope of winning the 'double' in their first season back in Division 1.

Final Division 1 Table

		P	W	D	L	F	A	Pts
1	MANCHESTER U	42	26	9	7	89	39	61
2	LEEDS UNITED	42	26	9	7	83	52	61
3	CHELSEA	42	24	8	10	89	54	56
4	EVERTON	42	17	15	10	69	60	49
5	NOTTINGHAM F	42	17	13	12	71	67	47
6	TOTTENHAM H	42	19	7	16	87	71	45
7	LIVERPOOL	42	17	10	15	67	73	44
8	SHEFFIELD W	42	16	11	15	57	55	43
9	WEST HAM U	42	19	4	19	82	71	42
10	BLACKBURN R	42	16	10	16	83	79	42
11	STOKE C	42	16	10	16	67	66	42
12	BURNLEY	42	16	10	16	70	70	42
13	ARSENAL	42	17	7	18	69	75	41
14	WBA	42	13	13	16	70	65	39
15	SUNDERLAND	42	14	9	19	64	74	37
16	ASTON VILLA	42	16	5	21	57	82	37
17	BLACKPOOL	42	12	11	19	67	78	35
18	LEICESTER C	42	11	13	18	69	85	35
19	SHEFFIELD U	42	12	11	19	50	64	35
20	FULHAM	42	11	12	19	60	78	34
21	WOLVERHAMPTON W	42	13	4	25	59	89	30
22	BIRMINGHAM C	42	8	11	23	64	96	27

Season 1965-66

Football League Division 1

DATE	OPPONENTS	SCORE	GOALSCORERS	ATTENDANCE
Aug 21	SUNDERLAND	W 1-0	Hunter	36,348
Aug 23	Aston Villa	W 2-0	Peacock, Cooper	33,836
Aug 28	West Ham United	L 1-2	Peacock	27,995
Sep 1	ASTON VILLA	W 2-0	Peacock 2	33,575
Sep 4	NOTTINGHAM FOREST	W 2-1	Bell, Lorimer	35,427
Sep 8	Tottenham Hotspur	L 2-3	Lorimer, Clayton o.g	48,114
Sep 11	SHEFFIELD UNITED	D 2-2	Bremner, Hunter	33,249
Sep 15	TOTTENHAM HOTSPUR	W 2-0	Bremner, Charlton	41,920
Sep 18	Leicester City	D 3-3	Peacock 2, Madeley	23,276
Sep 25	BLACKBURN ROVERS	W 3-0	Lorimer 2, Cooper	31,098
Oct 9	Sheffield Wednesday	D 0-0		35,105
Oct 16	NORTHAMPTON TOWN	W 6-1	Lorimer 2, Bremner, Charlton, Peacock, Storrie	33,748
Oct 23	Stoke City	W 2-1	Peacock, O'Grady	30,093
Oct 30	BURNLEY	D 1-1	Storrie	41,628
Nov 6	Chelsea	L 0-1		39,373
Nov 13	ARSENAL	W 2-0	Bremner, Giles	36,383
Nov 20	Everton	D 0-0		36,291
Dec 11	WEST BROMWICH ALBION	W 4-0	Giles 2, Storrie, O'Grady	33,140
Dec 27	Liverpool	W 1-0	Lorimer	53,430
Dec 28	LIVERPOOL	L 0-1		49,192
Jan 1	SHEFFIELD WEDNESDAY	W 3-0	Storrie, Peacock, Gray	34,841
Jan 8	West Bromwich Albion	W 2-1	Peacock, Giles (pen)	24,900
Jan 12	MANCHESTER UNITED	D 1-1	Storrie	49,762
Jan 15	STOKE CITY	D 2-2	O'Grady, Storrie	34,802
Jan 29	Sunderland	L 0-2		35,942
Feb 5	WEST HAM UNITED	W 5-0	Hunter 2, Lorimer, Bremner, Storrie	33,312
Feb 19	Nottingham Forest	W 4-0	Lorimer 2, Hibbitt, Giles (pen)	26,283
Feb 26	Sheffield United	D 1-1	Bell	35,682
Mar 5	Northampton Town	L 1-2	O'Grady	21,548
Mar 12	LEICESTER CITY	W 3-2	Charlton 2, Hunter	35,597
Mar 19	Blackburn Rovers	W 3-2	Bremner, Lorimer, Storrie	25,398
Mar 26	BLACKPOOL	L 1-2	Charlton	30,727
Mar 28	Blackpool	L 0-1		19,017
Apr 4	CHELSEA	W 2-0	Bremner, Hinton o.g	37,784
Apr 8	Fulham	W 3-1	Bremner, Johanneson, Storrie	38,960
Apr 12	FULHAM	L 0-1		33,968
Apr 16	EVERTON	W 4-1	Charlton, Lorimer, Storrie, Johanneson	25,200
Apr 30	NEWCASTLE UNITED	W 3-0	Lorimer, Storrie, McGrath o.g	29,531
May 5	Arsenal	W 3-0	Storrie 2, Greenhoff	4,554
May 7	Burnley	W 1-0	Elder o.g	33,238
May 16	Newcastle United	L 0-2		21,660
May 19	Manchester United	D 1-1	Reaney	35,008

FA Cup

Jan 22	BURY	(Rd 3) W 6-0	Lorimer 3, Reaney, Greenhoff, Giles	30,384
Feb 12	Chelsea	(Rd 4) L 0-1		57,847

League Cup

Sep 22	HARTLEPOOL UNITED	(Rd 2) W 4-2	Cooper, Johnson, Belfitt, Storrie	11,081
Oct 13	WEST BROMWICH ALBION	(Rd 3) L 2-4	Madeley, Belfitt	13,455

Inter-Cities Fairs Cup

Sep 29	TORINO	(Rd 1/FL) W 2-1	Bremner, Peacock	33,852
Oct 6	Torino	(Rd 1/SL) D 0-0		26,000
Nov 24	SC Leipzig	(Rd 2/FL) W 2-1	Lorimer, Bremner	8,000
Dec 1	SC LEIPZIG	(Rd 2/SL) D 0-0		32,111
Feb 2	VALENCIA	(Rd 3/FL) D 1-1	Lorimer	34,414
Feb 16	Valencia	(Rd 3/SL) W 1-0	O'Grady	45,000
Mar 2	UJPEST DOZSA	(Rd 4/FL) W 4-1	Cooper, Bell, Storrie, Bremner	40,462
Mar 9	Ujpest Dozsa	(Rd 4/SL) D 1-1	Lorimer	30,000
Apr 20	Real Zaragoza	(SF/FL) L 0-1		35,000
Apr 27	REAL ZARAGOZA	(SF/SL) W 2-1	Johanneson, Charlton	45,008
May 11	REAL ZARAGOZA	(R) L 1-3	Charlton	43,046

> **MANAGER:** Don Revie   **CAPTAIN:** Bobby Collins/Jack Charlton
> **TOP SCORER:** Peter Lorimer
> **BIGGEST WIN:** 6-0 v Bury, 22 January 1966, FA Cup, Round 3
> **HIGHEST ATTENDANCE:** 57,847 v Chelsea, 12 February 1966, lost 0-1, FA Cup, Round 4
> **MAJOR TRANSFERS IN:** Mike O'Grady from Huddersfield Town

League & Cup Appearances (substitute)

PLAYER	LEAGUE	CUP COMPETITION			TOTAL
		FA CUP	LC	ICFC	
Bates			1		1
Belfitt	3		2	1	6
Bell	33	2	1	9	45
Bremner	41	2		11	54
Charlton	40	2	1	11	54
Collins	10			2	12
Cooper	15 (3)		2	4	21 (3)
Davey				1	1
Giles	40	2	1	11	54
Gray	3 (1)			2	5 (1)
Greenhoff	10 (2)	1		3	14 (2)
Harvey	2		1		3
Hawkins			1		1
Hibbitt	0 (1)				0 (1)
Hunter	41	2	1	11	55
Johanneson	12	1		2	15
Johnson	2 (3)		2		4 (3)
Lorimer	34	2		9	45
Madeley	9 (4)	1	1	4	15 (4)
O'Grady	29	1		7	37
Peacock	24	1		3	28
Reaney	41	2	1	11	55
Sprake	40	1	1	11	53
Storrie	30	1	2	9	42
Weston	3		1		4
Williamson		1			1
Wright		1			1

Goalscorers

PLAYER	LEAGUE	CUP COMPETITION			TOTAL
		FA CUP	LC	ICFC	
Lorimer	13	3		3	19
Storrie	13		1	1	15
Bremner	8			3	11
Peacock	10			1	11
Charlton	6			2	8
Giles	5	1			6
Hunter	5				5
O'Grady	4		1		5
Cooper	2		1	1	4
Bell	2			1	3
Johanneson	2			1	3
Belfitt			2		2
Greenhoff	1	1			2
Madeley	1		1		2
Reaney	1	1			2
Johnson			1		1
Gray	1				1
Hibbitt	1				1
Opps' o.gs.	4				4

> ## Fact File
> New Year's Day saw Eddie Gray make a goal-scoring debut against Sheffield Wednesday.

Final Division 1 Table

		P	W	D	L	F	A	Pts
1	LIVERPOOL	42	26	9	7	79	34	61
2	LEEDS UNITED	42	23	9	10	79	38	55
3	BURNLEY	42	24	7	11	79	47	55
4	MANCHESTER U	42	18	15	9	84	59	51
5	CHELSEA	42	22	7	13	65	53	51
6	WBA	42	19	12	11	91	69	50
7	LEICESTER C	42	21	7	14	80	65	49
8	TOTTENHAM H	42	16	12	14	75	66	44
9	SHEFFIELD U	42	16	11	15	56	59	43
10	STOKE C	42	15	12	15	65	64	42
11	EVERTON	42	15	11	16	56	62	41
12	WEST HAM U	42	15	9	18	70	83	39
13	BLACKPOOL	42	14	9	19	55	65	37
14	ARSENAL	42	12	13	17	62	75	37
15	NEWCASTLE U	42	14	9	19	50	63	37
16	ASTON VILLA	42	15	6	21	69	80	36
17	SHEFFIELD W	42	14	8	20	56	66	36
18	NOTTINGHAM F	42	14	8	20	56	72	36
19	SUNDERLAND	42	14	8	20	51	72	36
20	FULHAM	42	14	7	21	67	85	35
21	NORTHAMPTON T	42	10	13	19	55	92	33
22	BLACKBURN R	42	8	4	30	57	88	20

Season 1966-67

Football League Division 1

DATE	OPPONENTS	SCORE	GOALSCORERS	ATTENDANCE
Aug 20	Tottenham Hotspur	L 1-3	Giles	43,844
Aug 24	WEST BROMWICH ALBION	W 2-1	Bell, Giles	35,102
Aug 27	MANCHESTER UNITED	W 3-1	Reaney, Lorimer, Madeley	45,092
Aug 31	West Bromwich Albion	L 0-2		22,303
Sep 3	Burnley	D 1-1	Gray	30,757
Sep 7	SUNDERLAND	W 2-1	Giles (pen), Johanneson	37,646
Sep 10	NOTTINGHAM FOREST	D 1-1	Gray	35,634
Sep 17	Fulham	D 2-2	Lorimer, Johanneson	19,985
Sep 24	EVERTON	D 1-1	Giles (pen)	38,486
Oct 1	Stoke City	D 0-0		28,987
Oct 8	Aston Villa	L 0-3		19,188
Oct 15	ARSENAL	W 3-1	Bell, Madeley, Giles	31,481
Oct 29	SOUTHAMPTON	L 0-1		32,232
Nov 5	Arsenal	W 1-0	Charlton	24,227
Nov 12	LEICESTER CITY	W 3-1	Giles 2, Greenhoff	33,803
Nov 19	Liverpool	L 0-5		50,764
Nov 26	WEST HAM UNITED	W 2-1	Giles, Johanneson	37,382
Dec 3	Sheffield Wednesday	D 0-0		35,264
Dec 10	BLACKPOOL	D 1-1	Greenhoff	28,466
Dec 17	TOTTENHAM HOTSPUR	W 3-2	Greenhoff 2, Gray	29,853
Dec 24	Newcastle United	W 2-1	O'Grady, Johanneson	29,160
Dec 26	NEWCASTLE UNITED	W 5-0	Lorimer 2, Charlton, Storrie, Cooper	40,680
Dec 31	Manchester United	D 0-0		53,486
Jan 7	BURNLEY	W 3-1	Greenhoff, Johanneson 2	37,465
Jan 14	Nottingham Forest	L 0-1		43,899
Jan 21	FULHAM	W 3-1	Giles, Greenhoff, Johanneson	32,015
Feb 4	Everton	L 0-2		48,738
Feb 11	STOKE CITY	W 3-0	Bell, Lorimer, Belfitt	37,370
Feb 25	ASTON VILLA	L 0-2		34,398
Mar 4	Southampton	W 2-0	Charlton, Giles	26,150
Mar 18	MANCHESTER CITY	D 0-0		34,366
Mar 25	Blackpool	D 0-0		22,548
Mar 27	Sheffield United	W 4-1	Giles, Peacock, Bremner, Matthewson o.g.	25,701
Mar 28	SHEFFIELD UNITED	W 2-0	Charlton, Peacock	38,755
Apr 1	CHELSEA	W 1-0	Lorimer	39,728
Apr 10	Leicester City	D 0-0		15,437
Apr 22	West Ham United	W 1-0	Lorimer	25,500
May 3	LIVERPOOL	W 2-1	Giles (pen), Greenhoff	36,457
May 6	Chelsea	D 2-2	Lorimer, Belfitt	35,882
May 8	Manchester City	L 1-2	Belfitt	24,924
May 13	Sunderland	W 2-0	Gray, Lorimer	23,686
May 15	SHEFFIELD WEDNESDAY	W 1-0	Hibbitt	23,052

FA Cup

Jan 28	CRYSTAL PALACE	(Rd 3) W 3-0	O'Grady, Bell, Johanneson	37,768
Feb 18	WEST BROMWICH ALBION	(Rd 4) W 5-0	Lorimer 2, Madeley, Belfitt 2	41,329
Mar 11	Sunderland	(Rd 5) D 1-1	Charlton	55,763
Mar 15	SUNDERLAND*	(R) D 1-1	Giles	57,892
Mar 20	Sunderland**	(R) W 2-1	Belfitt, Giles (pen)	40,546
Apr 8	MANCHESTER CITY	(Rd 6) W 1-0	Charlton	48,887
Apr 29	Chelsea†	(SF) L 0-1		62,378

*aet. **Played at Boothferry Park, Hull. †Played at Villa Park, Birmingham.

League Cup

Sep 13	NEWCASTLE UNITED	(Rd 2) W 1-0	Peacock	18,131
Oct 4	Preston North End	(Rd 3) D 1-1	Storrie	15,049
Oct 12	PRESTON NORTH END	(R) W 3-0	Lorimer 2 (1 pen), Greenhoff	17,221
Nov 7	West Ham United	(Rd 4) L 0-7		27,474

Inter-Cities Fairs Cup

Oct 18	DWS Amsterdam	(Rd 2/FL) W 3-1	Bremner, Johanneson, Greenhoff	7,000
Oct 26	DWS AMSTERDAM	(Rd 2/SL) W 5-1	Johanneson 3, Giles, Madeley	27,096
Jan 18	VALENCIA	(Rd 3/FL) D 1-1	Greenhoff	40,644
Feb 8	Valencia	(Rd 3/SL) W 2-0	Giles, Lorimer	48,000
Mar 22	Bologna	(Rd 4/FL) L 0-1		20,000
Apr 19	BOLOGNA*	(Rd 4/SL) W 1-0	Giles (pen)	42,148
May 19	KILMARNOCK	(SF/FL) W 4-2	Belfitt 3, Giles (pen)	43,000
May 24	Kilmarnock	(SF/SL) D 0-0		28,000
Aug 30	Dynamo Zagreb	(F/FL) L 0-2		40,000
Sep 6	DYNAMO ZAGREB	(F/SL) D 0-0		35,604

*Won on toss of disc.

MANAGER: Don Revie **CAPTAIN:** Billy Bremner **TOP SCORER:** Johnny Giles
BIGGEST WIN: 5-0 v Newcastle United, 26 December 1966, League;
5-0 v West Bromwich Albion, 18 February 1967, FA Cup, Round 4

League & Cup Appearances (substitute)

PLAYER	LEAGUE	CUP COMPETITION			TOTAL
		FA CUP	LC	ICFC	
Bates	8 (1)	0 (1)	1	1	10 (2)
Belfitt	10 (2)	5	1	7	23 (2)
Bell	38	7	4	7	56
Bremner	36 (1)	6	4	10	56 (1)
Charlton	28	6	4	7	45
Collins	7			1	8
Cooper	20 (4)	2 (1)		6	28 (5)
Giles	29	7	3	10	49
Gray	29	4	1	6	40
Greenhoff	27 (2)	5 (1)	3	4	39 (3)
Harvey	3		2		5
Hawkins	1				1
Hibbitt	3 (1)			1	4 (1)
Hunter	40	7	3	10	60
Johanneson	22	2	2	2	28
Johnson	3				
Lorimer	27 (2)	5 (1)	2	5	39 (3)
Lumsden	1				1
Madeley	27 (1)	4 (1)	4	8	43 (2)
O'Grady	14	2	2	4	22
Peacock	6	1	2		9
Reaney	41	7	4	9	61
Sibbald	0 (1)				0 (1)
Sprake	39	7	2	10	58
Storrie	3 (3)		1	1	5 (3)

Goalscorers

PLAYER	LEAGUE	CUP COMPETITION			TOTAL
		FA CUP	LC	ICFC	
Giles	12	2		4	18
Lorimer	9	2	2	1	13
Johanneson	7	1		4	12
Greenhoff	7		1	2	10
Belfitt	3	3		3	9
Charlton	5	2			7
Bell	3	1			4
Gray	4				4
Madeley	2	1		1	4
Bremner	2			1	3
Peacock	2		1		3
O'Grady	1	1			2
Storrie	1			1	2
Cooper	1				1
Hibbitt	1				1
Reaney	1				1
Opps' o.g.	1				1

Fact File

The FA Cup semi-final against Chelsea will be remembered for Peter Lorimer's free kick two minutes from time. The referee disallowed the goal, claiming the kick had been taken too quickly.

Final Division 1 Table

		P	W	D	L	F	A	Pts
1	MANCHESTER U	42	24	12	6	84	45	60
2	NOTTINGHAM F	42	23	10	9	64	41	56
3	TOTTENHAM H	42	24	8	10	71	48	56
4	LEEDS UNITED	42	22	11	9	62	42	55
5	LIVERPOOL	42	19	13	10	64	47	51
6	EVERTON	42	19	10	13	65	46	48
7	ARSENAL	42	16	14	12	58	47	46
8	LEICESTER C	42	18	8	16	78	71	44
9	CHELSEA	42	15	14	13	67	62	44
10	SHEFFIELD U	42	16	10	16	52	59	42
11	SHEFFIELD W	42	14	13	15	56	47	41
12	STOKE C	42	17	7	18	63	58	41
13	WBA	42	16	7	19	77	73	39
14	BURNLEY	42	15	9	18	66	76	39
15	MANCHESTER C	42	12	15	15	43	52	39
16	WEST HAM U	42	14	8	20	80	84	36
17	SUNDERLAND	42	14	8	20	58	72	36
18	FULHAM	42	11	12	19	71	83	34
19	SOUTHAMPTON	42	14	6	22	74	92	34
20	NEWCASTLE U	42	12	9	21	39	81	33
21	ASTON VILLA	42	11	7	24	54	85	29
22	BLACKPOOL	42	6	9	27	41	76	21

Season 1967-68

Football League Division 1

DATE	OPPONENTS	SCORE	GOALSCORERS	ATTENDANCE
Aug 19	SUNDERLAND	D 1-1	Greenhoff	36,252
Aug 23	Manchester United	L 0-1		53,016
Aug 26	Wolverhampton W	L 0-2		35,368
Sep 2	FULHAM	W 2-0	Belfitt 2	25,760
Sep 9	Southampton	D 1-1	Lorimer	25,522
Sep 16	Everton	W 1-0	Gray	53,159
Sep 20	BURNLEY	W 2-1	Lorimer 2	32,944
Sep 23	LEICESTER CITY	W 3-2	Lorimer 2 (1 pen), Greenhoff	37,084
Sep 30	West Ham United	D 0-0		28,940
Oct 7	CHELSEA	W 7-0	Johanneson, Greenhoff, Charlton, Gray, Lorimer, Bremner, Hinton o.g.	40,460
Oct 14	West Bromwich Albion	L 0-2		21,300
Oct 25	NEWCASTLE UNITED	W 2-0	Lorimer, Johanneson	30,347
Oct 28	Manchester City	L 0-1		39,713
Nov 4	ARSENAL	W 3-1	Lorimer (pen), Jones, Gray	31,632
Nov 8	MANCHESTER UNITED	W 1-0	Greenhoff	43,999
Nov 11	Sheffield United	L 0-1		24,715
Nov 18	COVENTRY CITY	D 1-1	Lorimer	32,469
Nov 25	Nottingham Forest	W 2-0	Greenhoff, Lorimer	29,750
Dec 2	STOKE CITY	W 2-0	Lorimer, Madeley	29,988
Dec 9	Liverpool	L 0-2		39,675
Dec 16	Sunderland	D 2-2	Greenhoff, Gray	21,189
Dec 23	WOLVERHAMPTON W	W 2-1	Jones, Charlton	28,376
Dec 26	Sheffield Wednesday	W 1-0	Giles (pen)	51,055
Dec 30	SHEFFIELD WEDNESDAY	W 3-2	Greenhoff, Gray, Hunter	36,409
Jan 6	Fulham	W 5-0	Greenhoff 3, Jones 2	24,419
Jan 13	SOUTHAMPTON	W 5-0	Madeley 2, Lorimer, Jones, Hibbitt	31,474
Jan 29	EVERTON	W 2-0	Jones, Giles (pen)	44,119
Feb 3	Leicester City	D 2-2	Madeley, Giles	30,081
Feb 10	WEST HAM UNITED	W 2-1	Lorimer 2	41,814
Mar 13	NOTTINGHAM FOREST	D 1-1	Bremner	32,508
Mar 16	Newcastle United	D 1-1	Hunter	45,190
Mar 20	Chelsea	D 0-0		47,470
Mar 23	MANCHESTER CITY	W 2-0	Charlton, Giles	51,818
Apr 6	SHEFFIELD UNITED	W 3-0	Madeley, Giles 2 (pen)	31,059
Apr 12	Tottenham Hotspur	L 1-2	Madeley	56,597
Apr 13	Coventry City	W 1-0	Hibbitt	38,778
Apr 17	TOTTENHAM HOTSPUR	W 1-0	Lorimer (pen)	50,000
Apr 20	WEST BROMWICH ALBION	W 3-1	Gray (pen), Madeley, Charlton	38,334
Apr 23	Stoke City	L 2-3	Charlton, Greenhoff	23,999
May 4	LIVERPOOL	L 1-2	Jones	44,553
May 7	Arsenal	L 3-4	Lorimer, Jones, Giles	25,043
May 11	Burnley	L 0-3		13,247

FA Cup

Jan 27	DERBY COUNTY	(Rd 3) W 2-0	Charlton, Lorimer	39,753
Feb 17	NOTTINGHAM FOREST	(Rd 4) W 2-1	Jones, Giles	51,739
Mar 9	BRISTOL CITY	(Rd 5) W 2-0	Jones, Lorimer	45,227
Mar 30	SHEFFIELD UNITED	(Rd 6) W 1-0	Madeley	48,322
Apr 27	Everton*	(SF) L 0-1		63,000

*Played at Old Trafford, Manchester.

League Cup

Sep 13	LUTON TOWN	(Rd 2) W 3-1	Lorimer 3 (1 pen)	11,473
Oct 11	BURY	(Rd 3) W 3-0	Charlton, Johanneson, Greenhoff	20,927
Nov 15	Sunderland	(Rd 4) W 2-0	Greenhoff 2	29,536
Dec 13	STOKE CITY	(Rd 5) W 2-0	Bremner, Lorimer	24,558
Jan 17	Derby County	(SF FL) W 1-0	Giles (pen)	31,904
Feb 7	DERBY COUNTY	(SF SL) W 3-2	Belfitt 2, Gray	29,367
Mar 2	Arsenal†	(F) W 1-0	Cooper	97,887

†Played at Wembley.

Inter-Cities Fairs Cup

Oct 3	Spora Luxembourg	(Rd 1/FL) W 9-0	Lorimer 4, Bremner, Jones, Greenhoff 2, Madeley	2,500
Oct 17	SPORA LUXEMBOURG	(Rd 1/SL) W 7-0	Johanneson 3, Greenhoff 2, Cooper, Lorimer	15,196
Nov 29	Partizan Belgrade	(Rd 2/FL) W 2-1	Lorimer, Belfitt	10,000
Dec 6	PARTIZAN BELGRADE	(Rd 2/SL) D 1-1	Lorimer	34,258
Dec 20	HIBERNIAN	(Rd 3/FL) W 1-0	Gray	31,522
Jan 10	Hibernian	(Rd 3/SL) D 1-1	Charlton	30,000
Mar 26	Rangers	(Rd 4/FL) D 0-0		80,000
Apr 9	RANGERS	(Rd 4/SL) W 2-0	Giles (pen), Lorimer	50,498
May 1	Dundee	(SF/FL) D 1-1	Madeley	30,000
May 15	DUNDEE	(SF/SL) W 1-0	Gray	23,830
Aug 7	FERENCVAROS	(F/FL) W 1-0	Jones	25,268
Sep 11	Ferencvaros	(F/SL) D 0-0		76,000

League & Cup Appearances (substitute)

PLAYER	LEAGUE	CUP COMPETITION			TOTAL
		FA CUP	LC	ICFC	
Bates	6 (1)		0 (3)	0 (3)	6 (7)
Belfitt	11 (3)		5 (1)	2 (2)	18 (6)
Bell	3		1		4
Bremner	36	5	6	11	58
Charlton	34	4	5	11	54
Cooper	37	5	6	12	60
Davey	2				2
Giles	20	5	3	7	35
Gray	32	3	7	6	48
Greenhoff	35 (2)	3	7	9 (1)	54 (3)
Harvey	6			4	10
Hawkins	1		1		2
Hibbitt	12 (4)	1	2	3	18 (4)
Hunter	40	5	7	12	64
Johanneson	8 (1)		1	1 (1)	10 (2)
Johnson	0 (1)		1 (1)		1 (2)
Jones	25	5			30
Lorimer	36 (1)	5	6	12	59 (1)
Lumsden	1				1
Madeley	33 (3)	3 (2)	5	10 (1)	51 (6)
O'Grady	6	1		1	8
Reaney	40 (1)	6	7	12	64 (1)
Sibbald	1				1
Sprake	36	5	7	8	56

Goalscorers

PLAYER	LEAGUE	CUP COMPETITION			TOTAL
		FA CUP	LC	ICFC	
Lorimer	16	2	4	8	30
Greenhoff	11		3	4	18
Jones	8	2		2	12
Giles	7	1	1	1	10
Madeley	7	1		2	10
Gray	6		1	2	9
Charlton	5	1	1	1	8
Johanneson	2		1	3	6
Belfitt	2		2	1	5
Bremner	2		1	1	4
Cooper			1	1	2
Hibbitt	2				2
Hunter	2				2
Opps' o.gs.	1				1

Fact File

Going into the last week of April, Leeds were on course for four trophies.

Final Division 1 Table

		P	W	D	L	F	A	Pts
1	MANCHESTER C	42	26	6	10	86	43	58
2	MANCHESTER U	42	24	8	10	89	55	56
3	LIVERPOOL	42	22	11	9	71	40	55
4	LEEDS UNITED	42	22	9	11	71	41	53
5	EVERTON	42	23	6	13	67	40	52
6	CHELSEA	42	18	12	12	62	68	48
7	TOTTENHAM H	42	19	9	14	70	59	47
8	WBA	42	17	12	13	75	62	46
9	ARSENAL	42	17	10	15	60	56	44
10	NEWCASTLE U	42	13	15	14	54	67	41
11	NOTTINGHAM F	42	14	11	17	52	64	39
12	WEST HAM U	42	14	10	18	73	69	38
13	LEICESTER C	42	13	12	17	64	69	38
14	BURNLEY	42	14	10	18	64	71	38
15	SUNDERLAND	42	13	11	18	51	61	37
16	SOUTHAMPTON	42	13	11	18	66	83	37
17	WOLVERHAMPTON W	42	14	8	20	66	75	36
18	STOKE C	42	14	7	21	50	73	35
19	SHEFFIELD W	42	11	12	19	51	63	34
20	COVENTRY C	42	9	15	18	51	71	33
21	SHEFFIELD U	42	11	10	21	49	70	32
22	FULHAM	42	10	7	25	56	98	27

Season 1968-69

Football League Division 1

DATE	OPPONENTS	SCORE	GOALSCORERS	ATTENDANCE
Aug 10	Southampton	W 3-1	Lorimer, Jones, Hibbitt	25,479
Aug 14	QUEENS PARK RANGERS	W 4-1	Jones, Giles, Reaney, Hibbitt	31,612
Aug 17	STOKE CITY	W 2-0	Jones, Johanneson	30,383
Aug 20	Ipswich Town	W 3-2	O'Grady, Belfitt, Hibbitt	30,382
Aug 28	SUNDERLAND	D 1-1	Belfitt	37,797
Aug 31	LIVERPOOL	W 1-0	Jones	38,929
Sep 7	WOLVERHAMPTON W	W 2-1	Cooper, Charlton	31,227
Sep 14	Leicester City	D 1-1	Madeley	28,564
Sep 21	ARSENAL	W 2-0	Charlton, O'Grady	39,946
Sep 28	Manchester City	L 1-3	O'Grady	45,000
Oct 5	Newcastle United	W 1-0	Charlton	41,915
Oct 9	Sunderland	W 1-0	Jones	33,853
Oct 12	WEST HAM UNITED	W 2-0	Giles (pen), Lorimer	40,786
Oct 19	Burnley	L 1-5	Bremner	26,423
Oct 26	WEST BROMWICH ALBION	D 0-0		33,926
Nov 2	Manchester United	D 0-0		55,839
Nov 9	TOTTENHAM HOTSPUR	D 0-0		38,995
Nov 16	Coventry City	W 1-0	Madeley	33,224
Nov 23	EVERTON	W 2-1	Giles (pen), Gray	41,716
Nov 30	Chelsea	D 1-1	Gray	43,286
Dec 7	SHEFFIELD WEDNESDAY	W 2-0	Lorimer 2	32,718
Dec 14	West Ham United	D 1-1	Gray	27,418
Dec 21	BURNLEY	W 6-1	Lorimer 2, Bremner, Jones, Giles, Gray	31,409
Dec 26	NEWCASTLE UNITED	W 2-1	Lorimer (pen), Madeley	42,000
Jan 11	MANCHESTER UNITED	W 2-1	Jones, O'Grady	48,145
Jan 18	Tottenham Hotspur	D 0-0		42,396
Jan 24	Queens Park Rangers	W 1-0	Jones	26,163
Feb 1	COVENTRY CITY	W 3-0	O'Grady, Bremner 2	32,314
Feb 12	IPSWICH TOWN	W 2-0	Belfitt, Jones	24,229
Feb 15	CHELSEA	W 1-0	Lorimer	35,789
Feb 25	Nottingham Forest	W 2-0	Lorimer, Jones	36,249
Mar 1	SOUTHAMPTON	W 3-2	Giles (pen), Jones, Kirkup o.g	33,205
Mar 8	Stoke City	W 5-1	Jones, Bremner 2, O'Grady 2	24,327
Mar 29	Wolverhampton W	D 0-0		27,986
Apr 1	Sheffield Wednesday	D 0-0		34,278
Apr 5	MANCHESTER CITY	W 1-0	Giles	43,176
Apr 9	West Bromwich Albion	D 1-1	Gray	28,959
Apr 12	Arsenal	W 2-1	Jones, Giles	43,715
Apr 19	LEICESTER CITY	W 2-0	Jones, Gray	38,391
Apr 22	Everton	D 0-0		59,000
Apr 28	Liverpool	D 0-0		53,750
Apr 30	NOTTINGHAM FOREST	W 1-0	Giles	46,508

FA Cup

Jan 4	Sheffield Wednesday	(Rd 3) D 1-1	Lorimer (pen)	52,111
Jan 8	SHEFFIELD WEDNESDAY	(R) L 1-3	Johanneson	48,234

League Cup

Sep 4	CHARLTON ATHLETIC	(Rd 2) W 1-0	Jones	18,860
Sep 25	BRISTOL CITY	(Rd 3) W 2-1	Johanneson, Jones	16,359
Oct 16	Crystal Palace	(Rd 4) L 1-2	Madeley	26,217

Inter-Cities Fairs Cup

Sep 18	Standard Liege	(Rd 1/FL) D 0-0		35,000
Oct 23	STANDARD LIEGE	(Rd 1/SL) W 3-2	Charlton, Lorimer, Bremner	24,178
Nov 13	NAPOLI	(Rd 2/FL) W 2-0	Charlton 2	26,967
Nov 27	Napoli*	(Rd 2/SL) L 0-2		15,000
Dec 18	HANNOVER 96	(Rd 3/FL) W 5-1	O'Grady, Hunter, Lorimer 2, Charlton	25,162
Feb 4	Hannover 96	(Rd 3/SL) W 2-1	Belfitt, Jones	15,000
May 5	UJPEST DOSZA	(Rd 4/FL) L 0-1		
May 19	Ujpest Dosza	(Rd 4/SL) L 0-2		40,000

*Won on toss of disc.

League & Cup Appearances (substitute)

PLAYER	LEAGUE	CUP COMPETITION			TOTAL
		FA CUP	LC	ICFC	
Bates	3	2	1	0 (1)	6 (1)
Belfitt	6 (2)	0 (1)	1	3	10 (3)
Bremner	42	2	2	8	54
Charlton	41	2	2	7	52
Cooper	34 (1)		3	5	42 (1)
Giles	32		2	4	38
Gray	32 (1)	2		5 (1)	41 (2)
Greenhoff	3				3
Hibbitt	9 (3)		1	2 (2)	12 (5)
Hunter	42	2	2	8	54
Johanneson	0 (1)	1	1		2 (1)
Jones	40	2	3	8	53
Lorimer	25 (4)	2	3	6 (1)	36 (5)
Madeley	31	2	2	7	42
O'Grady	38	1	3	7	49
Reaney	42	2	3	7	54
Sprake	42	2	3	8	55
Yorath				0 (1)	0 (1)

Goalscorers

PLAYER	LEAGUE	CUP COMPETITION			TOTAL
		FA CUP	LC	ICFC	
Jones	14		2	1	17
Lorimer	9	1		3	13
O'Grady	8			1	9
Giles	8				8
Bremner	6			1	7
Charlton	3			4	7
Gray	5				5
Belfitt	3			1	4
Madeley	3		1		4
Hibbitt	3				3
Johanneson	1		1	1	3
Cooper	1				1
Hunter				1	1
Reaney	1				1
Opps' o.gs.	1				1

Fact File

Leeds won the championship at Anfield, prompting a remarkably sporting chant of 'Champions!' from the Liverpool Kop.

Final Division 1 Table

		P	W	D	L	F	A	PTS
1	LEEDS UNITED	42	27	13	2	66	26	67
2	Liverpool	42	25	11	6	63	24	61
3	Everton	42	21	15	6	77	36	57
4	Arsenal	42	22	12	8	56	27	56
5	Chelsea	42	20	10	12	73	53	50
6	Tottenham H	42	14	17	11	61	51	45
7	Southampton	42	16	13	13	57	48	45
8	West Ham U	42	13	18	11	66	50	44
9	Newcastle U	42	15	14	13	61	55	44
10	WBA	42	16	11	15	64	67	43
11	Manchester U	42	15	12	15	57	53	42
12	Ipswich T	42	15	11	16	59	60	41
13	Manchester C	42	15	10	17	64	55	40
14	Burnley	42	15	9	18	55	82	39
15	Sheffield W	42	10	16	16	41	54	36
16	Wolverhampton W	42	10	15	17	41	58	35
17	Sunderland	42	11	12	19	43	67	34
18	Nottingham F	42	10	13	19	45	57	33
19	Stoke C	42	9	15	18	40	63	33
20	Coventry C	42	10	11	21	46	64	31
21	Leicester C	42	9	12	21	39	68	30
22	QPR	42	4	10	28	39	95	18

MANAGER: Don Revie

CAPTAIN: Billy Bremner

TOP SCORER: Mick Jones

BIGGEST WIN: 6-1 v Burnley, 21 December 1968, League

HIGHEST ATTENDANCE: 59,000 v Everton, 22 April 1969, drew 0-0, League

MAJOR TRANSFERS OUT: Jimmy Greenhoff to Birmingham City

Season 1969-70

Football League Division 1

DATE	OPPONENTS	SCORE	GOALSCORERS	ATTENDANCE
Aug 9	TOTTENHAM HOTSPUR	W 3-1	Bremner, Clarke, Giles (pen)	35,804
Aug 13	ARSENAL	D 0-0		37,164
Aug 16	Nottingham Forest	W 4-1	Clarke, Giles (pen), Gray, Lorimer	34,290
Aug 19	Arsenal	D 1-1	Lorimer	45,160
Aug 23	NEWCASTLE UNITED	D 1-1	Jones	40,403
Aug 26	Burnley	D 1-1	Jones	28,000
Aug 30	Everton	L 2-3	Bremner, Clarke	51,797
Sep 6	MANCHESTER UNITED	D 2-2	Sadler o.g, Bremner	44,271
Sep 13	Sheffield Wednesday	W 2-1	Clarke, Gray	31,998
Sep 20	CHELSEA	W 2-0	Giles (pen), Lorimer	33,130
Sep 27	Coventry City	W 2-1	Clarke, Gray	36,091
Oct 4	STOKE CITY	W 2-1	Giles (2 pen)	35,860
Oct 11	West Bromwich Albion	D 1-1	Jones	33,688
Oct 18	Crystal Palace	D 1-1	Lorimer	31,910
Oct 25	DERBY COUNTY	W 2-0	Clarke 2	44,183
Oct 29	NOTTINGHAM FOREST	W 6-1	Lorimer 3, Charlton, Bates, Hibbitt	29,636
Nov 1	Sunderland	D 0-0		31,842
Nov 8	IPSWICH TOWN	W 4-0	Giles, Jones, Hunter, Gray	26,497
Nov 15	Southampton	D 1-1	Jones	23,963
Nov 19	SUNDERLAND	W 2-0	Jones, Lorimer	25,890
Nov 22	LIVERPOOL	D 1-1	Giles (pen)	43,293
Nov 29	Manchester City	W 2-1	Gray, Jones	44,590
Dec 6	WOLVERHAMPTON W	W 3-1	Holsgrove o.g, Charlton, Clarke	33,090
Dec 13	SHEFFIELD WEDNESDAY	W 2-0	Clarke 2	31,114
Dec 17	WEST HAM UNITED	W 4-1	Lorimer 2, Clarke, Giles	30,699
Dec 26	Newcastle United	L 1-2	Giles	54,527
Dec 27	EVERTON	W 2-1	Jones 2	46,770
Jan 10	Chelsea	W 5-2	Clarke, Cooper, Giles (pen), Lorimer, Jones	57,221
Jan 17	COVENTRY CITY	W 3-1	Clarke 2, Charlton	34,295
Jan 26	Manchester United	D 2-2	Jones, Bremner	60,514
Jan 31	Stoke City	D 1-1	Giles	35,908
Feb 10	WEST BROMWICH ALBION	W 5-1	Gray, Jones, Giles 2, Lorimer	31,515
Feb 14	Tottenham Hotspur	D 1-1	Lorimer	41,713
Feb 28	CRYSTAL PALACE	W 2-0	Jones 2	37,138
Mar 7	Liverpool	D 0-0		51,435
Mar 21	Wolverhampton W	W 2-1	Jones, Clarke	35,057
Mar 28	SOUTHAMPTON	L 1-3	Lorimer	38,370
Mar 30	Derby County	L 1-4	Kennedy	41,011
Apr 2	West Ham United	D 2-2	Clarke 2	26,140
Apr 4	BURNLEY	W 2-1	Gray 2	24,691
Apr 18	MANCHESTER CITY	L 1-3	Belfitt	22,932
Apr 21	Ipswich Town	L 2-3	Hibbitt, Gray	16,875

FA Cup

Jan 3	SWANSEA TOWN	(Rd 3) W 2-1	Giles, Jones	30,246
Jan 24	Sutton United	(Rd 4) W 6-0	Clarke 4, Lorimer 2	14,000
Feb 7	MANSFIELD TOWN	(Rd 5) W 2-0	Giles, Clarke	48,093
Feb 21	Swindon Town	(Rd 6) W 2-0	Clarke 2	27,500
Mar 14	Manchester United*	(SF) D 0-0		55,000
Mar 23	Manchester United**	(R) D 0-0		62,500
Mar 26	Manchester United†	(SR) W 1-0	Bremner	56,000
Apr 11	Chelsea#	(F) D 2-2	Charlton, Jones	100,000
Apr 29	Chelsea•	(R) L 1-2	Jones	62,078

*Played at Hillsborough, Sheffield. **aet – played at Villa Park, Birmingham.
†Played at Burnden Park, Bolton. #aet – played at Wembley.
•aet – played at Old Trafford, Manchester.

League Cup

Sep 3	Fulham	(Rd 2) W 1-0	Charlton	20,446
Sep 24	CHELSEA	(Rd 3) D 1-1	Madeley	21,933
Sep 31	Chelsea	(R) L 0-2		38,485

European Cup

Sep 17	LYN OSLO	(Rd 1/FL) W 10-0	O'Grady, Jones 3, Clarke 2, Giles 2, Bremner 2	25,979
Oct 1	Lyn Oslo	(Rd 1/SL) W 6-0	Hibbitt 2, Belfitt 2, Jones, Lorimer	7,595
Nov 12	FERENCVAROS	(Rd 2/FL) W 3-0	Giles, Jones 2	37,291
Nov 26	Ferencvaros	(Rd 2/SL) W 3-0	Jones 2, Lorimer	5,400
Mar 4	Standard Liege	(Rd 3/FL) W 1-0	Lorimer	38,000
Mar 11	STANDARD LIEGE	(Rd 3/SL) W 1-0	Giles (pen)	48,775
Apr 1	CELTIC	(SF/FL) L 0-1		45,505
Apr 15	Celtic	(SF/SL) L 1-2	Bremner	136,505

Charity Shield

Aug 2	MANCHESTER CITY	W 2-1	Charlton, Gray	39,835

League & Cup Appearances (substitute)

PLAYER	LEAGUE	CUP COMPETITION					TOTAL
		FA CUP	LC	EC	OTHER		
Bates	13 (3)	0 (1)	1 (1)	2 (3)			16 (8)
Belfitt	6 (1)		3	1			10 (1)
Bremner	35	9	2	8	1		55
Charlton	32	9	2	7	1		51
Clarke	28	9		5	1		43
Cooper	29 (1)	9	2	7	1		49 (1)
Davey	5						5
Faulkner	2						2
Galvin	3			0 (1)			3 (1)
Giles	32	9	1	7	1		50
Gray	30	6 (1)	2	5	1		44 (1)
Harvey	5	2	2	0 (1)			9 (1)
Hibbitt	8 (3)		2	1			11 (3)
Hunter	35	7	2	6	1		51
Johanneson	2						2
Jones	32	9	3	8	1		53
Kennedy	2						2
Lorimer	36 (3)	8	3	7	1		55 (3)
Lumsden	1 (1)						1 (1)
Madeley	39	8	3	8	1		59
O'Grady	3 (1)			1			4 (1)
Peterson	3 (1)						3 (1)
Reaney	37	7	3	7	1		55
Sprake	37	7	1	8	1		54
Yorath	7 (4)						7 (4)

Goalscorers

PLAYER	LEAGUE	CUP COMPETITION				TOTAL
		FA CUP	LC	EC	OTHER	
Clarke	17	7		2		26
Jones	15	3		8		26
Giles	13	2		4		19
Lorimer	14	2		3		19
Gray	9				1	10
Bremner	4	1		3		8
Charlton	3	1	1		1	6
Hibbitt	2			2		4
Belfitt	1			2		3
Bates	1					1
Cooper	1					1
Hunter	1					1
Kennedy	1					1
Madeley			1			1
O'Grady				1		1
Opps' o.gs.	2					

Fact File

Paul Reaney broke his leg in the match against West Ham in April. He missed the FA Cup final, the second leg of the European Cup semi-final and England's World Cup campaign in Mexico.

Final Division 1 Table

		P	W	D	L	F	A	Pts
1	EVERTON	42	29	8	5	72	34	66
2	LEEDS UNITED	42	21	15	6	84	49	57
3	CHELSEA	42	21	13	8	70	50	55
4	DERBY CO	42	22	9	11	64	37	53
5	LIVERPOOL	42	20	11	11	65	42	51
6	COVENTRY C	42	19	11	12	58	48	49
7	NEWCASTLE U	42	17	13	12	57	35	47
8	MANCHESTER U	42	14	17	11	66	61	45
9	STOKE C	42	15	15	12	56	52	45
10	MANCHESTER C	42	16	11	15	55	48	43
11	TOTTENHAM H	42	17	9	16	54	55	43
12	ARSENAL	42	12	18	12	51	49	42
13	WOLVERHAMPTON W	42	12	16	14	55	57	40
14	BURNLEY	42	12	15	15	56	61	39
15	NOTTINGHAM F	42	10	18	14	50	71	38
16	WBA	42	14	9	19	58	66	37
17	WEST HAM U	42	12	12	18	51	60	36
18	IPSWICH T	42	10	11	21	40	63	31
19	SOUTHAMPTON	42	6	17	19	46	67	29
20	CRYSTAL PALACE	42	6	15	21	34	68	27
21	SUNDERLAND	42	6	14	22	30	68	26
22	SHEFFIELD W	42	8	9	25	40	71	25

Season 1970-71

Football League Division 1

DATE	OPPONENTS	SCORE	GOALSCORERS	ATTENDANCE
Aug 15	Manchester United	W 1-0	Jones	59,365
Aug 19	Tottenham Hotspur	W 2-0	Giles, Gray	39,927
Aug 22	EVERTON	W 3-2	Bremner 2, Giles	46,718
Aug 26	WEST HAM UNITED	W 3-0	Jones, Giles (pen), Belfitt	42,677
Aug 29	Burnley	W 3-0	Clarke 2, Jones	26,006
Sep 1	Arsenal	D 0-0		47,749
Sep 5	CHELSEA	W 1-0	Clarke	47,662
Sep 12	Stoke City	L 0-3	-	22,592
Sep 19	SOUTHAMPTON	W 1-0	Giles (pen)	32,713
Sep 26	Nottingham Forest	D 0-0		31,537
Oct 3	HUDDERSFIELD TOWN	W 2-0	Lorimer 2 (1 pen)	36,498
Oct 10	West Bromwich Albion	D 2-2	Clarke, Jones	37,255
Oct 17	MANCHESTER UNITED	D 2-2	Belfitt, Charlton	50,190
Oct 24	Derby County	W 2-0	Lorimer, Clarke	32,797
Oct 31	COVENTRY CITY	W 2-0	Charlton, Giles	31,670
Nov 7	Crystal Palace	D 1-1	Lorimer	37,963
Nov 14	BLACKPOOL	W 3-1	Madeley, Charlton, Giles	32,921
Nov 18	STOKE CITY	W 4-1	Madeley, Clarke, Lorimer, Giles (pen)	30,549
Nov 21	Wolverhampton W	W 3-2	Madeley, Clarke, Hollsgrove o.g.	41,048
Nov 28	MANCHESTER CITY	W 1-0	Clarke	43,511
Dec 5	Liverpool	D 1-1	Madeley	51,357
Dec 12	IPSWICH TOWN	D 0-0		29,675
Dec 19	Everton	W 1-0	Charlton	47,393
Dec 26	NEWCASTLE UNITED	W 3-0	Clarke, Giles (2 pen)	46,758
Jan 9	TOTTENHAM HOTSPUR	L 1-2	Clarke	43,907
Jan 16	West Ham United	W 3-2	Hunter, Giles, Belfitt	34,396
Jan 30	Manchester City	W 2-0	Clarke, Charlton	43,517
Feb 6	LIVERPOOL	L 0-1		48,425
Feb 20	WOLVERHAMPTON W	W 3-0	Madeley, Clarke, Giles (pen)	37,273
Feb 23	Ipswich Town	W 4-2	Lorimer, Clarke 2, Giles (pen)	27,264
Feb 26	Coventry City	W 1-0	Lorimer	20,686
Mar 6	DERBY COUNTY	W 1-0	Lorimer	36,467
Mar 13	Blackpool	D 1-1	Lorimer	27,401
Mar 20	CRYSTAL PALACE	W 2-1	Lorimer, Giles	31,876
Mar 27	Chelsea	L 1-3	Cooper	58,462
Apr 3	BURNLEY	W 4-0	Clarke 4	31,192
Apr 10	Newcastle United	D 1-1	Lorimer	49,640
Apr 12	Huddersfield Town	D 0-0		43,011
Apr 17	WEST BROMWICH ALBION	L 1-2	Clarke	36,812
Apr 24	Southampton	W 3-0	Hollywood o.g., Jones 2	30,001
Apr 26	ARSENAL	W 1-0	Charlton	48,350
May 1	NOTTINGHAM FOREST	W 2-0	Bremner, Lorimer	43,083

FA Cup

Jan 11	Rotherham United	(Rd 3) D 0-0		24,000
Jan 18	ROTHERHAM UNITED	(R) W 3-2	Lorimer 2, Giles	36,890
Jan 23	SWINDON TOWN	(Rd 4) W 4-0	Jones 3, Clarke	36,985
Feb 13	Colchester United	(Rd 5) L 2-3	Hunter, Giles	16,000

League Cup

Sep 8	Sheffield United	(Rd 2) L 0-1		29,573

Inter-Cities Fairs Cup

Sep 15	Sarpsborg	(Rd 1/FL) W 1-0	Lorimer	10,000
Sep 29	SARPSBORG	(Rd 1/SL) W 5-0	Charlton 2, Bremner 2, Lorimer	19,283
Oct 21	DYNAMO DRESDEN	(Rd 2/FL) W 1-0	Lorimer	21,292
Nov 4	Dynamo Dresden	(Rd 2/SL) L 1-2	Jones	35,000
Dec 2	SPARTA PRAGUE	(Rd 3/FL) W 6-0	Clarke, Bremner, Gray 2, Charlton, Chovanec o.g.	25,843
Dec 9	Sparta Prague	(Rd 3/SL) W 3-2	Gray, Clarke, Belfitt	30,000
Mar 10	VITORIA SETUBAL	(Rd 4/FL) W 2-1	Lorimer, Giles (pen)	27,143
Mar 24	Vitoria Setubal	(Rd 4/SL) D 1-1	Lorimer	30,000
Apr 14	Liverpool	(SF/FL) W 1-0	Bremner	52,877
Apr 28	LIVERPOOL	(SF/SL) D 0-0		40,462
May 28	Juventus	(F/FL) D 2-2	Madeley, Bates	45,000
Jun 3	JUVENTUS*	(F/SL) D 1-1	Clarke	42,483

*Won on away goals rule.

MANAGER: Don Revie   **CAPTAIN:** Billy Bremner

TOP SCORER: Allan Clarke

BIGGEST WIN: 6-0 v Sparta Prague, 2 December 1970, Inter-Cities Fairs Cup, Round 3

HIGHEST ATTENDANCE: 52,877 v Liverpool, 14 April 1971, drew 0-0, Inter-Cities Fairs Cup, semi-final

League & Cup Appearances (substitute)

PLAYER	LEAGUE	CUP COMPETITION			TOTAL
		FA CUP	LC	ICFC	
Bates	29 (2)	2 (1)	1	6 (2)	38 (5)
Belfitt	3 (7)	1	0 (1)	6	10 (8)
Bremner	25	2	1	10	38
Charlton	40	4	1	10	55
Clarke	41	4	1	10	56
Cooper	41	3	1	10	55
Davey	6 (1)	1		3 (1)	10 (2)
Galvin	1	0 (1)		1	2 (1)
Giles	34	4		8	46
Gray	19		1	5	25
Harvey	7			3 (1)	10 (1)
Hibbitt	0 (3)			1	1 (3)
Hunter	42	4	1	11	58
Jones	39	3	1	9	52
Jordan				0 (2)	0 (2)
Kennedy				1	1
Lorimer	38	4	1	10	53
Madeley	41	4	1	11 (1)	57 (1)
Reaney	19 (2)	4		5 (3)	28 (5)
Sprake	35	4	1	9	49
Yorath	2 (1)			0 (2)	2 (3)

Goalscorers

PLAYER	LEAGUE	CUP COMPETITION			TOTAL
		FA CUP	LC	ICFC	
Clarke	19	1		3	23
Lorimer	12	2		5	19
Giles	13	2		1	16
Jones	6	3		1	10
Charlton	6			3	9
Bremner	3			4	7
Madeley	5			1	6
Belfitt	3			2	5
Gray	1			3	4
Hunter	1	1			2
Cooper	1				1
Opps' o.gs.	2			1	3

Fact File

The match against West Bromwich Albion in April was one of the most controversial in the club's history. Despite a linesman flagging for offside, referee Tinkler allowed the game to continue and West Brom to score. Leeds lost the match and conceded the Championship to 'lucky' Arsenal.

Final Division 1 Table

		P	W	D	L	F	A	Pts
1	ARSENAL	42	29	7	6	71	29	65
2	LEEDS UNITED	42	27	10	5	72	30	64
3	TOTTENHAM H	42	19	14	9	54	33	52
4	WOLVERHAMPTON W	42	22	8	12	64	54	52
5	LIVERPOOL	42	17	17	8	42	24	51
6	CHELSEA	42	18	15	9	52	42	51
7	SOUTHAMPTON	42	17	12	13	56	44	46
8	MANCHESTER U	42	16	11	15	65	66	43
9	DERBY CO	42	16	10	16	56	54	42
10	COVENTRY C	42	16	10	16	37	38	42
11	MANCHESTER C	42	12	17	13	47	42	41
12	NEWCASTLE U	42	14	13	15	44	46	41
13	STOKE C	42	12	13	17	44	48	37
14	EVERTON	42	12	13	17	54	60	37
15	HUDDERSFIELD T	42	11	14	17	40	49	36
16	NOTTINGHAM F	42	14	8	20	42	61	36
17	WBA	42	10	15	17	58	75	35
18	CRYSTAL PALACE	42	12	11	19	39	57	35
19	IPSWICH T	42	12	10	20	42	48	34
20	WEST HAM U	42	10	14	18	47	60	34
21	BURNLEY	42	7	13	22	29	63	27
22	BLACKPOOL	42	4	15	23	34	66	23

Season 1971-72

Football League Division 1

DATE	OPPONENTS	SCORE	GOALSCORERS	ATTENDANCE
Aug 14	Manchester City	W 1-0	Lorimer	38,556
Aug 17	Sheffield United	L 0-3		40,725
Aug 21	WOLVERHAMPTON W	D 0-0		20,686
Aug 25	TOTTENHAM HOTSPUR	D 1-1	Bremner	25,099
Aug 28	Ipswich Town	W 2-0	Lorimer, Belfitt	26,689
Sep 1	NEWCASTLE UNITED	W 5-1	Charlton, Lorimer, Giles (pen), Yorath, Madeley	18,623
Sep 4	CRYSTAL PALACE	W 2-0	Madeley, Giles (pen)	18,715
Sep 11	Arsenal	L 0-2		51,196
Sep 18	LIVERPOOL	W 1-0	Lorimer	41,381
Sep 25	Huddersfield Town	L 1-2	Charlton	26,340
Oct 2	WEST HAM UNITED	D 0-0		30,942
Oct 9	Coventry City	L 1-3	Parker o.g	32,182
Oct 16	MANCHESTER CITY	W 3-0	Clarke, Jones, Lorimer	36,004
Oct 23	EVERTON	W 3-2	Cooper, Charlton, Lorimer	34,208
Oct 30	Manchester United	W 1-0	Lorimer	53,960
Nov 6	LEICESTER CITY	W 2-1	Bremner, Lorimer	39,877
Nov 13	Southampton	L 1-2	Giles	25,331
Nov 20	STOKE CITY	W 1-0	Lorimer	32,012
Nov 27	Nottingham Forest	W 2-0	Lorimer, Clarke	29,463
Dec 4	WEST BROMWICH ALBION	W 3-0	Giles 2, Lorimer	32,521
Dec 11	Chelsea	D 0-0		45,867
Dec 18	Crystal Palace	D 1-1	Lorimer	31,456
Dec 27	DERBY COUNTY	W 3-0	Gray, Lorimer 2	44,214
Jan 1	Liverpool	W 2-0	Clarke, Jones	53,847
Jan 8	IPSWICH TOWN	D 2-2	Bremner, Clarke	32,194
Jan 22	SHEFFIELD UNITED	W 1-0	Clarke	41,038
Jan 29	Tottenham Hotspur	L 0-1		46,774
Feb 12	Everton	D 0-0		45,935
Feb 19	MANCHESTER UNITED	W 5-1	Jones 3, Clarke, Lorimer	45,399
Mar 4	SOUTHAMPTON	W 7-0	Clarke 2, Lorimer 3, Charlton, Jones	34,275
Mar 11	COVENTRY CITY	W 1-0	Charlton	43,154
Mar 22	Leicester City	D 0-0		32,152
Mar 25	ARSENAL	W 3-0	Clarke, Jones, Lorimer	45,399
Mar 27	NOTTINGHAM FOREST	W 6-1	Lorimer 2, Gray 2, Clarke 2	40,866
Mar 31	West Ham United	D 2-2	Gray 2	41,003
Apr 1	Derby County	L 0-2		39,450
Apr 5	HUDDERSFIELD TOWN	W 3-1	Jones, Lorimer, Gray	46,148
Apr 8	Stoke City	W 3-0	Jones 2, Lorimer	35,123
Apr 19	Newcastle United	L 0-1		42,006
Apr 22	West Bromwich Albion	W 1-0	Giles (pen)	39,724
May 1	CHELSEA	W 2-0	Bremner, Jones	46,565
May 8	Wolverhampton W	L 1-2	Bremner	53,379

FA Cup

Jan 15	BRISTOL ROVERS	(Rd 3) W 4-1	Giles 2, Lorimer 2	33,565
Feb 5	Liverpool	(Rd 4) D 0-0		56,300
Feb 9	LIVERPOOL	(R) W 2-0	Clarke 2	45,821
Feb 26	Cardiff City	(Rd 5) W 2-0	Giles 2	50,000
Mar 18	TOTTENHAM HOTSPUR	(Rd 6) W 2-1	Clarke, Charlton	43,937
Apr 15	Birmingham City*	(SF) W 3-0	Jones 2, Lorimer	55,000
May 6	Arsenal†	(F) W 1-0	Clarke	100,000

*Played at Hillsborough, Sheffield. †Played at Wembley.

League Cup

Sep 8	Derby County	(Rd 2) D 0-0		34,023
Sep 27	DERBY COUNTY	(R) W 2-0	Lorimer 2	29,132
Oct 6	West Ham United	(Rd 3) D 0-0		35,890
Oct 20	WEST HAM UNITED#	(R) L 0-1		26,504

#Result after extra time.

UEFA Cup

Sep 15	Lierse SK	(Rd 1 FL) W 2-0	Galvin, Lorimer	17,000
Sep 29	LIERSE SK	(Rd 1 SL) L 0-4		18,680

Inter-Cities Fairs Cup Play-off

(between first and last winners of the competition for the for retention of trophy)

Sep 22	Barcelona		L 1-2	Jordan	35,000

MANAGER: Don Revie

CAPTAIN: Billy Bremner

TOP SCORER: Peter Lorimer

BIGGEST WIN: 7-0 v Southampton, 4 March 1972, League

HIGHEST ATTENDANCE: 100,000 v Arsenal, 6 May 1972, won 1-0, FA Cup final

---

League & Cup Appearances (substitute)

PLAYER	LEAGUE	CUP COMPETITION				TOTAL
		FA CUP	LC	UEFA	OTHER	
Bates	6 (3)	2		2		10 (3)
Belfitt	10 (1)		3	2	1	16 (1)
Bremner	41	7	4	2	1	54
Charlton	41	5	4	1	1	51
Clarke	35	6	2			43
Cooper	34	5	4	1		43
Davey			1	1	1	2
Edwards	0 (1)					0 (1)
Faulkner				2		2
Galvin	2 (1)	0 (1)		2	1	5 (2)
Giles	38	7	4	2	1	51
Gray	25 (1)	6	0 (1)			31 (2)
Harvey	7	2	2			11
Hunter	42	7	4	2 (1)	1	55 (1)
Jones	24	5	1			30
Jordan	5 (7)	1 (1)			1	7 (8)
Lorimer	42	7	4	2	1	56
Madeley	42	7	4	1		54
Mann	1		0 (1)	1		2 (1)
Reaney	29 (4)	5 (1)	3	2	1	40 (5)
Shaw			1			1
Sprake	35	5		2 (1)	1	44 (1)
Yorath	3 (4)		3	2		8 (4)

Goalscorers

PLAYER	LEAGUE	CUP COMPETITION				TOTAL
		FA CUP	LC	UEFA	OTHER	
Lorimer	23	3	2	1		29
Clarke	11	4				15
Jones	11	2				13
Giles	6	4				10
Gray	6					6
Charlton	5	1				6
Bremner	5					5
Madeley	2					2
Belfitt	1					1
Cooper	1					1
Yorath	1					1
Galvin				1		1
Jordan				1		1
Opps' o.gs.	1					1

Fact File

Two days after the FA Cup final, Leeds travelled to Molineux needing only a draw to win the 'double'. But they lost 2-1.

Final Division 1 Table

		P	W	D	L	F	A	Pts
1	DERBY CO	42	24	10	8	69	33	58
2	LEEDS UNITED	42	24	9	9	73	31	57
3	LIVERPOOL	42	24	9	9	64	30	57
4	MANCHESTER C	42	23	11	8	77	45	57
5	ARSENAL	42	22	8	12	58	40	52
6	TOTTENHAM H	42	19	13	10	63	42	51
7	CHELSEA	42	18	12	12	58	49	48
8	MANCHESTER U	42	19	10	13	69	61	48
9	WOLVERHAMPTON W	42	18	11	13	65	57	47
10	SHEFFIELD U	42	17	12	13	61	60	46
11	NEWCASTLE U	42	15	11	16	49	52	41
12	LEICESTER C	42	13	13	16	41	46	39
13	IPSWICH T	42	11	16	15	39	53	38
14	WEST HAM U	42	12	12	18	47	51	36
15	EVERTON	42	9	18	15	37	48	36
16	WBA	42	12	11	19	42	54	35
17	STOKE C	42	10	15	17	39	56	35
18	COVENTRY C	42	9	15	18	44	67	33
19	SOUTHAMPTON	42	12	7	23	52	80	31
20	CRYSTAL PALACE	42	8	13	21	39	65	29
21	NOTTINGHAM F	42	8	9	25	47	81	25
22	HUDDERSFIELD T	42	6	13	23	27	59	25

Season 1972-73

Football League Division 1

DATE	OPPONENTS	SCORE	GOALSCORERS	ATTENDANCE
Aug 12	Chelsea	L 0-4		51,102
Aug 15	Sheffield United	W 2-0	Colquhoun o.g., Giles (pen)	40,159
Aug 19	WEST BROMWICH ALBION	W 2-0	Clarke, Giles (pen)	36,555
Aug 23	IPSWICH TOWN	D 3-3	Jordan 2, Giles (pen)	32,461
Aug 26	Tottenham Hotspur	D 0-0		41,191
Aug 30	SOUTHAMPTON	W 1-0	Bremner	31,401
Sep 2	NORWICH CITY	W 2-0	Jordan, Charlton	34,261
Sep 9	Stoke City	D 2-2	Lorimer, Clarke	26,705
Sep 16	LEICESTER CITY	W 3-1	Clarke, Jones, Bates	33,930
Sep 23	Newcastle United	L 2-3	Clarke, Jones	38,962
Sep 30	LIVERPOOL	L 1-2	Jones	46,468
Oct 7	DERBY COUNTY	W 5-0	Giles 2, Clarke, Bremner, Lorimer	36,477
Oct 14	Everton	W 2-1	Jones, Jordan	47,821
Oct 21	COVENTRY CITY	D 1-1	Charlton	36,240
Oct 28	Wolverhampton W	W 2-0	E Gray, Lorimer	33,731
Nov 4	Ipswich Town	D 2-2	Charlton, Lorimer	27,566
Nov 11	SHEFFIELD UNITED	W 2-1	Clarke 2	31,600
Nov 18	Crystal Palace	D 2-2	Jones, Giles	30,107
Nov 25	MANCHESTER CITY	W 3-0	Cherry, Lorimer, Clarke	39,879
Dec 2	Arsenal	L 1-2	Lorimer (pen)	39,108
Dec 9	WEST HAM UNITED	W 1-0	Jones	30,270
Dec 16	BIRMINGHAM CITY	W 4-0	Clarke 2, Lorimer, Jones	25,285
Dec 23	Manchester United	D 1-1	Clarke	46,382
Dec 26	NEWCASTLE UNITED	W 1-0	Jordan	45,486
Jan 6	TOTTENHAM HOTSPUR	W 2-1	Jones, Lorimer (pen)	32,404
Jan 20	Norwich City	W 2-1	Jordan, Clarke	27,447
Jan 27	STOKE CITY	W 1-0	Clarke	33,487
Feb 10	Leicester City	L 0-2		35,976
Feb 17	CHELSEA	D 1-1	Jones	41,781
Mar 3	Derby County	W 3-2	Lorimer (2 pen), Clarke	38,100
Mar 10	EVERTON	W 2-1	Clarke, Lorimer	39,663
Mar 24	WOLVERHAMPTON W	D 0-0		39,078
Mar 28	West Bromwich Albion	D 1-1	Clarke	33,057
Mar 31	Manchester City	L 0-1		35,772
Apr 2	Coventry City	W 1-0	Reaney	24,383
Apr 14	West Ham United	D 1-1	Clarke	38,804
Apr 18	MANCHESTER UNITED	L 0-1		45,450
Apr 21	CRYSTAL PALACE	W 4-0	Bremner, Lorimer, F Gray, Clarke	31,173
Apr 23	Liverpool	L 0-2		55,738
Apr 28	Southampton	L 1-3	Hunter	24,108
Apr 30	Birmingham City	L 1-2	Jordan	34,449
May 9	ARSENAL	W 6-1	Lorimer 3 (1 pen), Bremner, Jordan 2	25,088

FA Cup

Jan 13	Norwich City	(Rd 3) D 1-1	Lorimer	32,310
Jan 17	NORWICH CITY**	(R) D 1-1	Giles	36,087
Jan 29	Norwich City#	(2nd R) W 5-0	Clarke 3, Jones, Lorimer	33,225
Feb 3	PLYMOUTH ARGYLE	(Rd 4) W 2-1	Clarke, Bates	38,374
Feb 24	WEST BROMWICH ALBION	(Rd 5) W 2-0	Clarke 2	39,229
Mar 17	Derby County	(Rd 6) W 1-0	Lorimer	38,350
Apr 7	Wolverhampton W*	(SF) W 1-0	Bremner	52,505
May 5	Sunderland†	(F) L 0-1		100000

**Result after extra time. #Played at Villa Park, Birmingham.
*Played at Maine Road, Manchester. †Played at Wembley.

League Cup

Sep 6	BURNLEY	(Rd 2) W 4-0	Lorimer 2, Jones, Cherry	20,857
Oct 4	ASTON VILLA	(Rd 3) D 1-1	Lorimer	46,185
Oct 11	Aston Villa	(R) W 2-0	Nicholl o.g., Jones	28,894
Oct 31	Liverpool	(Rd 4) D 2-2	Jones, Lorimer	44,609
Nov 22	LIVERPOOL	(R) L 0-1		34,856

European Cup-Winners' Cup

Sep 13	Ankaragucu	(Rd 1/FL) D 1-1	Jordan	20,000
Sep 27	ANKARAGUCU	(Rd 1/SL) W 1-0	Jones	22,411
Oct 25	Carl Zeiss Jena	(Rd 2/FL) D 0-0		18,000
Nov 8	CARL ZEISS JENA	(Rd 2/SL) W 2-0	Cherry, Jones	26,885
Mar 7	RAPID BUCHAREST	(Rd 3/FL) W 5-0	Giles, Clarke, Lorimer 2, Jordan	25,702
Mar 21	Rapid Bucharest	(Rd 3/SL) W 3-1	Bates, Jones, Jordan	25,000
Apr 11	HAJDUK SPLIT	(SF/FL) W 1-0	Clarke	32,051
Apr 25	Hajduk Split	(SF/SL) D 0-0		30,000
May 16	AC Milan*	(F) L 0-1		45,000

*Played at Salonika, Greece.

League & Cup Appearances (substitute)

PLAYER	LEAGUE	CUP COMPETITION			TOTAL
		FA CUP	LC	ECWC	
Bates	26 (3)	4 (1)	4	6	40 (4)
Bremner	38	7	5	7	57
Charlton	18	1	4	2	25
Cherry	38 (1)	8	5	8	59 (1)
Clarke	36	8	4	5	53
Ellam	6 (1)		1	2	9 (1)
Galvin	1			1	2
Giles	33	8	1	6 (1)	48 (1)
Gray E	16 (1)	3	3	2	24 (1)
Gray F	3 (1)			1 (1)	4 (2)
Hampton	2				2
Harvey	41	8	5	9	63
Hunter	32	7	5	9	53
Jones	27 (1)	8	4 (1)	6	45 (2)
Jordan	16 (10)	0 (1)	1 (1)	6 (1)	23 (13)
Liddell	1		1		2
Lorimer	41	8	5	9	63
Madeley	4	8	5	34	51
Mann	1				1
McGinley	0 (1)				0 (1)
McQueen	6			2 (1)	8 (1)
Reaney	29	8	2	9	48
Sprake				1	1
Yorath	16 (6)	2 (2)	1 (1)	4 (3)	23 (12)

Goalscorers

PLAYER	LEAGUE	CUP COMPETITION			TOTAL
		FA CUP	LC	ECWC	
Clarke	18	6		2	26
Lorimer	15	3	3	2	23
Jones	9	1	3	3	16
Jordan	9			3	12
Giles	6	1		1	8
Bremner	4	1			5
Charlton	3		1		4
Bates	1	1		1	3
Cherry	1		1	1	3
Gray E	1				1
Gray F	1				1
Hunter	1				1
Reaney	1				1
Opps' o.gs.	1		1		2

Final Division 1 Table

		P	W	D	L	F	A	Pts
1	LIVERPOOL	42	25	10	7	72	42	60
2	ARSENAL	42	23	11	8	57	43	57
3	LEEDS UNITED	42	21	11	10	71	45	53
4	IPSWICH T	42	17	14	11	55	45	48
5	WOLVERHAMPTON W	42	18	11	13	66	54	47
6	WEST HAM U	42	17	12	13	67	53	46
7	DERBY CO	42	19	8	15	56	54	46
8	TOTTENHAM H	42	16	13	13	58	48	45
9	NEWCASTLE U	42	16	13	13	60	51	45
10	BIRMINGHAM C	42	15	12	15	53	54	42
11	MANCHESTER C	42	15	11	16	57	60	41
12	CHELSEA	42	13	14	15	49	51	40
13	SOUTHAMPTON	42	11	18	13	47	52	40
14	SHEFFIELD U	42	15	10	17	51	59	40
15	STOKE C	42	14	10	18	61	56	38
16	LEICESTER C	42	10	17	15	40	46	37
17	EVERTON	42	13	11	18	41	49	37
18	MANCHESTER U	42	12	13	17	44	60	37
19	COVENTRY C	42	13	9	20	40	55	35
20	NORWICH C	42	11	10	21	36	63	32
21	CRYSTAL PALACE	42	9	12	21	41	58	30
22	WBA	42	9	10	23	38	62	28

Season 1973-74

Football League Division 1

DATE	OPPONENTS	SCORE	GOALSCORERS	ATTENDANCE
Aug 25	EVERTON	W 3-1	Bremner, Giles, Jones	39,325
Aug 28	Arsenal	W 2-1	Lorimer, Madeley	47,429
Sep 1	Tottenham Hotspur	W 3-0	Bremner 2, Clarke	42,801
Sep 5	WOLVERHAMPTON W	W 4-1	Lorimer 2 (1 pen), Jones, Bremner	39,946
Sep 8	BIRMINGHAM CITY	W 3-0	Lorimer 3 (1pen)	39,736
Sep 11	Wolverhampton W	W 2-0	Jones, Clarke	36,980
Sep 15	Southampton	W 2-1	Clarke 2	27,770
Sep 22	MANCHESTER UNITED	D 0-0		47,058
Sep 29	Norwich City	W 1-0	Giles	31,993
Oct 6	STOKE CITY	D 1-1	Jones	36,562
Oct 13	Leicester City	D 2-2	Jones, Bremner	36,978
Oct 20	LIVERPOOL	W 1-0	Jones	44,911
Oct 27	Manchester City	W 1-0	Bates	45,346
Nov 3	WEST HAM UNITED	W 4-1	Bates, Jones 2, Clarke	36,869
Nov 10	Burnley	D 0-0		37,894
Nov 17	COVENTRY CITY	W 3-0	Clarke, Jordan, Bremner	35,552
Nov 24	Derby County	D 0-0		36,003
Dec 1	QUEENS PARK RANGERS	D 2-2	Bremner, Jones	32,194
Dec 8	Ipswich Town	W 3-0	Yorath, Jones, Clarke	27,110
Dec 15	Chelsea	W 2-1	Jordan, Jones	40,768
Dec 22	NORWICH CITY	W 1-0	Yorath	34,747
Dec 26	Newcastle United	W 1-0	Madeley	54,474
Dec 29	Birmingham City	D 1-1	Jordan	50,451
Jan 1	TOTTENHAM HOTSPUR	D 1-1	Jones	46,545
Jan 12	SOUTHAMPTON	W 2-1	Jones, Jordan	35,000
Jan 19	Everton	D 0-0		55,811
Feb 2	CHELSEA	D 1-1	Cherry	41,510
Feb 5	ARSENAL	W 3-1	Simpson o.g., Jordan 2	26,778
Feb 9	Manchester United	W 2-0	Jones, Jordan	60,025
Feb 23	Stoke City	L 2-3	Bremner, Clarke	39,598
Feb 26	LEICESTER CITY	D 1-1	Lorimer (pen)	30,489
Mar 2	NEWCASTLE UNITED	D 1-1	Clarke	46,611
Mar 9	MANCHESTER CITY	W 1-0	Lorimer (pen)	36,578
Mar 16	Liverpool	L 0-1		56,003
Mar 23	BURNLEY	L 1-4	Clarke	39,335
Mar 30	West Ham United	L 1-3	Clarke	37,480
Apr 6	DERBY COUNTY	W 2-0	Lorimer, Bremner	37,838
Apr 13	Coventry City	D 0-0		35,182
Apr 15	SHEFFIELD UNITED	D 0-0		41,140
Apr 16	Sheffield United	W 2-0	Lorimer 2 (1 pen)	39,972
Apr 20	IPSWICH TOWN	W 3-2	Lorimer, Bremner, Clarke	44,015
Apr 27	Queens Park Rangers	W 1-0	Clarke	35,353

FA Cup

Jan 5	Wolverhampton W	(Rd 3)	D 1-1	Lorimer	38,132
Jan 9	WOLVERHAMPTON W	(R)	W 1-0	Jones	42,747
Jan 26	Peterborough United	(Rd 4)	W 4-1	Lorimer, Jordan 2, Yorath	28,000
Feb 16	Bristol City	(Rd 5)	D 1-1	Bremner	37,000
Feb 19	BRISTOL CITY	(R)	L 0-1		47,128

League Cup

Oct 8	Ipswich Town	(Rd 2)	L 0-2	26,385

UEFA Cup

Sep 19	Stromsgodset	(Rd 1 FL)	D 1-1	Clarke	16,276
Oct 3	STROMSGODSET	(Rd 1 SL)	W 6-1	Clarke 2, Jones 2, F Gray, Bates	18,711
Oct 24	HIBERNIAN	(Rd 2 FL)	D 0-0		27,145
Nov 7	Hibernian*	(Rd 2 SL)	D 0-0		36,051
Nov 28	VITORIA SETUBAL	(Rd 3 FL)	W 1-0	Cherry	14,196
Dec 12	Vitoria Setubal	(Rd 3 SL)	L 1-3	Liddell	25,000

*Won 5-4 on penalties.

MANAGER: Don Revie

CAPTAIN: Billy Bremner

TOP SCORER: Mick Jones

BIGGEST WIN: 6-1 v Stromsgodset, 3 October 1974, UEFA Cup, Round 1

HIGHEST ATTENDANCE: 60,025 v Manchester United, 9 February 1974, won 2-0, League

MAJOR TRANSFERS OUT: Jack Charlton to Middlesbrough

League & Cup Appearances (substitute)

PLAYER	LEAGUE	CUP COMPETITION			TOTAL
		FA CUP	LC	UEFA	
Bates	23			5	28
Bremner	42	5	1	4	52
Cherry	37	5	1	6	49
Clarke	34	1 (1)		5	40 (1)
Cooper	1 (1)			2	3 (1)
Davey			0 (1)		0 (1)
Ellam	3 (1)	2		4	10 (1)
Giles	17	2			19
Gray E	8			1	9
Gray F	3 (3)	0 (1)	1	5 (1)	9 (5)
Hampton			1		1
Harvey	39	4	1	3	47
Hunter	42	5	1	1	49
Jones	28 (3)	4	1	3	36 (3)
Jordan	25 (8)	4 (1)		3 (1)	32 (10)
Letheran				0 (1)	0 (1)
Liddell	0 (1)		1	1 (1)	2 (2)
Lorimer	37	5		5	47
Madeley	39	5	1	2	47
Mann				1	1
McGinley			0 (1)		0 (1)
McQueen	36	3		3	42
O'Neill			0 (1)	0 (2)	0 (3)
Reaney	36	3	1	4	44
Shaw			1		1
Sprake			1		1
Stewart	3			1	4
Yorath	23 (5)	3 (1)	1	6	33 (6)

Goalscorers

PLAYER	LEAGUE	CUP COMPETITION			TOTAL
		FA CUP	LC	UEFA	
Jones	14	1		2	17
Clarke	13			3	16
Lorimer	12	2			14
Bremner	10	1			11
Jordan	7	2			9
Bates	2			1	3
Yorath	2	1			3
Giles	2				2
Madeley	2				2
Cherry	1			1	2
Gray F				1	1
Liddell				1	1
Opps' o.gs.	1				1

Fact File

The 2-3 reverse against Stoke City in February was Leeds' first league defeat of the season. This ended a record-breaking 29-match unbeaten run.

Final Division 1 Table

		P	W	D	L	F	A	Pts
1	LEEDS UNITED	42	24	14	4	66	31	62
2	LIVERPOOL	42	22	13	7	52	31	57
3	DERBY CO	42	17	14	11	52	42	48
4	IPSWICH T	42	18	11	13	67	58	47
5	STOKE C	42	15	16	11	54	42	46
6	BURNLEY	42	16	14	12	56	53	46
7	EVERTON	42	16	12	14	50	48	44
8	QPR	42	13	17	12	56	52	43
9	LEICESTER C	42	13	16	13	51	41	42
10	ARSENAL	42	14	14	14	49	51	42
11	TOTTENHAM H	42	14	14	14	45	50	42
12	WOLVERHAMPTON W	42	13	15	14	49	49	41
13	SHEFFIELD U	42	14	12	16	44	49	40
14	MANCHESTER C	42	14	12	16	39	46	40
15	NEWCASTLE U	42	13	12	17	49	48	38
16	COVENTRY C	42	14	10	18	43	54	38
17	CHELSEA	42	12	13	17	56	60	37
18	WEST HAM U	42	11	15	16	55	60	37
19	BIRMINGHAM C	42	12	13	17	52	64	37
20	SOUTHAMPTON	42	11	14	17	47	68	36
21	MANCHESTER U	42	10	12	20	38	48	32
22	NORWICH C	42	7	15	20	37	62	29

Season 1974-75

Football League Division 1

DATE	OPPONENTS	SCORE	GOALSCORERS	ATTENDANCE
Aug 17	Stoke City	L 0-3		33,534
Aug 21	QUEENS PARK RANGERS	L 0-1		31,497
Aug 24	BIRMINGHAM CITY	W 1-0	Clarke	30,820
Aug 27	Queens Park Rangers	D 1-1	Yorath	24,965
Aug 31	Manchester City	L 1-2	Clarke	37,919
Sep 7	LUTON TOWN	D 1-1	Clarke	26,450
Sep 14	Burnley	L 1-2	Lorimer	25,122
Sep 21	SHEFFIELD UNITED	W 5-1	Clarke 2, McQueen, Lorimer, Yorath	33,382
Sep 28	Everton	L 2-3	Clarke, Yorath	41,824
Oct 5	ARSENAL	W 2-0	McKenzie 2	32,784
Oct 12	Ipswich Town	D 0-0		29,815
Oct 15	Birmingham City	L 0-1		36,513
Oct 19	WOLVERHAMPTON W	W 2-0	Clarke, McKenzie	31,224
Oct 26	Liverpool	L 0-1		54,996
Nov 2	DERBY COUNTY	L 0-1		33,551
Nov 9	Coventry City	W 3-0	O'Hare, Hindley o.g., Bremner	25,414
Nov 16	MIDDLESBROUGH	D 2-2	McKenzie 2	45,488
Nov 23	Carlisle United	W 2-1	Jordan, McKenzie	19,975
Nov 30	CHELSEA	W 2-0	Cherry, Clarke	30,441
Dec 4	TOTTENHAM HOTSPUR	W 2-1	McKenzie, Lorimer (pen)	25,832
Dec 7	West Ham United	L 1-2	McKenzie	39,562
Dec 14	STOKE CITY	W 3-1	McQueen, Lorimer, Yorath	34,685
Dec 21	Newcastle United	L 0-3		32,535
Dec 26	BURNLEY	D 2-2	Jordan, Lorimer	34,724
Dec 28	Leicester City	W 2-0	F Gray, McKenzie	29,699
Jan 11	WEST HAM UNITED	W 2-1	Clarke, McKenzie	40,099
Jan 18	Chelsea	W 2-0	McKenzie, Yorath	34,733
Feb 1	COVENTRY CITY	D 0-0		33,901
Feb 8	Derby County	D 0-0		33,641
Feb 22	Middlesbrough	W 1-0	Clarke	39,500
Feb 25	CARLISLE UNITED	W 3-1	Lorimer, Clarke, E Gray	32,346
Mar 1	MANCHESTER CITY	D 2-2	Lorimer 2	47,489
Mar 15	EVERTON	D 0-0		50,084
Mar 22	Luton Town	L 1-2	Jordan	23,048
Mar 29	NEWCASTLE UNITED	D 1-1	Clarke	40,994
Mar 31	LEICESTER CITY	D 2-2	Clarke, Giles	29,898
Apr 1	Sheffield United	D 1-1	Madeley	38,442
Apr 5	LIVERPOOL	L 0-2		34,971
Apr 12	Arsenal	W 2-1	Clarke, Hunter	36,619
Apr 19	IPSWICH TOWN	W 2-1	Cherry, Harris	30,174
Apr 26	Wolverhampton W	D 1-1	F Gray	34,875
Apr 28	Tottenham Hotspur	L 2-4	Jordan, Lorimer	49,886

FA Cup

Jan 4	CARDIFF CITY	(Rd 3)	W 4-1	E Gray, Clarke 2, McKenzie	31,572
Jan 24	WIMBLEDON	(Rd 4)	D 0-0		46,230
Feb 10	Wimbledon*	(R)	W 1-0	Bassett o.g.	45,071
Feb 18	Derby County	(Rd 5)	W 1-0	Nish o.g.	35,298
Mar 8	Ipswich Town	(Rd 6)	D 0-0		38,010
Mar 11	IPSWICH TOWN**	(R)	D 1-1	McKenzie	50,074
Mar 25	Ipswich Town†	(2nd R)	D 0-0		35,195
Mar 27	Ipswich Town#	(3rd R)	L 2-3	Clarke, Giles	19,510

*Played at Selhurst Park, London. **Result after extra time.
†Result after extra time, played at Filbert Street, Leicester. #Played at Filbert Street.

League Cup

Sep 10	Huddersfield Town	(Rd 2)	D 1-1	Lorimer	15,013
Sep 24	HUDDERSFIELD TOWN	(R)	D 1-1	Clarke	18,496
Oct 7	Huddersfield Town	(2nd R)	W 2-1	Bates, Lorimer	14,599
Oct 9	Bury	(Rd 3)	W 2-1	Lorimer, Cherry	16,354
Nov 11	Chester	(Rd 4)	L 0-3		19,000

*Result after extra time.

European Cup

Sep 28	FC ZURICH	(Rd 1/FL)	W 4-1	Clarke 2, Lorimer (pen), Jordan	20,012
Oct 2	FC Zurich	(Rd 1/SL)	L 1-2	Clarke	16,500
Oct 23	Ujpest Dosza	(Rd 2/FL)	W 2-1	Lorimer, McQueen	20,000
Nov 6	UJPEST DOZSA	(Rd 2/SL)	W 3-0	McQueen, Bremner, Yorath	28,091
Mar 5	ANDERLECHT	(Rd 3/FL)	W 3-0	Jordan, McQueen, Lorimer	43,195
Mar 19	Anderlecht	(Rd 3/SL)	W 1-0	Bremner	37,000
Apr 9	BARCELONA	(SF/FL)	W 2-1	Bremner, Clarke	50,393
Apr 24	Barcelona	(SF/SL)	D 1-1	Lorimer	110,000
May 28	Bayern Munich*	(F)	L 0-2		48,374

*Played in Paris.

Charity Shield

Aug 10	Liverpool		D 1-1	Cherry	67,000

Played at Wembley, lost 6-5 on penalties.

League & Cup Appearances (substitute)

PLAYER	LEAGUE	CUP COMPETITION				TOTAL
		FA CUP	LC	EUROPEAN	OTHER	
Bates	2 (1)		2 (2)	1		5 (3)
Bremner	27	8	2	6	1	44
Cherry	24 (3)	0 (1)	5	2 (1)	1	32 (5)
Clarke	33 (1)	7	3	8	1	52 (1)
Cooper	11		2	3		16
Giles	26 (3)	7	2	6	1	42 (3)
Gray E	12	6		2 (1)	1	21 (1)
Gray F	18	8	0 (1)	6		32 (1)
Hampton	0 (2)			0 (1)		0 (3)
Harris	1 (2)			0 (1)		1 (3)
Harvey	27	3	4	4	1	39
Hunter	25	4	4	8	1	42
Jordan	26 (3)	6	4	8	1	45 (3)
Letheran	1					1
Liddell	1					1
Lorimer	35 (1)	4	5	8	1	53 (1)
Madeley	38	8	4 (1)	9		59 (1)
McGovern	4					4
McKenzie	26 (1)	4 (3)	3	1	1	35 (4)
McQueen	33	4	4	7	1	49
O'Hare	6	1				7
Reaney	39	7	5	7	1	59
Stevenson	1					1
Stewart	14	5	1	5		25
Thomas	0 (1)					0 (1)
Yorath	32 (1)	7	4	8 (1)		51 (2)

Goalscorers

PLAYER	LEAGUE	CUP COMPETITION				TOTAL
		FA CUP	LC	EUROPEAN	OTHER	
Clarke	14	3	1	4		22
Lorimer	9		3	4		16
McKenzie	11	2				13
Yorath	5			1		6
Jordan	4			2		6
McQueen	2			3		5
Bremner	1			3		4
Cherry	2		1		1	4
Gray F	2					2
Giles	1	1				2
Gray E	1	1				2
Harris	1					1
Hunter	1					1
Madeley	1					1
O'Hare	1					1
Bates			1			1
Opps' o.gs.	1	2				3

Fact File

Leeds received a two-year ban from Europe after violence at the European Cup final in Paris.

Final Division 1 Table

		P	W	D	L	F	A	Pts
1	Derby Co	42	21	11	10	67	49	53
2	Liverpool	42	20	11	11	60	39	51
3	Ipswich T	42	23	5	14	66	44	51
4	Everton	42	16	18	8	56	42	50
5	Stoke C	42	17	15	10	64	48	49
6	Sheffield U	42	18	13	11	58	51	49
7	Middlesbrough	42	18	12	12	54	40	48
8	Manchester C	42	18	10	14	54	54	46
9	Leeds United	42	16	13	13	57	49	45
10	Burnley	42	17	11	14	68	67	45
11	QPR	42	16	10	16	54	54	42
12	Wolverhampton W	42	14	11	17	57	54	39
13	West Ham U	42	13	13	16	58	59	39
14	Coventry C	42	12	15	15	51	62	39
15	Newcastle U	42	15	9	18	59	72	39
16	Arsenal	42	13	11	18	47	49	37
17	Birmingham C	42	14	9	19	53	61	37
18	Leicester C	42	12	12	18	46	60	36
19	Tottenham H	42	13	8	21	52	63	34
20	Luton T	42	11	11	20	47	65	33
21	Chelsea	42	9	15	18	42	72	33
22	Carlisle U	42	12	5	25	43	59	29

Season 1975-76

Football League Division 1

DATE	OPPONENTS	SCORE	GOALSCORERS	ATTENDANCE
Aug 16	Aston Villa	W 2-1	Lorimer 2 (1pen)	46,026
Aug 20	Norwich City	D 1-1	Cherry	25,301
Aug 23	IPSWICH TOWN	W 1-0	Lorimer	30,912
Aug 26	LIVERPOOL	L 0-3		36,186
Aug 30	Sheffield United	W 2-0	McKenzie, Clarke	29,996
Sep 6	WOLVERHAMPTON W	W 3-0	McQueen, Clarke, McKenzie	24,460
Sep 13	Stoke City	L 2-3	Lorimer 2 (1pen)	23,139
Sep 20	TOTTENHAM HOTSPUR	D 1-1	Lorimer	27,372
Sep 27	Burnley	W 1-0	Cherry	23,190
Oct 4	QUEENS PARK RANGERS	W 2-1	Clarke, Lorimer	30,943
Oct 11	MANCHESTER UNITED	L 1-2	Clarke	40,264
Oct 18	Birmingham City		Cherry, Hunter	33,775
Oct 25	COVENTRY CITY	W 2-0	Yorath, Clarke	25,946
Nov 1	Derby County	L 2-3	Cherry, McKenzie	33,107
Nov 8	NEWCASTLE UNITED	W 3-0	McKenzie 2, Yorath	39,304
Nov 15	Middlesbrough	D 0-0		33,000
Nov 22	BIRMINGHAM CITY	W 3-0	Bremner, McKenzie 2	26,640
Nov 29	EVERTON	W 5-2	Lorimer 2 (1 pen), E Gray, Clarke 2	30,879
Dec 6	Arsenal	W 2-1	McKenzie 2	36,003
Dec 13	Ipswich Town	L 1-2	McKenzie	26,858
Dec 20	ASTON VILLA	W 1-0	Clarke	29,118
Dec 26	Manchester City	W 1-0	Madeley	48,077
Dec 27	LEICESTER CITY	W 4-0	Clarke, McKenzie 2, Lorimer	45,139
Jan 10	STOKE CITY	W 2-0	McKenzie, Bremner	36,906
Jan 17	Wolverhampton W	D 1-1	McAlle o.g.	34,925
Jan 31	NORWICH CITY	L 0-3		27,254
Feb 7	Liverpool	L 0-2		54,525
Feb 21	MIDDLESBROUGH	L 0-2		32,994
Feb 23	West Ham United	D 1-1	McKenzie	28,025
Feb 28	Coventry City	W 1-0	F Gray	25,563
Mar 2	DERBY COUNTY	D 1-1	F Gray (pen)	40,608
Mar 9	WEST HAM UNITED	D 1-1	Jordan	28,453
Mar 13	Manchester United	L 2-3	Cherry, Bremner	59,429
Mar 20	Everton	W 3-1	Bremner, Jordan, Harris	28,566
Mar 27	ARSENAL	W 3-0	Clarke 2, Bremner	26,657
Mar 31	Newcastle United	W 3-2	Oates o.g., Cherry, Harris	32,685
Apr 3	BURNLEY	W 2-1	McKenzie, Hampton	25,384
Apr 10	Tottenham Hotspur	D 0-0		40,359
Apr 14	SHEFFIELD UNITED	L 0-1		22,799
Apr 17	MANCHESTER CITY	W 2-1	McNiven, Harris	33,514
Apr 20	Leicester City	L 1-2	McKenzie	24,240
Apr 24	Queens Park Rangers	L 0-2		31,002

FA Cup

Jan 3	Notts County	(Rd 3) W 1-0	Clarke	31,129
Jan 24	CRYSTAL PALACE	(Rd 4) L 0-1		43,116

League Cup

Sep 9	IPSWICH TOWN	(Rd 2) W 3-2	McKenzie, Lorimer, Clarke	15,318
Oct 8	NOTTS COUNTY	(Rd 3) L 0-1		19,122

League & Cup Appearances (substitute)

PLAYER	LEAGUE	CUP COMPETITION		TOTAL
		FA CUP	LC	
Bates	4			4
Bremner	34	2	2	38
Cherry	40	2	2	44
Clarke	35 (1)	2	1	38 (1)
Gray E	27 (2)	1	2	30 (2)
Gray F	42	2	2	46
Hampton	0 (1)			0 (1)
Harris	9 (5)		0 (1)	9 (6)
Harvey	40	2	2	44
Hunter	31	1 (1)	2	34 (1)
Jordan	15 (2)			15 (2)
Lorimer	27 (2)	2	2	31 (2)
Madeley	39	2	2	43
McKenzie	38 (1)	2	2	42 (1)
McNiven	0 (2)		1	1 (2)
McQueen	10			10
Parkinson	3 (1)			3 (1)
Reaney	31 (1)	2	1	34 (1)
Stevenson	0 (1)			0 (1)
Stewart	2			2
Yorath	35	2	1	38

Goalscorers

PLAYER	LEAGUE	CUP COMPETITION		TOTAL
		FA CUP	LC	
McKenzie	16		1	17
Clarke	11	1	1	13
Lorimer	11		1	12
Cherry	6			6
Bremner	5			5
Harris	3			3
Gray F	2			2
Jordan	2			2
Yorath	2			2
Gray E	1			1
Hampton	1			1
Hunter	1			1
Madeley	1			1
McNiven	1			1
McQueen	1			1
Opps' o.gs.	2			2

Fact File

Coach Syd Owen moved on to Birmingham City. He had been at Elland Road since 1959 and was a key figure in the nurturing of Leeds' young talent.

MANAGER: Jimmy Armfield
CAPTAIN: Billy Bremner
TOP SCORER: Duncan McKenzie
BIGGEST WIN: 4-0 v Leicester City, 27 December 1975, League
HIGHEST ATTENDANCE: 59,429 v Manchester United, 13 March 1976, lost 2-3, League
MAJOR TRANSFERS IN: Tony Currie from Sheffield United
MAJOR TRANSFERS OUT: John O'Hare and John McGovern to Nottingham Forest, Terry Cooper to Middlesbrough, Mick Jones (retired), Johnny Giles to West Bromwich Albion

Final Division 1 Table

		P	W	D	L	F	A	Pts
1	LIVERPOOL	42	23	14	5	66	31	60
2	QPR	42	24	11	7	67	33	59
3	MANCHESTER U	42	23	10	10	68	42	56
4	DERBY CO	42	21	11	10	75	58	53
5	LEEDS UNITED	42	21	9	12	65	46	51
6	IPSWICH T	42	16	14	12	54	48	46
7	LEICESTER C	42	13	19	10	48	51	45
8	MANCHESTER C	42	16	12	15	64	46	43
9	TOTTENHAM H	42	14	15	13	63	63	43
10	NORWICH C	42	16	10	16	58	58	42
11	EVERTON	42	15	12	15	60	66	42
12	STOKE C	42	15	11	16	48	50	41
13	MIDDLESBROUGH	42	15	10	17	46	45	40
14	COVENTRY C	42	13	14	15	47	57	40
15	NEWCASTLE U	42	15	9	18	71	62	39
16	ASTON VILLA	42	11	17	14	51	59	39
17	ARSENAL	42	13	10	19	47	53	36
18	WEST HAM U	42	13	10	19	48	71	36
19	BIRMINGHAM C	42	13	7	22	57	75	33
20	WOLVERHAMPTON W	42	10	10	22	51	68	30
21	BURNLEY	42	9	10	23	43	66	28
22	SHEFFIELD U	42	6	10	26	33	82	22

Season 1976-77

Football League Division 1

DATE	OPPONENTS	SCORE	GOALSCORERS	ATTENDANCE
Aug 21	WEST BROMWICH ALBION	D 2-2	Harris, Clarke	40,248
Aug 24	Birmingham City	D 0-0		35,399
Aug 28	Coventry City	L 2-4	F Gray, Currie	18,227
Sep 4	DERBY COUNTY	W 2-0	E Gray, Cherry	33,352
Sep 11	Tottenham Hotspur	L 0-1		35,525
Sep 18	NEWCASTLE UNITED	D 2-2	McNiven, Harris	35,089
Sep 25	Middlesbrough	L 0-1		25,000
Oct 2	MANCHESTER UNITED	L 0-2		44,512
Oct 6	West Ham United	W 3-1	E Gray, Lorimer, Harris	21,909
Oct 16	Norwich City	W 2-1	F Gray, E Gray	25,217
Oct 23	LIVERPOOL	D 1-1	McNiven	44,696
Oct 30	ARSENAL	W 2-1	Cherry, Jordan	33,566
Nov 6	Everton	W 2-0	McQueen, Jordan	32,618
Nov 10	STOKE CITY	D 1-1	Lorimer	29,199
Nov 20	Ipswich Town	D 1-1	McQueen	30,096
Nov 27	LEICESTER CITY	D 2-2	Lorimer, McNiven	29,713
Dec 11	ASTON VILLA	L 1-3	McNiven	31,232
Dec 27	MANCHESTER CITY	L 0-2		48,708
Dec 29	Sunderland	W 1-0	Jordan	26,999
Jan 3	Arsenal	D 1-1	Clarke	44,090
Jan 22	West Bromwich Albion	W 2-1	E Gray, McQueen	25,958
Feb 2	BIRMINGHAM CITY	W 1-0	McQueen	22,805
Feb 5	COVENTRY CITY	L 1-2	Jordan	26,058
Feb 12	Derby County	W 1-0	Jordan	28,350
Feb 19	TOTTENHAM HOTSPUR	W 2-1	Jordan, Clarke	26,858
Mar 2	Newcastle United	L 0-3		31,995
Mar 5	MIDDLESBROUGH	W 2-1	McQueen 2	32,152
Mar 8	Queens Park Rangers	D 0-0		20,386
Mar 12	Manchester United	L 0-1		60,612
Mar 23	NORWICH CITY	W 3-2	Reaney, Hampton, Jordan	18,700
Apr 2	Liverpool	L 1-3	McQueen	48,791
Apr 8	Manchester City	L 1-2	Jordan	47,727
Apr 9	SUNDERLAND	D 1-1	Cherry	32,966
Apr 12	Stoke City	L 1-2	Jordan	17,960
Apr 16	IPSWICH TOWN	W 2-1	McGhie, Clarke (pen)	28,578
Apr 26	WEST HAM UNITED	D 1-1	Jordan	16,891
Apr 30	BRISTOL CITY	W 2-0	Thomas, E Gray	21,461
May 4	EVERTON	D 0-0		22,175
May 7	Aston Villa	L 1-2	McNiven	38,205
May 10	Bristol City	L 0-1		23,587
May 14	QUEENS PARK RANGERS	L 0-1		22,226
May 16	Leicester City	W 1-0	F Gray	13,642

FA Cup

Jan 8	NORWICH CITY	(Rd 3) W 5-2	Clarke, Reaney, Jordan, McQueen, Hampton	28,130
Jan 29	Birmingham City	(Rd 4) W 2-1	Jordan, Clarke	38,000
Feb 26	MANCHESTER CITY	(Rd 5) W 1-0	Cherry	47,731
Mar 19	Wolverhampton W	(Rd 6) W 1-0	E Gray	50,000
Apr 23	Manchester United*	(SF) L 1-2	Clarke	55,000

*Played at Hillsborough, Sheffield.

League Cup

Sep 1	Stoke City	(Rd 2) L 1-2	Currie	22,559

League & Cup Appearances (substitute)

PLAYER	LEAGUE	CUP COMPETITION		TOTAL
		FA CUP	LC	
Bremner	4		1	5
Cherry	42	4	1	47
Clarke	20	5	1	26
Currie	35	5	1	41
Gray E	37	5		42
Gray F	41	5	1	47
Hampton	30 (1)	5		35 (1)
Hankin	4			4
Harris	7 (9)		1	8 (9)
Harvey	26	3		29
Hunter	9		1	10
Jordan	32	5	1	38
Lorimer	21 (5)	1 (1)		22 (6)
Madeley	38	5	1	44
McGhie	2			2
McNiven	13 (5)			13 (5)
McQueen	34	1		39
Reaney	34	5	1	40
Stevenson	10			10
Stewart	16	2		18
Thomas	5 (2)			5 (2)
Whyte	1 (1)			1 (1)
Yorath	1			1

Goalscorers

PLAYER	LEAGUE	CUP COMPETITION		TOTAL
		FA CUP	LC	
Jordan	10	2		12
McQueen	7	1		8
Clarke	4	3		7
Gray E	5	1		6
McNiven	5			5
Cherry	3	1		4
Gray F	3			3
Harris	3			3
Lorimer	3			3
Currie	1		1	2
Hampton	1	1		2
Reaney	1	1		2
McGhie	1			1
Thomas	1			1

Fact File

The matches in the autumn against Newcastle and West Ham saw the last appearances in Leeds' colours of both Billy Bremner and Norman Hunter.

MANAGER: Jimmy Armfield

CAPTAIN: Trevor Cherry

TOP SCORER: Joe Jordan

BIGGEST WIN: 5-2 v Norwich City, 8 January 1977, FA Cup, Round 3

HIGHEST ATTENDANCE: 60,612 v Manchester United, 12 March 1977, lost 1-0, League

MAJOR TRANSFERS OUT: Billy Bremner to Hull City, Norman Hunter to Bristol City, Terry Yorath to Coventry City

Final Division 1 Table

		P	W	D	L	F	A	Pts
1	LIVERPOOL	42	23	11	8	62	33	57
2	MANCHESTER C	42	21	14	7	60	34	56
3	IPSWICH T	42	22	8	12	66	39	56
4	ASTON VILLA	42	22	7	13	76	50	51
5	NEWCASTLE U	42	18	13	11	64	49	49
6	MANCHESTER U	42	18	11	13	71	62	47
7	WBA	42	16	13	13	62	56	45
8	ARSENAL	42	16	11	15	64	59	43
9	EVERTON	42	14	14	14	62	64	42
10	LEEDS UNITED	42	15	12	15	48	51	42
11	LEICESTER C	42	12	18	12	47	60	42
12	MIDDLESBROUGH	42	14	13	15	40	45	41
13	BIRMINGHAM C	42	13	12	17	63	61	38
14	QPR	42	13	12	17	47	52	38
15	DERBY CO	42	9	19	14	50	55	37
16	NORWICH C	42	14	9	19	47	64	37
17	WEST HAM U	42	11	14	17	46	65	36
18	BRISTOL C	42	11	13	18	38	48	35
19	COVENTRY C	42	10	15	17	48	59	35
20	SUNDERLAND	42	11	12	19	46	54	34
21	STOKE C	42	10	14	18	28	51	34
22	TOTTENHAM H	42	12	9	21	48	72	33

Season 1977-78

Football League Division 1

DATE	OPPONENTS	SCORE	GOALSCORERS	ATTENDANCE
Aug 20	Newcastle United	L 2-3	Hankin, Lorimer (pen)	36,491
Aug 24	WEST BROMWICH ALBION	D 2-2	Jordan, McQueen	21,000
Aug 27	BIRMINGHAM CITY	W 1-0	Hankin	24,551
Sep 3	Coventry City	D 2-2	Hankin, McQueen	21,479
Sep 10	IPSWICH TOWN	W 2-1	Hankin 2	24,280
Sep 17	Derby County	D 2-2	Lorimer, Graham	24,274
Sep 24	MANCHESTER UNITED	D 1-1	Hankin	33,514
Oct 1	Chelsea	W 2-1	Lorimer, Hankin	35,427
Oct 5	ASTON VILLA	D 1-1	McQueen	27,797
Oct 8	Bristol City	L 2-3	Hankin 2	26,215
Oct 15	LIVERPOOL	L 1-2	Thomas	45,500
Oct 22	Middlesbrough	L 1-2	Harris	27,516
Oct 29	Leicester City	D 0-0		20,128
Nov 5	NORWICH CITY	D 2-2	Lorimer 2	24,345
Nov 12	Manchester City	W 3-2	Jordan, Graham, Hankin	42,651
Nov 19	NOTTINGHAM FOREST	W 1-0	Hankin	42,925
Nov 26	West Ham United	W 1-0	Hankin	26,883
Dec 3	QUEENS PARK RANGERS	W 3-0	Needham o.g., Flynn, Currie	26,597
Dec 10	Arsenal	D 1-1	McQueen	40,162
Dec 17	MANCHESTER CITY	W 2-0	McQueen, Cherry	37,380
Dec 26	Wolverhampton W	L 1-3	Jordan	27,704
Dec 27	EVERTON	W 3-1	Hankin 2, Lorimer	45,560
Dec 31	West Bromwich Albion	L 0-1		24,249
Jan 2	NEWCASTLE UNITED	L 0-2		36,643
Jan 14	Birmingham City	W 3-2	Graham 3	23,703
Jan 21	COVENTRY CITY	W 2-0	Hankin, Harris	27,062
Feb 4	Ipswich Town	W 1-0	E Gray	24,023
Feb 25	CHELSEA	W 2-0	F Gray, Currie	25,263
Mar 1	Manchester United	W 1-0	Clarke	49,101
Mar 4	BRISTOL CITY	L 0-2		24,830
Mar 11	Liverpool	L 0-1		48,233
Mar 18	MIDDLESBROUGH	W 5-0	Hankin, Graham 2, Clarke 2	25,158
Mar 25	Everton	L 0-2		45,020
Mar 27	WOLVERHAMPTON W	W 2-1	Graham, Hankin	24,440
Mar 28	LEICESTER CITY	W 5-1	Hankin, F Gray, E Gray 3	21,145
Apr 1	Norwich City	L 0-3		19,615
Apr 8	WEST HAM UNITED	L 1-2	Graham	22,953
Apr 12	DERBY COUNTY	W 2-0	E Gray, Hankin	16,531
Apr 15	Nottingham Forest	D 1-1	F Gray (pen)	38,662
Apr 22	ARSENAL	L 1-3	Currie	33,263
Apr 26	Aston Villa	L 1-3	Hankin	30,524
Apr 29	Queens Park Rangers	D 0-0		23,993

FA Cup

Jan 7	MANCHESTER CITY	(Rd 3) L 1-2	F Gray (pen)	38,517

League Cup

Aug 31	Rochdale	(Rd 2) W 3-0	Jordan, Cherry, Harris	8,644
Oct 26	COLCHESTER UNITED	(Rd 3) W 4-0	Jordan, Graham, Lorimer, Hankin	17,713
Nov 30	Bolton Wanderers	(Rd 4) W 2-0	Graham, Jordan, F Gray	33,766
Jan 18	EVERTON	(Rd 5) W 4-1	Currie, Lorimer 2 (1 pen), E Gray	35,020
Feb 8	NOTTINGHAM FOREST	(SF/FL) L 1-3	E Gray	43,222
Feb 22	Nottingham Forest	(SF/SL) L 2-4	F Gray, Graham	38,131

Fact File

After acts of hooliganism at Elland Road in the FA Cup tie against Manchester City, the FA punished Leeds by making them play all of their games in next season's competition away from home.

MANAGER: Jimmy Armfield

CAPTAIN: Trevor Cherry

TOP SCORER: Ray Hankin

BIGGEST WIN: 5-0 v Middlesbrough, 18 March 1978, League

HIGHEST ATTENDANCE: 48,233 v Liverpool, 11 March 1978, lost 1-0, League

MAJOR TRANSFERS IN: Arthur Graham from Aberdeen, Brian Flynn and Ray Hankin from Burnley, Paul Hart from Blackpool

MAJOR TRANSFERS OUT: Joe Jordan and Gordon McQueen to Manchester United

League & Cup Appearances (substitute)

PLAYER	LEAGUE	CUP COMPETITION		TOTAL
		FA CUP	LC	
Cherry	41	1	6	48
Clarke	8 (1)		1	9 (1)
Currie	35	1	5	41
Flynn	28	1		29
Graham	40	1	6	47
Gray E	24 (3)		4	28 (3)
Gray F	40 (1)	1	6	47 (1)
Hampton	10 (1)		1 (1)	11 (2)
Hankin	33	1	6	40
Harris	16 (3)	1	2 (2)	19 (5)
Hart	12			12
Harvey	25	1	4	30
Jordan	20		3	23
Lorimer	26 (2)		4	30 (2)
Madeley	38	1	6	45
McNiven	2			2
McQueen	21	1	1	23
Parker	0 (1)			0 (1)
Parkinson	6 (2)		4	10 (2)
Reaney	15	1	5	21
Stevenson	3 (2)			3 (2)
Stewart	17		2	19
Thomas	2 (1)			2 (1)

Goalscorers

PLAYER	LEAGUE	CUP COMPETITION		TOTAL
		FA CUP	LC	
Hankin	20		1	21
Graham	9		3	12
Lorimer	6		3	9
Gray E	5		2	7
Gray F	3	1	2	6
Jordan	3		3	6
McQueen	5			5
Currie	3		1	4
Clarke	3			3
Harris	2		1	3
Cherry	1		1	2
Flynn	1			1
Thomas	1			1
Opps' o.gs.	1			1

Final Division 1 Table

1	NOTTINGHAM F	42	25	14	3	69	24	64
2	Liverpool	42	24	9	9	65	34	57
3	Everton	42	22	11	9	76	45	55
4	Manchester C	42	20	12	10	74	51	52
5	Arsenal	42	21	10	11	60	37	52
6	WBA	42	18	14	10	62	53	50
7	Coventry C	42	18	12	12	75	62	48
8	Aston Villa	42	18	10	14	57	42	46
9	Leeds United	42	18	10	14	63	53	46
10	Manchester U	42	16	10	16	67	63	42
11	Birmingham C	42	16	9	17	55	60	41
12	Derby Co	42	14	13	15	54	59	41
13	Norwich C	42	11	18	13	52	66	40
14	Middlesbrough	42	12	15	15	42	54	39
15	Wolverhampton W	42	12	12	18	51	64	36
16	Chelsea	42	11	14	17	46	69	36
17	Bristol C	42	11	13	18	49	53	35
18	Ipswich T	42	11	13	18	47	61	35
19	QPR	42	9	15	18	47	64	33
20	West Ham U	42	12	8	22	52	69	32
21	Newcastle U	42	6	10	26	42	78	22
22	Leicester C	42	5	12	25	26	70	22

Season 1978-79

Football League Division 1

DATE	OPPONENTS	SCORE	GOALSCORERS	ATTENDANCE
Aug 19	Arsenal	D 2-2	Currie, Cherry	42,057
Aug 23	MANCHESTER UNITED	L 2-3	Hart, F Gray	36,845
Aug 26	WOLVERHAMPTON W	W 3-0	Hankin, F Gray, Currie	26,267
Sep 2	Chelsea	W 3-0	Graham, Hawley 2	30,099
Sep 9	Manchester City	L 0-3		40,125
Sep 16	TOTTENHAM HOTSPUR	L 1-2	Graham	36,062
Sep 23	Coventry City	D 0-0		27,365
Sep 30	BIRMINGHAM CITY	W 3-0	Flynn, F Gray, Hankin	23,331
Oct 7	Bolton Wanderers	L 1-3	Graham	27,751
Oct 14	WEST BROMWICH ALBION	L 1-3	Stevenson	25,931
Oct 21	Norwich City	D 2-2	F Gray, Hawley	19,981
Oct 28	DERBY COUNTY	W 4-0	Flynn, Hart, Hankin, Hawley	25,449
Nov 4	Liverpool	D 1-1	Hawley	51,857
Nov 11	ARSENAL	L 0-1		33,961
Nov 18	Wolverhampton W	D 1-1	Currie	18,961
Nov 22	CHELSEA	W 2-1	Graham, Hankin	24,088
Nov 25	SOUTHAMPTON	W 4-0	Graham, Currie, Golac o.g., Madeley	23,592
Dec 2	Ipswich Town	W 3-2	Hankin, Harris, Cherry	22,526
Dec 9	BRISTOL CITY	D 1-1	Flynn	22,529
Dec 16	Everton	D 1-1	Hawley	37,997
Dec 23	MIDDLESBROUGH	W 3-1	Hawley, F Gray, Currie	27,146
Dec 26	Aston Villa	D 2-2	E Gray 2	40,973
Dec 30	Queens Park Rangers	W 4-1	Hawley 2, Harris, E Gray	17,435
Jan 13	MANCHESTER CITY	D 1-1	Hawley	36,303
Jan 20	Tottenham Hotspur	W 2-1	Hart, Hankin	36,828
Feb 3	COVENTRY CITY	W 1-0	Currie	22,928
Feb 10	Birmingham City	W 1-0	F Gray (pen)	17,620
Feb 24	West Bromwich Albion	W 2-1	Graham 2	26,426
Mar 3	NORWICH CITY	D 2-2	Hawley 2	23,038
Mar 10	Derby County	W 1-0	Hawley	22,800
Mar 24	Manchester United	L 1-4	Hankin	51,191
Mar 31	Southampton	D 2-2	Hawley 2	21,805
Apr 7	IPSWICH TOWN	D 1-1	Cherry	24,153
Apr 10	Middlesbrough	L 0-1		23,260
Apr 14	ASTON VILLA	W 1-0	Hart	24,281
Apr 16	Nottingham Forest	D 0-0		37,397
Apr 21	EVERTON	W 1-0	Currie	29,125
Apr 25	BOLTON WANDERERS	W 5-1	Cherry, F Gray (pen), Hart, Harris, Hawley	20,218
Apr 28	Bristol City	D 0-0		25,388
May 4	QUEENS PARK RANGERS	W 4-3	Graham, Hankin 2, Cherry	20,121
May 15	NOTTINGHAM FOREST	L 1-2	Cherry	33,544
May 17	LIVERPOOL	L 0-3		41,324

FA Cup

Jan 18	Hartlepool United	(Rd 3) W 6-2	Hart, Graham, E Gray 2, Harris, F Gray	16,000
Feb 26	WEST BROMWICH ALBION*	(Rd 4) D 3-3	F Gray, Graham, Harris	34,000
Mar 1	West Bromwich Albion**	(R) L 0-2		31,101

*Played at the Hawthorns, West Bromwich. **Result after extra time.

League Cup

Aug 29	West Bromwich Albion	(Rd 2) D 0-0		25,064
Sep 6	WEST BROMWICH ALBION†	(R) D 0-0		29,316
Oct 2	West Bromwich Albion#	(2nd R) W 1-0	Hart	8,164
Oct 10	Sheffield United	(Rd 3) W 4-1	Currie, F Gray, E Gray 2	40,899
Nov 7	Queens Park Rangers	(Rd 4) W 2-0	Hawley, Hankin	22,769
Dec 13	LUTON TOWN	(Rd 5) W 4-1	Cherry, Currie, E Gray, F Gray	28,177
Jan 24	SOUTHAMPTON	(SF/FL) D 2-2	Currie, Hankin	33,415
Jan 30	Southampton	(SF/SL) L 0-1		23,645

†Result after extra time. #Played at Maine Road, Manchester.

MANAGER: Jock Stein/Maurice Lindley (caretaker)/Jimmy Adamson

CAPTAIN: Trevor Cherry

TOP SCORER: John Hawley

BIGGEST WIN: 6-2 v Hartlepool United, 18 January 1979, FA Cup, Round 3

HIGHEST ATTENDANCE: 51,857 v Liverpool, 4 November 1978, drew 1-1, League

MAJOR TRANSFERS IN: Kevin Hird from Blackburn Rovers

MAJOR TRANSFERS OUT: Paul Reaney to Bradford City, Allan Clarke to Barnsley

League & Cup Appearances (substitute)

PLAYER	LEAGUE	CUP COMPETITION		TOTAL
		FA CUP	LC	
Cherry	38	3	7	48
Currie	32	3	7	42
Flynn	41	3	8	52
Graham	39	3	7	49
Gray E	25 (3)	1	6 (1)	32 (4)
Gray F	41	3	8	52
Hampton	4		2	6
Hankin	29 (1)		8	37 (1)
Harris	29 (2)	3	1 (2)	33 (4)
Hart	40	2	8	50
Harvey	39	3	6	48
Hawley	29 (3)	3	6	38 (3)
Hird	13 (1)			13 (1)
Lorimer	3		1	4
Madeley	39	3	7	49
Parkinson	3 (2)	1		4 (2)
Stevenson	14 (1)	2	4	20 (1)
Stewart	3		2	5
Thomas	1 (1)	1	1	3 (1)

Goalscorers

PLAYER	LEAGUE	CUP COMPETITION		TOTAL
		FA CUP	LC	
Hawley	16		1	17
Hankin	9		2	11
Currie	8		3	11
Gray F	7	2	2	11
Graham	8	2		10
Gray E	3	2	3	8
Cherry	6		1	7
Hart	5	1	1	7
Harris	2	2		4
Flynn	3			3
Madeley	1			1
Stevenson	1			1
Opps' o.gs.	1			1

Fact File

The 2-2 draw with Norwich in October marked the beginning of a run that saw Leeds lose only three times in 23 league matches.

Final Division 1 Table

		P	W	D	L	F	A	PTS
1	LIVERPOOL	42	30	8	4	85	16	68
2	NOTTINGHAM F	42	21	18	3	61	26	60
3	WBA	42	24	11	7	72	35	59
4	EVERTON	42	17	17	8	52	40	51
5	LEEDS UNITED	42	18	14	10	70	52	50
6	IPSWICH T	42	20	9	13	63	49	49
7	ARSENAL	42	17	14	11	61	48	48
8	ASTON VILLA	42	15	16	11	59	49	46
9	MANCHESTER U	42	15	15	12	60	63	45
10	COVENTRY C	42	14	16	12	58	68	44
11	TOTTENHAM H	42	13	15	14	48	61	41
12	MIDDLESBROUGH	42	15	10	17	57	50	40
13	BRISTOL C	42	15	10	17	47	51	40
14	SOUTHAMPTON	42	12	16	14	47	53	40
15	MANCHESTER C	42	13	13	16	58	56	39
16	NORWICH C	42	7	23	12	51	57	37
17	BOLTON W	42	12	11	19	54	75	35
18	WOLVERHAMPTON W	42	13	8	21	44	68	34
19	DERBY CO	42	10	11	21	44	71	31
20	QPR	42	6	13	23	45	73	25
21	BIRMINGHAM C	42	6	10	26	37	64	22
22	CHELSEA	42	5	10	27	44	92	20

Season 1979-80

Football League Division 1

DATE	OPPONENTS	SCORE	GOALSCORERS	ATTENDANCE
Aug 18	Bristol City	D 2-2	Curtis 2	22,845
Aug 22	EVERTON	W 2-0	Hird, Harris	30,000
Aug 25	Norwich City	L 1-2	Hart	18,444
Sep 1	ARSENAL	D 1-1	Hart	23,245
Sep 8	Nottingham Forest	D 0-0		26,914
Sep 15	LIVERPOOL	D 1-1	Curtis	39,779
Sep 22	Bolton Wanderers	D 1-1	Gray (pen)	21,724
Sep 29	MANCHESTER CITY	L 1-2	Hankin	29,592
Oct 6	IPSWICH TOWN	W 2-1	Cherry, Hird (pen)	19,342
Oct 13	Brighton & Hove Albion	D 0-0		27,002
Oct 20	TOTTENHAM HOTSPUR	L 1-2	Hankin	25,203
Oct 27	Southampton	W 2-1	Entwistle, Curtis	23,259
Nov 3	BRISTOL CITY	L 1-3	Gray	17,376
Nov 10	Coventry City	L 0-3		19,402
Nov 13	Everton	L 1-5	Hird	23,000
Nov 17	WEST BROMWICH ALBION	W 1-0	Connor	17,481
Nov 24	Aston Villa	D 0-0		29,376
Dec 1	CRYSTAL PALACE	W 1-0	Hird	21,330
Dec 8	Manchester United	D 1-1	Connor	57,478
Dec 15	WOLVERHAMPTON W	W 3-0	Connor, Graham, Hamson	21,227
Dec 21	Stoke City	W 2-0	Connor, Harris	16,878
Dec 26	Middlesbrough	L 1-3	Entwistle	23,259
Dec 29	NORWICH CITY	D 2-2	Hird, Hankin	23,493
Jan 1	DERBY COUNTY	W 1-0	Hird	24,271
Jan 12	Arsenal	W 1-0	Connor	32,799
Jan 19	NOTTINGHAM FOREST	L 1-2	Connor	29,816
Feb 9	BOLTON WANDERERS	D 2-2	Hird (pen), Graham	16,428
Feb 16	Manchester City	D 1-1	Graham	34,392
Feb 23	BRIGHTON & HOVE ALBION	D 1-1	Flynn	17,216
Mar 1	Tottenham Hotspur	L 1-2	Chandler	35,331
Mar 8	SOUTHAMPTON	W 2-0	Hart, Parlane	21,169
Mar 14	Ipswich Town	L 0-1		23,140
Mar 19	Liverpool	L 0-3		37,008
Mar 22	COVENTRY CITY	D 0-0		14,967
Mar 29	West Bromwich Albion	L 1-2	Chandler	18,898
Apr 2	MIDDLESBROUGH	W 2-0	Cherry, Flynn	17,906
Apr 5	Derby County	L 0-2		22,745
Apr 8	STOKE CITY	W 3-0	Parlane, Harris 2	15,451
Apr 12	Crystal Palace	L 0-1		25,318
Apr 19	ASTON VILLA	D 0-0		15,840
Apr 26	Wolverhampton W	L 1-3	Flynn	22,746
May 3	MANCHESTER UNITED	W 2-0	Parlane, Hird (pen)	39,625

FA Cup

Jan 5	NOTTINGHAM FOREST	(Rd 3)	L	1-4	Lloyd o.g.	35,945

League Cup

Aug 29	ARSENAL	(Rd 2/FL)	D	1-1	Stevenson (pen)	23,421
Sep 4	Arsenal	(Rd 2/SL)	L	0-7		35,129

UEFA Cup

Sep 19	Valetta	(Rd 1/FL)	W	4-0	Graham 3, Hart	18,000
Oct 3	VALETTA	(Rd 1/SL)	W	3-0	Curtis, Hankin, Hart	13,682
Oct 24	Uni. Craiova	(Rd 2/FL)	L	0-2		40,000
Nov 7	UNI. CRAIOVA	(Rd 2/SL)	L	0-2		14,438

MANAGER: Jimmy Adamson

CAPTAIN: Trevor Cherry

TOP SCORER: Kevin Hird

BIGGEST WIN: 4-0 v Valetta, 19 September 1979, UEFA Cup, Round 1

HIGHEST ATTENDANCE: 57,478 v Manchester United, 8 December 1979, drew 1-1, League

MAJOR TRANSFERS IN: Alan Curtis from Swansea City, Brian Greenhoff from Manchester United, Derek Parlane from Rangers, Alex Sabella from Sheffield United

MAJOR TRANSFERS OUT: Tony Currie to Queens Park Rangers, John Hawley to Sunderland

League & Cup Appearances (substitute)

PLAYER	LEAGUE	CUP COMPETITION			TOTAL
		FA CUP	LC	UEFA	
Chandler	13 (4)				13 (4)
Cherry	39	1	2	4	46
Connor	20 (3)	1			21 (3)
Curtis	22	1	2	4	29
Dickinson	6				6
Entwistle	7 (4)	0 (1)			7 (5)
Firm	3				3
Flynn	24		2	4	30
Graham	26 (1)		2	3	31 (1)
Gray E	30	1		3	34
Greenhoff	22 (2)		2		24 (2)
Hampton	17		2	2	21
Hamson	18 (1)	1		1 (1)	20 (2)
Hankin	16		1	4	21
Harris	13 (2)	1	1 (1)	1 (2)	16 (5)
Hart	30	1	2	4	37
Harvey	9		2	1	12
Hawley	1				1
Hird	39	1	2	3	45
Lukic	33	1		3	37
Madeley	25	1		3	29
Parkinson	10 (1)			2	12 (1)
Parlane	11				11
Stevenson	25 (1)	1	2	2	30 (1)
Thomas	3				3

Goalscorers

PLAYER	LEAGUE	CUP COMPETITION			TOTAL
		FA CUP	LC	UEFA	
Hird	8				8
Connor	6				6
Graham	3			3	6
Hart	3			2	5
Curtis	4			1	5
Harris	4				4
Hankin	3			1	4
Flynn	3				3
Parlane	3				3
Chandler	2				2
Cherry	2				2
Entwistle	2				2
Gray E	2				2
Hamson	1				1
Stevenson			1		1
Opps' o.gs.		1			1

Fact File

17-year-old Terry Connor scores on his debut against West Bromwich Albion at Elland Road. He went on to score six goals in his first 11 matches.

Final Division 1 Table

		P	W	D	L	F	A	Pts
1	LIVERPOOL	42	25	10	7	81	30	60
2	MANCHESTER U	42	24	10	8	65	35	58
3	IPSWICH T	42	22	9	11	68	39	53
4	ARSENAL	42	18	16	8	52	36	52
5	NOTTINGHAM F	42	20	8	14	63	43	48
6	WOLVERHAMPTON W	42	19	9	14	58	47	47
7	ASTON VILLA	42	16	14	12	51	50	46
8	SOUTHAMPTON	42	18	9	15	65	53	45
9	MIDDLESBROUGH	42	16	12	14	50	44	44
10	WBA	42	11	19	12	54	50	41
11	LEEDS UNITED	42	13	14	15	46	50	40
12	NORWICH C	42	13	14	15	58	66	40
13	CRYSTAL PALACE	42	12	16	14	41	50	40
14	TOTTENHAM H	42	15	10	17	52	62	40
15	COVENTRY C	42	16	7	19	56	66	39
16	BRIGHTON & HA	42	11	15	16	47	57	37
17	MANCHESTER C	42	12	13	17	43	66	37
18	STOKE C	42	13	10	19	44	58	36
19	EVERTON	42	9	17	16	43	51	35
20	BRISTOL C	42	9	13	20	37	66	31
21	DERBY CO	42	11	8	23	47	67	30
22	BOLTON W	42	5	15	22	38	73	25

Season 1980-81

Football League Division 1

DATE	OPPONENTS	SCORE	GOALSCORERS	ATTENDANCE
Aug 16	ASTON VILLA	L 1-2	Stevenson (pen)	23,401
Aug 19	Middlesbrough	L 0-3		19,470
Aug 23	Norwich City	W 3-2	Hart, Graham, Cooper	17,890
Aug 30	LEICESTER CITY	L 1-2	Hart	18,530
Sep 6	Stoke City	L 0-3		12,729
Sep 13	TOTTENHAM HOTSPUR	D 0-0		21,947
Sep 20	MANCHESTER UNITED	D 0-0		32,539
Sep 27	Sunderland	L 1-4	Parlane	29,619
Oct 4	Ipswich Town	D 1-1	Sabella	24,087
Oct 8	MANCHESTER CITY	W 1-0	Harris	19,134
Oct 11	EVERTON	W 1-0	Curtis	25,601
Oct 18	Wolverhampton W	L 1-2	Connor	20,699
Oct 22	Nottingham Forest	L 1-2	Harris	25,033
Oct 25	CRYSTAL PALACE	W 1-0	Connor	19,208
Nov 1	Coventry City	L 1-2	Connor	13,970
Nov 8	ARSENAL	L 0-5		20,855
Nov 12	MIDDLESBROUGH	W 2-1	Hird 2 (1 pen)	17,382
Nov 15	Aston Villa	D 1-1	Sabella	29,106
Nov 22	Southampton	L 1-2	Graham	20,278
Nov 29	BRIGHTON & HOVE ALBION	W 1-0	Harris	14,333
Dec 6	West Bromwich Albion	W 2-1	Harris, Graham	17,771
Dec 13	NOTTINGHAM FOREST	W 1-0	Greenhoff	21,882
Dec 20	Manchester City	L 0-1		31,866
Dec 26	BIRMINGHAM CITY	D 0-0		19,214
Dec 27	Liverpool	D 0-0		44,086
Jan 10	SOUTHAMPTON	L 0-3		21,007
Jan 17	Leicester City	W 1-0	Hart	16,094
Jan 31	NORWICH CITY	W 1-0	Harris	15,836
Feb 7	Tottenham Hotspur	D 1-1	Harris	32,372
Feb 14	STOKE CITY	L 1-3	Flynn	16,530
Feb 21	SUNDERLAND	W 1-0	Harris	23,236
Feb 28	Manchester United	W 1-0	Flynn	45,733
Mar 14	Everton	W 2-1	Parlane, Harris	23,014
Mar 21	WOLVERHAMPTON W	L 1-3	Harris	19,252
Mar 28	Crystal Palace	W 1-0	Parlane	15,053
Mar 31	IPSWICH TOWN	W 3-0	Hird, Harris, Hart	26,462
Apr 4	COVENTRY CITY	W 3-0	Stevenson, Parlane, Flynn	15,882
Apr 11	Arsenal	D 0-0		29,339
Apr 18	LIVERPOOL	D 0-0		39,206
Apr 21	Birmingham City	W 2-0	Parlane, Hird (pen)	14,505
May 2	Brighton & Hove Albion	L 0-2		27,577
May 6	WEST BROMWICH ALBION	D 0-0		17,218

FA Cup

Jan 3	COVENTRY CITY	(Rd 3) D 1-1	Hird	24,523
Jan 6	Coventry City	(R) L 0-1		22,057

League Cup

Aug 27	Aston Villa	(Rd 2/FL) L 0-1		24,238
Sep 3	ASTON VILLA	(Rd/SL) L 1-3	Graham	12,236

League & Cup Appearances (substitute)

PLAYER	LEAGUE	CUP COMPETITION		TOTAL
		FA CUP	LC	
Butterworth	0 (1)			0 (1)
Chandler	8 (1)	1	1	10 (1)
Cherry	41	2	2	45
Connor	25 (2)	1	2	28 (2)
Curtis	6			6
Dickinson	0 (1)			0 (1)
Firm	5 (1)	5		10 (1)
Flynn	41	2	2	45
Graham	40	2	2	44
Gray E	38	2		40
Greenhoff	36	1	2	39
Hamson	7 (4)	1 (1)	1	9 (5)
Harris	33 (4)		0 (1)	33 (5)
Hart	38	2	2	42
Hird	32 (1)	2		34 (1)
Lukic	42	2	2	46
Madeley	6		2	8
Parkinson	3			3
Parlane	22 (4)	2	1	25 (4)
Sabella	22 (1)	2	2	26 (1)
Stevenson	17 (1)			17 (1)
Thomas	0 (2)		1	1 (2)

Goalscorers

PLAYER	LEAGUE	CUP COMPETITION		TOTAL
		FA CUP	LC	
Harris	10			10
Parlane	5			5
Hird	4	1		5
Hart	4			4
Graham	3		1	4
Connor	3			3
Flynn	3			3
Sabella	2			2
Stevenson	2			2
Cooper	1			1
Curtis	1			1
Greenhoff	1			1

Fact File

Eddie Gray moved to full back after the embarrassing 0-5 defeat by Arsenal at Elland Road in November.

MANAGER: Jimmy Adamson (until September)/Maurice Lindley (Caretaker until October)/Allan Clarke

CAPTAIN: Trevor Cherry

TOP SCORER: Carl Harris

BIGGEST WIN: 3-0 v Ipswich Town, 31 March 1981, League; 3-0 v Coventry City, 4 April 1981, League

HIGHEST ATTENDANCE: 45,733 v Manchester United, 26 February 1977, won 1-0, League

MAJOR TRANSFERS IN: Kenny Burns from Nottingham Forest, Frank Worthington from Birmingham City

MAJOR TRANSFERS OUT: Alan Curtis to Swansea City, Peter Hampton to Stoke City

Final Division 1 Table

		P	W	D	L	F	A	Pts
1	ASTON VILLA	42	26	8	8	72	40	60
2	IPSWICH T	42	23	10	9	77	43	56
3	ARSENAL	42	19	15	8	61	45	53
4	WBA	42	20	12	10	60	42	52
5	LIVERPOOL	42	17	17	8	62	46	51
6	SOUTHAMPTON	42	20	10	12	76	56	50
7	NOTTINGHAM F	42	19	12	11	62	44	50
8	MANCHESTER U	42	15	18	9	51	36	48
9	LEEDS UNITED	42	17	10	15	39	47	44
10	TOTTENHAM H	42	14	15	13	70	68	43
11	STOKE C	42	12	18	12	51	60	42
12	MANCHESTER C	42	14	11	17	56	59	39
13	BIRMINGHAM C	42	13	12	17	50	61	38
14	MIDDLESBROUGH	42	16	5	21	53	61	37
15	EVERTON	42	13	10	19	55	58	36
16	COVENTRY C	42	13	10	19	48	68	36
17	SUNDERLAND	42	14	7	21	52	53	35
18	WOLVERHAMPTON W	42	13	9	20	43	55	35
19	BRIGHTON & HA	42	14	7	21	54	67	35
20	NORWICH C	42	13	7	22	49	73	33
21	LEICESTER C	42	13	6	23	40	67	32
22	CRYSTAL PALACE	42	6	7	29	47	83	19

Season 1981-82

Football League Division 1

DATE	OPPONENTS	SCORE	GOALSCORERS	ATTENDANCE
Aug 30	Swansea City	L 1-5	Parlane	23,489
Sep 2	EVERTON	D 1-1	Graham	26,502
Sep 5	WOLVERHAMPTON W	W 3-0	Graham 3	20,216
Sep 12	Coventry City	L 0-4		13,065
Sep 19	ARSENAL	D 0-0		21,410
Sep 23	Manchester City	L 0-4		35,077
Sep 26	Ipswich Town	L 1-2	Barnes	22,319
Sep 30	Manchester United	L 0-1		47,019
Oct 3	ASTON VILLA	D 1-1	Balcombe	21,065
Oct 10	Liverpool	L 0-3		35,840
Oct 17	WEST BROMWICH ALBION	W 3-1	Graham, Cherry, Connor	19,164
Oct 24	SUNDERLAND	W 1-0	E Gray	25,220
Oct 31	Nottingham Forest	L 1-2	Butterworth	25,272
Nov 7	NOTTS COUNTY	W 1-0	Butterworth	19,552
Nov 21	Southampton	L 0-4		21,127
Nov 28	WEST HAM UNITED	D 3-3	Graham, Hird (pen), Cherry	25,637
Dec 5	Stoke City	W 2-1	Graham, Hamson	13,901
Dec 12	TOTTENHAM HOTSPUR	D 0-0		28,780
Jan 16	SWANSEA CITY	W 2-0	Stevenson, Butterworth	18,700
Jan 30	Arsenal	L 0-1		22,408
Feb 6	COVENTRY CITY	D 0-0		16,385
Feb 20	IPSWICH TOWN	L 0-2		20,287
Feb 27	LIVERPOOL	L 0-2		33,689
Mar 2	Brighton & Hove Albion	L 0-1		12,857
Mar 10	MANCHESTER CITY	L 0-1		20,797
Mar 13	Sunderland	W 1-0	Worthington	20,285
Mar 16	Wolverhampton W	L 0-1		11,729
Mar 20	NOTTINGHAM FOREST	D 1-1	Worthington (pen)	18,036
Mar 27	Notts County	L 1-2	Worthington	13,316
Apr 3	MANCHESTER UNITED	D 0-0		31,118
Apr 6	Middlesbrough	D 0-0		15,494
Apr 10	Birmingham City	W 1-0	Hart	14,497
Apr 13	MIDDLESBROUGH	D 1-1	Parlane	20,458
Apr 17	SOUTHAMPTON	L 1-3	Worthington	21,353
Apr 24	West Ham United	L 3-4	Connor, Graham, Flynn	24,748
Apr 28	Aston Villa	W 4-1	Graham, Worthington 2, Connor	20,566
May 1	STOKE CITY	D 0-0		17,775
May 4	Everton	L 0-1		17,137
May 8	Tottenham Hotspur	L 1-2	Worthington	35,020
May 12	BIRMINGHAM CITY	D 3-3	Worthington 2 (1 pen), Connor	18,583
May 19	BRIGHTON & HOVE ALBION	W 2-1	Hamson, Hird	19,831
May 22	West Bromwich Albion	L 0-2		23,118

FA Cup

Jan 2	Wolverhampton W	(Rd 3)	W 3-1	Hamson, Hird, E Gray	20,923
Jan 23	Tottenham Hotspur	(Rd 4)	L 0-1		46,126

League Cup

Oct 21	IPSWICH TOWN	(Rd 2/FL)	L 0-1	16,994
Oct 22	Ipswich Town	(Rd 2/SL)	L 0-3	16,494

League & Cup Appearances (substitute)

PLAYER	LEAGUE	CUP COMPETITION		TOTAL
		FA CUP	LC	
Arins	0 (1)			0 (1)
Aspin	1			1
Balcombe	1			1
Barnes	31		2	33
Burns	22 (1)	2	1	25 (1)
Butterworth	13 (1)	2		15 (1)
Cherry	38	2	1	41
Connor	23 (4)		1	24 (4)
Firm	3			3
Flynn	16	0 (1)		16 (1)
Graham	38	2	2	42
Gray E	31	2	2	35
Gray F	34	2	2	38
Greenhoff	10 (2)		1	11 (2)
Hamson	17 (1)	2	1	20 (1)
Harris	15 (3)		2	17 (3)
Hart	32	2	2	36
Hird	35 (3)	2	2	39 (3)
Lukic	42	2	2	46
Parlane	12			12
Stevenson	18 (1)	2	1 (1)	21 (2)
Thomas	13 (2)			13 (2)
Worthington	17			17

Goalscorers

PLAYER	LEAGUE	CUP COMPETITION		TOTAL
		FA CUP	LC	
Graham	9			9
Worthington	9			9
Connor	4			4
Butterworth	3			3
Hamson	2	1		3
Hird	2	1		3
Cherry	2			2
Parlane	2			2
Gray E	1	1		2
Balcombe	1			1
Barnes	1			1
Flynn	1			1
Hart	1			1
Stevenson	1			1

Fact File

Two nights after Leeds' defeat at the Hawthorns, Stoke City beat West Bromwich Albion – consigning Leeds to the Second Division after 17 years in the top flight.

MANAGER: Allan Clarke

CAPTAIN: Trevor Cherry

TOP SCORERS: Arthur Graham and Frank Worthington

BIGGEST WIN: 4-1 v Aston Villa, 28 April 1982, League

HIGHEST ATTENDANCE: 47,019 v Manchester United, 30 September 1981, lost 1-0, League

MAJOR TRANSFERS IN: Frank Gray from Nottingham Forest, Peter Barnes from West Bromwich Albion

MAJOR TRANSFERS OUT: Jeff Chandler to Bolton Wanderers

Final Division 1 Table

		P	W	D	L	F	A	Pts
1	LIVERPOOL	42	26	9	7	80	32	87
2	IPSWICH T	42	26	5	11	75	53	83
3	MANCHESTER U	42	22	12	8	59	29	78
4	TOTTENHAM H	42	20	11	11	67	48	71
5	ARSENAL	42	20	11	11	48	37	71
6	SWANSEA C	42	21	6	15	58	51	69
7	SOUTHAMPTON	42	19	9	14	72	67	66
8	EVERTON	42	17	13	12	56	50	64
9	WEST HAM U	42	14	16	12	66	57	58
10	MANCHESTER C	42	15	13	14	49	50	58
11	ASTON VILLA	42	15	12	15	55	53	57
12	NOTTINGHAM F	42	15	12	15	42	48	57
13	BRIGHTON & HA	42	13	13	16	43	52	52
14	COVENTRY C	42	13	11	18	56	62	50
15	NOTTS CO	42	13	8	21	61	69	47
16	BIRMINGHAM C	42	10	14	18	53	61	44
17	WBA	42	11	11	20	46	57	44
18	STOKE C	42	12	8	22	44	63	44
19	SUNDERLAND	42	11	11	20	38	58	44
20	LEEDS UNITED	42	10	12	20	39	61	42
21	WOLVERHAMPTON W	42	10	10	22	32	63	40
22	MIDDLESBROUGH	42	8	15	19	34	52	39

Season 1982-83

Football League Division 2

DATE	OPPONENTS	SCORE	GOALSCORERS	ATTENDANCE
Aug 28	Grimsby Town	D 1-1	Connor	16,137
Sep 4	WOLVERHAMPTON W	D 0-0		16,462
Sep 8	Leicester City	W 1-0	Butterworth	12,963
Sep 11	Sheffield Wednesday	W 3-2	Worthington 2, Butterworth	29,050
Sep 18	DERBY COUNTY	W 2-1	F Gray, Worthington	16,889
Sep 25	Fulham	L 2-3	Thomas, Graham	12,798
Oct 2	CAMBRIDGE UNITED	W 2-1	Butterworth, Hird	14,910
Oct 9	Chelsea	D 0-0		25,358
Oct 16	CARLISLE UNITED	D 1-1	Hart	14,141
Oct 20	BURNLEY	W 3-1	Worthington, Butterworth, Hird	13,827
Oct 23	Blackburn Rovers	D 0-0		12,040
Oct 30	NEWCASTLE UNITED	W 3-1	Worthington, Burns, Butterworth	26,750
Nov 6	CHARLTON ATHLETIC	L 1-2	Connor	15,148
Nov 13	Crystal Palace	D 1-1	Connor	11,673
Nov 20	MIDDLESBROUGH	D 0-0		18,482
Nov 27	Barnsley	L 1-2	Butterworth	21,530
Dec 4	QUEENS PARK RANGERS	L 0-1		11,528
Dec 11	Rotherham United	W 1-0	Gavin	13,034
Dec 18	SHREWSBURY TOWN	D 1-1	Hird	8,741
Dec 26	Oldham Athletic	D 2-2	Burns, Sheridan	15,658
Dec 28	BOLTON WANDERERS	D 1-1	Graham	16,180
Jan 1	Middlesbrough	D 0-0		17,000
Jan 3	Wolverhampton W	L 0-3		22,567
Jan 15	GRIMSBY TOWN	W 1-0	Butterworth	13,583
Jan 22	Derby County	D 3-3	Graham 2, Hart	17,005
Feb 12	Cambridge United	D 0-0		6,909
Feb 19	CHELSEA	D 3-3	Butterworth, F Gray (pen), Graham	19,365
Feb 26	Carlisle United	D 2-2	Connor, Butterworth	6,419
Mar 5	BLACKBURN ROVERS	W 2-1	F Gray (pen), Hird	12,280
Mar 12	Newcastle United	L 1-2	Connor	24,580
Mar 19	Charlton Athletic	W 1-0	Sheridan	8,229
Mar 26	CRYSTAL PALACE	W 2-1	Ritchie, F Gray (pen)	13,973
Apr 2	Bolton Wanderers	W 2-1	Butterworth, Hart	10,784
Apr 5	OLDHAM ATHLETIC	D 0-0		18,442
Apr 9	Burnley	W 2-1	Ritchie, Scott o.g.	12,149
Apr 16	FULHAM	D 1-1	Wright	24,328
Apr 23	Queens Park Rangers	L 0-1		19,573
Apr 27	SHEFFIELD WEDNESDAY	L 1-2	Ritchie	16,591
Apr 30	BARNSLEY	D 0-0		15,344
May 2	LEICESTER CITY	D 2-2	O'Neill o.g., F Gray (pen)	14,442
May 7	Shrewsbury Town	D 0-0		6,052
May 14	ROTHERHAM UNITED	D 2-2	Butterworth, Donnelly	14,958

FA Cup

Jan 8	PRESTON NORTH END	(Rd 3)	W 3-0	Sheridan, Connor, Graham	16,816
Jan 29	Arsenal	(Rd 4)	D 1-1	Nicholas o.g.	33,930
Feb 2	ARSENAL*	(R)	D 1-1	Butterworth	24,410
Feb 9	Arsenal	(2nd R)	L 1-2	Connor	26,802

*Result after extra time.

League Cup

Oct 6	NEWCASTLE UNITED	(Rd 2/FL)	L 0-1		24,012
Oct 27	Newcastle United**	(Rd 2/SL)	W 4-1	Saunder o.g., Worthington, Butterworth, Connor	24,173
Nov 10	HUDDERSFIELD TOWN	(Rd 3)	L 0-1		24,215

**Result after extra time.

MANAGER: Eddie Gray

CAPTAIN: Trevor Cherry/David Harvey

TOP SCORER: Aidan Butterworth

BIGGEST WIN: 4-1 v Newcastle United, 27 October 1982, League Cup, Round 2 Second Leg

HIGHEST ATTENDANCE: 33,390 v Arsenal, 9 February 1983, drew 1-1, FA Cup, Round 4

MAJOR TRANSFERS IN: Andy Ritchie from Brighton

MAJOR TRANSFERS OUT: John Lukic to Arsenal, Terry Connor to Brighton, Paul Hart to Nottingham Forest

League & Cup Appearances (substitute)

PLAYER	LEAGUE	CUP COMPETITION		TOTAL
		FA CUP	LC	
Aspin	14 (1)	4		18 (1)
Brown	1			1
Burns	19 (1)	1	3	23 (1)
Butterworth	37 (1)	4	3	44 (1)
Cherry	15 (1)		3	18 (1)
Connor	15 (4)	4	1 (2)	20 (6)
Dickinson	31	3		34
Donnelly	13 (1)			13 (1)
Flynn	2			2
Gavin	3 (4)			3 (4)
Graham	39	4	3	46
Gray E	20 (1)	4	3	27 (1)
Gray F	42	3	3	48
Hamson			1	1
Harvey	13			13
Hart	39	4	3	46
Hird	30 (9)	1 (2)	1 (2)	32 (13)
Lukic	29	4	3	36
McNab	5	1		6
Parlane	0 (1)			0 (1)
Ritchie	10			10
Sellars	1			1
Sheridan	27	2		29
Thomas	39	4	3	46
Wright	3 (1)			3 (1)
Worthington	15		3	18

Goalscorers

PLAYER	LEAGUE	CUP COMPETITION		TOTAL
		FA CUP	LC	
Butterworth	11	1	1	13
Connor	5	2	1	8
Graham	5	1		6
Worthington	5		1	6
Gray F	5			5
Hird	4			4
Hart	3			3
Ritchie	3			3
Sheridan	2	1		3
Burns	2			2
Donnelly	1			1
Gavin	1			1
Thomas	1			1
Wright	1			1
Opps' o.gs.	2	1	1	4

Fact File

The Elland Road Kop was closed for two matches as punishment after a ball bearing was thrown at Kevin Keegan during the home match with Newcastle.

Final Division 2 Table

		P	W	D	L	F	A	Pts
1	QPR	42	26	7	9	77	36	85
2	WOLVERHAMPTON W	42	20	15	7	68	44	75
3	LEICESTER C	42	20	10	12	72	44	70
4	FULHAM	42	20	9	13	64	47	69
5	NEWCASTLE U	42	18	13	11	75	53	67
6	SHEFFIELD W	42	16	15	11	60	47	63
7	OLDHAM ATH	42	14	19	9	64	47	61
8	LEEDS UNITED	42	13	21	8	51	46	60
9	SHREWSBURY T	42	15	14	13	48	48	59
10	BARNSLEY	42	14	15	13	57	55	57
11	BLACKBURN R	42	15	12	15	58	58	57
12	CAMBRIDGE U	42	13	12	17	42	60	51
13	DERBY CO	42	10	19	13	49	58	49
14	CARLISLE U	42	12	12	18	68	70	48
15	CRYSTAL PALACE	42	12	12	18	43	52	48
16	MIDDLESBROUGH	42	11	15	16	46	67	48
17	CHARLTON ATH	42	13	9	20	63	86	48
18	CHELSEA	42	11	14	17	51	61	47
19	GRIMSBY T	42	12	11	19	45	70	47
20	ROTHERHAM U	42	10	15	17	45	68	45
21	BURNLEY	42	12	8	22	56	66	44
22	BOLTON W	42	11	11	20	42	61	44

DERBY v FULHAM ABANDONED AFTER 88 MINUTES BUT 1-0 RESULT ALLOWED TO STAND.

Season 1983-84

Football League Division 2

DATE	OPPONENTS	SCORE	GOALSCORERS	ATTENDANCE
Aug 27	NEWCASTLE UNITED	L 0-1		30,806
Aug 29	BRIGHTON & HOVE ALBION	W 3-2	Watson, F Gray, Sheridan	13,303
Sep 3	Middlesbrough	D 2-2	F Gray (pen), McCluskey	12,793
Sep 6	Grimsby Town	L 0-2		8,000
Sep 10	CARDIFF CITY	W 1-0	McCluskey	12,336
Sep 17	Fulham	L 1-2	Ritchie	10,055
Sep 24	MANCHESTER CITY	L 1-2	Ritchie	21,918
Oct 1	Shrewsbury Town	L 1-5	Ritchie	6,289
Oct 8	Sheffield United	L 1-3	F Gray (pen)	26,814
Oct 14	CAMBRIDGE UNITED	W 3-1	Hird, Watson, Donnelly	9,923
Oct 22	Barnsley	W 2-0	Donnelly, Barnes	18,236
Oct 29	PORTSMOUTH	W 2-1	Watson, Barnes	16,254
Nov 5	CRYSTAL PALACE	D 1-1	McCluskey	14,847
Nov 12	Blackburn Rovers	D 1-1	Donnelly	9,556
Nov 19	Derby County	D 1-1	Ritchie	16,726
Nov 26	CHELSEA	D 1-1	McCluskey	20,680
Dec 3	Carlisle United	L 0-1		6,845
Dec 15	Charlton Athletic	L 0-2		6,285
Dec 26	HUDDERSFIELD TOWN	L 1-2	Wright	23,791
Dec 27	Oldham Athletic	L 2-3	Wright, F Gray	8,393
Dec 31	MIDDLESBROUGH	W 4-1	Sellars, McCluskey 2, Wright	14,215
Jan 2	Manchester City	D 1-1	Bond o.g.	34,441
Jan 21	FULHAM	W 1-0	Watson	11,421
Feb 4	SHREWSBURY TOWN	W 3-0	Watson 2, Brown	10,628
Feb 11	Cardiff City	W 1-0	McCluskey	9,407
Feb 15	SWANSEA CITY	W 1-0	Lorimer	10,031
Feb 18	Portsmouth	W 3-2	Wright, Watson, Lorimer (pen)	13,911
Feb 25	BARNSLEY	L 1-2	Wright	19,138
Mar 3	Crystal Palace	D 0-0		8,077
Mar 10	BLACKBURN ROVERS	W 1-0	Butterworth	12,857
Mar 17	GRIMSBY TOWN	W 2-1	Aspin, Sellars	14,412
Mar 24	Brighton & Hove Albion	L 0-3		12,605
Mar 28	Newcastle United	L 0-1		30,877
Mar 31	SHEFFIELD WEDNESDAY	D 1-1	Ritchie	25,343
Apr 7	Cambridge United	D 2-2	Barnes, Sellars	4,700
Apr 14	DERBY COUNTY	D 0-0		12,549
Apr 21	Huddersfield Town	D 2-2	Wright, Barnes	16,270
Apr 24	OLDHAM ATHLETIC	W 2-0	Ritchie, Lorimer (pen)	9,576
Apr 28	Chelsea	L 0-5		33,447
May 5	CARLISLE UNITED	W 3-0	Gavin, Ritchie, McCluskey	8,278
May 7	Swansea City	D 2-2	Wright, Lorimer	5,498
May 12	CHARLTON ATHLETIC	W 1-0	Wright	13,254

FA Cup

Jan 7	SCUNTHORPE UNITED	(Rd 3) D 1-1	Wright	17,130
Jan 10	Scunthorpe United*	(R) D 1-1	Wright	13,129
Jan 16	Scunthorpe United	(2nd R) L 2-4	Wright, Ritchie	13,312

*Result after extra time.

League Cup

Oct 5	CHESTER CITY	(Rd 2/FL) L 0-1		8,106
Oct 26	Chester City	(Rd 2/SL) W 4-1	Ritchie 2, Burns, Barnes	8,044
Nov 9	OXFORD UNITED	(Rd 3) D 1-1	McCluskey	13,349
Nov 23	Oxford United	(R) L 1-4	Burns	13,389

Fact File

The match against Fulham in January saw Leeds legend Peter Lorimer's return to the club.

MANAGER: Eddie Gray

CAPTAIN: David Harvey

TOP SCORER: Tommy Wright

BIGGEST WIN: 4-1 v Chester City, 26 October 1983, League Cup, Round 2 Second Leg; 4-1 v Middlesbrough, 31 December 1983, League

HIGHEST ATTENDANCE: 34,441 v Manchester City, 2 January 1984, drew 1-1, League

League & Cup Appearances (substitute)

PLAYER	LEAGUE	CUP COMPETITION		TOTAL
		FA CUP	LC	
Aspin	21	3	2	26
Barnes	25 (2)	1	3	2 (2)
Brown	22			22
Burns	13		4	17
Butterworth	4 (7)		1	5 (7)
Dickinson	34	2	4	40
Donnelly	23 (2)	1	3	27 (2)
Gavin	10 (2)		1 (1)	11 (3)
Gray E	4			4
Gray F	24	2	4	30
Hamson	23 (2)	3		26 (2)
Harvey	40	3	4	47
Hird	16 (2)		1	17 (2)
Hughes	2			2
Irwin	12		1	13
Lorimer	20 (2)	2 (1)		22 (2)
McCluskey	24 (8)	3	3 (1)	30 (9)
McGoldrick	7	3	2	12
Ritchie	38	3	4	45
Sellars	19	2		21
Sheridan	11			11
Thomas	16 (1)		4	20 (1)
Thompson	1			1
Watson	30 (1)	1	4	35 (1)
Wright	23 (2)	3	0 (1)	26 (3)

Goalscorers

PLAYER	LEAGUE	CUP COMPETITION		TOTAL
		FA CUP	LC	
Wright	8	3		11
Ritchie	7	1	2	10
McCluskey	8		1	9
Watson	7			7
Barnes	4		1	5
Gray F	4			4
Lorimer	4			4
Donnelly	3			3
Sellars	3			3
Burns	2		2	2
Aspin	1			1
Brown	1			1
Butterworth	1			1
Gavin	1			1
Hird	1			1
Sheridan	1			1
Opps' o.gs.	1			1

Final Division 2 Table

		P	W	D	L	F	A	Pts
1	CHELSEA	42	25	13	4	90	40	89
2	SHEFFIELD W	42	26	10	6	72	34	89
3	NEWCASTLE U	42	24	8	10	85	53	80
4	MANCHESTER C	42	20	10	12	66	48	70
5	GRIMSBY T	42	19	13	10	60	47	70
6	BLACKBURN R	42	17	16	9	57	46	67
7	CARLISLE U	42	16	16	10	48	41	64
8	SHREWSBURY T	42	17	10	15	49	53	61
9	BRIGHTON & HA	42	17	9	16	69	60	60
10	LEEDS UNITED	42	16	12	14	55	56	60
11	FULHAM	42	15	12	15	60	53	57
12	HUDDERSFIELD T	42	14	15	13	56	49	57
13	CHARLTON ATH	42	16	9	17	53	64	57
14	BARNSLEY	42	15	7	20	57	53	52
15	CARDIFF C	42	15	6	21	53	66	51
16	PORTSMOUTH	42	14	7	21	73	64	49
17	MIDDLESBROUGH	42	12	13	17	41	47	49
18	CRYSTAL PALACE	42	12	11	19	42	52	47
19	OLDHAM ATH	42	13	8	21	47	73	47
20	DERBY CO	42	11	9	22	36	72	42
21	SWANSEA C	42	7	8	27	36	85	29
22	CAMBRIDGE U	42	4	12	26	28	77	24

Season 1984-85

Football League Division 2

DATE	OPPONENTS	SCORE	GOALSCORERS	ATTENDANCE
Aug 25	Notts. County	W 2-1	Wright 2	12,196
Aug 27	FULHAM	W 2-0	McCluskey, Wright	14,207
Sep 1	WOLVERHAMPTON W	W 3-2	Wright 2, Lorimer	17,843
Sep 8	Grimsby Town	W 2-0	McCluskey, Lorimer	13,290
Sep 12	Cardifff City	L 1-2	Sellars	6,893
Sep 15	PORTSMOUTH	L 0-1		19,438
Sep 22	Crystal Palace	L 1-3	Sellars	19,460
Sep 29	OLDHAM ATHLETIC	W 6-0	Wright, Ritchie 3, Sheridan, Linighan	14,290
Oct 6	SHEFFIELD UNITED	D 1-1	Lorimer (pen)	25,547
Oct 13	Barnsley	L 0-1		16,199
Oct 20	Huddersfield Town	L 0-1		15,257
Oct 27	MIDDLESBROUGH	W 2-0	Lorimer (pen), Ritchie	14,838
Nov 3	Charlton Athletic	W 3-2	Sheridan, McCluskey, Gavin	6,950
Nov 10	CARLISLE UNITED	D 1-1	Dickinson	13,327
Nov 17	BRIGHTON & HOVE ALBION	W 1-0	Ritchiee	13,127
Nov 24	Oxford United	L 2-5	Wright, Lorimer	12,192
Dec 1	WIMBLEDON	W 5-2	Wright, Ritchie 3, Sellars	10,899
Dec 8	Shrewsbury Town	W 3-2	Ritchie 2, Linighan	6,358
Dec 15	BIRMINGHAM CITY	L 0-1		15,584
Dec 22	Wolverhampton W	W 2-0	F Gray, McCluskey	9,259
Dec 26	Blackburn Rovers	L 1-2	McCluskey	20,149
Dec 29	CARDIFF CITY	D 1-1	Lorimer (pen)	11,798
Jan 1	MANCHESTER CITY	D 1-1	Lorimer (pen)	22,626
Jan 19	NOTTS. COUNTY	W 5-0	Sheridan, Wright 3, Irwin	11,369
Feb 2	Oldham Athletic	D 1-1	Lorimer (pen)	8,824
Feb 9	GRIMSBY TOWN	D 0-0		12,517
Feb 23	CHARLTON ATHLETIC	W 1-0	Lorimer	10,644
Feb 26	Carlisle United	D 2-2	Wright, Aspin	5,484
Mar 2	Middlesbrough	D 0-0		8,781
Mar 9	HUDDERSFIELD TOWN	D 0-0		18.607
Mar 12	Portsmouth	L 1-3	Sheridan	16,208
Mar 16	BARNSLEY	W 2-0	Lorimer, Sellars	13,091
Mar 23	Sheffield United	L 1-2	Ritchie	21,468
Mar 30	Fulham	W 2-0	Wright 2	7,901
Apr 6	BLACKBURN ROVERS	D 0-0		15,289
Apr 8	Manchester City	W 2-1	Baird, Sellars	33,553
Apr 13	CRYSTAL PALACE	W 4-1	Baird, Sellars, Sheridan 2	12,286
Apr 20	Brighton & Hove Albion	D 1-1	Sellars	17,279
Apr 27	OXFORD UNITED	W 1-0	Baird	17,992
May 4	Wimbledon	D 2-2	Baird 2	6,638
May 6	SHREWSBURY TOWN	W 1-0	Baird	12,423
May 11	Birmingham City	L 0-1		24,847

FA Cup

Jan 4	EVERTON	(Rd 3) L 0-2		21,211

League Cup

Sep 25	Gillingham	(Rd 2/FL) W 2-1	Wright, Ritchie	8,881
Oct 10	GILLINGHAM	(Rd 2/SL) W 3-2	Gavin, Sellars, Lorimer	11,109
Oct 31	WATFORD	(Rd 3) L 0-4		21,221

League & Cup Appearances (substitute)

PLAYER	LEAGUE	CUP COMPETITION		TOTAL
		FA CUP	LC	
Aspin	32	1		33
Baird	10			10
Brown	1			1
Day	18		3	21
Dickinson	22		3	25
Donnelly	0 (1)			0 (1)
Eli	0 (1)			0 (1)
Gavin	7 (4)	0 (1)	3	10 (5)
Gray F	39	1	3	43
Hamson	31	1		32
Harvey	20			20
Hughes	4	1		5
Irwin	41	1	3	45
Linighan	42	1	3	46
Lorimer	40	1	3	44
McCluskey	13 (6)	1	0 (1)	14 (7)
Ritchie	22 (6)		3	25 (6)
Sellars	39		3	42
Sheridan	42	1	3	46
Simmonds	0 (1)			0 (1)
Stiles	1			1
Watson	7			7
Wright	41 (1)	1	3	45 (1)

Goalscorers

PLAYER	LEAGUE	CUP COMPETITION		TOTAL
		FA CUP	LC	
Wright	14		1	15
Ritchie	12		1	13
Lorimer	9		1	10
Sellars	7		1	8
Baird	6			6
Sheridan	6			6
McCluskey	5			5
Linighan	2			2
Gavin	1		1	2
Aspin	1			1
Dickinson	1			1
Gray F	1			1
Irwin	1			1

Fact File

Leeds could have earned promotion by winning at St. Andrews in the last match of the season.

MANAGER: Eddie Gray

CAPTAIN: Peter Lorimer

TOP SCORER: Tommy Wright

BIGGEST WIN: 6-0 v Oldham Athletic, 29 September 1984, League

HIGHEST ATTENDANCE: 33,553 v Manchester City, 8 April 1985, won 2-1, League

MAJOR TRANSFERS IN: Andy Linighan from Hartlepool United, Ian Baird from Southampton

Final Division 2 Table

		P	W	D	L	F	A	Pts
1	OXFORD U	42	25	9	8	84	36	84
2	BIRMINGHAM C	42	25	7	10	59	33	82
3	MANCHESTER C	42	21	11	10	66	40	74
4	PORTSMOUTH	42	20	14	8	69	50	74
5	BLACKBURN R	42	21	10	11	66	41	73
6	BRIGHTON & HA	42	20	12	10	54	34	72
7	LEEDS UNITED	42	19	12	11	66	43	69
8	SHREWSBURY T	42	18	11	13	66	53	65
9	FULHAM	42	19	8	15	68	64	65
10	GRIMSBY T	42	18	8	16	72	64	62
11	BARNSLEY	42	14	16	12	42	42	58
12	WIMBLEDON	42	16	10	16	71	75	58
13	HUDDERSFIELD T	42	15	10	17	52	64	55
14	OLDHAM ATH	42	15	8	19	49	67	53
15	CRYSTAL PALACE	42	12	12	18	46	65	48
16	CARLISLE U	42	13	8	21	50	67	47
17	CHARLTON ATH	42	11	12	19	51	63	45
18	SHEFFIELD U	42	10	14	18	54	66	44
19	MIDDLESBROUGH	42	10	10	22	41	57	40
20	NOTTS CO	42	10	7	25	45	73	37
21	CARDIFF C	42	9	8	25	47	79	35
22	WOLVERHAMPTON W	42	8	9	25	37	79	33

Season 1985-86

Football League Division 2

DATE	OPPONENTS	SCORE	GOALSCORERS	ATTENDANCE
Aug 17	Fulham	L 1-3	Lorimer	5,772
Aug 21	WIMBLEDON	D 0-0		12,426
Aug 24	HULL CITY	D 1-1	Baird	16,689
Aug 26	Stoke City	L 2-6	Aspin, Snodin	7,047
Aug 31	CHARLTON ATHLETIC	L 1-2	Lorimer (pen)	10,862
Sep 4	Brighton & Hove Albion	W 1-0	McCluskey	9,798
Sep 7	Shrewsbury Town	W 3-1	Wright, Mcluskey, Baird	4,168
Sep 14	SUNDERLAND	D 1-1	Sheridan	19,693
Sep 21	BRADFORD CITY	W 2-1	Lorimer, Sellars	21,104
Sep 28	SHEFFIELD UNITED	D 1-1	Baird	15,622
Oct 5	Huddersfield Town	L 1-3	Baird	9,983
Oct 12	MIDDLESBROUGH	W 1-0	Lorimer (pen)	14,117
Oct 19	GRIMSBY TOWN	D 1-1	Baird	11,244
Oct 27	Barnsley	L 0-3		8,302
Nov 2	PORTSMOUTH	W 2-1	Simmonds 2 (1 pen)	15,672
Nov 9	Millwall	L 1-3	Ritchie	9,158
Nov 16	CRYSTAL PALACE	L 1-3	McCluskey	10,378
Nov 23	Carlisle United	W 2-1	Linighan, Ritchie	3,504
Nov 30	NORWICH CITY	L 0-2		11,480
Dec 7	Wimbledon	W 3-0	Snodin, Baird, Dickinson	3,492
Dec 14	FULHAM	W 1-0	Sheridan	9,998
Dec 22	Hull City	L 1-2	Sheridan	11,852
Dec 26	Blackburn Rovers	L 0-2		8,666
Dec 28	BRIGHTON & HOVE ALBION	L 2-3	Baird, Snodin	13,110
Jan 1	OLDHAM ATHLETIC	W 3-1	Baird 2, Ritchie	10,830
Jan 11	Sunderland	L 2-4	Baird, Sheridan	15,139
Jan 18	Charlton Athletic	L 0-4		4,333
Feb 1	STOKE CITY	W 4-0	Stiles, Baird, Swan 2	10,425
Feb 8	Grimsby Town	L 0-1		6,338
Feb 15	BARNSLEY	L 0-2		11,765
Mar 8	HUDDERSFIELD TOWN	W 2-0	Ormsby, Snodin	14,667
Mar 15	Middlesbrough	D 2-2	Simmonds, Rennie	6,899
Mar 22	SHREWSBURY TOWN	D 1-1	Rennie	9,641
Mar 28	Oldham Athletic	L 1-3	Ritchie	4,937
Mar 31	BLACKBURN ROVERS	D 1-1	Ritchie	9,919
Apr 5	Portsmouth	W 3-2	Ritchie 2, Baird	14,430
Apr 9	Bradford City	W 1-0	Aspin	10,751
Apr 12	MILLWALL	W 3-1	Sellars, Swan, Ritchie	15,067
Apr 19	Crystal Palace	L 0-3		6,285
Apr 22	Sheffield United	L 2-3	Ritchie, Snodin	9,158
Apr 26	CARLISLE UNITED	W 2-0	Ritchie 2	13,868
May 3	Norwich City	L 0-4		17,942

FA Cup

Jan 4	Peterborough United	(Rd 3) L 0-1		10,137

Milk Cup

Sep 25	WALSALL	(Rd 2/FL) D 0-0		8,869
Oct 8	Walsall	(Rd 2/SL) W 3-0	Linighan, Snodin 2	7,085
Oct 30	ASTON VILLA	(Rd 3) L 0-3		15,444

Full Members Cup

Oct 14	Manchester City	(Gp 3) L 1-6	Lorimer (pen)	4,029
Oct 16	SHEFFIELD UNITED	(Gp 3) D 1-1	Sellars	2,274

League & Cup Appearances (substitute)

PLAYER	LEAGUE	CUP COMPETITION			TOTAL
		FA CUP	MILK	OTHER	
Aspin	38	1	1	2	42
Baird	34 (1)	1	3	2	40 (1)
Caswell	8				8
Day	40	1	3	2	46
Dickenson	17 (2)	1	3		21 (2)
Eli	1				1
Hamson	30	1	2	1	34
Harle	3				3
Irwin	19	1	2	2	24
Linighan	24	1	3	2	30
Lorimer	14		2	2	18
McCluskey	20 (2)		2 (1)	1	23 (3)
McGregor	5				5
Ormsby	12				12
Phelan	12 (2)		3	2	17 (2)
Rennie	16				16
Ritchie	28 (1)	1	2		31 (1)
Robinson	16				16
Sellars	13 (4)	1	1	2	17 (4)
Sheridan	31 (1)	0 (1)	3	2	36 (2)
Simmonds	6 (2)			1 (1)	7 (3)
Snodin	37	1	3		41
Stiles	11 (1)			0 (1)	11 (2)
Swan	16	1		0 (2)	17 (2)
Swinburne	2				2
Taylor	2				2
Thompson	1				1
Wright	6 (4)		0 (1)		6 (5)

Goalscorers

PLAYER	LEAGUE	CUP COMPETITION			TOTAL
		FA CUP	MILK	OTHER	
Baird	12				12
Ritchie	11				11
Snodin	5		2		7
Lorimer	4			1	5
Sheridan	4				4
McCluskey	3				3
Simmonds	3				3
Swann	3				3
Aspin	2				2
Rennie	2				2
Sellars	2			1	3
Linighan	1	1			2
Dickenson	1				1
Ormsby	1				1
Stiles	1				1
Wright	1				1

Fact File

The season's average attendance at Elland Road was down to 13,265 – the lowest since 1922-23.

MANAGER: Eddie Gray (until October)/Billy Bremner

CAPTAIN: Ian Snodin

TOP SCORER: Ian Baird

BIGGEST WIN: 4-0 v Stoke City, 1 February 1986, League

HIGHEST ATTENDANCE: 21,104 v Bradford City, 21 September 1985, won 2-1, League

MAJOR TRANSFERS OUT: Frank Gray to Sunderland, Scott Sellars to Blackburn Rovers

Final Division 2 Table

		P	W	D	L	F	A	Pts
1	NORWICH C	42	25	9	8	84	37	84
2	CHARLTON ATH	42	22	11	9	78	45	77
3	WIMBLEDON	42	21	13	8	58	37	76
4	PORTSMOUTH	42	22	7	13	69	41	73
5	CRYSTAL PALACE	42	19	9	14	57	52	66
6	HULL C	42	17	13	12	65	55	64
7	SHEFFIELD U	42	17	11	14	64	63	62
8	OLDHAM ATH	42	17	9	16	62	61	60
9	MILLWALL	42	17	8	17	64	65	59
10	STOKE C	42	14	15	13	48	50	57
11	BRIGHTON & HA	42	16	8	18	64	64	56
12	BARNSLEY	42	14	14	14	47	50	56
13	BRADFORD C	42	16	6	20	51	63	54
14	LEEDS UNITED	42	15	8	19	56	72	53
15	GRIMSBY T	42	14	10	18	58	62	52
16	HUDDERSFIELD T	42	14	10	18	51	67	52
17	SHREWSBURY T	42	14	9	19	52	64	51
18	SUNDERLAND	42	13	11	18	47	61	50
19	BLACKBURN R	42	12	13	17	53	62	49
20	CARLISLE U	42	13	7	22	47	71	46
21	MIDDLESBROUGH	42	12	9	21	44	53	45
22	FULHAM	42	10	6	26	45	69	36

Season 1986-87

Football League Division 2

DATE	OPPONENTS	SCORE	GOALSCORERS	ATTENDANCE
Aug 23	Blackburn Rovers	L 1-2	Ritchie	8,346
Aug 25	STOKE CITY	W 2-1	Sheridan, Baird	13,334
Aug 30	SHEFFIELD UNITED	L 0-1		18,294
Sep 2	Barnsley	W 1-0	Baird	6,839
Sep 6	Huddersfield Town	D 1-1	Sheridan	9,306
Sep 13	READING	W 3-2	Edwards, Ritchie, Buckley	12,248
Sep 20	Bradford City	L 0-2		13,525
Sep 27	HULL CITY	W 3-0	Ritchie (pen), Baird, Ormsby	13,551
Oct 4	Plymouth Argyle	D 1-1	Baird	11,923
Oct 11	CRYSTAL PALACE	W 3-0	Sheridan (pen), Ormsby, Edwards	14,316
Oct 18	PORTSMOUTH	W 3-1	Sheridan (pen), Ritchie, Baird	21,364
Oct 25	Grimsby Town	D 0-0		7,168
Nov 1	SHREWBURY TOWN	W 1-0	Aspin	14,966
Nov 8	Millwall	L 0-1		6,869
Nov 15	OLDHAM ATHLETIC	L 0-2		21,052
Nov 21	Birmingham City	L 1-2	Sheridan	7,836
Nov 29	DERBY COUNTY	W 2-0	Sheridan, Edwards	19,129
Dec 6	West Bromwich Albion	L 0-3		9,853
Dec 13	BRIGHTON & HOVE ALBION	W 3-1	Sheridan, Snodin, Baird	12,014
Dec 21	Stoke City	L 2-7	Baird, Sheridan (pen)	12,358
Dec 26	SUNDERLAND	D 1-1	Bennett o.g.	21,286
Dec 27	Oldham Athletic	W 1-0	Ritchie	8,477
Jan 1	Ipswich Town	L 0-2		14,125
Jan 3	HUDDERSFIELD TOWN	D 1-1	Baird	17,983
Jan 24	BLACKBURN ROVERS	D 0-0		14,452
Feb 7	Sheffield United	D 0-0		12,494
Feb 14	BARNSLEY	D 2-2	Baird, Sheridan	14,216
Feb 28	BRADFORD CITY	W 1-0	Edwards	21,802
Mar 7	GRIMSBY TOWN	W 2-0	Ritchie, Sheridan (pen)	14,270
Mar 10	Portsmouth	D 1-1	Adams	13,745
Mar 21	Crystal Palace	L 0-1		8,781
Mar 28	PLYMOUTH ARGYLE	W 4-0	Sheridan (pen), Baird 3	18,618
Apr 4	MILLWALL	W 2-0	Baird, Ritchie	18,304
Apr 8	Hull City	D 0-0		9,531
Apr 14	Shrewsbury Town	W 2-0	Sheridan, Pearson	4,186
Apr 18	IPSWICH TOWN	W 3-2	McDonald, Sheridan, Ormsby	24,839
Apr 20	Sunderland	D 1-1	Pearson	14,725
Apr 22	Reading	L 1-2	Pearson	7,415
Apr 25	BIRMINGHAM CITY	W 4-0	Sheridan, Baird 2, Edwards	19,100
May 2	Derby County	L 1-2	Ashurst	20,087
May 4	WEST BROMWICH ALBION	W 3-2	Sheridan (pen), Pearson, Ormsby	24,688
May 9	Brighton & Hove Albion	W 1-0	Edwards	8,139

Play-offs

May 14	OLDHAM ATHLETIC	(SF/FL)	W 1-0	Edwards	29,472
May 17	Oldham Athletic	(SF/SL)	L 1-2	Edwards	19,216
May 23	Charlton Athletic	(F/FL)	L 0-1		16,680
May 25	CHARLTON ATHLETIC	(F/SL)	W 1-0	Ormsby	31,395
May 29	Charlton Athletic†	(R)	L 1-2	Sheridan	18,000

†Played at Birmingham, result after extra time.

FA Cup

Jan 11	Telford United*	(Rd 3)	W 2-1	Baird 2	6,560
Feb 3	Swindon Town	(Rd 4)	W 2-1	Quinn o.g., Baird	14,031
Feb 21	QUEENS PARK RANGERS	(Rd 5)	W 2-1	Baird, Ormsby	31,324
Mar 15	Wigan Athletic	(Rd 6)	W 2-0	Stiles, Adams	12,250
Apr 12	Coventry City**	(SF)	L 2-3	Rennie, Edwards	51,372

*Played at the Hawthorns, West Bromwich. **Played at Hillsborough, Sheffield.

Littlewoods Cup

Sep 23	Oldham Athletic	(Rd 2/FL)	L 2-3	Aspin, Taylor	5,569
Oct 8	OLDHAM ATHLETIC	(Rd 2/SL)	L 0-1		11,449

Full Members Cup

Oct 1	BRADFORD CITY	(Rd 1)	L 0-1		3,960

MANAGER: Billy Bremner **CAPTAIN:** Brendan Ormsby

TOP SCORER: Ian Baird

BIGGEST WIN: 4-0 v Plymouth Argyle, 28 March 1987, League; 4-0 v Birmingham City, 25 April 1987, League

HIGHEST ATTENDANCE: 51,372 v Coventry City, 12 April 1987, lost 3-2, FA Cup semi-final

---

League & Cup Appearances (substitute)

PLAYER	LEAGUE	CUP COMPETITION			TOTAL
		FA CUP	LITTLEWOODS	OTHER	
Adams	17	4		5	26
Ashurst	41	5	2	6	54
Aspin	41	5	2	5	53
Baird	40	4	1	6	51
Buckley	6 (3)	0 (1)		1	7 (4)
Caswell	1				1
Day	34	5	1	6	46
Doig	2 (2)	1			3 (2)
Edwards	24 (6)	2 (3)	2	1 (4)	29 (13)
Haddock	10 (1)	0 (1)		1	11 (2)
McDonald	17			5	22
Ormsby	33	4	1	5	43
Pearson	18	4		4	26
Rennie	24	5	2	1	32
Ritchie	29 (2)	5	2	3 (1)	39 (3)
Robinson	11			0 (1)	11 (1)
Snodin	14				14
Stiles	26 (3)	5	1	2	34 (3)
Sheridan	40	5	2	5 (1)	52 (1)
Sinclair	8	1			9
Swan	5 (2)	1		1	8 (2)
Taylor	2		1 (1)	2	5 (1)
Thompson	4 (1)		2	1	7 (1)
Wright		0 (1)		1	1 (1)

Goalscorers

PLAYER	LEAGUE	CUP COMPETITION			TOTAL
		FA CUP	LITTLEWOODS	OTHER	
Baird	15	4			19
Sheridan	15			1	16
Edwards	6	1		2	9
Ritchie	7				7
Ormsby	4	1		1	6
Pearson	4				4
Adams	1	1			2
Aspin	1		1		2
Ashurst	1				1
Buckley	1				1
McDonald	1				1
Snodin	1				1
Rennie		1			1
Stiles		1			1
Taylor			1		1
Opps' o.gs.	1	1			2

Fact File

John Stiles, youth team graduate and son of World Cup winner Nobby, fought his way into the first team as a regular this season.

Final Division 2 Table

		P	W	D	L	F	A	Pts
1	DERBY CO	42	25	9	8	64	38	84
2	PORTSMOUTH	42	23	9	10	53	28	78
3	OLDHAM ATH	42	22	9	11	65	44	75
4	LEEDS UNITED	42	19	11	12	58	44	68
5	IPSWICH T	42	17	13	12	59	43	64
6	CRYSTAL PALACE	42	19	5	18	51	53	62
7	PLYMOUTH ARG	42	16	13	13	62	57	61
8	STOKE C	42	16	10	16	63	53	58
9	SHEFFIELD U	42	15	13	14	50	49	58
10	BRADFORD C	42	15	10	17	62	62	55
11	BARNSLEY	42	14	13	15	49	52	55
12	BLACKBURN R	42	15	10	17	45	55	55
13	READING	42	14	11	17	52	59	53
14	HULL C	42	13	14	15	41	55	53
15	WBA	42	13	12	17	51	49	51
16	MILLWALL	42	14	9	19	39	45	51
17	HUDDERSFIELD T	42	13	12	17	54	61	51
18	SHREWSBURY T	42	15	6	21	41	53	51
19	BIRMINGHAM C	42	11	17	14	47	59	50
20	SUNDERLAND	42	12	12	18	49	59	48
21	GRIMSBY T	42	10	14	18	39	59	44
22	BRIGHTON & HA	42	9	12	21	37	54	39

Season 1987-88

Football League Division 2

DATE	OPPONENTS	SCORE	GOALSCORERS	ATTENDANCE
Aug 16	Barnsley	D 1-1	Taylor	9,778
Aug 19	LEICESTER CITY	W 1-0	Sheridan (pen)	21,034
Aug 22	READING	D 0-0		19,286
Aug 29	Bradford City	D 0-0		11,428
Aug 31	WEST BROMWICH ALBION	W 1-0	Sheridan	19,847
Sep 5	Ipswich Town	L 0-1		11,016
Sep 12	HULL CITY	L 0-2		18,205
Sep 15	Huddersfield Town	D 0-0		9,085
Sep 19	Middlesbrough	L 0-2		12,051
Sep 26	MANCHESTER CITY	W 2-0	De Mange, Snodin	25,358
Sep 30	STOKE CITY	D 0-0		17,208
Oct 3	Blackburn Rovers	D 1-1	Taylor	7,675
Oct 10	ASTON VILLA	L 1-3	Taylor	20,741
Oct 17	Plymouth Argyle	L 3-6	Taylor, Snodin 2	9,358
Oct 20	Oldham Athletic	D 1-1	Swan	6,312
Oct 24	BOURNEMOUTH	W 3-2	Taylor, Swan, Rennie	15,253
Oct 31	Sheffield United	D 2-2	Snodin, Swan	12,095
Nov 7	SHREWSBURY TOWN	W 2-1	Stiles, Taylor	13,760
Nov 14	Millwall	L 1-3	McLeary o.g.	8,014
Nov 21	SWINDON TOWN	W 4-2	Rennie, Taylor, Davison, Haddock	15,457
Nov 28	Crystal Palace	L 0-3		8,749
Dec 5	BIRMINGHAM CITY	W 4-1	Sheridan, Davison, Swan, Taylor	15,977
Dec 12	Reading	W 1-0	Sheridan (pen)	6,505
Dec 19	HUDDERSFIELD TOWN	W 3-0	Sheridan 2, Davison	20,111
Dec 26	Manchester City	W 2-1	Redmond o.g., Batty	30,153
Dec 28	MIDDLESBROUGH	W 2-0	Davison, Swan	33,606
Jan 1	BRADFORD CITY	W 2-0	Williams G, Snodin	36,004
Jan 3	Hull City	L 1-3	Swan	14,694
Jan 16	BARNSLEY	L 0-2		19,028
Jan 30	West Bromwich Albion	W 4-1	Sheridan, Williams G, Pearson, Davison	9,008
Feb 6	IPSWICH TOWN	W 1-0	Pearson	19,564
Feb 13	Leicester City	L 2-3	Williams G, Sheridan (pen)	11,937
Feb 23	Stoke City	L 1-2	Pearson	10,129
Feb 27	BLACKBURN ROVERS	D 2-2	Sheridan, Snodin	23,843
Mar 5	PLYMOUTH ARGYLE	W 1-0	Baird	18,115
Mar 12	Aston Villa	W 2-1	Swan, Taylor	19,677
Mar 19	SHEFFIELD UNITED	W 5-0	Swan, Pearson 3, Sheridan	22,376
Mar 26	Bournemouth	D 0-0		9,147
Apr 2	Shrewsbury Town	L 0-1		7,369
Apr 6	MILLWALL	L 1-2	Sheridan (pen)	24,241
Apr 23	OLDHAM ATHLETIC	D 1-1	Snodin	13,442
Apr 30	Swindon Town	W 2-1	Baird 2	8,229
May 2	CRYSTAL PALACE	W 1-0	Sheridan (pen)	13,217
May 6	Birmingham City	D 0-0		6,024

FA Cup

Jan 9	ASTON VILLA	(Rd 3)	L 1-2	Davison	29,002

Littlewoods Cup

Sep 23	YORK CITY	(Rd 2/FL)	D 1-1	Snodin	11,527
Oct 6	York City	(Rd 2/SL)	W 4-0	Sheridan 2, Taylor, Mumby	5,996
Oct 28	OLDHAM ATHLETIC	(Rd 3)	D 2-2	Swan 2	15,600
Nov 4	Oldham Athletic*	(R)	L 2-4	Snodin, Taylor	7,058

*Result after extra time.

Simod Cup

Nov 25	SHEFFIELD UNITED	(Rd 1)	W 3-0	Taylor, Noteman, Rennie	4,425
Dec 8	Millwall	(Rd 2)	L 0-2		5,034

Fact File

18-year-old David Batty made his debut against Swindon in November. Shortly after, Leeds began a run of six successive victories.

MANAGER: Billy Bremner

CAPTAIN: Mark Aizlewood//Jack Ashurst

TOP SCORER: John Sheridan

BIGGEST WIN: 5-0 v Sheffield United, 19 March 1988, League

HIGHEST ATTENDANCE: 36,004 v Bradford City, 1 January 1988, won 2-0, League

MAJOR TRANSFERS IN: Glynn Snodin from Sheffield Wednesday, Gary Williams from Aston Villa, Bobby Davison from Derby County

League & Cup Appearances (substitute)

PLAYER	LEAGUE	CUP COMPETITION			TOTAL
		FA CUP	LITTLEWOODS	OTHER	
Adams	40	1	3	1	45
Aizlewood	16 (1)				16 (1)
Ashurst	41	1	4	2	48
Aspin	25 (1)	1	2	1	29 (1)
Baird	10				10
Batty	22 (1)	1			25 (1)
Brockie	2				2
Buckley	0 (1)				0 (1)
Davison	15 (1)	1		2	18 (1)
Day	44	1	4	2	51
De Mange	14 (1)		3	2	19 (1)
Doig	1 (1)		1 (2)		2 (3)
Edwards	4 (4)				4 (4)
Grayson	2			1	3
Haddock	38 (2)	1	3	2	44 (2)
Maguire	2				2
McDonald	1	1			2
Melrose	3 (1)	0 (1)	0 (1)		3 (3)
Mumby	3 (2)		0 (2)		3 (4)
Noteman	0 (1)			1	1 (1)
Pearson	21 (7)		2	0 (1)	23 (8)
Rennie	25 (3)		2	1	28 (3)
Sheridan	36 (2)	1	4	1	42 (2)
Snodin	33 (2)	1	4	1	39 (2)
Stiles	7 (6)		2 (2)	0 (1)	9 (9)
Swan	21 (4)		2	1	24 (4)
Taylor	27 (5)	1	4	2	34 (5)
Williams G	31	1	3		35

Goalscorers

PLAYER	LEAGUE	CUP COMPETITION			TOTAL
		FA CUP	LITTLEWOODS	OTHER	
Sheridan	12		2		14
Taylor	9		2	1	12
Swan	8		2		10
Snodin	7		2		9
Pearson	6				6
Davison	5	1			6
Baird	3				3
Williams G	3				3
Rennie	2				2
Batty	1				1
De Mange	1				1
Haddock	1				1
Stiles	1				1
Mumby			1		1
Noteman				1	1
Rennie				1	1
Opps' o.gs.	2				2

Final Division 2 Table

		P	W	D	L	F	A	Pts
1	MILLWALL	44	25	7	12	72	52	82
2	ASTON VILLA	44	22	12	10	68	41	78
3	MIDDLESBROUGH	44	22	12	10	63	36	78
4	BRADFORD C	44	22	11	11	74	54	77
5	BLACKBURN R	44	21	14	9	68	52	77
6	CRYSTAL PALACE	44	22	9	13	86	59	75
7	LEEDS UNITED	44	19	12	13	61	51	69
8	IPSWICH T	44	19	9	16	61	52	66
9	MANCHESTER C	44	19	8	17	80	60	65
10	OLDHAM ATH	44	18	11	15	72	64	65
11	STOKE C	44	17	11	16	50	57	62
12	SWINDON T	44	16	11	17	73	60	59
13	LEICESTER C	44	16	11	17	62	61	59
14	BARNSLEY	44	15	12	17	61	62	57
15	HULL C	44	14	15	15	54	60	57
16	PLYMOUTH ARG	44	16	8	20	65	67	56
17	BOURNEMOUTH	44	13	10	21	56	68	49
18	SHREWSBURY T	44	11	16	17	42	54	49
19	BIRMINGHAM C	44	11	15	18	41	66	48
20	WBA	44	12	11	21	50	69	47
21	SHEFFIELD U	44	13	7	24	45	74	46
22	READING	44	10	12	22	44	70	42
23	HUDDERSFIELD T	44	6	10	28	41	100	2

Season 1988-89

Football League Division 2

DATE	OPPONENTS	SCORE	GOALSCORERS	ATTENDANCE
Aug 27	OXFORD UNITED	D 1-1	Snodin	20,697
Sep 3	Portsmouth	L 0-4		15,263
Sep 10	MANCHESTER CITY	D 1-1	Blake	23,122
Sep 17	Bournemouth	D 0-0		7,922
Sep 21	BARNSLEY	W 2-0	Davison, Hilaire	17,390
Sep 24	CHELSEA	L 0-2		26,080
Oct 1	Brighton & Hove Albion	L 1-2	Baird	7,109
Oct 3	Sunderland	L 1-2	Davison	12,671
Oct 8	WATFORD	L 0-1		15,657
Oct 16	Swindon Town	D 0-0		9234
Oct 22	LEICESTER CITY	D 1-1	Hilaire	17,263
Oct 26	Bradford City	D 1-1	Davison	13,048
Oct 29	HULL CITY	W 2-1	Sheridan, Baird	17,536
Nov 5	Ipswich Town	W 1-0	Sheridan (pen)	11,755
Nov 12	WEST BROMWICH ALBION	W 2-1	Aizlewood, Baird	20,442
Nov 19	Oldham Athletic	D 2-2	Davison 2	8,824
Nov 22	Birmingham City	D 0-0		6,168
Nov 26	STOKE CITY	W 4-0	Baird 2, Davison, Sheridan (pen)	19,933
Dec 3	Walsall	W 3-0	Davison 2, Whitlow	6,885
Dec 10	SHREWSBURY TOWN	L 2-3	Sheridan (pen), Davison	19,967
Dec 17	Crystal Palace	D 0-0		9,847
Dec 26	BLACKBURN ROVERS	W 2-0	Baird, Davison	31,622
Dec 31	PLYMOUTH ARGYLE	W 2-0	Baird, Snodin	24,043
Jan 2	Manchester City	D 0-0		33,034
Jan 14	BIRMINGHAM CITY	W 1-0	Hilaire	21,837
Jan 21	Oxford United	L 2-3	Blake, Hilaire	7,926
Feb 4	SUNDERLAND	W 2-0	Davison, Sheridan (pen)	31,985
Feb 11	Watford	D 1-1	Pearson	13,439
Feb 18	Leicester City	W 2-1	Davison, Snodin	14,151
Feb 25	SWINDON TOWN	D 0-0		22,651
Mar 1	BRADFORD CITY	D 3-3	Blake, Hilaire, Baird	33,325
Mar 5	West Bromwich Albion	L 1-2	Adams	15,964
Mar 11	IPSWICH TOWN	L 2-4	Hilaire, Blake	19,639
Mar 14	Hull City	W 2-1	Baird, Davison	8,887
Mar 19	Barnsley	D 2-2	Aizlewood, Sheridan (pen)	11,578
Mar 25	PORTSMOUTH	W 1-0	Baird	27,049
Mar 27	Blackburn Rovers	L 0-2		11,533
Apr 1	BOURNEMOUTH	W 3-0	Shutt 3	21,095
Apr 5	CRYSTAL PALACE	L 1-2	Shutt	25,604
Apr 9	Plymouth Argyle	L 0-1		9,365
Apr 15	BRIGHTON & HOVE ALBION	W 1-0	Williams G	14,915
Apr 22	Chelsea	L 0-1		30,337
Apr 29	Stoke City	W 3-2	Sheridan (pen), Davison, Strachan	9,051
May 1	WALSALL	W 1-0	Aizlewood	13,280
May 6	OLDHAM ATHLETIC	D 0-0		14,459
May 13	Shrewsbury Town	D 3-3	Strachan 2 (1 pen), Rennie	4,693

FA Cup

Jan 6	Brighton & Hove Albion	(Rd 3) W 2-1	Baird 2	10,900
Jan 28	Nottingham Forest	(Rd 4) L 0-2		28,107

Littlewoods Cup

Sep 27	Peterborough United	(Rd 2/FL) W 2-1	Snodin, Baird	4,979
Oct 12	PETERBOROUGH UNITED	(Rd 2/SL) W 3-1	Davison, Hilaire, Sheridan (pen)	8,894
Nov 2	LUTON TOWN	(Rd 3) L 0-2		19,447

Simod Cup

Nov 9	SHREWSBURY TOWN	(Rd 1) W 3-1	Aizlewood, Davison 2	3,220
Nov 29	Millwall	(Rd 2) L 0-2		4,242

MANAGER: Billy Bremner (until September)/Howard Wilkinson

CAPTAIN: Mark Aizlewood

TOP SCORER: Bobby Davison

BIGGEST WIN: 4-0 v Stoke City, 26 November 1988, League

HIGHEST ATTENDANCE: 33,325 v Bradford City, 4 April 1989, drew 3-3, League

MAJOR TRANSFERS IN: Gordon Strachan from Manchester United, Carl Shutt from Bristol City, Noel Blake and Vince Hilaire from Portsmouth, Mike Whitlow from Whitton Albion, Chris Fairclough from Tottenham, Andy Williams from Rotherham

League & Cup Appearances (substitute)

PLAYER	LEAGUE	CUP COMPETITION			TOTAL
		FA CUP	LITTLEWOODS	OTHER	
Adams	15 (1)	1	1		17 (1)
Aizlewood	34 (4)	1	3	2	40 (4)
Andrews	1				1
Ashurst	6 (1)				6 (1)
Aspin	31 (2)	2	2	2	37 (2)
Baird	43	2	3	2	50
Batty	25 (3)	1	3	1	30 (3)
Blake	44	2	3	2	51
Davison	37 (2)	1	2 (1)	2	42 (3)
Day	45	2	3	2	52
Fairclough	11				11
Haddock	8 (4)		0 (1)	0	8 (4)
Hilaire	42	2	3	2	49
Kerr	1 (2)				1 (2)
Mumby	0 (1)				0 (1)
Ormsby	1				1
Pearson	6 (27)		1 (2)	0 (1)	7 (30)
Rennie	30 (3)	2	3	2	37 (3)
Sheridan	38 (2)	2	2	2	44 (2)
Shutt	3				3
Snodin	33 (2)	2	3	1	39 (2)
Speed	1				1
Stiles	6 (4)		0 (2)		6 (6)
Strachan	11				11
Swan	1	1			2
Taylor	2 (4)				2 (4)
Whitlow	18 (2)			2	20 (2)
Williams A	7	1			8
Williams G	8	0 (1)	0		9 (1)

Goalscorers

PLAYER	LEAGUE	CUP COMPETITION			TOTAL
		FA CUP	LITTLEWOODS	OTHER	
Davison	14		1	2	17
Baird	10	2	1		13
Sheridan	7		1		8
Hilaire	6		1		7
Aizlewood	3			1	4
Blake	4				4
Shutt	4				4
Snodin	3		1		4
Strachan	3				3
Adams	1				1
Pearson	1				1
Rennie	1				1
Whitlow	1				1
Williams G	1				1

Fact File

Don Revie, Leeds United's greatest manager, died in May 1989.

Final Division 2 Table

		P	W	D	L	F	A	Pts
1	CHELSEA	46	29	12	5	96	50	99
2	MANCHESTER C	46	23	13	10	77	53	82
3	CRYSTAL PALACE	46	23	12	11	71	49	81
4	WATFORD	46	22	12	12	74	48	78
5	BLACKBURN R	46	22	11	13	74	59	77
6	SWINDON T	46	20	16	10	68	53	76
7	BARNSLEY	46	20	14	12	66	58	74
8	IPSWICH T	46	22	7	17	71	61	73
9	WBA	46	18	18	10	65	41	72
10	LEEDS UNITED	46	17	16	13	59	50	67
11	SUNDERLAND	46	16	15	15	60	60	63
12	BOURNEMOUTH	46	18	8	20	53	62	62
13	STOKE C	46	15	14	17	57	72	59
14	BRADFORD C	46	13	17	16	52	59	56
15	LEICESTER C	46	13	16	17	56	63	55
16	OLDHAM ATH	46	11	21	14	75	72	54
17	OXFORD U	46	14	12	20	62	70	54
18	PLYMOUTH ARG	46	14	12	20	55	66	54
19	BRIGHTON & HA	46	14	9	23	57	66	51
20	PORTSMOUTH	46	13	12	21	53	62	51
21	HULL C	46	11	14	21	52	68	47
22	SHREWSBURY T	46	8	18	20	40	67	42
23	BIRMINGHAM C	46	8	11	27	31	76	35
24	WALSALL	46	5	16	25	41	80	31

Season 1989-90

Football League Division 2

DATE	OPPONENTS	SCORE	GOALSCORERS	ATTENDANCE
Aug 19	Newcastle United	L 2-5	Davison, Baird	24,482
Aug 23	MIDDLESBROUGH	W 2-1	Davison, Parkinson o.g.	25,004
Aug 26	BLACKBURN ROVERS	D 1-1	Fairclough	25,045
Sep 2	Stoke City	D 1-1	Strachan	14,570
Sep 9	IPSWICH TOWN	D 1-1	Jones	22,972
Sep 16	Hull City	W 1-0	Davison	11,620
Sep 23	SWINDON TOWN	W 4-0	Strachan 3 (1 pen), Davison	21,694
Sep 27	OXFORD UNITED	W 2-1	Davison, Sterland	24,097
Sep 30	Port Vale	D 0-0		11,156
Oct 7	West Ham United	W 1-0	Jones	23,539
Oct 14	SUNDERLAND	W 2-0	Davison, Fairclough	27,815
Oct 17	Portsmouth	D 3-3	Davison, Whitlow, Sterland	9,000
Oct 21	WOLVERHAMPTON W	W 1-0	Davison	28,204
Oct 28	Bradford City	W 1-0	Davison	12,527
Nov 1	PLYMOUTH ARGYLE	W 2-1	Strachan (pen), Davison	26,791
Nov 4	BOURNEMOUTH	W 3-0	Baird, Strachan, Fairclough	26,484
Nov 11	Leicester City	L 3-4	Baird, Williams A, Strachan (pen)	18,032
Nov 18	WATFORD	W 2-1	Fairclough, Williams A	26,921
Nov 25	West Bromwich Albion	L 1-2	Fairclough	15,116
Dec 2	NEWCASTLE UNITED	W 1-0	Baird	31,715
Dec 9	Middlesbrough	W 2-0	Shutt, Fairclough	19,686
Dec 16	BRIGHTON & HOVE ALBION	W 3-0	Strachan, Hendrie, Jones	24,070
Dec 26	Sheffield United	D 2-2	Sterland, Shutt	31,602
Dec 30	Barnsley	L 0-1		14,841
Jan 1	OLDHAM ATHLETIC	D 1-1	Hendrie	30,217
Jan 13	Blackburn Rovers	W 2-1	Chapman, Strachan	14,485
Jan 20	STOKE CITY	W 2-0	Strachan (pen), Hendrie	29,313
Feb 4	Swindon Town	L 2-3	Strachan (pen), Hendrie	16,208
Feb 10	HULL CITY	W 4-3	Hendrie, Jones, Varadi, Strachan	29,997
Feb 17	Ipswich Town	D 2-2	Chapman 2	17,102
Feb 24	WEST BROMWICH ALBION	D 2-2	Kamara, Chapman	30,004
Mar 3	Watford	L 0-1		13,468
Mar 7	PORT VALE	D 0-0		28,756
Mar 10	Oxford United	W 4-2	Chapman 2, Varadi, Fairclough	8,397
Mar 17	WEST HAM UNITED	W 3-2	Chapman 2, Strachan	32,536
Mar 20	Sunderland	W 1-0	Sterland	17,851
Mar 24	PORTSMOUTH	W 2-0	Jones, Chapman	27,600
Mar 31	Wolverhampton W	L 0-1		22,419
Apr 8	BRADFORD CITY	D 1-1	Speed	32,316
Apr 10	Plymouth Argyle	D 1-1	Chapman	11,382
Apr 13	Oldham Athletic	L 1-3	Davison	16,292
Apr 16	SHEFFIELD UNITED	W 4-0	Strachan 2, Chapman, Speed	32,727
Apr 21	Brighton & Hove Albion	D 2-2	Speed, Chapman o.g.	11,359
Apr 25	BARNSLEY	L 1-2	Fairclough	31,700
Apr 28	LEICESTER CITY	W 2-1	Sterland, Strachan	32,597
May 5	Bournemouth	W 1-0	Chapman	9,918

FA Cup

Jan 6	IPSWICH TOWN	(Rd 3) L 0-1		26,768

Littlewoods Cup

Sep 19	Oldham Athletic	(Rd 2/FL) L 1-2	Strachan	8,415
Oct 3	OLDHAM ATHLETIC	(Rd 2/SL) L 1-2	Fairclough	18,092

Zenith Data Systems Cup

Nov 7	BLACKBURN ROVERS	(Rd 1) W 1-0	Davison	5,070
Nov 28	Barnsley	(Rd 2) W 2-1	Strachan (pen), Williams A	6,136
Dec 19	Stoke City*	(Rd 3) D 2-2	Shutt 2	5,792
Jan 17	Aston Villa	(SF/N) L 0-2		17,543

*Won 5-4 on pens.

MANAGER: Howard Wilkinson **CAPTAIN:** Gordon Strachan

TOP SCORER: Gordon Strachan **BIGGEST WIN:** 4-0 v Swindon Town, 23 September 1989, League; 4-0 v Sheffield United, 4 April 1990, League

HIGHEST ATTENDANCE: 32,727 v Sheffield United, 16 April 1990, won 4-0, League

MAJOR TRANSFERS IN: Mel Sterland from Sheffield Wednesday, John Hendrie from Newcastle United, John McClelland from Watford, Vinnie Jones from Wimbledon, Lee Chapman from Nottingham Forest

MAJOR TRANSFERS OUT: John Sheridan to Nottingham Forest, Neil Aspin to Port Vale, Mark Aizlewood to Bradford City

---

League & Cup Appearances (substitute)

PLAYER	LEAGUE	CUP COMPETITION			TOTAL
		FA CUP	LITTLEWOODS	OTHER	
Baird	23 (1)	1	2	4	30 (1)
Batty	39 (3)	1	2	4	46 (3)
Beglin	18 (1)			1	19 (1)
Blake	7		1 (1)	2	10 (1)
Chapman	21				21
Davison	25 (4)		2	2	29 (4)
Day	44	1	2	3	50
Fairclough	42	1	1 (1)	3	47 (1)
Haddock	40	1	2	4	47
Hendrie	22 (5)	1	1	2	26 (5)
Hilaire	0 (2)				0 (2)
Jones	43 (2)	1	2	4	50 (2)
Kamara	10 (1)				10 (1)
Kerr	2 (3)	1		0 (3)	3 (6)
McClelland	3 (1)				3 (1)
O'Donnell	0 (1)				0 (1)
Pearson	2 (5)	0 (1)		1 (1)	3 (7)
Shutt	6 (14)	1		0 (1)	7 (15)
Snodin	3 (1)	0 (1)			3 (2)
Speed	12 (13)		0 (1)	0 (1)	12 (15)
Sterland	41 (1)	1	2	3	47 (1)
Strachan	46	1	2	4	53
Thomas	3				3
Turner	2				2
Varadi	12 (1)				12 (1)
Whitlow	27 (2)		2	4	33 (2)
Williams	13 (3)		1 (1)	2	16 (4)

Goalscorers

PLAYER	LEAGUE	CUP COMPETITION			TOTAL
		FA CUP	LITTLEWOODS	OTHER	
Strachan	16		1	1	18
Chapman	12				12
Davison	11			1	12
Fairclough	8		1		9
Hendrie	5				5
Jones	5				5
Sterland	5				5
Baird	4				4
Shutt	2			2	4
Speed	3				3
Williams A	2		1		3
Varadi	2				2
Kamara	1				1
Whitlow	1				1
Opps' o.gs.	2				2

Fact File

Leeds went to Bournemouth for the last game of the season needing a victory for promotion and the Championship.

Final Division 2 Table

		P	W	D	L	F	A	Pts
1	LEEDS UNITED	46	24	13	9	79	52	85
2	SHEFFIELD U	46	24	13	9	78	58	85
3	NEWCASTLE U	46	22	14	10	80	55	80
4	SWINDON T	46	20	14	12	79	59	74
5	BLACKBURN R	46	19	17	10	74	59	74
6	SUNDERLAND	46	20	14	12	70	64	74
7	WEST HAM U	46	20	12	14	80	57	72
8	OLDHAM ATH	46	19	14	13	70	57	71
9	IPSWICH T	46	19	12	15	67	66	69
10	WOLVERHAMPTON W	46	18	13	15	67	60	67
11	PORT VALE	46	15	16	15	62	57	61
12	PORTSMOUTH	46	15	16	15	62	65	61
13	LEICESTER C	46	15	14	17	67	79	59
14	HULL C	46	14	16	16	58	65	58
15	WATFORD	46	14	15	17	58	60	57
16	PLYMOUTH ARG	46	14	13	19	58	63	55
17	OXFORD U	46	15	9	22	57	66	54
18	BRIGHTON & HA	46	15	9	22	56	72	54
19	BARNSLEY	46	13	15	18	49	71	54
20	WBA	46	12	15	19	67	71	51
21	MIDDLESBROUGH	46	13	11	22	52	63	50
22	BOURNEMOUTH	46	12	12	22	57	76	48
23	BRADFORD C	46	9	14	23	44	68	41
24	STOKE C	46	6	19	21	35	63	37

Season 1990-91

Football League Division 1

DATE	OPPONENTS	SCORE	GOALSCORERS	ATTENDANCE
Aug 25	Everton	W 3-2	Fairclough, Speed, Varadi	34,412
Aug 28	MANCHESTER UNITED	D 0-0		29,728
Sep 1	NORWICH CITY	W 3-0	Chapman 2, Varadi	25,802
Sep 8	Luton Town	L 0-1		10,185
Sep 15	TOTTENHAM HOTSPUR	L 0-2		30,602
Sep 23	Sheffield United	W 2-0	Pearson, Strachan	26,078
Sep 29	ARSENAL	D 2-2	Chapman, Strachan (pen)	29,885
Oct 6	Crystal Palace	D 1-1	Speed	21,676
Oct 20	QUEENS PARK RANGERS	L 2-3	Chapman, Whyte	27,443
Oct 27	Aston Villa	D 0-0		24,219
Nov 3	NOTTINGHAM FOREST	W 3-1	Chapman, Strachan, McAllister	30,733
Nov 11	Manchester City	W 3-2	Chapman, Shutt, Strachan	27,782
Nov 17	DERBY COUNTY	W 3-0	Chapman, Strachan, Speed	27,868
Nov 24	Coventry City	D 1-1	Chapman	16,183
Dec 1	SOUTHAMPTON	W 2-1	Fairclough, Shutt	29,341
Dec 8	Manchester United	D 1-1	Sterland	40,927
Dec 16	EVERTON	W 2-0	Strachan (pen), Shutt	27,775
Dec 23	Sunderland	W 1-0	Sterland	23,773
Dec 26	CHELSEA	W 4-1	Sterland, Chapman 2, Whitlow	30,893
Dec 29	WIMBLEDON	W 3-0	Chapman, Speed, Sterland	29,292
Jan 1	Liverpool	L 0-3		36,975
Jan 12	Norwich City	L 0-2		17,786
Jan 19	LUTON TOWN	W 2-1	Strachan (pen), Fairclough	27,160
Feb 2	Tottenham Hotspur	D 0-0		32,253
Mar 2	Southampton	L 0-2		16,585
Mar 9	COVENTRY CITY	W 2-0	Davison, Whyte	28,880
Mar 17	Arsenal	L 0-2		26,218
Mar 23	CRYSTAL PALACE	L 1-2	Speed	28,556
Mar 30	Chelsea	W 2-1	Shutt, Fairclough	17,585
Apr 2	SUNDERLAND	W 5-0	Chapman 2, Speed 2, Shutt	28,132
Apr 6	Wimbledon	W 1-0	Chapman	6,805
Apr 10	MANCHESTER CITY	L 1-2	McAllister	28,757
Apr 13	LIVERPOOL	L 4-5	Chapman 3, Shutt	31,460
Apr 17	Queens Park Rangers	L 0-2		10,998
Apr 23	Derby County	W 1-0	Shutt	12,666
May 4	ASTON VILLA	W 5-2	Price o.g., Chapman 2, Whyte, Shutt	29,188
May 8	SHEFFIELD UNITED	W 2-1	Sterland, Shutt	28,978
May 11	Nottingham Forest	L 3-4	Chapman 2, Shutt	25,067

FA Cup

Jan 5	Barnsley	(Rd 3) D 1-1	Sterland	22,424
Jan 8	BARNSLEY	(R) W 4-0	Smith o.g., Chapman, McAllister, Strachan	21,377
Jan 27	Arsenal	(Rd 4) D 0-0		30,905
Jan 30	ARSENAL*	(R) D 1-1	Chapman	27,753
Feb 13	Arsenal*	(2nd R) D 0-0		34,050
Feb 16	ARSENAL	(3rd R) L 1-2	Chapman	27,190

*Results after extra time.

Rumbelows Cup

Sep 26	Leicester City	(Rd 2/FL) L 0-1		13,774
Oct 10	LEICESTER CITY	(Rd 2/SL) W 3-0	Walsh o.g., Speed, Strachan	19,090
Oct 31	OLDHAM ATHLETIC	(Rd 3) W 2-0	Chapman, Speed	26,327
Nov 27	Queens Park Rangers	(Rd 4) W 3-0	McAllister, Fairclough, Chapman	15,832
Jan 16	ASTON VILLA	(Rd 5) W 4-1	Chapman 2, McAllister, Speed	28,176
Feb 10	Manchester United	(SF/FL) L 1-2	Whyte	34,050
Feb 24	MANCHESTER UNITED	(SF/SL) L 0-1		32,014

Zenith Data Systems Cup

Dec 19	Wolverhampton W	(Rd 2) W 2-1	Varadi, McAllister	11,080
Jan 22	DERBY COUNTY	(Rd 3) W 2-1	Shutt, Chapman	6,334
Feb 20	MANCHESTER CITY	(SF/N) W 2-0	Williams A, Strachan	11,898
Mar 19	EVERTON	(F/N) D 3-3	Sterland, Chapman 2	13,387
Mar 21	Everton	(R) L 1-3	Sterland	12,603

MANAGER: Howard Wilkinson

CAPTAIN: Gordon Strachan

TOP SCORER: Lee Chapman

BIGGEST WIN: 5-0 v Sunderland, 2 April 1990, League

HIGHEST ATTENDANCE: 40,927 v Manchester United, 8 December 1990, drew 1-1, League

League & Cup Appearances (substitute)

PLAYER	LEAGUE	CUP COMPETITION			TOTAL
		FA CUP	RUMBELOWS	OTHER	
Batty	37	6	6	4	53
Beglin				1	1
Chapman	38	6	7	4	55
Davison	2 (3)	0 (2)		1 (1)	3 (6)
Day		1	1		2
Fairclough	34	6	7	4	51
Haddock	10 (5)	3	4 (1)	2	19 (6)
Jones	1				1
Kamara	5 (2)		1 (1)		6 (3)
Kerr				0 (1)	0 (1)
Lukic	38	6	6	4	54
McAllister	38	6	7	4	55
McClelland	3	2			5
Pearson	4 (9)	1	2 (3)	1	8 (12)
Shutt	25 (3)	5	3 (1)	3 (1)	36 (5)
Snodin	14 (6)	2	2 (1)	2	20 (7)
Speed	35 (3)	6	7	3 (2)	51 (5)
Sterland	38	6	6	5	55
Strachan	34	6	7	5	52
Varadi	5 (1)		1	1 (1)	7 (2)
Whitlow	14 (4)	1 (3)	2 (1)	3	20 (8)
Whyte	38	4	7	4	53
Williams A	5 (7)		1 (1)	3 (2)	9 (10)

Goalscorers

PLAYER	LEAGUE	CUP COMPETITION			TOTAL
		FA CUP	RUMBELOWS	OTHER	
Chapman	21	3	4	3	31
Shutt	10			1	11
Speed	7		3		10
Strachan	7	1	1	1	10
Sterland	5	1		2	8
McAllister	2	1	2	1	6
Fairclough	4		1		5
Whyte	3		1		4
Varadi	2			1	3
Davison	1				1
Pearson	1				1
Whitlow	1				1
Williams A			1		1
Opps' o.gs.	1	1	1		3

Fact File

Leeds' 4-5 defeat by Liverpool in April was one of the great games of the season. From 0-4 down, a Lee Chapman hat-trick inspired a magnificent comeback and only a disallowed equaliser stopped him notching a fourth goal.

Final Division 1 Table

		P	W	D	L	F	A	Pts
1	ARSENAL	38	24	13	1	74	18	83
2	LIVERPOOL	38	23	7	8	77	40	76
3	CRYSTAL PALACE	38	20	9	9	50	41	69
4	LEEDS UNITED	38	19	7	12	65	47	64
5	MANCHESTER C	38	17	11	10	64	53	62
6	MANCHESTER U	38	16	12	10	58	45	59
7	WIMBLEDON	38	14	14	10	53	46	56
8	NOTTINGHAM F	38	14	12	12	65	50	54
9	EVERTON	38	13	12	13	50	46	51
10	TOTTENHAM H	38	11	16	11	51	50	49
11	CHELSEA	38	13	10	15	58	69	49
12	QPR	38	12	10	16	44	53	46
13	SHEFFIELD U	38	13	7	18	36	55	46
14	SOUTHAMPTON	38	12	9	17	58	69	45
15	NORWICH C	38	13	6	19	41	64	45
16	COVENTRY C	38	11	11	16	42	49	44
17	ASTON VILLA	38	9	14	15	46	58	41
18	LUTON T	38	10	7	21	42	61	37
19	SUNDERLAND	38	8	10	20	38	60	34
20	DERBY CO	38	5	9	24	37	75	24

ARSENAL HAD TWO POINTS DEDUCTED, MANCHESTER UNITED HAD ONE POINT DEDUCTED BOTH FOR DISIPLINARY REASONS.

Season 1991-92

Football League Division 1

DATE	OPPONENTS	SCORE	GOALSCORERS	ATTENDANCE
Aug 20	NOTTINGHAM FOREST	W 1-0	McAllister	29,457
Aug 24	SHEFFIELD WEDNESDAY	D 1-1	Hodge	30,260
Aug 28	Southampton	W 4-0	Speed 2, Strachan (2 pens)	15,862
Aug 31	Manchester United	D 1-1	Chapman	43,778
Sep 3	ARSENAL	D 2-2	Strachan (pen), Chapman	29,396
Sep 7	MANCHESTER CITY	W 3-0	Dorigo, Batty, Strachan (pen)	29,986
Sep 14	Chelsea	W 1-0	Shutt	23,439
Sep 18	Coventry City	D 0-0		15,488
Sep 21	LIVERPOOL	W 1-0	Hodge	32,917
Sep 28	Norwich City	D 2-2	Dorigo, Speed	15,828
Oct 1	Crystal Palace	L 0-1		18,250
Oct 5	SHEFFIELD UNITED	W 4-3	Hodge 2, Sterland 2	28,362
Oct 19	Notts County	W 4-2	Chapman, Hodge, Whyte, McAllister	12,964
Oct 26	OLDHAM ATHLETIC	W 1-0	Kilkline o.g.	28,109
Nov 2	Wimbledon	D 0-0		7,025
Nov 16	QUEENS PARK RANGERS	W 2-0	Sterland, Wallace	27,087
Nov 24	Aston Villa	W 4-1	Wallace, Sterland, Chapman 2	23,713
Nov 30	EVERTON	W 1-0	Wallace	30,043
Dec 7	Luton Town	W 2-0	Wallace, Speed	11,550
Dec 14	TOTTENHAM HOTSPUR	D 1-1	Speed	31,404
Dec 22	Nottingham Forest	D 0-0		27,170
Dec 26	SOUTHAMPTON	D 3-3	Hodge 2, Speed	29,052
Dec 29	MANCHESTER UNITED	D 1-1	Sterland (pen)	32,638
Jan 1	West Ham United	W 3-1	Chapman 2, McAllister	21,766
Jan 12	Sheffield Wednesday	W 6-1	Chapman 3, Dorigo, Whitlow, Wallace	32,228
Jan 18	CRYSTAL PALACE	D 1-1	Fairclough	27,717
Feb 1	NOTTS COUNTY	W 3-0	Sterland, Batty, Wallace	27,224
Feb 8	Oldham Athletic	L 0-2		18,409
Feb 23	Everton	D 1-1	Shutt	19,248
Feb 29	LUTON TOWN	W 2-0	Cantona, Chapman	28,231
Mar 3	ASTON VILLA	D 0-0		28,886
Mar 7	Tottenham Hotspur	W 3-1	Wallace, Newsome, McAllister	27,622
Mar 11	Queens Park Rangers	L 1-4	Speed	14,641
Mar 14	WIMBLEDON	W 5-1	Wallace, Chapman 3, Cantona	26,760
Mar 22	Arsenal	D 1-1	Chapman	27,844
Mar 28	WEST HAM UNITED	D 0-0		31,101
Apr 4	Manchester City	L 0-4		30,239
Apr 11	CHELSEA	W 3-0	Wallace, Chapman, Cantona	31,363
Apr 18	Liverpool	D 0-0		37,186
Apr 20	COVENTRY CITY	W 2-0	Fairclough, McAllister (pen)	26,582
Apr 26	Sheffield United	W 3-2	Wallace, Newsome, Gayle o.g.	31,082
May 2	NORWICH CITY	W 1-0	Wallace	32,673

FA Cup

Jan 15	Manchester United	(Rd 3) L 0-1		31,819

Rumbelows Cup

Sep 24	Scunthorpe United	(Rd 2/FL) D 0-0		8,392
Oct 8	SCUNTHORPE UNITED	(Rd 2/SL) W 3-0	Sterland, Chapman, Speed	14,558
Oct 29	TRANMERE ROVERS	(Rd 3) W 3-1	Chapman 2, Shutt	18,265
Dec 4	Everton	(Rd 4) W 4-1	Speed, Chapman, Wallace 2	25,467
Jan 8	MANCHESTER UNITED	(Rd 5) L 1-3	Speed	28,886

Zenith Data Systems Cup

Oct 22	Nottingham Forest	(Rd 1) L 1-3	Wallace	6,145

MANAGER: Howard Wilkinson

CAPTAIN: Gordon Strachan

TOP SCORER: Lee Chapman

BIGGEST WIN: 6-1 v Sheffield Wednesday, 12 January 1992, League

HIGHEST ATTENDANCE: 43,778 v Manchester United, 31 August 1991, drew 1-1, League

MAJOR TRANSFERS IN: Ray Wallace and Rod Wallace from Southampton, Steve Hodge from Nottingham Forest, Eric Cantona from Nimes, Tony Dorigo from Chelsea, Jon Newsome and David Wetherall from Sheffield Wednesday

---

League & Cup Appearances (substitute)

PLAYER	LEAGUE	CUP COMPETITION			TOTAL
		FA CUP	RUMBELOWS	OTHER	
Agana	1 (1)				1 (1)
Batty	40		4	1	45
Cantona	6 (9)				6 (9)
Chapman	38	1	5		44
Davison	0 (2)	0 (1)			0 (3)
Dorigo	38	1	5	1	45
Fairclough	30 (1)	1	3 (1)	1	35 (2)
Grayson				0 (1)	0 (1)
Hodge	12 (11)	1	3 (2)		16 (13)
Kamara	2		0 (1)	1	3 (1)
Kellly	0 (2)		0 (1)		0 (3)
Lukic	42	1	5	1	49
McAllister	41 (1)	1	4		46 (1)
McClelland	16 (2)		2 (1)		18 (3)
Newsome	7 (3)			1	8 (3)
Shutt	6 (9)		2 (1)	1	9 (10)
Snodin				1	1
Speed	41	1	4	1	47
Sterland	29 (2)	1	5	1	36 (2)
Strachan	35 (1)		4		39 (1)
Varadi	2 (1)				2 (1)
Wallace Rod	34	1	3	0 (1)	38 (1)
Wetherall	0 (1)				0 (1)
Whitlow	3 (7)	0 (1)			3 (8)
Whyte	41	1	5	1	48
Williams A	1		0 (1)		1 (1)

Goalscorers

PLAYER	LEAGUE	CUP COMPETITION			TOTAL
		FA CUP	RUMBELOWS	OTHER	
Chapman	16		4		20
Wallace Rod	10		2		12
Speed	7		3		10
Hodge	7				7
Sterland	6		1		7
McAllister	5				5
Strachan	4				4
Cantona	3				3
Dorigo	3				3
Shutt	2		1		3
Batty	2				2
Fairclough	2				2
Newsome	2				2
Williams A	1			1	2
Whitlow	1				1
Whyte	1				1
Opps' o.gs.	2				2

Fact File

Leeds win the Championship three hours after beating Sheffield United, as Manchester United lost their match against Liverpool.

Final Division 1 Table

		P	W	D	L	F	A	Pts
1	LEEDS UNITED	42	22	16	4	74	37	82
2	MANCHESTER U	42	21	15	6	63	33	78
3	SHEFFIELD W	42	21	12	9	62	49	75
4	ARSENAL	42	19	15	8	81	46	72
5	MANCHESTER C	42	20	10	12	61	48	70
6	LIVERPOOL	42	16	16	10	47	40	64
7	ASTON VILLA	42	17	9	16	48	44	60
8	NOTTINGHAM F	42	16	11	15	60	58	59
9	SHEFFIELD U	42	16	9	17	65	63	57
10	CRYSTAL PALACE	42	14	15	13	53	61	57
11	QPR	42	12	18	12	48	47	54
12	EVERTON	42	13	14	15	52	51	53
13	WIMBLEDON	42	13	14	15	53	53	53
14	CHELSEA	42	13	14	15	50	60	53
15	TOTTENHAM H	42	15	7	20	58	63	52
16	SOUTHAMPTON	42	14	10	18	39	55	52
17	OLDHAM ATH	42	14	9	19	63	67	51
18	NORWICH C	42	11	12	19	47	63	45
19	COVENTRY C	42	11	11	20	35	44	44
20	LUTON T	42	10	12	20	38	71	42
21	NOTTS CO	42	10	10	22	40	62	40
22	WEST HAM U	42	9	11	22	37	59	38

Season 1992-93

Premier League

DATE	OPPONENTS	SCORE	GOALSCORERS	ATTENDANCE
Aug 15	WIMBLEDON	W 2-1	Chapman 2	25,795
Aug 19	Aston Villa	D 1-1	Speed	29,151
Aug 22	Middlesbrough	L 1-4	Cantona	18,469
Aug 25	TOTTENHAM HOTSPUR	W 5-0	Wallace, Cantona 3, Chapman	28,218
Aug 29	LIVERPOOL	D 2-2	McAllister, Chapman	29,598
Sep 1	Oldham Athletic	D 2-2	Cantona 2	14,857
Sep 6	Manchester United	L 0-2		31,296
Sep 13	ASTON VILLA	D 1-1	Hodge	27,815
Sep 19	Southampton	D 1-1	Speed	16,229
Sep 26	EVERTON	W 2-0	McAllister (pen), Chapman	27,915
Oct 3	Ipswich Town	L 2-4	Chapman, Speed	21,200
Oct 17	SHEFFIELD UNITED	W 3-1	Chapman, Speed, Whyte	29,706
Oct 24	Queens Park Rangers	L 1-2	Strachan	19,326
Oct 31	COVENTRY CITY	D 2-2	Chapman, Fairclough	28,018
Nov 7	Manchester City	L 0-4		27,225
Nov 21	ARSENAL	W 3-0	Fairclough, Chapman, McAllister	30,516
Nov 29	Chelsea	L 0-1		24,345
Dec 5	NOTTINGHAM FOREST	L 1-4	Speed	29,364
Dec 12	SHEFFIELD WEDNESDAY	W 3-1	Speed, Chapman, Varadi	29,770
Dec 20	Crystal Palace	L 0-1		14,462
Dec 26	Blackburn Rovers	L 1-3	McAllister	19,910
Dec 28	NORWICH CITY	D 0-0		30,282
Jan 9	SOUTHAMPTON	W 2-1	Fairclough, Speed	26,071
Jan 16	Everton	L 0-2		21,031
Jan 30	MIDDLESBROUGH	W 3-0	Strandli, Batty, Fairclough	30,344
Feb 6	Wimbledon	L 0-1		6,704
Feb 8	MANCHESTER UNITED	D 0-0		34,166
Feb 13	OLDHAM ATHLETIC	W 2-0	McAllister (pen), Chapman	27,654
Feb 20	Tottenham Hotspur	L 0-4		32,040
Feb 24	Arsenal	D 0-0		21,061
Feb 27	IPSWICH TOWN	W 1-0	Dorigo (pen)	28,848
Mar 13	MANCHESTER CITY	W 1-0	Rocastle	30,840
Mar 21	Nottingham Forest	D 1-1	Wallace	25,148
Mar 24	CHELSEA	D 1-1	Wetherall	28,135
Apr 6	Sheffield United	L 1-2	Strandli	20,562
Apr 10	BLACKBURN ROVERS	W 5-2	Strachan 3, Wallace, Chapman	31,789
Apr 14	Norwich City	L 2-4	Chapman, Wallace	18,613
Apr 17	CRYSTAL PALACE	D 0-0		27,545
Apr 21	Liverpool	L 0-2		34,992
May 1	QUEENS PARK RANGERS	D 1-1	Hodge	31,408
May 4	Sheffield Wednesday	D 1-1	Chapman	26,855
May 8	Coventry City	D 3-3	Wallace 3	19,591

FA Cup

Jan 2	CHARLTON ATHLETIC	(Rd 3) D 1-1	Speed	21,827
Jan 13	Charlton Athletic	(R) W 3-1	Speed, Garland o.g., McAllister	8,337
Jan 25	Arsenal	(Rd 4) D 2-2	Speed, Chapman	26,516
Feb 3	ARSENAL*	(R) L 2-3	Shutt, McAllister	26,449

*Result after extra time.

Coca-Cola Cup

Sep 22	SCUNTHORPE UNITED	(Rd 2/FL) W 4-1	Strachan, Chapman, Speed, Shutt	10,113
Oct 27	Scunthorpe United	(Rd 2/SL) D 2-2	Wallace, Chapman	7,410
Nov 2	Watford	(Rd 3) L 1-2	McAllister	18,035

European Cup

Sep 16	Vfb Stuttgart	(Rd 1/FL) L 0-3		38,000
Sep 30	Vfb STUTTGART	(Rd 1/SL) W 4-1	Speed, McAllister, Cantona, Chapman	20,457
Oct 9	Vfb Stuttgart**	(Play-off) W 2-1	Strachan, Shutt	7,400
Oct 21	Glasgow Rangers	(Rd 2/SL) L 1-2	McAllister	43,251
Nov 4	GLASGOW RANGERS	(Rd 2/SL) L 1-2	Cantona	25,118

**Play-off as Stuttgart played an ineligible player, match played at Barcelona.

Charity Shield

Aug 8	Liverpool		W 4-3	Cantona 3, Dorigo	61,291

MANAGER: Howard Wilkinson   **CAPTAIN:** Gordon Strachan

TOP SCORER: Lee Chapman

BIGGEST WIN: 5-0 v Tottenham Hotspur, 25 August 1992, League

MAJOR TRANSFERS IN: Mark Beeney from Brighton & Hove Albion

MAJOR TRANSFERS OUT: Eric Cantona to Manchester United

League & Cup Appearances (substitute)

PLAYER	LEAGUE	CUP COMPETITION				TOTAL
		FA	COCA-COLA	EUROPEAN	OTHER	
Batty	30	3	2	4	1	40
Beeney	1					1
Bowman	3 (1)					3 (1)
Cantona	12 (1)		1	5	1	19 (1)
Chapman	36 (4)	4	3	5	1	49 (4)
Day	2	1				3
Dorigo	33	4	1	5	1	44
Fairclough	29 (1)	3 (1)	2	5		40 (2)
Forrester	5 (1)					5 (1)
Hodge	9 (14)		0 (1)	0 (2)	0 (1)	9 (18)
Kerr	3 (2)		2			5 (2)
Kerslake	8					8
Lukic	39	3	3	5	1	51
McAllister	32	4	3	5	1	45
Newsome	30 (7)	0 (1)	2	3	1	36 (8)
Rocastle	11 (7)	0 (3)	0 (2)	2 (1)		13 (13)
Sellars	6 (1)		1 (1)	1		8 (2)
Sharp	4					4
Shutt	6 (8)			0 (2)		10 (10)
Speed	39	4	3	5	1	52
Sterland	3	2				5
Strachan	25 (6)	4	3	5	0 (1)	37 (7)
Strandli	5 (5)					5 (5)
Tinkler	5 (2)					5 (2)
Varadi	4					4
Wallace Ray	5 (1)					5 (1)
Wallace Rod	31 (1)	1 (3)	2	0 (2)	1	35 (6)
Wetherall	13	4	2			19
Whyte	34	3	2 (1)	5	1	45 (1)

Goalscorers

PLAYER	LEAGUE	CUP COMPETITION				TOTAL
		FA	COCA-COLA	EUROPEAN	OTHER	
Chapman	14	1	2	1		18
Speed	7	3	1	1		12
Cantona	6			2	3	11
McAllister	5	2	1	2		10
Wallace Rod	7					8
Strachan	4		1	1		6
Fairclough	4					4
Shutt	1		1	1		3
Dorigo	1				1	2
Hodge	2					2
Strandli	2					2
Batty	1					1
Rocastle	1					1
Varadi	1					1
Wetherall	1					1
Whyte	1					1
Opps' o.g.			1			1

Fact File

Eric Cantona scored a Wembley hat-trick as Leeds beat Liverpool in the Charity Shield.

Final Premier League Table

		P	W	D	L	F	A	Pts
1	MANCHESTER U	42	24	12	6	67	31	84
2	ASTON VILLA	42	21	11	10	57	40	74
3	NORWICH C	42	21	9	12	61	65	72
4	BLACKBURN R	42	20	11	11	68	46	71
5	QPR	42	17	12	13	63	55	63
6	LIVERPOOL	42	16	11	15	62	55	59
7	SHEFFIELD W	42	15	14	13	55	51	59
8	TOTTENHAM H	42	16	11	15	60	66	59
9	MANCHESTER C	42	15	12	15	56	51	57
10	ARSENAL	42	15	11	16	40	38	56
11	CHELSEA	42	14	14	14	51	54	56
12	WIMBLEDON	42	14	12	16	56	55	54
13	EVERTON	42	15	8	19	53	55	53
14	SHEFFIELD U	42	14	10	18	54	53	52
15	COVENTRY C	42	13	13	16	52	57	52
16	IPSWICH T	42	12	16	14	50	55	52
17	LEEDS UNITED	42	12	15	15	57	62	51
18	SOUTHAMPTON	42	13	11	18	54	61	50
19	OLDHAM ATH	42	13	10	19	63	74	49
20	CRYSTAL PALACE	42	11	16	15	48	61	49
21	MIDDLESBROUGH	42	11	11	20	54	75	44
22	NOTTINGHAM F	42	10	10	22	41	62	40

Season 1993-94

Premier League

DATE	OPPONENTS	SCORE	GOALSCORERS	ATTENDANCE
Aug 14	Manchester City	D 1-1	Deane	32,366
Aug 17	WEST HAM UNITED	W 1-0	Speed	34,588
Aug 21	NORWICH CITY	L 0-4		32,008
Aug 24	Arsenal	L 1-2	Strachan	29,042
Aug 28	Liverpool	L 0-2		44,068
Aug 30	OLDHAM ATHLETIC	W 1-0	Strachan	28,717
Sep 11	Southampton	W 2-0	Deane, Speed	13,511
Sep 18	SHEFFIELD UNITED	W 2-1	McAllister, Strachan	33,892
Sep 25	Coventry City	W 2-0	Wallace 2	13,934
Oct 2	WIMBLEDON	W 4-0	Speed 2, McAllister 2	30,020
Oct 17	Ipswich Town	D 0-0		17,548
Oct 23	BLACKBURN ROVERS	D 3-3	McAllister 2, Newsome	37,827
Oct 30	Sheffield Wednesday	D 3-3	Fairclough, Wallace, Speed	31,892
Nov 6	CHELSEA	W 4-1	Deane, Wallace 2, Rocastle	35,022
Nov 20	Tottenham Hotspur	D 1-1	Deane	31,275
Nov 23	Everton	D 1-1	Wallace	17,066
Nov 27	SWINDON TOWN	W 3-0	Deane, Wallace, Speed	32,630
Dec 4	MANCHESTER CITY	W 3-2	Wallace, Speed, Deane	33,821
Dec 8	West Ham United	W 1-0	Wallace	20,468
Dec 13	Norwich Cty	L 1-2	Wallace	16,586
Dec 18	ARSENAL	W 2-1	McAllister, Adams o.g.	37,515
Dec 22	Newcastle United	D 1-1	Fairclough	36,388
Dec 29	QUEENS PARK RANGERS	D 1-1	Hodge	39,106
Jan 1	Manchester United	D 0-0		44,724
Jan 15	IPSWICH TOWN	D 0-0		31,317
Jan 23	Blackburn Rovers	L 1-2	Speed	16,938
Feb 6	Aston Villa	L 0-1		26,919
Feb 19	LIVERPOOL	W 2-0	Wetherall, McAllister	40,053
Feb 28	Oldham Athletic	D 1-1	McAllister	11,136
Mar 5	SOUTHAMPTON	D 0-0		30,890
Mar 13	Sheffield United	D 2-2	Speed, Deane	19,250
Mar 16	ASTON VILLA	W 2-0	Wallace, Deane	33,120
Mar 19	COVENTRY CITY	W 1-0	Wallace	30,023
Mar 26	Wimbledon	L 0-1		9,035
Apr 1	NEWCASTLE UNITED	D 1-1	Fairclough	40,005
Apr 4	Queens Park Rangers	W 4-0	Deane, Wallace, White 2	13,365
Apr 17	TOTTENHAM HOTSPUR	W 2-0	Wallace 2	33,658
Apr 23	Chelsea	D 1-1	Speed	18,544
Apr 27	MANCHESTER UNITED	L 0-2		41,125
Apr 30	EVERTON	W 3-0	McAllister, Watson o.g., White	35,487
May 3	SHEFFIELD WEDNESDAY	D 2-2	White, Wallace	33,806
May 7	Swindon Town	W 5-0	Deane 2, White, Wallace, Fairclough	17,539

FA Cup

Jan 8	CREWE ALEXANDRA	(Rd 3) W 3-1	Deane, Forrester 2	23,475
Jan 29	Oxford United	(Rd 4) D 2-2	Speed, Wetherall	11,029
Feb 9	OXFORD UNITED	(R) L 2-3	Strachan, White	22,167

Coca-Cola Cup

Sep 21	SUNDERLAND	(Rd 2/FL) L 1-2	Speed	17,101
Oct 6	Sunderland	(Rd 2/SL) L 1-2	Whelan	22,265

League & Cup Appearances (substitute)

PLAYER	LEAGUE	CUP COMPETITION		TOTAL
		FA CUP	COCA COLA	
Batty	8 (1)			8 (1)
Beeney	22	3	2	27
Deane	41	3	2	46
Dorigo	37	3	2	42
Fairclough	40	3	2	45
Ford	0 (1)			0 (1)
Forrester	2 (1)	1 (1)		3 (2)
Hodge	7 (1)	1 (1)	1	9 (2)
Kelly	42	3	2	47
Lukic	20			20
McAllister	42	3	2	47
Newsome	25 (4)	3		29 (4)
O'Leary	10			10
Pemberton	6 (3)			6 (3)
Rocastle	6 (1)		0 (1)	6 (2)
Sharp	7 (3)			7 (3)
Speed	35 (1)	2	2	39 (1)
Strachan	32 (1)	3	2	37 (1)
Strandli	0 (4)	1	0 (1)	1 (5)
Tinkler	0 (3)			0 (3)
Wallace Ray	0 (1)			0 (1)
Wallace Rod	34 (3)	1	1	36 (3)
Wetherall	31 (1)	0 (2)	2	33 (3)
Whelan	6 (10)		1	7 (10)
White	9 (6)	3		12 (6)

Goalscorers

PLAYER	LEAGUE	CUP COMPETITION		TOTAL
		FA CUP	COCA COLA	
Wallace Rod	17			17
Deane	11	1		12
Speed	10	1	1	12
McAllister	9			9
White	5	1		6
Fairclough	4			4
Strachan	3	1		4
Wetherall	1	1		2
Forrester		2		2
Hodge	1			1
Newsome	1			1
Rocastle	1			1
Whelan			1	1
Opps' o.gs.	2			2

Fact File

Rod Wallace's mazy run and spectacular goal against Tottenham Hotspur in April won him *Match of the Day*'s Goal of the Season award.

MANAGER: Howard Wilkinson

CAPTAIN: Gordon Strachan

TOP SCORER: Rod Wallace

BIGGEST WIN: 5-0 v Swindon Town, 7 May 1994, League

HIGHEST ATTENDANCE: 44,724 v Manchester United, 1 January 1994, drew 0-0, League

MAJOR TRANSFERS IN: Brian Deane from Sheffield Wednesday, David O'Leary from Arsenal, David White from Manchester City, John Pemberton from Sheffield United

MAJOR TRANSFERS OUT: Mel Sterland (retired), Chris Whyte to Birmingham City, Lee Chapman to Portsmouth

Final Premier League Table

		P	W	D	L	F	A	PTS
1	MANCHESTER U	42	27	11	4	80	38	92
2	BLACKBURN R	42	25	9	8	63	36	84
3	NEWCASTLE U	42	23	8	11	82	41	77
4	ARSENAL	42	18	17	7	53	28	71
5	LEEDS UNITED	42	18	16	8	65	39	70
6	WIMBLEDON	42	18	11	13	56	53	65
7	SHEFFIELD W	42	16	16	10	76	54	64
8	LIVERPOOL	42	17	9	16	59	55	60
9	QPR	42	16	12	14	62	61	60
10	ASTON VILLA	42	15	12	15	46	50	57
11	COVENTRY C	42	14	14	14	43	45	56
12	NORWICH C	42	12	17	13	65	61	53
13	WEST HAM U	42	13	13	16	47	58	52
14	CHELSEA	42	13	12	17	49	53	51
15	TOTTENHAM H	42	11	12	19	54	59	45
16	MANCHESTER C	42	9	18	15	38	49	45
17	EVERTON	42	12	8	22	42	63	44
18	SOUTHAMPTON	42	12	7	23	49	66	43
19	IPSWICH T	42	9	16	17	35	58	43
20	SHEFFIELD U	42	8	18	16	42	60	42
21	OLDHAM ATH	42	9	13	20	42	68	40
22	SWINDON T	42	5	15	22	47	100	30

Season 1994-95

Premier League

DATE	OPPONENTS	SCORE	GOALSCORERS	ATTENDANCE
Aug 20	West Ham United	D 0-0		18,610
Aug 23	ARSENAL	W 1-0	Whelan	34,218
Aug 27	CHELSEA	L 2-3	Whelan, Masinga	32,212
Aug 30	Crystal Palace	W 2-1	White, Whelan	13,654
Sep 11	MANCHESTER UNITED	W 2-1	Wetherall, Deane	39,396
Sep 17	Coventry City	L 1-2	Speed	15,389
Sep 26	Sheffield Wednesday	D 1-1	McAllister	23,227
Oct 1	MANCHESTER CITY	W 2-0	Whelan 2	30,938
Oct 8	Norwich City	L 1-2	Wallace	17,390
Oct 15	TOTTENHAM HOTSPUR	D 1-1	Deane	39,224
Oct 24	LEICESTER CITY	W 2-1	McAllister, Whelan	28,547
Oct 29	Southampton	W 3-1	Maddison o.g., Wallace 2	15,202
Nov 1	Ipswich Town	L 0-2		15,546
Nov 5	WIMBLEDON	W 3-1	Wetherall, Speed, White	27,284
Nov 19	Queens Park Rangers	L 2-3	McDonald o.g., Deane	17,416
Nov 26	NOTTINGHAM FOREST	W 1-0	Whelan	38,191
Dec 5	Everton	L 0-3		25,897
Dec 10	WEST HAM UNITED	D 2-2	Worthington, Deane	28,897
Dec 17	Arsenal	W 3-1	Masinga 2, Deane	38,098
Dec 26	NEWCASTLE UNITED	D 0-0		39,387
Dec 31	LIVERPOOL	L 0-2		38,563
Jan 2	Aston Villa	D 0-0		35,038
Jan 14	SOUTHAMPTON	D 0-0		28,953
Jan 24	QUEENS PARK RANGERS	W 4-0	Masinga 2, White, Deane	28,780
Feb 1	Blackburn Rovers	D 1-1	McAllister	25,561
Feb 4	Wimbledon	D 0-0		10,211
Feb 22	EVERTON	W 1-0	Yeboah	30,793
Feb 25	Manchester City	D 0-0		22,892
Mar 4	SHEFFIELD WEDNESDAY	L 0-1		33,750
Mar 11	Chelsea	W 3-0	Yeboah 2, McAllister	20,174
Mar 15	Leicester City	W 3-1	Yeboah 2, Palmer	20,068
Mar 18	COVENTRY CITY	W 3-0	Yeboah, Gould o.g., Wallace	29,179
Mar 22	Nottingham Forest	L 0-3		26,299
Apr 2	Manchester United	D 0-0		43,712
Apr 5	IPSWICH TOWN	W 4-0	Yeboah 3, Speed	28,600
Apr 9	Liverpool	W 1-0	Deane	37,454
Apr 15	BLACKBURN ROVERS	D 1-1	Deane	39,426
Apr 17	Newcastle United	W 2-1	McAllister (pen), Yeboah	35,626
Apr 29	ASTON VILLA	W 1-0	Palmer	32,955
May 6	NORWICH CITY	W 2-1	McAllister (pen), Palmer	31,982
May 9	CRYSTAL PALACE	W 3-1	Yeboah 2, Wetherall	30,942
May 14	Tottenham Hotspur	D 1-1	Deane	33,040

FA Cup

Jan 7	Walsall	(Rd 3) D 1-1	Wetherall	8,619
Jan 17	WALSALL	(R) W 5-2	Deane, Wetherall, Masinga 3	17,881
Jan 28	OLDHAM ATHLETIC	(Rd 4) W 3-2	White, Palmer, Masinga	25,010
Feb 19	Manchester United	(Rd 5) L 1-3	Yeboah	42,744

Coca-Cola Cup

Sep 21	MANSFIELD TOWN	(Rd 2/FL) L 0-1		7,844
Oct 4	Mansfield Town	(Rd 2/SL) D 0-0		7,227

MANAGER: Howard Wilkinson

CAPTAIN: Gary McAllister

TOP SCORER: Tony Yeboah

BIGGEST WIN: 4-0 v Queens Park Rangers, 24 January 1995, League; 4-0 v Ipswich Town, 5 April 1995, League

HIGHEST ATTENDANCE: 43,712 v Manchester United, 2 April 1995, drew 0-0, League

MAJOR TRANSFERS IN: Phil Masinga from Mamelodi Sundowns, Lucas Radebe from Kaizer Chiefs, Tony Yeboah from Eintracht Frankfurt, Carlton Palmer from Sheffield Wednesday

MAJOR TRANSFERS OUT: David Batty to Blackburn Rovers, David Rocastle to Manchester City, Gordon Strachan to Coventry City, Jon Newsome to Norwich City

League & Cup Appearances (substitute)

PLAYER	LEAGUE	CUP COMPETITION		TOTAL
		FA CUP	COCA COLA	
Couzens	2 (2)			2 (2)
Deane	33 (2)	3	1 (1)	37 (3)
Dorigo	28	1	0 (1)	29 (1)
Fairclough	1 (4)			23 (4)
Kelly	42	4	2	48
Lukic	42	4	2	48
Masinga	15 (7)	2 (2)	1	18 (9)
McAllister	41	4	2	47
Palmer	39	3	2	44
Pemberton	22 (5)	4		26 (5)
Radebe	9 (3)	1 (1)	0 (1)	10 (5)
Sharp	0 (2)			0 (2)
Speed	39	4	2	45
Strachan	5 (1)			6 (1)
Tinkler	3			3
Wallace Rod	30 (3)	2 (1)	2	34 (3)
Wetherall	38	4	1	43
Whelan	18 (5)	2	2	22 (5)
White	18 (5)	3		21 (5)
Worthington	21 (6)	3 (1)	2	26 (7)
Yeboah	16 (2)	0 (2)		16 (4)

Goalscorers

PLAYER	LEAGUE	CUP COMPETITION		TOTAL
		FA CUP	COCA COLA	
Yeboah	12	1		13
Deane	9	1		10
Masinga	5	4		9
Whelan	7			7
McAllister	6			6
Wetherall	3	2		5
Palmer	3	1		4
Wallace Rod	4			4
White	3	1		4
Speed	3			3
Worthington	1			1
Opps' o.gs.	3			3

Fact File

Phil Masinga came on as a substitute and scored a hat-trick in just nine minutes against Walsall in the FA Cup.

Final Premier League Table

		P	W	D	L	F	A	Pts
1	BLACKBURN R	42	27	8	7	80	39	89
2	MANCHESTER U	42	26	10	6	77	28	88
3	NOTTINGHAM F	42	22	11	9	72	43	77
4	LIVERPOOL	42	21	11	10	65	37	74
5	LEEDS UNITED	42	20	13	9	59	38	73
6	NEWCASTLE U	42	20	12	10	67	47	72
7	TOTTENHAM H	42	16	14	12	66	58	62
8	QPR	42	17	9	16	61	59	60
9	WIMBLEDON	42	15	11	16	48	65	56
10	SOUTHAMPTON	42	12	18	12	61	63	54
11	CHELSEA	42	13	15	14	50	55	54
12	ARSENAL	42	13	12	17	52	49	51
13	SHEFFIELD W	42	13	12	17	49	57	51
14	WEST HAM U	42	13	11	18	44	48	50
15	EVERTON	42	11	17	14	44	51	50
16	COVENTRY C	42	12	14	16	44	62	50
17	MANCHESTER C	42	12	13	17	53	64	49
18	ASTON VILLA	42	11	15	16	51	56	48
19	CRYSTAL PALACE	42	11	12	19	34	49	45
20	NORWICH C	42	10	13	19	37	54	43
21	LEICESTER C	42	6	11	25	45	80	29
22	IPSWICH T	42	7	6	29	36	93	27

Season 1995-96

Premier League

DATE	OPPONENTS	SCORE	GOALSCORERS	ATTENDANCE
Aug 19	West Ham United	W 2-1	Yeboah 2	22,901
Aug 21	LIVERPOOL	W 1-0	Yeboah	35,852
Aug 26	ASTON VILLA	W 2-0	Speed, White	35,086
Aug 30	Southampton	D 1-1	Dorigo	15,212
Sep 9	Tottenham Hotspur	L 1-2	Yeboah	30,034
Sep 16	QUEENS PARK RANGERS	L 1-3	Wetherall	31,504
Sep 23	Wimbledon	W 4-2	Palmer, Yeboah 3	13,307
Sep 30	SHEFFIELD WEDNESDAY	W 2-0	Yeboah, Speed	34,076
Oct 14	ARSENAL	L 0-3		38,322
Oct 21	Manchester City	D 0-0		26,390
Oct 28	COVENTRY CITY	W 3-1	McAllister 3	30,161
Nov 4	Middlesbrough	D 1-1	Deane	29,467
Nov 18	CHELSEA	W 1-0	Yeboah	36,209
Nov 25	Newcastle United	L 1-2	Deane	36,572
Dec 2	MANCHESTER CITY	L 0-1		33,249
Dec 9	WIMBLEDON	D 1-1	Jobson	27,984
Dec 16	Sheffield Wednesday	L 2-6	Brolin, Wallace	24,573
Dec 24	MANCHESTER UNITED	W 3-1	McAllister (pen), Yeboah, Deane	39,801
Dec 27	Bolton Wanderers	W 2-0	Brolin, Wetherall	18,414
Dec 30	Everton	L 0-2		40,009
Jan 1	BLACKBURN ROVERS	D 0-0		31,285
Jan 13	WEST HAM UNITED	W 2-0	Brolin 2	30,658
Jan 20	Liverpool	L 0-5		40,254
Jan 31	Nottingham Forest	L 1-2	Palmer	24,465
Feb 3	Aston Villa	L 0-3		35,982
Mar 2	BOLTON WANDERERS	L 0-1		30,106
Mar 6	Queens Park Rangers	W 2-1	Yeboah 2	13,991
Mar 13	Blackburn Rovers	L 0-1		23,358
Mar 17	EVERTON	D 2-2	Deane 2	29,422
Mar 30	MIDDLESBROUGH	L 0-1		31,778
Apr 3	SOUTHAMPTON	W 1-0	Deane	26,077
Apr 6	Arsenal	L 1-2	Deane	37,619
Apr 8	NOTTINGHAM FOREST	L 1-3	Wetherall	29,220
Apr 13	Chelsea	L 1-4	McAllister	22,131
Apr 17	Manchester United	L 0-1		48,382
Apr 29	NEWCASTLE UNITED	L 0-1		38,862
May 2	TOTTENHAM HOTSPUR	L 1-3	Wetherall	30,061
May 5	Coventry City	D 0-0		22,757

FA Cup

Jan 7	Derby County	(Rd 3) W 4-2	Speed, Deane, McAllister, Yeboah	16,155
Feb 14	Bolton Wanderers	(Rd 4) W 1-0	Wallace	16,694
Feb 21	PORT VALE	(Rd 5) D 0-0		18,607
Feb 27	Port Vale	(R) W 2-1	McAllister 2	14,023
Mar 10	LIVERPOOL	(Rd 6) D 0-0		34,632
Mar 20	Liverpool	(R) L 0-3		30,812

Coca-Cola Cup

Sep 19	NOTTS COUNTY	(Rd 2/FL) D 0-0		12,384
Oct 3	Notts County	(Rd 2/SL) W 3-2	McAllister, Couzens, Speed	12,477
Oct 25	Derby County	(Rd 3) W 1-0	Speed	16,030
Nov 29	BLACKBURN ROVERS	(Rd 4) W 2-1	Deane, Yeboah	26,006
Jan 10	READING	(Rd 5) W 2-1	Masinga, Speed	21,023
Feb 11	Birmingham City	(SF/FL) W 2-1	Yeboah, White o.g.	24,781
Feb 25	BIRMINGHAM CITY	(SF/SL) W 3-0	Masinga, Yeboah, Deane	35,435
Mar 24	Aston Villa*	(F) L 0-3		77,065

*Played at Wembley

UEFA Cup

Sep 12	Monaco	(Rd 1/FL) W 3-0	Yeboah 3	14,000
Sep 26	MONACO	(Rd 1/SL) L 0-1		24,501
Oct 17	PSV EINDHOVEN	(Rd 2/FL) L 3-5	Speed, Palmer, McAllister	24,846
Oct 31	PSV Eindhoven	(Rd 2/SL) L 0-3		25,750

MANAGER: Howard Wilkinson **CAPTAIN:** Gary McAllister

TOP SCORER: Tony Yeboah

BIGGEST WIN: 3-0 v Monaco, 12 September 1996, UEFA Cup, Round 1 First leg; 3-0 v Birmingham City, 25 February 1997, Coca-Cola Cup, semi-final First Leg

HIGHEST ATTENDANCE: 77,065 v Aston Villa, 24 March 1996, lost 0-3, Coca-Cola Cup final

MAJOR TRANSFERS IN: Paul Beesley from Sheffield United, Tomas Brolin from Parma, Richard Jobson from Oldham Athletic

MAJOR TRANSFERS OUT: Noel Whelan to Coventry City

League & Cup Appearances (substitute)

PLAYER	LEAGUE	CUP COMPETITION			TOTAL
		FA CUP	COCA COLA	UEFA	
Beeney	10	1	1		12
Beesley	8 (2)	4	4 (1)	2 (2)	18 (5)
Blunt	2 (1)				2 (1)
Bowman	1 (2)		0 (1)	1	2 (3)
Brolin	17 (2)	1 (1)	2 (2)		20 (5)
Chapman	2				2
Couzens	8 (6)		1 (1)	0 (2)	9 (9)
Deane	30 (4)	3 (3)	5 (2)	3	41 (9)
Dorigo	17	3	4	2	26
Ford	12	5	4	0 (1)	21 (1)
Gray	12 (3)	0 (2)		1 (1)	13 (6)
Harte	2 (2)		0 (1)		2 (3)
Jackson	0 (1)				0 (1)
Jobson	12	1			13
Kelly	34	5	8	4	51
Kewell	2				2
Lukic	28	5	7	4	44
Masinga	5 (4)	1	2		8 (4)
McAllister	36	6	8	4	54
Palmer	35	6	8	4	53
Pemberton	16 (1)	1 (1)	3	4	24 (2)
Radebe	10 (3)	3 (1)	1 (1)		14 (5)
Sharp	0			0 (1)	0 (1)
Speed	29	4	7	4	44
Tinkler	5 (4)		1	0 (1)	6 (5)
Wallace	12 (12)	3 (1)	3	0 (1)	18 (14)
Wetherall	34	5	8	4	51
Whelan	3 (5)		0 (2)	3	6 (7)
White	1 (3)		1	1 (1)	3 (4)
Worthington	12 (4)	3	2 (1)		17 (5)
Yeboah	22	6	7	4	39

Goalscorers

PLAYER	LEAGUE	CUP COMPETITION			TOTAL
		FA CUP	COCA COLA	UEFA	
Yeboah	12	1	3	3	19
Deane	7	1	2		10
McAllister	5	3	1	1	10
Speed	2	1	3	1	7
Brolin	4				4
Wetherall	4				4
Palmer	2			1	3
Wallace	1	1			2
Masinga			2		2
Dorigo	1				1
Jobson	1				1
White	1				1
Couzens			1		1
Opps' o.gs.			1		1

Fact File

Tony Yeboah hit two hat-tricks in 11 days in September against Wimbledon and Monaco.

Final Premier League Table

		P	W	D	L	F	A	Pts
1	MANCHESTER U	38	25	7	6	73	35	82
2	NEWCASTLE U	38	24	6	8	66	37	78
3	LIVERPOOL	38	20	11	7	70	34	71
4	ASTON VILLA	38	18	9	11	52	35	63
5	ARSENAL	38	17	12	9	49	32	63
6	EVERTON	38	17	10	11	64	44	61
7	BLACKBURN R	38	18	7	13	61	47	61
8	TOTTENHAM H	38	16	13	9	50	38	61
9	NOTTINGHAM F	38	15	13	10	50	54	58
10	WEST HAM U	38	14	9	15	43	52	51
11	CHELSEA	38	12	14	12	46	44	50
12	MIDDLESBROUGH	38	11	10	17	35	50	43
13	LEEDS UNITED	38	12	7	19	40	57	43
14	WIMBLEDON	38	10	11	17	55	70	41
15	SHEFFIELD W	38	10	10	18	48	61	40
16	COVENTRY C	38	8	14	16	42	60	38
17	SOUTHAMPTON	38	9	11	18	34	52	38
18	MANCHESTER C	38	9	11	18	33	58	38
19	QPR	38	9	6	23	38	57	33
20	BOLTON W	38	8	5	25	39	71	29

The Essential History of Leeds United

Season 1996-97

Premier League

DATE	OPPONENTS	SCORE	GOALSCORERS	ATTENDANCE
Aug 17	Derby County	D 3-3	Laurson o.g., Harte, Bowyer	17,927
Aug 20	SHEFFIELD WEDNESDAY	L 0-2		31,011
Aug 26	WIMBLEDON	W 1-0	Sharpe	25,860
Sep 4	Blackburn Rovers	W 1-0	Harte	23,226
Sep 7	MANCHESTER UNITED	L 0-4		39,694
Sep 14	Coventry City	L 1-2	Couzens	17,297
Sep 21	NEWCASTLE UNITED	L 0-1		36,070
Sep 28	Leicester City	L 0-1		20,359
Oct 12	NOTTINGHAM FOREST	W 2-0	Wallace 2	29,225
Oct 19	Aston Villa	L 0-2		39,051
Oct 26	Arsenal	L 0-3		38,076
Nov 2	SUNDERLAND	W 3-0	Ford, Sharpe, Deane	31,667
Nov 16	LIVERPOOL	L 0-2		39,981
Nov 23	Southampton	W 2-0	Kelly, Sharpe	15,241
Dec 1	CHELSEA	W 2-0	Deane, Rush	32,671
Dec 7	Middlesbrough	D 0-0		30,018
Dec 14	TOTTENHAM HOTSPUR	D 0-0		33,783
Dec 21	Everton	D 0-0		36,954
Dec 26	COVENTRY CITY	L 1-3	Deane	36,465
Dec 28	Manchester United	L 0-1		55,256
Jan 1	Newcastle United	L 0-3		36,489
Jan 11	LEICESTER CITY	W 3-0	Bowyer, Rush 2	29,486
Jan 20	West Ham United	W 2-0	Kelly, Bowyer	19,441
Jan 29	DERBY COUNTY	D 0-0		27,549
Feb 1	ARSENAL	D 0-0		35,502
Feb 19	Liverpool	L 0-4		38,957
Feb 22	Sunderland	W 1-0	Bowyer	21,890
Mar 1	WEST HAM UNITED	W 1-0	Sharpe	30,575
Mar 8	EVERTON	W 1-0	Molenaar	32,055
Mar 12	SOUTHAMPTON	D 0-0		25,913
Mar 15	Tottenham Hotspur	L 0-1		33,040
Mar 22	Sheffield Wednesday	D 2-2	Sharpe, Wallace	30,373
Apr 7	BLACKBURN ROVERS	D 0-0		27,264
Apr 16	Wimbledon	L 0-2		7,979
Apr 19	Nottingham Forest	D 1-1	Deane	25,565
Apr 22	ASTON VILLA	D 0-0		26,897
May 3	Chelsea	D 0-0		28,279
May 11	MIDDLESBROUGH	D 1-1	Deane	38,567

FA Cup

Jan 14	Crystal Palace	(Rd 3) D 2-2	Deane, Andersen o.g.	21,052
Jan 25	CRYSTAL PALACE	(R) W 1-0	Wallace	21,903
Feb 4	Arsenal	(Rd 4) W 1-0	Wallace	38,115
Feb 15	PORTSMOUTH	(Rd 5) L 2-3	Bowyer 2	35,604

Coca-Cola Cup

Sep 18	DARLINGTON	(Rd 2/FL) D 2-2	Wallace 2	15,711
Sep 24	Darlington	(Rd 2/SL) W 2-0	Wallace, Harte	6,298
Oct 23	ASTON VILLA	(Rd 3) L 1-2	Sharpe	15,890

League & Cup Appearances (substitute)

PLAYER	LEAGUE	CUP COMPETITION		TOTAL
		FA CUP	COCA COLA	
Beeney	1			1
Beesley	11	1	1	13
Blunt	0 (1)		0 (1)	0 (2)
Bowyer	32	4		36
Boyle	0 (1)			0 (1)
Couzens	7 (3)		3	10 (3)
Deane	27 (1)	4		31 (1)
Dorigo	15 (3)	4		19 (3)
Evans	1			1
Ford	15 (1)		3	18 (1)
Gray	1 (6)		2	3 (6)
Halle	20	3		23
Harte	10 (4)	1	2 (1)	13 (5)
Hateley	5 (1)			5 (1)
Jackson	11 (6)	4		15 (6)
Jobson	10		3	13
Kelly	34 (2)	4	3	41 (2)
Kewell	0 (1)			0 (1)
Laurent	2 (2)			2 (2)
Lilley	4 (2)			4 (2)
Martyn	37	4	3	44
Molenaar	12	2		14
Palmer	26 (2)	3	2	31 (2)
Radebe	28 (4)	3	1	32 (4)
Rush	34 (2)	2 (2)	2	38 (4)
Sharpe	26	0 (1)	3	29 (1)
Shepherd	0 (1)			0 (1)
Tinkler	1 (2)			1 (2)
Wallace	17 (5)	4	3	24 (5)
Wetherall	25 (4)	1 (1)	2 (1)	28 (6)
Yeboah	6 (1)			6 (1)

Goalscorers

PLAYER	LEAGUE	CUP COMPETITION		TOTAL
		FA CUP	COCA COLA	
Wallace	3	2	3	8
Deane	5	1		6
Sharpe	5		1	6
Bowyer	4	2		6
Rush	3			3
Harte	2		1	3
Kelly	2			2
Couzens	1			1
Ford	1			1
Molenaar	1			1
Opps' o.gs.	1	1		2

Fact File

A Leeds' team, including Harry Kewell, Stephen McPhail, Jonathan Woodgate and Matthew Jones, won the FA Youth Cup.

MANAGER: Howard Wilkinson (until September)/George Graham

CAPTAIN: Lucas Radebe

TOP SCORER: Rod Wallace

BIGGEST WIN: 3-0 v Sunderland, 2 November 1996, League; 4-1 v Leicester City, 11 January 1997, League

HIGHEST ATTENDANCE: 39,981 v Manchester United, 28 December 1997, lost 1-0, League

MAJOR TRANSFERS IN: Ian Rush from Liverpool, Lee Bowyer from Charlton, Nigel Martyn from Crystal Palace, Lee Sharpe from Manchester United, Gunnar Halle from Oldham, Robert Molenaar from Volendam, Derek Lilley from Morton, Pierre Laurent from Bastia

MAJOR TRANSFERS OUT: Phil Masinga to FC Gallen

Final Premier League Table

		P	W	D	L	F	A	Pts
1	MANCHESTER U	38	21	12	5	76	44	75
2	NEWCASTLE U	38	19	11	8	73	40	68
3	ARSENAL	38	19	11	8	62	32	68
4	LIVERPOOL	38	19	11	8	62	37	68
5	ASTON VILLA	38	17	10	11	47	34	61
6	CHELSEA	38	16	11	11	58	55	59
7	SHEFFIELD W	38	14	15	9	50	51	57
8	WIMBLEDON	38	15	11	12	49	46	56
9	LEICESTER C	38	12	11	15	46	54	47
10	TOTTENHAM H	38	13	7	18	44	51	46
11	LEEDS UNITED	38	11	13	14	28	38	46
12	DERBY CO	38	11	13	14	45	58	46
13	BLACKBURN R	38	9	15	14	42	43	42
14	WEST HAM U	38	10	12	16	39	48	42
15	EVERTON	38	10	12	16	44	57	42
16	SOUTHAMPTON	38	10	11	17	50	56	41
17	COVENTRY C	38	9	14	15	38	54	41
18	SUNDERLAND	38	10	10	18	35	53	40
19	MIDDLESBROUGH	38	10	12	16	51	60	39
20	NOTTINGHAM F	38	6	16	16	31	59	34

MIDDLESBROUGH WERE DEDUCTED THREE POINTS FOR FAILURE TO FULFIL A FIXTURE ON A GIVEN DATE.

Season 1997-98

Premier League

DATE	OPPONENTS	SCORE	GOALSCORERS	ATTENDANCE
Aug 9	ARSENAL	D 1-1	Hasselbaink	37,993
Aug 12	Sheffield Wednesday	W 3-1	Wallace 2, Riberio	31,520
Aug 23	CRYSTAL PALACE	L 0-2		29,076
Aug 26	LIVERPOOL	L 0-2		39,775
Aug 30	Aston Villa	L 0-1		39,027
Sep 14	Blackburn Rovers	W 4-3	Wallace 2, Molenaar, Hopkin	21,956
Sep 20	LEICESTER CITY	L 0-1		29,620
Sep 24	Southampton	W 2-0	Molenaar, Wallace	15,102
Sep 27	MANCHESTER UNITED	W 1-0	Wetherall	39,952
Oct 4	Coventry City	D 0-0		17,770
Oct 18	NEWCASTLE UNITED	W 4-1	Riberio, Beresford o.g., Kewell, Wetherall	39,834
Oct 25	Wimbledon	L 0-1		15,718
Nov 1	Tottenham Hotspur	W 1-0	Wallace	26,441
Nov 8	DERBY COUNTY	W 4-3	Wallace, Kewell, Hasselbaink, Bowyer	33,572
Nov 23	WEST HAM UNITED	W 3-1	Hasselbaink 2, Haaland	30,031
Nov 29	Barnsley	W 3-2	Haaland, Wallace, Lilley	18,690
Dec 6	EVERTON	D 0-0		34,869
Dec 13	Chelsea	D 0-0		34,690
Dec 20	BOLTON WANDERERS	W 2-0	Riberio, Hasselbaink	31,163
Dec 26	Liverpool	L 1-3	Haaland	43,854
Dec 28	ASTON VILLA	D 1-1	Hasselbaink	36,287
Jan 10	Arsenal	L 1-2	Hasselbaink	38,018
Jan 17	SHEFFIELD WEDNESDAY	L 1-2	Pembridge o.g.	33,166
Jan 31	Crystal Palace	W 2-0	Wallace, Hasselbaink	25,248
Feb 6	Leicester City	L 0-1		21,244
Feb 22	Newcastle United	D 1-1	Wallace	36,511
Feb 28	SOUTHAMPTON	L 0-1		28,791
Mar 4	TOTTENHAM HOTSPUR	W 1-0	Kewell	31,394
Mar 11	BLACKBURN ROVERS	W 4-0	Bowyer, Hasselbaink, Haaland 2	32,933
Mar 15	Derby County	W 5-0	Halle o.g., Bowyer, Kewell, Hasselbank	30,217
Mar 30	West Ham United	L 0-3		24,107
Apr 4	BARNSLEY	W 2-1	Hasselbaink, Moses o.g.	37,749
Apr 8	CHELSEA	W 3-1	Hasselbaink 2, Wetherall	37,276
Apr 11	Everton	L 0-2		37,099
Apr 18	Bolton Wanderers	W 3-2	Haaland, Halle, Hasselbaink	25,000
Apr 20	FULHAM	D 3-3	Hasselbaink 2, Kewell	36,522
May 4	Manchester United	L 0-3		55,167
May 10	WIMBLEDON	D 1-1	Haaland	38,172

FA Cup

Jan 3	OXFORD UNITED	(Rd 3) W 4-0	Radebe, Hasselbaink, Kewell 2	20,568
Jan 24	GRIMSBY TOWN	(Rd 4) W 2-0	Molenaar, Hasselbaink	29,598
Feb 14	BIRMINGHAM CITY	(Rd 5) W 3-2	Wallace, Hasselbaink 2	35,463
Mar 7	WOLVERHAMPTON W	(Rd 6) L 0-1		39,902

Coca-Cola Cup

Sep 17	BRISTOL CITY	(Rd 2/FL) W 3-1	Wetherall, Hasselbaink, Riberio	8,806
Sep 30	Bristol City	(Rd 2/SL) L 1-2	Hasselbaink	10,857
Oct 15	Stoke City*	(Rd 3) W 3-1	Kewell, Wallace 2,	16,203
Nov 18	READING	(Rd 4) L 2-3	Wetherall, Bowyer	15,069

*Result after extra time.

MANAGER: George Graham

CAPTAIN: Lucas Radebe

TOP SCORER: Jimmy Floyd Hasselbaink

BIGGEST WIN: 5-0 v Derby County, 15 March 1998, League

HIGHEST ATTENDANCE: 55,167 v Manchester United, 4 May 1998, lost 0-3, League

MAJOR TRANSFERS IN: David Hopkin from Crystal Palace, Jimmy Floyd Hasselbaink from Boavista, Bruno Ribeiro from Vitoria Setubal, David Robertson from Glasgow Rangers, Alf-Inge Haaland from Nottingham Forest, Martin Hiden from Rapid Vienna

MAJOR TRANSFERS OUT: Brian Deane to Middlesbrough, Carlton Palmer to Southampton

League & Cup Appearances (substitute)

PLAYER	LEAGUE	CUP COMPETITION		TOTAL
		FA CUP	COCA COLA	
Beeney	1	0 (1)		1 (1)
Bowyer	21 (4)	3	2 (1)	26 (5)
Haaland	26 (6)	2	3	31 (6)
Halle	31 (2)	3	2 (1)	36 (3)
Harte	12	1 (2)		13 (2)
Hasselbaink	30 (3)	4	3	37 (3)
Hiden	11	1		12
Hopkin	22 (3)	1	4	27 (3)
Jackson	0 (1)			0 (1)
Kelly	34	3 (1)	3	40 (1)
Kewell	26 (3)	4	2	32 (3)
Lilley	0 (13)	0 (1)	0 (3)	0 (17)
Martyn	37	4	4	45
Matthews	0 (3)			0 (3)
Maybury	9 (3)	2	1	12 (3)
McPhail	0 (4)			0 (4)
Molenaar	18 (4)	3	2 (1)	23 (4)
Radebe	26 (1)	2	4	32 (1)
Ribeiro	26 (1)	3	2 (1)	31 (2)
Robertson	24 (2)	1	4	29 (2)
Wallace	29 (2)	4	4	37 (2)
Wetherall	33 (1)	3	4	40 (1)

Goalscorers

PLAYER	LEAGUE	CUP COMPETITION		TOTAL
		FA CUP	COCA COLA	
Hasselbaink	16	4	2	22
Wallace	10	1	2	13
Kewell	5	2	1	8
Haaland	7			7
Wetherall	3		2	5
Bowyer	3		1	4
Ribeiro	3		1	4
Molenaar	2	1		3
Halle	2			2
Hopkin	1			1
Lilley	1			1
Radebe		1		1
Opps' o.gs.	4			4

Fact File

A Jimmy Floyd Hasselbaink penalty miss two minutes from time against Wolves in the quarter-final ended Leeds' FA Cup run.

Final Premier League Table

		P	W	D	L	F	A	Pts
1	ARSENAL	38	23	9	6	68	33	78
2	MANCHESTER U	38	23	8	7	73	26	77
3	LIVERPOOL	38	18	11	9	68	42	65
4	CHELSEA	38	20	3	15	71	43	63
5	LEEDS UNITED	38	17	8	13	57	46	59
6	BLACKBURN R	38	16	10	12	57	52	58
7	ASTON VILLA	38	17	6	15	49	48	57
8	WEST HAM U	38	16	8	14	56	57	56
9	DERBY CO	38	16	7	15	52	49	55
10	LEICESTER C	38	13	14	11	51	41	53
11	COVENTRY C	38	12	16	10	46	44	52
12	SOUTHAMPTON	38	14	6	18	50	55	48
13	NEWCASTLE U	38	11	11	16	35	44	44
14	TOTTENHAM H	38	11	11	16	44	56	44
15	WIMBLEDON	38	10	14	14	34	46	44
16	SHEFFIELD W	38	12	8	18	52	67	44
17	EVERTON	38	9	13	16	41	56	40
18	BOLTON W	38	9	13	16	41	61	40
19	BARNSLEY	38	10	5	23	37	82	35
20	CRYSTAL PALACE	38	8	9	21	37	71	33

Season 1998-99

Premier League

DATE	OPPONENTS	SCORE	GOALSCORERS	ATTENDANCE
Aug 15	Middlesbrough	D 0-0		34,162
Aug 24	BLACKBURN ROVERS	W 1-0	Hasselbaink	30,652
Aug 29	Wimbledon	D 1-1	Bowyer	16,437
Sep 8	SOUTHAMPTON	W 3-0	Marshall o.g., Harte, Wijnhard	30,637
Sep 12	Everton	D 0-0		36,687
Sep 19	ASTON VILLA	D 0-0		33,446
Sep 26	Tottenham Hotspur	D 3-3	Halle, Hasselbaink, Wijnhard	35,535
Oct 3	LEICESTER CITY	L 0-1		32,606
Oct 17	Nottingham Forest	D 1-1	Halle	23,911
Oct 25	CHELSEA	D 0-0		36,292
Oct 31	Derby County	D 2-2	Molenaar, Kewell	27,034
Nov 8	SHEFFIELD WEDNESDAY	W 2-1	Hasselbaink, Woodgate	30,012
Nov 14	Liverpool	W 3-1	Smith, Hasselbaink 2	44,305
Nov 21	CHARLTON ATHLETIC	W 4-1	Bowyer, Kewell, Hasselbaink, Smith	32,487
Nov 29	Manchester United	L 2-3	Hasselbaink, Kewell	55,172
Dec 5	WEST HAM UNITED	W 4-0	Bowyer 2, Hasselbaink, Molenaar	36,320
Dec 14	COVENTRY CITY	W 2-0	Hopkin, Bowyer	31,802
Dec 20	Arsenal	L 1-3	Hasselbaink	38,025
Dec 26	Newcastle United	W 3-0	Kewell, Hasselbaink, Bowyer	36,783
Dec 29	WIMBLEDON	D 2-2	Ribeiro, Hopkin,	39,816
Jan 9	Blackburn Rovers	L 0-1		27,620
Jan 16	MIDDLESBROUGH	W 2-0	Bowyer, Smith	37,473
Jan 30	Southampton	L 0-3		15,236
Feb 6	NEWCASTLE UNITED	L 0-1		40,202
Feb 17	Aston Villa	W 2-1	Hasselbaink 2	37,510
Feb 20	EVERTON	W 1-0	Korsten	36,344
Mar 1	Leicester City	W 2-1	Kewell, Smith	18,101
Mar 10	TOTTENHAM HOTSPUR	W 2-0	Kewell, Smith	34,521
Mar 13	Sheffield Wednesday	W 2-0	Hasselbaink, Hopkin	28,142
Mar 20	DERBY COUNTY	W 4-1	Harte, Bowyer, Korsten, Hasselbaink	38,971
Apr 3	NOTTINGHAM FOREST	W 3-1	Harte, Smith, Hasselbaink	39,645
Apr 12	LIVERPOOL	D 0-0		39,451
Apr 17	Charlton Athletic	D 1-1	Woodgate	20,043
Apr 25	MANCHESTER UNITED	D 1-1	Hasselbaink	40,255
May 1	West Ham United	W 5-1	Hasselbaink, Smith, Harte (pen), Bowyer, Haaland	25,997
May 5	Chelsea	L 0-1		34,762
May 11	ARSENAL	W 1-0	Hasselbaink	40,124
May 16	Coventry City	D 2-2	Wijnhard, Hopkin	25,049

FA Cup

Jan 2	Rushden & Diamonds	(Rd 3) D 0-0		6,431
Jan 13	RUSHDEN & DIAMONDS	(R) W 3-1	Smith 2, Hasselbaink	39,159
Jan 23	Portsmouth	(Rd 4) W 5-1	Harte, Wetherall, Riberio, Kewell, Wijnhard	18,864
Feb 13	TOTTENHAM HOTSPUR	(Rd 5) D 1-1	Harte	34,521
Feb 24	Tottenham Hotspur	(R) L 0-2		32,307

Worthington Cup

Oct 28	BRADFORD CITY	(Rd 3) W 1-0	Kewell	27,561
Nov 11	Leicester City	(Rd 4) L 1-2	Kewell	20,161

UEFA Cup

Sep 15	CS MARITIMO	(Rd 1/FL) W 1-0	Hasselbaink	38,033
Sep 29	CS Maritimo*	(Rd 1/SL) L 0-1		10,000
Oct 20	AS Roma	(Rd2/FL) L 0-1		41,892
Nov 3	AS ROMA	(Rd2/SL) D 0-0		39,161

*Leeds won 4-1 on penalties.

MANAGER: George Graham (until September)/David O'Leary

CAPTAIN: Lucas Radebe

TOP SCORER: Jimmy Floyd Hasselbaink

BIGGEST WIN: 5-1 v Portsmouth, 23 January 1999, FA Cup, Round 4; 5-1 v West Ham United, 1 May 1999, League

HIGHEST ATTENDANCE: 55,172 v Manchester United, 29 November 1998, lost 2-3, League

MAJOR TRANSFERS IN: Clyde Wijnhard from Willem II, Danny Granville from Chelsea, David Batty from Newcastle United

League & Cup Appearances (substitute)

PLAYER	LEAGUE	CUP COMPETITION			TOTAL
		FA CUP	WORTHINGTON	UEFA	
Batty	10				10
Bowyer	35	4	2	4	45
Granville	7 (2)	3	1	0 (1)	11 (3)
Haaland	24 (5)	3 (1)		2 (1)	29 (7)
Halle	14 (3)	2	1	2	19 (3)
Harte	34 (1)	5	1	3	43 (1)
Hasselbaink	36	5	2	4	47
Hiden	14		1	4	19
Hopkin	32 (2)	5	2	4	43 (2)
Jones	3 (5)	0 (1)			3 (6)
Kewell	36 (2)	5	2	4	47 (2)
Knarvik		0 (1)			0 (1)
Korston	4 (3)				4 (3)
Lilley	0 (2)			0 (1)	0 (3)
Martyn	34	5	1	4	44
McPhail	11 (6)		1	2	14 (6)
Molenaar	17		2	4	23
Radebe	29	3	1	3	36
Ribeiro	6 (6)	1 (1)	1	1 (1)	9 (8)
Robinson	4 (1)		1		5 (1)
Smith	15 (7)	2 (1)			17 (8)
Wetherall	14 (7)	4			18 (7)
Wijnhard	11 (7)	1 (1)	1	1 (3)	14 (11)
Woodgate	25	5	2	1	33

Goalscorers

PLAYER	LEAGUE	CUP COMPETITION			TOTAL
		FA CUP	WORTHINGTON	UEFA	
Hasselbaink	18	1		1	20
Bowyer	9				9
Smith	7	2			9
Kewell	6	1	2		9
Harte	4	2			6
Hopkin	4				4
Wijnhard	3	1			4
Halle	2				2
Korsten	2				2
Molenaar	2				2
Woodgate	2				2
Haaland	1				1
Ribeiro	1	1			2
Wetherall		1			1
Opps' o.gs.	1				1

Fact File

George Graham left after the Tottenham Hotspur game in September. David O'Leary took over as caretaker manager and was subsequently appointed to the post.

Final Premier League Table

		P	W	D	L	F	A	Pts
1	MANCHESTER UNITED	38	22	13	3	80	37	79
2	ARSENAL	38	22	12	4	59	17	78
3	CHELSEA	38	20	15	3	57	30	67
4	LEEDS UNITED	38	18	13	7	62	34	67
5	WEST HAM UNITED	38	16	9	13	46	53	57
6	ASTON VILLA	38	15	10	13	51	46	55
7	LIVERPOOL	38	15	9	14	68	49	54
8	DERBY COUNTY	38	13	13	12	40	45	52
9	MIDDLESBROUGH	38	12	15	11	48	54	51
10	LEICESTER CITY	38	12	13	13	40	46	49
11	TOTTENHAM HOTSPUR	38	11	14	13	47	50	47
12	SHEFFIELD WEDNESDAY	38	13	7	18	41	42	46
13	NEWCASTLE UNITED	38	11	13	14	48	54	46
14	EVERTON	38	11	10	17	42	47	43
15	COVENTRY CITY	38	11	9	18	39	51	42
16	WIMBLEDON	38	10	12	16	40	63	42
17	SOUTHAMPTON	38	11	8	19	37	64	41
18	CHARLTON ATHLETIC	38	8	12	18	41	56	36
19	BLACKBURN ROVERS	38	7	14	17	38	52	35
20	NOTTINGHAM FOREST	38	7	9	22	35	69	30

Season 1999-2000

Premier League

DATE	OPPONENTS	SCORE	GOALSCORERS	ATTENDANCE
Aug 7	DERBY COUNTY	D 0-0		40,118
Aug 11	Southampton	W 3-0	Bridges 3	15,206
Aug 14	Manchester United	L 0-2		55,187
Aug 21	SUNDERLAND	W 2-1	Bowyer, Mills	39,064
Aug 23	LIVERPOOL	L 1-2	Song o.g.	39,703
Aug 28	Tottenham Hotspur	W 2-1	Smith, Harte	36,012
Sep 11	Coventry City	W 4-3	Bowyer, Harte, Huckerby, Bridges	21,532
Sep 19	MIDDLESBROUGH	W 2-0	Bridges, Kewell	34,122
Sep 25	NEWCASTLE UNITED	W 3-2	Bowyer, Kewell, Bridges	40,192
Oct 3	Watford	W 2-1	Bridges, Kewell	19,677
Oct 16	SHEFFIELD WEDNESDAY	W 2-0	Smith 2	39,437
Oct 24	Everton	D 4-4	Bridges 2, Kewell, Woodgate	37,355
Oct 30	WEST HAM UNITED	W 1-0	Harte	40,190
Nov 7	Wimbledon	L 0-2		18,747
Nov 20	BRADFORD CITY	W 2-1	Smith, Harte (pen)	39,937
Nov 28	SOUTHAMPTON	W 1-0	Bridges	39,288
Dec 5	Derby County	W 1-0	Harte (pen)	29,455
Dec 19	Chelsea	W 2-0	McPhail 2	35,106
Dec 26	LEICESTER CITY	W 2-1	Bridges, Bowyer	40,105
Dec 28	Arsenal	L 0-2		38,096
Jan 3	ASTON VILLA	L 1-2	Kewell	40,027
Jan 23	Sunderland	W 2-1	Wilcox, Bridges	41,947
Feb 5	Liverpool	L 1-3	Bowyer	44,793
Feb 12	TOTTENHAM HOTSPUR	W 1-0	Kewell	40,127
Feb 20	MANCHESTER UNITED	L 0-1		40,160
Feb 26	Middlesbrough	D 0-0		34,800
Mar 5	COVENTRY CITY	W 3-0	Kewell, Bridges, Wilcox	38,710
Mar 12	Bradford City	W 2-1	Bridges 2	18,276
Mar 19	WIMBLEDON	W 4-1	Bakke 2, Harte (pen), Kewell	39,256
Mar 26	Leicester City	L 1-2	Kewell	21,095
Apr 1	CHELSEA	L 0-1		40,162
Apr 9	Aston Villa	L 0-1		33,889
Apr 16	ARSENAL	L 0-4		39,307
Apr 23	Newcastle United	D 2-2	Bridges, Wilcox	36,460
Apr 30	Sheffield Wednesday	W 3-0	Hopkin, Bridges, Kewell	23,416
May 3	WATFORD	W 3-1	Bridges, Duberry, Huckerby	36,324
May 8	EVERTON	D 1-1	Bridges	37,713
May 14	West Ham United	D 0-0		26,044

FA Cup

Dec 12	PORT VALE	(Rd 3) W 2-0	Bakke 2	11,912
Jan 9	Manchester City	(Rd 4) W 5-2	Bakke, Smith, Kewell 2, Bowyer	29,240
Jan 30	Aston Villa	(Rd 5) L 2-3	Harte, Bakke	30,026

Worthington Cup

Oct 13	BLACKBURN ROVERS	(Rd 3) W 1-0	Mills	24,353
Dec 15	Leicester City*	(Rd 4) D 0-0		16,125

*Lost 4-2 on pens.

UEFA Cup

Sep 14	Partizan Belgrade†	(Rd 1/FL) W 3-1	Bowyer 2, Radebe	4,950
Sep 30	PARTIZAN BELGRADE	(Rd 1/SL) W 1-0	Huckerby	39,806
Oct 21	LOKOMOTIV MOSCOW	(Rd 2/FL) W 4-1	Bowyer 2, Smith, Kewell	37,814
Nov 4	Lokomotiv Moscow	(Rd 2/SL) W 3-0	Harte (pen), Bridges 2	8,000
Dec 2	Spartak Moscow#	(Rd 3/FL) L 1-2	Kewell	6,000
Dec 9	SPARTAK MOSCOW*	(Rd 3/SL) W 1-0	Radebe	39,732
Mar 2	AS Roma	(Rd 4/FL) D 0-0		37,726
Mar 9	AS ROMA	(Rd 4/SL) W 1-0	Kewell	39,149
Mar 16	SLAVIA PRAGUE	(QF/FL) W 3-0	Wilcox, Kewell, Bowyer	39,519
Mar 23	Slavia Prague	(QF/SL) L 1-2	Kewell	13,460
Apr 6	Galatasaray	(SF/FL) L 0-2		30,000
Apr 20	GALATASARAY	(SF/SL) D 2-2	Bakke 2	38,406

†Played at Heerenveen. #Played at Sofia. *Won on away goals rule.

MANAGER: David O'Leary

CAPTAIN: Lucas Radebe   TOP SCORER: Michael Bridges

BIGGEST WIN: January 9, 2000 5-2 v Manchester City, FA Cup Round 4

HIGHEST ATTENDANCE: August 14, 1999 55,187 v Manchester United, lost 0-2, Premier Division

MAJOR TRANSFERS IN: Michael Bridges from Sunderland, Darren Huckerby from Coventry, Danny Mills from Charlton, Michael Duberry from Chelsea, Eirik Bakke from Songdal, Jason Wilcox from Blackburn

MAJOR TRANSFERS OUT: Jimmy Floyd Hasselbaink to Atletico Madrid, David Wetherall and Gunnar Halle to Bradford City

League & Cup Appearances (substitute)

PLAYER	LEAGUE	CUP COMPETITION			TOTAL
		FA CUP	WORTHINGTON	UEFA	
Bakke	24 (5)	3	2	9 (1)	38 (6)
Batty	16		2	4	22
Bowyer	31 (2)	3	1	11	46 (2)
Bridges	32 (2)	1 (1)	2	12	47 (3)
Duberry	12 (1)	1	0 (1)	1	14 (2)
Haaland	7 (6)			5 (1)	12 (7)
Harte	33	3		12	49
Hiden	0 (1)				0 (1)
Hopkin	10 (4)	1		2 (2)	13 (6)
Huckerby	9 (24)	1 (2)	0 (1)	1 (8)	11 (35)
Jones	5 (6)	0 (1)	0 (1)	3 (2)	8 (10)
Kelly	28 (3)	3	2	11	44 (3)
Kewell	36	3	2	12	53
Martyn	38	3	2	12	55
McPhail	22 (1)	3	1 (1)	9	35 (2)
Mills	16 (1)	0 (1)	1	2	19 (2)
Radebe	31	2	2	12	47
Smith	20 (6)	2 (1)	1	2	25 (7)
Wilcox	15 (5)	2	0	3 (1)	20 (6)
Woodgate	32 (2)	3	2	10	47 (2)

Goalscorers

PLAYER	LEAGUE	CUP COMPETITION			TOTAL
		FA CUP	WORTHINGTON	UEFA	
Bridges	19			2	21
Kewell	10	2		5	17
Bowyer	5	1		5	11
Bakke	2	4		2	8
Harte	6	1		1	8
Smith	4	1		1	6
Wilcox	3			1	4
Huckerby	2		1		3
McPhail	2				2
Mills	1		1		2
Radebe				2	2
Duberry	1				1
Hopkin	1				1
Woodgate	1				1
Opps' o.g.s.	1				1

Fact File

Six goals in as many games during the autumn launched Michael Bridges' Elland Road career and earned him an England call-up.

Final Premier League Table

		P	W	D	L	F	A	Pts
1	MANCHESTER UNITED	38	28	7	3	97	45	91
2	ARSENAL	38	22	7	9	73	43	73
3	LEEDS UNITED	38	21	6	11	58	43	69
4	LIVERPOOL	38	19	10	9	51	30	67
5	CHELSEA	38	18	11	9	53	34	65
6	ASTON VILLA	38	15	13	10	46	35	58
7	SUNDERLAND	38	16	10	12	57	56	58
8	LEICESTER CITY	38	16	7	15	55	55	55
9	WEST HAM UNITED	38	15	10	13	52	53	55
10	TOTTENHAM HOTSPUR	38	15	8	15	57	49	53
11	NEWCASTLE UNITED	38	14	10	14	63	54	52
12	MIDDLESBROUGH	38	14	10	14	46	52	52
13	EVERTON	38	12	14	12	59	49	50
14	COVENTRY CITY	38	12	8	18	47	54	44
15	SOUTHAMPTON	38	12	8	18	45	62	44
16	DERBY COUNTY	38	9	11	18	44	57	38
17	BRADFORD CITY	38	9	9	20	38	68	36
18	WIMBLEDON	38	7	12	19	46	74	33
19	SHEFFIELD WEDNESDAY	38	8	7	23	38	70	31
20	WATFORD	38	6	6	26	35	77	24

Season 2000-2001

Premier League

DATE	OPPONENTS	SCORE	GOALSCORERS	ATTENDANCE
Aug 19	EVERTON	W 2-0	Smith 2	40,010
Aug 26	Middlesbrough	W 2-1	Bowyer, Smith	31,626
Sep 5	MANCHESTER CITY	L 1-2	Bowyer	40,055
Sep 9	Coventry City	D 0-0		20,377
Sep 16	IPSWICH TOWN	L 1-2	Bowyer	33,446
Sep 23	Derby County	D 1-1	Harte	26,248
Sep 30	TOTTENHAM HOTSPUR	W 4-3	Viduka 2, Smith 2	37,562
Oct 14	CHARLTON ATHLETIC	W 3-1	Smith, Viduka 2	38,837
Oct 21	Manchester United	L 0-3		67,525
Oct 29	Bradford City	D 1-1	Viduka	17,364
Nov 4	LIVERPOOL	W 4-3	Viduka 4	40,055
Nov 11	Chelsea	D 1-1	Viduka	35,121
Nov 18	WEST HAM UNITED	L 0-1		40,005
Nov 26	ARSENAL	W 1-0	Dacourt	38,084
Dec 2	Leicester City	L 1-3	Viduka	21,486
Dec 9	Southampton	L 0-1		15,225
Dec 16	SUNDERLAND	W 2-0	Bowyer, Viduka	40,053
Dec 23	ASTON VILLA	L 1-2	Woodgate	39,714
Dec 26	Newcastle United	L 1-2	Dacourt	52,118
Jan 1	MIDDLESBROUGH	D 1-1	Keane (pen)	39,251
Jan 13	Manchester City	W 4-0	Bakke, Bowyer, Keane 2	34,288
Jan 20	NEWCASTLE UNITED	L 1-3	Keane	40,005
Jan 24	Aston Villa	W 2-1	Bowyer, Harte (pen)	29,335
Jan 31	COVENTRY CITY	W 1-0	Keane	36,555
Feb 3	Ipswich Town	W 2-1	Venus o.g., Keane	22,015
Feb 7	Everton	D 2-2	Harte, Dacourt	34,224
Feb 10	DERBY COUNTY	D 0-0		38,789
Feb 24	Tottenham Hotspur	W 2-1	Harte (pen), Bowyer	36,070
Mar 3	MANCHESTER UNITED	D 1-1	Viduka	40,055
Mar 17	Charlton Athletic	W 2-1	Viduka, Smith	20,043
Mar 31	Sunderland	W 2-0	Smith, Viduka	48,285
Apr 7	SOUTHAMPTON	W 2-0	Kewell, Keane	39,267
Apr 13	Liverpool	W 2-1	Ferdinand, Bowyer	44,116
Apr 21	West Ham United	W 2-0	Keane, Ferdinand	26,041
Apr 28	CHELSEA	W 2-0	Keane, Viduka	39,253
May 5	Arsenal	L 1-2	Harte	38,142
May 13	BRADFORD CITY	W 6-1	Viduka, Harte, Bakke, Smith, Kewell, Bowyer	38,300
May 19	LEICESTER CITY	W 3-1	Smith 2, Harte	39,105

FA Cup

Jan 2	BARNSLEY	(Rd 3) W 1-0	Viduka	32,386
Jan 13	LIVERPOOL	(Rd 4) L 0-2		37,628

Worthington Cup

Oct 31	Tranmere Rovers	(Rd 3) L 2-3*	Huckerby 2	11,681

*Result after extra time.

European Champions League

Aug 9	TSV 1860 MUNICH	(QR3/FL) W 2-1	Smith, Harte (pen)	33,769
Aug 9	TSV 1860 Munich	(QR3/SL) W 1-0	Smith	56,000
Sep 13	Barcelona	(FP/Gp H) L 0-4		85,000
Sep 19	AC MILAN	(FP/Gp H) W 1-0	Bowyer	35,398
Sep 26	BESIKTAS	(FP/Gp H) W 6-0	Bowyer 2, Viduka, Matteo, Bakke, Huckerby	34,435
Oct 18	Besiktas	(FP/Gp H) D 0-0		20,000
Oct 24	BARCELONA	(FP/Gp H) D 1-1	Bowyer	36,721
Nov 8	AC Milan	(FP/Gp H) D 1-1	Matteo	52,289
Nov 3	REAL MADRID	(SP/Gp D) L 0-2		36,794
Dec 5	Lazio	(SP/Gp D) W 1-0	Smith	42,450
Feb 13	ANDERLECHT	(SP/Gp D) W 2-1	Harte, Bowyer	36,068
Feb 21	Anderlecht	(SP/Gp D) W 4-1	Smith 2, Viduka, Harte (pen)	28,000
Mar 6	Real Madrid	(SP/Gp D) L 2-3	Smith, Viduka	40,000
Mar 14	LAZIO	(SP/Gp D) D 3-3	Bowyer, Wilcox, Viduka	36,741
Apr 4	DEPORTÍVO LA CORUÑA	(QF/FL) W 3-0	Harte, Smith, Ferdinand	35,508
Apr 17	Deportívo La Coruña	(QF/SL) L 0-2		35,600
May 2	VALENCIA	(SF/FL) D 0-0		35,437
May 2	Valencia	(SF/SL) L 0-3		53,000

MANAGER: David O'Leary

CAPTAIN: Lucas Radebe/Gary Kelly   **TOP SCORER:** Mark Viduka

BIGGEST WIN: 6-0 v Besiktas, 26 September 2000, Champions League, First Group Phase   **HIGHEST ATTENDANCE:** 85,000 v Barcelona, 13 September 2000, drew 1-1, Champions League, First Group Phase

MAJOR TRANSFERS IN: Olivier Dacourt from Lens, Mark Viduka from Celtic, Dominic Matteo from Liverpool, Rio Ferdinand from West Ham

MAJOR TRANSFERS OUT: Darren Huckerby and Alf Inge Haaland to Manchester City, Matthew Jones to Leicester City

League & Cup Appearances (substitute)

PLAYER	LEAGUE	FA CUP	WORTHINGTON	CL	TOTAL
Bakke	24 (5)	2	1	10 (2)	37 (7)
Batty	13 (3)	2		7 (1)	22 (4)
Bowyer	38	1		15	54
Bridges	6 (1)			4	10
Burns	3 (1)		1	3 (1)	7 (2)
Dacourt	33	1		14	48
Evans	0 (1)			0 (1)	0 (2)
Ferdinand	23	2		7	32
Hackworth			0 (1)	0 (2)	0 (3)
Harte	29	1	1	17	48
Hay	2 (2)		1	0 (1)	3 (3)
Huckerby	2 (5)		1	0 (2)	3 (7)
Jones	3 (1)		1	1	5 (1)
Keane	12 (6)	2			14 (6)
Kelly	22 (2)	1	1	11 (1)	35 (3)
Kewell	36 (2)	5	2	4	47 (2)
Martyn	23		1	12	36
Matteo	30	2	1	15	48
Maybury				1	1
McPhail	3 (4)			1 (2)	4 (6)
Mills	20 (3)	1		15 (1)	36 (4)
Radebe	19 (1)	1	0 (1)	10	30 (2)
Robinson	15 (1)	1	1	6	23 (1)
Smith	26 (7)	1 (1)	0 (1)	16	43 (9)
Viduka	34	2	1	16	53
Wilcox	7 (10)	0 (1)		2 (3)	9 (14)
Woodgate	14	1	2	5	22

Goalscorers

PLAYER	LEAGUE	FA CUP	WORTHINGTON	CL	TOTAL
Viduka	17	1		4	22
Smith	11			7	18
Bowyer	9			6	15
Harte	7			4	11
Keane	9				9
Bakke	2		1		3
Dacourt	3				3
Ferdinand	2			1	3
Huckerby			2	1	3
Kewell	2				2
Matteo				2	2
Wilcox				1	1
Woodgate	1				1
Opps' o.gs.	1				1

Fact File

Harry Kewell, Mark Viduka and reserve goalkeeper Danny Milosevic were all named in Australia's Olympic squad (Kewell later pulled out because of an injury), but the Aussie team failed to progress beyond the group stage.

Final Premier League Table

		P	W	D	L	F	A	Pts
1	MANCHESTER UNITED	38	24	8	6	79	31	80
2	ARSENAL	38	20	10	8	63	38	70
3	LIVERPOOL	38	20	9	9	71	39	69
4	LEEDS UNITED	38	20	8	10	64	43	68
5	IPSWICH TOWN	38	20	6	12	57	42	66
6	CHELSEA	38	17	10	11	68	45	61
7	SUNDERLAND	38	15	12	11	46	41	57
8	ASTON VILLA	38	13	15	10	46	43	54
9	CHARLTON ATHLETIC	38	14	10	14	50	57	52
10	SOUTHAMPTON	38	14	10	14	40	48	52
11	NEWCASTLE UNITED	38	14	9	15	44	50	51
12	TOTTENHAM HOTSPUR	38	13	10	15	47	54	49
13	LEICESTER CITY	38	14	6	18	39	51	48
14	MIDDLESBROUGH	38	9	15	14	44	44	42
15	WEST HAM UNITED	38	10	12	16	45	50	42
16	EVERTON	38	11	9	18	45	59	42
17	DERBY COUNTY	38	10	12	16	37	59	42
18	MANCHESTER CITY	38	8	10	20	41	65	34
19	COVENTRY CITY	38	8	10	20	36	63	34
20	BRADFORD CITY	38	5	11	22	30	70	26

Season 2001-2002

Premier League

DATE	OPPONENTS	SCORE	GOALSCORERS	ATTENDANCE
Aug 18	SOUTHAMPTON	W 2-0	Bowyer, Smith	39,715
Aug 21	Arsenal	W 2-1	Harte, Viduka	38,062
Aug 25	West Ham United	D 0-0		24,517
Sep 8	BOLTON WANDERERS	D 0-0		40,153
Sep 16	Charlton Athletic	W 2-0	Keane, Mills	20,451
Sep 23	DERBY COUNTY	W 3-0	Bakke, Kewell 2	39,155
Sep 30	Ipswich Town	W 2-1	Keane, Venus o.g.	22,643
Oct 13	Liverpool	D 1-1	Kewell	44,352
Oct 21	CHELSEA	D 0-0		40,171
Oct 27	Manchester United	D 1-1	Viduka	67,555
Nov 4	TOTTENHAM HOTSPUR	W 2-1	Harte, Kewell	40,203
Nov 20	Sunderland	L 0-2		48,005
Nov 25	ASTON VILLA	D 1-1	Smith	40,159
Dec 2	Fulham	D 0-0		20,918
Dec 9	Blackburn Rovers	W 2-1	Kewell 2	28,309
Dec 16	LEICESTER CITY	D 2-2	Kewell, Viduka	38,237
Dec 19	EVERTON	W 3-2	Viduka, Fowler 2	40,201
Dec 22	NEWCASTLE UNITED	L 3-4	Bowyer, Viduka, Harte	40,287
Dec 26	Bolton Wanderers	W 3-0	Fowler 3	27,060
Dec 29	Southampton	W 1-0	Bowyer	31,622
Jan 1	WEST HAM UNITED	W 3-0	Viduka 2, Fowler	39,322
Jan 12	Newcastle United	L 1-3	Smith	52,130
Jan 20	ARSENAL	D 1-1	Fowler	40,143
Jan 30	Chelsea	L 0-2		40,614
Feb 3	LIVERPOOL	L 0-4		40,216
Feb 9	Middlesbrough	D 2-2	Bakke, Fowler	30,221
Feb 24	CHARLTON ATHLETIC	D 0-0		39,374
Mar 3	Everton	D 0-0		33,226
Mar 6	IPSWICH TOWN	W 2-0	Fowler, Harte (pen)	39,414
Mar 17	BLACKBURN ROVERS	W 3-1	Fowler 2, Kewell	39,857
Mar 23	Leicester City	W 2-0	Viduka, Fowler	18,976
Mar 30	MANCHESTER UNITED	L 3-4	Viduka, Harte, Bowyer	40,058
Apr 1	Tottenham Hotspur	L 1-2	Viduka	35,167
Apr 7	SUNDERLAND	W 2-0	Craddock o.g., Keane	39,195
Apr 13	Aston Villa	W 1-0	Viduka	40,039
Apr 20	FULHAM	L 0-1		39,111
Apr 27	Derby County	W 1-0	Bowyer	30,735
May 11	MIDDLESBROUGH	W 1-0	Smith	40,218

FA Cup

Dec 12	Cardiff City	(Rd 3) L 1-2	Viduka	22,009

Worthington Cup

Oct 9	Leicester City	(Rd 3) W 6-0	Keane 3, Bakke, Viduka Kewell	16,316
Nov 28	CHELSEA	(Rd 4) L 0-2		33,841

UEFA Cup

Sep 20	CS Maritimo	(Rd 1/FL) L 0-1		10,500
Sep 27	CS MARITIMO	(Rd 1/SL) W 3-0	Keane, Kewell, Bakke	38,125
Oct 18	TROYES	(Rd 2/FL) W 4-2	Viduka 2, Bowyer 2	40,015
Nov 1	Troyes	(Rd 2/SL) L 3-2	Viduka, Keane, Bakke	15,079
Nov 22	Grasshopper-club	(Rd 3/FL) W 2-1	Harte, Smith	15,000
Dec 6	GRASSHOPPER-CLUB	(Rd 3/SL) D 2-2	Kewell, Keane	40,014
Feb 21	PSV Eindhoven	(Rd 4/FL) D 0-0		32,000
Feb 28	PSV EINDHOVEN	(Rd 4/SL) L 0-1		39,755

MANAGER: David O'Leary

CAPTAIN: Rio Ferdinand

TOP SCORER: Mark Viduka

BIGGEST WIN: 6-0 v Leicester City, 9 October 2001, Worthington Cup Round 3

HIGHEST ATTENDANCE: 67,555 v Manchester United, 27 October 2001, drew 1-1, League

MAJOR TRANSFERS IN: Seth Johnson from Derby County, Robbie Fowler from Liverpool

MAJOR TRANSFERS OUT: Tony Hackworth to Notts County, Alan Maybury to Heart of Midlothian

---

League & Cup Appearances (substitute)

PLAYER	LEAGUE	CUP COMPETITION			TOTAL
		FA CUP	WORTHINGTON	UEFA	
Bakke	20 (7)		2	6 (1)	31 (8)
Batty	30 (6)	1	1	5 (1)	37 (7)
Bowyer	24 (1)	1	1	3	29 (1)
Dacourt	16 (1)		2	6	24 (1)
Duberry	3	0 (1)	0 (2)	1	4 (3)
Ferdinand	31	1	2	7	41
Fowler	22	1			23
Harte	34 (2)	1	2	8	45 (2)
Johnson	12 (2)				12 (2)
Keane	16 (9)		2	6	24 (9)
Kelly	19 (1)	1	0 (1)	3	23 (2)
Kewell	26 (1)		1	7	34 (1)
Martyn	38	1	2	8	49
Matteo	32		1	7	40
Maybury	0 (1)				0 (1)
McPhail	0 (1)		0 (2)	1	1 (3)
Mills	28	1	2	8	39
Smith	19 (4)	1	1 (1)	4 (1)	25 (6)
Viduka	33	1	1	7	42
Wilcox	4 (9)		1	1 (2)	6 (11)
Woodgate	11 (2)	1	1		13 (2)

Goalscorers

PLAYER	LEAGUE	CUP COMPETITION			TOTAL
		FA CUP	WORTHINGTON	UEFA	
Viduka	11	1	1	3	16
Fowler	12				12
Kewell	8		1	2	11
Keane	3		3	3	9
Bowyer	5			2	7
Harte	5			1	6
Smith	4			1	5
Bakke	2		1	1	4
Mills	1				1
Opps' o.gs.	2				2

Fact File

Olivier Dacourt (France), Rio Ferdinand, Robbie Fowler, Nigel Martyn and Danny Mills (England), Lucas Radebe (South Africa) and Ian Harte, Robbie Keane and Gary Kelly (Republic of Ireland) were Leeds' representatives at the 2002 World Cup in Japan and South Korea.

Final Premier League Table

		P	W	D	L	F	A	Pts
1	ARSENAL	38	26	9	3	79	36	87
2	LIVERPOOL	38	24	8	6	67	30	80
3	MANCHESTER UNITED	38	24	5	9	87	45	77
4	NEWCASTLE UNITED	38	21	8	9	74	52	71
5	LEEDS UNITED	38	18	12	8	53	37	66
6	CHELSEA	38	17	13	8	66	38	64
7	WEST HAM UNITED	38	15	8	15	48	57	53
8	ASTON VILLA	38	12	14	12	46	47	50
9	TOTTENHAM HOTSPUR	38	14	8	16	49	53	50
10	BLACKBURN ROVERS	38	12	10	16	55	51	46
11	SOUTHAMPTON	38	12	9	17	46	54	45
12	MIDDLESBROUGH	38	12	9	17	35	47	45
13	FULHAM	38	10	14	14	36	44	44
14	CHARLTON ATHLETIC	38	10	14	14	38	49	44
15	EVERTON	38	11	10	17	45	57	43
16	BOLTON WANDERERS	38	9	13	16	44	62	40
17	SUNDERLAND	38	10	10	18	29	51	40
18	IPSWICH TOWN	38	9	9	20	41	64	36
19	DERBY COUNTY	38	8	6	24	33	63	30
20	LEICESTER CITY	38	5	13	20	30	64	28

Complete Players' Career Records

(records include Leeds United players 1919-2002)

FAC = FA Cup, **LC** = League Cup, **Other** = Charity Shield, Inter-Cities Fairs Cup, European Cup/Champions League, UEFA Cup, European Cup-Winners' Cup, Full Members Cup, Simod Cup, Zenith Data Systems Cup and Simod Cup.

Player		Birthplace	From	Year Joined	Year Left	To
Abel	Robert	Manchester	Junior	1931	1936	Bradford C
Adams	Mickey	Sheffield	Coventry C	1987	1989	Southampton
Addy	Mike	Knottingley	Junior	1962	1967	Corby T
Ainsley	George	South Shields	Bolton W	1936	1947	Bradford
Aizlewood	Mark	Newport	Charlton A	1987	1989	Bradford C
Alderson	Tom	West Auckland	Huddersfield T	1930	1933	Darlington
Allan	Jimmy	Airdrie	Airdrie	1925	1928	Third Lanark
Allen	Jack	Newburn	Prudhoe Castle	1922	1924	Brentford
Andrews	Ian	Nottingham	Celtic	1988	1988	Loan
Arins	Tony	Chesterfield	Burnley	1976	1980	Scunthorpe U
Armand	John	Sabathu, India	West Stanley	1922	1929	Swansea T
Armes	Sammy	New Seaham	Blackpool	1936	1939	Middlesbrough
Armitage	Len	Sheffield	Sheffield W	1920	1923	Wigan
Ashall	Jimmy	Chesterfield	Junior	1951	1961	Weymouth
Ashurst	Jack	Coatbridge	Carlisle U	1986	1988	Doncaster R
Aspin	Neil	Gateshead	Junior	1982	1989	Port Vale
Atkinson	Josh	Blackpool	Blackpool	1924	1928	Chester
Baird	Hugh	New Monklan	Airdrie	1957	1958	Aberdeen
Baird	Ian	Rotherham	Southampton	1985	1988	Portsmouth ⎫
			Portsmouth	1987	1990	Middlesbrough ⎭
Baker	Aaron	Basford Green	Ilkeston T	1927	1927	Sheffield W
Baker	Jim	Basford Green	Huddersfield T	1920	1926	Nelson
Baker	Lawrie	Sheffield	Blackpool	1923	1925	Barnsley
Bakke	Eirik	Songdal, Norway	Songdal	1999	–	Still at club
Balcombe	Steve	Bangor, Wales	Home Farm	1978	1982	Home Farm
Bannister	Eddie	Leyland	Preston NE	1946	1950	Barnsley
Barnes	Peter	Manchester	West Brom A	1981	1984	Coventry C
Barritt	Ron	Huddersfield	Frickley Coll	1950	1952	York C
Bates	Mick	Doncaster	Junior	1964	1976	Walsall
Batey	Bob	Haltwhistle	Preston NE	1946	1947	Southport
Batty	David	Leeds	Junior	1987	1993	Blackburn R ⎫
			Newcastle U	1998	–	Still at club ⎭
Beeney	Mark	Tunbridge Wells	Brighton	1993	–	Retired, injured
Beesley	Paul	Liverpool	Sheffield U	1995	1997	Manchester C
Beglin	Jim	Waterford	Liverpool	1989	–	Retired, injured
Belfitt	Rod	Doncaster	Junior	1963	1971	Ipswich T
Bell	Albert	Sunderland	West Stanley	1922	1927	Durham C
Bell	Tom	Gateshead	Birtley	1922	1925	Southend U
Bell	Willie	Johnstone	Queens Park	1960	1967	Leicester C
Bennett	Willie	Manchester	Winsford U	1928	1933	Southport
Best	Jerry	Northumberland	Newcastle U	1920	1920	Non-league club
Blake	Noel	Kingston, Jamaica	Portsmouth	1988	1990	Stoke C
Boardman	Billy	Manchester	Eccles	1920	1922	Doncaster R
Blunt	Jason	Penzance	Junior	1994	1996	Blackpool
Bowman	Robert	Durham C	Junior	1992	1997	Rotherham U
Bowyer	Lee	London	Charlton A	1996	–	Still at club
Boyle	Wesley	Portadown	Junior	1996	–	Still at club
Bremner	Billy	Stirling	Junior	1959	1976	Hull C
Bridges	Michael	North Shields	Sunderland	1999	–	Still at club
Brock	John	Edinburgh	Junior	1920	1921	Released
Brockie	Vince	Greenock	Junior	1985	1989	Doncaster R
Brolin	Tomas	Hudiksvall, Sweden	Parma	1995	1997	Crystal P
Brook	Harold	Sheffield	Sheffield U	1954	1958	Lincoln C
Brown	George	Northumberland	Burnley	1935	1936	Darlington
Brown	Tony	Bradford	Thackley	1983	1990	Rochdale
Brown	Vic	Bedford	Bedford T	1929	1933	Coventry C
Browne	Bobby	Londonderry	Derry City	1935	1947	York C
Browning	Len	Leeds	Junior	1946	1951	Sheffield U
Buck	Teddy	County Durham	West Stanley	1927	1929	Grimsby T
Buckley	Arthur	Oldham	Oldham A	1936	–	World War II
Buckley	John	East Kilbride	Doncaster R	1986	1987	Rotherham U
Bullions	Jim	Stirling	Derby C	1947	1950	Shrewsbury T
Burbanks	Eddie	Doncaster	Hull City	1953	–	Retired
Burden	Tommy	Andover	Chester	1948	1954	Bristol C
Burgin	Ted	Sheffield	Doncaster R	1958	1961	Rochdale

Complete Players' Career Records: Abel – Burgin

League			FAC			LC			Other			Total		
Apps	Sub	Goals	Apps	Sub	Goals	Apps	Sub	Goals	Apps	Sub	Goals	Apps	Sub	Goals
1		0	0		0	0		0	0		0	1		0
77		2	6		1	4		0	1		0	88		3
2		0	0		0	0		0	0		0	2		0
91		30	6		3	0		0	0		0	97		33
70	5	3	1		0	3		0	2		1	76	5	4
4		2	0		0	0		0	0		0	4		2
70		0	4		0	0		0	0		0	74		0
2		0	0		0	0		0	0		0	2		0
1		0	0		0	0		0	0		0	1		0
	1	0	0		0	0		0	0		0	0	1	0
74		23	5		1	0		0	0		0	79		24
79		8	3		1	0		0	0		0	82		9
48		11	5		3	0		0	0		0	53		14
89		0	2		0	0		0	0		0	91		0
93	1	1	6		0	6		0	3		0	108	1	1
208	3	5	17		0	9		1	6		0	240	3	6
52		0	1		0	0		0	0		0	53		0
45		22	0		0	0		0	0		0	45		22
165	2	50	8		6	9		1	8		0	190	2	57
2		0	0		0	0		0	0		0	2		0
200		2	8		0	0		0	0		0	208		2
11		0	0		0	0		0	0		0	11		0
68	17	6	5		4	5		1	25	3	4	103	20	15
1	1	0	0		0	1		0	0	2	0	2	3	0
44		1	0		0	0		0	0		0	44		1
56	2	5	1		0	5		1	0		0	62	2	6
6		1	0		0	0		0	0		0	6		1
106	15	4	10	4	1	9	8	1	26	9	3	151	36	9
8		0	0		0	0		0	0		0	8		0
270	19	4	15		0	20		0	33	2	0	338	21	4
35		3	4	1	0	3		0	0		0	42	1	3
19	3	0	5		0	5	1	0	2	2	0	31	6	0
18	1	0	0		0	0		0	2		0	20	1	0
57	18	17	6	1	3	17	2	5	24	2	8	104	23	33
1		0	0		0	0		0	0		0	1		0
1		0	0		0	0		0	0		0	1		0
204		15	24		1	15		1	17		1	260		18
10		4	1		0	0		0	0		0	11		4
11		1	0		0	0		0	0		0	11		1
51		4	2		0	4	1	0	4		0	61	1	4
4		0	0		0	0		0	0		0	4		0
2	1	0	0		0	0		0	0		0	2	1	0
4	3	0	0		0	0	1	0	1		0	5	4	0
181	7	35	16		3	6	1	1	33		13	236	8	52
0	1	0	0		0	0		0	0		0	0	1	0
586	1	90	69		6	38		3	79		16	772	1	115
38	3	19	1	1	0	2		0	16		2	57	4	21
6		0	0		0	0		0	0		0	6		0
2		0	0		0	0		0	0		0	2		0
15	2	4	1	1	0	2	2	0	0		0	18	5	4
102		46	4		1	0		0	0		0	106		47
37		19	4		2	0		0	0		0	41		21
24		1	0		0	0		0	0		0	24		1
1		0	0		0	0		0	0		0	1		0
110		0	4		0	0		0	0		0	114		0
97		42	8		4	0		0	0		0	105		46
8		0	0		0	0		0	0		0	8		0
83		20	3		2	0		0	0		0	86		22
6	4	1	0	1	0	0		0	1		0	7	5	1
35		0	2		0	0		0	0		0	37		0
13		1	0		0	0		0	0		0	13		1
243		13	16		0	0		0	0		0	259		13
58		0	0		0	1		0	0		0	59		0

Player		Birthplace	From	Year Joined	Year Left	To
Burns	Jacob	Sydney, Australia	Parramatta Power	2000	–	Still at club
Burns	Kenny	Glasgow	Nottingham F	1981	1984	Derby C
Butler	Walter	Leeds	Leeds Steelworks	1920	1921	Doncaster R
Butterworth	Aiden	Leeds	Junior	1980	1984	Retired
Butterworth	Frank	Barking	Barnet	1942	–	World War II
Caldwell	Terry	Wakefield	Junior	1959	1961	Carlisle U
Cameron	Bobby	Greenock	Q.P.R.	1959	1962	Gravesend
Cantona	Eric	Paris, France	Nimes	1991	1992	Manchester U
Carling	Terry	Otley	Junior	1956	1962	Lincoln C
Carr	Jimmy	Segefield	Spennymoor	1934	1938	York C
Casey	Terry	Swansea	Junior	1960	1962	Contract ended
Casey	Tom	Bangor, NI	Bangor	1949	1950	Bournemouth
Caswell	Brian	Wednesbury	Doncaster R	1985	–	Retired
Chadwick	Wilf	Bury	Everton	1925	1926	Wolves
Chandler	Jeff	Hammersmith	Blackpool	1979	1981	Bolton W
Chapman	Lee	Lincoln	Nottingham F	1988	1993	Portsmouth ⎫
			Ipswich	1996	1996	Loan ⎭
Charles	John	Swansea	Junior	1949	1957	Juventus ⎫
			Juventus	1962	1962	Roma ⎭
Charlton	Jack	Ashington	Junior	1952	1973	Retired
Cherry	Trevor	Huddersfield	Huddersfield T	1972	1982	Bradford C
Chisholm	Ken	Glasgow	Partick T	1948	1948	Leicester C
Clark	James	County Durham	Newcastle U	1924	1925	Swindon T
Clark	Wallace	Jarrow	Middlesbrough	1921	1923	Birmingham C
Clarke	Allan	Short Heath	Leicester C	1969	1978	Barnsley
Clarke	Harry	Northumberland	Darlington	1947	1947	Darlington
Coates	Walter	County Durham	Leadgate Park	1921	1925	Newport C
Cochrane	David	Portadown	Portadown	1937	1950	Retired
Cochrane	Tom	Newcastle	Doncaster	1928	1936	Middlesbrough
Collins	Bobby	Glasgow	Everton	1962	1967	Bury
Connor	Terry	Leeds	Junior	1979	1983	Brighton
Cooper	Terry	Brotherton	Junior	1961	1975	Middlesbrough
Copping	Wilf	Barnsley	Junior	1929	1934	Arsenal ⎫
			Arsenal	1939	1942	Retired ⎭
Coutts	Tom	County Durham	Dunstan	1927	1928	Southampton
Couzens	Andy	Shipley	Junior	1993	1997	Carlisle U
Coyne	Cyril	Barnsley	Barnsley Main	1944	1946	Stalybridge Celtic
Crowe	Chris	Newcastle	Junior	1956	1960	Blackburn R
Currie	Tony	Edgware	Sheffield U	1976	1979	Q.P.R.
Curtis	Alan	Ton Pentre	Swansea C	1979	1980	Swansea C
Cush	Wilbur	Lurgan, NI	Glenavon	1957	1960	Portadown
Dacourt	Oliver	Montreuil, France	Lens	2000	–	Still at club
Daniels	John	Leeds	Ashton	1933	1935	Stockport
Danskin	Bob	Newcastle	Wallsend	1929	1932	Bradford
Dark	Alf	Bristol	Newcastle U	1921	1923	Port Vale
Davey	Nigel	Garforth	Junior	1964	1974	Rotherham U
Davies	Byron	Llanelli	Llanelli	1952	1956	Newport C
Davison	Bobby	South Shields	Derby C	1987	1993	Leicester C
Dawson	Bobby	South Shields	South Shields	1953	1955	Gateshead
Day	Mervyn	Chelmsford	Aston Villa	1985	1993	Carlisle U
Deane	Brian	Leeds	Sheffield U	1993	1997	Sheffield U
De Mange	Ken	Dublin	Liverpool	1987	1988	Hull C
Depear	Roly	Spalding	Boston U	1948	1949	Newport C
Dickinson	Martin	Leeds	Junior	1980	1986	West Brom A
Doig	Russell	Millport	St Mirren	1986	1988	Peterborough
Donnelly	John	Glasgow	Dumbarton	1983	1984	Partick T
Dorigo	Tony	Melboune, Australia	Chelsea	1991	1997	Torino
Down	Billy	Sunderland	Ashington	1920	1925	Doncaster R
Duberry	Michael	Enfield	Chelsea	1999	–	Still at club
Dudley	Frank	Southend	Southend U	1949	1951	Southampton
Duffield	Bert	Owston Ferry	Castleford T	1920	1925	Bradford
Duggan	Harry	Dublin	Richmond U	1925	1936	Newport C
Dunderdale	Len	Gainsborough	Watford	1939	1946	Watford
Dunn	Jimmy	Rutherglen	Rutherglen	1947	1959	Darlington
Duxbury	Tom	Accrington	Preston NE	1924	1926	Fleetwood
Edwards	Keith	Stockton	Sheffield U	1986	1987	Aberdeen
Edwards	Neil	Aberdare	Junior	1989	1991	Stockport C
Edwards	Walter	Mansfield	Mansfield T	1949	1950	Rochdale
Edwards	Willis	Alfreton	Chesterfield	1925	1939	Retired
Eli	Roger	Bradford	Junior	1982	1985	Wolves

League			FAC			LC			Other			Total		
Apps	Sub	Goals	Apps	Sub	Goals	Apps	Sub	Goals	Apps	Sub	Goals	Apps	Sub	Goals
3	1	0	0		0	1		0	3	1	0	7	2	0
54	2	2	3	0	0	7		2	0		0	64	2	4
1		0	2		3	0		0	0		0	3		3
54	10	15	6		1	4		1	0		0	64	10	17
2		0	0	0	0	0		0	0		0	2		0
20		0	0	0	0	2		0	0		0	22		0
58		9	2	0	0	4		2	0		0	64		11
18	10	9	0	0	0	1		0	6		5	25	10	14
5		0	0	0	0	1		0	0		0	6		0
2		0	0	0	0	0		0	0		0	2		0
3		0	0	0	0	1		0	0		0	4		0
4		0	0	0	0	0		0	0		0	4		0
9		0	0	0	0	0		0	0		0	9		0
16		3	0		0	0		0	0		0	16		3
21	5	2	1		0	1		0	0		0	23	5	2
137	**4**	**63**	**11**		**4**	**15**		**10**	**10**		**4**	**173**	**4**	**81**
308		153	19		4	0		0	0		0	327		157
629		70	52		8	35		7	57		11	773		96
393	3	24	28	1	1	35		4	21	1	3	477	5	32
40		17	0		0	0		0	0		0	40		17
3		0	0		0	0		0	0		0	3		0
13		0	0		0	0		0	0		0	13		0
270	3	110	43	2	25	13		2	35		14	361	5	151
14	1	0	0		0	0		0	0		0	14	1	0
47		3	3		1	0		0	0		0	50		4
175		28	10		4	0		0	0		0	185		32
244		23	15		4	0		0	0		0	259		27
149		24	13		0	2		1	3		0	167		25
83	13	19	6	2	0	4		2	1		1	94	15	22
240	10	7	30	1	0	21		2	48		2	339	11	11
174		4	9		0	0		0	0		0	183		4
1		0	0		0	0		0	0		0	1		0
17	11	1	0	0	0	4	1	1	0	2	0	21	14	2
0		0	0		0	0	2	0	0	2	0	0		0
95		27	3		0	0		0	0		0	98		27
102		11	9		0	13		5	0		0	124		16
28		5	1		0	2		0	4		1	35		6
87		9	3		0	0		0	0		0	90		9
49	1	3	1	0	0	2		0	20		0	72	1	3
1		0	0		0	0		0	0		0	1		0
5		1	1		0	0		0	0		0	6		1
3		0	0		0	0		0	0		0	3		0
13	1	0	1		0	2		0	4	2	0	20	3	0
1		0	0		0	0		0	0		0	1		0
79	12	31	2	4	1	4		1	7	2	3	92	18	36
1		0	0		0	0		0	0		0	1		0
227		0	11		0	14		0	10		0	262		0
131	7	32	13	3	4	8	3	2	3		0	156	13	38
14	1	1	0		0	3		0	2		0	19	1	1
4		0	0		0	0		0	0		0	5		0
100	2	2	6		0	10		0	0		0	116	2	2
3	3	0	1		0	1		0	0	2	0	5	5	0
36	4	4	1		0	3		0	0		0	40	4	4
168	3	5	16		0	12	1	0	9		1	205	4	6
96		0	5		0	0		0	0		0	101		0
20	1	1	1	1	0	0	3	0	6		0	27	5	1
64		23	7		4	0		0	0		0	71		27
203		0	8		0	0		0	0		0	211		0
187		45	9		4	0		0	0		0	196		49
4		0	0		0	0		0	0		0	4		0
422		1	21		0	0		0	0		0	443		1
3		0	0		0	0		0	0		0	3		0
29	14	8	2	3	1	2		0	1		0	34	17	9
0		0	0		0	0		0	0	1	0	0	1	0
2		0	0		0	0		0	0		0	2		0
417		6	27		0	0		0	0		0	444		6
1	1	0	0		0	0		0	0		0	1	1	0

Player		Birthplace	From	Year Joined	Year Left	To
Ellam	Roy	Hemsworth	Huddersfield T	1972	1974	Huddersfield T
Ellson	Merton	Thrapston	Frickley Coll	1920	1922	Frickley Coll
Entwistle	Wayne	Bury	Sunderland	1979	1980	Blackpool
Evans	Gareth	Leeds	Junior	–	2001	Huddersfield Town
Fairclough	Chris	Nottingham	Tottenham H	1989	1995	Bolton W
Faulkner	John	Orpington	Sutton U	1970	1972	Luton T
Fearnley	Harry	Morley	Junior	1941	1949	Halifax T
Fell	John	County Durham	Durham C	1925	1927	Southend U
Ferdinand	Rio	Peckham	West Ham	2000	2002	Manchester U
Fidler	Frank	Middleton	Wrexham	1950	1952	Bournemouth
Finlay	John	Glasgow	New Brighton	1951	1952	Yeovil
Firm	Neil	Bradford	Junior	1976	1982	Peterborough
Firth	Joe	Glasshoughton	Junior	1927	1935	Southend U
Fitzgerald	Peter	Waterford	Sparta Rotterdam	1960	1961	Chester
Flynn	Brian	Port Talbot	Burnley	1977	1982	Burnley
Flynn	Peter	Glasgow	Petershill	1953	1957	Bradford
Ford	Mark	Pontefract	Junior	1993	1997	Burnley
Forrest	Bobby	Rossington	Retford T	1952	1957	Notts C
Forrester	Jamie	Bradford	Auxerre	1992	1995	Grimsby
Fowler	Alan	Rothwell	Junior	1927	1934	Swindon T
Fowler	Robbie	Liverpool	Liverpool	2001	–	Still at club
Francis	Cliff	Merthyr	Aberawan	1935	1938	Swindon T
Francis	Gerry	Johannesburg, SA	Amateur	1957	1961	York C
Frew	Jimmy	Fife	Hearts	1920	1924	Retired, injured
Frost	Desmond	Congleton	Congleton T	1949	1951	Halifax T
Fullam	Bob	Dublin	Shamrock R	1923	1929	Shamrock R
Furness	Billy	County Durham	Unsworth Coll	1928	1937	Norwich C
Gadsby	Ken	Chesterfield	Middlecliffe R	1934	1948	Kings Lynn
Galvin	Chris	Huddersfield	Junior	1968	1973	Hull C
Gascoigne	Tom	Newcastle	Scotswood	1921	1926	Bradford C
Gavin	Mark	Glasgow	Junior	1980	1985	Carlisle U
Gibson	Archie	Girvan	Junior	1950	1961	Scunthorpe
Giles	John	Dublin	Manchester U	1963	1975	West Brom A
Goldthorpe	Ernie	Leeds	Bradford C	1920	1922	Bradford C
Goodwin	Freddie	Heywood	Manchester U	1960	1964	Scunthorpe
Graham	Arthur	Glasgow	Aberdeen	1977	1983	Manchester U
Grainger	Colin	Wakefield	Sunderland	1960	1961	Port Vale
Grainger	Dennis	Royston	South Kirby	1945	1947	Wrexham
Graver	Fred	County Durham	West Stanley	1924	1925	Southend U
Granville	Danny	London	Chelsea	1998	1999	Manchester C
Gray	Andy	Harrogate	Junior	1995	1998	Nottingham F
Gray	Eddie	Glasgow	Junior	1963	1982	Player manager
Gray	Frank	Glasgow	Junior	1971	1979	Nottingham F ⎫
			Nottingham F	1981	1985	Sunderland ⎭
Grayson	Simon	Ripon	Junior	1988	1992	Leicester C
Green	Harry	Sheffield	Mexborough	1930	1934	Bristol C
Greenhoff	Brian	Barnsley	Manchester U	1979	1983	Rochdale
Greenhoff	Jimmy	Barnsley	Junior	1963	1968	Birmingham C
Gribben	Bill	Glasgow	Beeston	1928	1929	Harrogate
Haaland	Alfie	Stavangar, Norway	Nottingham F	1997	–	Still at club
Hackworth	Tony	Durham	Junior	–	2001	Notts County
Haddock	Peter	Newcastle	Newcastle U	1986	–	Retired, injured
Hair	Grenville	Burton On Trent	Newhall U	1948	1964	Wellington T
Halle	Gunnar	Oslo, Norway	Oldham A	1996	1999	Bradford C
Hallett	Tom	Glynneath	Junior	1956	1963	Swindon T
Hampson	Tom	Salford	Droylesdon	1934	1939	Oldham A
Hampton	Peter	Oldham	Junior	1971	1980	Stoke C
Hamson	Gary	Nottingham	Sheffield U	1979	1986	Bristol C
Hankin	Ray	Wallsend	Burnley	1976	1980	Vancouver W
Hargreaves	Jack	Rotherham	Junior	1934	1945	Bristol C
Harle	David	Denaby	Doncaster R	1985	1986	Bristol C
Harris	Carl	Neath	Junior	1973	1982	Charlton A
Harris	Joe	Glasgow	Bristol C	1922	1925	Fulham
Harrison	Peter	Sleaford	Peterborough	1948	1952	Bournemouth
Harrison	Ralph	Blackburn	Great Harwood	1949	1949	Great Harwood
Hart	Ernie	Burton On Trent	Junior	1920	1936	Mansfield T
Hart	Paul	Manchester	Blackpool	1978	1983	Nottingham F
Harte	Ian	Drogheda	Junior	1995	–	Still at club
Harvey	David	Leeds	Junior	1965	1980	Vancouver W ⎫
			Vancouver W	1983	–	Retired ⎭

Complete Players' Career Records: Ellam – Harvey

League			FAC			LC			Other			Total		
Apps	Sub	Goals	Apps	Sub	Goals	Apps	Sub	Goals	Apps	Sub	Goals	Apps	Sub	Goals
9	2	0	2		0	2		0	6		0	19	2	0
37		8	0		0	0		0	0		0	37		8
7	4	2	0	1	0	0		0	0		0	7	5	2
0	1	0	0		0	0		0	0	1	0	0	2	0
187	6	21	14	1	0	17	2	2	14		0	232	9	23
2		0	0		0	0		0	2		0	4		0
28		0	1		0	0		0	0		0	29		0
13		1	0		0	0		0	0		0	13		1
54		2	3		0	2		0	14		1	73		3
22		8	1		0	0		0	0		0	23		8
1		0	0		0	0		0	0		0	1		0
11	1	0	0		0	0		0	0		0	11	1	0
72		25	3		0	0		0	0		0	75		25
8		0	0		0	0		0	0		0	8		0
152	2	11	6	1	0	12		0	4		0	174	3	11
1		0	0		0	0		0	0		0	1		0
27	2	1	5		0	7		0	0	1	0	39	3	1
119		36	2		1	0		0	0		0	121		37
7	2	0	1	1	2	0		0	0		0	8	3	2
15		8	0		0	0		0	0		0	15		8
22		12	1		0	0		0	0		0	23		12
1		0	0		0	0		0	0		0	1		0
46		9	1		0	3		0	0		0	50		9
96		0	3		0	0		0	0		0	99		0
10		2	0		0	0		0	0		0	10		2
7		2	0		0	0		0	0		0	7		2
243		62	14		4	0		0	0		0	257		66
81		0	6		0	0		0	0		0	87		0
6	1	1	0	2	0	1		0	4	2	1	11	5	2
20		0	0		0	0		0	0		0	20		0
20	10	3	0		0	4	1	1	0		0	24	11	4
169		5	5		0	0		0	0		0	174		5
380	3	88	61		15	19		1	63	1	11	523	4	115
6		2	0		0	0		0	0		0	6		2
107		2	4		0	9		0	0		0	120		2
222	1	37	12		3	22		4	3		3	259	1	47
33		5	1		0	3		1	0		0	37		6
37		5	3		1	0		0	0		0	40		6
3		0	0		0	0		0	0		0	3		0
7	2	0	3		0	1		0	0	1	0	11	3	0
13	9	0	0	2	0	3	1	0	0		0	16	12	0
441	13	52	46	1	5	33	2	6	41	2	6	561	18	69
327	5	32	27	1	3	30	1	4	12	2	1	396	8	35
2		0	0		0	0		0	1	1	0	3	1	0
19		4	0		0	0		0	0		0	19		4
68	4	1	1		0	5		0	0		0	74	4	1
88	6	21	10	1	2	12		4	18	1	6	128	8	33
3		0	0		0	0		0	0		0	3		0
57	17	8	5	1	0	3		0	7	2	0	72	20	8
0		0	0		0	0	1	0	0	2	0	0	3	0
96	7	1	2	2	0	5	1	0	7	1	0	110	11	1
443		1	21		1	10		0	0		0	474		2
65	5	4	8	1	0	3	1	0	2		0	78	7	4
1		0	0		0	0		0	0		0	1		0
2		0	0		0	0		0	0		0	2		0
63	5	2	5		0	5	1	0	3	1	0	76	7	2
126	8	3	10	1	1	4		0	2	1	0	142	10	4
82	1	32	1		0	15		3	4		1	102	1	36
46		10	2		1	0		0	0		0	48		11
3		0	0		0	0		0	0		0	3		0
123	30	26	5		2	7	7	1	1	3	0	136	40	29
126		14	8		0	0		0	0		0	134		14
65		9	2		0	0		0	0		0	67		9
2		0	0		0	0		0	0		0	2		0
447		14	25		1	0		0	0		0	472		15
191		16	11		1	17		1	4		2	223		20
154	9	24	12	2	3	7	2	1	40		6	213	13	34
350		0	31		0	38		0	26	2	0	445	2	0

Player		Birthplace	From	Year Joined	Year Left	To
Hasselbaink	Jimmy Floyd	Surinam	Boavista	1997	1999	Atletico Madrid
Hastie	Ken	Cape Town, SA	Clyde A	1952	1953	Contract ended
Hawkins	Dennis	Swansea	Junior	1964	1968	Shrewsbury T
Hawksby	John	York	Junior	1959	1964	Lincoln C
Hawley	John	Withernsea	Hull C	1978	1979	Sunderland
Hay	Danny	Auckland, New Zealand	Perth Glory	1999	2002	Walsall
Heaton	Billy	Leeds	Junior	1937	1949	Southampton
Henderson	John	Glasgow	Rotherham U	1955	1956	Weymouth
Henderson	Tommy	Larkhall	Hearts	1962	1965	Bury
Hendrie	John	Lennox Town	Newcastle U	1989	1990	Middlesbrough
Henry	Gerry	Hemsworth	Junior	1937	1947	Bradford
Hibbitt	Terry	Bradford	Junior	1964	1971	Newcastle U
Hiden	Martin	Stainz, Austria	Rapid Vienna	1998	–	Still at club
Hilaire	Vince	Forest Hill	Portsmouth	1988	1990	Stoke C
Hill	George	Sheffield	Rotherham T	1920	1921	Contract ended
Hilton	Joe	Bromborough	Junior	1948	1949	Scarborough
Hindle	Tom	Keighley	Junior	1943	1948	York C
Hird	Kevin	Colne	Blackburn R	1979	1984	Burnley
Hodge	Steve	Nottingham	Nottingham F	1991	1994	Q.P.R.
Hodgkinson	Eddie	Ilkeston	Junior	1946	1948	Halifax T
Hodgson	Gordon	Johannesburg, SA	Aston Villa	1937	–	World War II
Hodgson	John	County Durham	Murton Coll	1944	1948	Middlesbrough
Holley	Tom	Wolverhampton	Barnsley	1936	1949	Retired
Hopkin	David	Greenock	Crystal P	1997	–	Still at club
Hornby	Cyril	West Bromwich	Oakengates T	1929	1936	Sunderland
Howarth	Tommy	Bury	Bristol C	1921	1922	Bristol R
Huckerby	Darren	Nottingham	Coventry C	1999	2001	Manchester C
Hudson	Billy	Swansea	Pembroke Dock	1951	1952	Sheffield U
Hughes	Charlie	Manchester	Junior	1950	1951	Contract ended
Hughes	Phil	Manchester	Manchester U	1983	1985	Bury
Humphreys	Alan	Chester	Shrewsbury	1960	1962	Gravesend
Humphries	Billy	Belfast	Ards	1958	1959	Ards
Hunter	Norman	County Durham	Junior	1960	1976	Bristol C
Hutchinson	George	Castleford	Tottenham H	1955	1957	Halifax T
Hydes	Arthur	Barnsley	Ardsley Rec	1930	1938	Newport C
Iggleden	Ray	Hull	Leicester C	1948	1955	Exeter C
Ingham	Tony	Harrogate	Junior	1947	1950	Q.P.R.
Irwin	Dennis	Cork	Junior	1982	1986	Oldham A
Jacklin	Harold	Chesterfield	Blackpool	1920	1922	Doncaster R
Jackson	Billy	Farnworth	Sunderland	1925	1927	West Ham U
Jackson	Mark	Barnsley	Junior	1995	2000	Scunthorpe
Jennings	Tom	Strathaven	Middlesbrough	1925	1931	Chester
Jobson	Richard	Holdeness	Oldham A	1995	1998	Manchester C
Johnneson	Albert	Johannesburg, SA	Germiston	1961	1970	York C
Johnson	Bill	Sheffield	Wombwell	1923	1931	Chester
Johnson	Rod	Leeds	Junior	1962	1968	Doncaster R
Johnson	Seth	Birmingham	Derby County	2001	–	Still at club
Jones	Alf	Liverpool	Marine	1960	1962	Lincoln C
Jones	Matthew	Llanelli	Junior	1997	2001	Leicester C
Jones	Mick	Worksop	Sheffield U	1967	1975	Retired, injured
Jones	Vinnie	Watford	Wimbledon	1989	1990	Sheffield U
Jordan	Joe	Carluke	Morton	1970	1978	Manchester U
Kamara	Chris	Miidlesbrough	Stoke C	1988	1991	Luton T
Kane	Bob	Lanarkshire	St Rochs	1935	1947	Retired
Keane	Robbie	Dublin	Inter Milan	2001	–	Still at club
Keetley	Charlie	Derby	Alvaston	1927	1934	Bradford C
Kelly	Dominic	Sandbach	Sandbach R	1935	1938	Newcastle U
Kelly	Gary	Drogheda	Home Farm	1991	–	Still at club
Kelly	Jack	Hetton-Le-Hole	Newcastle U	1935	1938	Birmingham C
Kelly	Mick	Sandbach	Accrington S	1933	1935	Barnsley
Kemp	John	Clydebank	Clyde	1957	1959	Barrow
Kennedy	David	Sunderland	Junior	1968	1971	Lincoln C
Kerfoot	Eric	Ashton Under Lyne	Stalybridge Celtic	1949	1959	Chesterfield
Kerr	Dylan	Valletta, Malta	Arcadia Shepherds	1988	1993	Reading
Kerslake	David	Stepnet	Swindon T	1993	1994	Tottenham H
Kewell	Harry	Smithfield, Australia	Australia Academy	1995	–	Still at club
Kilford	John	Derby	Notts C	1959	1962	Tonbridge
Kirby	Dennis	Leeds	Junior	1942	1950	Halifax T
Kirk	Roy	Shuttlewood	Bolsover Coll	1948	1953	Coventry C
Kirkpatrick	Jim	Annan	Workington	1924	1927	Watford

League			FAC			LC			Other			Total		
Apps	Sub	Goals	Apps	Sub	Goals	Apps	Sub	Goals	Apps	Sub	Goals	Apps	Sub	Goals
66	3	34	9		5	5		2	4		1	84	3	42
4		2	0		0	0		0	0		0	4		2
2		0	0		0	2		0	0		0	4		0
37		2	1		0	7		0	0		0	45		2
30	3	16	3		0	6		1	0		0	39	3	17
2	2	0	0		0	1		0	0	1	0	3	3	0
59		6	1		0	0		0	0		0	60		6
15		4	0		0	0		0	0		0	15		4
24		2	6		0	4		0	0		0	34		2
22	5	5	1		0	1		0	2		0	26	5	5
44		4	3		1	0		0	0		0	47		5
32	15	9	1		0	5		0	8	2	2	46	17	11
25	1	0	1		0	1		0	4		0	31	1	0
42	3	6	2		0	3		1	2		0	49	3	7
7		0	1		0	0		0	0		0	8		0
1		0	0		0	0		0	0		0	1		0
43		2	3		0	0		0	0		0	46		2
165	16	19	6	2	2	7	1	0	3		0	181	19	21
28	26	10	2	1	0	4	3	0	0	3	0	34	33	10
2		0	0		0	0		0	0		0	2		0
82		51	4	2	0	0		0	0		0	86		53
20		0	2		0	0		0	0		0	22		0
164		1	5		0	0		0	0		0	169		1
64	9	6	6		0	7		0	6	1	0	83	10	6
88		5	1		0	0		0	0		0	89		5
45		19	1		0	0		0	0		0	46		19
11	29	2	1	2	0	1	0	2	0	2	1	13	33	5
4		0	0		0	0		0	0		0	4		0
21		2	2		0	0		0	0		0	23		2
6		1	0		0	0		0	0		0	7		0
40		0	1		0	3		0	0		0	44		0
25		2	1		0	0		0	0		0	26		2
540		18	65	1	1	39		1	80	1	1	724	2	21
11		5	0		0	0		0	0		0	11		5
127		74	10	8	0	0		0	0		0	137		82
169		47	12	3	0	0		0	0		0	181		50
3		0	0		0	0		0	0		0	3		0
72		1	3		0	5		0	2		0	82		1
3		0	2		0	0		0	0		0	5		0
38		2	1		0	0		0	0		0	39		2
11	8	0	4		0	0		0	0		0	15	8	0
167		112	7		5	0		0	0		0	174		117
22		1	1		0	3		0	0		0	26		1
170	2	48	14		5	8		6	5	1	8	200	2	67
72		0	1		0	0		0	0		0	73		0
18	4	4	1		1	6	1	1	0		0	26	5	6
12	2	0	0		0	0		0	0		0	12	12	0
25		0	1		0	3		0	0		0	29		0
11	12	0	0	2	0	1	1	1	4	2	0	16	17	0
216	4	77	36		12	13	1	5	43		17	308	5	111
44	2	5	1		0	2		0	4		0	51	2	5
139	30	35	16	3	4	9	1	3	19	4	6	177	38	48
15	5	1	0		0	1	2	0	0	1	0	16	8	1
58		0	3		0	0		0	0		0	61		0
28	15	12	2		0	2		3	6		3	38	115	18
160		108	9	2	0	0		0	0		0	169		110
4		0	0		0	0		0	0		0	4		0
255	10	2	24	1	0	21	2	0	29	1	0	329	14	2
59		17	5		1	0		0	0		0	64		18
4		0	0		0	0		0	0		0	4		0
1		0	0		0	0		0	0		0	1		0
2		1	0		0	0		0	1		0	3		1
336		9	13		1	0		0	0		0	349		10
3	5	0	0		0	0	1	0	0	4	0	3	10	0
8		0	0		0	0		0	0		0	8		0
138	12	31	12		5	7		4	29	3	7	186	15	47
21		0	0		0	2		0	0		0	23		0
8		0	0		0	0		0	0		0	8		0
34		1	5		3	0		0	0		0	39		4
10		0	0		0	0		0	0		0	10		0

Player		Birthplace	From	Year Joined	Year Left	To
Knarvik	Tommy	Bergen, Norway	Skjeijard	2000	2000	Brann Bergen
Korsten	Willem	Buxtell, Holland	Vitesse Arnheim	1999	1999	Loan
Lambert	Jack	Rotherham	Methley P	1924	1924	Doncaster R
Lamph	Tommy	Gateshead	Derby C	1921	1922	Retired, ill health
Langley	Jim	Kilburn	Guildford	1952	1953	Brighton
Laurent	Pierre	Tulle, France	Bastia	1997	1998	Bastia
Lawson	Ian	County Durham	Burnley	1962	1966	Crystal P
Letheran	Glan	Llanelli	Junior	1973	1977	Chesterfield
Liddell	Gary	Bannockburn	Junior	1971	1977	Grimsby T
Lilley	Derek	Paisley	Morton	1997	1999	Oxford U
Linighan	Andy	Hartlepool	Hartlepool U	1984	1986	Oldham A
Lomas	Albert	Bolton	Bolton W	1948	1949	Mossley
Longden	Eric	Rotherham	Doncaster R	1929	1930	Hull C
Lorimer	Peter	Dundee	Junior	1962	1979	Toronto B
			Vancouver W	1983	–	Retired
Lukic	John	Chesterfield	Junior	1978	1990	Arsenal
			Arsenal	1983	1994	Arsenal
Lumsden	Jimmy	Glasgow	Junior	1964	1970	Southend U
Lydon	Mickey	Sunderland	Sunderland	1954	1955	Gateshead
Lyon	Jack	Prescott	Hull C	1920	1921	New Brighton
McAdam	David	Hereford	Stapenhil Wmc	1948	1950	Wrexham
McAdams	Billy	Belfast	Bolton W	1961	1962	Brentford
McAllister	Gary	Motherwell	Leicester C	1990	1996	Coventry C
McCabe	Jim	Derry	Middlesbrough	1948	1954	Peterborough U
McCall	Andy	Hamilton	West Brom A	1952	1955	Lovells A
McClelland	John	Belfast	Watford	1989	1992	Retired, injured
McCluskey	George	Hamilton	Celtic	1983	1986	Hibernian
McCole	John	Glasgow	Bradford C	1959	1961	Bradford C
McConnell	Peter	Stockport	Junior	1954	1962	Carlisle U
McDonald	Bobby	Aberdeen	Oxford U	1987	1988	VS Rugby
McDougall	Jock	Port Glasgow	Sunderland	1934	1937	Retired
McGhie	Billy	Dumfries	Junior	1956	1959	Contract ended
McGinley	Billy	Dumfries	Junior	1972	1974	Huddersfield T
McGoldrick	John	Laarkshire	Celtic	1983	1985	Motherwell
McGovern	John	Montrose	Derby C	1974	1975	Nottingham F
McGregor	John	Airdrie	Liverpool	1985	1987	Rangers
McGugan	John	Airdrie	St Mirren	1960	1961	Tranmere R
McInroy	Albert	Preston	Sunderland	1935	1937	Gateshead
McKenna	Frank	Blaydon	Bishop Auckland	1956	1958	Carlisle U
McKenzie	Duncan	Grimsby	Nottingham F	1974	1976	Anderlecht
McMorran	Eddie	Larne	Manchester C	1949	1950	Barnsley
McNab	Neil	Greenock	Brighton	1982	1982	Loan
McNeish	Sam	West Lothian	Linlithgow	1951	1952	Contract ended
McNestry	George	County Durham	Doncaster R	1928	1929	Sunderland
McNiven	David	Lanarkshire	Junior	1972	1978	Bradford C
McPhail	Stephen	London	Junior	1996	–	Still at club
McQueen	Gordon	Kilbirnie	St Mirren	1972	1978	Manchester U
Madeley	Paul	Leeds	Junior	1962	1980	Retired
Maguire	Peter	Holmfirth	Junior	1986	1989	Huddersfield T
Mahon	Johnny	Gillingham	Junior	1929	1935	West Brom A
Makinson	James	Wigan	Clitheroe	1935	1944	Retired
Mangnall	Dave	Wigan	Maltby Coll	1927	1929	Huddersfield T
Mann	Jimmy	Goole	Junior	1969	1974	Bristol C
Marsden	Jack	Leeds	Osmondthorpe	1948	1959	Barrow
Marsh	Cliff	Atherton	Winsford U	1948	1949	Bournemouth
Martin	Con	Dublin	Glentoran	1946	1948	Aston Villa
Martin	Geoff	New Tupton	Chesterfield	1960	1961	Darlington
Martin	John	Gateshead	Darlington	1924	1926	Accrington S
Martyn	Nigel	St Austell	Crystal P	1996	–	Still at club
Masinga	Philomen	South Africa	Mamelodi S	1994	1996	Young Boys Berne
Mason	Bobby	Sunderland	Whitburn	1922	1927	Bristol R
Mason	Cliff	York	Sheffield U	1962	1964	Scunthorpe U
Mason	George	Church Gresley	Frickley Coll	1920	1923	Swindon T
Matteo	Dominic	Dunfries	Liverpool	2000	–	Still at club
Matthews	Lee	Middlesbrough	Junior	1996	–	Still at club
Maybury	Alan	Dublin	Junior	1995	2001	Heart of Midlothian
Mayers	Derek	Liverpool	Preston NE	1961	1962	Bury
Mears	Frank	Manchester	Stalybridge Celtic	1924	1928	Barnsley
Meek	George	Glasgow	Hamilton A	1952	1960	Leicester C
Melrose	Jim	Glasgow	Charlton A	1987	1988	Shrewsbury T

Complete Players' Career Records: Knarvik – Melrose

League			FAC			LC			Other			Total		
Apps	Sub	Goals	Apps	Sub	Goals	Apps	Sub	Goals	Apps	Sub	Goals	Apps	Sub	Goals
0		0	0	1	0	0		0	0		0	0	1	0
4	3	2	2	1	0	0		0	0		0	6	4	2
1		0	0		0	0		0	0		0	1		0
6		0	0		0	0		0	0		0	6		0
9		3	0		0	0		0	0		0	9		3
2	2	0	0		0	0		0	0		0	2	2	0
44		17	3		1	4		3	0		0	51		21
1		0	0		0	0		0	0	1	0	1	1	0
2	1	0	0		0	1		0	1	1	1	4	2	1
4	17	1	0	1	0	0	3	0	0	1	0	4	22	1
66		3	2		0	6		1	2		0	76		4
1		0	0		0	0		0	0		0	1		0
28		7	0		0	0		0	0		0	28		7
503	22	168	56	3	20	41	1	19	77	2	31	677	8	238
327		0	28		0	30		0	14		0	399		0
3	1	0	0		0	0		0	0		0	3	1	0
4		1	0		0	0		0	0		0	4		1
33		3	0		0	0		0	0		0	33		3
24		0	0		0	0		0	0		0	24		0
11		3	2		1	0		0	0		0	13		4
230	1	31	24		6	26		5	14		4	294	1	46
152		0	9		0	0		0	0		0	161		0
62		8	2		0	0		0	0		0	64		8
22	2	0	2		0	2	1	0	0		0	26	3	0
57	6	16	4		0	5	3	1	1		0	67	9	17
78		45	2		1	5		7	0		0	85		53
48		4	2		0	3		1	0		0	53		5
23		1	0		0	1		0	0		0	24		1
52		0	7		1	0		0	0		0	59		1
2		1	0		0	0		0	0		0	2		1
0	1	0	0		0	0		0	0	1	0	0	2	0
7		0	3		0	2		0	0		0	12		0
4		0	0		0	0		0	0		0	4		0
5		0	0		0	0		0	0		0	5		0
1		0	0		0	0		0	0		0	1		0
67		0	4		0	0		0	0		0	71		0
6		4	0		0	0		0	0		0	6		4
64	2	27	6	3	2	5		1	1	1	0	76	6	30
38		6	2		0	0		0	0		0	40		6
5		0	1		0	0		0	0		0	6		0
1		0	0		0	0		0	0		0	1		0
3		0	0		0	0		0	0		0	3		0
15	7	6	0		0	1		0	0		0	16	7	6
36	16	2	3		0	2	1	0	2	2	0	43	19	2
140		15	13		1	5		0	13	1	3	171	1	19
528	8	25	64	3	2	49	1	3	71	1	4	712	13	34
1		0	0		0	0		0	0		0	1		0
78		20	6		3	0		0	0		0	84		26
68		0	2		0	0		0	0		0	70		0
9		6	0		0	0		0	0		0	9		6
2		0	0		0	0	1	0	2		0	4	1	0
71		0	4		0	0		0	0		0	75		0
4		1	1		0	0		0	0		0	5		1
47		1	2		0	0		0	0		0	49		1
1		0	0		0	0		0	0		0	1		0
2		0	0		0	0		0	0		0	2		0
207		0	18		0	12		0	36		0	273	0	0
20	11	5	3	2	4	3		2	0		0	26	13	11
15		0	0		0	0		0	0		0	15		0
31		0	0		0	2		0	0		0	33		0
65		5	1		0	0		0	0		0	66		5
62		0	2		0	2		0	22	2	0	86		2
0	3	0	0		0	0	1	0	2		0	0	4	0
10	4	0	2		0	2		0	0		0	14	4	0
20		5	2		0	2		0	0		0	24		5
2		0	1		0	0		0	0		0	3		0
195		19	4		0	0		0	0		0	199		19
3	1	0	0	1	0	0	1	0	0		0	3	3	0

Player		Birthplace	From	Year Joined	Year Left	To
Menzies	Bill	Aberdeen	Mugiemoss	1922	1933	Goole
Milburn	George	Ashington	Ashington	1928	1937	Chesterfield
Milburn	Jim	Ashington	Ashington	1935	1952	Bradford C
Milburn	Jack	Ashington	Junior	1927	1947	Bradford C
Miller	George	South Africa	Arcadia FC	1950	1952	Workington
Mills	Danny	Norwich	Charlton A	1999	–	Still at club
Mills	Don	Rotherham	Cardiff C	1951	1952	Torquay U
Mills	Fred	Hanley	Port Vale	1934	1939	Retired
Mitchell	Ron	Morecombe	Morecombe	1958	1959	Contract ended
Mitchell	Tom	Spennymoor	Newcastle U	1926	1931	York VC
Molenaar	Robert	Zaandam, Holland	Volendam	1997	–	Still at club
Mollatt	Ron	Edwinstowe	Junior	1950	1955	York C
Moore	Bill	Sunderland	Seaham Coll	1924	1925	Southend U
Moore	Jim	County Durham	Southampton	1921	1922	Brighton
Moore	Stan	Worksop	Worksop T	1931	1935	Swansea T
Morton	Norman	Barnsley	Wooley Coll	1945	1946	Contract ended
Moss	Jack	Bolton	Rochdale	1949	1950	Halifax
Mumby	Peter	Bradford	Junior	1987	1989	Burnley
Murray	Tommy	Airdrie	Queen of South	1960	1961	Tranmere R
Musgrove	Robert	Sunderland	Durham C	1920	1921	Durham C
Neal	Tom	Gateshead	Usworth Coll	1931	1936	Hull C
Newsome	John	Sheffield	Sheffield W	1989	1994	Hull C
Nightingale	Albert	Rotherham	Blackburn R	1952	1956	Retired, injured
Nimmo	Willie	Forth	Alloa A	1956	1958	Doncaster R
Noble	Alan	Southampton	Bournemouth	1922	1925	Brentford
Noteman	Kevin	Preston	Junior	1987	1989	Doncaster R
O'Brien	George	Dunfermline	Dunfermline	1957	1959	Southampton
O'Donnell	Chris	Newcastle	Ipswich T	1989	1992	Northampton
O'Grady	Harry	Tunstall	Southampton	1932	1933	Burnley
O'Grady	Mike	Leeds	Huddersfield T	1965	1969	Wolves
O'Hare	John	Renton	Derby C	1974	1975	Nottingham F
O'Leary	David	London	Arsenal	1993	–	Retired, injured
O'Neill	Jimmy	Belfast	Junior	1969	1974	Chesterfield
Ormsby	Brendan	Birmingham	Aston Villa	1986	–	Retired, injured
Overfield	Jack	Leeds	Junior	1953	1960	Sunderland
Palmer	Carlton	Rowley Regis	Sheffield W	1994	1997	Southampton
Parker	Neil	Blackburn	Junior	1975	1981	Scarborough
Parkinson	Keith	Preston	Junior	1973	1981	Doncaster R
Parlane	Derek	Helensburgh	Rangers	1980	1983	Manchester C
Parry	Bill	Denaby	Frickley Coll	1937	1939	Chelmsford
Peacock	Alan	Middlesbrough	Middlesbrough	1964	1967	Plymouth A
Pearson	John	Sheffield	Charlton A	1987	1991	Barnsley
Pemberton	John	Oldham	Sheffield U	1990	1994	Crewe A
Peterson	Paul	Luton	Junior	1969	1971	Swindon T
Peyton	Noel	Dublin	Shamrock R	1958	1963	York C
Phelan	Terry	Manchester	Junior	1983	1986	Swansea C
Potts	Jimmy	Ashington	Blyth Spartans	1926	1934	Port Vale
Potts	Joe	Newcastle	Portsmouth	1921	1923	Chesterfield
Powell	Aubrey	Pontardawe	Swansea	1935	1948	Everton
Powell	Sam	Rotherham	Thornhill	1921	1925	Sheffield W
Poyntz	Bill	Tylerstown	Llanelli	1921	1923	Doncaster R
Price	Arthur	County Durham	Consett	1945	1947	Contract ended
Radebe	Lucas	Johannesburg, SA	Kaizer Chiefs	1994	–	Still at club
Reaney	Paul	Fulham	Junior	1961	1978	Bradford C
Reed	George	Wakefield	Altofts	1924	1931	Plymouth A
Rennie	David	Edinburgh	Leicester C	1986	1989	Bristol C
Revie	Don	Middlesbrough	Sunderland	1958	1961	Club manager
Riberio	Bruno	Setubal, Portugal	Vittoria Setubal	1997	1999	Sheffield U
Richmond	Joe	Leasingthorpe	Shildon	1922	1926	Barnsley
Riley	Valentine	South Shields	Hebburn	1924	1928	Newport C
Ripley	Keith	Normanton	Junior	1952	1958	Norwich C
Ritchie	Andy	Manchester	Brighton	1983	1987	Oldham A
Roberts	Harry	Wakefield	Castleford T	1925	1937	Bristol R
Robertson	David	Aberdeen	Rangers	1997	–	Retired, injured
Robinson	David	Dumfries	Carlisle U	1926	1928	Southend U
Robinson	Paul	Beverley	Junior	1997	–	Still at club
Robinson	Ronnie	Sunderland	Ipswich T	1985	1987	Doncaster R
Robson	Cuthbert	County Durham	Cockfield A	1924	1926	Southend U
Robson	William	Shildon	Junior	1921	1924	Ashington
Rocastle	David	London	Arsenal	1992	1993	Manchester C

Complete Players' Career Records: Menzies – Rocastle

League			FAC			LC			Other			Total		
Apps	Sub	Goals	Apps	Sub	Goals	Apps	Sub	Goals	Apps	Sub	Goals	Apps	Sub	Goals
248		1	10		1	0		0	0		0	258		2
157		1	9		0	0		0	0		0	166		1
208		15	12		2	0		0	0		0	220		17
386		28	22		2	0		0	0		0	408		30
13		1	1		0	0		0	0		0	14		1
48	3	1	2		0	2		0	23	1	0	75	4	1
34		9	3		1	0		0	0		0	37		10
67		2	3		0	0		0	0		0	70		2
4		0	0		0	0		0	0		0	4		0
142		19	10		2	0		0	0		0	152		21
47	4	5	5	1	0	4		1	4		0	60	5	6
17		0	0		0	0		0	0		0	17		0
6		0	0		0	0		0	0		0	6		0
27		4	1		0	0		0	0		0	28		4
78		0	5		0	0		0	0		0	83		0
2		0	0		0	0		0	0		0	2		0
23		2	0		0	0		0	0		0	23		2
3	3	0	0		0	0	2	1	0		0	3	5	1
7		2	0		0	0		0	0		0	7		2
36		2	0		0	0		0	0		0	36		2
20		0	3		0	0		0	0		0	23		0
62	14	3	3	1	0	3		0	5		0	73	15	3
130		48	5		0	0		0	0		0	135		48
1		0	0		0	0		0	0		0	1		0
60		4	3		0	0		0	0		0	63		4
0	1	0	0		0	0		0	1		1	1	1	1
44		6	0		0	0		0	0		0	44		6
0	1	0	0		0	0		0	0		0	0	1	0
8		2	1		0	0		0	0		0	9		2
90	1	12	5		1	5		0	20		3	120	1	16
6	1	0	0		0	1		1	0		0	7	1	1
10		0	0		0	0		0	0		0	10		0
0	1	0	0		0	0		0	0	2	0	0	3	0
51		6	1		0	4		1	1		0	57		7
159		20	4		0	0		0	0		0	163		20
100	2	5	12		1	12		0	4		1	128	2	7
0	1	0	0		0	0		0	0		0	0	1	0
4		0	0		0	0		0	2		0	6		0
45	5	10	2		0	1		0	0		0	48	5	10
6		0	2		0	0		0	0		0	8		0
54		27	6		2	2		1	3		1	65		31
55	48	12	5	2	0	5	4	0	2	3	0	67	57	12
44	9	0	5	1	0	3	1	0	4		0	56	11	0
3	1	0	0		0	0		0	0		0	3	1	0
105		17	3		1	9		2	0		0	117		20
12	2	0	0		0	3		0	2		0	17	2	0
247		0	15		0	0		0	0		0	262		0
10		0	0		0	0		0	0		0	10		0
114		25	5		0	0		0	0		0	119		25
28		7	0		0	0		0	0		0	28		7
29		7	0		0	0		0	0		0	29		7
6		0	1		0	0		0	0		0	7		0
152	12	0	15	2	1	9	4	0	25		2	201	18	3
549	8	6	72	1	3	39		0	76	3	0	736	12	9
141		2	9		1	0		0	0		0	150		3
95	6	5	7		1	7		0	4		1	113	6	7
76		11	1		0	3		1	0		0	80		12
36	7	4	4	1	3	1	1	1	1		0	43	9	6
56		19	4		0	0		0	0		0	60		19
0		0	1		0	0		0	0		0	1		0
67		15	2		0	0		0	0		0	69		15
129	10	40	9		1	11		3	0		0	149	10	44
84		2	3		0	0		0	0		0	87		2
24	2	0	1		0	4		0	0		0	29	2	0
5		0	0		0	0		0	0		0	5		0
19	2	0	1		0	2		0	11	1	0	33	3	0
16		0	0		0	0		0	0		0	16		0
17		4	0		0	0		0	0		0	17		4
10		0	1		0	0		0	0		0	11		0
17	8	2	0	3	0	0	3	0	2	1	0	19	15	2

Player		Birthplace	From	Year Joined	Year Left	To
Searson	Harry	Mansfield	Mansfield T	1949	1952	York City
Rodgerson	Ralph	Sunderland	Huddersfield T	1921	1923	Dundee
Roper	Harry	Stockport	New Mills	1929	1935	Cardiff C
Ross	Bobby	Lanarkshire	Workington	1950	1954	Stockport C
Rudd	Jimmy	Hull	Manchester C	1949	1949	Rotherham U
Rush	Ian	St Asaph	Liverpool	1996	1997	Newcastle U
Russell	David	Dunfermline	Doncaster R	1925	1926	Watford
Sabella	Alex	Buenos Aires, Arg	Sheffield U	1980	1984	Estudiantes
Savage	Reg	Eccles	Stalybridge C	1931	1939	Queen of South
Scaife	George	Bradford	Junior	1936	1939	Millwall
Scott	John	Crosby	Workington	1950	1956	Workington
Sellars	Scott	Sheffield	Junior	1983	1986	Blackburn R ⎫
			Blackburn R	1992	1993	Newcastle U ⎭
Shackleton	Alan	Burnley	Burnley	1958	1959	Everton
Sharp	Kevin	Canada	Auxerre	1992	1995	Wigan A
Sharpe	Ivan	St Albans	Glossop NE	1920	1923	Retired
Sharpe	Lee	Halesowen	Manchester U	1996	1999	Bradford C
Shaw	John	Stirling	Junior	1971	1974	Bristol C
Sheridan	John	Manchester	Junior	1982	1989	Nottingham F
Sherwin	Harry	Walsall	Sunderland	1921	1925	Barnsley
Short	John	Gateshead	St Hildas	1937	1948	Millwall
Shutt	Carl	Sheffield	Bristol C	1989	1993	Birmingham C
Shepherd	Paul	Leeds	Junior	1995	1998	Ayr U
Sibbald	Bobby	County Durham	Junior	1965	1969	York C
Simmonds	Lyndon	Pontypool	Junior	1983	1987	Rochdale
Sinclair	Ronnie	Stirling	Nottingham F	1986	1989	Bristol C
Sissons	Albert	Kiveton Park	Doncaster R	1925	1928	Southport
Smelt	Alf	Rotherham	Mexborough T	1920	1921	Contract ended
Smith	Alan	Wakefield	Junior	1998	–	Still at club
Smith	Barry	Hemsworth	Farsley C	1951	1955	Bradford
Smith	Eric	Glasgow	Celtic	1960	1964	Morton
Smith	Len	Birmingham	Redditch	1922	1926	Bristol R
Snodin	Glynn	Rotherham	Sheffield W	1987	1992	Hearts
Snodin	Ian	Rotherham	Doncaster R	1985	1987	Everton
Speak	George	Blackburn	Preston NE	1923	1925	Retired
Speed	Gary	Mancot	Junior	1987	1996	Everton
Sprake	Gary	Swansea	Junior	1962	1973	Birmingham C
Sproston	Bert	Sandbach	Sandbach	1933	1938	Tottenham H
Stacey	Alex	London	New Mills	1927	1933	Sheffield U
Stephenson	Eric	Bexleyheath	Junior	1933	–	World War II
Sterland	Mel	Sheffield	Rangers	1989	1994	Retired, injured
Stevenson	Byron	Llanelli	Junior	1973	1982	Birmingham C
Stevenson	Ernie	Rotherham	Southampton	1951	1952	Wisbech T
Stewart	David	Glasgow	Ayr U	1973	1978	West Brom A
Stewart	Gordon	Durban, SA	Parkhill	1951	1953	Returned to SA
Stiles	John	Manchester	Vancouver W	1984	1989	Doncaster R
Storrie	Jim	Kirkintilloch	Airdrie	1962	1967	Rotherham U
Strachan	Gordon	Edinburgh	Manchester U	1989	1995	Coventry C
Stuart	George	Fife	Dundee	1920	1921	Contract ended
Sutherland	Harry	Salford	Sedgely Park	1938	1947	Exeter C
Swan	Jack	County Durham	Huddersfield T	1921	1925	Watford
Swan	Peter	Leeds	Junior	1985	1989	Hull C
Swinburne	Trevor	County Durham	Brentford	1985	1986	Lincoln C
Taylor	Frank	Londonderry	Bangor NI	1949	1950	Contract ended
Strandli	Frank	Norway	Kristiansand	1993	1994	Brann Bergen
Taylor	Bob	County Durham	Horden Cw	1985	1989	Bristol C
Taylor	Brian	Rossington	Worksop T	1951	1953	Kings Lynn
Thom	Jock	Hurlford	Workington	1924	1927	Bristol R
Thomas	Gwyn	Swansea	Junior	1975	1984	Barnsley
Thomas	Mickey	Mochdre	Shrewsbury T	1989	1990	Stoke C
Thompson	Nigel	Leeds	Junior	1984	1988	Chesterfield
Thompson	Robert	Eldon	Durham City	1920	1921	Ashington
Thomson	John	Edinburgh	Loanhead Steel	1924	1939	Grimsby T
Thornton	Richard	County Durham	Bearpark	1925	1928	Accrington S
Tillotson	Arthur	Hunslet	Castleford T	1920	1920	Castleford T
Tinkler	Mark	Bishop Auckland	Junior	1991	1997	York C
Toner	Jim	Glasgow	Dundee	1954	1955	Contract ended
Townsley	Tom	Stirling	Falkirk	1925	1931	Falkirk
Trainor	John	Norham On Tweed	Ashington	1935	1938	Southend U
Turnbull	Bobby	Middlesbrough	Bradford	1925	1932	Rhyl

League			FAC			LC			Other			Total		
Apps	Sub	Goals	Apps	Sub	Goals	Apps	Sub	Goals	Apps	Sub	Goals	Apps	Sub	Goals
104		0	12		0	0		0	0		0	116		0
27		0	1		0	0		0	0		0	28		0
18		3	0		0	0		0	0		0	18		3
5		0	0		0	0		0	0		0	5		0
18		1	0		0	0		0	0		0	18		1
34	2	3	2	2	0	2		0	0		0	38	4	3
9		0	0		0	0		0	0		0	9		0
22	1	2	2		0	2		0	0		0	26	1	2
79		0	5		0	0		0	0		0	84		0
9		0	0		0	0		0	0		0	9		0
111		0	3		0	0		0	0		0	114		0
78	5	12	4		0	5	1	1	3		1	90	6	14
30		16	1		1	0		0	0		0	31		17
11	6	0	0		0	0		0	0	1	0	11	7	0
1		0	0		0	0		0	0		0	1		0
28	2	5	0	1	0	3		1	1	2	0	32	5	6
0		0	0		0	0		0	2		0	2		0
230	5	48	11	1	1	14		3	6		0	261	6	52
98		2	9		0	0		0	0		0	107		2
60		18	3		1	0		0	0		0	63		19
46	33	17	10		1	6	2	2	4	5	4	66	40	24
1		0	0		0	0		0	0		0	1		0
1	1	0	0		0	0		0	0		0	1	1	0
6	3	3	0		0	0		0	1	1	0	7	4	0
8		0	0		0	1		0	0		0	9		0
30		1	1		0	0		0	0		0	31		1
1		0	0		0	0		0	0		0	1		0
80	24	26	6	3	4	2	2	0	22	1	6	110	30	36
2	1	0	0		0	0		0	0		0	2	1	0
65		3	3		0	0		0	0		0	68		3
32		0	3		0	0		0	0		0	35		0
85	11	10	5	1	0	9	1	3	5		0	102	13	13
51		6	1		0	3		2	0		0	55		8
28		0	4		0	0		0	0		0	32		0
231	17	39	21		5	25	1	11	14	3	2	291	21	57
380		0	45		0	22		0	58	2	0	505	2	0
130		1	10		0	0		0	0		0	140		1
51		0	0		0	0		0	0		0	51		0
111		21	4		1	0		0	0		0	115		22
111	3	16	10		1	13		1	9		2	143	3	20
88	7	4	5		0	7	1	1	2		0	102	8	5
16	5	0	0		0	0		0	0		0	16	5	0
55		0	8		0	6		0	5		0	74		0
9		2	2		0	0		0	0		0	11		2
51	15	2	5		1	4	2	0	1	2	0	61	19	3
123	3	58	12		3	8		5	10		1	153	3	67
188	9	37	14		2	19		3	14	1	3	235	10	45
1		0	2		0	0		0	0		0	3		0
3		1	0		0	0		0	0		0	3		1
108		47	8		3	0		0	0		0	116		50
43	8	11	3		0	3	2	1	2		0	50	10	13
2		0	0		0	0		0	0		0	2		0
3		0	0		0	0		0	0		0	3		0
5	9	2	1		0	0	1	0	0		0	6	10	2
34	9	9	1		0	5	1	3	3	1	1	43	11	13
11		0	0		0	0		0	0		0	11		0
7		3	0		0	0		0	0		0	7		3
79	10	3	4	1	0	9		0	0		0	92	11	3
3		0	0		0	0		0	0		0	3		0
6	1	0	0		0	2		0	1	1	0	9	2	0
23		11	2		1	0		0	0		0	25		12
41		11	0		0	0		0	0		0	41		11
1		0	0		0	0		0	0		0	1		0
2		0	0		0	0		0	0		0	2		0
14	11	0	0		0	1		0	0	1	0	15	12	0
7		1	0		0	0		0	0		0	7		1
159		2	8		0	0		0	0		0	167		2
3		0	1		0	0		0	0		0	4		0
204		45	11		1	0		0	0		0	215		46

Player		Birthplace	From	Year Joined	Year Left	To
Turner	Charlie	Manchester	Stalybridge Celtic	1933	1935	Southend U
Turner	Chris	Sheffield	Sheffield W	1989	1989	Loan
Turner	John	Worksop	Junior	1935	1937	Mansfield T
Twomey	Jim	Newry, NI	Newry T	1937	1949	Halifax T
Tyrer	Arthur	Manchester	Junior	1950	1954	Peterborough
Underwood	Ben	Alfreton	Doncaster R	1928	1931	Coventry C
Varadi	Imre	London	Sheffield W	1990	1993	Rotherham
Vickers	Peter	Doncaster	Junior	1951	1956	Kings Lynn
Viduka	Mark	Melbourne, Australia	Celtic	1999	–	Still at club
Wainscoat	Russell	East Retford	Middlesbrough	1925	1931	Hull C
Wakefield	Albert	Pudsey	Stanningley Wks	1942	1949	Southend U
Wallace	Ray	Greenwich	Southampton	1991	1994	Stoke C
Wallace	Rod	Greenwich	Southampton	1991	1998	Rangers
Walton	Jimmy	County Durham	West Stanley	1920	1923	Bristol R
Watson	Andy	Aberdeen	Aberdeen	1983	1984	Hearts
Webb	Bobby	Castleford	Junior	1951	1955	Bradford C
Weston	Don	Mansfield	Rotherham	1962	1965	Huddersfield T
Wetherall	David	Sheffield	Sheffield W	1991	1999	Bradford C
Whalley	Fred	Bolton	Grimsby T	1921	1924	Fulham
Wharton	Norman	Askham In Furness	York C	1939	1939	Retired
Wheatley	Tom	County Durham	Amble	1953	1953	Lincoln C
Whelan	Noel	Leeds	Junior	1993	1995	Coventry C
Whipp	Percy	Glasgow	Sunderland	1922	1927	Orient
White	David	Manchester	Manchester C	1993	1995	Sheffield U
White	John	Coatbridge	Hearts	1927	1930	Hearts
Whitlow	Mike	Davenham	Witton A	1988	1992	Leicester C
Whyte	Chris	London	West Brom A	1990	1993	Birmingham C
Whyte	David	Dunfermline	Junior	1977	1979	Hibernian
Wijnhard	Clyde	Surinam	Willem II	1998	1999	Huddersfield T
Wilcox	Jason	Farnworth	Blackburn R	1999	–	Still at club
Wilkins	George	Hackney	Nottingham F	1949	1949	Retired
Wilkinson	Charlie	County Durham	Consett	1928	1933	Sheffield U
Williams	Andy	Birmingham	Rotherham U	1988	1992	Notts Co
Williams	Gary	Wolverhampton	Aston Villa	1987	1990	Watford
Williams	Harold	Briton Ferry	Newport C	1949	1957	Newport C
Williams	John	Doncaster	Denaby U	1948	1950	Denaby U
Williamson	Brian	Blyth	Crewe A	1962	1966	Nottingham F
Willingham	Ken	Sheffield	Sunderland	1947	1948	Retired
Willis	George	County Durham	Evenwood T	1953	1954	Hartlepool
Wilson	George	Kilmarnock	Huddersfield T	1929	1930	Chesterfield
Wilson	James	Garforth	Rothwell Am	1928	1930	Halifax T
Windle	Billy	Maltby	Denaby U	1947	1948	Lincoln C
Wood	Basil	Sheffield	Crook T	1920	1922	Sheffield W
Wood	Roy	Wallasey	Clitheroe	1952	1959	Retired
Woodgate	Jonathan	Middlesbrough	Junior	1997	–	Still at club
Worsley	Bert	Stockport	Manchester NE	1932	1935	Fulham
Worthington	Frank	Halifax	Birmingham	1982	1982	Sunderland
Worthington	Nigel	Ballymena	Sheffield W	1994	1996	Stoke C
Wright	Barrie	Bradford	Junior	1962	1964	New York Generals
Wright	Ronnie	Falkirk	Shettleston R	1959	1960	St Johnstone
Wright	Tommy	Dunfermline	Junior	1982	1987	Oldham A
Yeboah	Anthony	Ghana	Eintracht F	1995	1997	Hamburg
Yorath	Terry	Cardiff	Junior	1967	1976	Coventry C
Younger	Tommy	Edinburgh	Stoke C	1961	1962	Retired

Top Five Transfers

In

Amount	Player	From	Date
£18,000,000	Rio Ferdinand	West Ham United	November 2000
£12,000,000	Robbie Keane	Inter Milan	December 2000
£11,000,000	Robbie Fowler	Liverpool	November 2001
£7,200,000	Olivier Dacourt	Lens	May 2000
£7,000,000	Seth Johnson	Derby County	October 2001

Complete Players' Career Records: Turner – Younger

League			FAC			LC			Other			Total		
Apps	Sub	Goals	Apps	Sub	Goals	Apps	Sub	Goals	Apps	Sub	Goals	Apps	Sub	Goals
13		0	0		0	0		0	0		0	13		0
2		0	0		0	0		0	0		0	2		0
14		0	0		0	0		0	0		0	14		0
109		0	2		0	0		0	0		0	111		0
39		4	3		0	0		0	0		0	42		4
6		0	0		0	0		0	0		0	6		0
21	5	4	0		0	1		0	1	1	1	23	6	5
20		4	1		0	0		0	0		0	21		4
67		28	3		2	2		1	23		7	95		38
215		87	11		6	0		0	0		0	226		93
49		23	1		0	0		0	0		0	50		23
5	2	0	0		0	0		0	0		0	5	2	0
187	25	53	16	5	4	18	1	8	3	1	2	224	32	67
69		4	2		0	0		0	0		0	71		4
37	1	7	1		0	4		0	0		0	42	1	7
3		0	0		0	0		0	0		0	3		0
68		24	7		1	3		1	0		0	78		26
174	7	12	17	3	3	19	1	2	4		0	214	11	17
87		0	4		0	0		0	0		0	91		0
2		0	0		0	0		0	0		0	2		0
6		0	0		0	0		0	0		0	6		0
28	20	7	2		0	3	2	1	3		0	36	22	8
145		44	9		3	0		0	0		0	154		47
28	14	9	6	1	1	1		0	1		0	36	15	10
102		36	6		2	0		0	0		0	108		38
62	15	4	1	4	0	4	1	0	9		0	76	20	4
113		5	8		0	14	1	1	11		0	146	1	6
1	1	0	0		0	0		0	0		0	1	1	0
11	7	3	1	1	1	1		0	1	3	0	14	11	4
16	24	3	1	1	0	1		0	6	6	2	24	31	5
3		0	0		0	0		0	0		0	3		0
3		0	0		0	0		0	0		0	3		0
25	21	3	1		0	3	3	0	5	3	2	34	27	5
39		3	1	1	0	4		0	0		0	44	1	3
211		32	17		3	0		0	0		0	228		35
1		0	0		0	0		0	0		0	1		0
5		0	1		0	2		0	0		0	8		0
35		0	1		0	0		0	0		0	36		0
3		0	0		0	0		0	0		0	3		0
3		0	0		0	0		0	0		0	3		0
3		0	1		0	0		0	0		0	4		0
2		0	0		0	0		0	0		0	2		0
56	2	0	0		0	0		0	0		0	56	2	0
196		0	7		0	0		0	0		0	203		0
82	3	5	10		0	6		0	16		0	114	3	5
3		0	0		0	0		0	0		0	3		0
32		14	0		0	3		1	0		0	35		15
33	10	1	6	1	0	4	1	0	0		0	43	12	1
5		0	0		0	3		0	0		0	8		0
1		0	0		0	1		0	0		0	2		0
73	8	24	4	3	3	3	1	1	0		0	80	12	28
44	3	24	6	2	2	7		3	4		3	61	5	32
121	21	10	14	3	1	10	1	0	20	7	1	165	32	12
37		0	2		0	3		0	0		0	42		0

Out

Amount	Player	To	Date
£30,000,000	Rio Ferdinand	Manchester United	July 2002
£12,000,000	Jimmy Floyd Hasselbaink	Atlético Madrid	August 1999
£3,500,000	Gary Speed	Everton	June 1996
£3,250,000	Matthew Jones	Leicester City	December 2000
£3,000,000	Gary McAllister	Coventry City	July 1996

Player of the Year
Award winners

1970-71	Norman Hunter	
1971-72	Peter Lorimer	
1972-73	Allan Clarke	
1973-74	Mick Jones	
1974-75	Gordon McQueen	
1975-76	Paul Madeley	
1976-77	Gordon McQueen	
1977-78	Tony Currie	
1978-79	Brian Flynn	
1979-80	John Lukic	
1980-81	Trevor Cherry	
1981-82	Eddie Gray	
1982-83	Kenny Burns	
1983-84	Tommy Wright	
1984-85	Neil Aspin	
1985-86	Ian Snodin	
1986-87	John Sheridan	
1987-88	Peter Haddock	
1988-89	Ian Baird	
1989-90	Chris Fairclough	
1990-91	David Batty	
1991-92	Tony Dorigo	
1992-93	Gordon Strachan	
1993-94	Gary McAllister	
1994-95	Brian Deane	
1995-96	Tony Yeboah	
1996-97	Nigel Martyn	
1997-98	Jimmy Floyd Hasselbaink	
1998-99	Lee Bowyer	
1999-2000	Harry Kewell	
2000-01	Lee Bowyer	
2001-02	Rio Ferdinand	

Total Appearances
(including as substitute)

1.	Jack Charlton	773
2.	Billy Bremner	773
3.	Paul Reaney	748
4.	Norman Hunter	726
5.	Paul Madeley	725
6.	Peter Lorimer	685
7.	Eddie Gray	579
8.	Johnny Giles	527
9.	Gary Sprake	507
10.	Trevor Cherry	482

League Appearances
(including as substitute)

1.	Jack Charlton	629
2.	Billy Bremner	587
3.	Paul Reaney	557
4.	Norman Hunter	558
5.	Paul Madeley	536
6.	Peter Lorimer	525
7.	Eddie Gray	454
8.	Ernie Hart	447
9.	Grenville Hair	443
10.	Jimmy Dunn	422

Top Ten Overall Scorers

1.	Peter Lorimer	238
2.	John Charles	157
3.	Allan Clarke	151
4.	Tom Jennings	117
5.	Billy Bremner	115
6.	Johnny Giles	115
7.	Mick Jones	111
8.	Charlie Keetley	110
9.	Jack Charlton	96
10.	Russell Wainscoat	93

Top Ten League Scorers

1.	Peter Lorimer	168
2.	John Charles	153
3.	Tom Jennings	112
4.	Allan Clarke	110
5.	Charles Keetley	108
6.	Billy Bremner	90
7.	Johnny Giles	88
8.	Russell Wainscoat	87
9.	Mick Jones	77
10.	Arthur Hydes	74

A HISTORY OF ELLAND ROAD

Elland Road Stadium is sited on land that in the 19th century stood on the road to the nearby town of Elland. The land, owned by Bentley's Brewery, was known as the Old Peacock Ground, named after a pub standing opposite the playing field. It was from this pub that the club took its nickname of the Peacocks, after being known as the Citizens during the days of Leeds City.

1897
Holbeck Rugby Club purchase the ground for £1,100 with a condition that it remained a football ground for at least seven years and that the catering rights should be held by Bentley's.
1898
On 23 April, 3,400 people watch Hunslet beat Harrogate 1-0 in the West Yorkshire Cup final.
1902
Leeds League side, Leeds Woodville, share the ground with Holbeck for the 1902-03 season.
1904
Holbeck fold and the ground is put up for sale. Leeds City sign the lease on 13 October, paying £4,500 and an annual rent of £75. Two days after giving the all-clear to sign the lease, Leeds City played their first game at Elland Road losing 2-0 to Hull City in a friendly.
1905
In August work begins on a covered stand for 5,000 people on the west side of the ground.
1906
In February City buy 3,961 square yards of land on the Churwell and Gelderd Road side of the ground, for £420, from the Monk's Bridge Iron Company.
1909
Elland Road is chosen as the venue for England's amateur international against Ireland.
1910
Elland Road hosts the FA Cup semi-final between Barnsley and Everton. Crowd control is a fiasco as an estimated 36,000 attended the match and thousands more are locked outside.
1912
Leeds City fall into the hands of the Receiver.
1914
On 14 August a Leeds business syndicate guarantee to pay £1,000 and an annual ground rent of £250 to keep City at Elland Road.
1915-18
Elland Road was used for army drilling and shooting practice.
1919
In October Leeds City are disbanded, plans are laid to utilize Elland Road's rich mineral deposits and turn it into a brickyard.
1920s
The Elland Road terrace is covered with a wooden barrel-shaped roof which became known as the Scratching Shed.
1932
56,796 watch United and Arsenal fight out a goalless draw on 27 December. This record attendance would stand for the next 35 years.
1938
54,112 attend Elland Road to see Leeds play Hunslet in the Rugby Championship final.
1939-45
Elland Road is requisitioned by the War Office for administrative purposes.
1950
Huddersfield Town play two matches at Elland Road after their main stand was destroyed by fire.
1953
On 9 November, in a friendly against Hibernian, floodlights costing £7,000, are switched on for the first time.
1956
On Tuesday 18 September fish and chip shop owner Arnold Price, whose premises were opposite the main gates, raises the alarm as a blaze sweeps through the West Stand. The fire, causing damage estimated at £100,000, destroys the stand, dressing-rooms, offices, directors' rooms and press-box and club records. The following saturday saw Leeds and Villa players change in the dressing-rooms of the Petty's sports ground in Lowfields Road and catch a coach to the ground.

1957
In August a new stand is opened at a cost of £180,000, £60,000 of which was met by public appeal.
1958
The West Stand is once again hit by fire but major damage is avoided as directors and officials man the hose pipes and put the fire out.
1965
On 20 March BBC *Match of the Day* cameras visit Elland Road for the first time as Leeds beat Everton 4-1.
1967
A record crowd of 57,892 watches the FA Cup Fifth Round replay against Sunderland.
1968
The North Stand – formerly referred to as the Kop (also known as the Gelderd End) – is rebuilt and roofed. As a result of the space created the pitch is moved 30 feet (9.144 metres) towards the Kop end.
1970
New building links the Kop with the West Stand and Lowfields Road.
1971
Elland Road, often a winter quagmire, is re-seeded. This year also sees Don Revie call in a gypsy to lift a curse that had been supposedly laid on the ground. Due to crowd disturbances, Leeds are banned from playing at Elland Road for the first four games of the 1971-72 season.
1972
The Leeds United Sports and Souvenir Shop opens on 30 September.
1974
The old Scratching Shed is dismantled and replaced by a £500,000 South Stand with 16 Executive Boxes, 3,500 seats and a terrace holding 4,000 people.
1974
New floodlights are installed - at 260 feet (79 m) high they are the highest in Europe.
1978
Leeds are banned from staging FA Cup games at Elland Road for the next three seasons after trouble flares during a cup-tie with Manchester City.
1979
The Kop is closed for two matches after objects are thrown on the pitch in a League match against Nottingham Forest.
1980
Record receipts of £346,483 are received, as Elland Road hosts the FA Cup semi-final replay between West Ham United and Everton.
1982
The pop group Queen play a concert at Elland Road.
1985
Bradford City play three home games at Leeds after the tragic fire closes Valley Parade. In November, Elland Road stages a Great Britain v New Zealand Rugby League Test Match.
1987
Apart from football, the stadium is host to a gaelic football match between Dublin and Mayo, and a three-day Jehovah's Witnesses' convention.
1989
An additional 16 boxes are built in the South Stand and the South and East stands are linked providing a section for visiting fans.
1994
The new East Stand replaces the existing Lowfields Road Stand. It is the biggest cantilever stand in the world. The bottom tier holds 10,000 *Yorkshire Evening Post* Family Stand members.
7,000 seats are installed in the North (now Revie) Stand making Elland Road an all-seater stadium.
1995
The FA Cup semi-final between Tottenham Hotspur and Everton at Elland Road on 9 April brings in new record gate receipts of £1,006,000.
1996
Elland Road is one of the eight English venues for Euro '96, hosting Spain's matches against Bulgaria, France and Romania.
2000
The average attendance for the 1999-2000 season is 39,155, the highest ever at Elland Road.
2002
Chairman Peter Ridsdale unveils plans for a new state-of-the-art 50,000-seater stadium on the outskirts of the city. Leeds United would expect to leave Elland Road by the start of the 2004-05 season.